STATISTICAL CONCEPTS
FOR THE
BEHAVIORAL SCIENCES

STATISTICAL CONCEPTS FOR THE BEHAVIORAL SCIENCES

SECOND EDITION

Harold O. Kiess

Framingham State College

Allyn and Bacon

Boston • London • Toronto • Sydney • Tokyo • Singapore

Vice President, Publisher, Social Science: Susan Badger
Executive Editor: Laura Pearson
Executive Marketing Manager: Joyce Nilsen
Production Administrator: Marjorie Payne
Editorial Assistant: Jennifer Normandin
Cover Administrator: Linda Knowles
Composition/Prepress Buyer: Linda Cox
Manufacturing Buyer: Megan Cochran
Editorial-Production Service: Raeia Maes

Copyright © 1996, 1989 by Allyn & Bacon
A Simon & Schuster Company
Needham Heights, Massachusetts 02194

Library of Congress Cataloging-in-Publication Data

Kiess, Harold O.
    Statistical concepts for the behavioral sciences / Harold O.
Kiess. —2nd ed.
        p.   cm.
    Includes bibliographical references and indexes.
    ISBN 0-205-16648-2
    1. Social sciences—Statistical methods.   2. Statistics.
I. Title.
HA29.K4857   1996
519.5—dc20   95-12845
                                                             CIP

Printed in the United States of America

10 9 8 7 6 5 4 3 2 1   00 99 98 97 96 95

Brief Contents

Contents

Preface

My objective for the first edition of this text was to provide a conceptual development of basic statistical methods in the context of their use in behavioral science. To achieve this goal, I placed a strong emphasis on utilizing contemporary research problems in the behavioral sciences. I believe that real problems more adequately illustrate the immediate relevance of statistical analysis in scientific research. This second edition represents a substantial revision of the first, yet I have tried to attain the same objective while improving on the weaknesses of my first attempt.

ORGANIZATION OF THE TEXT

The organization of this edition is designed for continuity in the concepts presented. The uses of statistics are developed and presented in a conceptually logical progression. The first five chapters introduce the need for statistics, the measurement of behavior, displaying scores in frequency distributions and graphically, and measures of central tendency and variability. Chapters 6 and 7 introduce the normal distribution, probability, sampling distributions, and using statistics for estimation of parameters. The basics of statistical hypothesis testing are introduced with the z test and the one-sample t test in Chapter 8. Chapters 9 to 12 deal with hypothesis testing for the difference between means using parametric tests. The analysis of variance is emphasized, for analysis of variance is currently the most widely used statistical test in the behavioral sciences, and students clearly need to be familiar with its use. A thorough introduction is provided for the one-factor between-subjects, one-factor within-subjects, and the factorial between-subjects analysis of variance, including the use of multiple comparison tests and strength of effect measures. In addition, considerable attention is given to the interpretation of an interaction in a factorial design. Hypothesis testing is continued in Chapter 13 with three nonparametric statistical tests, the chi-square, Mann–Whitney U, and the Wilcoxon signed ranks. Chapters 14 and 15 deal with correlation and regression. The first of these chapters introduces both the Pearson and Spearman correlation coefficients. Statistical hypothesis testing with each correlation coefficient is also developed. The second of these chapters provides an overview of the basics of simple linear regression. The placement of these chapters at the end of the text is somewhat unusual, for many texts include these chapters following a discussion of descriptive statistics. But I believe this common placement poses conceptual difficulties for students. Descriptive statistics, such as the mean and standard deviation, lead naturally to a discussion of statistical tests for the difference between sample means. Interposition of correlation and regression between descriptive statistics and statistical hypothesis testing interrupts this continuity of thought. I thus elected to maintain the continuity of conceptual development and place the correlation and regression material at the end of the text.

FEATURES

Many problems are encountered by students attempting to grasp the sometimes difficult conceptual basis of statistics. To help overcome these problems, the text uses a variety of features to keep the material tied to actual research problems and to permit students to assess their understanding of the material as they proceed through a chapter.

Realistic Problems

All statistical methods are introduced in the context of a problem from behavioral research. Many problems are based on studies drawn from contemporary published research. These studies are referenced fully so that the interested student may read the original research.

Conceptual Development of Statistics

The various statistics are introduced conceptually, often by use of a definitional formula. A problem is then worked using this conceptual approach so that students may see what the statistic does with the data. Using this format, I have tried not to overwhelm students mathematically when introducing a statistic. The mathematics required for elementary statistics is simple, yet many students are intimidated by a first chapter that reviews basic mathematics with no immediate connection to the statistics that use the mathematics. Thus I have introduced and explained the necessary mathematical concepts when they are needed. For those who need a more complete review of basic mathematical operations, however, such a review is provided in Appendix B.

Testing Your Knowledge and Review Questions

Each chapter contains interspersed *Testing Your Knowledge* sections and end-of-chapter *Review Questions*. The questions in these sections provide an opportunity for students to review and test their understanding of the text material. Many of the questions asked focus on actual research problems. Thus, not only do these questions provide a review, but they also give examples of the uses of the various statistical methods. I strongly encourage students to complete these exercises whenever they are encountered before continuing on in the chapter or to the next chapter.

Statistics in Use

After a statistical method has been introduced, its use in actual research is described in a *Statistics in Use* section. Each Statistics in Use presents a brief summary of recently published research and a description of how the statistical method was employed in that research.

Sample Journal Formats

For many statistical tests a sample journal report of a statistical analysis is presented with an explanation of the information contained in the report. The sample is followed by exercises on extracting information from journal presentations of the results of a study. The second edition expands this feature to include a greater variety of statistics and to provide the requirements of the fourth edition of the *Publication Manual of the American Psychological Association* (1994).

Marginal Definitions and Terms Glossary

Marginal definitions of important terms and a glossary of these terms are included in this edition. Important terms are boldfaced and defined in the text material. These definitions are supplemented by marginal definitions to reinforce learning of the material. A glossary of all these terms is provided in Appendix C.

Statistical Symbols

It is easy to become overwhelmed by the variety of symbols used in statistics. To aid in learning the language of statistics, Appendix D provides a glossary of all the symbols used in this text. Students may thus easily refresh themselves of the meaning of symbols they encounter.

Readability

The text is written so that it may be read and studied without interruption by boxed features or optional reading. Each section of the text follows from the previous material. To enhance this continuity, raw score computational formulas for the analysis of variance have been placed in chapter supplements at the end of the chapter. Thus instructors who omit computational formulas in favor of one of the many programs available for computerized statistical analysis may readily do so without loss of continuity in the text material.

I hope that you will find that this text leads to an interesting and rewarding study of statistics. If you have any comments or suggestions on the text, please write me at the Department of Psychology, Framingham State College, Box 2000, Framingham, MA 01701 or Internet hkiess@compsvc.frc.mass.edu.

ACKNOWLEDGMENTS

A number of individuals contributed to the development of this text. The idea for the first edition came from Allen Workman of Allyn and Bacon, who suggested that I use the approach taken in a psychological research methods text, *Psychological Research Methods,*

A Conceptual Approach, I coauthored with my colleague, Dr. Douglas W. Bloomquist, and extend it to a statistics text. Consequently, many of the conceptual ideas used in this text are similar to those developed in that research methods text. I thank Doug Bloomquist for his contributions to the development of those ideas and material and for his willingness to let me use that material in this text. Susan Badger, Vice-President and Publisher at Allyn and Bacon, endorsed the preparation of a second edition and provided the impetus for carrying the project to completion. Laura Pearson, Allyn and Bacon Executive Editor for psychology, had an important role in shaping this end product. Her ideas and suggestions have been most useful in revising the text. Jennifer Normandin, Editorial Assistant, cheerfully and capably dealt with my many questions concerning the preparation of the manuscript. And, Bill Barke, President at Allyn and Bacon, again deserves acknowledgment; it was his encouragement and confidence some twelve or more years ago that led me to even attempt to write a college-level text.

The actual production process was handled most capably by Cynthia Newby of Chestnut Hill Enterprises, Inc., and Raeia Maes of Maes Associates. Raeia's many phone calls kept me apprised of what I could expect next in the production schedule and helped me put some order into my life. William O. Thomas was a most conscientious copy editor, who not only improved my writing but also shared part of his six cats with me. I express my gratitude to them.

Various professional colleagues were also involved in the development of this text. Some responded to a detailed questionnaire offering suggestions regarding content and approach. Others reviewed part or all of the manuscript; their careful scrutiny helped me immensely in clarifying the presentation and avoiding conceptual and mathematical errors. Of course, any inaccuracies remaining are my responsibility alone. I am grateful to the following for their assistance: Paul Amrhein, University of New Mexico; Dennis Cogan, Texas Tech University; Mark Fineman, Southern Connecticut State University; Mike Grelle, Central Missouri State University; Rick Hoyle, University of Kentucky; Arthur D. Kemp, Central Missouri State University; Melanie M. Kercher, Sam Houston State University; Robert Lange, University of Central Florida; J. W. Moore, Jr., Marshall University; Jon Rich, California State University at Fullerton; Richard Serkes, Tulsa Junior College; N. C. Silver, University of Central Florida; David D. Simpson, Carroll College; Michael Tirrell, Stonehill College; and Paul Yarnold, Northwestern University Medical School.

I also thank CRC Press, Inc., for their gracious permission to use many of the statistical tables in the appendix.

A final acknowledgment is to those who have been affected most by the work required to write a book, my children, Kimberley and Jeffrey, and my wife, Sandra. Without their understanding, tolerance, encouragement and love, this book would never have reached completion.

H.O.K.

STATISTICAL CONCEPTS
FOR THE
BEHAVIORAL SCIENCES

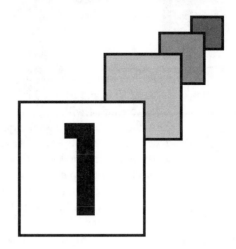

Introduction to Statistics

"Oh that blasted alarm" you mutter as you push the snooze button for a second time. What a short night! As you stumble out of bed, you realize that only a quick shower and a fast breakfast will let you be on time for your 8:00 A.M. class. As you walk to your car, you notice what a pleasant, warm day seems to be in store for this early spring day. Much nicer than yesterday's cold rain and drizzle. As you pull onto the expressway, the traffic is heavier than usual and it's not moving as fast as you had expected. Will you be late for your class? Fortunately, you make your class on time; the lecture today is one of the best of the semester. But, you dread your 9:00 A.M. science lab; often it runs so long you don't have time for lunch. But today is different, everything goes smoothly, and you get out in time to have a leisurely, fun lunch with two of your best friends. After lunch it's off to work at the Big Bargain Department Store. The customers today seem very pleasant in contrast to yesterday, you think maybe it's because of the nice weather. The pleasant customers make the afternoon pass quickly, and soon you are again on the expressway heading for home. Traffic now is lighter than most days; maybe everyone left work earlier today. You have a great deal of school work to do, so after dinner you settle at your desk, hoping for a productive night of studying. And so it is, at least in comparison to many of your attempts to study after dinner. You really feel prepared for that statistics exam coming up at the end of the week. To reward yourself, you watch an hour of television and then you go to bed. Maybe if you go to bed a bit earlier, the night will seem longer.

Perhaps this short vignette represents a typical day in your life, perhaps it does not. In any event, you are probably wondering what does this vignette have to do with statistics? Well, for one, it illustrates that you have recognized certain regularities or consistencies in the events of your life: The typical amount of time you have for a shower or breakfast, the normal weather for an early spring day, the characteristic amount of traffic on your drive to college and how long it takes you to get there, the general interest level of a class, the average length of a science lab, the normal amount of fun you have at lunch, the typical behavior of a department store customer, and the normal productivity of a night of studying. The fact that you recognize there are consistencies or regularities in the occurrences of your life indicates you also recognize that there is variability or variation about these regularities. Some nights seem longer than others, showers and breakfasts vary in length from day to day, the weather rarely is normal for the time of the year (in fact as I write this material it is 61 degrees in early January in New England; the normal temperature should be in the mid-30s), traffic may be lighter or heavier, classes vary in interest level from day to day (and from course to course), science labs are sometimes longer and other times shorter than average, the behavior of shoppers is quite variable from person to person, and some study sessions are more productive than others.

Variable: Any environmental condition or event, stimulus, personal characteristic or attribute, or behavior that can take on different values at different times or with different people.

This variation among events implies the existence of variables in the environment. A **variable** is any environmental condition or event, stimulus, personal characteristic or attribute, or behavior that can take on different values at different times or with different people. The amount of sleep you obtain, the length of your shower, the amount of traffic on the expressway, the interest level of a class, the length of a science lab, the mood of shoppers, and the productivity of study sessions are all variables. Statistics is the discipline that quantifies the consistency found in a variable and the variability about this consistency. Although this definition of statistics is informal and incomplete, it will serve for the moment.

TABLE 1-1

Conviction rates in French courts as a function of year and the ability of the defendant to read and write.

Ability of Accused to Read or Write	Year			Average
	1828	1829	1830	
Unable to read or write	0.63	0.63	0.62	0.627
Able to read and write imperfectly	0.62	0.60	0.58	0.600
Able to read and write well	0.56	0.55	0.52	0.543
Has a superior education	0.35	0.48	0.37	0.400

After data of Quetelet. Adapted from Table 5–2, p. 176, *The History of Statistics: The Measurement of Uncertainty before 1900* by S. M. Stigler. Copyright 1986 by the President and Fellows of Harvard College.

You, of course, are not the only person to note the regularity of events in the world. Lambert Adolphe Jacques Quetelet (1796–1874), a Belgian professor with wide-ranging interests, believed that such regularities in variables have causes and that if he could identify the regularities he could then identify their causes. He thus set out to identify these regularities. His initial work was to characterize what he called an "average man." To do so, he obtained anthropometric data (that is, bodily measurements) on variables such as height and weight from a large number of French soldiers (Stigler, 1986). His hope was that by characterizing an average person he could find regularities in human attributes and then compare these averages between males and females, or across nationalities, localities, ages, or races. Quetelet's interest in the average person extended also to what he called "moral statistics," regularities in variables such as suicide rates or crime and conviction rates. For example, Quetelet studied conviction rates in French courts over a period of years and categorized the rate of conviction by the accused's ability to read and write. His results are presented in Table 1–1. The numerical values in Table 1–1 represent probabilities. For example, if you were being tried in a French court in 1829 and you were able to read and write only imperfectly, the probability of your being convicted would be .60 (or 6 chances out of 10). Notice there appears to be a clear relationship (or consistency) between the accused's reading and writing abilities and the likelihood that he or she would be convicted of a crime. Quetelet often is called the father of social science for initiating these statistical studies (Dudycha & Dudycha, 1972).

STUDYING STATISTICS: HOW TO USE THIS TEXT

As the introduction illustrates, the study of statistics deals with both the regularities and variability of events that all of us have noticed in our lives. Thus in one sense we are all novice statisticians. Nevertheless, many people are intimidated by the ideas of statistics and dread the thought of an entire course in statistics. This fear need not be the case, however. Learning statistics is similar to learning a new language. The language of statistics is composed of words, symbols, and formulas. As with any new language it requires serious study to master its components. But with practice and experience it should become as natural to you as your native language. Several features of this text will help you with your study of statistics.

Important Terms and Symbols

Important terms are **boldfaced** when they are introduced in the text. They are then highlighted in a marginal definition. When you encounter a boldfaced term, you should recognize that it is important to understanding statistics. Don't proceed with your study until you have learned the term. Also, a glossary of terms is provided in Appendix C. If you encounter a term whose meaning you have forgotten, consult this glossary to refresh your memory. A glossary of statistical symbols is provided in Appendix D.

Testing Your Knowledge Sections

Each chapter contains interspersed *Testing Your Knowledge* sections. These sections provide an opportunity for you to review and test your understanding of the material before you move on to the next section of the chapter. Many of the questions focus on actual research problems; thus they provide examples of uses of the statistical methods you are studying. Answers for many of the *Testing Your Knowledge* questions are given in Appendix E, *Answers for Computational Problems*, at the end of the text.

Statistics in Use

Each chapter contains descriptions of the actual use of statistical methods in the *Statistics in Use* sections. By carefully studying these examples you will increase your understanding of how statistics are put to actual use.

Review Questions

Review questions are provided at the end of each chapter. As with the Testing Your Knowledge questions, I encourage you to complete the chapter review questions and then compare your answers to those given in Appendix E, *Answers for Computational Problems*.

Mathematics Review

The mathematics used in this text is elementary, requiring only the operations of addition, subtraction, multiplication, and division. Mathematical symbols and operations are explained as they are needed. If you encounter difficulties with any of the mathematical operations, a *Mathematics Review* is provided in Appendix B. This review provides a summary of basic mathematical symbols and operations.

WHAT IS STATISTICS?

Data: The scores or measurements of behavior or characteristics obtained from observations of a sample of people or animals.

Statistics: The methods or procedures used to summarize, analyze, and draw inferences from data.

Statistic: A single number used to describe a set of data from a sample or to analyze those data more fully.

Following in the footsteps of Quetelet, behavioral scientists attempt to understand and explain human and animal behavior. They do so by collecting data. **Data** (*data* is plural, *datum* is singular) are the scores or measurements of behavior or characteristics obtained from observations of people or animals. To identify both the consistencies and variability in these data, procedures called *statistics* are applied to the data. **Statistics** thus refers to the methods or procedures used to summarize, analyze, and reach conclusions from data. A **statistic** is a single number that may be used to describe a set of data from a sample or to analyze those data more fully.

USING STATISTICS: THREE EXAMPLES

Statistical procedures are used in many different ways in behavioral science. The remainder of this chapter provides examples of three uses of statistical methods in behavioral science. A number of terms are introduced, and you should study and learn these terms, for you will encounter them throughout the text. Don't worry, however, if you don't understand all the details of the examples provided; the use of each approach is discussed more fully in later chapters.

Description and Inference

From our everyday reading, we are familiar with statistical descriptions of large sets of data. For example, the national newspaper, *USA Today*, offered a description of the activities of typical individuals in the United States in the mid-1980s ("The Way," 1985). One characterization offered was that in the average household a television is turned on 7.12 hours per day. This numerical value illustrates two important uses of statistical methods: description and inference. Although the value of 7.12 hours is intended to characterize the population of all U.S. households on the variable of the duration that a television is turned on per day, it was not obtained by observing and measuring all the households in the country. Rather, only a portion, or sample, of all households was observed and measured. The number of hours that each household included in the sample had a television on in a day was recorded, providing a set of data. The data from the different households in the sample were then summarized by calculating a single number, a descriptive statistic, 7.12 hours. This statistic is intended to describe the daily amount of time that a typical household in the sample had a television turned on. The number of hours the television was on per day for a typical household in the population of all households in the United States was then inferred, or estimated, from this statistic.

Population: A complete set of people, animals, objects, or events that share a common characteristic.

Our discussion has used the terms *populations* and *samples*. A **population** is a complete set of people, animals, objects, or events that share a common characteristic. For example, all the college students in the United States constitute a population. The common characteristic of this population is that all the individuals included in it are enrolled in college. Other examples are all the households in the United States, all the adult females in North Carolina, the farmers in Nebraska, all individuals who commute on a daily basis to New York City, or all the people who have one or more bank credit cards; each comprises a population. Any group of individuals may be thought of as a population as long as all those possessing the characteristic common to the population are included in the group.

Sample: A subset, or subgroup, selected from a population.

Random sample: A sample in which individuals are selected so that each member of the population has an equal chance of being selected for the sample, and the selection of one member is independent of the selection of any other member of the population.

Behavioral scientists often want to characterize populations with statements such as "the typical American household has a television on 7.12 hours per day" or "the average U.S. male earns $19,438 per year, whereas a female earns only $9,584 per year" ("The Way," 1985). But it should be obvious that in most instances these characterizations cannot be obtained from measuring all members of the population. Rather, scientists typically use only a sample of the population.

Descriptive statistics: Statistical procedures used to summarize and describe the data from a sample.

Statistical inference: Estimating population values from statistics obtained from a sample.

Parameter: A number that describes a characteristic of a population.

A **sample** is a subset, or subgroup, selected from a population, often by following a set of rules to ensure that the sample is representative of the population. One common form of selecting a sample is random sampling. In a simple **random sample** individuals are selected so that each member of the population has an equal chance of being selected for the sample, and the selection of one member is independent of the selection of any other member of the population. Data are then obtained from members of the sample, and a **descriptive statistic** is calculated to describe the data. This descriptive statistic is then used to infer a characteristic of the population. The word *infer* implies reasoning from something known to something unknown. Thus **statistical inference** is the process of reaching conclusions about unknown population values (e.g., the number of hours per day that a television is turned on in the typical U.S. household), called **parameters**, from statistics obtained from a sample. I discuss the procedures involved in the selection and description of samples and inference to a population more fully in Chapters 3 through 7.

STATISTICS IN USE 1–1

Health-seeking Behaviors: Estimation and Inference

We are often urged by the popular media to change our behavior to improve our health. Public service announcements suggest that people should not smoke, or that we should drink alcoholic beverages in moderation, or that our blood pressure should be checked regularly. But how does the public perceive the importance of such behaviors to the maintenance of good health? Bausell (1986), as part of a larger study, sampled 1254 adults in the United States and asked them to rate the perceived importance of a variety of potential health-improving behaviors. For example, individuals were asked how important they believed not driving after drinking is to good health. They rated each behavior on a scale similar to the one illustrated next.

1	2	3	4	5	6	7	8	9	10
Low				Moderate				Utmost	
importance				importance				importance	

Bausell reports that, on the average, individuals in the sample rated "not driving after drinking" as 9.3, "exercising regularly" as 8.3, and "drinking in moderation" as 6.6. Each of these values is a *descriptive statistic*, a number describing the typical response of members of the sample. Because each person in the sample did not give the same rating to an item, however, Bausell also presented other descriptive statistics, called *measures of variability*. These statistics indicate the amount of variation in the ratings given. From these descriptive statistics Bausell inferred that, among the public, not driving after drinking is perceived as more important for maintaining good health than is exercising regularly, and exercising regularly is rated as more important than drinking in moderation. Because of Bausell's method of sampling from the population, he can be quite confident that the inferences made from the sample to the population are correct. I discuss methods of sampling and other problems of inference more fully in Chapter 7.

TESTING YOUR KNOWLEDGE 1-1

1. Define: data, parameter, population, random sample, sample, statistic, statistical inference, statistics, variable.
2. In a recent election, 600 potential voters of a congressional district were polled to discover who they planned to vote for in an upcoming election. The results indicated that 312 voters, or 52 percent of the sample, planned to vote for candidate A, 240 voters, or 40 percent, planned to vote for candidate B, and 48 voters, or 8 percent, said they did not plan to vote or had no preference among the candidates. Based on the results of the poll, the researchers estimated that candidate A would win the election with about 52 percent of the total vote.
    a. Explain why descriptive statistics are necessary to summarize the results of this research.
    b. What inferences to a population were made from the statistics obtained?

Experimentation and Statistical Hypothesis Testing

Independent variable: A variable manipulated in an experiment to determine its effect on the dependent variable.

Behavioral scientists are interested not only in describing and characterizing samples and populations, but they also want to find the causes of behavior for individuals or groups. One approach to this task is to perform an experiment. To conduct an experiment, a researcher identifies a variable, called an **independent variable**, that he or she thinks

Dependent variable: The variable in an experiment that depends on the independent variable. In most instances the dependent variable is some measure of a behavior.

Research hypothesis: A statement of an expected, or predicted, relationship between two or more variables. In an experiment, a research hypothesis is a predicted relationship between an independent variable and a dependent variable.

Subject: The person who participates in an experiment.

Equivalent groups: Groups of subjects that are not expected to differ in any consistent or systematic way prior to receiving the independent variable of the experiment.

Between-subjects design: A research design in which two or more groups are created.

Score: The measurement obtained on the subject's performance of a task.

Raw data: The scores obtained from all the subjects before the scores have been analyzed statistically.

affects a person's behavior. The behavior that is expected to be affected by this independent variable is called the **dependent variable**.

For example, I might expect alcohol consumption to affect a person's response to violence: People under the influence of alcohol are expected to be more accepting of violence than people who are not under the influence of alcohol (Gustafson, 1987a). In this instance, alcohol consumption is the independent variable. An experimenter has control over whether a person does or does not consume alcohol, and he or she expects it to affect the acceptance of violence. A measure of the person's acceptance of violence is the dependent variable. Acceptance of violence is presumed to depend on whether or not a person has consumed alcohol. The statement of the researcher's expectation that alcohol consumption will affect the acceptance of violence is called a research hypothesis. A **research hypothesis** is a statement of an expected, or predicted, relationship between two or more variables. In an experiment, a research hypothesis is a predicted relationship between an independent variable and a dependent variable.

The simplest experiment that could be performed to test a research hypothesis relating alcohol consumption to acceptance of violence begins by creating two equivalent groups of people. Scientists refer to the people who participate in research studies as **subjects** or **participants**. **Equivalent groups** are groups of subjects that are not expected to differ in any consistent or systematic way prior to receiving the independent variable of the experiment. An experiment in which two or more groups are created is called a **between-subjects design**. After equivalent groups are created, the researcher manipulates, or varies, the independent variable and measures the dependent variable, while controlling all other variables that may affect the dependent variable. In this example, the experimenter might give subjects in the first group 0.8 milliliter of alcohol per kilogram of body weight mixed with an equal amount of orange juice. Subjects in the second group might be given 1.6 milliliters of plain orange juice per kilogram of body weight. The difference in the drink is the only way in which the two groups are allowed to vary. The dependent variable may be measured by having the subjects watch a violent movie and then rate the movie on the acceptability of the violence shown. A score on the rating task is obtained for each subject. A **score** is the measurement obtained on the subject's performance of a task. This score is the dependent variable, for we expect it to depend on whether or not the subject had consumed alcohol prior to watching the movie. The scores obtained from all the subjects provide the **raw data** for the experiment. From these raw data the researcher must decide if the independent variable of consumption of alcohol affected the subjects' rating of the acceptability of violence in the movie.

The process by which the experimenter decides if the independent variable had an effect or not involves several steps. The first step is to describe the ratings of each of the two groups by calculating descriptive statistics presenting the typical ratings of subjects in each group. This step is identical to the process of description of data discussed earlier in this chapter. Most likely you are already familiar with some common descriptive statistics such as the mode, the median, or the mean.

The second step involves deciding if any observed difference in the descriptive statistics for the two groups of scores is large enough to be attributed to the effect of the independent variable. This step requires using **statistical hypothesis testing**. The purpose of statistical hypothesis testing is to determine the anticipated size of chance differences between the groups.

Chance difference: A difference between equivalent groups occurring by accident or for no predictable reason.

In an experiment, equivalent groups will always differ in some unpredictable way that I will call a **chance difference**. Chance differences occur between groups in an experiment even if the independent variable has no effect on the dependent variable. In statistical hypothesis testing the difference actually observed between the two groups in the experiment is compared to expected chance differences between the groups. If the possibility of obtaining a chance difference as large as the actual difference found is sufficiently small, then the researcher decides that the observed difference is not a chance difference. Rather, the observed difference is attributed to the effect of the independent variable.

Statistical testing is used widely in the behavioral sciences. To understand the concepts involved, however, requires building on knowledge of descriptive statistics and statistical inference and estimation, topics discussed in Chapters 3 through 7. I discuss statistical testing in Chapters 8 through 13.

STATISTICS IN USE 1-2

Errors in Perception: Experimentation and Statistical Hypothesis Testing

Scientists have long been interested in the question of how experience affects our perception of the world. For example, when asked to judge the size of an object that is a considerable distance away, we may let the expected or familiar size of the object affect our perception of it. To gain greater understanding of how experience affects perception, Predebon (1987) conducted an experiment that required subjects to estimate the size of an object. The independent variable manipulated was the type of object viewed. Two different objects were used. The first was a 7.1 centimeters (cm) high reproduction of a "nine of spades" playing card. This reproduced card was only 80 percent of the size of a regular playing card, which is 8.9 cm high. The other object was a blank white card that was the same size as the reproduced nine of spades card (i.e., 7.1 cm). Two equivalent groups of 12 subjects each were formed; one group (identified as the experimental group) estimated the height of the reproduced nine of spades card; the other group (identified as the control group) estimated the height of the blank white card. For the size estimates, the card was placed about 27 feet from the subject in a darkened room so that common distance cues could not be used to aid the size judgments. The estimated size of the card was the dependent variable. Predebon hypothesized that the reproduced playing card would be estimated as larger than the blank white card. He expected this relationship because the familiar size of a playing card would influence a subject's perception of the reproduced playing card, but not the blank white card.

The mean or average height estimates were 6.8 cm for the control group and 8.6 cm for the experimental group. To determine if these observed estimates differed by more than chance, Predebon used a statistical test called the t. This test indicated that the estimates of the two groups differed by more than expected from chance differences alone. Thus, although the cards were actually the same physical size, the subjects in the experimental group judged the reproduced playing card to be larger than the subjects in the control group, who judged the blank white card. These results agreed with the research hypothesis and indicate that thought processes influence visual perception.

1. Define: between-subjects design, chance difference, dependent variable, equivalent groups, independent variable, raw data, research hypothesis, score, subjects.
2. Students learning the basic positions of ballet often have difficulty assuming the correct foot positions. One problem is that of foot pronation, letting the feet roll in when the heels are placed together and the toes pointed laterally outward. To help students overcome this problem, Clarkson, James, Watkins, and Foley (1986) formed two equivalent groups of females who had not previously had ballet training. Both groups were then taught basic ballet positions, and the amount of time the feet pronated was measured. For one group, a buzzer was sounded when the students allowed their feet to pronate. The other group of subjects, however, was not given any feedback about foot pronation. For one test period, the researchers found that subjects given the buzzer feedback had 3.1 seconds of foot pronation, whereas the subjects in the no feedback group had 21.8 seconds of foot pronation. A statistical test confirmed that the difference in foot pronation time between the groups was a real and not a chance difference.
   a. Identify the independent variable manipulated by Clarkson et al.
   b. Identify the dependent variable measured.
   c. Explain why this study is an experiment.
   d. Explain why statistical hypothesis testing is necessary in this experiment.

Correlation and Regression

Covary: Two variables covary when a change in one variable is related to a consistent change in the other variable.

In many instances of behavioral science research an experimenter does not want to manipulate an independent variable, but is interested only in finding whether two or more characteristics of individuals are related to each other or covary. Two variables are said to **covary** if a change in one variable is related to a consistent change in the other variable. For example, if a person's typical level of anxiety is related to his or her use of alcohol, such that high levels of anxiety are related to high use of alcohol and low levels of anxiety are related to low use of alcohol, then anxiety and alcohol usage covary.

Correlation coefficient: A statistic that provides a numerical description of the extent of the relatedness of two sets of scores and the direction of the relationship.

To find if two variables covary, we measure a sample of people and obtain two scores from each person, an anxiety score and an alcohol use score. Then a *correlation coefficient* is calculated. A **correlation coefficient** is a statistic that provides a numerical description of the extent of the relatedness of two sets of scores and the direction of the relationship. Values of this coefficient may range from −1.00 to +1.00.

Statistical hypothesis testing also enters into use with the correlation coefficient. There will always be some chance or accidental relationship between scores on two different variables. Thus the question arises of whether an observed relation, given by the numerical value of the correlation coefficient, is greater than would be expected from chance alone. A statistical test on the correlation coefficient provides an answer for this question.

Regression analysis: The use of statistical methods to predict one set of scores from a second set of scores.

If the two sets of scores are related beyond chance occurrence, then we may be interested in attempting to predict one score from the other. If you knew a person's anxiety score, could you predict his or her use of alcohol score? And, if you could predict the use of alcohol score, how accurate would your prediction be? Predicting a score on one variable from a score on a second variable involves using **regression analysis**.

Correlation and regression analysis techniques are used widely in many areas of behavioral science. One prominent use is in standardized test construction, for the purpose of many standardized tests is to predict future behaviors in school or on the job. I discuss correlation and regression in Chapters 14 and 15.

STATISTICS IN USE 1–3

Are Lonely People Also Depressed? Using Correlational Statistics

Are any of your friends lonely people? Do they appear depressed also? Loneliness and depression among individuals seem to be related characteristics. But, are they actually related? And, if so, how strong is the relationship? To answer these questions, Ouellet and Joshi (1986) used paper-and-pencil rating scales to measure the loneliness and depression of 81 college undergraduates. Each student provided two scores: a loneliness score and a depression score. Ouellet and Joshi calculated a correlation coefficient on the two scores and obtained a value of +.41. A statistical test indicated that this correlation is not simply a chance relationship. Loneliness and depression vary together. Lonely people typically are depressed, and nonlonely individuals usually are not depressed. Consequently, Ouellet and Joshi confirmed with actual measurements the relationship between depression and loneliness that many of us have observed casually.

TESTING YOUR KNOWLEDGE 1–3

1. Define: correlation coefficient, covary, regression analysis.
2. Many people believe in paranormal phenomena, such as precognition, extrasensory perception, and psychokinesis. Is the extent of belief in such phenomena related to the type of high school courses taken by such individuals? Tobacyk, Miller, and Jones (1984) measured the belief in paranormal phenomena of 193 eleventh-grade high school students. They also recorded the total number of science courses each student had taken. When relating the number of science courses to belief in paranormal phenomena, they discovered an inverse relationship. The more science courses a student had taken, the weaker the belief in paranormal phenomena.
   a. Explain why correlational statistics are needed in this study.
   b. What two sets of measures are used in this study?

WHY ARE STATISTICS NECESSARY?

I have presented three common uses of statistical analysis in behavioral science research. Nagging at you, however, may be the discomforting question of why statistical methods are necessary in the behavioral sciences in the first place. The answer is quite straightforward and the same for each statistical procedure I have presented: It is a delightful fact of life that people differ on many characteristics in varying degrees. It would be a tiresome world if every person were identical to every other person, but such an environment would possess the advantage of requiring no need for statistical techniques. Why? Consider the various uses of statistics that I have introduced.

The first deals with describing numerical measurements obtained from individuals. If all people were alike, then a measurement taken on any one person would describe all other people. Everyone, for example, would earn exactly $19,438 per year. To make an inference to a population, only one person would need to be measured. Accordingly, there would be no need for descriptive statistics to represent a typical score for members of the sample.

The second use discussed deals with statistical hypothesis testing to answer the question of whether an independent variable has an effect on behavior. Think how easy it would be to decide if an independent variable has an effect on behavior if every person's behavior were identical to every other person's. Suppose, for example, that you wanted to know if a particular drug lowers heart rate. Without the drug, everyone's heart rate is 60 beats per minute, and with the drug, everyone's heart rate is 55 beats per minute. Is there any question of whether the drug lowers heart rate? Because there is no chance variation from person to person, there would be no doubt that the drug lowered heart rate. Statistical hypothesis testing would be unnecessary.

Finally, the third use deals with the problem of correlation and regression analysis. Are two behaviors related and, if so, can I predict the occurrence of one behavior from the occurrence of the other? This question only arises because people are different from one another and behave differently in the same situation. If every person were identical to every other person on all behaviors, then all behaviors would be perfectly predictable. Because there would be no variability in behaviors among people, I could predict all behaviors perfectly without using correlation and regression statistics.

An environment with no variability among people and animals would eliminate the need for statistical analysis, but what a boring place it would be. Fortunately, we do not have such a world. But a life with both regularities and variability among its peoples requires statistical techniques in order to describe and explain behavior.

SUMMARY

- Statistics refers to the methods or procedures used to summarize, analyze, and draw inferences from data.
- A statistic is a number that may be used to describe the scores from a sample.
- A statistic may also be used to infer the value of a population parameter.
- Statistical hypothesis testing is used to determine if an observed difference between two groups in an experiment is large enough to be attributed to the effect of an independent variable, rather than to chance.
- Correlational statistics are used to determine if two sets of scores are related.
- Regression statistics are used to predict one set of scores from another set of scores.

KEY TERMS AND SYMBOLS

between-subjects design
chance difference
correlation coefficient
covary
data
dependent variable
descriptive statistics
equivalent groups

independent variable
parameter
population
random sample
raw data
regression analysis
research hypothesis
sample

score
statistic
statistical hypothesis test
statistical inference
statistics
subjects
variable

REVIEW QUESTIONS

1. Identify four events or occurrences in your life that possess regularity (e.g., the typical amount of sleep you obtain or the typical number of hours you work each day).

2. Think of three different populations. What is the common characteristic possessed by the members of each population?

3. Crews, Shirreffs, Thomas, Krahenbuhl, and Helfrich (1986) measured the percentage of body fat in 23 professional female golfers. They related this measure to the golfer's average score for a year of competitive play and found that they could predict golf scores from percentage of body fat. A low percentage of body fat was related to a low average golf score, whereas higher percentages of body fat were associated with higher average golf scores.
   a. Which statistical methods discussed in this chapter are used in this study?
   b. Explain why correlational statistics are needed in this study.
   c. What two sets of measures are used in this study?

4. Kawasaki syndrome is a disease of childhood characterized by fever, fissured lips, a bright red tongue, redness of the palms and soles, and a rash. Typical therapy has involved taking aspirin. Recent research, however, has suggested that gamma globulin plus aspirin may be more effective than aspirin alone. To test this research hypothesis, Newburger et al. (1986) randomly assigned 168 children with Kawasaki syndrome to one of two treatment conditions: aspirin or aspirin plus gamma globulin. They found that after one day of treatment the temperature of children in the aspirin plus gamma globulin treatment group fell an average of 2.3°F, whereas the temperature of the children in the aspirin-only treatment group fell 0.8°F. A statistical test indicated that the difference in the temperature decreases was not a chance difference between the two groups; the aspirin plus gamma globulin group had a greater temperature decrease than the aspirin-only group.

      a. Which statistical methods discussed in this chapter are used in this study?

      b. Identify the independent variable manipulated by Newburger et al.

      c. Identify the dependent variable measured.

      d. Explain why this study is an experiment.

      e. Explain why statistical hypothesis testing is necessary in this experiment.

5. Gurnack and Werbie (1985) analyzed the court records of 3941 individuals arrested for drunken driving in Wisconsin. They discovered that about 40 percent of the individuals were under 25 years old, about 40 percent were between 26 to 44 years old, and about 20 percent were older than 44 years. They also found that about 50 percent of those arrested were unskilled workers.

      a. Which statistical methods discussed in this chapter are used in this study?

      b. Explain why descriptive statistics are necessary to summarize the results of this research.

      c. What descriptive statistic was used in this study?

6. For each of the following statements, indicate whether it describes raw data, a statistic, or an inference to a population parameter.

      a. Linda commutes 36 minutes to her work each day.

      b. The average male commuter in the United States spends 42 minutes commuting each day.

      c. A sample of 75 commuters gave an average daily commuting time of 46 minutes.

      d. Benjamin and Anita Houston have $5126 in their bank savings account.

      e. The typical American adult has $6024 in a bank savings account.

      f. A random sample of 50 residents of a small southwestern town provided an average bank savings account of $5692.

7. Think of an instance where your score on one variable is used to predict your score on a second variable (e.g., your cholesterol level, which is used to predict the chance of heart disease).

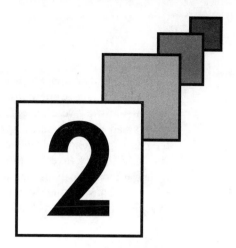

2

Scientific Research

Statistical methods have developed over several thousand years to solve practical problems. In fact, the word *statistics* derives from the Latin *status* or state, for the earliest uses of statistics were for obtaining knowledge of the state or empire. Roman emperors always had a census taken whenever a new territory was conquered. Information from the census, which provided statistics about the population and the valuation of property, was used to levy taxes on the population. Although statistics are still used in this way, their use today has expanded to include methods used in the study of human and animal behavior. Thus, to understand modern statistical methods, we need to know the basics of the scientific study of behavior.

WHAT IS SCIENCE?

Science is a method for the acquisition of knowledge. It involves identifying a question, proposing a tentative answer to the question in the form of a research hypothesis, formulating a research design to empirically test the hypothesis, collecting data, analyzing the data, and reaching a conclusion about the hypothesis from the analyzed data.

Scientific Questions

Empirical data: Scores or measurements based on observation and sensory experience.

A scientific question is one that allows an answer to be obtained by the collection of empirical data. The word *empirical* refers to sensory experience or observation; thus **empirical data** are scores or measurements based on systematic observation and sensory experience. Each example in Chapter 1 presented research based on a scientific question, for each example allowed an answer to be obtained by collecting empirical data.

If I cannot put a question or problem to a test that allows the collection of empirical data, then it is not a question open to scientific investigation. For example, Pope John Paul II proposed that angels have intellect and free will ("Pope says," 1986). This statement is not open to scientific inquiry, for there currently is no known way of making observations of the intellect of angels. As another example, a psychologist suggested that spiritualists believe that "Those who die suddenly are supposedly disoriented for a while after dying. This has been reported to be true of suicides also." (Lester, 1981–82, p. 46). Again, there currently is no known way of empirically studying a person's orientation after death. Thus the problem of a person's orientation after death is not open to scientific investigation.

Often an experimenter will offer a tentative answer to the question in the form of a research hypothesis. In Chapter 1 a research hypothesis was defined as a statement of an expected, or predicted, relationship between two or more variables. For example, Ouellet and Joshi (1986) hypothesized that loneliness and depression are related characteristics in individuals (see Statistics in Use 1–3). Because a research hypothesis identifies the variables and indicates how they are expected to be related, it directs the researcher in the selection of a research design and the collection of data.

Research Methods

Research method: An approach used to collect data.

Collecting empirical data to test a research hypothesis requires using a research method. A **research method** is an approach the scientist uses to collect data. A variety of methods is used in the behavioral sciences; here I provide only a brief overview of four basic methods. For each of these methods, statistics are used to summarize and analyze the data collected.

Naturalistic Observation

Naturalistic observation: Research involving the observation of behaviors occurring in natural settings.

Naturalistic observation refers to observing behaviors occurring in natural settings without intruding into the situation. As an example of naturalistic observation, Trinkaus (1982, 1983, 1988, 1993) has systematically observed the behavior of drivers at one intersection over a 10-year period. One of his findings is that compliance with a stop sign has decreased over the observation period. In these observations, the experimenter remained unobtrusive; drivers were not aware that their compliance with a stop sign was being observed. Had the drivers been aware of this observation, they likely would have altered their behavior.

Archival Records

Archival records: Research using existing records.

Archival records research involves answering questions by using existing records. Societies typically collect a variety of information about their members: birth, marriage, and death records; crime reports; census records; and so on. These existing records may provide the data necessary to answer a scientific question. For example, John Graunt (1620–1674), a London shopkeeper, used existing records on births and deaths to identify differences in the causes of death for men and women. More recently, Zusne (1986–87), interested in the question of whether dying individuals may attempt to delay their death until after an approaching birthday, examined the birthday and deathday records for over 3000 people. These records indicated that such a relationship may exist, but it differs for males and females.

As another example, Thorson (1993) analyzed data from the National Center for Health Statistics on homicide rates in the United States. This research indicated that the homicide rate is greatest in the District of Columbia; about 39 of every 1000 deaths in the District of Columbia are homicides. The rate is lowest in Iowa, where only two deaths of every 1000 are homicides.

Survey Research

Survey research: Research involving obtaining data from either oral or written interviews with people.

Survey research involves obtaining data from either oral or written interviews with people. Survey research is widespread in society. If you have ever filled out a card at a restaurant that asked questions on the quality of the meal or service, or if you have ever completed a product warranty card that asked questions about your income, marital status, and hobbies, then you have participated in survey research. Another familiar example is the surveys at election times that result in political polls. The research in Statistics in Use 1–1 describes the results of a survey on health-related behaviors.

Experiment

Experiment: A controlled situation in which one or more independent variables are manipulated to observe the effects on the dependent variable.

An **experiment** is a carefully controlled situation in which a scientist manipulates one or more independent variables to observe their effect on the dependent variable. Statistics in Use 1–2 presented an example of an experiment. The independent variable in this experiment was the type of card shown a subject, either a reproduced playing card or a blank white card. The dependent variable was the estimated size of the card. The conditions in which the experiment was conducted were carefully controlled so that no variables other than the type of card affected the subject's estimate of its size. Experiments allow scientists to reach cause-and-effect conclusions of the effect of the independent variable on the dependent variable. If the two types of cards are judged to be different in size, the cause for this difference must be the independent variable, the type of card. I discuss experiments more fully in Chapter 9, in which the statistical methods needed to analyze an experiment are introduced.

Operational Definitions

Operational definition: A specification of the operations used to make observations, to manipulate an independent variable, or to measure the dependent variable.

Scientific knowledge gained from application of the various research designs must be repeatable and subject to agreement among different observers. Scientific knowledge of a behavior gains strength and generality when other scientists can replicate the behavior in different settings and locations with different participants. For knowledge to be scientific, there must be full communication of ideas and results so that findings can be replicated, criticized, and extended by others. A crucial step in this communication process is specifying the operations that were used to make observations, to manipulate independent variables, or to measure the dependent variable. Scientists refer to this process as **operationally defining** the procedures used in research. As an example, in Statistics in Use 1–3, Ouellet and Joshi operationally defined loneliness as the subject's score on the UCLA loneliness scale (Russell, Peplau, & Cutrona, 1980). Thus, if another scientist wants to extend this research, he or she will know how loneliness was measured by Ouellet and Joshi.

TESTING YOUR KNOWLEDGE 2–1

1. Define: archival records, empirical data, experiment, naturalistic observation, operational definition, research method, research hypothesis, survey research.
2. For each of the following questions, name the type of research method that you expect would be used to find an answer to the question asked.
   a. What is the opinion of a community concerning the siting of a hazardous waste processing plant within its boundaries?
   b. What is the effect of type of message, either fear inducing or factual, on attitude change?
   c. What is the average age of fathers of firstborn children in Arizona?
   d. How often do 4-year-old children play in groups of three in a nursery school?
3. Refer to Statistics in Use 1–1. How did Bausell operationally define how important his subjects believed not driving after drinking is to good health?

MEASUREMENT

Measurement: Assigning numbers to variables following a set of rules.

Answering scientific questions requires measurement. **Measurement** is a process of assigning numbers to variables following a set of rules. Each research method described requires making measurements of characteristics or behaviors of subjects. Typically, measurements are classified into one of four scales or levels of measurement: nominal, ordinal, interval, or ratio measurements.

Scales of Measurement

Nominal Measurement

Nominal measurement: A classification of the measured variable into different categories.

Nominal measurement is a classification of the measured variable into different categories. As an example, with a nominal measure of the variable of ethnic origin of a person, people may be categorized as Native American, Asian American, African American, Caucasian, or Hispanic and then a number is assigned to name the category (hence the term *nominal*, which means *to name*), such as 1 = Native American, 2 = Asian American, 3 = African American, 4 = Caucasian, and 5 = Hispanic. Each individual assigned to the same category will be assigned the same number. The number, however, conveys no numerical information; a letter could have been used to identify the category as easily as a number. Many behavioral scientists do not regard nominal measures as actual measurements because the numbers assigned serve the purpose of identification only; they do not provide quantitative information about the variable measured.

STATISTICS IN USE 2–1

First Class Attendance and Academic Performance: Using Nominal Measurement

Is attendance on the first day of class related to course grades? Assuming that the more motivated the students are, the more likely they would attend the first class meeting and would also do well in a course, Buckalew, Daly, and Coffield (1986) assigned students who attended the first class day a category of 1 and those who were absent a category of 0. This measurement of class attendance was nominal; attendance was recorded as one of two categories: present, 1, or absent, 0. The assigned number is used only to identify the category of attendance. No mathematical operations can be performed on the numbers beyond tabulating frequencies of responses. It would have been as reasonable to assign a 0 to a student present on the first class day and a 1 to a student absent on this day. In fact, numbers need not be assigned to the response categories at all for nominal measurement; I simply can tabulate the behaviors as present or absent. You might be interested in knowing that the course grades of students attending the first class day were higher than the course grades of those not attending.

Ordinal Measurement

Ordinal measurement: The amount of a variable is placed in order of magnitude along a dimension.

When the amount of a variable is placed in order of magnitude along a dimension, then an **ordinal measurement scale** is used. For example, people may be asked to arrange a series of cartoons on a funniness scale from most to least funny. Often a numerical value of 1 is assigned to the stimulus or individual possessing the greatest amount of the characteristic being measured, a value of 2 to that person or stimulus that exhibits the next greatest amount, and so forth. If, for example, anxiety is measured with an ordinal scale, then the person exhibiting the most anxiety is assigned a 1, the person showing the next largest amount of anxiety a 2, the next a 3, and so on, producing an ordering of people from most to least anxious.

Ordinal scales essentially produce a ranking in which someone or something assigned a rank of 1 possesses more of a variable than one given a rank of 2. Ordinal measures do not, however, permit determining how much of a difference exists in the measured variable between ranks. A small difference in the variable being measured may exist between ranks 1 and 2, but a large difference may exist between ranks 2 and 3. For example, the times for the first three runners of a marathon may be 3 hours 19 minutes, 3 hours 20 minutes, and 3 hours 36 minutes, respectively. The rank order of the finish of these runners is 1, 2, and 3. But the time difference between the first and second finisher is 1 minute, whereas it is 16 minutes between the second- and third-place contestants.

Ordinal scales do not indicate how much of the measured variable exists; they provide information only about the order of individuals or objects on the variable measured. I cannot assume that a rank of 1 necessarily corresponds to a large amount of the variable being measured. Nor can I assume that the lowest-ranked object or person possesses little of the property being measured. A person who is asked to rank order cartoons from most to least funny may find no humor in any of them. Yet a rank of 1 assigned to a cartoon by this individual conveys the same information as a rank of 1 assigned a cartoon by another person who may regard all the cartoons as very funny. Despite their deficiencies, however, ordinal measures are a first step in the development of more precise measures, as Statistics in Use 2–2 illustrates.

STATISTICS IN USE 2–2

Measuring Autistic Behavior with an Ordinal Scale

Autism is a developmental disorder that affects a child's language development, thought processes, and responsiveness to social and physical stimulation. However, there has been little research on how children diagnosed as autistic may vary from each other. As a first step in this direction, Dihoff, Hetznecker, Brosvic, Carpenter, and Hoffman (1993) developed an ordinal measurement of the extent of autistic behavior that a child may demonstrate. In this scale, six components of behavior are measured: language ability, responsiveness to the environment, responsiveness to social stimulation, responsiveness to physical stimulation, adaptiveness to the use of materials, and cognitive functioning. Within each component, five levels of functioning were identified, the levels differing on an ordinal scale from the lowest level to the highest level of functioning. For example, the levels within the component of language development are the following:

None
Gestures
Communicative intent
Communicative intent plus words
Other-directed communication

Gestures show greater language development than no language development at all, and communicative intent plus words shows greater language development than only gestures. But I do not know how large the differences are between the categories; hence the measurement is ordinal.

Applying the scale to a group of children allows an ordering of the amount of autistic behavior displayed. As an example, assume that five autistic children were measured using this scale and the outcome of the ordering from most to least autistic behavior was as follows:

Ordering	Person
1	Gordon
2	Elizabeth
3	Marisa
4	Rivka
5	Michael

Notice that Gordon was ordered as having the most autistic behavior and Michael the least. But this ordering does not indicate whether Gordon's autistic behavior is severe or not; it indicates only that he is the most autistic among the children measured. The ordering indicates also that Gordon has more severe autistic behavior than does Elizabeth. I cannot tell, however, how much more severe Gordon's autism is compared to Elizabeth or any of the others. Furthermore, I cannot determine if the difference in autistic behavior between Gordon and Elizabeth is the same as the difference between Elizabeth and Marisa or between Rivka and Michael. I can be confident only that one child demonstrates greater autistic behavior than another; I do not know if the differences between adjacent individuals correspond to equal differences in amount of autistic behavior. Although ordinal measures possess these deficiencies, Dihoff et al. (1993) point out that the scale is useful in identifying homogeneous groups of autistic children and placing them into appropriate program levels.

TESTING YOUR KNOWLEDGE 2–2

1. Define: measurement, nominal measurement, ordinal measurement.
2. Name the four scales of measurement.
3. Identify one deficiency of nominal measurements.
4. What information is provided by a rank of 2 assigned to an individual on a ranking of motivation to achieve?
5. On a rank ordering of 13 people for depression proneness from most to least, Jennifer was ranked 1, Debbi 2, Ena 12, and Marty 13.

a. Explain why you cannot conclude that Jennifer is very prone to depression and Marty is not at all depression prone.

b. Is it appropriate to conclude that the difference in depression proneness between Jennifer and Debbi is the same as the difference in depression proneness between Ena and Marty? Explain your answer.

Interval Measurement

Interval measurement: The amount of a variable is ordered along a dimension, and the differences between the assigned numbers represent equal amounts in the magnitude of the variable measured. The zero point of an interval scale is an arbitrary starting point.

If the requirements for ordinal measurement are met, and in addition the differences between the assigned numbers represent equal amounts in the magnitude of the variable measured, then an **interval measurement** is created. An interval measurement, however, has no true zero point for which a value of zero represents the complete absence of the variable measured. A zero value on an interval measurement is an arbitrary starting point that could be replaced by any other value as a starting point.

The Fahrenheit and Celsius temperature scales are examples of interval measurements. Zero degrees does not represent an absence of temperature for either scale. Neither scale contains a true zero point because measured temperatures may fall below zero degrees. It is accurate to state that the difference in temperature between 20°C and 40°C is equivalent to the difference in temperature between 40°C and 60°C, but it is not appropriate to say that 40°C is twice as high a temperature as 20°C. We can see why this difficulty arises by comparing several equivalent Celsius and Fahrenheit temperatures, as follows:

Equivalent Temperatures	
°C	°F
20	68
40	104
60	140

Notice that a difference of 20°C is always equal to a difference of 36°F. But because each scale starts with an arbitrary zero point, adjacent scores on one scale do not form ratios equal to adjacent scores on the other scale. For example, a ratio of 40°C/20°C = 2.0, whereas a corresponding temperature ratio of 104°F/68°F = 1.5.

STATISTICS IN USE 2–3

Rating Scales Treated as Interval Measurements

Examples of measurements in the behavioral sciences that definitely achieve an interval level are infrequent. But rating scales, which frequently are used to measure attributes of people, such as personality characteristics, attitudes, marital happiness, fear of objects, motivation to achieve, or leadership ability, are often treated as yielding interval measurement. Rating scales generally present a statement and then a response scale with two extremes and several points between the extremes. For example, in attitude measurement a person may be asked to respond to a statement such as "Strong gun control laws reduce crime" by making a check mark on the scale:

| Strongly agree | Agree | Uncertain | Disagree | Strongly disagree |

Other forms of rating scales may ask you to rate a person on a set of bipolar adjectives, such as

Dishonest ____ : ____ : ____ : ____ : ____ : ____ : ____ Honest

Attractive ____ : ____ : ____ : ____ : ____ : ____ : ____ Unattractive

Cold ____ : ____ : ____ : ____ : ____ : ____ : ____ Warm

Rating scales may have any number of categories between the extremes; and the scales may be referred to as 5-point, 7-point, or 9-point scales, depending on the number of categories provided. Often the favorability of the adjectives at the end points of the scale is reversed for half the items. Thus half the favorable adjectives are at the left of the scale and half at the right. This reversal helps to avoid problems of response set, such as checking only the items on the right side of the scale.

After a person has responded on the scale, a numerical value is assigned to each category on the scale, such as

Dishonest ____ : ____ : ____ : ____ : ____ : ____ : ____ Honest
       1   2   3   4   5   6   7

Attractive ____ : ____ : ____ : ____ : ____ : ____ : ____ Unattractive
       7   6   5   4   3   2   1

Cold ____ : ____ : ____ : ____ : ____ : ____ : ____ Warm
       1   2   3   4   5   6   7

In many instances, a series of scales is presented, and the scores on the separate scales are added to yield one score for a person. These scales are called *summated rating scales*. As an illustration, Rotton and Kelly (1985) developed a scale for assessing belief in the effect of a full moon on behavior, the Belief in Lunar Effects Scale. The scale consists of nine statements. For each statement the respondent indicates agreement with the statement by choosing a number between 1 (*strong disagreement*) to 9 (*strong agreement*). For example, one statement on the scale is as follows and is reproduced with permission of authors and publisher from J. Rotton & I. W. Kelly, "A scale for assessing belief in lunar effects: reliability and concurrent validity," *Psychological Reports*, 1985, *57*, 239–245, © *Psychological Reports* 1985.

It is a good idea to stay at home when the moon is full.

1	2	3	4	5	6	7	8	9
Strongly disagree			Neither agree nor disagree				Strongly agree	

A score is obtained by summing over the nine statements to yield a total score for the rating scale. The possible range of scores is from 9 (obtained by responding with a 1 to all nine statements) to 81 (obtained by responding with a 9 to all nine statements). Notice that the range of scores that this scale can assume is arbitrary; if the anchor points for each statement ranged from 10 to 90, then the range of the summated rating scale would be 90 to 810.

What level of measurement is represented by scores on the Belief in Lunar Effects Scale and other similar rating scales? It should be clear that the rating for each statement represents at least ordinal measurement. A score of 4 indicates more of a particular characteristic described by the statement than does a 3, and a 3 reflects more than a 2; however, I cannot be certain that the difference between a 4 and 3 represents the same difference in a characteristic as that between 3 and 2. Such ratings do seem to provide more than merely ordinal information, however. I might expect that a respondent subjectively divides the categories into roughly equal intervals between the ends of the scale. Moreover, if the ratings obtained from a person on a number of separate scales are summed, then it seems reasonable to assume that the resulting score provides more than just ordinal information. Gardner (1975) argues that scores from summated scales are in a gray region between ordinal and interval. Thus a measurement may not necessarily fit neatly into one of the four measurement scales. For statistical analysis, however, researchers often treat rating scales as representing interval measurement.

Ratio Measurement

Ratio measurement: The amount of a variable is ordered along a dimension, the differences between the assigned numbers represent equal amounts in the magnitude of the variable measured, and a true zero point exists, which represents the absence of the characteristic measured.

A **ratio measurement scale** replaces the arbitrary zero point of the interval scale with a true zero starting point that corresponds to the absence of the variable being measured. With a ratio scale it is possible to state that one thing (e.g., a stimulus, an event, or an individual) has twice, or half, or three times as much of the variable measured than another. Ratio measurement is used in the behavioral sciences when measures such as reaction time or the amount of time spent on a task are measured. These measures have a true zero point, and the intervals between the units of measurement are equal. For example, if the amount of time a person spends solving a puzzle is measured, the difference between 15 seconds and 25 seconds (i.e., 10 seconds) is equal to the difference between 50 seconds and 60 seconds (again 10 seconds). Furthermore, someone who spends 60 seconds solving a puzzle spends twice as long as someone who spends only 30 seconds.

STATISTICS IN USE 2–4

Which Line Is Longer? Using Ratio Measurement

The magnitude of perceptual illusions may often be measured with a ratio scale. An illusion occurs when our perception of a stimulus does not correspond to its physical characteristics; we misperceive what actually exists. A familiar example is the Müller–Lyer illusion, illustrated in Figure 2–1. Here you perceive (or most likely perceive) line A to be longer than line B. Both lines are physically equal in length, however. Your perception is in error. The magnitude of this illusion can be measured by finding how much the perceived length of the stimulus differs from its actual length. Perceptual error measured in millimeters (mm) represents a ratio measurement. It is possible for a person to have an error of 0 mm (i.e., no error) when the perceived length of the stimulus does not differ from the actual length. The difference between an error of 5 mm and an error of 8 mm is the same as the difference between errors of 10 mm and 13 mm; in each case the difference is 3 mm. Moreover, an error of 10 mm represents an illusion magnitude that is twice as great as an error of 5 mm.

As an example of the use of such a measurement, LeTourneau (1976) hypothesized that the extent to which a person perceives an illusion depends on the person's spatial abilities and specialized training. To test this hypothesis, he compared architectural-design students with optometry students on their perception of the Müller–Lyer illusion. Presumably, architectural-design students possess greater spatial visualization skills and also have had more training using these skills than optometry students. He found, in agreement with his hypothesis, that architectural-design students typically were about 13.1 mm in error in their perception of the illusion, whereas optometry students perceived the illusion with a typical error of 24.2 mm.

FIGURE 2–1
The Müller–Lyer illusion.

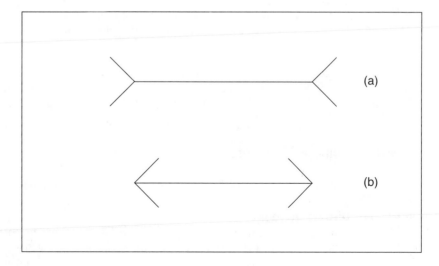

Qualitative and Quantitative Data

Qualitative data: Data obtained from nominal measurement indicating that variables differ in quality.

Nominal measurement uses numbers to name or assign people or objects to different categories; it does not provide numerical information about the variables categorized. Thus nominal measurements provide **qualitative data**; the people or objects categorized differ in some quality. Ordinal, interval, and ratio measurements provide **quantitative data**; the numbers assigned to a variable express the amount or quantity of the variable measured. Of the three quantitative measures, behavioral scientists prefer to use interval and ratio measurements, for these measures allow more precise quantification of the underlying attribute or characteristic being measured than do ordinal measurements. Furthermore, because interval and ratio measures permit the use of mathematical procedures such as addition, subtraction, multiplication, and division, they allow the application of more versatile statistical techniques. Consequently, many of the statistical techniques presented in this text are for scores measured on an interval or ratio scale.

Quantitative data: Data obtained from ordinal, interval, or ratio measurements indicating how much of a variable exists.

TESTING YOUR KNOWLEDGE 2–3

1. Define: interval measurement, qualitative data, quantitative data, ratio measurement.
2. The following scores were obtained on an interval measure of leadership ability: Rosana, 84; Eva, 78; Pierce, 71; Victoria, 65; Nancy, 42; and William, 0.
   a. Is it accurate to conclude that the difference in leadership ability between Rosana and Eva is the same as the difference between Pierce and Victoria? Explain your answer.
   b. Is it accurate to conclude that Rosana possesses twice as much leadership ability as Nancy? Explain your answer.
   c. Is it accurate to conclude that, because of his score of zero, William totally lacks leadership ability? Explain your answer.
3. Several college students participated in a study on sleep in which the amount of time (in minutes) spent in rapid-eye-movement sleep (REM sleep, the dream sleep stage) was measured using an electroencephalogram. On one night, the durations of REM sleep were Dominic, 204 minutes; Greta, 194 minutes; Andre, 175 minutes; Jody, 165 minutes; and Carmen, 102 minutes.
   a. Is it appropriate to conclude that the difference in the amount of REM sleep between Dominic and Greta is the same as the difference between Andre and Jody? Explain your answer.
   b. Is it appropriate to conclude that Dominic spent twice as much time in REM sleep as Carmen? Explain your answer.
   c. Suppose another student, Mandie, spent zero minutes in REM sleep. Is it appropriate to conclude that she had no REM sleep that night? Explain your answer.

Discrete and Continuous Variables

Variables may also be characterized as discrete or continuous.

Discrete variable: A variable that can take on only a finite or potentially countable set of values.

Discrete Variables

A **discrete variable** is one that can take on only a finite or potentially countable set of values. The word *finite* means a definite set of possible values. The number of students at your college is a discrete variable: there may be 5652 students or 5653 students, but not $5652\frac{1}{2}$ students. The number of students may increase or decrease by one whole student, not one-half or one-third student. Thus the number of students takes on a definite countable set of values. Typically, variables whose possible values can be counted are discrete variables: the number of people living in a city, the number of children in a family, the number of burglaries in a year, the number of automobiles registered in a state, and so forth.

Continuous Variables

Continuous variable: A variable that can take on an infinite set of values between any two levels of the variable.

A **continuous variable** is one that can take on an infinite set of values between any two levels of the variable. A continuous variable thus has an unlimited set of values in the range within which it varies. A measurement of your weight is an example, for you may weigh 135.6 pounds or 135.64 pounds. Your weight is not limited to discrete values such as 135 pounds or 136 pounds. Notice that I am referring to the underlying variable that is being measured when I identify discrete and continuous variables. It is possible that you may have a scale that indicates your weight only in whole pounds, such as 135 or 136 pounds. Yet your weight is not limited to these specific values. It may take on any value between 135 and 136 pounds. Similarly, many psychological variables, such as anxiety or intelligence, exist as continuous variables, although they may be measured by scales that assign discrete scores to a person.

Real Limits of a Measurement.   When measurements are made of a continuous variable, specific numerical values are assigned to the amount of the variable present. But the assigned measures only approximate the actual amount of the variable. Consequently, we must be aware of the accuracy of our measurements, regardless of the scale of measurement that we are using. And the accuracy of measurement of a continuous variable is contained in the real limits of the number assigned.

Real limits of a number: The points midway between the number and the next lower and the next higher numbers on the scale used to make the measurements.

Real limits of a measurement are easily understood using measurements of the variable of time. Suppose that you are measuring the amount of time that a person can hold his or her hand in a tub of 40°F water. This task is often used to induce pain safely in experiments dealing with relaxation strategies to increase pain tolerance. Suppose for one subject that you measured a time of 37 seconds by observing the second hand on a stopwatch. How accurate is this measurement? Because you measured to the nearest whole second, the time could not have been 36 or 38 seconds. But might the actual duration have been 37.2 seconds or 36.7 seconds? The answer is yes; for you may have rounded either 36.7 seconds or 37.2 seconds to 37 seconds. The accuracy of this measurement of 37 seconds is given by the real limits of this number. The **real limits of a number** are the points that are midway between the number and the next lower and the next higher numbers on the scale used to make the measurements. For a measured value of 37 seconds, then, the *real lower limit* is 36.5 seconds and the *real upper limit* is 37.5 seconds. The real lower limit of 36.5 seconds is midway between 36 seconds, the next lower measured value on the scale used, and 37 seconds. The real upper limit of 37.5 seconds is midway between 37 seconds and 38 seconds, the next higher measured value on the scale used.

Suppose now that you had measured the duration with an electronic stopwatch that provided measurements to the nearest $\frac{1}{100}$ second, such as 37.21 seconds. What are the real upper and lower limits of this measurement? Again, the rule is to find the midpoint between the next lower and the next higher value on the measuring scale used. Thus the real lower limit is the midpoint between 37.20 (the next lower number) and 37.21 seconds, or 37.205 seconds. The real upper limit is the midpoint between 37.21 seconds and 37.22 seconds (the next upper value), or 37.215 seconds.

Every numerical measurement of a continuous variable has real upper and lower limits associated with it. For example, suppose that I am using the 7-point rating scale illustrated in Figure 2–2. Assume that a person checked a response of 3 on this scale. Following the rules presented earlier, the real lower and upper limits for this score are 2.5 and 3.5, respectively.

The real limits of a measurement are important when plotting frequency distributions of scores and when rounding values in statistical computations. I discuss frequency distributions in Chapter 3.

Rounding: Answers to Computations.   Suppose that you asked three friends to complete the scale shown in Figure 2–2 and obtained the following responses: 4, 4, and 3. To describe the typical response, you found the sum of these numbers, 11, and divided it by 3, or $\frac{11}{3} = 3.666\overline{6}$. The bar ($^-$) over the last 6 indicates that the 6s continue endlessly. How many decimal places should you present in your answer?

One convention is that the final value of a computation should be rounded to two decimal places beyond the value to which the original scores were measured. In the example, the scores were given to the ones (or units) place; a person could check 3 or 4, but not 3.2 or 4.6. Following this rule, the final value of the computation is rounded to two decimal places beyond the ones place, or to 3.67.

Others follow a convention of rounding the final value of a computation to one decimal place beyond the value to which the original scores were measured. Following

FIGURE 2–2
Real upper and lower limits for a response (indicated by the $\sqrt{}$) on a 7-point rating scale.

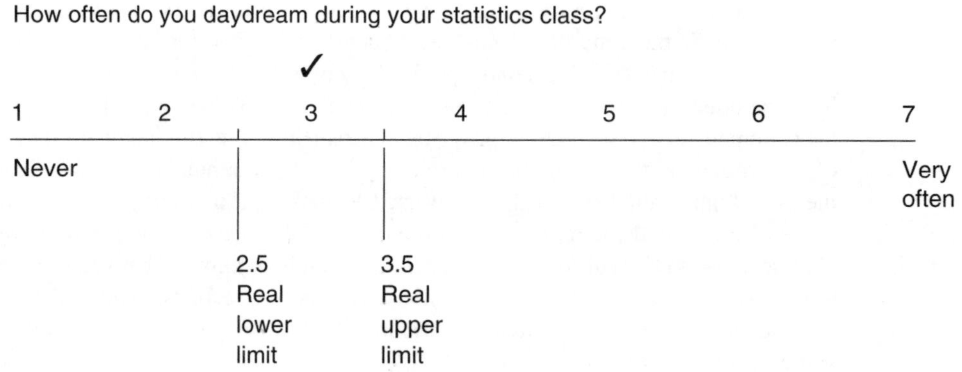

How often do you daydream during your statistics class?

1	2	3	4	5	6	7

Never

Very often

2.5
Real
lower
limit

3.5
Real
upper
limit

this approach, the final value of the computation for the example is rounded to one decimal place beyond the ones place, or to 3.7. I illustrate both approaches in text examples.

Rounding: Intermediate Steps in Computations. If computations require a number of steps prior to obtaining the final answer, then intermediate numerical values should be carried to at least two decimal places beyond the number of decimal places needed for the final answer. For example, if the value of $\frac{11}{3}$ were to enter into further computations, I would not round its value to 3.67. Rather, I carry it to two additional places, 3.6667, for the additional computations. This approach minimizes rounding error in computations.

Rounding Rules. Suppose that I have an answer to a computation such as $3.6AB$, where the A and B are possible numerical values. For example, if $A = 2$ and $B = 9$, then $3.6AB = 3.629$. I wish to round this number to two decimal places. Several rules typically are followed when rounding numbers:

- If the number represented by the letter B is greater than 5, increase A by 1 and drop the B value. Following this rule, 3.629 (here $A = 2$ and $B = 9$) is rounded to 3.63.
- If the number represented by the letter B is less than 5, leave the A value as is and drop the B value. Following this rule, 3.623 (here $A = 2$ and $B = 3$) is rounded to 3.62.
- If the number represented by the letter B is exactly 5, increase A by 1 if A is an odd number, but leave its value as is if it is an even number; then drop B. Following this rule, 3.635 (here $A = 3$ and $B = 5$) is rounded to 3.64, but 3.625 (here $A = 2$ and $B = 5$) is rounded to 3.62. Notice, however, that if the number is 3.6251 it is rounded to 3.63, not 3.62.

TESTING YOUR KNOWLEDGE 2–4

1. Define: continuous variable, discrete variable, real limits of a number, real lower limit, real upper limit.
2. Identify each of the following variables being measured as discrete or continuous.
   a. A person's handgrip strength measured in pounds.
   b. The eye contact of an accuser with a defendant in a courtroom measured in seconds.
   c. The number of stotts (leaping vertically with four legs off the ground simultaneously) made by a Thompson's gazelle in a 1-hour period.
   d. The length of song (in seconds) by a male songbird during courtship.
   e. The funniness of a set of cartoons measured by the amount of time (in seconds) subjects laugh at them.
   f. The number of altruistic behaviors observed in nursery school children in a one-day period.
   g. The number of friends a child has.
   h. The number of items correct on a statistics examination.

3. Provide the real lower and real upper limits for each of the scores presented.
   a. A height of 152.4 centimeters.
   b. A duration of eye contact of 17.3 seconds.
   c. An assigned rating of 4 on a 7-point scale.
   d. A reaction time of 0.437 second.
   e. An error of 6.9 millimeters on the Müller–Lyer illusion.
   f. A handgrip strength of 67.81 pounds.
4. Round the following values to the number of decimal places indicated.
   a. 27.436 (two decimal places)
   b. 119.0278 (three decimal places)
   c. 1.445 (two decimal places)
   d. 1263.75915 (four decimal places)
   e. 0.352 (two decimal places)
   f. 13.2659 (two decimal places)

SUMMARY

- Statistics are tools used in the scientific study of behavior.
- Scientific research begins by asking a question that can be answered by obtaining empirical data.
- A research method is an approach used to collect data. Four types of research methods are naturalistic observation, archival records, survey research, and experiments.
- Naturalistic observation is research involving the observation of behaviors occurring in natural settings.
- Archival records research uses existing records.
- Survey research involves obtaining data from either oral or written interviews with people.
- An experiment is a carefully controlled situation in which a scientist manipulates one or more independent variables to observe their effect on the dependent variable.
- An operational definition identifies the operations or steps followed to make an observation or to manipulate a variable.
- Measurement is a process of assigning numbers to variables according to a set of rules.
- Nominal measurement is a classification of the measured variable into different categories. Nominal measurement provides qualitative data.
- Ordinal measurement scales place a variable in an ordered set along a dimension.
- Interval scales create equal increments in the magnitude of the variable measured, but they do not have a true zero.
- Ratio scales possess the properties of the interval scale plus a true zero point.
- Ordinal, interval, and ratio measurements provide quantitative data.

- A discrete variable can take on only a finite or potentially countable set of values.
- A continuous variable can take on an infinite set of values between any two levels of the variable.
- The real limits of a number are the points that are midway between the number and the next lower and the next higher numbers on the scale used to make the measurements.

KEY TERMS AND SYMBOLS

archival records
continuous variable
discrete variable
empirical data
experiment
interval measurement
measurement

naturalistic observation
nominal measurement
operational definition
ordinal measurement
qualitative data
quantitative data
ratio measurement

real limits of a number
real lower limit of a number
real upper limit of a number
research design
research hypothesis
survey research
variable

REVIEW QUESTIONS

1. Suppose that you were asked to collect data to answer each of the following questions. For each question, indicate what type of research design you would choose and why.
   a. What is the typical amount of time spent on homework by the members of your statistics class?
   b. How often does a basketball player make a free shot when a time-out is called immediately before the shot is made?
   c. Does a sales training program increase the amount of sales by people who have completed the program?
   d. What are the common behaviors of a young child in the check-out line of a supermarket?
2. Suppose that you were asked to measure job stress in a group of employees. How would you operationally define your measure of job stress?
3. The career orientation of police officers was measured by having police officers order four paragraphs describing various career orientations from 1, the paragraph closest to the individual's career orientation, to 4, the paragraph furthest from the individual's career orientation.
   a. What is the underlying variable being measured in this study?
   b. What level of measurement is achieved by the measure used?

4. Professional female golfers were weighed to determine if body weight was related to their game.
   a. What is the underlying variable being measured in this study?
   b. What level of measurement is achieved by the measure used?
   c. The weight of one golfer was reported as 134.6 pounds. What are the real upper and lower limits of this measurement?
   d. Six golfers were weighed to the nearest pound. Their average weight was 127.648 pounds. Round this value.

5. Parents of first-grade children were measured on a personality trait of emotional stability using a rating scale.
   a. What is the underlying variable being measured in this study?
   b. What level of measurement is achieved by the measure used?
   c. Suppose that a person assigned a rating of 8 on a 9-point rating scale for agreement or disagreement with a statement. What are the real lower and upper limits of this measurement?
   d. Suppose that you measured six people on this statement and found their typical rating to be 5.833. Is this result correctly reported with respect to the number of decimal places given? Explain your answer.

6. You are investigating how much time students spend doing homework each day. One student reported she spent 97 minutes working on chemistry.
   a. What level of measurement is achieved by the measure used?
   b. What are the real lower and upper limits of the 97 minutes the student reported spending on homework?
   c. Three students reported spending 97, 68, and 83 minutes on homework, respectively. The average of these three scores is 82.66666. Round this value.

7. Interpersonal values of an individual were measured by having the person order 12 value statements from most to least important. What level of measurement is achieved by the measure used?

8. The behavioral interactions of children at a nursery school with other children at the school were categorized as agonistic (i.e., argumentative or fighting), neutral (i.e., not interacting), or altruistic (i.e., helpful). What level of measurement is achieved by the measure used?

9. Identify each of the following measured variables as discrete or continuous.
   a. The number of students in your statistics class.
   b. The weight loss in pounds by people who have completed a diet and exercise workshop.
   c. The number of left-handed people in a group of 100.
   d. A person's blood pressure measured in millimeters of mercury.

10. Provide the real lower and real upper limits for each of the scores presented.
    a. A weight of 141.3 pounds.
    b. A duration of 34 minutes playing a video game.
    c. A golf drive of 175.6 yards.
    d. A body temperature of 98.2°F.
    e. A systolic blood pressure of 109 millimeters of mercury.

11. Round the following values to two decimal places.
    a. 42.255   e. 13.895
    b. 1.165   f. 24.6250
    c. 163.651   g. 19.2751
    d. 27.426

12. A restaurant leaves cards for its patrons to complete after finishing a meal. Each card asks patrons to rate the restaurant on the quality of food, friendliness of service, speed of service, and cleanliness on 5-point scales ranging from poor to excellent. An overall score from 4 to 20 is obtained from each card. What level of measurement is used here? Explain your answer.

13. A psychologist studied how well people could tolerate pain by placing their hand in a bucket of 40°F water and measuring how long they could keep their hand in the water. She performed two studies.
    a. In study 1, subjects were ranked on the duration that they could hold their hand in the water as follows: Lisa, 1; Stacia, 2; Maritza, 3; Robin, 4; and Jody, 5. What level of measurement is used here?
    b. In study 2, the duration of tolerance was measured in seconds with the following results: Lisa, 111.3 seconds; Stacia, 97.8 seconds; Maritza, 71.3 seconds; Robin, 18.7 seconds; and Jody, 13.6 seconds. What level of measurement is used here?

14. A recent survey of car owners on problems in the first 90 days with their new cars indicated that the first three cars in rank with the fewest problems were Lexus, Toyota, and Infiniti, respectively.
    a. If you buy a new Lexus, can you be sure you will have no problems in the first 90 days? Explain your answer.
    b. If you buy a new Lexus, how many problems can you expect in the first 90 days?
    c. Toyota was ranked between Lexus and Infiniti. Can you conclude that if you buy a Toyota you will have many more problems than if you buy a Lexus, but many fewer than if you buy an Infiniti? Explain your answer.
    d. In this summary, Oldsmobile was ranked 13th. What does this ranking tell you about the number of problems you may encounter if you buy an Oldsmobile?

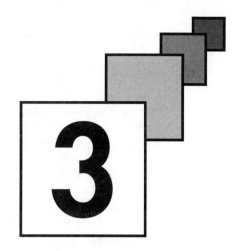

3

Describing Data: Frequency Distributions and Graphs

Have you ever thought, "If only I could get my anxiety under control I could do much better on examinations"? If so, you are not alone. In recent years, counselors and psychologists have identified test anxiety as a contributor to poor performance for many students. To measure test anxiety, Spielberger (1980) developed the *Test Anxiety Inventory* (TAI). The TAI is composed of 20 statements similar to "I become very uneasy and upset before a big examination." For each statement, the student completing the inventory chooses one of the alternatives, *almost never, sometimes, often, almost always*, that best applies to him or her. After the inventory is completed, a numerical value is assigned to each alternative: *almost never* = 1; *sometimes* = 2; *often* = 3; *almost always* = 4. A score is obtained by adding the numerical values of the alternatives selected. This inventory is thus a summated rating scale (see Statistics in Use 2–3) with a score ranging from 20 to 80. A score of 20 indicates the minimum level of anxiety possible on the TAI and a score of 80 the maximum level. As observed in Chapter 2, summated rating scales probably are in a gray area of measurement. Yet, for statistical purposes, scores from rating scales are often treated as representing interval measurements. I follow this custom with this example.

N: The total number of scores in a set of scores.

Suppose a college counselor administers the Test Anxiety Inventory to a sample of 20 students seeking assistance in controlling test anxiety. The scores obtained are portrayed in Table 3–1. Such scores are called **raw data** or **raw scores**, for they are exactly as collected and have not been subjected to statistical analysis. The letter N is used to indicate the total number of scores obtained; thus N for this example is 20.

Behavioral scientists often collect a large number of scores, such as the TAI scores, in their research. The first step in analyzing these scores and drawing information from them is to arrange the data as a frequency distribution. I first discuss the presentation of quantitative data from interval or ratio measurements.

FREQUENCY DISTRIBUTIONS WITH UNGROUPED SCORES

Simple Frequency Distributions

Frequency distribution: A table showing each score in a set of scores and how frequently each score occurred.

A **frequency distribution** is a table showing each score and its frequency of occurrence. Table 3–2 illustrates an ungrouped frequency distribution for the Test Anxiety Inventory

TABLE 3–1
Hypothetical Test Anxiety Inventory scores from 20 students.

61	57
67	55
63	59
60	59
62	59
67	64
59	65
60	62
68	59
64	60

TABLE 3–2

Ungrouped frequency distribution for Test Anxiety Inventory scores of Table 3–1.

(a) Score	(b) Tally	(c) Frequency (f)	(d) Relative Frequency (rf)	(e) Percentage Frequency ($\%f$)
68	/	1	.05	5
67	//	2	.10	10
66		0	.00	0
65	/	1	.05	5
64	//	2	.10	10
63	/	1	.05	5
62	//	2	.10	10
61	/	1	.05	5
60	///	3	.15	15
59	/////	5	.25	25
58		0	.00	0
57	/	1	.05	5
56		0	.00	0
55	/	1	.05	5

Ungrouped frequency distribution: A frequency distribution constructed by listing all possible score values between the lowest and highest scores obtained and then placing a tally mark (/) beside a score each time it occurs.

f: The simple frequency of occurrence of each score in a frequency distribution.

scores presented in Table 3–1. This **ungrouped frequency distribution** was constructed by listing all possible score values between the lowest and highest scores obtained (column a of Table 3–2) and then placing a tally mark (/) beside a score each time it occurred (shown in column b of Table 3–2). Notice that all possible scores in the range from the lowest to the highest score obtained are included in column a, even if the score did not occur. Scores that do not occur in the set of scores obtained are not given a tally mark. The number of tally marks for each score was counted and entered into column c as the **simple frequency of occurrence of each score** (symbolized by f).

Relative Frequency Distributions

Relative frequency (rf): The frequency of a score divided by the total number of scores obtained.

The frequency of occurrence of scores in an ungrouped frequency distribution may also be presented as relative frequencies. A **relative frequency distribution** is obtained by dividing the frequency of each score by the total number of scores in the distribution. Thus a **relative frequency** (symbolized by rf) is expressed as

$$rf \text{ of a score} = f \text{ of a score}/N.$$

As an example, the relative frequency of occurrence of the score of 59 in Table 3–2 is found by dividing its frequency (i.e., $f = 5$) by the total number of scores ($N = 20$), which equals .25.[1] The relative frequency of the TAI scores is presented in column d of Table 3–2.

Percentage Frequency Distributions

Percentage frequency (%f): The relative frequency of a score multiplied by 100.

A **percentage frequency distribution** expresses the frequency of occurrence of a score as a percentage of the total number of scores obtained. The **percentage frequency of a score** (symbolized by *%f*) is found by multiplying the relative frequency of a score by 100, or

$$\textit{%f} \textbf{ of a score} = (\textit{rf} \textbf{ of score}) \times 100.$$

The percentage frequency of scores is presented in column e of Table 3–2. Notice that columns c, d, and e of this table present equivalent information about the distribution of scores in Table 3–1. The advantage of having frequencies presented as relative or percentage frequencies is that these values are independent of the total number of scores obtained. Thus, if you had a second sample of 35 scores ($N = 35$) from another group of students, it would be easier to compare the frequency distributions from the two different size samples if the frequency distributions were expressed as either relative or percentage frequencies, rather than as simple frequencies alone.

Obtaining Information from a Frequency Distribution

The simple frequencies, relative frequencies, or percentage frequencies presented in Table 3–2 produce several impressions of the Test Anxiety Inventory scores that are not readily apparent from the unorganized raw data of Table 3–1. For example, from each distribution you can notice the following:

- The lowest score is 55.
- The highest score is 68.
- The most frequently occurring score is 59.
- Fifteen of the scores are between 59 and 65.

Obviously, organizing raw data in a frequency distribution makes it easier to see important characteristics of these data.

[1]When presenting decimal fractions in this text, I will follow the guidelines of the *Publication Manual of the American Psychological Association* (1994), which indicate that if a decimal fraction cannot be greater than 1, a zero is not used before the decimal point. Thus relative frequencies are reported without a zero before the decimal point.

Example Problem 3-1

Constructing Ungrouped Frequency Distributions

Problem

Psychologists are interested in the perception of ambiguous figures, for they believe that understanding how we perceive these figures will provide knowledge about perception of the everyday world. The Mach pyramid shown in Figure 3–1 is an example of an ambiguous figure, for it is reversible in perspective. You may see this figure either as a pyramid with the small square appearing to project out of the page toward you or as a room in perspective with the small square being the far wall. Suppose you timed 25 subjects over a 1-minute period to see how long each subject could see the figure as a pyramid and found the following times (to the nearest whole second):

2, 7, 10, 5, 5, 3, 9, 11, 5, 8, 2, 4, 7, 6, 10, 7, 3,

9, 7, 11, 4, 6, 3, 1, and 8.

Construct an ungrouped simple frequency distribution, relative frequency distribution, and percentage frequency distribution for these scores. What conclusions about the scores may you reach from these distributions?

FIGURE 3–1
The Mach pyramid.

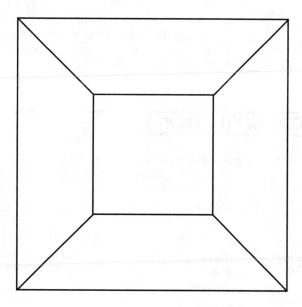

Solution   The requested frequency distributions are shown in the following table:

Score	Tally	f	rf	$\%f$
11	//	2	.08	8
10	//	2	.08	8
9	//	2	.08	8
8	//	2	.08	8
7	////	4	.16	16
6	//	2	.08	8
5	///	3	.12	12
4	//	2	.08	8
3	///	3	.12	12
2	//	2	.08	8
1	/	1	.04	4

Conclusions   The scores range from 1 to 11 seconds and the most frequently occurring score is 7 seconds. With the exception of the most frequently occurring score of 7, the scores occur about equally throughout their range.

TESTING YOUR KNOWLEDGE 3–1

1. Define: frequency distribution, percentage frequency distribution, $\%f$, raw data, raw scores, relative frequency distribution, rf, ungrouped frequency distribution.
2. Good and Good (1973) developed a scale to measure fear of success. Individuals high in the fear of success are thought to avoid being too successful in their endeavors for fear of antagonizing others. Scores on the fear of success scale may range from 0, indicating no measured fear of success, to 29, indicating the greatest fear of success measurable on this scale. Suppose you administered the scale to 20 people and obtained the following scores: 6, 13, 4, 19, 3, 12, 9, 8, 5, 11, 6, 8, 15, 5, 8, 10, 9, 14, 4, and 8.
    a. Construct an ungrouped simple frequency distribution, relative frequency distribution, and percentage frequency distribution for these scores.
    b. What are the lowest and highest scores obtained?
    c. What is the most frequently occurring score?

GROUPED FREQUENCY DISTRIBUTIONS

Grouped frequency distribution: A frequency distribution in which scores are grouped together in class intervals and the frequency of scores occurring within each class is tabulated.

If a large number of scores is collected or if there is a wide range of score values in the data, an ungrouped frequency distribution as illustrated in Table 3–2 can become spread out, making it difficult to see clear patterns in the data. It is useful, then, to construct a **grouped frequency distribution** in which scores are grouped together in class intervals. The class intervals are arranged from highest to lowest, and the frequency of scores occurring within each class is tallied and tabulated. To illustrate grouped frequency distributions, suppose the counselor decided to measure test anxiety in a sample of 100 students who had not sought assistance for the control of this anxiety. The scores she obtained are presented in Table 3–3.

TABLE 3–3
Hypothetical Test Anxiety Inventory scores
from 100 students.

42	44	41	36	39	50
28	38	44	34	40	46
37	41	22	48	39	37
45	41	32	43	36	60
58	38	35	46	25	60
41	37	41	43	31	47
39	50	38	42	40	36
52	40	47	28	39	73
40	31	52	41	38	43
34	50	48	38	45	46
25	41	55	41	70	37
43	46	41	65	36	46
49	37	28	42	44	34
45	40	36	46	39	29
48	38	41	34	42	40
42	26	44	38	44	37
44	41	55	40		

Constructing Grouped Frequency Distributions

Class interval: The width of the interval used to group raw scores in a grouped frequency distribution. The size or width of the interval is represented by *i*.

A grouped frequency distribution places raw scores into class intervals. A **class interval** is a range of score values into which the raw scores are grouped. Table 3–4 presents several grouped frequency distributions of the scores in Table 3–3 using a class interval of size 5. Constructing grouped frequency distributions, such as Table 3–4, requires two decisions: (1) the number of class intervals to be used and (2) the size (or width) of the class interval.

Number of Class Intervals

The number of class intervals to be used is determined by the range of the scores, with 10 to 20 class intervals ordinarily used. The number of intervals usually is chosen so that the size of the class interval is 1, 2, 3, 5, or a multiple of 5. The range of scores in Table 3–3 is from 22 (the lowest score) to 73 (the highest score), or 51. With this range of scores, 10 intervals appear sufficient to group the data.

Size of Class Intervals

After the number of intervals is determined, the size or width of the interval is found by dividing the difference between the largest and smallest score by the number of class intervals to be used. Hence the **size of the class interval**, represented by *i*, is found by

$$i = \frac{X_{\text{highest}} - X_{\text{lowest}}}{\text{number of intervals}}.$$

TABLE 3–4
Grouped frequency distributions for the Test Anxiety Inventory scores of Table 3–3.

(a)	(b) Real Limits		(c)	(d)	(e)	(f)	(g)	(h)	(i)	(j)
Class Interval	Lower	Upper	Midpoint of Class	Tally	f	rf	%of	cf	crf	c%of
70–74	69.5	74.5	72	//	2	.02	2	100	1.00	100
65–69	64.5	69.5	67	/	1	.01	1	98	.98	98
60–64	59.5	64.5	62	//	2	.02	2	97	.97	97
55–59	54.5	59.5	57	///	3	.03	3	95	.95	95
50–54	49.5	54.5	52	/////	5	.05	5	92	.92	92
45–49	44.5	49.5	47	///////////////	15	.15	15	87	.87	87
40–44	39.5	44.5	42	/////////////////////////////////	33	.33	33	72	.72	72
35–39	34.5	39.5	37	////////////////////////	24	.24	24	39	.39	39
30–34	29.5	34.5	32	///////	7	.07	7	15	.15	15
25–29	24.5	29.5	27	///////	7	.07	7	8	.08	8
20–24	19.5	24.5	22	/	1	.01	1	1	.01	1

Here $X_{highest}$ indicates the highest score and X_{lowest} the lowest score in the distribution. Using the raw data of Table 3–3, with $X_{highest} = 73$ and $X_{lowest} = 22$, and 10 class intervals, the size of the class interval equals

$$i = \frac{73 - 22}{10} = \frac{51}{10} = 5.10.$$

If this formula leads to a decimal value, such as 5.10, we round to the nearest recommended class size (i.e., 1, 2, 3, 5, or a multiple of 5). For the example, I round i to 5. Should scores be decimals less than 1.0, then I do not round the interval to a whole number. Rather, a decimal interval such as 0.3, 0.5, 0.03, or 0.05 is used.

Constructing the Class Intervals

Two guidelines are used to construct class intervals:

- The lowest interval must contain the lowest score.
- The lower limit of the first interval, that is, the lowest possible score value in the first interval, should be evenly divisible by the size of the class interval.

For the scores of Table 3–3, the lowest score is 22. Accordingly, the lowest class interval in column a of Table 3–4 begins with a lower limit of 20, because 20 is the first score less than 22 that is evenly divisible by the class interval of 5.0. The first class interval is then from 20 to 24. Notice that it is possible for five score values to fall into this interval: 20, 21, 22, 23, and 24; thus its size or width is 5. The next class interval is

25 to 29. Additional class intervals are calculated up to the point needed to include the highest score, in the example, a class interval of 70 to 74.

Stated limits of a class interval: The highest and lowest scores that could fall into that class interval.

Stated Limits of a Class Interval.   Each interval in column a of Table 3–4 has upper and lower stated limits (also called *nominal limits* or *score limits*). The **upper and lower stated limits of a class interval** are the highest and lowest scores that could fall into that class interval. For example, for the class interval of 40 to 44, the lower stated limit is 40 and the upper stated limit is 44. A numerical score of 40 is the lowest score that may be placed in the interval, and a score of 44 is the highest that may be placed in the interval. Figure 3–2 illustrates the lower and upper stated limits for the class interval of 40 to 44.

Real limit of a class interval: The point midway between the stated limit of a class interval and the stated limit of the next lower or upper class interval.

Real Limits of a Class Interval.   The real limits of a number were defined in Chapter 2 as the points that are midway between the number and the next lower and higher numbers on the scale used to make the measurements. Real limits exist for the intervals of a grouped frequency distribution also, and these real limits are found similarly to the real limits of a number. The **lower real limit of a class interval** is the point midway between the lower stated limit of the class interval and the upper stated limit of the next lower

FIGURE 3–2
Illustration of lower and upper stated limits, lower and upper real limits, and the midpoint of a class interval of a grouped frequency distribution.

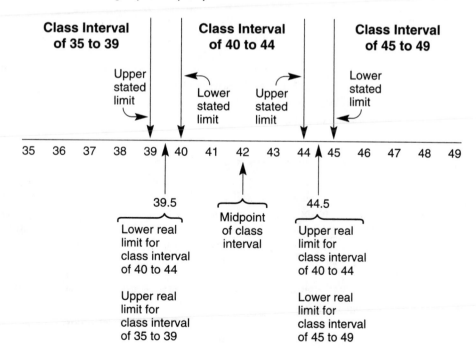

class interval. For example, I find the lower real limit of the class interval of 40 to 44 in Table 3–4. The lower stated limit of this interval is 40. The upper stated limit of the next lower class interval (i.e., the interval of 35 to 39) is 39. Accordingly, the real lower limit of the class interval of 40 to 44 is the midpoint between 39 and 40, or 39.5. This lower real limit is also illustrated in Figure 3–2.

Similarly, the **upper real limit of a class interval** is the point midway between the upper stated limit of that class interval and the lower stated limit of the next higher class interval. The upper real limit of the class interval of 40 to 44 is found by obtaining the midpoint of the upper stated limit of the interval of 40 to 44 (i.e., 44) and the lower stated limit of the next higher class interval, the interval of 45 to 49. The lower stated limit of this interval is 45; thus the upper real limit of the class interval of 40 to 44 is the midpoint of 44 and 45, or 44.5. This upper real limit is also shown in Figure 3–2. Notice that the upper real limit for the class interval of 40 to 44 is also the lower real limit for the next class interval of 45 to 49. The upper and lower real limits of the class intervals are presented in column b of Table 3–4.

Midpoint of a class interval: The point midway between the real limits of the class interval.

Midpoints of Class Intervals.   Each class interval also has a midpoint. The **midpoint of a class interval** is the point midway between the real limits of the class interval. The midpoint of the class interval 40 to 44 is 42, because 42 is the midpoint between 39.5 and 44.5. Midpoints of a class interval can be found by adding the values of the real limits of a class interval and dividing the sum by 2. For the class interval of 40 to 44, the midpoint is found by

$$\frac{39.5 + 44.5}{2} = \frac{84}{2} = 42.$$

The midpoints of each class interval are shown in column c of Table 3–4. Although I included both the real upper and lower limits and the midpoint of the class interval in Table 3–4, grouped frequency distributions often are presented with only the class intervals of column a.

Grouped Simple Frequency Distribution

A grouped simple frequency distribution is obtained by tallying scores into the class interval in which they fall (see column d of Table 3–4). For example, a score of 35 is tallied into the class interval of 35 to 39, and a score of 52 is tallied into the class interval of 50 to 54. The tallies in an interval are then summed to obtain the simple frequency (f) for that interval (given in column e of Table 3–4).

Grouped Relative Frequency and Percentage Frequency Distributions

Relative frequency distributions and percentage frequency distributions may also be obtained for grouped frequency distributions. The procedures are similar to those used for an ungrouped frequency distribution.

Grouped relative frequency distribution: A grouped frequency distribution in which the frequency of scores in an interval is divided by the total number of scores in the distribution.

Grouped Relative Frequency Distribution. A **grouped relative frequency distribution** is found by dividing the frequency of scores in an interval by the total number of scores in the distribution. Thus

$$rf \text{ of scores in an interval} = \frac{f \text{ of scores in interval}}{N}.$$

A grouped relative frequency distribution for the test anxiety scores is presented in column f of Table 3–4.

Grouped percentage frequency distribution: A grouped frequency distribution obtained by multiplying the relative frequency values by 100 to obtain percentages.

Grouped Percentage Frequency Distribution. A **grouped percentage frequency distribution** is obtained by

$$\%f \text{ of scores in an interval} = \frac{f \text{ of scores in interval}}{N} \times 100.$$

The grouped percentage frequency distribution of the Test Anxiety Inventory scores is presented in column g of Table 3–4.

Cumulative Frequency Distributions

Cumulative frequency of a score: The frequency of occurrence of that score plus the sum of the frequencies of all the scores of lower value.

Cumulative Grouped Simple Frequency Distribution. Each form of frequency distribution discussed—a simple frequency, relative frequency, and percentage frequency—may also be presented as a cumulative frequency distribution. The **cumulative frequency of a score** (symbolized as *cf* or *cum f*) is the frequency of occurrence of that score plus the sum of the frequencies of all the scores of lower value. In a grouped distribution, the **cumulative frequency of a class interval** is the frequency of occurrence of scores in that interval plus the sum of the frequencies of scores of lower class intervals. For example, the cumulative frequency of the class interval of 30 to 34 in Table 3–4 is 15, because a total of 15 scores occur in the intervals 20 to 24 (1 score), 25 to 29 (7 scores), and 30 to 34 (7 scores). The simple cumulative frequency of each class interval is shown in column h of Table 3–4.

Cumulative frequency of a class interval: The frequency of occurrence of scores in that interval plus the sum of the frequencies of scores of lower class intervals.

Cumulative grouped relative frequency of a class interval: The relative frequency of the scores in that interval plus the sum of the relative frequencies of class intervals of lower value.

Cumulative grouped percentage frequency of a class interval: The percentage frequency of the scores in that interval plus the sum of the percentage frequencies of all the class intervals of lower value.

Cumulative Grouped Relative and Percentage Frequency Distributions. Relative frequencies and percentage frequencies may be presented as cumulative frequencies also. The **cumulative grouped relative frequency of a class interval** (symbolized as *crf* or *cum rf*) is the relative frequency of the scores in that interval plus the sum of the relative frequencies of scores of lower class intervals.

Similarly, the **cumulative grouped percentage frequency of a class interval** (symbolized as *c%f* or *cum %f*) is the percentage frequency of the scores in that interval plus the sum of the percentage frequencies of scores of all lower class intervals. The cumulative grouped relative frequencies and percentage frequencies for each class interval of Table 3–4 are presented in columns i and j, respectively.

Obtaining Information from a Grouped Frequency Distribution

The several grouped frequency distributions in Table 3–4 indicate that the majority of scores are between 30 to 54. Furthermore, the distributions indicate that about one-third (33 out of 100) of the anxiety scores are in the interval from 40 to 44. However, the exact numerical value of scores is lost in Table 3–4. I cannot determine the exact lowest or highest scores or the most frequently occurring score. But this loss of information is often offset by the greater ease with which we can perceive the general shape of the distribution.

PERCENTILES AND PERCENTILE RANKS

Percentile: The score at or below which a specified percentage of scores in a distribution falls.

Percentile rank of a score: The percentage of scores in a distribution that are equal to or less than that score.

Cumulative frequency distributions are frequently used to find percentiles and percentile ranks. A **percentile** is the score at or below which a specified percentage of scores in a distribution fall. For example, if the 35th percentile on an examination is 70, 35 percent of the scores on the examination are equal to or less than 70. The **percentile rank of a score** indicates the percentage of scores in the distribution that are equal to or less than that score. Thus, in the example, the percentile rank of a test score of 70 is 35. Thirty-five percent of the scores are equal to or less than 70.

The benefit of providing a percentile or the percentile rank for a score is that it provides information about the location of the score with respect to the other scores in the distribution. Suppose that you were one of the 100 students who took the TAI and your score was 41. Simply knowing your score does not give you any information about your test anxiety level. Is 41 high or low compared to other students? But if you were told that 41 was the 49th percentile, or the percentile rank for a score of 41 was 49, then you would know that 49 percent of the scores were equal to or less than 41.

Finding the Percentile Rank of a Score

Suppose I want to find the percentile rank of a score of 41 in the distribution portrayed in Table 3–4. This score falls into the class interval of 40 to 44. The cumulative percentage frequency of scores up to the lower real limit of this interval is 39 (from column j, the $c\%f$), and the cumulative percentage frequency of scores to the upper real limit of this interval is 72 (from column j). Thus the percentile rank of 41 will be between 39 and 72. To find the exact percentile rank, I must interpolate the value of 41 in the interval of 40 to 44. The following formula provides this interpolation and calculates the percentile rank of a score:

$$P_X = \frac{cf_L + [(X - X_L) / i] f_i}{N} \times 100,$$

where P_X = percentile rank of a score of X.

cf_L = cumulative frequency of scores up to the lower real limit of the interval containing X.

X = the score for which the percentile rank is being found.

X_L = lower real limit of the interval containing X.

i = size of the class interval.

f_i = frequency of scores in the interval containing X.

N = total number of scores in the distribution.

For a score of 41 in Table 3–4, the values for this formula are

$$P_X = P_{41},$$

$$cf_L = 39 \quad \text{(from column h of Table 3–4)},$$

$$X = 41,$$

$$X_L = 39.5 \text{ (from column b of Table 3–4)},$$

$$i = 5,$$

$$f_i = 33 \quad \text{(from column e of Table 3–4)},$$

$$N = 100.$$

Substituting these values into the formula, I obtain

$$P_{41} = \frac{39 + [(41 - 39.5)/5]33}{100} \times 100$$

$$= \frac{39 + [(1.5/5)(33)]}{100} \times 100$$

$$= \frac{39 + [(.3)(33)]}{100} \times 100$$

$$= \frac{39 + 9.9}{100} \times 100$$

$$= \frac{48.9}{100} \times 100$$

$$= 48.9.$$

Typically, a percentile rank is rounded to a whole number; thus

$$P_{41} = 49.$$

The percentile rank of a score of 41 is 49; 49 percent of the scores in Table 3–4 are equal to or less than 41. This formula may also be applied to an ungrouped frequency distribution by using $i = 1$.

Finding a Percentile of a Distribution

A second problem is finding a score that corresponds to a specified percentile in a distribution. For example, suppose that I want to find the 49th percentile of the distribution in Table 3–4. I notice that this percentile is a score in the class interval of 40 to 44, for 39 percent of the scores fall below the lower real limit of this interval and 72 percent of the scores fall below the upper real limit. Again I must interpolate to find the exact score that is the 49th percentile. The following formula provides this interpolation and calculates the percentile:

$$X_P = X_L + \left(\frac{P(N) - cf_L}{f_i} \right) i,$$

where

X_P = score at a specified percentile (i.e., the score we want to find).

X_L = lower real limit of the interval containing the specified percentile.

P = required percentile given as a proportion between 0 to 1.00.

N = total number of scores in the distribution.

cf_L = cumulative frequency of scores up to the lower real limit of the interval containing X_P.

f_i = frequency of scores in the interval containing X_P.

i = size of the class interval.

For the 49th percentile, these values are

$$X_P = X_{49},$$

$$X_L = 39.5 \text{ (from column b of Table 3–4)},$$

$$P = .49,$$

$$N = 100,$$

$$cf_L = 39 \quad \text{(from column h of Table 3–4)},$$

$$f_i = 33 \quad \text{(from column e of Table 3–4)},$$

$$i = 5.$$

Substituting these values into the formula, I obtain

$$X_{49} = 39.5 + \left(\frac{.49(100) - 39}{33} \right) 5$$

$$= 39.5 + \left(\frac{49 - 39}{33} \right) 5$$

$$= 39.5 + \left(\frac{10}{33} \right) 5$$

$$= 39.5 + 1.52$$

$$= 41.02.$$

Rounding this value to a whole number, $X_{49} = 41$. The 49th percentile is a score of 41. Forty-nine percent of the scores in the distribution are equal to or less than 41. Again this formula may be used with an ungrouped distribution by using $i = 1$.

Example Problem 3–2

Grouped Frequency Distributions

Problem

Suppose that I investigated the problem of perception of ambiguous figures discussed in Example Problem 3–1 and measured the duration that subjects could see the pyramid in the Mach pyramid figure. I used 50 subjects and obtained the following scores (to the nearest whole second): 18, 2, 7, 23, 16, 10, 5, 30, 5, 15, 17, 3, 31, 9, 11, 13, 5, 13, 8, 19, 16, 2, 14, 4, 7, 7, 6, 2, 10, 6, 7, 24, 3, 8, 9, 7, 19, 7, 11, 9, 4, 7, 6, 1, 3, 10, 1, 26, 8, and 5.

    a. Construct the following grouped distributions for these scores: simple frequency, relative frequency, percentage frequency, simple cumulative frequency, cumulative relative frequency, and cumulative percentage frequency distribution. Include the real lower and upper limits of the class intervals, and the midpoint of each class interval.

    b. What conclusions about the scores may you reach from these distributions?

    c. Find the percentile rank of a score of 16 seconds.

    d. What is the 25th percentile for this distribution?

Solution   **a.** The solution requires choosing the number of class intervals to be used, finding the size of the class interval, and then constructing a grouped frequency distribution using these class intervals.

    Number of Class Intervals: The range of scores is from 1 to 31 seconds, or 30 seconds. Ten class intervals seem sufficient to group the data.

    Size of Class Intervals: $i = (31 - 1)/10 = 3.0$.

    Constructing the Distribution: The lowest score obtained is 1 second, and the class interval to be used is 3 seconds. The first class interval then is 0 to 2. This interval contains the lowest score, and the lower stated limit of this interval (i.e., 0) is divisible evenly by the size of the class interval (i.e., 3). The class intervals of the grouped frequency distribution are presented in column a of the following table. The upper and lower real limits for each interval are obtained by finding the points midway between adjacent class intervals. For example, upper and lower real limits for the class interval of 24 to 26 are the points mid-way between 23 and 24 (lower real limit) and midway between 26 and 27 (upper real limit), respectively. The real limits of each class interval are shown in column b of the table. Midpoints for each class interval are presented in column c. The scores are tallied in column d, and the grouped frequency distributions are presented in columns e through j of the table.

(a)	(b)		(c)	(d)	(e)	(f)	(g)	(h)	(i)	(j)
Class Interval	Real Limits		Midpoint of Interval	Tally	f	rf	$\%f$	cf	crf	$c\%f$
	Lower	Upper								
30–32	29.5–32.5		31	//	2	.04	4	50	1.00	100
27–29	26.5–29.5		28		0	.00	0	48	.96	96
24–26	23.5–26.5		25	//	2	.04	4	48	.96	96
21–23	20.5–23.5		22	/	1	.02	2	46	.92	92
18–20	17.5–20.5		19	///	3	.06	6	45	.90	90
15–17	14.5–17.5		16	////	4	.08	8	42	.84	84
12–14	11.5–14.5		13	///	3	.06	6	38	.76	76
9–11	8.5–11.5		10	////////	8	.16	16	35	.70	70
6–8	5.5–8.5		7	/////////////	13	.26	26	27	.54	54
3–5	2.5–5.5		4	/////////	9	.18	18	14	.28	28
0–2	−0.5–2.5		1	/////	5	.10	10	5	.10	10

b. Conclusions: From the simple frequencies (column e), relative frequencies (column f), or percentage frequencies (column g), we see that scores in the interval of 6 to 8 seconds occurred most frequently. The cumulative frequency distributions indicate that .70 or 70 percent of the scores were durations of 11 seconds or less.

c. The percentile rank of a score is found using the formula

$$P_X = \frac{cf_L + [(X - X_L)/i]f_i}{N} \times 100.$$

The values needed to find the percentile rank of a score of 16 are

$$P_X = P_{16},$$
$$cf_L = 38,$$
$$X = 16,$$
$$X_L = 14.5,$$
$$i = 3,$$
$$f_i = 4,$$
$$N = 50.$$

Substituting these values, I obtain

$$P_{16} = \frac{38 + [(16 - 14.5)/3]4}{50} \times 100$$

$$= \frac{38 + [(1.5/3]4}{50} \times 100$$

$$= \frac{38 + (.5)4}{50} \times 100$$

$$= \frac{38 + 2}{50} \times 100$$

$$= \frac{40}{50} \times 100$$

$$= .80 \times 100 = 80.$$

The percentile rank of a score of 16 seconds is 80. Eighty percent of the durations are equal to or less than 16 seconds.

d. The 25th percentile is found using the formula

$$X_P = X_L + \left(\frac{P(N) - cf_L}{f_i}\right) i.$$

The numerical values needed to find the 25th percentile are

$$X_P = X_{25},$$
$$X_L = 2.5,$$
$$P = .25,$$
$$N = 50,$$
$$cf_L = 5,$$
$$f_i = 9,$$
$$i = 3.$$

Substituting these values, I obtain

$$P_{16} = 2.5 + \left(\frac{.25(50) - 5}{9}\right) 3$$

$$= 2.5 + \left(\frac{12.5 - 5}{9}\right) 3$$

$$= 2.5 + \left(\frac{7.5}{9}\right) 3$$

$$= 2.5 + 2.5$$

$$= 5.0.$$

A score of 5 seconds is the 25th percentile.

TESTING YOUR KNOWLEDGE 3-2

1. Define: class interval, cumulative frequency of a class interval, cumulative frequency of a score, cumulative percentage frequency of a class interval, cumulative relative frequency of a class interval, cf, c%f, crf, cum f, cum %f, cum rf, grouped frequency distribution, lower real limit of a class interval, lower stated limit of a class interval, midpoint of a class interval, percentile, percentile rank, upper real limit of a class interval, upper stated limit of a class interval.

2. What is the recommended number of class intervals to use when constructing a grouped frequency distribution?

3. The largest score in a distribution is 88 and the smallest is 14. You plan to construct a grouped distribution with 15 intervals. What will be the size of your class interval?

4. The largest score in a distribution is 95 and the smallest is 62. You want the class interval to be 3. How many intervals will you use?

5. What are the two guidelines for constructing grouped distributions?

6. A grouped frequency distribution has class intervals of 120 to 122, 123 to 125, 126 to 128, 129 to 131, and 132 to 134.

   a. Identify the lower and upper stated limits for the class interval of 123 to 125.

   b. Identify the lower and upper stated limits for the class interval of 129 to 131.

   c. Identify the lower and upper real limits for the class interval of 123 to 125.

   d. Identify the lower and upper real limits for the class interval of 129 to 131.

   e. Find the midpoint of the class interval of 120 to 122.

   f. What is the value of i for this distribution?

7. When approached by a predator, Thompson's gazelles leap straight up with all four feet simultaneously off the ground. This behavior, known as stotting, appears costly to the gazelle, for it delays the onset of flight from the predator. To learn more about stotting, Caro (1986) used naturalistic observation to study gazelles in Serengeti National Park, Tanzania. One measure obtained was the estimated distance of a predator, such as a cheetah, from a gazelle before the first stott occurred. Suppose that he observed 50 instances of a cheetah approaching a gazelle and recorded the following estimated distances (in meters) between the cheetah and the gazelle before the first stott occurred: 47, 61, 72, 63, 56, 54, 67, 75, 91, 72, 83, 140, 31, 37, 25, 38, 57, 62, 49, 205, 66, 39, 43, 81, 66, 72, 42, 29, 190, 64, 76, 54, 38, 67, 61, 33, 48, 55, 59, 68, 18, 49, 37, 83, 70, 154, 91, 50, 58, and 66.

   a. Construct the following grouped distributions for these scores: simple frequency, relative frequency, percentage frequency, cumulative simple frequency, cumulative relative frequency, and cumulative percentage frequency distribution. Include the lower and upper real limits of the class intervals and the midpoint of each class interval. Use 20 class intervals.

   b. What conclusions about stotting distances are you able to reach from the information in the grouped frequency distributions?

   c. Find the percentile rank of a distance of 68 meters.

   d. What is the 50th percentile for this distribution?

PRESENTING FREQUENCY DISTRIBUTIONS GRAPHICALLY

Frequency distributions provide a systematic way of looking at data to understand their characteristics. To further this understanding, the information contained in a frequency distribution is often displayed in the form of a graph, such as a histogram, a frequency polygon, or a stem-and-leaf display. First, however, I review some of the common rules for constructing graphs.

- Graphs are most easily and accurately drawn on graph paper.
- The two axes of the graph are drawn at right (90°) angles to each other. The horizontal axis is identified as the *x axis* or the *abscissa*. The vertical axis is called the *y axis* or *ordinate*.
- The possible scores, or the class intervals of the possible scores in a grouped frequency distribution, are located along the *x* axis. The measure of frequency (e.g., simple frequency, relative frequency, percentage frequency, cumulative frequency, etc.) is placed on the *y* axis.
- Each axis is labeled so that the reader knows what information is being graphed.
- The origin of each axis is normally at zero. If a part of the scale between the zero origin and the first recorded score or frequency of a score is left off the axis, then a break, indicated by -/ /-, is inserted into the axis.
- A scale should be chosen for the *y* axis such that the maximum height of the frequency measure is about two-thirds to three-fourths of the width of the *x* axis.

Histograms

Histogram: A form of bar graph in which the frequency of occurrence of scores in a class interval is given by the height of the bar, and the size of each class interval is represented by the width of the bar on the abscissa.

A **histogram** uses the height of a vertical bar to show the frequency of occurrence of scores in a class interval. The size of each class interval is represented by the width of the bar on the abscissa. Histograms are usually drawn only for grouped frequency distributions, and the measure of frequency typically used is either the simple frequency tabulation or the relative frequency for a class interval (columns e and f of Table 3–4, respectively). A histogram of the grouped simple frequency of the Test Anxiety Inventory scores is presented in Figure 3–3. To construct a histogram, the midpoints of the class intervals or the class intervals themselves are plotted on the abscissa. The bar that represents the frequency of each interval is centered on the midpoint of the class interval, and the vertical sides of each bar are drawn at the real limits of each class interval. Scores on the abscissa are usually indicated by the numerical value of the midpoint of each class interval, as illustrated in Figure 3–3 and Figure 3–5. The frequency of occurrence of scores is plotted on the ordinate and the height of each bar is drawn to the frequency of the class interval it represents.

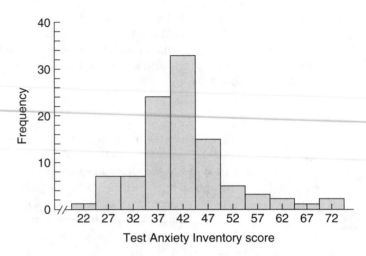

FIGURE 3–3
Simple frequency histogram of Test Anxiety Inventory scores of Table 3–3.

Frequency Polygons

Frequency polygon: A graph constructed by placing the midpoints of each class interval of a frequency distribution on the abscissa and indicating the frequency of a class interval by placing a dot at the appropriate frequency above the midpoint. The dots are connected with straight lines.

A **frequency polygon** is constructed by placing the midpoints of each class interval on the abscissa and indicating the frequency of a class interval by placing a dot at the appropriate frequency above the midpoint. The dots are then connected by straight lines. Figure 3–4 portrays a frequency polygon of the grouped Test Anxiety Inventory scores of Table 3–4. The frequency measure used is the simple frequency tabulation in column e of the table. Notice in Figure 3–4 that one extra class interval containing no scores has been included at each end of the distribution, and the frequency polygon has been brought to zero at each end of the graph (at the midpoints of 17 and 77). This practice is commonly followed in the construction of frequency polygons.

Relative Frequency Histograms and Polygons

Histograms and frequency polygons may be constructed using relative frequencies in place of the simple frequencies used in Figures 3–3 and 3–4. A histogram and a frequency polygon of the Test Anxiety Inventory scores using relative frequencies (from column f of Table 3–4) are presented in Figures 3–5 and 3–6, respectively.

The benefit of using relative frequencies for a histogram or frequency polygon is that the relative frequency values indicate the proportion of scores falling in the various class intervals. Thus, if two different frequency distributions, each based on a different total number of scores, are being compared, relative frequencies make direct comparison easier than simple frequencies.

FIGURE 3–4

Simple frequency polygon of Test Anxiety Inventory scores of Table 3–3.

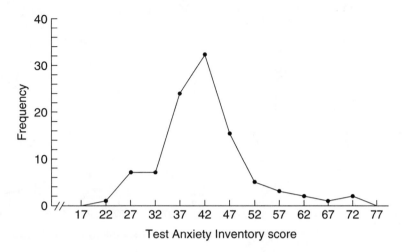

FIGURE 3–5

Relative frequency histogram of Test Anxiety Inventory scores of Table 3–3.

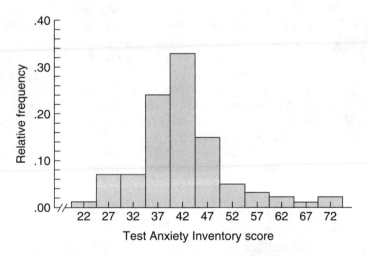

Obtaining Information from a Histogram or a Frequency Polygon

The histogram and frequency polygon present the same information as does a frequency distribution. The advantage of histograms and frequency polygons is that the information presented is often more easily grasped visually. From any of Figures 3–3, 3–4, 3–5, or 3–6, you can see that the peak of the distribution of the anxiety scores is in the low 40s, and more scores are closer to the bottom of the anxiety scale score (i.e., 20) than to the top (i.e., 80). A few scores, however, tail off in the direction of high test anxiety.

FIGURE 3–6
Relative frequency polygon of Test Anxiety Inventory scores of Table 3–3.

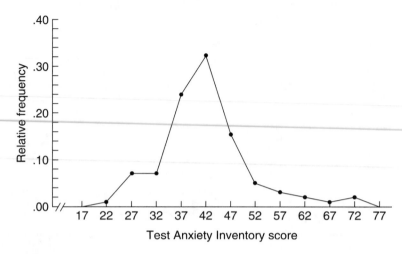

Stem-and-Leaf Displays

Stem-and-leaf display: A display of data in which the first (or second) digit of a score is the stem and the second (or last) digit is the leaf.

The **stem-and-leaf display**, developed by Tukey (1977), combines the qualities of a frequency distribution and a graphic display of the data. Table 3–5 presents a stem-and-leaf display of the Test Anxiety Inventory scores of Table 3–3. In this display, the numbers in the column to the left are the **stems** and represent the first digit of a score. For example, 3 is the stem for a score of 35. Stems are usually ordered with the lowest stem (in the example, 2) at the bottom of the display and the largest stem (in the example, 7) at the top. The numbers in the right column are the **leaves** and represent the second digit of the score, in the example of 35, a 5. For example, the topmost row with a stem of 7 and leaves of 0 and 3 represents the scores of 70 and 73, respectively. If scores involve three digits, such as a score of 321 seconds, then the first two digits (i.e., 32) are used to form the stem, and the last digit (i.e., 1) is the leaf.

Stem-and-leaf displays are constructed easily from the raw data, and no information is lost in the process, as occurs in a grouped frequency distribution; all the raw scores

TABLE 3–5
Stem-and-leaf display of Test Anxiety Inventory scores presented in Table 3–3.

Stem	Leaf
7	03
6	005
5	00022558
4	00000001111111111112222233334444445555666666778889
3	112444456666677777788888899999
2	25568889

can be reconstructed from the display. From an examination of Table 3–5 and simply counting the number of scores, you can quickly determine that the scores vary from 22 to 73 and that scores in the 40s occur most frequently, with 41 the most frequent score with 11 occurrences.

STATISTICS IN USE 3–1

Belief in Lunar Effects: Using a Stem-and-Leaf Display

I offered the example of a summated rating scale called the Belief in Lunar Effects Scale in Statistics in Use 2–3. This scale was developed by Rotton and Kelly (1985) to measure belief in the effect of a full moon on behavior. Recall that the minimum score on this scale is 9, indicating minimal or no belief in lunar effects, and the maximum score is 81, indicating maximum belief in lunar effects. Rotton and Kelly administered this scale to 157 undergraduate college students, and the scores they obtained are portrayed in the following stem-and-leaf display, which is adapted with permission of authors and publisher from Rotton, J., & Kelly, I. W., "A scale for assessing belief in lunar effects: reliability and concurrent validity," *Psychological Reports*, 1985, 57, 239–245, © *Psychological Reports* 1985.

Stem		Leaf
7	.	12
	*	59
6	.	0011114
	*	5666668999
5	.	000111111222334
	*	5555555555666678888899
4	.	0011111223333344444
	*	56666677788899999
3	.	00001122223344444
	*	55667777899999
2	.	00001122234444
	*	556666778888899
1	.	122334

The stem represents the 10s value of the score and the leaf the 1s value of the score. Thus a stem of 3 and a leaf of 7 is a score of 37. Rotton and Kelly added several refinements to their stem-and-leaf plot. Notice the column of periods and asterisks next to the stem column. For a particular stem value, the period is used to denote leaf values from 0 through 4, and the asterisk is used to indicate leaf values from 5 through 9. For example, scores with a stem of 1 are given in the table as

	*	556666778888899
1	.	122334

The leaf values in the row preceded by the period range from 1 to 4. When preceded by their stem of 1, these values become scores of 11, 12, 12, 13, 13, and 14, respectively. The leaf values in the row preceded by the asterisk (*) also have a stem of 1, but they are leaf values from 5 through 9. When preceded by their stem of 1, these values become 15, 15, 16, 16, 16, 16, 17, 17, 18, 18, 18, 18, 18, 19, and 19, respectively. The use of the periods to indicate leaf values from 0 through 4 and asterisks to denote leaf values from 5 through 9 provides for a more compact table, which is useful when a large number of scores is involved.

From this stem-and-leaf display we can see that the range of scores obtained was from 11 to 72, and the most frequently occurring score was 45, with nine occurrences. No information is lost in this display, for each of the 157 scores may be reconstructed from the display.

GRAPHIC PRESENTATION OF QUALITATIVE DATA

The discussion to this point has dealt with the graphic presentation of quantitative data. Qualitative data, however, indicate only that the variable measured differs in quality. As an example, Trinkaus, in a series of studies using naturalistic observation (1982, 1983, 1988, 1993), categorized driver's behavior at a highway stop sign into one of three categories: 1, coming to a full stop; 2, coming to a rolling stop; and 3, not stopping at all. These categories differ qualitatively; they label the behavior, but they do not tell us how it differs in amount. Trinkaus counted the number of occurrences of each behavior and found the percentage frequencies of occurrence of each category. These percentage frequencies can be presented graphically in the form of a **bar graph**, as shown in Figure 3–7, which presents data representative of those reported by Trinkaus.

A bar graph is similar to a histogram, except the bars are separated on the X axis to indicate that the categories do not represent a continuous measurement. The distance between the bars is arbitrary, but the same for each bar. Either simple frequencies, relative frequencies, or percentage frequencies (as illustrated in Figure 3–7) may be used to indicate the frequency of occurrence of each category. From this graph we easily note that the most frequently occurring behavior at the intersections observed was category 3, not stopping at all.

TESTING YOUR KNOWLEDGE 3-3

1. Question 7a of Testing Your Knowledge 3–2 required you to construct a frequency distribution of the estimated distance of a predator from a gazelle when the gazelle first stotted. Use that frequency distribution to answer question 1a and b.
   a. Construct a histogram and a frequency polygon for the estimated distances using the simple frequencies of a grouped distribution with a class interval of 10 meters.
   b. Construct a relative frequency histogram and a relative frequency polygon from the grouped distribution of question 1a.
   c. What conclusions do you reach about stotting distances from the graphs that you have constructed?
2. Construct a stem-and-leaf plot of the 50 distance estimates given in question 7 of Testing Your Knowledge 3–2.
   a. What is the shortest distance recorded?
   b. What is the longest distance recorded?
   c. What is the most frequently occurring distance?

FIGURE 3–7
Percentage frequency of occurrence of three categories of stop sign behavior representative of that reported by Trinkaus (1982, 1983, 1988, 1993).

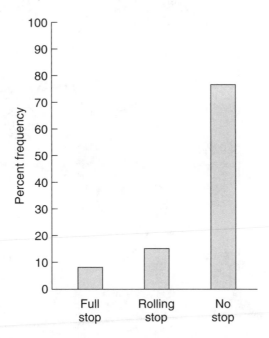

SHAPES OF FREQUENCY DISTRIBUTIONS

A distribution of scores may take on any of a variety of shapes. Thus there usually is no simple way to describe precisely the shape of a frequency distribution in a word or two. There are, however, some general descriptive terms that apply to the shape of a distribution and that help to describe a distribution in words. To illustrate, Figure 3–8 presents examples of several different shaped frequency polygons.

Symmetrical Frequency Distributions

Symmetrical frequency distribution: A frequency distribution that, when folded in half about a midpoint, produces two halves identical in shape.

A **symmetrical frequency distribution**, if it were folded in half about a midpoint, would produce two halves identical in shape. One side of the distribution is a mirror image of the other. Distributions (a), (b), and (c) in Figure 3–8 are symmetrical distributions, but distributions (d) and (e) are not symmetrical; they are **asymmetrical**. The symmetrical bell-shaped or **normal distribution** shown in Figure 3–8a is of special importance in the behavioral sciences. I discuss it more fully in Chapter 6.

FIGURE 3–8
Shapes of hypothetical frequency distributions.

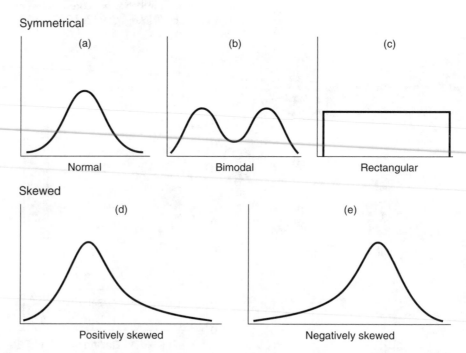

Symmetrical

(a)   (b)   (c)

Normal   Bimodal   Rectangular

Skewed

(d)   (e)

Positively skewed   Negatively skewed

Skewness

Skewed distribution: A frequency distribution in which scores are clustered at one end of the distribution, with scores occurring infrequently at the other end of the distribution.

It is rare to obtain a perfectly symmetrical distribution of raw data for a given measure. Instead, a frequency distribution is likely to be asymmetrical or skewed. In a **skewed distribution,** scores are clustered at one end of the distribution, with scores occurring infrequently at the other end (or tail) of the distribution. A distribution is described as **positively skewed** if the tail occurs for the high scores at the right of the distribution (Figure 3–8d) or **negatively skewed** if the tail occurs for the low scores at the left of the distribution (Figure 3–8e).

Modality

Mode: The most frequently occurring score in a distribution of scores.

Distributions are also described in terms of the number of modes possessed. The **mode** is the most frequently occurring score in a distribution of scores. A **unimodal distribution** has just one most frequently occurring score (see Figures 3–8a, d, and e). A frequency distribution that has two modes is described as **bimodal** (illustrated in Figure 3–8b). Many behavioral scientists consider a distribution bimodal if it has two distinct peaks, even if the peaks do not represent scores with equal frequencies of occurrence. A **multimodal distribution** has three or more score values that are the most frequently occurring scores. Again, a distribution may be considered multimodal if it has three or more peaks, even

FIGURE 3–9
Frequency distributions for question 2.

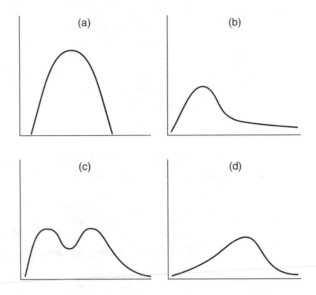

if the frequencies of occurrence of each peak are not equal. There is no mode in the flat rectangular distribution illustrated in Figure 3–8c; in such distributions, each score occurs an equal number of times or nearly so.

TESTING YOUR KNOWLEDGE 3-4

1. Define: asymmetrical distribution, bimodal distribution, mode, multimodal distribution, negatively skewed distribution, positively skewed distribution, skewed distribution, symmetrical distribution, unimodal distribution.
2. Describe the frequency distributions in Figure 3–9 with respect to symmetry, skewness, and modality.

SUMMARY

- A frequency distribution is a table showing each score obtained by a group of individuals and how frequently each score occurred.
- Frequency distributions are used to organize raw data.
- An ungrouped frequency distribution may be used when there is not a large number of scores in the data set.
- Grouped frequency distributions are used when the number of scores becomes large or the scores extend over a wide range of values.
- Ungrouped or grouped frequency distributions may be portrayed as simple, relative, or percentage frequencies.

- A percentile is the score at or below which a specified percentage of scores in a distribution fall.
- The percentile rank of a score indicates the percentage of scores in the distribution that are equal to or less than that score.
- Frequency distributions may be presented graphically as histograms, frequency polygons, or stem-and-leaf displays.
- Qualitative data may be presented graphically in a bar graph.
- Shapes of frequency distributions are described in terms of their symmetry, skewness, and modality.

KEY TERMS AND SYMBOLS

asymmetrical distribution
bar graph
bimodal distribution
class interval
cumulative frequency of a class
   interval
cumulative frequency of a score
cumulative percentage frequency
cumulative relative frequency
cf or *cum f*
crf or *cum rf*
c%f or *cum%f*
frequency distribution
frequency polygon
grouped frequency distribution
histogram

lower real limit of a class
   interval
lower stated limit of a class
   interval
midpoint of a class interval
mode
multimodal distribution
negatively skewed distribution
percentage frequency
   distribution
%f
percentile
percentile rank
positively skewed distribution
raw data
raw scores

real limits of a class interval
relative frequency distribution
rf
skewed distribution
stated limits of a class interval
stem-and-leaf display
symmetrical distribution
ungrouped frequency
   distribution
unimodal distribution
upper real limit of a class
   interval
upper stated limit of a class
   interval

REVIEW QUESTIONS

1. One survey ("The Way," 1985) found that the average man sleeps for 7 hours and 43 minutes (or 463 minutes) per night. You are curious if this figure holds also for male college students. Hence you ask 50 college males to record how long they slept for one night. The sleeping times you obtained, in minutes, were 440, 223, 309, 427, 463, 275, 315, 290, 356, 407, 399, 263, 417, 328, 377, 406, 275, 316, 391, 350, 422, 431, 382, 350, 371, 410, 295, 305, 327, 400, 227, 275, 340, 364, 279, 300, 412, 388, 296, 320, 342, 371, 258, 470, 496, 384, 439, 284, 351, 417.

   a. Construct a grouped percentage frequency distribution and grouped cumulative percentage frequency distribution for these scores. Use 14 class intervals.

   b. Which class interval contains the most scores? Is the midpoint of this interval in agreement with the 463 minutes reported in the survey?

   c. Estimate from the grouped cumulative frequency distribution the amount of time that divides the distribution in half, that is, the amount of time that places 25 people above it and 25 people below it.

   d. Find the 50th percentile of this distribution. Does it agree with your estimate from question 1c?

   e. What is the percentile rank of a score of 431 minutes?

   f. Construct a histogram and a frequency polygon using simple frequencies from the distribution you found in question 1a.

   g. Describe the shape of the distribution in terms of its skewness and modality.

2. Male bowerbirds build elaborate nests decorated with shells, colorful leaves, and blue feathers from parrots, for success in mating is related to the number of decorations on the bower. It has often been observed that male bowerbirds steal decorations from the bowers of other birds and use them to decorate their own nest. Borgia and Gore (1986) observed this stealing behavior among 59 bowerbirds in New South Wales, Australia. They marked feathers in a bower and recorded which feathers had been stolen from other bowers. Suppose that over the duration of their observation period they recorded the following number of feathers stolen by each bird: 0, 8, 17, 0, 21, 2, 6, 14, 1, 10, 3, 0, 26, 37, 47, 4, 0, 6, 21, 3, 6, 6, 51, 8, 11, 0, 0, 4, 2, 5, 9, 4, 6, 24, 4, 1, 18, 63, 1, 5, 6, 4, 7, 12, 5, 3, 4, 3, 15, 46, 0, 5, 0, 26, 5, 17, 1, 58, 9.

   a. Construct a grouped relative frequency distribution and a cumulative grouped relative frequency distribution for these scores. Use 13 class intervals.

   b. Which class interval contains the most scores?

   c. Find the 50th percentile of this distribution.

   d. What is the percentile rank of a score of 24?

   e. Construct a stem-and-leaf plot for this distribution. What are the lowest and highest scores in this distribution? What is the most frequently occurring score?

   f. Construct a histogram and a frequency polygon using simple frequencies from the distribution that you found in question 1a.

   g. Describe the shape of the distribution in terms of its skewness.

3. Suppose that you observed male and female drivers in a mall parking lot and counted the frequency with which they illegally parked in handicapped parking areas. Over a 3-day period you observed that 12 of every 100 male drivers and 7 of every 100 female drivers parked illegally. Construct a bar graph of the relative frequency of illegal parking in handicapped spaces by male and female drivers.

4. Sturgeon and Beer (1990) report that an attendance policy of rewarding students who attend school regularly by exempting them from semester tests increases attendance in comparison to no such policy. Suppose that you compare attendance at two high schools, one that has a reward policy in effect and one that does not, and you obtain the following simple frequency distribution of absences:

Number of Days Absent	Reward Policy School	No Reward Policy School
More than 25	2	6
24–25	0	6
22–23	2	1
20–21	0	8
18–19	1	0
16–17	0	4
14–15	2	22
12–13	0	10
10–11	3	18
8–9	8	20
6–7	4	3
4–5	13	14
2–3	23	34
0–1	42	54
Total	100	200

a. Construct a relative frequency distribution for each school.
b. What is the 50th percentile for each school?
c. What is the percentile rank for four absences at each school?
d. Do the schools appear to differ in absence rates? Describe the distributions.

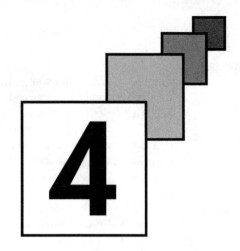

Describing Data: Measures of Central Tendency

Frequency distributions and graphs present a great deal of information about the shape of a distribution of scores and the range of scores obtained. Often, however, a scientist needs to describe a distribution of scores with only one number. These numbers are **descriptive statistics** for they describe the raw data in a single number. Two types of descriptive statistics are commonly used. One type, called *measures of central tendency*, describes the typical score obtained, and the other, called *measures of variability* or *measures of dispersion*, indicates the amount of variation or dispersion around the typical score.

Descriptive statistics have two uses. Their first is to describe the scores of a sample. Their second use is to estimate or infer characteristics of a population from the sample. For example, the researcher of Chapter 3 may be interested in estimating the typical level of test anxiety in the population of students at her college. She would base this estimate on a descriptive statistic obtained from the scores of her sample of 100 females.

The remainder of this chapter is concerned with the descriptive use of measures of central tendency. Measures of variability and the use of descriptive statistics for inferring population characteristics are introduced in Chapters 5 and 7, respectively.

Measures of central tendency are numbers that represent the average or typical score obtained from a sample. Three measures of central tendency are in common use: the mode, median, and arithmetic mean.

Measures of central tendency: Numbers that represent the average or typical score obtained from measurements of a sample.

MODE

Mode: The most frequently occurring score in a distribution of scores.

Unimodal: A distribution with one mode.

Bimodal: A distribution with two modes.

Multimodal: A distribution with more than two modes.

The **mode** is the most frequently occurring score in a distribution of scores. The mode is found by inspecting a simple, ungrouped frequency distribution and observing which score occurs most often. For example, in Table 3–2 (page 37) the most frequently occurring test anxiety score is 59, with five occurrences. Accordingly, the mode for this distribution is 59. Because there is only one mode for this set of scores, this distribution is said to be **unimodal**. A distribution of scores may be **bimodal** (i.e., have two modes) or even **multimodal** (i.e., have more than two modes). Recall that one way of describing the shape of a frequency distribution is on the basis of modality. Unimodal and bimodal distributions are shown in Figure 3–8.

Although the mode is computed easily from a simple ungrouped frequency distribution, it is rarely used or reported as a measure of central tendency in behavioral science research. One reason for this rarity of use is that a distribution may have more than one mode. And, if more than one mode exists, which is a more typical score? Thus the mode may not provide one typical score to characterize a distribution.

A second reason for the infrequent use of the mode is that a change in only one score may change the mode of a distribution dramatically. Suppose, for example, that you gave individuals a test of short-term memory by asking a person to repeat back as many as possible of 10 digits from a list. Assume that you obtained the following numbers of digits given back from six subjects:

Subject	Number of Digits
1	5
2	6
3	7
4	7
5	8
6	9

The mode of this distribution is 7, for two subjects repeated back seven digits. Suppose, however, that subject 4 repeated back only five digits instead of seven. Now the mode of the distribution is 5 rather than 7. The change of only one score shifted the mode considerably. As another instance, suppose subject 3 had recalled ten digits instead of seven. Now the distribution possesses no mode, for each score occurs an equal number of times. Because the mode is so dependent on only a few scores, it is not a stable measure of central tendency.

MEDIAN

Median (Mdn): A score value in the distribution with an equal number of scores above and below it. The median is the 50th percentile in a distribution.

The **median** (abbreviated *Mdn*) corresponds to a score value in the distribution that has an equal number of scores above and below it. The median thus represents the 50th percentile in a distribution. For most distributions of scores, there are simple ways of finding the median.

Calculating the Median with an Odd Number of Scores: No Tied Scores near the Median

For an odd number of scores in a distribution with no tied scores near the median, the median is usually determined by finding the middle score in the frequency distribution. As an example, for seven Test Anxiety Inventory scores of 22, 34, 36, 37, 38, 44, 72, the median is 37. This value is the fourth score and falls in the middle of the distribution of the seven scores. Three scores are less than 37 and three scores are greater than 37. Notice, essentially, that a counting procedure is used to determine a median. The numerical values of the scores that go into the count are not utilized in determining the value of the median.

Calculating the Median with an Even Number of Scores: No Tied Scores near the Median

With an even number of scores in a distribution and no tied scores near the median, the median is conventionally taken as the value that lies midway between the two middle scores in the frequency distribution. Consider, for example, six Test Anxiety Inventory scores: 34, 35, 37, 38, 44, 72. The median for these scores is 37.5, a value that falls halfway between 37 (the third score) and 38 (the fourth score). One-half of the six scores lie below a value of 37.5 and one-half lie above it.

Example Problem 4–1

Finding the Median

Problem
Studies investigating visual perception of real-world scenes sometimes present an individual with a picture of a scene for study and then ask the person to recall details of the scene. Suppose that you followed this procedure with 18 subjects and found the following number of details recalled by each person: 7, 3, 7, 9, 6, 10, 14, 3, 6, 9, 14, 9, 8, 5, 4, 6, 9, 13. Find the median.

Solution   Eighteen scores are given in the distribution; thus the median is the score with nine scores on either side of it. Accordingly, the median is midway between the ninth and tenth score when the scores are placed in a frequency distribution, as shown next.

Score	f		
14	2		
13	1		
12	0		
11	0		9 scores
10	1		
9	4		
8	1		
7	2		7.5 = median
6	3		
5	1		
4	1		9 scores
3	2		
2	0		
1	0		
0	0		

The ninth score is 7 and the tenth score is 8; thus the median is 7.5, midway between the scores of 7 and 8.

Calculating the Median with the Percentile Formula

When there are identical (i.e., tied) scores in the region of the median, the simple methods for obtaining the median will not work. In this instance a formula may be applied to obtain the median. The median is the 50th percentile in a distribution. Recall from

Chapter 3 that a percentile represents the value below which a certain percentage of scores in a distribution lies. For a median, 50 percent of the scores fall below its value. Accordingly, the median may be obtained from a grouped frequency distribution using the percentile formula given in Chapter 3:

$$Mdn = X_{.50} = X_L + \left(\frac{.50(N) - cf_L}{f_i} \right) i,$$

where $X_{.50}$ = median score we want to find.

X_L = lower real limit of the interval containing the 50th percentile.

N = total number of scores in the distribution.

cf_L = cumulative frequency of scores up to the lower real limit of the interval containing the median.

f_i = frequency of scores in the interval containing the median.

i = size of the class interval.

Characteristics of the Median

The median essentially is obtained by counting scores, ignoring numerical values except for the score that is the median. Therefore, the median is not influenced by the numerical value of extreme scores in a distribution. As an example, the median for each distribution shown next is 37:

Distribution

A	B	C
22	34	22
34	34	34
35	35	35
37	37	37
39	39	39
44	44	44
44	109	117

The median ignores the extreme scores in the tails of distributions B and C. This characteristic makes the median a desirable measure of central tendency for a skewed distribution. For example, the median is often reported for the typical income for a population because incomes are heavily positively skewed. There are only a few people who have incomes in the many millions of dollars. If the numerical values of these incomes were included in the measure of typical income, it would be too high to be representative of an average person. The median, however, is not affected by these few large incomes and thus provides a measure of central tendency representative of a typical income.

STATISTICS IN USE 4–1

What Year Would You Like to Know About?

What do adolescents think about the future? To find out, Tismer (1985) told 247 adolescents to suppose that a seer exists who can foretell the future. They were then asked to state what year in the future they would like the seer to tell them about. The subjects replied with a year, such as 2006 or 2013. This score offers the possibility of a positively skewed distribution. The lower bound of a response is provided by the year that has just passed, a year already known about. On the other hand, there is no upper bound to the year that someone may want to know about, for example, 3076 or 4121. Realistically, most adolescents will choose a future year in which they expect to be alive, such as 2015 or 2023. To describe his results, Tismer chose the median as a measure of central tendency; the median is not affected by a few large scores. With regard to knowing about the world as a whole, the median year named by males was 2003, whereas the median year named by females was 2000. Tismer found that these results concur with others indicating that boys may have a more distant future orientation than girls.

TESTING YOUR KNOWLEDGE 4–1

1. Define: bimodal distribution, descriptive statistics, measures of central tendency, median, mode, multimodal distribution, unimodal distribution.
2. Identify two uses of descriptive statistics.
3. Assume that a researcher measured self-esteem in 25 seventh-grade girls. The girls rated their self-esteem on a scale ranging from 10 (lowest self-esteem) to 70 (highest self-esteem). The scores obtained were 49, 53, 67, 20, 27, 36, 49, 27, 61, 17, 49, 50, 29, 56, 65, 27, 48, 24, 49, 15, 32, 66, 46, 24, and 38.
   a. Find the mode for this distribution.
   b. Is this distribution unimodal, bimodal, or multimodal?
4. Assume that one of the girls with a score of 49 in question 3 had instead obtained a score of 27.
   a. Find the mode for this distribution.
   b. Is this distribution unimodal, bimodal, or multimodal?
5. Assume that one of the girls with a score of 49 in question 3 had instead obtained a score of 24.
   a. Find the mode for this distribution.
   b. Is this distribution unimodal, bimodal, or multimodal?
6. What limitation of the mode as a descriptive statistic is illustrated by your answers to questions 4 and 5?
7. Find the median for the set of scores in question 3.
8. Assume that the experimenter measured one additional seventh-grader in question 3 and obtained a score of 28. Include this score in the distribution and find the median of the distribution.
9. Assume the original distribution of 25 scores in question 3. Suppose, however, that the scores of 61, 65, 66, and 67 were changed to 51, 55, 56, and 57, respectively. What is the median of this new distribution of scores?
10. Compare your answers to questions 7 and 8 and to questions 7 and 9. What limitations of the median as a measure of central tendency are illustrated by your answers?

SAMPLE MEAN

Sample mean ($\overline{X}$): The sum of a set of scores divided by the number of scores summed.

The most familiar measure of central tendency is the sample mean. The **sample mean**, often called the **arithmetic mean** or simply the **mean**, is the sum of a set of scores divided by the number of scores summed. Stated in statistical notation,

$$\overline{X} = \frac{\sum_{i=1}^{N} X_i}{N}$$

where

$\overline{X}$ (pronounced "ex-bar") indicates the mean.

$\sum$ (the Greek capital letter sigma) is a summation sign; it indicates the summing or adding up of a set of numbers. The limits over which the scores are added are indicated by the $i = 1$ and the N in the summation. These limits indicate that the summation should be over all scores, from the first subject $i = 1$ to the last subject (the Nth subject).

X_i represents a score for any individual, with the subscripted i used to indicate a particular person (thus X_1 indicates person 1, X_2 person 2, X_{10} person 10, and so on).

N is the number of individuals or scores in the sample.

When it is clear that the summation is over all N scores in a sample, then the limits on the summation sign are not included and the subscripted i is omitted; the formula for the mean then becomes

$$\overline{X} = \frac{\sum X}{N}.$$

In most instances I use this simplified notation.

Calculating the Sample Mean

Assume that I obtained the following six Test Anxiety Inventory scores: 34, 35, 37, 38, 44, and 40. The sample mean for this set of scores is obtained as follows.

First, I find the sum of the scores, or

$$\sum X = 34 + 35 + 37 + 38 + 44 + 40 = 228.$$

The number of scores, N, equals 6. To find the mean of the scores, I divide the sum, 228, by 6, or

$$\overline{X} = \frac{\sum X}{N} = \frac{228}{6} = 38.00.$$

The mean of the 100 TAI scores in Table 3–3 is found by summing the 100 scores and then dividing the sum by 100. In notation,

$$\overline{X} = \frac{42 + 28 + 37 + \cdots + 29 + 40 + 37}{100}$$

$$= \frac{4164}{100} = 41.64.$$

Example Problem 4–2
Calculating the Mean

Problem
Suppose that you obtained the following 18 scores in a picture recall task, as discussed in Example Problem 4–1: 7, 3, 7, 9, 6, 10, 14, 3, 6, 9, 14, 9, 8, 5, 4, 6, 9, 13. Find the mean of these scores.

Statistic to Be Used: $\overline{X} = \dfrac{\Sigma X}{N}.$

Solution   The first step is to obtain ΣX, which equals

$$7 + 3 + 7 + 9 + 6 + 10 + 14 + 3 + 6 + 9 + 14 + 9 + 8 + 5 + 4 + 6 + 9 + 13 = 142.$$

N is the number of scores added, or 18 in this example. Accordingly,

$$\overline{X} = \frac{\Sigma X}{N} = \frac{142}{18} = 7.89.$$

Characteristics of the Sample Mean

Computing the mean utilizes the numerical value of every score in the distribution. Thus any change of a score in a distribution will necessarily change the value of the mean for that distribution. For example, consider seven TAI scores: 26, 26, 26, 30, 34, 40, 42. The mode of this distribution is 26, the median 30, and the mean 32. If only one score, for example, 40, changes to a 43, the mode remains 26 and the median 30, but the mean is now 32.4. Because the mean depends on the magnitude of each score, extreme scores in a distribution affect the value of the mean and distort its value as a measure of central tendency. Suppose, for instance, that the 40 in the distribution of seven TAI scores changes not to a 44, but to a 78. The mode and the median of the distribution remain 26 and 30, respectively. But the mean has increased to 37.4. Accordingly, if a distribution includes a few extreme scores, the mean may not be a representative typical score.

A second characteristic of the mean is that the differences of a set of scores about the mean of those scores sum to zero. Notationally,

$$\Sigma(X - \overline{X}) = 0.$$

This notation indicates that I subtract the mean from each score in a set of scores and then sum the differences. If I do so, the sum of the differences will be zero. Table 4–1 illustrates this relation. Column a of Table 4–1 portrays seven Test Anxiety Inventory scores with a mean of 35.0. The numerical value of the mean is subtracted from each of the seven scores in column b of the table. The sum of column b, $\Sigma(X - \overline{X})$, is zero.

Sum of squares (SS): A numerical value obtained by subtracting the mean of a distribution from each score in the distribution, squaring each difference, and then summing the differences.

For any set of scores, the value of $\Sigma(X - \overline{X})$ will always be zero. But the value of $\Sigma(X - \overline{X})^2$ will not be zero unless each score in the distribution is equal to the mean. This value is calculated in column c of the table, where each difference (often referred to as a *deviation*) of a score from the mean is squared (i.e., multiplied by itself). For example, the score of 22 differs from $\overline{X}$ by -13, and $(-13)^2 = 169$. The total of the scores in column c, $\Sigma(X - \overline{X})^2$, is 264. The value of $\Sigma(X - \overline{X})^2$ is used frequently in statistical calculations and is called a **sum of squares** (abbreviated SS). Thus

$$SS = \Sigma(X - \overline{X})^2.$$

It can be demonstrated mathematically that the sum of the squared deviations of the scores from the mean [i.e., $\Sigma(X - \overline{X})^2$] is smaller than the squared deviation of the scores from any other statistic, such as the median or the mode. This property allows the mean to be used in several very important statistical techniques discussed in later chapters.

TABLE 4–1

Set of seven scores (column a) with a mean of 35.0.
Column b shows the value of $X - \overline{X}$ for each score. In column c the $X - \overline{X}$ deviation is squared for each score.

	(a) X	(b) $X - \overline{X}$	(c) $(X - \overline{X})^2$
	22	$22 - 35 = -13$	169
	34	$34 - 35 = -1$	1
	35	$35 - 35 = 0$	0
	35	$35 - 35 = 0$	0
	37	$37 - 35 = +2$	4
	38	$38 - 35 = +3$	9
	44	$44 - 35 = +9$	81
$\overline{X}$	35.0	Sum 0	264

STATISTICS IN USE 4–2

The Attractiveness and Perceived Competence of Political Candidates as Factors in Voting

The last several presidential elections have produced considerable speculation about the importance of the physical attractiveness and perceived competence of candidates in determining voter behavior. Speculation in the popular media has been that female voters may be swayed more by physical attractiveness than male voters. To investigate whether such a relationship exists, Lewis and Bierly (1990) had male and female subjects view black-and-white photographs of 22 female and 22 male politicians. The photographs were of members of the United States House of Representatives who were unknown to the subjects. The subjects rated each photograph on both the competence and physical attractiveness of the politician pictured. The rating scale used was a horizontal line, 9 centimeters long, with anchors at each end, as follows:

Physical attractiveness

Unattractive   Attractive

_____

Perceived competence

Incompetent   Competent

_____

The subject marked each line for each photograph. The rating was scored from 1 to 9; each numerical rating represented the distance of the rating mark to the nearest centimeter.

Male and female subjects rated the attractiveness of male politicians similarly; the mean for the female subjects was 4.48 and the mean for the male subjects was 4.50. For female politicians, however, the female subjects rated them as more attractive ($\overline{X} = 5.42$) than did the male subjects ($\overline{X} = 4.82$). With respect to perceived competence, the ratings of the female and male subjects of male politicians were similar ($\overline{X} = 5.63$ for female subjects and $\overline{X} = 5.55$ for male subjects). For female politicians, however, the female subjects rated them as more competent ($\overline{X} = 6.13$) than did the male subjects ($\overline{X} = 5.42$).

These results indicate that both males and females judge male political candidates similarly, but females judge female candidates as more competent and attractive than do males. Voters may use judgments of physical attractiveness and perceived competence of candidates to determine their voting behavior, but the nature of the judgment depends on both the gender of the voter and the candidate.

Journal Presentation of the Sample Mean

Statisticians typically use $\overline{X}$ to indicate the sample mean. Scientific journals, however, often use symbols different from those used by statisticians. Many behavioral science journals follow the editorial style of the *Publication Manual of the American Psychological Association* (American Psychological Association, 1994). The sample mean is represented by an italicized *M* in this style. Thus in a journal publication you may expect to find a presentation such as

> The mean rating of the competence of female politicians by females ($M = 6.13$) was greater than the mean rating by male subjects ($M = 5.42$).

In a typewritten or word-processed manuscript, underlining is used to indicate a statistical symbol; thus in a manuscript such as a laboratory report the presentation would appear as

> The mean rating of the competence of female politicians by females ($\underline{M} = 6.13$) was greater than the mean rating by male subjects ($\underline{M} = 5.42$).

TESTING YOUR KNOWLEDGE 4–2

1. Define: M, N, Σ, ΣX, $\overline{X}$.
2. Assume that you obtained the following scores: 97, 90, 86, 93, 76, and 86. Find the mean for the scores.
   a. Demonstrate that $\Sigma(X - \overline{X}) = 0$ for these scores.
   b. Find the value of $\Sigma(X - \overline{X})^2$ for these scores.
3. Assume that a researcher measured self-esteem in seventh-grade girls and obtained the scores 49, 53, 67, 20, 27, 36, 49, 27, 61, and 28.
   a. Find the mean of these scores.
   b. Suppose that the experimenter measured one additional seventh-grader and obtained a score of 17. Include this score in the previous distribution and find the mean of the distribution.
   c. Suppose that the score of 67 was changed to 27 so that the scores obtained were 49, 53, 27, 20, 27, 36, 49, 27, 61, and 28. What is the mean of this new set of scores?
   d. Compare your answers for questions 3a, b, and c. What characteristic of the mean is illustrated by your answers?

COMPARING MEASURES OF CENTRAL TENDENCY

Which is the "best" average score? There is no simple answer to this question. Which measure of central tendency is best depends on the intended use for the statistic. Measures of central tendency have both descriptive and inferential uses.

Descriptive Uses of Measures of Central Tendency

The choice of which measure of central tendency to use as a descriptive statistic depends on the scale of measurement realized in the scores and the shape of the frequency distribution of the scores.

Scale of Measurement of the Scores

Nominal Scale.   A nominal measurement merely places responses into categories; a response occurred or it did not occur. The only measure of central tendency that may be used with a nominal measurement is the mode—the category that occurs most frequently.

Ordinal Scale.   Ordinal measures place scores in order of magnitude, but there is no assurance that on the underlying variable being measured the intervals between adjacent scores are equal. Consequently, a median score may be obtained. The median divides the distribution of scores into two equal halves. A modal score, should one occur, may also be obtained.

Interval and Ratio Scales.   In both interval and ratio measures the intervals between adjacent scores are assumed to represent equal intervals on the variable being measured. Thus it is appropriate to compute a mean on scores that represent either interval or ratio measurement. It is also appropriate to find the median and the mode for scores at this level.

Shape of the Distribution of Scores

How well a measure of central tendency characterizes a distribution also depends on the shape of the distribution. Figure 3–8 presented shapes of several typical distributions of scores. If a distribution is unimodal and symmetric, such as the normal distribution of Figure 3–8a, then the mode, median, and mean are identical values. Each statistic characterizes the distribution of scores equally well. Often, however, obtained distributions are not unimodal and symmetric; they may be either positively or negatively skewed. In a skewed distribution, the mode, median, and mean will differ from each other. Because the mean is responsive to the extreme scores of a skewed distribution, it will move more in the direction of the extreme scores than either the mode or the median. Thus the direction of the difference between the mean and median will reveal whether the distribution is positively or negatively skewed. In a negatively skewed distribution the mean will have a lower value than the median; similarly, a few extreme high scores in a positively skewed distribution will increase the value of the mean with respect to the median. Figure 4–1 illustrates the relative locations of the median and mean in positively and negatively skewed distributions. As you can see from this figure, if a distribution is seriously skewed, with a large difference between the mean and median values, the median usually provides a better measure of central tendency than does the mean. A distribution of the salaries of major league baseball players illustrates this point. For one American League team, the range of annual salaries is from $109,000 to $5,155,250 (Cafardo, 1994). The mean of this distribution is $1,357,163, but the median is $500,000. The distribution is severely positively skewed; only 8 of the 25 players on the team earn more than the mean. Thus, characterizing the typical salary of the players on this team by the mean provides a misleading representation, for half the players earn $500,000 or less (Fudin & Levinson, 1994).

Whenever description is important, I recommend presentation of all three measures of central tendency for a distribution of scores. As you read behavioral sciences literature, however, you will find that the mean is the most widely presented descriptive measure of

FIGURE 4–1
The relative locations of the median and mean in positively and negatively skewed distributions.

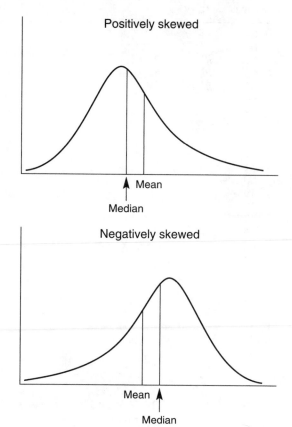

central tendency, and the mode is provided only rarely. This choice of the mean often is not based on its superior descriptive characteristics; rather the mean is the most useful of the three measures of central tendency as an inferential statistic. And, as you will see, inference is an important aspect of statistical analysis.

Do Some Distributions Not Have a Central Tendency?

Bimodal distributions cannot be adequately described by a single measure of central tendency, especially when the modal scores are widely separated. Suppose, for example, that a researcher obtains a distribution of Test Anxiety Inventory scores such as that shown in Table 4–2. This distribution is clearly bimodal, with a mode at 34 and another at 58. The median of the distribution is 45.5 and the mean is 45.8. But no one obtained scores near either the median or the mean. Neither the median nor the mean represents the test anxiety of a typical person in this sample. In this instance, the modes of 34 and 58 present the best description of typical scores.

TABLE 4–2
Bimodal distribution of 26 Test Anxiety Inventory scores.

Score	Tally	f	
61	/	1	
60			
59	//	2	
58	/////	5	Mode
57	///	3	
56	/	1	
55	/	1	
54			
53			
52			
51			
50			
49			
48			
47			
46			
45			$\overline{X} = 45.8,\quad Md = 45.5$
44			
43			
42			
41			
40			
39			
38			
37			
36	/	1	
35	///	3	
34	/////	5	Mode
33	//	2	
32	/	1	
31	/	1	

Consider another example. For a recent year the Department of Agriculture reported that the per capita consumption of chewing tobacco in the United States was 1.33 pounds per person. Does this statistic describe you? If you do not chew tobacco, this number is much too high. But if you do chew tobacco, the value likely is far too low. The distribution of chewing tobacco use is bimodal. A minority of the population uses chewing tobacco, and their consumption is considerably in excess of 1.33 pounds per year. The majority of the population does not chew tobacco, and their modal use is zero pounds per year.

Inferential Uses of Measures of Central Tendency

The choice of a measure of central tendency is determined in part by whether the statistic is to be used for subsequent inferential purposes. In Chapter 1, I indicated that population parameters are often estimated by statistics obtained from a sample. The sample mean, $\overline{X}$, is the best estimator of a population mean, represented by the Greek letter μ. Consequently, the sample mean enters into a number of important statistical tests. Because the mean is so useful for inference, then, behavioral scientists often use the mean to describe their data. I discuss the characteristics of the sample mean as an estimator of the population mean more fully in Chapter 7.

TESTING YOUR KNOWLEDGE 4-3

1. Which measure of central tendency would you choose to achieve each of the following?
   a. Provide a value that is the 50th percentile in a distribution.
   b. Minimize the sum of the squared difference of each score in the distribution from the measure of central tendency.
   c. Describe the most frequently occurring score in a distribution.
   d. Utilize the numerical value of each score in its computation.
2. A distribution is severely negatively skewed. Would you expect the mean to be smaller than, equal to, or larger than the median? Explain your answer.
3. The mean of a distribution is considerably larger than the median. Do you expect the distribution to be symmetrical, negatively skewed, or positively skewed? Why?

SUMMARY

- Measures of central tendency may be used for both descriptive and inferential purposes.
- The mode, median, and sample mean are the three commonly used measures of central tendency.
- The mode is the most frequently occurring score in a distribution of scores.
- The median is a score in the distribution with an equal number of scores above and below it.
- The sample mean is found from $\Sigma X/N$.
- The mean is the most used measure of central tendency for inferential purposes.
- The appropriate use of each statistic for descriptive purposes depends on the scale of measurement achieved and the shape of the frequency distribution of the scores.

KEY TERMS AND SYMBOLS

bimodal distribution	*Mdn*	measures of central tendency
descriptive statistics	μ (mu)	measures of variability
M	mean	median

mode	sample mean	$\overline{X}$
multimodal distribution	Σ (summation)	ΣX
population mean	unimodal distribution	$\Sigma(X - \overline{X})^2$

REVIEW QUESTIONS

1. Rotton and Kelly (1985) developed a scale called the Belief in Lunar Effects Scale to measure a person's belief in the effect of a full moon on behavior. Scores on this scale may range from 9 to 81. For one sample of individuals they report a mean of 37.9 and a median of 39. From this information, would you judge the distribution of scores to be approximately symmetrical or skewed? Why?

2. Davidson and Templin (1986) gathered data on the earnings of a sample of professional golfers. For 119 top money-winning golfers, they reported mean winnings of $118,016 and median winnings of $93,021. Is the distribution of winnings skewed? If you think it is skewed, in which direction is it skewed? Why?

3. Egli and Meyers (1984) surveyed 151 teenagers at a video-game arcade. The results revealed that the individuals played a mean of 5.2 hours per week, with a median of 2.5 hours per week. Is the distribution of hours played per week skewed? If you think it is skewed, in which direction is it skewed? Why?

4. Researchers in behavioral medicine are interested in psychological methods of controlling pain. To induce pain safely in their subjects, they may use the cold pressor task. One form of this task involves having a subject immerse a hand in cold water and then timing how long the subject can tolerate the pain induced. Suppose that an experimenter had each of 17 subjects place a hand in a tub of 40°F water and then timed how long the subject could hold his or her hand in the water before the pain became too intense to endure. The experimenter replicated the study four times and obtained the following four sets of scores (the scores represent time in seconds):

   Set 1: 35, 39, 38, 30, 37, 43, 30, 38, 41, 52, 25, 44, 33, 41, 38, 56, and 37.

   Set 2: 20, 28, 26, 29, 60, 21, 37, 30, 28, 57, 29, 25, 63, 26, 32, 30, and 28.

   Set 3: 45, 23, 57, 50, 47, 52, 20, 53, 50, 30, 52, 60, 52, 49, 52, 49, and 53.

   Set 4: 52, 23, 40, 60, 52, 21, 20, 52, 50, 23, 55, 26, 28, 53, 26, 49, and 26.

   For each set of scores:
   a. Construct an ungrouped simple frequency distribution. Use this frequency distribution to make a judgment about the shape of the distribution of the scores.

      b. Calculate the mode, median, and mean.

      c. Compare the measures of central tendency. Is the distribution skewed? Explain how you reached a decision. Does your answer from this comparison agree with your judgment from the frequency distribution constructed for question a?

      d. Do you think one of the measures of central tendency describes the scores better than the others? If so, which measure and why?

5. Your statistics professor plans to grade you on the basis of five examinations each worth 100 points. She informs you that your grade will be based on the central tendency of your scores and that you will have to choose whether you want your grade based on the modal, median, or mean score. Suppose the grades of three students in the class are as follows:

			Exam		
	1	2	3	4	5
Roberto	35	40	65	90	90
Dimitrios	10	50	65	80	85
Karen	56	56	67	78	98

If you were each of these students, which measure of central tendency would you choose to determine your course grade? Explain the reason for your choice for each student.

6. Gross (1993) surveyed students at a large midwestern university to find the extent of alcohol consumption among college males and females. One question on the survey asked the respondents to indicate the number of drinks consumed each week. Gross found that, among students 21 years or older, men reported having a mean of 23.9 drinks per week and women a mean of 7.5 drinks per week.

      a. Critique the use of a mean as a measure of central tendency of drinking behavior. Specifically, do you think the distribution of estimated drinks was skewed? If so, in which direction?

      b. Which measure of central tendency do you think may be a better measure to use in this instance?

7. Simple reaction time, the amount of time it takes to respond to a simple stimulus such as a light or tone, is a measure of a person's recovery from general anesthesia. Suppose that you measured eight surgery patients 2 hours after they received general anesthesia for minor surgery and found the following reaction times in milliseconds: 782, 793, 793, 817, 832, 847, 866, 893. A ninth patient was not sufficiently recovered to provide a reaction time; thus this subject was assigned an infinite reaction time.

      a. If you wanted to include the scores of all nine patients, which measure or measures of central tendency could you calculate?

      b. What is the numerical value of that measure?

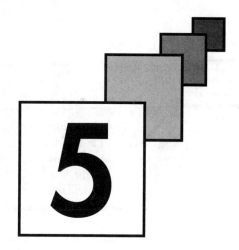

Describing Data: Measures of Variability

Variability refers to how much scores differ from each other and thus from the measure of central tendency in a distribution. The more the scores differ from each other, the more they will also differ from the measure of central tendency and the more variability there is in the distribution. Conversely, the less that scores differ from each other in a distribution, the less they will differ from the measure of central tendency and the less the variability of the distribution. Thus a measure of central tendency tells only part of the story about the scores obtained from a sample of individuals. From only this measure we cannot tell whether the scores are dispersed widely or clustered closely about the measure of central tendency. The mode, median, or mean alone do not indicate how much dispersion or variability there is among the scores in the distribution.

To illustrate the concept of variability, suppose that a researcher measured three different groups of nine subjects each on the amount of time that the subjects laughed while reading a book of cartoons. The scores she obtained, in seconds, are portrayed in Table 5–1. The mode, median, and mean for each group are 41.0. But it should be apparent that the distributions are very different, and the measures of central tendency are not equally representative of the scores in each group. In group 1 each score is equal to 41; thus there is no variability among the scores. Consequently, each measure of central tendency perfectly represents the scores in the distribution. But the scores in group 1 would be a rare outcome if actual duration-of-laughter scores were obtained from nine subjects. In group 2 there is little variability among the scores. The scores are clustered closely around the measure of central tendency; no score differs more than 3 seconds from 41 seconds. Each measure of central tendency is representative of all individuals in this group, for there is little variability among the individual scores.

TABLE 5–1
Duration-of-laughter scores in seconds for three groups of nine subjects each.

	Group		
	1	**2**	**3**
	41	38	21
	41	39	26
	41	40	33
	41	41	41
	41	41	41
	41	41	41
	41	42	50
	41	43	51
	41	44	65
Mode	41	41	41
Md	41	41	41
$\overline{X}$	41	41	41

The situation is different in group 3. Here there is more variability in the amount of laughter. The scores differ considerably from each other and in comparison to group 2, some scores differ by as much as 20 seconds from the measures of central tendency of 41 seconds. Clearly, any measure of central tendency for this set of scores is not as representative of the scores as are the measures of central tendency for groups 1 and 2.

As with measures of central tendency, the variability of scores must be quantified. Accordingly, there are several statistics to describe the variability of scores in a distribution.

RANGE MEASURES OF VARIABILITY

One form of a measure of variability provides an interval containing a certain percentage of the scores in a distribution. Three such measures are commonly used, the range, the interquartile range, and the semi-interquartile range.

Range

Range: The numerical difference between the lowest and highest scores in a distribution.

The simplest measure of variability for a set of scores, the **range**, is found by

$$\text{Range} = X_{\text{highest}} - X_{\text{lowest}},$$

where X_{highest} represents the highest score and X_{lowest}, the lowest score in a distribution. For group 3 of Table 5–1, $X_{\text{highest}} = 65$ and $X_{\text{lowest}} = 21$; thus the range for this group is $65 - 21$, or 44. The range for scores in group 2 is $44 - 38$, or 6, and the range of scores for group 1 is $41 - 41$, or 0. For the 100 Test Anxiety Inventory scores given in Table 3–3, the highest score is 73 and the lowest score is 22. Thus the range for this distribution is $73 - 22$, or 51 rating scale points.

Characteristics of the Range

The range describes the overall spread between the highest and lowest scores in a distribution. Any change in either the highest or lowest score will affect the range, even though all other scores may remain unchanged. Thus the range is a relatively unstable measure of variability. Moreover, the larger the size of the sample is, the more likely it is that one deviant score may be obtained to inflate the value of the range. The virtue of the range is its easy computation, but because of its lack of stability, it is not a frequently reported measure of variability.

Interquartile Range and Semi-interquartile Range

Interquartile range (*IQR*): The range of values for the middle 50 percent of the scores in a distribution.

The **interquartile range** (*IQR*) describes the range of values for the middle 50 percent of the scores in a distribution and is often used with ordinal measurements. It is obtained by subtracting the score corresponding to the 25th percentile (X_{25}) from the score that falls at the 75th percentile (X_{75}). In notation, the interquartile range is

$$IQR = X_{75} - X_{25}.$$

Values of X_{75} and X_{25} may be obtained using the formula in Chapter 3 for finding a specified percentile of a distribution (p. 48).

Semi-interquartile range (*SIQR*): One-half of the interquartile range.

The **semi-interquartile range** (*SIQR*) is one-half of the interquartile range, or

$$SIQR = IQR/2 = (X_{75} - X_{25})/2.$$

Characteristics of the *IQR* and the *SIQR*

The *IQR* provides the range of scores typical for the middle 50 percent of the individuals grouped around the median. Because the *IQR* excludes the top 25 percent and the bottom 25 percent of the scores in a distribution, its value is unaffected by extreme scores of a skewed distribution. Obviously, the interquartile range will be smaller than the range for a set of scores. For example, for the TAI scores of Table 3–3, $X_{75} = 45$ and $X_{25} = 37$ (rounded to the nearest whole number). Thus the *IQR* is

$$IQR = X_{75} - X_{25} = 45 - 37 = 8,$$

whereas the range for these scores is 51. Although the full range of the TAI scores of Table 3–3 is large, the range for the middle 50 percent of the scores is relatively small.

The *SIQR* describes the average spread of scores for 25 percent of the scores above and below the median. Only when the distribution is symmetrical, however, will the *SIQR* represent exactly the range of scores for the 25 percent of scores above the median and the 25 percent of scores below the median. As an example, for the TAI scores in Table 3–3, the *SIQR* is 8/2, or 4. This *SIQR* indicates that the middle 50 percent of the scores in the distribution does not extend more than about 4 rating points above or 4 rating points below the median. Notice that the preceding statement is qualified with the word *about*. Because the frequency distribution for the TAI scores is slightly skewed, this semi-interquartile range does not include exactly 25 percent of the scores on each side of the median.

STATISTICS IN USE 5–1

Using the *SIQR* to Describe Average Salaries

The United States Bureau of Labor Statistics maintains statistics on average salaries for a variety of jobs. One report for service-type jobs in the Boston, Massachusetts, area indicated a mean weekly salary for drafters of $486.00 with an *IQR* of $395.00 to $562.50

(Adams, 1986). For registered industrial nurses, the mean weekly salary was $490.50 with an *IQR* of $447.00 to $528.00. Although both jobs pay about the same mean salary, they differ considerably in variability of salary. The middle 50 percent of salaries for registered industrial nurses is more closely clustered together than is the middle 50 percent of salaries for drafters. For both occupations, the *IQR* excludes the very low or very high salaries that may occur infrequently.

TESTING YOUR KNOWLEDGE 5-1

1. Define: interquartile range, range, semi-interquartile range, variability, X_{25}, X_{75}.
2. The highest score on a class test is 98 and the lowest is 54. The 75th percentile score on the test is 92, and the 25th percentile score is 74. Find the range, *IQR*, and *SIQR* for these scores.
3. On a test of complex reaction time, the longest score is 929 milliseconds (ms) and the shortest score is 642 ms. The 75th percentile score is 809 ms and the 25th percentile score is 724 ms.
   a. Find the range, *IQR*, and *SIQR* for these scores.
   b. What information about the scores is given by the *IQR*?
   c. What information about the scores is given by the *SIQR*?
4. Explain why the range is a relatively unstable measure of variability.
5. Explain why the *IQR* is a more stable measure of variability than is the range.

MEASURES OF VARIABILITY ABOUT THE SAMPLE MEAN

The range, *IQR*, and *SIQR* each provide an interval containing a certain percentage of the scores (e.g., 100 percent for the range) around the central location in a distribution. But none of these statistics utilizes all the scores in the distribution for its computation. However, two important measures of variability, the variance and the standard deviation, utilize all the scores to measure variability about the mean.

In Chapter 4 I obtained the *deviation* or difference of each score in a distribution from the mean of the distribution. That is, I calculated $X - \overline{X}$ for each score. This deviation provides a measure of how much a score differs from a mean. If a score is equal to the mean, then $X - \overline{X}$ will be zero. But if the score is not equal to the mean, then $X - \overline{X}$ will take on a numerical value, and the more that X differs from $\overline{X}$, the larger $X - \overline{X}$ will become. We might then propose to obtain a measure of variability by adding up the deviations of all the scores in a distribution and dividing the sum by the number of scores. In notation, this measure of variability would be $\Sigma(X - \overline{X})/N$. But there is a problem with this proposed measure of variability. As illustrated in column b of Table 4–1, the sum of $X - \overline{X}$ deviations for a distribution of scores will always equal zero; that is, $\Sigma(X - \overline{X}) = 0$. To avoid this dead end, I could square each deviation value [i.e., $(X - \overline{X})^2$] before summing and dividing. Then the value of $\Sigma(X - \overline{X})^2$ will be zero only if each $X - \overline{X}$ value is zero. This procedure is used to derive the variance and, subsequently, the standard deviation. I first present the formulas for the variance and standard deviation and how to use them; then I discuss their interpretation.

Variance

Sample Variance

Sample variance (S^2): A measure of variability obtained by subtracting the mean of a distribution from each score in the distribution, squaring each difference, summing the differences, and then dividing the sum by the number of scores in the distribution.

The **sample variance** (represented in notation as S^2) is defined as

$$S^2 = \frac{\Sigma(X - \overline{X})^2}{N}.$$

To calculate the sample variance, this formula indicates the following:

1. Subtract the mean from each score [i.e., $(X - \overline{X})$].
2. Square each resulting difference [i.e., $(X - \overline{X})^2$].
3. Add all the squared difference values [i.e., $\Sigma(X - \overline{X})^2$].
4. Divide the sum by N, the number of scores in the distribution.

Estimated Population Variance

Estimated population variance (s^2): A measure of variability obtained by subtracting the mean of a distribution from each score in the distribution, squaring each difference, summing the differences, and then dividing the sum by the number of scores minus 1.

The formula I have just introduced describes the variance of a sample. As I indicated in Chapter 1, however, a researcher often needs to estimate a population variance from the variance obtained on a sample from the population. The sample variance found by S^2 consistently underestimates the actual value of the population variance, represented by σ^2 (the Greek letter sigma, squared), and provides a biased estimate of σ^2. This bias may be corrected by using $N - 1$ instead of N as the denominator in the preceding formula. Thus the **estimated population variance** is represented in notation as s^2 and defined as

$$s^2 = \frac{\Sigma(X - \overline{X})^2}{N - 1}.$$

To calculate the estimated population variance:

1. Subtract the mean from each score [i.e., $(X - \overline{X})$].
2. Square each resulting difference [i.e., $(X - \overline{X})^2$].
3. Add all the squared difference values [i.e., $\Sigma(X - \overline{X})^2$].
4. Divide the sum by $N - 1$, the number of scores minus 1.

For most purposes the estimated population variance, s^2, is more useful than the sample variance, S^2, and is much more widely used than S^2. Thus, from this point on when I discuss the variance, I will be referring to s^2 unless I specifically indicate that I am using S^2. I discuss the characteristics of s^2 and S^2 as estimates of σ^2 more fully in Chapter 7.

As noted in Chapter 4, the sum of squared deviations, $\Sigma(X - \overline{X})^2$, in the numerator of the formula for a variance is called the **sum of squares** and is represented by the symbol SS. Thus the estimated population variance also is defined as

$$s^2 = \frac{SS}{N - 1}.$$

Standard Deviation

Sample standard deviation (S): The square root of the sample variance.

The **sample standard deviation**, S, is the square root of the sample variance, or

$$S = \sqrt{S^2} = \sqrt{\frac{\Sigma(X - \overline{X})^2}{N}}.$$

Estimated population standard deviation (s): The square root of the estimated population variance.

The **estimated population standard deviation**, s, is the square root of the estimated population variance, or

$$s = \sqrt{s^2} = \sqrt{\frac{\Sigma(X - \overline{X})^2}{N - 1}}.$$

In sum of squares notation,

$$s = \sqrt{\frac{SS}{N - 1}}.$$

To calculate the estimated population standard deviation:

1. Subtract the mean from each score [i.e., $(X - \overline{X})$].
2. Square each resulting difference [i.e., $(X - \overline{X})^2$].
3. Add all the squared difference values [i.e., $\Sigma(X - \overline{X})^2$].
4. Divide the sum by $N - 1$, the number of scores minus 1.
5. Take the square root of the resulting quotient.

Again, for most purposes the estimated population standard deviation, s, is more useful than the sample standard deviation, S, and when I use the term *standard deviation*, I will be referring to s.

Example Problem 5–1

Calculating the Estimated Population Variance and Standard Deviation with the Definitional Formula

Problem
Find the estimated population variance and standard deviation of the nine duration-of-laughter scores of group 2 in Table 5–1 using the definitional formula for s^2.

Statistic to Be Used: $s^2 = \Sigma(X - \overline{X})^2/(N - 1)$.

Solution   The steps necessary in the calculation of s^2 and s are illustrated in the following table. I first find s^2. The formula requires obtaining the sum of squares, SS or $\Sigma(X - \overline{X})^2$. The nine scores are given in column a. The mean for these scores is 41, and this value is presented in column b. The first step is to subtract this mean from each score as illustrated in column c. The second step is to square the difference for each score as shown in column d. The squared differences are added together, and this sum, given at the bottom of column d, is 28. This sum is the $\Sigma(X - \overline{X})^2$, or SS, needed for the numerator of s^2. The last step is to divide the SS by $N - 1$. Because nine scores were used, $N = 9$ and $N - 1 = 8$. Accordingly, $s^2 = 28/8 = 3.50$. Notice that, because the deviation of each score from the mean is squared, s^2 must always be either zero or a positive number. A negative s^2 indicates a mistake in calculations.

(a) X	(b) $\overline{X}$	(c) $(X - \overline{X})$	(d) $(X - \overline{X})^2$
38	41	−3	9
39	41	−2	4
40	41	−1	1
41	41	0	0
41	41	0	0
41	41	0	0
42	41	+1	1
43	41	+2	4
44	41	+3	9
	Sum	0	28

The estimated population standard deviation, s, is the square root of s^2. Thus $s = \sqrt{3.50} = 1.87$ seconds. Notice that the units attached to s, seconds, are the same as those of the raw scores. It is important to remember to take the square root of s^2 when finding s, for a common error in calculating s is failing to take the square root of s^2.

Summary of Computational Steps

1. Find the mean of the scores in column a and then list this value in column b as shown.
2. Subtract the mean in column b from each score in column a. The difference is shown in column c.
3. Square each difference in column c. The result of this squaring is shown in column d.
4. Sum the squared differences of column d.
5. Divide the sum of column d by $N - 1$. The resulting value is s^2.
6. Take the square root of s^2 to obtain s.

Computational Formula for the Estimated Population Variance and Standard Deviation

The definitional formula for the variance best conveys conceptually what s^2 is. The formula is easy to use when only a few scores are involved and the scores and the mean of the scores are whole numbers. When decimal values are obtained with either the scores or the mean, or if a large number of scores is involved, the computations become more cumbersome. Then it is often easier to calculate s^2 with a formula that is equivalent algebraically to the definitional formula. The computational formula for s^2 is

$$s^2 = \frac{\Sigma X^2 - [(\Sigma X)^2/N]}{N-1}.$$

The estimated population standard deviation is obtained by taking the square root of s^2, or

$$s = \sqrt{s^2} = \sqrt{\frac{\Sigma X^2 - [(\Sigma X)^2/N]}{N-1}}.$$

Example Problem 5–2

Calculating the Variance and Standard Deviation with the Computational Formula

Problem
Find the variance and standard deviation of the nine duration-of-laughter scores of group 2 in Table 5–1 using the computational formula for s^2.

Statistic to Be Used:

$$s^2 = \frac{\Sigma X^2 - [(\Sigma X)^2/N]}{N-1}$$

Solution   The steps in calculating s^2 using this formula are illustrated in the following table. The nine scores are presented in column a. The formula requires obtaining two values from the scores, the sum of all the scores (i.e., ΣX) and the sum of the values of each score squared (i.e., ΣX^2). The sum of the scores, ΣX, is 369 and is presented at the bottom of column a. The value of each score squared is given in column b [e.g., $(38)^2 = 1,444$]. The sum of the squared scores, ΣX^2, is 15,157 and is shown at the bottom of column b. Nine scores were used; thus $N = 9$ and $N - 1 = 8$.

	(a) X	(b) X^2
	38	1,444
	39	1,521
	40	1,600
	41	1,681
	41	1,681
	41	1,681
	42	1,764
	43	1,849
	44	1,936
Sum	369	15,157

Substituting these values into the formula, I obtain

$$
\begin{aligned}
s^2 &= \frac{15{,}157 - [(369)^2/9]}{9-1} \\[6pt]
&= \frac{15{,}157 - (136{,}161/9)}{8} \\[6pt]
&= \frac{15{,}157 - 15{,}129}{8} \\[6pt]
&= \frac{28}{8} = 3.50.
\end{aligned}
$$

This value of s^2, 3.50, is identical to that obtained in Example Problem 5–1 using the definitional formula of s^2. Again, $s = \sqrt{s^2} = \sqrt{3.50} = 1.87$ seconds.

Review of Symbols and Formulas

I have introduced a number of symbols and formulas up to this point. They are reviewed here.

S^2 The variance of a sample. S^2 is a purely descriptive statistic for a sample.

S The standard deviation of a sample. S is a purely descriptive statistic for a sample.

s^2 The estimated population variance. This statistic is used to estimate a population variance.

s The estimated population standard deviation. This statistic is used to estimate a population standard deviation.

σ^2 The population variance. This parameter is discussed more fully in Chapter 6.

σ The population standard deviation, discussed more fully in Chapter 6.

The estimated population variance, s^2, and standard deviation, s, are the statistics typically calculated on a sample of scores. Table 5–2 presents the definitional, computational, and sum of squares formulas for both s^2 and s. Each formula provides the same numerical value of the statistic when applied to a set of data.

Interpreting the Variance and the Standard Deviation

The standard deviation is presented as a descriptive statistic in reports of research more often than the variance. One reason for this greater use is that, because the standard deviation is the square root of the variance, it provides a measure of the variability of scores in the original units of the scores. In Example Problems 5–1 and 5–2, s^2 is 3.50 seconds squared, a value not easily interpreted. The value of s, however, is 1.87 seconds, the same units (i.e., seconds) that the raw scores were measured in. Thus the focus in this section is on the interpretation of s. The variance, however, is used in statistical hypothesis testing methods and is discussed more fully in Chapters 10 through 12.

TABLE 5-2
Definitional, computational, and sum of squares formulas for the
estimated population variance and standard deviation.

| | **Formula** | | |
	Definitional	Computational	Sum of Squares
Variance, s^2	$\dfrac{\Sigma(X - \overline{X})^2}{N - 1}$	$\dfrac{\Sigma X^2 - [(\Sigma X)^2/N]}{N - 1}$	$\dfrac{SS}{N - 1}$
Standard deviation, $s = \sqrt{s^2}$	$\sqrt{\dfrac{\Sigma(X - \overline{X})^2}{N - 1}}$	$\sqrt{\dfrac{\Sigma X^2 - [(\Sigma X)^2/N]}{N - 1}}$	$\sqrt{\dfrac{SS}{N - 1}}$

The standard deviation provides a measure of the *average* of how much scores in a distribution differ from the mean. If all the scores in a distribution are equal to the mean, such as those of group 1 of Table 5–1, then s will equal zero. Thus the average amount by which the scores in group 1 differ from the mean is zero. In this case, if you use $\overline{X}$ to predict any of the scores in the distribution, there will be zero error in your prediction. If you see a value of s equal to zero, then you know that all scores in the distribution are equal to the sample mean, and the mean is a perfect predictor of all the scores.

On the other hand, if at least one score in the distribution is not equal to the mean, then s will take on a value greater than zero. And the value of s will increase as the variability of the scores increases. You can see this increase in s with increasing variability of scores by comparing the distributions of groups 2 and 3 of Table 5–1. Notice that the scores of group 3 are more variable about the mean of 41 than are the scores in group 2. For scores in group 2, $s = 1.87$ seconds, whereas in group 3, s is 13.44 seconds. Thus, for group 2 the average amount by which scores differ from $\overline{X}$ is 1.87 seconds, and in group 3 it is 13.44 seconds. If you use $\overline{X} = 41$ seconds to predict any of the scores in group 2, your prediction will be in error by about 1.87 seconds, whereas for group 3 such a prediction will be in error by about 13.44 seconds.

A second interpretation of s involves describing scores in terms of how many standard deviations they are away from the mean of a distribution. For many distributions, a majority of the scores are within one standard deviation of the mean. As an example, the mean for the 100 Test Anxiety Inventory scores of Table 3–3 is 41.64, and s for this distribution is 8.66. The scores within one standard deviation of $\overline{X}$ are scores from 32.98 to 50.30. These values are the distance encompassed by one standard deviation below the mean (i.e., $\overline{X} - 1s = 41.64 - 8.66 = 32.98$) to one standard deviation above the mean (i.e., $\overline{X} + 1s = 41.64 + 8.66 = 50.30$). Counting the scores of Table 3.3, I find that 79 of the 100 scores fall into this interval. If the distribution is normally shaped (as in Figure 3–7a), then knowledge of the standard deviation provides even more information about the scores in the distribution. This interpretation of s is discussed in Chapter 6.

Notice also that a score can be described by indicating how many standard deviations it is above or below the mean. For example, if a distribution of scores has a mean of

80 and a standard deviation of 6, then a score of 86 is one standard deviation above the mean and a score of 74 is one standard deviation below the mean. Again, Chapter 6 explains this use of the standard deviation more fully.

What Is a Large Amount of Variability?

No simple rule is used to determine whether a value for any measure of variability reflects a small or large amount of variability in a distribution of scores. Whether the variability is extensive or not is relative to the possible range of scores that can be obtained on the variable and the mean of the scores. For example, Senders (1958) points out that a standard deviation of 3 inches in the length of 100 electric utility poles would not be unusual, for the mean length of a utility pole is very large. If you were measuring the length of people's noses, however, a standard deviation of 3 inches would be alarming! You might expect you had found a new species of people. In relation to the average length of a person's nose, a standard deviation of 3 inches is very large.

STATISTICS IN USE 5–2

Describing Assaultive Husbands

Spousal abuse is a growing problem in society. To understand more fully the nature of such abuse, Browning and Dutton (1986) investigated reports of assaultive behavior by husbands in 30 couples who had been referred for therapy. To describe the sample of assaultive husbands studied, they reported the mean age of these husbands as 34.3 years, $s = 6.8$ years; the mean years married as 8.2 with $s = 5.4$ years; and the mean number of years of schooling as 11.0, $s = 2.2$ years. From these descriptive statistics, if I state that the typical assaultive husband studied in this research was 34.3 years old, I will be in error by an average of 6.8 years. But I can anticipate that the age of the majority of the husbands was within one standard deviation of the mean, or between 27.5 (i.e., $34.3 - 6.8$) to 41.1 (i.e., $34.3 + 6.8$) years old. It is unlikely that any of these husbands were in their 50s or 60s, for if husbands had been this old, then such large differences from the mean of 34.3 years would have increased the value of the standard deviation. On the other hand, the standard deviation of 5.4 for years of marriage is very large in comparison to the mean of 8.2 years of marriage. Hence there must be considerable variability in this measure: some couples were married for only a short time, others for a number of years.

Journal Presentation of Measures of Variability

The estimated population standard deviation, s, is the measure of variability commonly presented in journal presentations of research. Journals that follow the editorial style of the *Publication Manual of the American Psychological Association* (1994) use an italicized *SD* to indicate this standard deviation. Thus in a journal publication you may expect to find a presentation such as

The mean age of the assaultive husbands was 34.3 years $(SD = 6.8)$.

In a typewritten or word-processed manuscript, the presentation would appear as

The mean age of the assaultive husbands was 34.3 years ($\underline{SD} = 6.8$).

TESTING YOUR KNOWLEDGE 5-2

1. Define: standard deviation, sum of squares, s, s^2, SS, variance.
2. Homan, Topping, and Hall (1986) investigated the effect on test scores of a teacher's oral reading of a test to students compared to students reading the test by themselves. Suppose that you, too, were interested in this problem and created two different groups of students. One group of students read the test by themselves, whereas you read the test out loud to the other group of students. You obtained the following two sets of scores on the test (the minimum score is 0 and the maximum is 100):

<table>
<tr><td colspan="2" align="center">Group</td></tr>
<tr><th>Read by Themselves</th><th>Read by Teacher</th></tr>
<tr><td align="center">60</td><td align="center">51</td></tr>
<tr><td align="center">50</td><td align="center">74</td></tr>
<tr><td align="center">64</td><td align="center">64</td></tr>
<tr><td align="center">53</td><td align="center">63</td></tr>
<tr><td align="center">61</td><td align="center">52</td></tr>
<tr><td align="center">65</td><td align="center">45</td></tr>
<tr><td align="center">60</td><td align="center">50</td></tr>
</table>

   a. Find $\overline{X}$, s^2, and s for each group using the definitional formula for s^2 as illustrated in Example Problem 5–1.
   b. Find $\overline{X}$, s^2, and s for each group using the computational formula for s^2 as illustrated in Example Problem 5–2.
   c. From the values of s and s^2 obtained, which group has more variable scores?
   d. If you use $\overline{X}$ to predict a typical score in the read-by-teacher group, what would be the average error in your prediction?

3. Many psychologists are interested in the concept of personal space, the idea that each person has an invisible boundary or space around him or her that the individual does not want strangers to encroach upon. One approach to the investigation of this phenomenon has been to invade a person's personal space in a public place, such as a college library or cafeteria, by having an experimenter sit in an empty chair next to the person. An accomplice of the experimenter then covertly times how long the person remains seated next to the experimenter who has invaded his or her personal space. Suppose that a male experimenter invaded the personal space of 10 college-aged males and 10 college-aged females while they were seated in a library. The amount of time (in minutes) that each person stayed seated next to the experimenter was recorded as follows:

Gender of Person	
Male	**Female**
10.6	8.6
19.8	4.7
4.3	9.1
21.6	6.3
15.7	2.4
8.1	7.0
26.4	7.8
17.9	10.5

a. Find $\overline{X}$, s^2, and s for each group. Use the computational formula for s^2 as illustrated in Example Problem 5–2.

b. From the values of s and s^2 obtained, which group has more variable scores?

c. What is the average error in describing a male as taking 15.55 minutes to move after his personal space was invaded?

d. If you use the mean of a group to predict the typical behavior of a subject, will you make more accurate predictions for males or females? Explain your answer.

A COMPARISON OF MEASURES OF VARIABILITY

To aid in comparing measures of variability, Table 5–3 presents each measure of variability for the TAI scores of Table 3–3. It is evident that the values differ from each other considerably. Because each measure conveys different information about the scores, the numerical values of different measures are not directly comparable to each other. The range, *IQR*, and the *SIQR* provide intervals containing a certain percentage of participants' scores; 100 percent for the range, the middle 50 percent for the interquartile range, and 25 percent on each side of the median for the semi-interquartile range. The variance and standard deviation provide an index of the average amount by which

TABLE 5–3
Comparison of measures of variability for the 100 Test
Anxiety Inventory scores of Table 3–3.

Measure of Variability	Value
Range	51
Interquartile range (*IQR*)	8
Semi-interquartile range (*SIQR*)	4
Estimated population standard deviation (s)	8.66
Estimated population variance (s^2)	74.92

scores deviate from the mean. For all measures of variability, however, the smaller the value is the less dispersion there is among the scores. If all individuals had the same scores and there were no variability at all, then the value for each measure would be zero.

THE CHOICE OF DESCRIPTIVE STATISTICS

I have discussed a variety of statistics used to describe the average score and the variability of scores from a sample. Researchers, however, usually select only one measure of central tendency and one measure of variability to summarize their data from a study. The choice of which descriptive statistic to use to summarize data depends principally on three considerations: (1) the scale of measurement represented by the scores, (2) the shape of the frequency distribution of the scores, and (3) the intended use of the descriptive statistics for further statistical analysis. Table 5–4 summarizes the recommended measures depending on the scale of measurement and the shape of the distribution.

Scale of Measurement

Nominal Measurement

With nominal measurement, responses are classified into categories, and all responses within a category are equated behaviorally. Consequently, nominal data usually are described only in terms of frequencies (i.e., how many individuals in a group were assigned to one category or another) or percentages. Thus nominal measurement is not included in Table 5–4.

TABLE 5–4
Recommended measures of central tendency and variability given scales of measurement of the scores and the shape of the frequency distribution.

| | Shape of the Frequency Distribution | | | |
| | Approximately Symmetrical Unimodal | | Skewed Unimodal | |
Scale of Measurement	Measure of Central Tendency	Measure of Variability	Measure of Central Tendency	Measure of Variability
Ordinal	Mdn	SIQR	Mdn	SIQR
Interval or ratio	$\overline{X}$	s	Mdn	SIQR

Ordinal Measurement

With ordinal data the median is the most appropriate measure of central tendency, regardless of the shape of the frequency distribution or what further statistical analyses are intended. When the median is used as the measure of central tendency, typically the range, the interquartile range, or the semi-interquartile range is used as a measure of variability.

Interval and Ratio Measurement

When the frequency distribution of scores is approximately symmetric, the mean is the preferred measure of central tendency for interval and ratio measures. The estimated population standard deviation is the measure of variability commonly used with the mean.

Shape of the Frequency Distribution

The shape of the frequency distribution is usually a determinant in the choice of the descriptive statistics only when the dependent variable is measured with an interval or ratio scale of measurement. If the distribution of scores is approximately symmetrical, then the sample mean and standard deviation are the preferred statistics. But if the distribution of scores is considerably skewed, then the median and *SIQR* may be the descriptive statistics of choice.

Further Data Analysis

The choice of measures of central tendency and variability is also determined by whether the descriptive statistics are to be used for statistical inference. For inferential purposes, the mean, estimated population standard deviation, and estimated population variance are used because they are related to the known characteristics of the normal distribution. These relationships are discussed in Chapter 6. Hence behavioral scientists may use the sample mean and standard deviation to summarize their data when considerations of level of measurement and shape of the frequency distribution might dictate against it. The issue of making inferences from the data sometimes overrides these other considerations. For this reason, you will find that the mean and standard deviation are the most frequently utilized descriptive statistics in behavioral research.

TESTING YOUR KNOWLEDGE 5–3

1. For each of the following distributions of scores, indicate the measure of central tendency and variability that would provide the most appropriate description of the scores.
   a. The scores represent interval measurement and the distribution is heavily negatively skewed.
   b. The scores represent ordinal measurement and the distribution is approximately symmetric.

c. The scores represent ratio measurement and the distribution is approximately symmetric.
d. The scores represent ordinal measurement and the distribution is heavily positively skewed.
e. The scores represent interval measurement and the distribution is approximately symmetric.
f. The scores represent interval measurement and the distribution is heavily positively skewed.
g. The scores represent ratio measurement and the distribution is heavily negatively skewed.

SUMMARY

- Measures of variability quantify how much scores differ from each other and the measure of central tendency of a distribution.
- The range is found by $X_{\text{highest}} - X_{\text{lowest}}$.
- The interquartile range is the interval between the 25th and 75th percentiles of a distribution.
- The semi-interquartile range is one-half the interquartile range.
- The sample variance, S^2, is defined as $\Sigma(X - \overline{X})^2/N$.
- The estimated population variance, s^2, is defined as $\Sigma(X - \overline{X})^2/(N - 1)$.
- The square root of the variance provides the standard deviation. The square root of S^2 provides the sample standard deviation, and the square root of s^2 provides the estimated population standard deviation.
- The estimated population variance and standard deviation are the most frequently used measures of variability.
- The choice of a measure of variability depends on the scale of measurement represented in the scores, the shape of the frequency distribution of the scores, and what further data analysis is intended.

KEY TERMS AND SYMBOLS

estimated population standard deviation	S^2	semi-interquartile range
estimated population variance	S	$SIQR$
interquartile range	s^2	SS
IQR	s	sum of squares
population variance	σ^2	variability
range	sample standard deviation	X_{25}
	sample variance	X_{75}

REVIEW QUESTIONS

1. Is a student's perception of the expertness of a professor related to the professor's gender? Suppose that you had 20 male college juniors rate the expertness of a male professor giving a lecture. To rate expertness, you used the Teacher Rating Form, a summated rating scale (McCarthy & Schmeck, 1982). Scores on this scale may range from 12 (perceived as very inexpert) to 84 (perceived as very expert). The 20 scores you obtained were 50, 65, 44, 47, 52, 55, 35, 43, 43, 50, 60, 40, 45, 50, 45, 57, 47, 53, 54, and 57.
   a. Find the Mdn, $\overline{X}$, IQR, and s for this distribution.
   b. From a purely descriptive view, does the Mdn or $\overline{X}$ appear to be a better measure of central tendency for these scores? Explain your answer.
2. Suppose now that you had 20 male college juniors rate the expertness of a female professor giving the same lecture as the male professor of question 1, and you obtained the following expertness scores: 50, 80, 44, 47, 52, 55, 17, 43, 43, 50, 60, 40, 45, 50, 45, 57, 47, 53, 54, and 57.
   a. Find the Mdn, $\overline{X}$, IQR, and s for this distribution.
   b. From a purely descriptive view, does the Mdn or $\overline{X}$ appear to be a better measure of central tendency for these scores? Explain your answer.
   c. The value of s increased considerably in this set of scores compared with the value of s for question 1. The IQR did not change, however. Explain this outcome.
3. For each of the following statements, which measure of variability is described?
   a. It provides an interval that contains 100 percent of the scores.
   b. Its value is found by subtracting the 25th percentile score from the 75th percentile score.
   c. It provides an interval that contains about 25 percent of the scores above and below the median.
   d. It provides the average squared deviation of a score from the mean of the distribution and it estimates for the population.
   e. It provides the square root of the average squared deviation of a score from the mean of the distribution and it estimates for the population.
   f. It provides an interval that contains the middle 50 percent of the scores in a distribution.
   g. Its value depends on only two scores in the distribution.
   h. Its value is found by the formula $\Sigma(X - \overline{X})^2/N$.
   i. Its value is found by the formula $\Sigma(X - \overline{X})^2/(N - 1)$.
   j. Its value is found by the formula $\sqrt{\Sigma(X - \overline{X})^2/N}$.
   k. Its value is found by the formula $\sqrt{\Sigma(X - \overline{X})^2/(N - 1)}$.
   l. Its value is found by the formula $(X_{75} - X_{25})/2$.
4. Question 6 of the Review Questions for Chapter 4 presented partial results of a survey by Gross (1993) on drinking behavior by college students and reported that men over 21 years old estimated having a mean of 23.9 drinks per week and

women a mean of 7.5 drinks per week. The standard deviations associated with these means were 15.4 drinks per week for the men and 8.7 drinks per week for the women.

    a. If you predicted that the typical college male over 21 years old had 23.9 drinks per week, what would be the average error of your prediction?

    b. Would you judge these standard deviations to indicate a large or small amount of variation in the estimates given?

    c. What information do these standard deviations give you about the appropriateness of the mean as a measure of central tendency for the distributions of scores obtained in this survey?

5. Question 7 of the Review Questions for Chapter 4 presented simple reaction times of eight of nine surgical patients 2 hours after the administration of general anesthesia. The ninth patient was not recovered sufficiently to respond to a stimulus and was assigned an infinite reaction time. If you wanted to include the scores of all nine subjects, what measure of variability could you calculate on these scores? Explain your choice of measure.

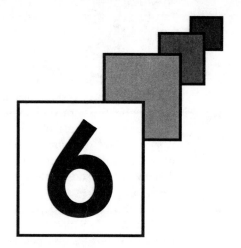

The Normal Distribution, Probability, and Standard Scores

To this point, I have discussed organizing and describing scores from a sample. I now turn to a discussion of populations and their characteristics, with emphasis on one population distribution, the normal distribution. In Chapter 1, I defined a **population** as a complete set of people, animals, objects, or events that possess a common characteristic. A **sample** is some subset or subgroup selected from a population. Chapters 3, 4, and 5 discussed organizing and describing the scores from a sample by using frequency distributions and descriptive statistics such as the median, mean, semi-interquartile range, and standard deviation.

Parameter: A number that describes a characteristic of a population.

The scores of a population, too, may be described by measures of central tendency and variability. Suppose that I could measure all the individuals in some population of interest. Following procedures developed in Chapters 4 and 5, I could summarize the scores by computing, for example, a mean and a standard deviation on the scores. Now, however, to indicate that I measured an entire population, I identify the mean as μ (mu, the twelfth letter of the Greek alphabet, pronounced "mew") and the standard deviation as σ (sigma, the eighteenth letter of the Greek alphabet). Moreover, I no longer call the values obtained *statistics*; rather I call them *parameters*. A **parameter** is a number, such as μ or σ, that describes a population.

The purpose of this change in terminology is to ensure that it is clear whether I am discussing a sample or a population. It is important to understand this distinction, for the normal distribution that I discuss next is characterized by μ and σ, rather than by $\overline{X}$ and s. This terminology is summarized in Table 6–1.

NORMAL DISTRIBUTION

Normal distribution: A theoretical mathematical distribution that specifies the relative frequency of a set of scores in a population.

One population distribution of importance to the behavioral sciences is the normal distribution. The **normal distribution** is a theoretical mathematical distribution that specifies the relative frequency of a population of scores. The frequency distribution for a normally distributed set of scores can be described completely by knowing only the mean (μ) and the standard deviation (σ) of the distribution. A normal distribution with $\mu = 70$ and $\sigma = 10$ is illustrated in Figure 6–1. The distribution shown is a mathematical distribution that does not represent any actually measured population of scores. No real population

TABLE 6–1
Notation for samples and populations.

	Sample	Population
Descriptive characteristics	Statistics	Parameters
Mean	$\overline{X}$	μ
Standard deviation	s	σ
Variance	s^2	σ^2

FIGURE 6–1
A normal distribution with $\mu = 70$ and $\sigma = 10$.

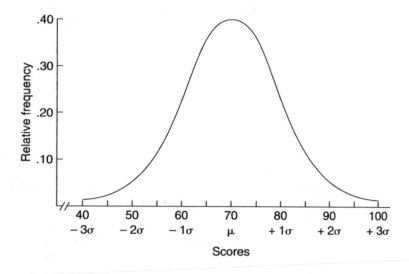

of scores is distributed so precisely that it will be exactly normal. But it will be useful at times to assume that some populations of scores are approximately normally distributed. In this chapter, however, I focus on the normal distribution as a theoretical mathematical distribution.

The Normal Distribution and the Behavioral Sciences

The normal distribution developed from the work of Jakob Bernoulli (1654–1705), Abraham de Moivre (1667–1754), Pierre Remond de Montmort (1678–1719), Karl Friedrich Gauss (1777–1855), and others. Their interests were in developing mathematical approximations for probabilities encountered in various games of chance or in the distribution of errors to be expected in observations, such as in astronomy or physics. The normal distribution soon became an important distribution to statisticians because many problems in statistics can be solved only if a normal distribution is assumed.

The normal distribution also gained importance for behavioral scientists because it is reasonable to assume that any behavioral measures determined by a large number of independent variables will be approximately normally distributed for a population. Many human capabilities, such as mathematical ability or verbal skills, are determined by a number of independent factors—genetic heritage, parental encouragement, schooling, a particular teacher, social class, cultural forces, and so forth. Consequently, measurements of such abilities are likely to be approximately normally distributed in a population. I stress the word *approximately*, for no actual set of scores is exactly normally distributed.

Properties of the Normal Distribution

The normal distribution possesses the properties of being symmetrical, asymptotic, and continuous.

Symmetrical

A theoretical normal distribution is **symmetrical** about its mode, median, and mean. In a normal distribution, then, the mode, median, and mean are equal to each other.

Asymptotic

Notice from Figure 6–1 that the tails of the normal distribution approach closer to the base line, or abscissa, as they get farther away from μ. The distribution, however, is **asymptotic**; the tails never touch the base line, regardless of the distance from μ.

Continuous

The normal distribution is **continuous** for all scores between plus and minus infinity. This means that, for any two scores, I can always obtain another score that lies between them.

Area under the Normal Distribution

The normal distribution is a theoretical relative frequency distribution. Recall from Chapter 3 that the relative frequency of a score is the frequency of occurrence of the score divided by the total number of scores in a distribution. Thus relative frequency is expressed as a proportion, and the total cumulative relative frequency in a distribution is 1.0 (see column i of Table 3–4). Because the normal distribution is a relative frequency distribution, the total area under the distribution is equal to 1.0. That is, the relative frequencies of the scores in a normal distribution cumulate to 1.0.

In all normal distributions, specific proportions of scores are within certain intervals about the mean. In any normally distributed population, .3413 of the scores is in an interval between μ and μ plus one standard deviation (i.e., between μ and $\mu + 1\sigma$). The proportion .3413 can be expressed as a percent by multiplying by 100; thus .3413 equals 34.13 percent. Hence I can say that 34.13 percent of the scores are in an interval between μ and μ plus one standard deviation. Because the distribution is symmetrical, the same proportion of scores is within an interval between μ and μ minus one standard deviation (i.e., between μ and $\mu - 1\sigma$). This relationship is shown in Figure 6–2. The interval from one to two standard deviations above the mean (i.e., the interval from $\mu + 1\sigma$ to $\mu + 2\sigma$) contains .1359 or 13.59 percent of the scores. Similarly, an interval from one to two standard deviations below the mean (i.e., the interval from $\mu - 1\sigma$ to $\mu - 2\sigma$) also contains .1359 of the scores. Because the normal distribution is symmetrical, corresponding intervals above and below the mean always contain equal areas. Notice from Figure 6–2 that scores more than two standard deviations above μ occur only .0228 of the time (i.e.,

FIGURE 6–2

Relative frequencies of scores in certain intervals of a normal distribution.

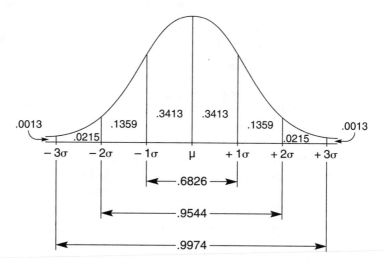

.0215 + .0013 = .0228), as do scores more than two standard deviations below μ. These relationships hold for any normal distribution regardless of the specific values of μ and σ.

The areas under the normal distribution may also be added so that, for example, the interval from the mean minus one standard deviation to the mean plus one standard deviation (i.e., from μ − 1σ to μ + 1σ) contains .3413 + .3413 or .6826 of the scores. Similarly, within plus or minus two standard deviations around the mean (the interval from μ − 2σ to μ + 2σ), .1359 + .3413 + .3413 + .1359 or .9544 of the scores occurs. Extending the range to three standard deviations around the mean (the interval from μ − 3σ to μ + 3σ) encompasses .0215 + .1359 + .3413 + .3413 + .1359 + .0215 or .9974 of the scores. These relationships also are illustrated in Figure 6–2. Again, the proportions remain the same regardless of the values of μ and σ.

To illustrate these relationships, suppose that a population of scores is normally distributed with μ = 100 and σ = 15. A score of 85 is one standard deviation below the mean (i.e., μ − 1σ = 100 − 15 = 85), and a score of 115 is one standard deviation above the mean (i.e., μ + 1σ = 100 + 15 = 115) in this distribution. Accordingly, .6826 of the scores in this distribution is within the interval of 85 to 115. Similarly, .9544 of the scores will have values between 70 and 130 (the interval from μ − 2σ to μ + 2σ), and .9974 of the scores will have values from 55 to 145 (the interval from μ − 3σ to μ + 3σ).

As another example, suppose that I have a second normally distributed population of scores with μ = 50 and σ = 5. In this distribution, .6826 of the scores is in the interval from 45 to 55 (the interval from μ − 1σ to μ + 1σ), .9544 in the interval from 40 to 60 (the interval from μ − 2σ to μ + 2σ), and .9974 in the interval from 35 to 65 (the interval from μ − 3σ to μ + 3σ).

To summarize, in a normal distribution the following relations hold between μ, σ, the proportion of scores, and the percentage of scores contained in certain intervals about the mean:

Interval	Proportion of Scores in Interval	Percentage of Scores in Interval
$\mu - 1\sigma$ to $\mu + 1\sigma$	.6826	68.26
$\mu - 2\sigma$ to $\mu + 2\sigma$	.9544	95.44
$\mu - 3\sigma$ to $\mu + 3\sigma$	.9974	99.74

In the next section you will learn to use a table to look up the proportion of scores that fall in certain intervals about the mean of a normal distribution; thus the values given here do not have to be memorized. It is useful to remember approximate values, however, so that when solving problems you can estimate answers to check on the correctness of your calculations. Thus, in solving problems it is helpful to remember the following approximations:

- The interval $\mu - 1\sigma$ to $\mu + 1\sigma$ contains approximately 68 percent of the scores.
- The interval $\mu - 2\sigma$ to $\mu + 2\sigma$ contains slightly more than 95 percent of the scores.
- The interval $\mu - 3\sigma$ to $\mu + 3\sigma$ contains over 99 percent of the scores.

TESTING YOUR KNOWLEDGE 6-1

1. Define: μ, normal distribution, parameter, population, s, sample, σ, statistic, $\overline{X}$.
2. Identify three properties of the normal distribution.
3. Why may scores obtained from an actual population of people never be exactly normally distributed? *Hint:* Think of the properties of the normal distribution.
4. Assume that you have a normally distributed population of scores with $\mu = 200$ and $\sigma = 20$. Indicate the proportions of scores that will be contained within each of the following intervals (use Figure 6-2).

Interval

a. 200 to 220
b. 200 to 240
c. 200 to 260
d. 180 to 200
e. 160 to 200
f. 140 to 200
g. 180 to 260
h. 160 to 240
i. 140 to 260
j. 220 to 240
k. 220 to 260
l. 140 to 160

STANDARD NORMAL DISTRIBUTION

Knowing the mean and standard deviation of a normal distribution provides precise information about the proportion of scores contained within certain intervals on that distribution. Because the normal distribution is defined by a mathematical equation, I can determine the exact relative frequency for any interval of scores on the distribution. A problem faced, however, is that I have to utilize a complex mathematical equation employing the value of μ and σ for the distribution of scores of interest. Fortunately, there is a simple way around this problem. The solution is to transform a normal distribution with mean μ and standard deviation σ (e.g., $\mu = 20$, $\sigma = 2$) into a standard form with $\mu = 0$ and $\sigma = 1$. Then, if I use only one standard normal distribution, with $\mu = 0$ and $\sigma = 1$, I can solve the equation for score values and table the relative frequencies found. Subsequently, I could simply look up the relative frequency or cumulative relative frequency of scores in a table, rather than using the equation of the normal distribution.

Standard normal distribution: A normal distribution with $\mu = 0$ and $\sigma = 1$.

The **standard normal distribution** (also called the *unit normal distribution*) has a mean of zero ($\mu = 0$) and a standard deviation of one ($\sigma = 1$). A score (e.g., X) from a normally distributed variable with any μ and σ may be transformed into a score on the standard normal distribution by employing the relation

$$z_{obs} = (X - \mu)/\sigma$$

Standard normal deviate: The value of z_{obs} when a score is transformed into a score on the standard normal distribution.

where z_{obs} is the value of z observed from the score, X is the original score, μ is the mean, and σ the standard deviation of the normal distribution from which the score X arose. The value of z_{obs} is the value of the score on the standard normal distribution; hence it is often called a **standard normal deviate**. A standard normal distribution is illustrated in Figure 6–3. The figure includes the proportion of scores between the illustrated z scores. Notice that, because $z = +1$ indicates a score one standard deviation above the mean, the proportion of scores between $z = 0$ and $z = +1$ is .3413, the same as the proportion of scores between μ and $\mu + 1\sigma$ in Figure 6–2.

To demonstrate the use of the standard normal distribution, suppose that a score of 115 (i.e., $X = 115$) is obtained from a normally distributed set of scores with $\mu = 100$ and $\sigma = 15$. This score is converted to a z_{obs} by

$$z_{obs} = \frac{X - \mu}{\sigma}$$
$$= \frac{115 - 100}{15}$$
$$= \frac{15}{15} = +1.0.$$

For the original score of 115, the transformed standard normal score is +1.0. The z_{obs} score of +1.0 indicates that the original score (i.e., 115) is one standard deviation (i.e., 15) above the mean (i.e., 100) of the normal distribution from which it was obtained.

The transformation of a score to a z score on the standard normal distribution locates the original score (i.e., X) in terms of how many standard deviations the score is

FIGURE 6–3
The standard normal distribution with $\mu = 0$ and $\sigma = 1.0$. The proportion of scores between the identified z values is shown.

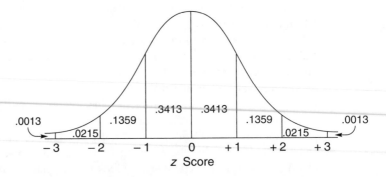

away from the mean. The score of 115 that I used as an example is $+1.0\sigma$ units away from the mean of its distribution. Consider the scores in Table 6–2 and their corresponding z_{obs} values. These scores were obtained from a normal distribution with $\mu = 75$ and $\sigma = 10$. Attempt to calculate some of the z_{obs} scores given. Notice that the z_{obs} value for any score is simply how many standard deviation units the score is above or below the mean of zero on the standard normal distribution.

A note of caution is in order here. Transforming a score, X, into a z score precisely locates the original score on the standard normal distribution only if the score is from a normally distributed set of scores. If the score is from a nonnormal distribution, such as a rectangular distribution or a bimodal distribution, then converting the score into a z score does not make the original score normally distributed.

TABLE 6–2
Transformation of scores from a normal distribution with $\mu = 75$ and $\sigma = 10$ to z scores on a standard normal distribution.

Score (X)	z
105	+3.0
100	+2.5
95	+2.0
90	+1.5
85	+1.0
80	+0.5
75	0.0
70	-0.5
65	-1.0
60	-1.5
55	-2.0
50	-2.5
45	-3.0

Using a Table of the Standard Normal Distribution

The advantage of transforming scores into z scores on a standard normal distribution is that the proportion of scores occurring between values of z is known and tabled. These proportions are presented in Table A–1 of the Appendix. A portion of Table A–1 is illustrated in Table 6–3. Column a lists values of z obtained when numerical values are substituted into the formula

$$z_{obs} = \frac{X - \mu}{\sigma}$$

Note that when I refer to z_{obs} I am discussing the z value obtained from a raw score (i.e., X). z without the subscripted *obs* always refers to the value of z in column a of Table A–1. Column b presents the area between $z = 0$ and the value of z listed in column a. The shaded area in the small figure at the top of the column illustrates this area. Column c provides the area beyond the value of z in column a to infinity. Again, the small figure at the top of the column illustrates this area. Because the normal distribution is symmetrical, negative values of z encompass areas identical to positive values of z. Thus negative values of z are not tabled.

To demonstrate using this table, consider a normally distributed set of scores with $\mu = 100$ and $\sigma = 15$. Suppose that a score of 115 is obtained on this distribution. What proportion of scores is equal to or less than 115? To solve this problem, I convert the score of 115 to a z score as follows:

$$z_{obs} = \frac{X - \mu}{\sigma}$$
$$= \frac{115 - 100}{15} = +1.0.$$

To help visualize the score I am attempting to find, it is useful to draw a figure of the standard normal distribution and indicate on it the raw scores and the z values of those scores. Accordingly, the raw scores of the distribution and the corresponding z scores are shown in Figure 6–4. The answer to the problem requires that I obtain the area of the distribution from $z = -\infty$ to $z = +1.0$. One-half (or .5000) of the scores in the distribution is below $z = 0$. Column b of Table 6–3 indicates that .3413 of the scores is between $z = 0$ and $z = +1.0$ (see the axis labeled c in Figure 6–4). Thus the answer to the problem is the proportion of scores from $z = -\infty$ to $z = 0$ (.5000) plus the proportion of scores from $z = 0$ to $z = +1.0$ (.3413 from column b of Table A–1), or .8413. The proportion of scores equal to or less than 115 is .8413 or 84.13 percent.

It is very easy to make mistakes reading Table A–1; hence it is always useful to estimate an answer to the problem and then check that the answer obtained by looking up the values in Table A–1 corresponds to the estimated answer. For this problem, you can estimate an answer by knowing that a little over one-third (i.e., slightly over 33 percent) of the scores is between the mean and one standard deviation in a normal distribution. Thus you would estimate your answer to be slightly more than 50 percent plus 33 percent, or slightly more than 83 percent total. The actual answer of 84.13 percent corresponds to this estimated answer.

TABLE 6–3
Proportion of area under the normal distribution between $z = 0.95$ and $z = 1.10$.

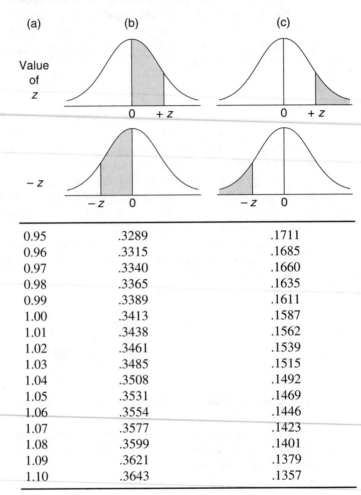

(a)	(b)	(c)
Value of z		
0.95	.3289	.1711
0.96	.3315	.1685
0.97	.3340	.1660
0.98	.3365	.1635
0.99	.3389	.1611
1.00	.3413	.1587
1.01	.3438	.1562
1.02	.3461	.1539
1.03	.3485	.1515
1.04	.3508	.1492
1.05	.3531	.1469
1.06	.3554	.1446
1.07	.3577	.1423
1.08	.3599	.1401
1.09	.3621	.1379
1.10	.3643	.1357

Excerpted and adapted from Table II.1, The Normal Probability Function and Related Functions. *CRC Handbook of Tables for Probability and Statistics* (2nd ed.). Copyright 1968, CRC Press, Inc., Boca Raton, Florida. Used by permission.

Suppose that I now want to know the proportion of scores equal to or greater than 115. I may obtain this proportion in one of two ways. First, because I have already found that 84.13 percent of the scores will be equal to or less than 115, the remaining area under the normal distribution must indicate the number of scores that will be equal to or greater than 115. I find this proportion by subtracting .8413 from 1.000, the total

FIGURE 6-4

Location of a score of 115 from a normal distribution with $\mu = 100$ and $\sigma = 15$ on the standard normal distribution. The labels on the X axis show (a) the raw scores, (b) z scores corresponding to the raw scores, and (c) the proportion of scores from $z = -\infty$ to $z = 0$ and from $z = 0$ to $z = +1$.

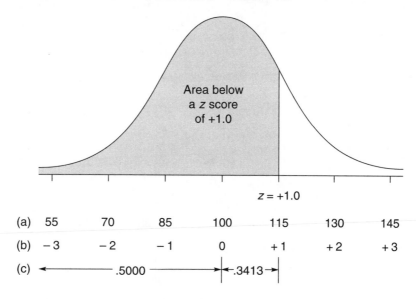

area of the distribution. Accordingly, $1.000 - .8413 = .1587$, the proportion of scores equal to or larger than 115.

If I had not previously found that .8413 of the scores is equal to or less than 115, then I could solve the problem by recognizing that the proportion requested is the area of the distribution beyond $z = +1.0$. Using Table 6–3, I find the value of $z = 1.00$ in column a. I then read across to column c, which presents the proportion of scores beyond z. For $z = +1.0$, this value is .1587. Thus .1587 of the scores, or 15.87%, is equal to or greater than 115.

Consider another problem from this distribution. What proportion of scores in this distribution is equal to or less than 82? Again I convert 82 to a z score, $z_{obs} = (82 - 100)/15 = -1.2$. This z_{obs} indicates that a score of 82 is 1.2 standard deviations below the mean of the distribution. The raw scores of the distribution and the $z_{obs} = -1.2$ are shown in Figure 6–5. I then obtain the proportion of scores below z equal to −1.2. Notice that from the figure alone I can estimate that this proportion will be very small. Because the standard normal distribution is symmetrical, as many scores lie beyond $z = -1.2$ as lie beyond $z = +1.2$; thus I look up $z = +1.2$. This value is not included in Table 6–3, however; thus I use the complete table of proportions of area under the normal distribution given in Table A–1. I find $z = 1.2$ in column a and read across to the value of .1151 in column c. Thus .1151 of the scores or 11.51 percent is equal to or less than 82. Other uses of the standard normal distribution are given in Example Problem 6–1.

FIGURE 6–5

Location of a score of 82 from a normal distribution with $\mu = 100$ and $\sigma = 15$ on the standard normal distribution. The labels on the X axis show (a) the raw scores, (b) z scores corresponding to the raw scores, and (c) the proportion of scores from $z = -\infty$ to $z = -1.2$.

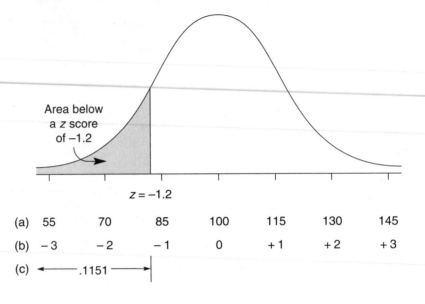

Area below
a z score
of –1.2

$z = -1.2$

(a)	55	70	85	100	115	130	145
(b)	– 3	– 2	– 1	0	+ 1	+ 2	+ 3
(c)	◀——— .1151 ———▶						

Example Problem 6–1

Using the Standard Normal Distribution

Assume a normally distributed population with $\mu = 80$ and $\sigma = 5$.

Problem

What proportion of scores in this distribution is equal to or greater than 88?

Statistic to Be Used: $z_{obs} = (X - \mu)/\sigma$.

Solution   The score of 88 must be converted into z_{obs}. Then Table A–1 is used to obtain the proportion of scores equal to or greater than z_{obs}. Substituting numerical values into the formula for z, I obtain

$$z_{obs} = \frac{88 - 80}{5} = \frac{8}{5} = +1.6.$$

Column c of Table A–1 indicates that the area of the standard normal distribution equal to or greater than $z = +1.6$ is .0548. Hence the proportion of scores equal to or greater than 88 is .0548 or 5.48%. Thus, out of every 1000 scores in the population, 54.8 are equal to or greater than 88.

Problem

What proportion of scores in this distribution is between 83 and 87?

Solution   Both 83 and 87 must be converted to z_{obs} scores. Then I obtain the area of the standard normal distribution between the two values of z_{obs}. Substituting numerical values, I obtain

$$z_{obs} \text{ for } 83 = \frac{83 - 80}{5} = \frac{3}{5} = +0.6,$$

$$z_{obs} \text{ for } 87 = \frac{87 - 80}{5} = \frac{7}{5} = +1.4.$$

The raw scores and the corresponding z_{obs} scores are shown in Figure 6–6. From column b of Table A–1, for $z_{obs} = +0.6$, the proportion of scores between $z = 0$ and $z = 0.6$ is .2257. For $z_{obs} = +1.4$, the proportion of scores between $z = 0$ and $z = +1.4$ is .4192. The area of the distribution between these two values of z provides the proportion of scores between 83 and 87. To obtain this area, I subtract .2257 from .4192. The result is .1935 (see the axis labeled c in Figure 6–6). Thus the proportion of scores that is in the interval from 83 to 87 is .1935 or 19.35 percent. For every 1000 scores, 193.5 are between scores of 83 to 87.

FIGURE 6–6

Location of scores of 83 and 87 from a normal distribution with $\mu = 80$ and $\sigma = 5$ on the standard normal distribution. The labels on the X axis show (a) the raw scores, (b) z scores corresponding to the raw scores, and (c) the proportion of scores from $z = 0$ to $z = +0.6$ and from $z = 0$ to $z = +1.4$.

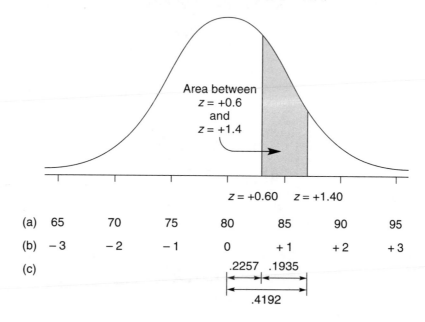

Problem

What proportion of scores is between 65 and 74?

Solution   This problem is solved identically to the previous problem. Both 65 and 74 must be converted to z_{obs} scores. Then I find the area of the standard normal distribution between the values of z_{obs} for the two scores. Substituting numerical values, I obtain

$$z_{obs} \text{ for } 65 = \frac{65 - 80}{5} = \frac{-15}{5} = -3.0,$$

$$z_{obs} \text{ for } 74 = \frac{74 - 80}{5} = \frac{-6}{5} = -1.2.$$

The raw scores and the corresponding z_{obs} scores are shown in Figure 6–7. Column b of Table A–1 indicates that .4987 of the scores is between $z = 0$ and $z = -3.0$. For $z_{obs} = -1.2$, .3849 of the scores is between $z = 0$ and $z = -1.2$. I obtain the proportion of scores between $z = -3.0$ and $z = -1.2$ by subtracting .3849 from .4987. This value is .1138 (see the axis labeled c in Figure 6–7). The proportion of scores in the interval from 65 to 74 is .1138 or 11.38 percent. For every 1000 scores in the population, 113.8 are between 65 to 74.

FIGURE 6–7

Location of scores of 65 and 74 from a normal distribution with $\mu = 80$ and $\sigma = 5$ on the standard normal distribution. The labels on the X axis show (a) the raw scores, (b) z scores corresponding to the raw scores, and (c) the proportion of scores from $z = 0$ to $z = -3.0$ and from $z = 0$ to $z = -1.2$.

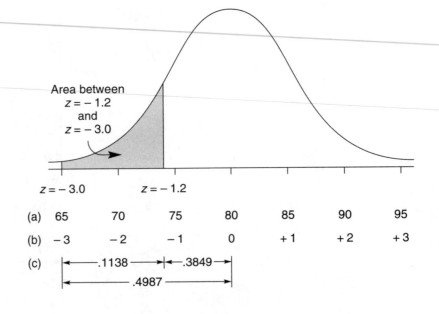

Problem

What range of scores includes the middle 80 percent of the scores on the distribution?

Solution   This problem is solved by finding areas in column b of Table A–1 that include a proportion of .40 or 40 percent of the scores on each side of the mean, determining the z value for these scores, and then solving the formula for z to obtain values of X. Figure 6–8 illustrates the proportions and scores that I need. To find the z that includes .40 of the scores between $z = 0$ and its value, I read down column b until I find the proportion closest to .40. This area is .3997, which corresponds to a z of 1.28. Thus scores that result in z values between 0 to +1.28 occur with a relative frequency of .3997, and scores that result in z values between 0 to −1.28 also occur with a relative frequency of .3997. The total area encompassed by scores between $z = -1.28$ to $z = +1.28$ is .3997 + .3997 = .7994, or approximately .80. The last step is to obtain the values of X that correspond to $z = -1.28$ and $z = +1.28$. To find these values, I substitute numerical values of z, μ, and σ into the formula $z_{\text{obs}} = (X - \mu)/\sigma$ and solve for X.

For $z_{\text{obs}} = +(1.28)$,

$$+1.28 = \frac{X - 80}{5}.$$

FIGURE 6–8

Illustration of finding scores that include the middle 80 percent of the scores from a normal distribution with $\mu = 80$ and $\sigma = 5$ on the standard normal distribution. The labels on the X axis show (a) the raw scores, (b) z scores corresponding to the raw scores, and (c) the proportion of scores from $z = 0$ to $z = -1.28$ and from $z = 0$ to $z = +1.28$.

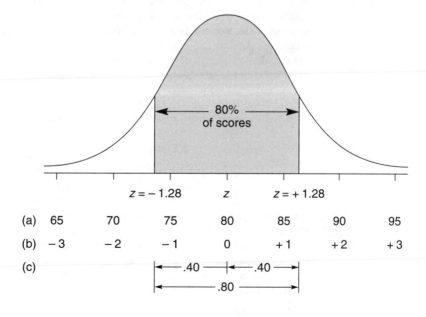

Solving this equation for X,

$$(+1.28)5 = X - 80$$
$$X = 5(1.28) + 80$$
$$= 6.4 + 80$$
$$= 86.4.$$

For $z_{obs} = -1.28$,

$$-1.28 = \frac{X - 80}{5}.$$

Solving this equation for X,

$$(-1.28)5 = X - 80$$
$$X = 5(-1.28) + 80$$
$$= -6.4 + 80$$
$$= 73.6.$$

Hence the middle 80 percent of the scores is between 73.6 to 86.4.

STATISTICS IN USE 6-1

Type A and Type B Behavior Patterns: Using the Standard Normal Distribution

Scores on tests standardized on a large number of people are often considered approximately normally distributed and are expressed as values of z. The knowledgeable user then knows exactly where a particular score lies with respect to the rest of the scores in the distribution. As an example, Yarnold, Grimm, and Mueser (1986) investigated whether Type A and Type B behavior patterns are related to social conformity. People characterized as Type A are thought of as extremely competitive, aggressive, impatient, and quickly irritated. Type B individuals, on the other hand, are characterized as noncompetitive, nonaggressive, patient, and calm in the face of delays and frustrations. One measure of Type A–Type B behavior patterns is the Jenkins Activity Survey (Jenkins, Zyzanski, & Rosenman, 1979). This survey is a paper-and-pencil questionnaire about typical activities with questions similar to this one:

When stuck in a traffic jam in your car,
do you ever blow the horn to express your frustration?

Never   Occasionally   Frequently   Almost always

Type A individuals are expected to answer with "frequently" or "almost always," whereas Type Bs are expected to answer with "occasionally" or "never."

Yarnold et al. hypothesized that Type A individuals would conform less to group consensus than Type B individuals when judging line length. To test this research hypothesis, they selected two groups of people, extreme Type A individuals and extreme Type B individuals, based on Jenkins Activity Survey scores. They report that the mean z score on the Jenkins

Activity Survey for the Type A individuals was +1.22 (positive z scores indicate Type A behavior), and the mean z score for Type B individuals was −1.38 (negative z scores indicate Type B behavior). This information on the mean z scores for each group permits us to precisely locate each group on the Type A–Type B dimension of the Jenkins Activity Survey. From column c of Table A–1, I find that only about .11 of the values of z on a standard normal distribution is equal to or exceeds $z = +1.22$. Thus a z of +1.22 places the group mean at the 89th percentile of scores in Type A behavior. Likewise, for a z of −1.38 I notice that only about .08 of the scores is below this value on the Type B dimension. The goal of achieving groups extreme in either Type A or Type B behavior was met. The results of the study supported the hypothesis; Type B individuals conformed to a group consensus twice as often as Type A subjects.

TESTING YOUR KNOWLEDGE 6–2

1. Define: standard normal deviate, standard normal distribution, z, z_{obs}.
2. For each of the following values of X, μ, and σ, obtain the value of z_{obs}. Then use Table A–1 to find the area between $z = 0$ and z and the area beyond z.

	μ	σ	X
a.	73	4.2	81
b.	127	11.6	121
c.	17	1.3	18
d.	50	6.0	39
e.	5	0.4	5.7
f.	256	35.0	212

3. Solve the following problems using the approach illustrated in Example Problem 6–1. You have conducted a large-scale testing project measuring students on a test of reasoning with verbal analogies. Assume that the distribution of test scores is normally distributed with $\mu = 72$ and $\sigma = 8$.
   a. What proportion of scores in the distribution is equal to or greater than 86?
   b. What proportion of scores in the distribution is between 80 and 90?
   c. What proportion of scores in the distribution is between 60 and 70?
   d. What range of scores includes the middle 90 percent of scores on the test?

PROBABILITY

I have discussed the normal distribution as a theoretical relative frequency distribution, but it also is a probability distribution of a continuous variable. In this section, I introduce the basics of probability needed to understand probability distributions and the use of probability in statistics.

The daily activities of living provide an intuitive sense of probability. For example, have you ever received a letter similar to the following example?

Urgent Notification—Reply Immediately. You are the lucky winner of one of the following prizes:

A Brand New Luxury Town Car, Value $36,000
A Two Week All Expenses Paid Vacation in Hawaii, Value $6,500
A Wide-Screen TV with Stereo Sound, Value $1995
An Easy Use Microwave Oven, Value $375
A Top Quality 35mm Camera, Value $75
A Whiz-Bang Home Computer, Value $749.

All you need to do to claim your prize is visit beautiful LAZY ACRES VACATION RESORT and see the MAGNIFICENT home sites available for your purchase. You will definitely win one of the above prizes when you visit our STUNNING resort.

Visions of a luxurious town car or a delightful two-week vacation may begin to fill your thoughts. Those beautiful visions are shattered, however, when you read the small print on the second page of the letter. Here you find your chances of winning each gift and often they are expressed as follows:

Prize		Number of Awards/ 1,000,000 Visitors
1	Car	1
2	Vacation	20
3	TV	34
4	Microwave	66
5	Camera	999,845
6	Computer	34

Assuming that each visitor has an equal chance of winning one prize, which prize do you think that it is most likely you will win? Which prize do you think that it is least likely that you will win? Even if you haven't studied probability formally, you likely will say, "Forget prize 1, the town car, I'll take a picture of it with my camera, prize 5." Only one visitor out of a million wins a car, whereas 999,845 visitors out of a million win a camera. Obviously, the chances are that you will win the camera, not the car.

Suppose that you are asked what the probability is that you will win a TV. It's likely that you will answer something similar to "I have 34 chances in a million." In effect, what you have indicated is that the probability of winning a specific prize is found by dividing the numbers of that prize to be awarded by the total number of prizes to be given, or

$$\text{Probability of winning a specific prize} = \frac{\text{Number of the specific prize to be awarded}}{\text{Total number of prizes awarded}}.$$

Applying this formula to prize 3, I obtain the probability of winning a TV as 34/1,000,000, or .000034. If I apply this formula to each of the prizes, I obtain the following probability distribution for the prizes:

Prize	Number of Awards/ 1,000,000 Visitors	Probability of Winning
1	1	.000001
2	20	.000020
3	34	.000034
4	66	.000066
5	999,845	.999845
6	34	.000034

You may have noticed that the formula for the probability of a prize looks much like the formula for relative frequency given in Chapter 3. Indeed, this probability formula is a specific application of the relative frequency formula. In a more general sense, if the occurrence of an event in a population is independent of the occurrence of other events in that population, then the **probability (p) of occurrence** of an event is defined as

$$p \text{ (event)} = \frac{\textbf{number of occurrences of the event in a population}}{\textbf{total number of possible events in a population}}.$$

The letter p is used to indicate the probability of occurrence of an event, and the result of applying this formula is usually expressed as a decimal, for example,

$$p(\text{prize } 4) = .000066.$$

Probability of a discrete event: p (event) = number of occurrences of the event in a population / total number of possible events in a population

This definition of probability is essentially that of a relative frequency except that it is based on all the events in a population, and not only on those that may occur in a sample of the population. This formula provides the **probability for discrete events**, events that have a countable set of values, such as the number of cars to be awarded per 1 million visitors. Thus the probabilities associated with the awarding of each prize constitute a discrete probability distribution.

Properties of Discrete Probability Distributions

Probability distributions possess properties that you likely are aware of already. The probability of an event ranges between 0 to +1. An event with $p(\text{event}) = 0$ is certain not to occur, and an event with $p(\text{event}) = 1$ is certain to occur. Figure 6–9 represents a probability scale and presents the probabilities of some events. Few events are absolutely certain in life and possess a probability equal to 1, and few are absolutely impossible and possess a probability equal to 0. This range of probability from 0 to 1 corresponds to the characteristic of a relative frequency distribution that the cumulative relative frequencies (crf) range from 0 to 1.0 (see column i of Table 3–4).

FIGURE 6–9

A probability scale and the probabilities of some events.

Probability

1.0		Probability that you will eventually die.
.9		
	.86	Probability that at birth a female will live to age 60 (86 out of every 100 live female births are alive at age 60, $p = 86/100 = .86$).[1]
.8	.81	Probability that at birth a male will live to age 60 (81 out of every 100 live male births are alive at age 60, $p = 81/100 = .81$).[1]
.7		
.6	.64	Probability that an adult resident of the United States chosen at random has at least one credit card.[2]
.5		Probability that a toss of a fair coin will result in a head $(p = 1/2 = .5)$.
.4		
.3		
.2		
.1		
	.077	Probability of drawing a king from a deck of playing cards $(p = 4/52 = .077)$.
	.000000005	Approximate probability of winning a national magazine sweepstakes.[3]
0		The probability that you will live forever.

[1] 1980 Commissioners Standard Ordinary (CSO) Mortality Table (The Wizards, 1989).
[2] The Way, 1985.
[3] Artis, 1993.

Theoretical Probability

There are two ways in which we can determine the probability of an event, theoretically and empirically. For certain events we can reason the probability of occurrence of that event. As a simple example, the probability of the toss of a fair coin resulting in a head showing can be reasoned out. There are two possible outcomes of a coin toss, a head or a tail. If the coin is fair, then each is equally likely. Hence the probability of a single toss resulting in a head showing is one outcome out of the two possible, or p(head showing) $= \frac{1}{2} = .5$. Theoretical probability models often are more complex than this. As an example, in a later section, I discuss the standard normal distribution as a theoretical probability distribution.

Empirical Probability

For some events I cannot reason a theoretical probability, such as the probability that if you are a female you will live to be 60 years old. To obtain this probability, we use empirical probabilities obtained by long-term occurrences of the event. As an example, the life insurance industry uses the Commissioners Standard Ordinary Mortality Table to determine longevity rates for residents of the United States (The Wizards, 1989). This table is developed empirically over a long duration by recording mortality rates at various ages for males and females. The table indicates that for every 10,000,000 live female births, 8,603,801 females are still alive at age 60. Thus the probability at birth that a female in the United States will live to age 60 is

$$p(\text{female living to age 60}) = \frac{8,603,801}{10,000,000} = .86.$$

Of course, this value of p will change as mortality rates change due to improved health care and nutrition.

Behavioral scientists have occasion to use both theoretical and empirical probabilities, but the emphasis in this text is on theoretical distributions such as the standard normal distribution.

The Standard Normal Distribution as a Probability Distribution

The normal distribution is a theoretical relative frequency distribution. Because the relative frequencies specified in the normal distribution are based on a population, the normal distribution is also a probability distribution. But it is a slightly different probability distribution than the discrete probability distribution just introduced. A score, X, in a normal distribution is a continuous variable, one that can take on an unlimited set of values in the range within which it varies. As an example, suppose that the scores to which a theoretical normal distribution is being applied are body weights. What is the probability of finding a person who weighs exactly 123 pounds? Weight is a continuous variable, however, and some people may weigh 123.3 pounds, or perhaps 123.36, or even 123.364 pounds. Conceptually, at least, I might find someone weighing 123.3642193 pounds if I could measure so precisely. Is a weight of 123.3 pounds to be considered 123 pounds?

What of a weight of 123.00001 pounds? In principle, I can never obtain a weight of exactly 123 pounds, for I could always measure weight to a greater degree of accuracy and find that it was not exactly 123 pounds.

Following this line of reasoning, the probability of occurrence of an exact value of a continuous score is zero. But the probability of the score falling within a certain interval is not zero. Although I cannot obtain a weight of exactly 123 pounds, I can obtain a weight in the interval between 122.5 and 123.5 pounds. For example, regardless of the number of decimal places to which I may carry my measurements, a weight of 123.36 (or even 123.3642193) will always fall into the interval between 122.5 and 123.5 pounds. Thus the probability function specified by the normal distribution does not provide probabilities for discrete values of X; rather it provides probabilities that the value of X will fall within a certain interval. The probability is provided by the area under the distribution encompassed by the interval.

As an example of the normal distribution used as a probability distribution, consider the following problem. Suppose you know that a set of scores is normally distributed with $\mu = 150$ and $\sigma = 8$. If you were to randomly select a score from this distribution, what is the probability of obtaining a score between 150 and 158? To answer this question, I first transform the distribution into the standard normal distribution with $\mu = 0$ and $\sigma = 1$ using $z = (X - \mu)/\sigma$. Thus the score of 150 becomes $z = 0$, and the score of 158 becomes $z = +1.0$. The question then resolves to what is the probability of obtaining a score with a value between $z = 0$ and $z = +1.0$? The answer is the area under the standard normal distribution between $z = 0$ and $z = +1.0$, or .3413 (obtained from column b of Table A–1). Accordingly, the probability of obtaining a score between 150 and 158 is .3413. I may phrase this conclusion in probability terms as $p(150 \leq X \leq 158) = .3413$. The $\leq$ is the "less than or equal to" symbol. The number preceding the $\leq$ is less than or equal to the number following the $\leq$. Hence this statement is read "the probability that X is equal to or greater than 150 (i.e., $150 \leq X$) and equal to or less than 158 (i.e., $X \leq 158$) is .3413."

Example Problem 6–2

Using the Standard Normal Distribution as a Probability Distribution

Assume that you have the normally distributed population described in Example Problem 6–1 with $\mu = 80$ and $\sigma = 5$. The problems that follow are identical to those in Example Problem 6–1 except that they ask for probabilities rather than proportions of scores. It may be useful to refer to the figures associated with Example Problem 6–1 to follow the solutions presented.

Problem
What is the probability that a score in this distribution is equal to or greater than 88?

Statistic to Be Used: $z_{obs} = (X - \mu)/\sigma.$

Solution   The score of 88 must be converted into a z_{obs}. Then Table A–1 is to be used to obtain the proportion of scores equal to or greater than z_{obs}. This proportion represents the probability requested. Substituting numerical values into the formula for z_{obs}, I obtain

$$z_{obs} = \frac{88 - 80}{5} = \frac{8}{5} = +1.6.$$

Column c of Table A–1 indicates that the area of the standard normal distribution equal to or greater than $z = +1.6$ is .0548. Thus the probability of a score being equal to or greater than 88 is .0548 or, written as a probability statement, $p(X \geq 88) = .0548$.

Problem
What is the probability that a score in this distribution is between 83 and 87?

Solution   Both 83 and 87 must be converted to z_{obs} scores. Then I find the area of the standard normal distribution between the two values of z_{obs} (see Figure 6–6). Substituting numerical values, I obtain

$$z_{obs} \text{ for } 83 = \frac{83 - 80}{5} = \frac{3}{5} = +0.6,$$

$$z_{obs} \text{ for } 87 = \frac{87 - 80}{5} = \frac{7}{5} = +1.4.$$

From column b of Table A–1, we see that for $z_{obs} = +0.6$ the proportion of scores between $z = 0$ and $z = +0.6$ is .2257. For $z_{obs} = +1.4$, the proportion of scores between $z = 0$ and $z = +1.4$ is .4192. The area of the distribution between these two values of z provides the proportion of scores between 83 and 87. To obtain this area, I subtract .2257 from .4192. The result is .1935. This proportion represents the probability requested. Thus the probability of a score falling into the interval from 83 to 87 is .1935. In probability terms, $p(83 \leq X \leq 87) = .1935$.

Problem
What is the probability that a score in this distribution is between 65 and 74?

Solution   Both 65 and 74 must be converted to z_{obs} scores. Then I find the area of the standard normal distribution between the two values of z_{obs} (see Figure 6–7). Substituting numerical values, I obtain

$$z_{obs} \text{ for } 65 = \frac{65 - 80}{5} = \frac{-15}{5} = -3.0,$$

$$z_{obs} \text{ for } 74 = \frac{74 - 80}{5} = \frac{-6}{5} = -1.2.$$

Consulting column b of Table A–1 and recalling that, because the standard normal distribution is symmetrical, the same relations hold for negative z scores as for positive z scores, I find that .4987 of the scores lies between $z = 0$ and $z = -3.0$. For $z_{obs} = -1.2$, .3849 of the scores lies between $z = 0$ and $z = -1.2$. Accordingly, I obtain the proportion of scores between $z = -3.0$ and $z = -1.2$ by subtracting .3849 from .4987, which equals .1138. This proportion represents the probability requested; hence $p(65 \leq X \leq 74) = .1138$.

STATISTICS IN USE 6–2

Playing the Lottery

Millions of people play state lotteries on a daily or weekly basis. One popular form of the lottery is the "million dollar" type in which only a few winners share a very large lottery prize, often as large as several million dollars. The probability of winning such a lottery with one ticket is exceedingly small. Probabilities of winning as small as .0000005 or even smaller often exist in these lotteries. A probability of .0000005 represents 5 chances out of 10,000,000 of winning the lottery, about the same as the probability of being struck and killed by lightning. It seems with such a small probability that no one would purchase a lottery ticket; there is virtually no chance of winning. Yet people continue to buy lottery tickets in record numbers. Why? Many behavioral scientists believe that people play lotteries because they cannot conceptualize the probabilities involved. I indicated earlier that most of us have an intuitive notion of probability. Indeed, this is likely the case for commonly encountered probabilities that we can easily conceptualize—the probability of .3 that rain will fall on a certain day or the probability of .5 that a flipped coin will land as a head. But it is very difficult to conceptualize a probability of .0000005. What does it mean to say that chances of winning are 5 in 10 million? Can you visualize this probability? You can visualize a coin being flipped and coming up heads or tails, but how can you visualize the occurrence of 5 events out of a possible 10 million events?

One behavioral scientist, David Bell, suggests that this probability could be visualized by imagining 10,000,000 playing cards placed face down, side by side, and top to bottom on an open field (Mehegan, 1985, October 17). To accommodate this many cards, the field would have to be approximately 1000 feet long and 700 feet wide (about the size of two and one-half football fields). Five of the cards are marked with an X on the face. Your task is to pick out the five cards with the X on the first try. If you visualize the probability of winning a lottery in this way, would you still continue to play?

TESTING YOUR KNOWLEDGE 6–3

1. Define: discrete event, empirical probability, probability of a discrete event, theoretical probability.

2. What is the formula for the probability of occurrence of a discrete event?

3. You have purchased a ticket for a raffle of a bicycle. The ticket states that one bicycle will be raffled off for every 700 tickets sold. What is the probability that you will win a bicycle in this raffle?

4. A recent survey based on a large random sample of adults in the United States indicated that 19 percent of American men report sleeping in the nude. If you were to ask a randomly chosen man about his sleeping attire, what is the probability he would report sleeping in the nude?

5. For each of the following values of X, μ, and σ, obtain the value of z. Then use Table A–1 to find the probability of a score being equal to or larger than the score given.

	μ	σ	X
a.	73	4.2	81
b.	127	11.6	121
c.	17	1.3	18
d.	50	6.0	39
e.	5	0.4	5.7
f.	256	35.0	212

6. You have conducted a large-scale testing project measuring students on a test of reasoning with verbal analogies. Assume that the distribution of test scores is normally distributed, with $\mu = 72$ and $\sigma = 8$.
   a. What is the probability of a score in the distribution being equal to or greater than 84?
   b. What is the probability of a score in the distribution falling between 78 and 86?
   c. What is the probability of a score in the distribution falling between 64 and 70?

STANDARD SCORES

We have seen that we can take a normally distributed raw score and transform it into a score on the standard normal distribution by using the formula

$$z_{obs} = \frac{X - \mu}{\sigma}.$$

The z_{obs} is a standard score that can be used for comparing scores from two different normal distributions. For example, suppose that a person obtained a score of 75 on a test with $\mu = 70$ and $\sigma = 5$ and a score of 110 on a second test with $\mu = 100$ and $\sigma = 10$. Assume that scores on both tests are normally distributed. For the scores of 75 and 110, z_{obs} is +1 for each. On both tests the individual scored one standard deviation above the mean. Accordingly, the person's standing in relation to other scores on the tests is identical for both tests; he or she has obtained a score one standard deviation above the mean.

It would be useful to make a similar transformation on scores from a sample, even if the scores were not normally distributed. I may make such a transformation using the formula

$$z = \frac{X - \overline{X}}{S},$$

where X = score of interest
         $\overline{X}$ = mean of the sample of scores
         S = sample standard deviation using the formula

$$S = \sqrt{\frac{\Sigma(X - \overline{X})^2}{N}}.$$

Standard score: A score
obtained by using the
transformation $z = (X - \overline{X})/S$.

The z value obtained from this formula is often called a **standard score**. This formula transforms a score into a number indicating how far away from the mean of the sample the score is in standard deviation units. To illustrate, suppose that I gave a statistics test and a history test to five students and obtained the raw and z scores given in Table 6–4. Standard scores were obtained using the formula given previously. For example, Amalia's raw score on the statistics test was 91. The mean on the test was 72.0 and S was 14.2. Thus Amalia's z score is found as

$$z_{obs} = \frac{X - \overline{X}}{S}$$
$$= \frac{91 - 72.0}{14.2}$$
$$= \frac{19.0}{14.2} = +1.34.$$

By knowing the standard score, I know Amalia's score with relation to the class mean; it is 1.34 standard deviations above the mean.

   With standard scores I can easily compare scores from one test to the other, something I cannot do from the raw scores alone. For example, Jeff is 1.06 standard deviation units above the mean on his statistics test, but 0.50 standard deviation units below the mean on his history test. Positive standard scores indicate scores above the sample mean, scores of 0 (such as the history score of Denise) are equal to the sample mean, and negative standard scores are below the sample mean. You should note, however, that, because this z is obtained from a sample of scores, it will not possess the same characteristics with respect to the normal distribution as the z obtained by $z = (X - \mu)/\sigma$. Nevertheless, standard scores are often used when reporting test results, for the score provides the person's relative standing with respect to others taking the same test. The standard score conversion does not change the shape of the distribution of scores, however. If

TABLE 6–4
Raw scores and standard scores for five students on a statistics test and a history test.

	Test			
	Statistics		**History**	
Person	**Raw Score**	**z Score**	**Raw Score**	**z Score**
Amalia	91	+1.34	93	+1.18
Denise	62	−0.70	79	0.00
Jeff	87	+1.06	73	−0.50
Hans	56	−1.13	90	+0.92
Matt	64	−0.56	60	−1.60
$\overline{X}$	72.0		79.0	
S	14.2		11.9	

the distribution of raw scores was skewed, then the distribution of standard scores will remain skewed.

SUMMARY

- The normal distribution is a theoretical relative frequency distribution; no measured scores are exactly normally distributed. It is often useful, however, to assume that some behavioral measures are approximately normally distributed.
- A normal distribution can be transformed into a standard normal distribution with $\mu = 0$ and $\sigma = 1$ by the relation $z = (X - \mu)/\sigma$.
- The probability of a discrete event is found by

$$p(\text{event}) = \frac{\text{number of occurrences of the event in a population}}{\text{total number of events in a population}} .$$

- The standard normal distribution is a probability distribution specifying the probabilities associated with scores falling into a certain interval of the distribution. It can be used with normally distributed scores to either obtain the proportion of scores that will fall within specified intervals or to find the probability of scores occurring within specified intervals.
- Raw scores from a sample may be transformed into standard scores using the formula

$$z = \frac{X - \overline{X}}{S} .$$

This formula transforms a score into a number indicating how far away from the mean the score is in standard deviation units. It does not change the shape of the distribution of the raw scores.

KEY TERMS AND SYMBOLS

discrete event	probability of a discrete event	standard score
empirical probability	sample	statistic
μ	σ	theoretical probability
normal distribution	s	$\overline{X}$
parameter	standard normal deviate	z
population	standard normal distribution	z_{obs}

REVIEW QUESTIONS

1. Intelligence tests often involve measures of digit span, ability to follow instructions, vocabulary, analogy completion, picture completion, logical reasoning, and mathematical calculation. Explain why you would expect intelligence test scores to be approximately normally distributed in the population.

2. Measures of reaction time, the amount of time that it takes to initiate a response after the onset of a stimulus, typically are not normally distributed. Rather, the distribution of obtained scores often looks like a reversed letter *J* with most scores relatively short and only a few long scores. Explain why you would expect these scores to be distributed as they are.

3. Over the years, thousands of scores have been collected for the Wechsler Adult Intelligence Scale. Assume that the distribution of these scores is normal with $\mu = 100$ and $\sigma = 15$.
   a. What proportion of intelligence scores is equal to or greater than 115?
   b. What proportion of intelligence scores is less than 70?
   c. What proportion of intelligence scores is less than 60?
   d. What proportion of scores is between 100 to 120?
   e. What proportion of scores is between 75 to 100?
   f. What interval of scores includes the middle 80 percent of scores on the test?
   g. If you select a person at random, what is the probability that his or her intelligence score will be between 90 to 120?
   h. If you select a person at random, what is the probability that his or her intelligence score will be equal to or less than 80?
   i. If you select a person at random, what is the probability that his or her intelligence score will be equal to or greater than 125?
   j. If you select a person at random, what is the probability that his or her intelligence score will be equal to or greater than 140?

4. You have been summoned, along with 64 other people, to a court house as a prospective jury member. To choose members of the jury, names are put in a box and drawn one at a time.
   a. What is the probability that your name will be the first chosen?
   b. If your name is not among the first eight chosen, what is the probability that it will be chosen ninth, assuming that the names of the first eight people chosen are removed from the box?

5. The national newspaper, *USA Today*, published a column entitled "Chances" (December 31, 1985) presenting the odds that certain events might happen to an individual in a year. For each of the following events, find the probability of the event occurring for an individual.
   a. Many firms often run sweepstakes contests. For one recent contest, one prize was given for every 3000 entries. What is the probability of an entrant winning a prize in this contest?

b. Times have been difficult for farmers in recent years. One farmer out of every 5314 went out of business in one year. What is the probability of a farmer going out of business in a year?

c. Many of us dream about writing a best-selling novel. But for every 4637 book-length fiction manuscripts submitted to publishers in a year, only one is published. You have written a novel. What is the probability that it will be published this year?

6. I discussed the research of Yarnold et al. (1986) comparing Type A and Type B individuals in Statistics in Use 6–1. To obtain Type A or Type B individuals, Yarnold et al. chose people based on their scores on the Jenkins Activity Survey. Assume that the population mean for the Jenkins Activity Survey is 0 and the population standard deviation is 10. Suppose that you were interested in following up on Yarnold's work. To obtain Type A subjects, you want to select people with Jenkins Activity Survey scores greater than +13, and to obtain Type B individuals, you want to select people with Jenkins Activity Survey scores less than −13. Assume that scores on the Jenkins Activity Survey are normally distributed.

a. What is the probability of selecting a person at random with a Jenkins Activity Survey score of +13 or more?

b. What is the probability of selecting a person at random with a Jenkins Activity Survey score of −13 or less?

c. What is the probability of selecting a person at random with a score between −13 and +13?

7. Assume that the mean weight of American males between 21 to 30 years old is 156 pounds with a standard deviation of 8 pounds.

a. What proportion of 21- to 30-year-old males weighs 144 pounds or less?

b. What proportion of 21- to 30-year-old males weighs 170 pounds or more?

c. What proportion of 21- to 30-year-old males weighs between 140 to 172 pounds?

d. If you select a 21- to 30-year-old male at random, what is the probability that his weight will be between 144 to 168 pounds?

e. If you select a 21- to 30-year-old male at random, what is the probability that his weight will be 150 pounds or less?

f. If you select a 21- to 30-year-old male at random, what is the probability that his weight will be 160 pounds or more?

8. Suppose that you observed six students on the mean amount of time spent playing video games per week (in hours) and their semester grade point average (GPA) and found the following values:

Student	Video Games	GPA
Alex	6	2.5
Lauren	8	2.0
Yvonne	0	3.9
Laval	15	3.4
Bonnie	3	3.1
Jason	16	1.3

a. Compute the mean and sample standard deviation for each set of scores and then transform each score into a standard score.

b. Lauren has a standard score of 0 for time spent playing video games. What does this score tell you about the time she spends playing video games each week?

c. What information does Yvonne's standard score for GPA tell you about her GPA?

d. What does a negative standard score for GPA indicate?

e. What does a positive standard score for video game playing time indicate?

9. You recently had examinations in both English Literature and World History. Your grades on the exams and the class mean and standard deviation (S) are as follows:

	English Literature	World History
Your score	88	70
Class mean	83	65
Class S	6	5

In comparison to other members of the class, on which exam did you do better? What is the reason for your answer?

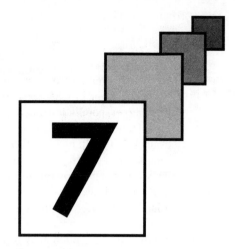

Using Statistics for Inference and Estimation

Statistical inference:
Estimating population values from statistics obtained from a sample.

In this chapter I discuss using descriptive statistics to estimate population parameters. As pointed out in Chapter 1, behavioral scientists often want to generalize their results to a larger population beyond the observations in the sample. For example, polling organizations want to predict the outcome of an election. But pollsters cannot possibly evaluate the opinions of all the members of a large voting population. They measure a sample from a voting population and then generalize to the population. Similarly, in many instances it is not possible to measure the amount of alcohol consumption, attitudes toward birth control, use of automobile seatbelts, or any other behaviors among all members of a large population. Estimates must be made from the descriptive statistics obtained from a sample of the population. Estimating population parameters from descriptive statistics requires making inferences from sample data. **Inference** is a process of reasoning from something known to something unknown. **Statistical inference** is estimating unknown population parameters from known sample statistics. I first discuss the characteristics of the sample mean ($\overline{X}$) as an estimate of a population mean (μ). Then I discuss the estimated population variance (s^2) and standard deviation (s) as estimates of the population variance (σ^2) and standard deviation (σ), respectively. Finally, I turn to determining the accuracy of $\overline{X}$ as an estimate of μ.

$\overline{X}$ AS A POINT ESTIMATOR OF μ

Point estimation: Estimating the value of a parameter as a single point from the value of a statistic.

The sample mean ($\overline{X}$) is often used as a point estimate of a population mean (μ). **Point estimation** is estimating the value of a parameter as a single point from the value of a statistic. Consider the measurement of test anxiety introduced in Chapter 3. The counselor selected 100 students from the population of students at her university and measured their test anxiety. The mean for the sample of scores presented in Table 3–3 is 41.64 and the standard deviation is 8.66. This sample mean of 41.64 may be used as an unbiased and consistent estimator of μ, the mean test anxiety of the population from which the sample was selected.

Unbiased Estimator

Unbiased estimator: A statistic with a mean value over an infinite number of random samples equal to the parameter it estimates.

An **unbiased estimator** is a statistic that, in the long run, equals the value of the parameter it estimates. Thus an unbiased estimator is one for which, if an infinite number of random samples of a certain size was obtained, the mean of the values of the statistic would equal the parameter being estimated. The sample mean, $\overline{X}$, is an unbiased estimator of μ because, if we take all possible random samples of size N from a population, then the mean of the sample means equals μ. The sample variance, S^2, is a biased estimator of σ^2 for it consistently underestimates σ^2. The estimated population variance, s^2, however, provides an unbiased estimate of σ^2.

Consistent Estimator

Consistent estimator: A statistic for which the probability that the statistic has a value closer to the parameter increases as the sample size increases.

A **consistent estimator** is a statistic for which the probability that the statistic has a value closer to the parameter increases as the sample size increases. Because it is a consistent estimator, a sample mean based on 25 scores has a greater probability of being closer to μ than does a sample mean based on only 5 scores. This characteristic makes intuitive sense for the sample mean. As sample size increases, more scores from the population are included in the calculation of $\overline{X}$, and I thus expect $\overline{X}$ to better estimate μ. If I were to sample the whole population of interest so that the sample comprised the entire population, then $\overline{X}$ would be the same as μ and there would be no error in the estimate.

Accuracy of Estimation

The sample mean is an unbiased and consistent estimator of μ. But we should not overlook the fact that an estimate is just an approximate calculation. It is unlikely in any estimate that $\overline{X}$ will be exactly equal to μ. Whether $\overline{X}$ is a good estimate of μ depends on the sampling method, the sample size, and the variability of scores in the population.

Sampling Method

Any sample from a population will provide some idea about characteristics of that population. Indeed, in the absence of any other information, $\overline{X}$ provides the "best guess" about the value of the corresponding μ. But to ensure that $\overline{X}$ is a good estimate of μ, the characteristics of the sample should be similar to those of the population of interest. The distribution of attributes, such as sex, age, intelligence, socioeconomic status, religion, political affiliation, anxiety, height, and weight, should occur in the sample much as they do in the population. A number of representative sampling methods has been developed in an attempt to ensure that the sample represents the population from which it is selected. I discuss two methods here.

Simple random sampling: Selecting members from a population such that each member of the population has an equal chance of being selected for the sample, and the selection of one member is independent of the selection of any other member of the population.

Simple Random Sampling.   **Simple random sampling** (often called **random sampling**) is defined as the process of selecting members from a population such that:

1. Each member of the population has an equal chance of being selected for the sample.
2. The selection of one member is independent of the selection of any other member of the population.

A random sample is one selected without bias; therefore, the characteristics of the sample should not differ in any systematic or consistent way from the population from which the sample was drawn. But random sampling does not guarantee that a particular sample will be exactly representative of a population. Because samples are usually much smaller than a population, we cannot expect the characteristics of the sample to be distributed exactly the same as in the population; some random samples will be more representative of the population than others. Random sampling does ensure, however, that in the long run (i.e., over an infinitely large number of samples) such samples will be representative of the population.

Stratified Random Sampling.   With **stratified random sampling**, members of a population are categorized into homogeneous subgroups called *strata*. The word *stratum* (stratum is singular, strata is plural) refers to a layer or level of similar things. Hence the members within a stratum are homogeneous or similar on some characteristic such as gender, age, or educational level. Members of the population are then randomly selected from the strata in the proportion to which the strata occur in the population. To illustrate, consider a population of students at a university. There are various possible homogeneous subgroups within this population, such as the subgrouping of year in college. The population may be stratified, or put into levels, on the basis of year in college—first, second, third, or fourth. The members of each college-year subgroup are homogeneous, or alike, on the characteristic of year in college. Obviously, there are many possible additional subgroupings, such as gender, academic major, or possessing a part-time job.

Suppose that I stratify the population of students based on their year in college and find the following percentage of students in each stratum (i.e., level or subgroup): first year, 40 percent; second year, 25 percent; third year, 20 percent; and fourth year, 15 percent. Simple random sampling from this population ensures that if I draw many samples the proportion of students in the population for each class year would be represented in similar proportions in the sample. But such proportionality would be unlikely to exist in any single sample. A stratified random sample, however, selects individuals in proportion to the frequency of the stratum in the population. If second-year students represent 25 percent of the population, then 25 percent of the sample will be randomly selected from this stratum. When strata can be identified in a population and when membership in a particular stratum is related to the behavior being measured, then a stratified random sample will likely provide a more representative sample than will simple random sampling.

Sample Size

The discussion of consistent estimators indicated that larger samples are more likely to produce a sample mean closer to the value of the population mean than are smaller samples. Thus, for consistent estimators, sample size is related to the accuracy of the estimate obtained.

Variability in Population Measures

Consider the unlikely possibility that the scores for all members of a population are exactly the same. Thus every score is equal to the mean of the population, and σ for the population is zero. Under this condition, it is evident that the $\overline{X}$ obtained from a sample of any size will equal μ. There will be no error in the sample estimate. On the other hand, consider a population that has extensive variation among the scores measured and σ is very large. Although it should occur infrequently, by chance alone the scores in one random sample may consist principally of low values. The resulting $\overline{X}$, then, would differ considerably from μ. Similarly, a relatively poor estimate of μ would be obtained if primarily high scores were randomly sampled from the population. Thus the accuracy of $\overline{X}$ as a point estimate of μ is related to the amount of variability in the population. The larger the population standard deviation is the less likely that a particular sample mean will be an accurate estimate of the population mean.

STATISTICS IN USE 7–1

Sampling for Surveys and Polls

Scientists conducting survey research estimate population parameters from measures of a sample. In Statistics in Use 1–1, I discussed the survey research of Bausell (1986), who was interested in the importance individuals attributed to certain behaviors in maintaining good health. Bausell selected one of his samples from the telephone-owning population of the continental United States. This sample involved 1254 adults who were contacted by telephone. To assure proportional geographic representation, the sample was stratified by geographical regions and metropolitan and nonmetropolitan residence. Within a stratum the sampling of individuals was done by simple random sampling. Because of this careful attention to sampling procedure, Bausell can be confident that this sample of individuals is representative of the larger population of telephone-owning adults in the United States.

Surveys reported in the popular media often may not pay careful attention to sampling procedures. As an example, one popular weekly tabloid reported that an "overwhelming majority" of their readers believe that nonviolent criminals should be whipped or agonizingly shocked instead of being sent to jail (Levy, June 7, 1983). This conclusion was based on the responses of 470 readers to a poll published in a previous issue. Of the 470 respondents, 84 percent (or 394 readers) stated that nonviolent criminals should be punished by beatings and shock. The author implied that the responses of these 470 readers were typical of the approximately 4.5 million readers of this tabloid. Is this inference reasonable? I think not. This sample was not selected by any procedure that would assure that the sample was representative of the population of readers. The respondents were those people sufficiently interested in the question to respond to the poll. Those most motivated to respond likely were individuals who believe in beating and shocking nonviolent criminals. People who recognize that such punishments are unconstitutional, or who regard the idea as absurd, did not respond. Thus it may be that out of the readership of about 4.5 million only 394 people believe in beating and shocking criminals, and they are the individuals who responded to this poll. Such a poll is scientifically useless.

TESTING YOUR KNOWLEDGE 7–1

1. Define: consistent estimator, simple random sampling, statistical inference, stratified random sampling, unbiased estimator.
2. Suppose that a population of individuals with anxiety disorders contains 27 percent generalized anxiety disorder, 23 percent agoraphobia, 19 percent simple phobia, 22 percent panic disorder, and 9 percent obsessive–compulsive disorder. You plan to draw a stratified random sample from this population using the types of disorders as strata.
   a. What proportion of your sample would be in each stratum?
   b. If you drew a sample of 100 individuals, how many people would be in each stratum?

ESTIMATING THE POPULATION VARIANCE AND STANDARD DEVIATION

Variance

The population variance, σ^2, is obtained by measuring all members of a population and then entering all scores into the formula

$$\sigma^2 = \frac{\Sigma(X - \mu)^2}{N_{pop}},$$

where X = individual score of a member of the population
          μ = population mean of the scores
          N_{pop} = total number of scores in the population.

As I have pointed out, however, it is usually impractical to measure all members of a population. Consequently, the population variance, σ^2, is typically estimated from a sample. As I discussed in Chapter 5, an **unbiased and consistent estimator of σ^2** is provided by

$$s^2 = \frac{\Sigma(X - \overline{X})^2}{N - 1}.$$

Notice in this formula that the denominator is $N - 1$ rather than N. As pointed out in Chapter 5, the sample variance given by

$$S^2 = \frac{\Sigma(X - \overline{X})^2}{N}$$

is a biased estimator of σ^2; typically, it underestimates the value of σ^2. Consequently, unless I indicate differently, s^2 is used as the variance.

Standard Deviation

The estimated population standard deviation, s, is used as an estimator of σ. In contrast to s^2 as an estimator of σ^2, s is not an unbiased estimator of σ. Rather, s slightly underestimates σ. But because the bias in s is small and becomes smaller as sample size increases, most researchers use s when it is necessary to estimate σ.

SAMPLING DISTRIBUTION OF THE MEAN: DETERMINING THE ACCURACY OF AN ESTIMATE

The accuracy of a point estimate of a population mean depends on both sample size and the population standard deviation. Unless the sample includes all the scores in the population or there is no variability of scores in the population, $\overline{X}$ will likely be in error in estimating μ. Although we never know for sure just how accurate a particular estimate of a population parameter is, we can determine the amount of error to be expected in the estimate by using the concept of a sampling distribution.

Sampling distribution: A theoretical probability distribution of values of a statistic resulting from drawing all possible samples of size N from a population.

Sampling distribution of the mean: The distribution of $\overline{X}$ values when all possible samples of size N are drawn from a population.

A **sampling distribution** is a theoretical probability distribution of values of a statistic resulting from drawing all possible samples of size N from a population. Thus the **sampling distribution of the mean** is the distribution of $\overline{X}$ values when all possible samples of size N are drawn from a population. Sampling distributions are determined theoretically from a mathematical equation, for I can never draw all possible samples from a population. Each statistical test introduced in the following chapters requires a knowledge of the sampling distribution for the statistic used. These sampling distributions are theoretical sampling distributions obtained from mathematical equations.

Although statistical tests use theoretical sampling distributions, I will generate several empirical sampling distributions of the mean to illustrate the concepts involved. The word *empirical* means observable or observed. Hence an empirical sampling distribution of the mean may be obtained by drawing a number of samples of size N from a population, calculating $\overline{X}$ for each sample, and then plotting a frequency distribution of the means obtained. For this illustration, I generated a population of 100 scores ranging from 8 to 20 with $\mu = 14.0$ and $\sigma = 2.14$. A frequency polygon of the 100 scores in the population is shown in Figure 7–1. As you can see, the distribution of scores in the population is symmetrical and unimodal.

Empirical sampling distributions of the mean were obtained for three different sample sizes, $N = 2$, $N = 5$, and $N = 10$, by drawing simple random samples from this population with the aid of a computer. For each sample size, 100 random samples were obtained, and the mean of each sample was calculated. Each sample mean for a particular sample size was then placed on an ungrouped frequency distribution, as shown in Figure 7–2. Each distribution, (a), (b), and (c), represents an empirical sampling distribution of the mean for a particular sample size ($N = 2$, $N = 5$, and $N = 10$, respectively).

Characteristics of the Sampling Distribution of the Mean

The empirical sampling distributions in Figure 7–2 illustrate several characteristics of the theoretical sampling distribution of the mean. Recall that a frequency distribution can be summarized in terms of its shape, measure of central tendency, and measure of variability. Because the sampling distribution of the mean is a frequency distribution, it, too, can be described in terms of its shape, mean, and standard deviation.

FIGURE 7–1
Frequency distribution for a population of 100 scores with μ = 14.0 and σ = 2.14.

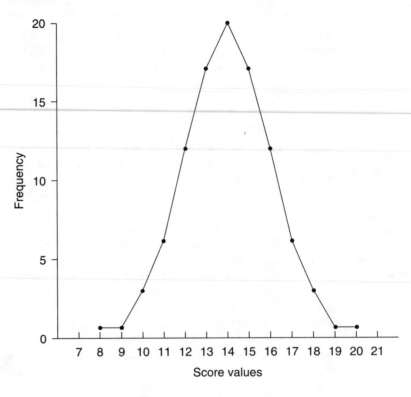

Shape of a Sampling Distribution of the Mean

Central limit theorem: A mathematical theorem stating that, as sample size increases, the sampling distribution of the mean approaches a normal distribution.

The three sampling distributions in Figure 7–2 are relatively symmetrical and unimodal. Any variations from symmetry are simply chance variation in the values of the sample means obtained in sampling. Notice that the distribution becomes more peaked and less spread out as the sample size increases (compare $N = 2$ to $N = 10$). A principle, known as the **central limit theorem**, applies to the shape of the sampling distribution of the mean: *As sample size increases, the sampling distribution of the mean will approach a normal distribution.* This approximation of the normal distribution by the sampling distribution of the mean occurs whether the shape of the distribution of individual scores in the population is symmetrical or skewed.

How large must N be before the sampling distribution of the mean approaches a normal distribution? The answer depends on the shape of the distribution of scores in the population. The population I sampled from is not normally distributed, but is unimodal and symmetrical (see Figure 7–1). From such a distribution the sampling distribution of the mean for sample sizes as small as $N = 5$ or $N = 10$ begins to approach the shape of a normal distribution (see Figures 7–2b and c). If the distribution of scores in the population is skewed, then the sample size must be larger for the sampling distribution

FIGURE 7–2

Three empirical sampling distributions of the mean for 100 samples drawn from the population of scores presented in Figure 7–1. The sample sizes are (a) $N = 2$, (b) $N = 5$, and (c) $N = 10$.

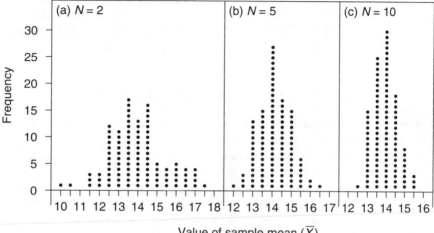

Value of sample mean ($\overline{X}$)

of the mean to approximate a normal distribution. For population distributions that are not heavily skewed, many statisticians consider a sample size of 30 ($N = 30$) to lead to a sampling distribution of the mean that will be approximately normally distributed.

A theoretical sampling distribution of the mean based on the central limit theorem is shown in Figure 7–3. Observe that this distribution is symmetrical, unimodal, and normal. I will use this and other theoretical sampling distributions in developing inferential statistical tests in following chapters. Empirical sampling distributions, such as those presented in Figure 7–2, are used only to help understand the concept of a sampling distribution.

FIGURE 7–3

Theoretical sampling distribution of the mean with mean $\mu_{\overline{X}}$ and standard error $\sigma_{\overline{X}}$.

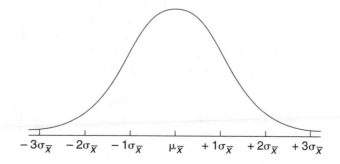

Mean of a Sampling Distribution of the Mean

The mean of the sample means (represented by $\mu_{\overline{X}}$) in a theoretical sampling distribution will be equal to the population mean (μ) of the individual scores. In an empirical sampling distribution of the mean, however, the mean of the sample means (represented by $\overline{X}_{\overline{X}}$) will not be exactly equal to the population mean. This point is illustrated by the empirical sampling distributions of Figure 7–2. The means of the sample means in the three sampling distributions are not exactly equal to 14.0, the mean of the parent population. The mean values are $\overline{X}_{\overline{X}} = 13.96$, $\overline{X}_{\overline{X}} = 14.14$, and $\overline{X}_{\overline{X}} = 13.99$ for distributions in parts (a), (b), and (c), respectively.

Sampling Error and the Standard Error of the Mean

Sampling Error.   Each sample mean in Figure 7–2 is an estimate of the population mean from which the sample was drawn ($\mu = 14$ in this example). As you can see, some of the sample means provide more accurate estimates of μ than do other sample means. **Sampling error** is the amount by which a particular sample mean differs from the population mean (i.e., $\overline{X} - \mu$). If $\overline{X}$ is exactly the same as μ, that is, if $\overline{X} = \mu$ and thus $\overline{X} - \mu = 0$, then there is no sampling error in the estimate. Figure 7–2 illustrates that sampling error is related to sample size; the larger the sample size is, the smaller the sampling error. The values of the 100 sample means in Figure 7–2a, with each mean based on two scores, are more variable than the sample means in Figures 7–2b and c, which were derived from either 5 or 10 scores, respectively. Thus more sampling error is evident in Figure 7–2a than in either Figure 7–2b or c.

Standard Error of the Mean.   The amount of variability among the sample means in a sampling distribution of the mean is described by the standard deviation computed on the values of the sample means. This standard deviation is called the **standard error of the mean**, or simply the **standard error**, to distinguish it from the standard deviation calculated on a population of raw scores. The standard error of the mean, symbolized as $\sigma_{\overline{X}}$, is equal to the standard deviation of the population divided by the square root of the size of the sample. In notation,

$$\sigma_{\overline{X}} = \sigma/\sqrt{N},$$

where σ represents the standard deviation of scores in the population and N is the size of the sample. The standard error of the mean, $\sigma_{\overline{X}}$, is a standard deviation, just as σ is a standard deviation. But $\sigma_{\overline{X}}$ is a standard deviation of a distribution of sample means, rather than a standard deviation of the raw scores in a population, as is σ.

Look at Figure 7–3, the theoretical sampling distribution of the mean. Notice that I have indicated its mean as $\mu_{\overline{X}}$ and its standard deviation as $\sigma_{\overline{X}}$. In Chapter 6, I discussed the area under the normal distribution and explained how to find the proportion of scores within certain areas of the distribution. Because the sampling distribution of the mean is a normal distribution, the same relationships hold for this distribution. In this instance, however, it is not raw scores that are contained in the intervals, but sample means. Thus, for example, the interval from one standard error below the mean of the sampling distribution to one standard error above the mean of the sampling distribution (i.e., the interval from $\mu_{\overline{X}} - 1\sigma_{\overline{X}}$ to $\mu_{\overline{X}} + 1\sigma_{\overline{X}}$) contains .6826 of the sample means, the interval from $\mu_{\overline{X}} - 2\sigma_{\overline{X}}$ to $\mu_{\overline{X}} + 2\sigma_{\overline{X}}$ contains .9544 of the sample means, and the interval

Sampling error: The amount by which a sample mean differs from the population mean.

Standard error of the mean, $\sigma_{\overline{X}}$: The standard deviation of the sampling distribution of the mean found by dividing σ by the square root of the size of the sample.

from $\mu_{\overline{X}} - 3\sigma_{\overline{X}}$ to $\mu_{\overline{X}} + 3\sigma_{\overline{X}}$ contains .9974 of the sample means. Notice that I have used $\mu_{\overline{X}}$ in these intervals because I am using the sampling distribution of the mean. Because $\mu_{\overline{X}}$ is equal to μ, however, I could write the relationships using μ in place of $\mu_{\overline{X}}$, as in the next example.

To illustrate the use of these relationships, suppose that a population of scores has a mean of $\mu = 50$ and $\sigma = 6$, and random samples of $N = 9$ are drawn from this population. The standard error of the mean for this sampling distribution is found by

$$\sigma_{\overline{X}} = \frac{\sigma}{\sqrt{N}}$$

or

$$\sigma_{\overline{X}} = \frac{6}{\sqrt{9}} = \frac{6}{3} = 2.$$

This value, $\sigma_{\overline{X}} = 2$, is the standard deviation of the sampling distribution of the mean for samples of size $N = 9$ from a population with $\sigma = 6$. Thus, in the theoretical sampling distribution of the mean for samples of $N = 9$ from this population, .6826 of the sample means is in the interval of $\mu - 1\sigma_{\overline{X}}$ (i.e., $50 - 2 = 48$) to $\mu + 1\sigma_{\overline{X}}$ (i.e., $50 + 2 = 52$), or the interval from 48 to 52. The interval of $\mu - 2\sigma_{\overline{X}}$ (i.e., $50 - 4 = 46$) to $\mu + 2\sigma_{\overline{X}}$ (i.e., $50 + 4 = 54$), or the interval from 46 to 54, contains .9544 of the sample means, and .9974 of the values of $\overline{X}$ will be in the interval of $\mu - 3\sigma_{\overline{X}}$ (i.e., $50 - 6 = 44$) to $\mu + 3\sigma_{\overline{X}}$ (i.e., $50 + 6 = 56$), or from 44 to 56. This knowledge will be useful in estimating the accuracy of $\overline{X}$ as an estimate of μ.

Using the Standard Normal Deviate with the Sampling Distribution of the Mean

The sampling distribution of the mean is normally distributed with mean, $\mu_{\overline{X}}$, and standard error, $\sigma_{\overline{X}}$. I may convert a value of $\overline{X}$ from a sampling distribution of the mean to a score on the standard normal distribution by

$$z_{\text{obs}} = \frac{\overline{X} - \mu_{\overline{X}}}{\sigma_{\overline{X}}}.$$

This z score may be used with the sample mean just as it was for an individual score in Chapter 6. Example Problem 7–1 illustrates its use.

Example Problem 7–1

Using the Sampling Distribution of the Mean

Problem

Suppose that we have a normally distributed population of scores with $\mu = 80$ and $\sigma = 12$. We plan to draw a large number of random samples of size 16 ($N = 16$) from this population and compute the mean for each sample. What proportion of the sample means will be equal to or greater than 82?

Solution   The solution to this problem requires recognizing that the sampling distribution of the mean is normally distributed with $\mu_{\overline{X}} = 80$ and $\sigma_{\overline{X}} = 12/\sqrt{16} = 12/4 = 3.0$. The proportion of sample means in any interval on the theoretical sampling distribution is found by converting the value of the sample mean (i.e., 82) to a value on the standard normal distribution and looking up the appropriate proportion in the standard normal table, Table A–1. The sample mean is converted to a z_{obs} value by

$$z_{obs} = \frac{\overline{X} - \mu_{\overline{X}}}{\sigma_{\overline{X}}}.$$

Substituting numerical values,

$$z_{obs} = \frac{82 - 80}{3.0} = \frac{2}{3.0} = +0.67.$$

Values of the sample means and the z_{obs} for a sample mean of 82 are shown in Figure 7–4. Column c of Table A–1 indicates that the area beyond $z = +0.67$ is .2514 (see the axis labeled c in Figure 7–4). Thus .2514 of the sample means is expected to be equal to or greater than 82. I may write this conclusion in probability terms as

$$p(\overline{X} \geq 82) = .2514.$$

FIGURE 7–4
Location of a sample mean of 82 on a sampling distribution of the mean with $\mu = 80$ and $\sigma_{\overline{X}} = 3$. The labels on the X axis show (a) values of the sample means, (b) z scores corresponding to values of the sample means, and (c) the proportion of sample means equal to or greater than 82.

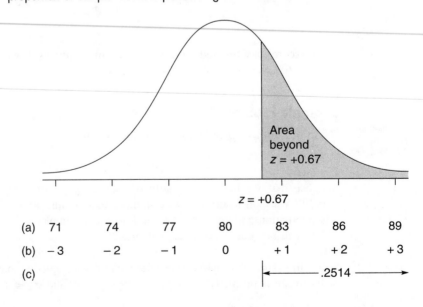

Area beyond z = +0.67

z = +0.67

(a) 71	74	77	80	83	86	89
(b) −3	−2	−1	0	+1	+2	+3
(c)				.2514		

TESTING YOUR KNOWLEDGE 7-2

1. Define: $\mu_{\overline{X}}$, sampling distribution of the mean, $\sigma_{\overline{X}}$, standard error of the mean.
2. Is the value of S^2 obtained by $S^2 = \Sigma(X - \overline{X})^2/N$ an unbiased estimator of σ^2? If it is biased, how is it biased?
3. Is the value of s^2 obtained by $s^2 = \Sigma(X - \overline{X})^2/(N-1)$ an unbiased estimator of σ^2? If it is biased, how is it biased?
4. Is the value of s obtained by $s = \sqrt{\Sigma(X - \overline{X})/(N-1)}$ an unbiased estimator of σ? If it is biased, how is it biased?
5. Distinguish between an empirical and a theoretical sampling distribution of the mean.
6. State the central limit theorem.
7. Suppose that you plan to draw 100 random samples of size 25 ($N = 25$) from a population of intelligence test scores with $\mu = 100$ and $\sigma = 15$.
   a. What proportion of the sample means do you expect to be between 97 and 103?
   b. What proportion of the sample means do you expect to be greater than 103?
   c. What proportion of the sample means do you expect to be less than 94?
   d. What proportion of the sample means do you expect to be greater than 105?
   e. What proportion of the sample means do you expect to be between 100 and 105?

ESTIMATING THE STANDARD ERROR OF THE MEAN

The sampling distribution of the mean provides a method of assessing the variability expected among sample means. But there is an apparent limit to the use of this knowledge. The population standard deviation, σ, is a population parameter, and any population parameter typically is unknown. How, then, can I determine the standard error of the mean, $\sigma_{\overline{X}}$, if I don't know σ?

Estimated standard error of the mean, $s_{\overline{X}}$: The standard error of the mean estimated by using s to estimate σ.

The answer to this question lies in estimating σ from the data of a sample, just as I have estimated μ from $\overline{X}$. In this instance the estimated population standard deviation (s) is used to estimate σ to obtain an estimated standard error of the mean. The **estimated standard error of the mean**, identified as $s_{\overline{X}}$, is based on the estimated population standard deviation and is expressed in notation as

$$\text{estimated } \sigma_{\overline{X}} = s_{\overline{X}} = \frac{s}{\sqrt{N}},$$

where s is obtained from the scores of a sample and N is the sample size. Thus $s_{\overline{X}}$ is the estimated standard deviation of the sampling distribution of the mean. In a journal report, the standard error is often identified as SE, rather than $s_{\overline{X}}$.

It is important to understand the distinction between $\sigma_{\overline{X}}$ and $s_{\overline{X}}$. The $\sigma_{\overline{X}}$ is a fixed value that can be determined when σ is known. Because I seldom know σ, however, I typically estimate $\sigma_{\overline{X}}$ by $s_{\overline{X}}$. The $s_{\overline{X}}$, because it is based on the value of s from a sample, will vary from sample to sample. Different random samples from the same population will produce different standard deviations because of the chance differences in scores that occur from one sample to another. Nevertheless, the scores of the sample provide the only basis for estimating $\sigma_{\overline{X}}$.

Factors Affecting the Value of $s_{\bar{X}}$

The formula for $s_{\bar{X}}$, $s/\sqrt{N}$, shows how the variability of sample means in a sampling distribution is related to (1) the variability of scores in the population and (2) the size of the sample. The more variable the scores in the population are, the larger the s of the scores in the sample. And, as s increases, $s_{\bar{X}}$ does also. However, increasing the sample size (N) increases the denominator of the formula for $s_{\bar{X}}$, which contributes to making the standard error smaller. Thus I can expect to obtain a smaller $s_{\bar{X}}$ with large random samples from populations in which the variability of scores is small. Although an investigator can control sample size, often little can be done to reduce the variation of scores in the population. Thus, to decrease the value of $s_{\bar{X}}$, behavioral scientists often resort to using larger sample sizes.

Use of $s_{\bar{X}}$

The standard error is used to measure the amount of sampling error in the sampling distribution of the mean. Therefore, $s_{\bar{X}}$ may be used to determine how well an obtained sample mean estimates a population mean. The smaller $s_{\bar{X}}$ is, the more confident I can be that $\bar{X}$ does not differ substantially from the population mean. In Chapter 8, I will use $s_{\bar{X}}$ to make precise statements about the accuracy with which $\bar{X}$ estimates μ. To simplify the discussion in the remainder of this chapter, however, I assume that $\sigma_{\bar{X}}$ is known to us. You should remember, however, that in practice $\sigma_{\bar{X}}$ will not be known and $s_{\bar{X}}$ must be used in its place.

Review of Types of Distributions

Table 7–1 summarizes the several types of distributions discussed to this point and the symbols used to identify the characteristics of the distributions. Distributions may be composed of either raw scores or of means of samples drawn from a population. A population distribution of raw scores is obtained by measuring all members of a population. If I were able to measure the population, I would be able to calculate the population mean, μ, standard deviation, σ, and variance, σ^2.

A sample distribution of raw scores is obtained by selecting a subgroup from a population. The scores in the sample are described by the sample mean, $\bar{X}$, standard deviation, s, and variance, s^2. These statistics may be used to estimate the corresponding parameter of the population from which the sample was selected.

A sampling distribution of the mean is a distribution of sample means drawn from a population. The theoretical sampling distribution of the mean for a given sample size is obtained from a mathematical equation. The mean of a theoretical sampling distribution of the mean is given by $\mu_{\bar{X}}$, which is equal to μ of the population from which the samples were selected. The standard deviation of a sampling distribution of

TABLE 7–1
Summary of types of distributions and their characteristics.

Type of Distribution	Obtained by:	Standard		
		Mean	Deviation	Variance
Raw scores				
Population	Measuring all members of the population	μ	σ	σ^2
Sample	Drawing and measuring a sample from a population	$\overline{X}$	s	s^2
Sampling distribution of the mean				
Theoretical	Theoretically from a mathematical equation	$\mu_{\overline{X}}$	$\sigma_{\overline{X}}$	$\sigma^2_{\overline{X}}$
Empirical	Empirically by drawing samples from a population	$\overline{X}_{\overline{X}}$	$s_{\overline{X}}$	$s^2_{\overline{X}}$

the mean is given by $\sigma_{\overline{X}}$ and the variance by $\sigma^2_{\overline{X}}$. Typically, μ and $\sigma_{\overline{X}}$ are estimated from $\overline{X}$ and $s_{\overline{X}}$. Empirical sampling distributions of the mean are obtained by actually drawing samples from a population and then plotting a frequency distribution of the sample means. The major function of empirical sampling distributions is to assist in understanding the concept of a sampling distribution; they typically are not used in actual research.

TESTING YOUR KNOWLEDGE 7-3

1. Suppose that you have a sample of scores for time on target of a tracking task. In this task, a person must track a moving target with a cursor on a video display tube. The amount of time that the person maintains the cursor on the target during a trial is recorded. The s for the distribution of these scores is 18.0 seconds.
   a. What is the value of $s_{\overline{X}}$ if the sample size is 4?
   b. What is the value of $s_{\overline{X}}$ if the sample size is 9?
   c. What is the value of $s_{\overline{X}}$ if the sample size is 36?
   d. What relationship between the value of $s_{\overline{X}}$ and sample size is illustrated by these samples?
2. Suppose that you have three different samples of scores on time on target during a tracking task as described in question 1. The values of s for the three samples are 10, 15, and 20 seconds, respectively. The sample size was 25 ($N = 25$).
   a. Find the value of $s_{\overline{X}}$ for each sample.
   b. What relationship between variability of scores and the value of $s_{\overline{X}}$ is illustrated by these samples?

3. You plan to draw equal-sized samples from two different populations of scores, A_1 and A_2. Population A_1 has a σ of 17.0, and population A_2 has a σ of 30.0. Which population, A_1 or A_2, do you expect will lead to a sample with a larger value of $s_{\overline{X}}$? Explain your answer.

INTERVAL ESTIMATION OF THE POPULATION MEAN

Confidence interval: A range of score values expected to contain the value of μ with a certain level of confidence.

Confidence limits: The lower and upper scores defining the confidence interval.

The sample mean is an unbiased and consistent estimator of μ. If we were to estimate the mean of a population from which a sample was drawn, the best point estimate of μ would be $\overline{X}$. But, as I have discussed, a point estimate of μ will likely be in error; the value of μ will not be equal to the value estimated by $\overline{X}$. To gain confidence about the accuracy of an estimate, we may estimate not only a point value for μ, but we may also construct a **confidence interval** for the estimate by providing a range of values expected to contain μ. For example, rather than estimating the population mean of Test Anxiety Inventory scores as exactly 41.64, a researcher may estimate that an interval from 39.94 to 43.34 contains the value of μ. A level of confidence, or probability value, can be attached to this estimate so that, for example, the scientist can be 95 percent confident that the interval encompasses μ. The lower (e.g., 39.9) and upper (e.g., 43.3) scores of the interval are called **confidence limits**. Let us see how such intervals are constructed and what it means to say that an experimenter is 95 percent confident that the interval includes the value of μ.

Constructing a Confidence Interval

Return to Figure 7–3, the theoretical sampling distribution of the mean. Recall that $\sigma_{\overline{X}}$ is the standard deviation of this sampling distribution and that the distribution is normally distributed. Using this knowledge, I illustrated earlier in this chapter that the interval from $\mu_{\overline{X}} - 1\sigma_{\overline{X}}$ to $\mu_{\overline{X}} + 1\sigma_{\overline{X}}$ contains .6826 of the sample means that could be drawn from this population. Suppose I now asked, if you were to draw one sample and find $\overline{X}$ for that sample, what is the probability that $\overline{X}$ would fall into the interval between $\mu_{\overline{X}} - 1\sigma_{\overline{X}}$ to $\mu_{\overline{X}} + 1\sigma_{\overline{X}}$? The answer is .6826, for .6826 of the sample means has values between $\mu_{\overline{X}} - 1\sigma_{\overline{X}}$ and $\mu_{\overline{X}} + 1\sigma_{\overline{X}}$. Accordingly, if you were to draw a sample, the probability that its mean would be between $\mu_{\overline{X}} - 1\sigma_{\overline{X}}$ and $\mu_{\overline{X}} + 1\sigma_{\overline{X}}$ is .6826. Notice that to answer the question I constructed an interval about $\mu_{\overline{X}}$ (or μ, because $\mu_{\overline{X}}$ is equal to μ) using values of $\sigma_{\overline{X}}$ and then applied known properties of the normal distribution. But in most instances μ is unknown, and I estimate μ with $\overline{X}$. Suppose that I follow the same procedure of constructing an interval around μ, but use $\overline{X}$ to estimate μ. Thus I obtain an interval of $\overline{X} - 1\sigma_{\overline{X}}$ to $\overline{X} + 1\sigma_{\overline{X}}$. The question I now ask is not whether this interval contains the value of $\overline{X}$, for I already know $\overline{X}$, but does the interval contain μ? I can answer this question with a probability statement also.

If the probability that the interval $\mu_{\overline{X}} - 1\sigma_{\overline{X}}$ to $\mu_{\overline{X}} + 1\sigma_{\overline{X}}$ contains $\overline{X}$ is .6826, then it is also true that the probability that the interval $\overline{X} - 1\sigma_{\overline{X}}$ to $\overline{X} + 1\sigma_{\overline{X}}$ contains μ is .6826.

The interval of $\overline{X} - 1\sigma_{\overline{X}}$ to $\overline{X} + 1\sigma_{\overline{X}}$ is a 68 percent (rounding .6826 and then multiplying by 100 to obtain percent) confidence interval. The limits, or extremes, of this interval, $\overline{X} - 1\sigma_{\overline{X}}$ and $\overline{X} + 1\sigma_{\overline{X}}$, are the confidence limits. I can interpret this interval by thinking that, if I were to repeatedly draw samples and calculate a mean for each sample and then construct an interval of plus or minus one $\sigma_{\overline{X}}$ about each $\overline{X}$, 68 percent of the intervals would contain the value of μ. Thus any one of the intervals has a probability of .68 (or a 68 percent chance) of including μ. Notice that, because μ is a population parameter and thus a specific value, it is either contained or not contained in the interval. Consider a numerical example to illustrate this discussion.

Suppose that I have a population with $\mu = 40$ and $\sigma = 10$. I draw a sample of size 25 ($N = 25$) from this population and obtain $\overline{X} = 41.5$. Then $\sigma_{\overline{X}} = \sigma/\sqrt{N} = 10/\sqrt{25}$, which equals 2.0. A 68 percent confidence interval for μ is obtained by finding the interval from $\overline{X} - 1\sigma_{\overline{X}}$ to $\overline{X} + 1\sigma_{\overline{X}}$. Substituting values of $\overline{X} = 41.5$ and $\sigma_{\overline{X}} = 2$, the resulting confidence interval is 39.5 (i.e., $\overline{X} - 1\sigma_{\overline{X}} = 41.5 - 2 = 39.5$) to 43.5 (i.e., $\overline{X} + 1\sigma_{\overline{X}} = 41.5 + 2 = 43.5$). I can be 68 percent confident that this interval contains the value of μ. And, in this instance, it does. Suppose, however, that $\overline{X}$ had been 44.0 rather than 41.5. Then the 68 percent confidence interval is 42.0 (i.e., $\overline{X} - 1\sigma_{\overline{X}} = 44 - 2 = 42.0$) to 46.0 (i.e., $\overline{X} + 1\sigma_{\overline{X}} = 44 + 2 = 46.0$). Again, I can be 68 percent confident that this interval contains μ. But in this instance the interval does not contain $\mu = 40$. In practice, of course, I cannot know for sure if the confidence interval contains μ or not, for I do not know the value of μ. If I did know μ, then I would not need to estimate its value. I can only have a certain level of confidence that the interval actually does contain the value of μ.

Confidence intervals used in actual research are typically 95 percent or 99 percent confidence intervals, rather than 68 percent confidence intervals. I find the limits for these intervals by using the properties of the standard normal distribution with $\mu = 0$ and $\sigma = 1$. From Table A–1, I find that an interval from $z = -1.96$ to 0 contains .4750 of the values of z, and an interval of $z = 0$ to $z = +1.96$ also contains .4750 of the values of z. Thus an interval of $z = -1.96$ to $z = +1.96$ will contain .95 of the values of z (i.e., $.4750 + .4750 = .95$). Accordingly, a **95 percent confidence interval for the population mean** is obtained by the interval

$$\overline{X} - 1.96\sigma_{\overline{X}} \text{ to } \overline{X} + 1.96\sigma_{\overline{X}}.$$

For a 99 percent confidence interval, I find that an interval from $z = -2.58$ to 0 contains .4951 of the values of z, and an interval of $z = 0$ to $z = +2.58$ also contains .4951 of the values of z. Thus an interval of $z = -2.58$ to $z = +2.58$ will contain .99 of the values of z (i.e., $.4951 + .4951 = .9902$, or .99). Hence, a **99 percent confidence interval for the population mean** is obtained by the interval

$$\overline{X} - 2.58\sigma_{\overline{X}} \text{ to } \overline{X} + 2.58\sigma_{\overline{X}}.$$

For the example with $\overline{X} = 41.5$ and $\sigma_{\overline{X}} = 2$, a 95 percent confidence interval equals

$$41.5 - 1.96(2) \text{ to } 41.5 + 1.96(2),$$

which equals

$$41.5 - 3.92 \text{ to } 41.5 + 3.92 \quad \text{or} \quad 37.58 \text{ to } 45.42.$$

The 99 percent confidence interval equals

$$41.5 - 2.58(2) \text{ to } 41.5 + 2.58(2),$$

which equals

$$41.5 - 5.16 \text{ to } 41.5 + 5.16 \quad \text{or} \quad 36.34 \text{ to } 46.66.$$

One aspect of this discussion may be puzzling. I have been estimating μ, a population parameter, because I cannot measure the population to obtain the value of this parameter. Yet, in constructing confidence intervals, I have used the value of σ, another parameter, to find $\sigma_{\overline{X}}$. Why should I know the value of σ when I do not know μ? The answer is that I would not; I would estimate $\sigma_{\overline{X}}$ from $s_{\overline{X}}$. I assumed knowledge of $\sigma_{\overline{X}}$ to simplify the introduction of interval estimation. But, in practice, $s_{\overline{X}}$, rather than $\sigma_{\overline{X}}$, is used to determine the confidence limits. When $s_{\overline{X}}$ is used, confidence intervals are slightly larger than those obtained using $\sigma_{\overline{X}}$. The concepts of interval estimation are identical, however, whether $\sigma_{\overline{X}}$ or $s_{\overline{X}}$ is used. I discuss using $s_{\overline{X}}$ in constructing confidence intervals in Chapter 8.

Example Problem 7–2

Constructing Confidence Intervals When $\sigma_{\overline{X}}$ Is Known

Problem
We have a sample of 30 scores from a population with $\sigma = 13.0$. The sample mean is 71.0. Find the 95 percent confidence interval for μ.

Solution   We find $\sigma_{\overline{X}}$ and then use Table A–1 to find the value of z that defines an interval containing 95 percent of the area on the standard normal distribution.

$$\sigma_{\overline{X}} = \frac{\sigma}{\sqrt{N}} = \frac{13.0}{\sqrt{30}} = \frac{13.0}{5.477} = 2.37.$$

From Table A–1, we find that an interval on the standard normal distribution from $z = -1.96$ to $z = +1.96$ contains 95 percent of the area of the distribution. Thus the 95 percent confidence interval for μ is given by

$$\overline{X} - 1.96\sigma_{\overline{X}} \text{ to } \overline{X} + 1.96\sigma_{\overline{X}}.$$

Substituting numerical values for $\overline{X}$ and $\sigma_{\overline{X}}$ provides an interval

$$71.0 - 1.96(2.37) \text{ to } 71.0 + 1.96(2.37)$$

or

$$71.0 - 4.65 \text{ to } 71.0 + 4.65,$$

which equals 66.35 to 75.65. The 95 percent confidence interval for μ is from 66.35 to 75.65.

TESTING YOUR KNOWLEDGE 7-4

1. Define: confidence interval, confidence limits, interval estimation, point estimation.
2. You have drawn a sample of 25 scores from a population with $\sigma = 10.0$. The value of $\overline{X}$ is 73.0.
   a. Provide a point estimate of μ.
   b. Construct a 95 percent confidence interval for μ.
   c. Construct a 99 percent confidence interval for μ.
   Assume for questions 2d, 2e, and 2f that the sample size was 100 ($N = 100$) rather than 25.
   d. Provide a point estimate of μ.
   e. Construct a 95 percent confidence interval for μ.
   f. Construct a 99 percent confidence interval for μ.
   g. The confidence intervals based on $N = 100$ are smaller than those based on $N = 25$. Explain why this difference occurs.

SUMMARY

- Statistical inference is a process of drawing conclusions about unknown population values from sample statistics.
- $\overline{X}$ is an unbiased and consistent estimator of μ.
- To provide accurate estimation, a sample should be representative of the population from which it is selected. Representativeness is determined by the method of sampling used.
- s^2 is an unbiased and consistent estimator of σ^2.
- s is used to estimate σ, although it slightly underestimates σ.
- The sampling distribution of the mean is the theoretical distribution of sample means for a given size sample.
- The standard error of the mean is the standard deviation of the sampling distribution of the mean.
- $\sigma_{\overline{X}}$ is found by $\sigma/\sqrt{N}$. In most cases it is estimated by $s_{\overline{X}} = s/\sqrt{N}$.

- The sampling distribution of the mean approaches a normal distribution as sample size increases. Thus $\sigma_{\overline{X}}$ can be used to find confidence intervals for estimates of μ from $\overline{X}$.
- A confidence interval is a range of score values expected to contain the value of μ with a certain level of confidence. The lower and upper scores defining the confidence interval are called the confidence limits.

KEY TERMS AND SYMBOLS

central limit theorem	sampling distribution of	simple random sampling
confidence interval	the mean	standard error of the mean
confidence limits	sampling error	statistical inference
consistent estimator	$\sigma_{\overline{X}}$	stratified random sampling
interval estimation	σ^2	unbiased estimator
$\mu_{\overline{X}}$	$s_{\overline{X}}$	variance
point estimation	s	$\overline{X}$
	s^2	$\overline{X}_{\overline{X}}$

CHAPTER SUPPLEMENT: REVIEW OF IMPORTANT SYMBOLS AND FORMULAS

Chapters 4 through 7 have introduced a number of important statistical symbols and formulas. To help your study and understanding of these materials, they are summarized in the following table.

Symbol	Formula	Definition
N		The number of scores in a sample, or the sample size.
N_{pop}		The number of scores in a population, or the population size.
X_i or X		An individual score in either a sample or a population.
$\overline{X}$	$\dfrac{\Sigma X}{N}$	The sample mean. X refers to the individual scores in the sample.
μ	$\dfrac{\Sigma X}{N_{\text{pop}}}$	The population mean. X refers to the individual scores in the population.
S^2	$\dfrac{\Sigma(X - \overline{X})^2}{N}$	The sample variance. This variance is a biased estimate of the population variance.

Symbol	Formula	Definition
S	$\sqrt{\dfrac{\Sigma(X-\overline{X})^2}{N}}$	The sample standard deviation. This standard deviation is descriptive of the sample, but it is not used to estimate the population standard deviation.
s^2	$\dfrac{\Sigma(X-\overline{X})^2}{N-1}$	The estimated population variance. This variance is an unbiased estimate of the population variance.
s	$\sqrt{\dfrac{\Sigma(X-\overline{X})^2}{N-1}}$	The estimated population standard deviation. This standard deviation is the formula most frequently used to calculate the standard deviation. Unless I indicate otherwise, it is the standard deviation used in this text.
SS	$\Sigma(X-\overline{X})^2$	The sum of squares.
σ^2	$\dfrac{\Sigma(X-\mu)^2}{N_{\text{pop}}}$	The population variance. X refers to individual scores in the population.
σ	$\sqrt{\dfrac{\Sigma(X-\mu)^2}{N_{\text{pop}}}}$	The population standard deviation. X refers to individual scores in the population.
$\mu_{\overline{X}}$		The mean of the theoretical sampling distribution of the mean. This mean is equal to the population mean, μ.
$\overline{X}_{\overline{X}}$		The mean of an empirical sampling distribution of the mean.
$\sigma_{\overline{X}}$	$\dfrac{\sigma}{\sqrt{N}}$	The standard error of the mean for a sample of size N. The standard error of the mean is the standard deviation of the sampling distribution of the mean.
$s_{\overline{X}}$	$\dfrac{s}{\sqrt{N}}$	The estimated standard error of the mean for a sample of size N.
z_{obs}	$\dfrac{X-\mu}{\sigma}$	The standard normal deviate. This formula converts a normally distributed raw score X to a z score in the standard normal distribution. The value of z_{obs} obtained with this formula can be used with the standard normal distribution of Table A–1.
z_{obs}	$\dfrac{X-\overline{X}}{S}$	A standard score. This formula converts a raw score into a z score that describes how far above or below the sample mean the raw score is. z scores obtained using this formula cannot be used with the standard normal distribution of Table A–1.
z_{obs}	$\dfrac{\overline{X}-\mu}{\sigma_{\overline{X}}}$	This formula converts a sample mean to a z score in the standard normal distribution. The value of z_{obs} obtained with this formula can be used with the standard normal distribution of Table A–1.

REVIEW QUESTIONS

1. Match the statistic with the parameter it estimates.

	Statistic	Parameter
a.	s	μ
b.	$\overline{X}$	$\sigma_{\overline{X}}$
c.	s^2	σ
d.	$s_{\overline{X}}$	σ^2

2. You select two samples from a population with mean μ. Sample 1 is of size $N = 10$. Sample 2 is of size $N = 24$. Which sample mean do you expect to be closer to the value of μ? Why?

3. A researcher is taking a poll to predict the outcome of a city election. She knows that the voting population of the city is composed of 34 percent registered Democrats, 29 percent registered Republicans, and 37 percent independents. Which type of sampling, simple or stratified random sampling, will more likely lead to a representative sample of voters? Why?

4. Many newspapers and tabloids run 900-number telephone polls in which a question is published and then readers may respond to the question by calling a 900 toll number. Using this approach to polling, one popular tabloid reported that about 80 percent of its readers believe that all people should be tested for AIDS ("4 in 5 Readers Say," 1987). They based this estimate on the responses of 6077 readers, 5022 of whom said that all people should be tested for AIDS. The total readership of this tabloid is about 4.5 million. Is it appropriate to conclude from this poll that about 80 percent of the readers of this tabloid favor AIDS testing for everyone? Explain your answer.

5. To estimate the number of cigarettes smoked per day by smokers in a high school population, you randomly sample 16 students from among those who identify themselves as smokers. You find that the sample mean for this group is 9.0 cigarettes per day.
   a. Provide a point estimate of the population mean.
   b. Suppose that $\sigma = 3.1$ cigarettes per day. Find the 95 percent confidence interval of the mean.

6. Suppose that the mean number of hours of sleep for a population of college students is 7.1 hours, with $\sigma = 1.2$ hours. You randomly sample 16 college students and determine the mean hours of sleep for this sample.
   a. What is the standard error of the mean for samples of size $N = 16$?
   b. What is the probability that the mean of your sample will be equal to or greater than 8.0 hours?
   c. What is the probability that the mean of your sample will be equal to or less than 6.8 hours?

d. What is the probability that the mean of your sample will be between 6.5 to 7.7 hours?

7. What is the difference between s and $s_{\bar{X}}$?

8. Zuckerman (1979) developed a scale to measure sensation seeking. People who are high in sensation seeking appear to be easily bored and have a high need to participate in new and sometimes risky activities. Scores on the scale can range from 10 to 40, with higher scores indicating a higher need for sensation seeking. Suppose that the population mean for college student athletes is 23.0, with $\sigma = 4.0$. You have measured five samples (samples A to E) of college-student athletes on this scale. Each of your samples was of a different size, as indicated next.

Sample	N
A	4
B	9
C	16
D	25
E	100

For each sample size:
   a. Calculate $\sigma_{\bar{X}}$.
   b. Find the probability that your sample mean will be equal to or greater than 25.
   c. What relationship between $\sigma_{\bar{X}}$ and N is illustrated in this example?
   d. For each sample size, find the probability that your sample mean will be between 23 and 25.

9. A light bulb manufacturer indicates that the mean life for a population of 75-watt bulbs is 750 hours with a $\sigma = 50$ hours. You buy a package of four bulbs.
   a. What is the probability that the mean life of your four bulbs will be equal to or greater than 800 hours?
   b. What is the probability that the mean life of your four bulbs will be equal to or less than 720 hours?

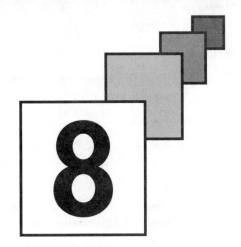

Introduction to Statistical Hypothesis Testing: The *z* Test and the One-sample *t* Test

In previous chapters I described the use of statistics for organizing and describing data and for estimating population parameters. In this chapter, I turn to the use of statistics for hypothesis testing.

Consider the following problem. Human factors is an area of behavioral science that attempts to match machines and technology to human capabilities. Human factors psychologists often take measurements of physical characteristics of people so that they can design seats, controls, or display devices to fit the person. As an example, assume that you are in charge of interior design for a major truck manufacturer. For years the seats in your trucks have been designed for a population of drivers with a mean popliteal height of 42.0 centimeters (cm) and a σ of 3.0 cm. Popliteal height (pronounced as three syllables: *pop lit eal*, with emphasis on *lit*), is the vertical distance from the underside of the thigh to the floor of a seated driver.

Recently, your company has begun selling its trucks worldwide and has received complaints that the seats are uncomfortable. You hypothesize that perhaps drivers in some countries differ in popliteal height from the population for which the seat is designed. To test this hypothesis, you obtain a sample of 25 drivers of your truck, sampled randomly and independently from the population of drivers in a country from which you have received complaints. The mean popliteal height for this sample of drivers is 44.0 cm. Obviously, this sample mean of 44.0 cm is not the same as the population mean of 42.0 cm. But what does this difference tell you about the population? There are two possibilities. The first is that the population from which the sample was drawn actually has a mean popliteal height of 42.0 cm, and your sample mean of 44.0 cm differs from this μ only because of sampling error. By chance you selected a sample with a mean popliteal height greater than 42.0 cm.

The second possibility is that the sample mean represents a population with a μ other than 42.0 cm. The population of drivers in this country has a mean popliteal height different from 42.0 cm. Which of these two possibilities should you select as representing the situation existing in the country from which the sample was selected?

I have posed a problem that requires statistical hypothesis testing to arrive at a choice of which of the two possible situations described is more probable. In statistical terms, this problem requires using a statistical hypothesis test to decide whether the sample mean of 44.0 cm differs significantly from a population mean of 42.0 cm. Figure 8–1 illustrates the problem.

STATISTICAL HYPOTHESIS TESTING

Parametric and Nonparametric Tests

Parametric Tests

Parametric test: A statistical test involving hypotheses that state a relationship about a population parameter.

Parametric statistical tests involve hypotheses that make a statement about a population parameter such as μ or $σ^2$. Parametric tests often assume certain conditions as true for the scores in the population from which a sample is drawn. As I introduce specific parametric tests, I also identify the assumptions of these tests. In this chapter, I introduce

FIGURE 8-1

Two possible situations that may give rise to an observed sample mean.

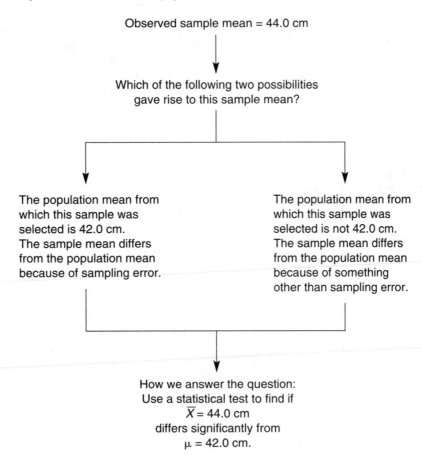

Observed sample mean = 44.0 cm

Which of the following two possibilities
gave rise to this sample mean?

The population mean from
which this sample was
selected is 42.0 cm.
The sample mean differs
from the population mean
because of sampling error.

The population mean from
which this sample was
selected is not 42.0 cm.
The sample mean differs
from the population mean
because of something
other than sampling error.

How we answer the question:
Use a statistical test to find if
$\overline{X}$ = 44.0 cm
differs significantly from
μ = 42.0 cm.

statistical hypothesis testing using two different parametric tests, the one-sample z and the one-sample t tests. Other parametric tests are introduced in Chapters 9 through 12.

Nonparametric Tests

Nonparametric test: A statistical test involving hypotheses that do not state a relationship about a population parameter.

Nonparametric tests involve hypotheses that do not make statements about a population parameter. Typically, nonparametric tests make no assumptions about the distribution of scores in the population from which the sample is drawn. For this reason, they are also referred to as *distribution-free tests*. Nonparametric tests are often used when the assumptions necessary for parametric tests are not met by the data. For many, but not all, parametric statistical tests, there are alternative nonparametric tests for analyzing the same data. Several nonparametric tests are presented in Chapter 13. The fundamental concepts of statistical hypothesis testing, though, are much the same for both parametric and nonparametric tests.

Statistical Hypotheses

Statistical hypothesis: A statement about a population parameter (for a parametric test).

Statistical hypothesis testing, parametric and nonparametric, begins with stating a statistical hypothesis. For a parametric test, a **statistical hypothesis** is a statement about a population parameter. This statement may or may not be true; it is made simply to establish a testable condition. For example, I may hypothesize that the mean for the population from which I obtained the sample of 25 popliteal height measures is 42.0 cm. In actuality, the population mean may or may not be 42.0 cm; I simply am proposing that it is 42.0 cm and that I will test this hypothesis. Statistical tests require that two hypotheses be formulated, the null and the alternative hypothesis.

Statistical Null Hypothesis

Statistical null hypothesis: A statement of a condition that a scientist tentatively holds to be true about a population; it is the hypothesis that is tested by a statistical test.

The **statistical null hypothesis**, often simply called the **null hypothesis**, is a statement of a condition that tentatively I hold to be true about a population; and it is the hypothesis that is tested by a statistical test. Null hypotheses usually are written in symbolic or notational form using H_0 to indicate that a hypothesis, such as $\mu = 42.0$ cm, is being offered. In statistical notation, the expression of the null hypothesis that $\mu = 42.0$ cm is H_0: $\mu = 42.0$ cm. The subscripted zero is often pronounced "naught"; thus we say "H naught: mu equals 42.0 centimeters."

Statistical Alternative Hypothesis

Statistical alternative hypothesis: A statement of what must be true if the null hypothesis is false.

The **statistical alternative hypothesis**, often simply called the **alternative hypothesis**, is a statement of what must be true if the null hypothesis is false. In the example, if H_0: $\mu = 42.0$ cm is not true, then the alternative must be μ does not equal 42.0 cm. This alternative hypothesis is identified as H_1 (or sometimes H_a) and written as H_1: $\mu \neq 42.0$ cm, where $\neq$ is the symbol for "does not equal." Hence H_1: $\mu \neq 42.0$ cm is read as "H one: mu does not equal 42.0 centimeters."

Properties of Statistical Hypotheses

Every statistical test requires the formulation of statistical null and alternative hypotheses. These hypotheses must be expressed so that:

- They are mutually exclusive. *Mutually exclusive* means both hypotheses cannot be true at the same time. For example, it is impossible for H_0: $\mu = 42.0$ cm and H_1: $\mu \neq 42.0$ cm to be true simultaneously for the same population.
- They include all possible values of the parameter involved in the hypothesis. The hypotheses H_0: $\mu = 42.0$ cm and H_1: $\mu \neq 42.0$ cm meet this requirement; between them they include all possible values of μ for the population of interest.

Because of these characteristics, one of the two hypotheses must represent the true condition in the population. For the example, the population mean either is 42.0 cm and H_0: $\mu = 42.0$ cm is true, or it is not, and the alternative hypothesis, H_1: $\mu \neq 42.0$ cm, is true.

In summary, for the example problem the statistical hypotheses are

$$H_0: \mu = 42.0 \text{ cm} \quad \text{(null hypothesis)}$$

$$H_1: \mu \neq 42.0 \text{ cm} \quad \text{(alternative hypothesis)}.$$

Function of the Statistical Hypotheses

The function of the null hypothesis in a statistical test is to establish a condition under which the sampling distribution of a statistic may be obtained. In Chapter 7, I defined a sampling distribution of the mean as the distribution of $\overline{X}$ values when all possible samples of size N were drawn from a population. For example, assuming that $H_0: \mu = 42.0 \text{ cm}$ is true and $\sigma = 3.0 \text{ cm}$, I may obtain the sampling distribution of $\overline{X}$ for samples of size 25 from this population. This sampling distribution, shown in Figure 8–2, is normally distributed with $\mu_{\overline{X}} = 42.0 \text{ cm}$ and a standard error equal to $\sigma_{\overline{X}}$, where

$$\sigma_{\overline{X}} = \frac{\sigma}{\sqrt{N}} = \frac{3.0}{\sqrt{25}} = \frac{3.0}{5} = 0.6.$$

In this distribution a sample mean of 44.0 cm falls beyond three standard errors of the mean away from $\mu_{\overline{X}}$. Accordingly, under the condition established by $H_0: \mu = 42.0 \text{ cm}$, a sample with a mean of 44.0 cm is a very infrequent occurrence if samples of size 25 are drawn from this population. Hence I might be inclined to reject the null hypothesis, $H_0: \mu = 42.0 \text{ cm}$, if I obtained a sample mean of 44.0 cm. This $\overline{X}$ is a statistically rare event if H_0 is true. But, before I can definitely make a decision on whether to treat H_0 as true, I must:

FIGURE 8–2
Theoretical sampling distribution of the mean for samples of $N = \cancel{100}\ 25$ from a population with $\mu_{\overline{X}} = 42.0 \text{ cm}$ and $\sigma_{\overline{X}} = 0.6 \text{ cm}$.

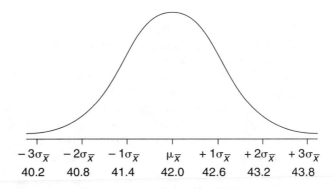

$-3\sigma_{\overline{X}}$	$-2\sigma_{\overline{X}}$	$-1\sigma_{\overline{X}}$	$\mu_{\overline{X}}$	$+1\sigma_{\overline{X}}$	$+2\sigma_{\overline{X}}$	$+3\sigma_{\overline{X}}$
40.2	40.8	41.4	42.0	42.6	43.2	43.8

Popliteal height (cm)

- Identify the probability of obtaining a value of $\overline{X}$ as large or larger than 44.0 cm if H_0: $\mu = 42.0$ cm is true. This step requires using a test statistic.
- Define what I mean by a statistically rare event. This step requires choosing a significance level.

A Test Statistic: z

Test statistic: A number calculated from the scores of the sample that allows testing a statistical null hypothesis.

A **test statistic** is a number calculated from the scores of the sample that allows us to test a statistical null hypothesis. For the example, we want a test to find the probability of occurrence of a sample mean as large or larger than 44.0 cm if H_0: $\mu = 42.0$ cm is true. Because the sampling distribution of the mean illustrated in Figure 8–2 is normally distributed with $\mu = 42.0$ cm and $\sigma_{\overline{X}} = 0.6$, I can transform any value of $\overline{X}$ into a value on the standard normal distribution by using the test statistic

$$z = \frac{\overline{X} - \mu}{\sigma_{\overline{X}}}$$

where $\overline{X}$ = sample mean
μ = hypothesized population mean
$\sigma_{\overline{X}}$ = standard error of the mean

The value of z locates the sample mean on the standard normal distribution. Notice that this formula is identical to that given for z in Chapter 7.

The value of z_{obs} with $\overline{X}$ of 44.0 cm, the value of μ hypothesized to be 42.0 cm, and $\sigma_{\overline{X}} = 0.6$ cm is

$$z_{obs} = \frac{\overline{X} - \mu}{\sigma_{\overline{X}}} = \frac{44.0 - 42.0}{0.6}$$

$$= \frac{2.0}{0.6} = +3.33.$$

The z statistic is identified as z_{obs} because it is observed from the value of $\overline{X}$ of the sample. From the sampling distribution of the z statistic given in Table A–1, I find that the probability of z being as large as or larger than +3.33 is .0004 (see column c of Table A–1 for $z = 3.33$). Consequently, the probability of obtaining $\overline{X} = 44.0$ cm or larger from a sample of size 25 is equal to .0004 if H_0: $\mu = 42.0$ cm is true. In other words, if I were to randomly select 10,000 samples of $N = 25$ from a population with $\mu = 42.0$ cm and $\sigma = 3.0$, I would expect only four of the 10,000 sample means to be as large as or larger than 44.0 cm. Thus, if H_0: $\mu = 42.0$ cm is true, obtaining a sample with $\overline{X}$ equal to 44.0 cm would be a statistically rare event. If I had obtained this $\overline{X}$, I certainly would reject the hypothesis that it was drawn from a population with a mean popliteal height of 42.0 cm, and I would accept the alternative hypothesis that $\mu \neq 42.0$ cm.

The logic of this decision making is that if the population mean is 42.0 cm then obtaining a sample with a mean of 44.0 cm would occur only four times out of every 10,000 samples selected. Although obtaining $\overline{X}$ = 44.0 cm is a possible event if μ = 42.0 cm, it is not a very probable event. It would be a more probable event if the population mean were something other than 42.0 cm. Thus I reject H_0 and accept H_1. This decision may be in error; it is possible to obtain $\overline{X}$ = 44.0 cm if μ = 42.0 cm, but it is not very probable.

Suppose, however, that I had observed a sample mean of 42.5 cm, instead of 44.0 cm. Here the value of z is

$$z_{obs} = \frac{42.5 - 42.0}{0.6} = \frac{0.5}{0.6} = +0.83.$$

From column c of Table A–1, I find that the probability of obtaining a value of z = +0.83 or larger is equal to .2033. Thus, if H_0 were true and I drew 10,000 samples of N = 25, 2033 of them would have values of $\overline{X}$ equal to or larger than 42.5 cm. Is a sample mean of 42.5 cm a statistically rare event if H_0: μ = 42.0 cm is true? What decision would you make about the null hypothesis in this instance? Would you reject H_0 : μ = 42.0 cm and accept H_1: $\mu \neq$ 42.0 cm? Or would you not reject H_0 and therefore not accept H_1? To answer these questions, I must define what value of z_{obs} will be considered a statistically rare outcome if H_0 is true. The definition of statistical rareness is given by the significance level adopted.

Significance Levels: Statistical Rareness

Significance level: A probability value that provides the criterion for rejecting a null hypothesis in a statistical test.

Alpha or α: The value of the significance level stated as a probability.

The **significance level** is a probability value that provides the criterion for rejecting a null hypothesis in a statistical test. Significance levels are given as values of **alpha** or α, the first letter of the Greek alphabet. Typically, behavioral scientists use alpha levels of either .05 or .01. Thus, if α = .05, values of z_{obs} occurring only 5 or fewer times in 100 occasions if H_0 is true are sufficiently rare that I am willing to reject H_0 and decide that H_1 is true.

Using the Test Statistic and the Significance Level to Decide about the Statistical Hypotheses

After choosing a test statistic and a significance level, we are ready to decide about the statistical hypotheses. Three steps are involved:

1. Locating a rejection region or regions in the sampling distribution of the test statistic
2. Calculating the value of the test statistic on the sample data
3. Deciding about the statistical hypotheses by observing whether the test statistic falls into a rejection region

Locating Rejection Regions

Rejection region: Values on the sampling distribution of the test statistic that have a probability equal to or less than α if H_0 is true. If the test statistic falls into the rejection region, H_0 is rejected.

Two-tailed test: A statistical test using rejection regions in both tails of the sampling distribution of the test statistic.

One-tailed test: A statistical test using a rejection region in only one tail of the sampling distribution of the test statistic.

The **rejection region** represents values on the sampling distribution of the test statistic that have a probability equal to or less than α if H_0 is true. For the example, the rejection region identifies the values of z that meet the criterion for rejecting H_0.

The sampling distribution of the z statistic with rejection regions located in each tail of the distribution is shown in Figure 8–3. Statistically rare values of z occur at either tail, or end, of the distribution. For example, z values of either +3.00 or −3.00 are equally improbable values of z if H_0 is true. Either large positive or negative values of z for the example problem would cast doubt on the truth of H_0: $\mu = 42.0$ cm. Thus rejection regions for the z statistic will be in either tail of the sampling distribution. A statistical test with rejection regions in both tails of the sampling distribution of the test statistic is identified as a **two-tailed** or a **nondirectional test**. A value of z_{obs} falling into either rejection region is improbable or rare if H_0 is true, but more likely to occur if H_1 is true. Therefore, if a value of z_{obs} falls into either rejection region, H_0 is rejected and H_1 accepted.

On occasion we may have reason to place the rejection region in only one tail of the sampling distribution of z. In this instance, a **one-tailed test** or **directional test** is used.

FIGURE 8–3

Sampling distribution of the z statistic illustrating rejection regions for a two-tailed test and $\alpha = .05$. A value of z_{obs} that falls into either rejection region leads to rejecting H_0.

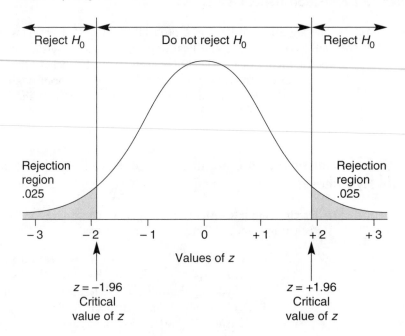

The benefit of a one-tailed test is that a smaller value of z_{obs} may fall into the rejection region. I discuss one-tailed tests more fully later in this chapter. For this example, I use a two-tailed test.

Critical value: The specific numerical values that define the boundaries of the rejection region.

Critical Values.   **Critical values** are the specific numerical values that define the boundaries of the rejection region. Critical values for z are given in column c of Table A–1. The first step in finding a critical value is to choose a significance level, such as $\alpha = .05$. For a two-tailed test, rejection regions are located in each tail of the sampling distribution of z. Accordingly, I want the area in each tail of the distribution to equal one-half of α, or .05/2, which equals .025. What values of z meet the requirement that .025 of the area of the sampling distribution of z lies beyond their values in each tail? Consulting Table A–1, I read down column c until I find the area beyond z equal to .025. When I find this area, I read the corresponding value of z in column a. This value of z is 1.96. Thus, for $\alpha = .05$ the two-tailed critical values are $z = -1.96$ and $z = +1.96$. These critical values of z (symbolized as z_{crit}) locate the rejection regions in the sampling distribution of z, as shown in Figure 8–3.

Decisions about the Statistical Hypotheses

We decide to reject or not reject H_0 by comparing the value of z_{obs} to z_{crit}. A value of z_{obs} equal to or less than $z_{crit} = -1.96$ or equal to or greater than $z_{crit} = +1.96$ falls into a rejection region. Values of z_{obs} that fall into a rejection region are statistically rare if H_0 is true, but are more common occurrences if H_1 is true. Thus a z_{obs} falling into a rejection region leads us to *reject H_0*. If I reject H_0, then I must *accept H_1*. If, however, z_{obs} does not fall into a rejection region, then I *fail to reject H_0*. And if I fail to reject H_0, then I *do not accept H_1*.

Notice that I use the value of z_{obs} to make a decision about H_0; I either reject H_0 or I fail to reject H_0. The decision about H_0 then dictates the decision to be made about H_1. If I reject H_0, then I must accept H_1. On the other hand, if I fail to reject H_0, I cannot accept H_1.

For the example on popliteal height, $z_{obs} = +3.33$ is larger than $z_{crit} = +1.96$; thus it falls into the upper rejection region. Accordingly, I reject H_0: $\mu = 42.0$ cm and accept H_1: $\mu \neq 42.0$ cm. I reject the null hypothesis that the sample was selected from a population with a mean of 42.0 cm. Because the sample mean, $\overline{X} = 44.0$ cm, is greater than the hypothesized population mean of 42.0 cm, I conclude that the mean popliteal height of the current drivers in the country from which I sampled is greater than 42.0 cm. The best point estimate I have of this population mean is the sample mean, $\overline{X} = 44.0$ cm. One reason the truck seats may be uncomfortable is because the population of drivers in some countries has longer popliteal heights than the seats were designed for.

To summarize decision making about the statistical hypotheses:

- If z_{obs} *falls into a rejection region*, then H_0 is rejected and H_1 is accepted.
- If z_{obs} *does not fall into a rejection region*, then H_0 is not rejected and H_1 is not accepted.

Statistically Significant Difference

Statistically significant difference: The observed value of the test statistic falls into a rejection region and H_0 is rejected.

A **statistically significant difference** occurs when the observed value of the test statistic falls into a rejection region and we reject H_0. For the z test, a statistically significant difference indicates that we have decided that the sample mean comes from a population with a mean different from the hypothesized population mean.

Statistically significant differences are often reported in the form $z_{obs} = +3.33, p \leq .05$. The symbol $\leq$ implies less than or equal to; thus $p \leq .05$ is read as "p less than or equal to .05." Often the less-than symbol ($<$) is used in place of the $\leq$ symbol, so the z is reported as $z_{obs} = +3.33, p < .05$. In either case, this report indicates that H_0 was rejected at the .05 significance level because the probability (p) of z_{obs} when H_0 is true is equal to or less than .05. The decisions and conclusions reached from a significant difference with the z test are summarized in the left column of Table 8–1.

Nonsignificant Difference

Nonsignificant difference: The observed value of the test statistic does not fall into a rejection region and the null hypothesis is not rejected.

A difference between a sample mean and a population mean is **nonsignificant** if the observed value of the test statistic does not fall into a rejection region. The null hypothesis is not rejected and the observed difference between $\overline{X}$ and the hypothesized μ is treated as due only to sampling error. A nonsignificant difference is indicated by $p > .05$ following the numerical value of z_{obs}. The decisions and conclusions reached from a nonsignificant difference with the z test are summarized in the right column of Table 8–1.

TABLE 8–1

Summary of decisions and conclusions in statistical hypothesis testing using the z test for testing a sample mean against an hypothesized population mean. A .05 significance level is used.

If z_{obs} **falls into a rejection region for $\alpha = .05$, then:**	If z_{obs} does *not* **fall into a rejection region for $\alpha = .05$, then:**
Probability of z_{obs} is less than or equal to .05, or $p \leq .05$.	Probability of z_{obs} is greater than .05, or $p > .05$.
H_0 is rejected.	H_0 is not rejected.
H_1 is accepted. The sample mean is from a population with a mean that is different from the hypothesized population mean.	H_1 is not accepted.
The difference between $\overline{X}$ and the hypothesized μ is statistically significant at the .05 level.	The difference between $\overline{X}$ and the hypothesized μ is nonsignificant at the .05 level.
It is decided that something other than sampling error is responsible for the difference between $\overline{X}$ and the hypothesized μ.	It is decided that sampling error is the most plausible explanation of the difference between $\overline{X}$ and the hypothesized μ.

Summary of the Steps of Statistical Hypothesis Testing

All statistical tests require the following:

- Selecting a test statistic, such as z
- Formulating two statistical hypotheses, H_0 and H_1
- Obtaining the sampling distribution of the test statistic assuming that H_0 is true
- Selecting a significance level
- Finding a critical value or values of the test statistic
- Locating a rejection region or regions in the sampling distribution of the test statistic
- Formulating decision rules regarding the statistical hypotheses
- Calculating the value of the test statistic on the sample data
- Deciding to reject or not reject H_0 based on whether the observed value of the test statistic does or does not fall into a rejection region
- Deciding to accept or not accept H_1 based on the decision for H_0

Although I have discussed these steps in the context of the z test, they apply to all the statistical tests discussed in the following chapters.

TESTING YOUR KNOWLEDGE 8-1

1. Define: alpha level, α, alternative hypothesis, critical value, H_0, H_1, nonsignificant difference, null hypothesis, one-tailed test, rejection region, significance level, statistical hypothesis, statistically significant difference, test statistic, two-tailed test, z_{crit}, z_{obs}.
2. Identify the two properties of statistical hypotheses.
3. Write H_0 and H_1 in notation for each of the following statements.
   a. The μ for scores on the Wechsler Adult Intelligence Test is 100.
   b. The mean number of murders per year is 8.3 for every 150,000 people.
   c. The mean reaction time of 19-year-old males to a simple stimulus is 423.0 milliseconds.
4. For each of the following, μ represents a population mean, $\sigma_{\overline{X}}$ the standard error of the mean for the population, and $\overline{X}$ a mean of a sample drawn from the population. For each set of values, formulate H_0 and H_1 and find the value of z_{obs}. Then, using Table A–1, determine whether the z_{obs} falls into a two-tailed rejection region at the .05 significance level and indicate your decision for H_0 and H_1.

	μ	$\sigma_{\overline{X}}$	$\overline{X}$
a.	50	4.7	40
b.	100	25.0	70
c.	143	0.4	143.9
d.	87	2.9	92

5. Complete the following problem using a .05 significance level and a two-tailed test. The population mean for an intelligence scale is 100 and $\sigma = 15$. You are the principal of

an elementary school in a rural county. For the 121 students in your school, $\overline{X}$ on this scale is 103.4. Does the mean of the students in your school differ significantly from the population mean? In your answer, indicate:

a. The statistic to be used
b. The statistical hypotheses
c. The significance level
d. z_{crit}
e. The location of the rejection regions
f. z_{obs}
g. Your decision about H_0 and H_1
h. Your conclusion regarding the mean of your students in relation to a population mean of 100

THE ONE-SAMPLE *t* TEST

In practice, σ usually is estimated by s, the standard deviation of the scores in the sample. Consequently, $\sigma_{\overline{X}}$ is also estimated from $s_{\overline{X}}$. When I estimate $\sigma_{\overline{X}}$ from $s_{\overline{X}}$, I obtain a new statistic, the t, defined as

$$t = \frac{\overline{X} - \mu}{s_{\overline{X}}}$$

or, substituting $s/\sqrt{N}$ for $s_{\overline{X}}$,

$$t = \frac{\overline{X} - \mu}{s/\sqrt{N}}$$

where
$\overline{X}$ = sample mean
μ = hypothesized population mean
$s_{\overline{X}}$ = estimated standard error of the mean obtained from the estimated population standard deviation s
N = sample size

One-sample *t* test: A *t* test used to test the difference between a sample mean and a hypothesized population mean for statistical significance when $\sigma_{\overline{X}}$ is estimated by $s_{\overline{X}}$.

This t statistic may be used to test the difference between a sample mean and a hypothesized population mean for statistical significance when $\sigma_{\overline{X}}$ is estimated by $s_{\overline{X}}$. Because only one sample mean is involved, the statistic is called the **one-sample *t*** to distinguish it from the t test involving two sample means introduced in Chapter 9.

The t statistic was developed by the British mathematician William Sealy Gosset shortly after the turn of the twentieth century. Gosset published his work under the pseudonym of "Student." Consequently, the t statistic is often identified as "Student's t."

Sampling Distribution of *t*

To use the t statistic, I must know its sampling distribution. The sampling distribution of the t differs from the sampling distribution of the z. The z statistic, because it uses the population parameter $\sigma_{\overline{X}}$, has only one sampling distribution, the distribution presented in Table A–1. The t statistic, however, uses s, the **estimated population standard deviation**, defined as

$$s = \sqrt{\frac{\Sigma(X - \overline{X})^2}{N - 1}}.$$

The calculation of s involves the sample size N; therefore, the sampling distribution of t varies with the sample size or, more specifically, the degrees of freedom of the sample.

Degrees of Freedom

Degrees of freedom: The number of scores free to vary when calculating a statistic.

Degrees of freedom (abbreviated *df*) are determined by the number of scores free to vary when calculating a statistic. Several examples will be helpful in understanding what is meant by "scores free to vary" when computing a statistic. Suppose that you are asked to choose three scores on a test. You may choose any three scores, say 75, 62, and 97. For this request there are no limitations on the scores that you may choose; each score is free to vary. Accordingly, there are N or 3 *df* for this set of scores. Consider a second request, however, where you are asked to choose three scores, but the sum of the three scores must be 254. Suppose you choose 81 and 78 as your first two scores; they can have any value you want. These two scores are free to vary. Is the third score also free to vary? It is not. Because the three scores must total 254, the third score must be 95; no other score provides a total of 254. Consequently, if you are told that the total of the scores is 254, two scores are free to vary, but the value of the third score is *fixed* by the value of the two scores free to vary and the total of the three scores. Accordingly, if you know the total of the three scores, then there are $N - 1 = 3 - 1 = 2$ degrees of freedom for the three scores.

Applying this reasoning to the calculation of the sample mean, $\overline{X}$ has N *df*. All scores in a set of scores are free to vary when calculating $\overline{X}$. To illustrate, you are asked to calculate the sample mean of a set of five scores, four of which are 7, 10, 3, and 6. Given only this information, you cannot find the mean. The fifth score may assume any value, and you cannot know the value of the fifth score from knowledge of the four scores. Thus all N scores (where $N = 5$ for this example) are free to vary when calculating the sample mean.

The degrees of freedom for s, however, are $N - 1$. To illustrate, suppose that you are asked to calculate s on a sample of five scores. The estimated population standard deviation is defined as

$$s = \sqrt{\frac{\Sigma(X - \overline{X})^2}{N - 1}}.$$

Suppose that four of the five scores have values of 13, 15, 13, and 12 and that the mean of the five scores is 13.4. I know also that $\Sigma(X - \overline{X}) = 0$. If I subtract $\overline{X}$ from each of the four known scores, I obtain

$$X - \overline{X}$$

$$13 - 13.4 = -0.4$$

$$15 - 13.4 = +1.6$$

$$13 - 13.4 = -0.4$$

$$12 - 13.4 = -1.4$$

Sum $\quad = -0.6$

The sum of these four $X - \overline{X}$ differences is -0.6. When the fifth score is included in the set, this sum must be zero. Thus the fifth score must result in an $X_5 - \overline{X}$ value of $+0.6$, for $+0.6$ added to -0.6 will equal zero. If $X_5 - 13.4 = +0.6$, then X_5 must equal 14. Accordingly, if $\overline{X}$ is known for the set of five scores, the values of only four of the five scores are free to vary. The value of the fifth score is not free to vary; its value is fixed by the restriction that the value of the mean imposes. Because $\overline{X}$ must be known to calculate s, all scores but one are free to vary in calculating s. Thus, when calculating either s or s^2, a set of N scores possesses $N - 1$ df.

We can apply this knowledge of degrees of freedom to the formula for s to write this formula more briefly. Because $\Sigma(X - \overline{X})^2$ is also called a *sum of squares* (SS), and $N - 1$ represents the degrees of freedom when obtaining a SS, the **estimated population standard deviation** can be expressed as the square root of a sum of squares divided by the degrees of freedom, or

$$s = \sqrt{\frac{SS}{df}}.$$

We will find this expression of s useful in later chapters.

Degrees of Freedom for the One-sample t Test

We now apply our knowledge of df to the t test. The estimated standard error of the mean, $s_{\overline{X}}$, is given by $s/\sqrt{N}$. Because s has $N - 1$ df, $s_{\overline{X}}$, too, has $N - 1$ df. Hence, the degrees of freedom for the sampling distribution of the one-sample t statistic are $N - 1$ also.

Sampling Distribution of the t

There is a different theoretical sampling distribution of t for each number of df. Because, potentially, any number of scores can be obtained in a sample, there is an unlimited number of df ranging from 1 to infinity for the t statistic. As examples of the potential sampling distributions, Figure 8–4 illustrates sampling distributions of t for 2, 4, and 60 df.

Although the shape of the t distribution changes with its degrees of freedom, it is similar to the normal distribution in several respects. Each t distribution is symmetrical and unimodal and has a mean equal to zero. Consider why these properties arise. When a null hypothesis, such as H_0: μ = some hypothesized value of the population mean, is true, the expected value of t will be zero, because the average $\overline{X} - \mu$ value in a sampling distribution from such a population will be zero. But, even when H_0 is true, values of $\overline{X} - \mu$ will vary around a mean of zero because of sampling error. Furthermore, I expect

FIGURE 8–4

Sampling distributions of the t statistic for 2, 4, and 60 df.

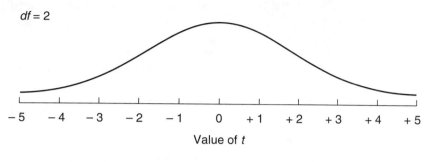

df = 2

Value of t

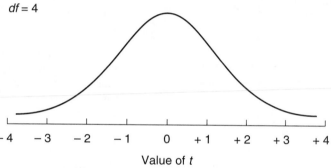

df = 4

Value of t

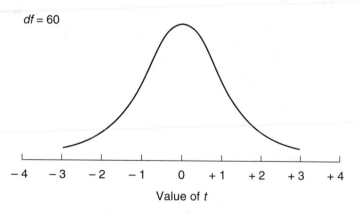

df = 60

Value of t

that $\overline{X}$ will be larger than μ about as often as it will be smaller than μ. In the long run, the $\overline{X} - \mu$ values will be positive and negative equally often when the null hypothesis is true. Consequently, the expected t values will be symmetrical around a mean of zero.

For an infinite number of degrees of freedom (a theoretical but not actual possibility), the sampling distribution of t is the same as the normal. All other t distributions are more spread out than a normal distribution. The flattest and widest t distributions are those based on the smallest sample sizes; for example, compare the distribution with 2 df (thus $N = 3$) with the distribution with 60 df (thus $N = 61$) in Figure 8–4.

Why Are Degrees of Freedom Used Rather Than N?   If the *df* for the one-sample *t* test are given by $N - 1$, why not present the sampling distribution of *t* in terms of *N* rather than *df*? For the one-sample *t* statistic, we have gained no advantage by using *df* rather than *N*, for the *df* are always one less than *N*. The advantage of using *df* becomes apparent in Chapter 9, however, when I introduce another *t* statistic used for comparing two sample means. For this *t*, the *df* are $N - 2$ rather than $N - 1$. For equal *df*, however, both *t* tests possess the same sampling distribution. We will encounter similar instances with other statistics in later chapters.

TESTING YOUR KNOWLEDGE 8-2

1. Write the formula for the one-sample *t* statistic.
2. Why is the *t* statistic sometimes called Student's *t*?
3. You are given seven scores: 73, 42, 51, 68, 49, 62, and 57. How many *df* does this set of scores possess for calculating (a) $\overline{X}$, (b) *s*, and (c) s^2?
4. You plan to compute the one-sample *t* statistic on samples of the following sizes. For each sample, find the *df*. (a) $N = 10$, (b) $N = 16$, (c) $N = 7$, (d) $N = 54$, (e) $N = 120$, (f) $N = 30$.
5. You have two theoretical sampling distributions of *t*, one with 13 *df* and one with 27 *df*. Which distribution will be wider and flatter?
6. Under what conditions will the sampling distribution of the *t* statistic be identical to the sampling distribution of *z*?

Statistical Hypothesis Testing with the One-sample *t*

The one-sample *t* allows us to determine whether an $\overline{X}$ differs from an hypothesized μ by more than expected from sampling error alone when σ is estimated by *s*. The procedure for statistical hypothesis testing with the *t* is identical to that for the *z* statistic. The necessary steps include the following:

- Formulating H_0 and H_1
- Obtaining the sampling distribution of the *t* statistic, assuming that H_0 is true
- Selecting a significance level
- Finding a critical value or values of *t*
- Locating a rejection region or regions in the sampling distribution of *t*
- Formulating decision rules regarding the statistical hypotheses
- Calculating the value of t_{obs} on the sample data
- Making decisions about H_0 and H_1 from the value of t_{obs}

I illustrate these steps with an example problem. Suppose that a child psychologist studying a group of 30 third-graders in an after-school care program found that for a weekday the children watched an average of 83.0 minutes of television with an *s* of 26.0 minutes. Suppose it is known also that the population mean for time spent watching television by third-graders on a weekday is 95.0 minutes. Does the sample mean of 83.0 minutes differ significantly from the population mean of 95.0 minutes? Because σ is estimated by *s*, the one-sample *t* test will be used to answer this question.

Formulating Statistical Hypotheses

The statistical hypotheses for the one-sample t statistic are identical to those of the z statistic. The **null hypothesis**, H_0, is stated as an hypothesized value of a population mean. The **alternative hypothesis**, H_1, is a statement that the population mean is not that hypothesized in H_0. For the example, the **statistical hypotheses expressed in notation** are

$$H_0: \mu = 95.0 \text{ minutes},$$

$$H_1: \mu \neq 95.0 \text{ minutes}.$$

Obtaining the Sampling Distribution of the *t* Statistic

The sampling distribution of t depends on the degrees of freedom for the t calculated on the sample scores. The *df* for the one-sample t are given by $N - 1$. For a mean based on 30 scores, the *df* for $t = 30 - 1$, or 29. After selecting a significance level and locating rejection regions, I will use these degrees of freedom with a table of the sampling distribution of t to find t_{crit}.

Selecting a Significance Level

The significance level is a probability value that provides the criterion for rejecting H_0. Either the .05 or .01 significance level is typically used in statistical hypothesis testing. For the example, I use $\alpha = .05$.

Locating Rejection Regions for *t*: Two-tailed Test

A rejection region consists of values in the sampling distribution of t that occur with a probability equal to or less than α when H_0 is true. Thus the rejection region defines values of t_{obs} that meet the criterion for rejecting H_0.

In a **two-tailed** or **nondirectional test**, rejection regions for the t test are located in either tail of the theoretical sampling distribution, as illustrated in Figure 8–5. When H_0 is true, most values of $\overline{X}$ will differ only slightly from μ, and thus most values of t will be clustered around zero in the middle of the distribution. Because of sampling error, however, some values of t will be at either end of the distribution even when H_0 is true. These values are obtained when the numerator of the t (i.e., the difference $\overline{X} - \mu$) is large compared to the denominator (i.e., $s_{\overline{X}}$). But these large values of t are rare occurrences if the null hypothesis is true.

On the other hand, if H_1 is true and $\overline{X}$ represents a sample from a population with a mean other than μ, then large values of $\overline{X} - \mu$, and thus of t, are expected to occur more frequently. Therefore, a rejection region is located in each tail of the theoretical sampling distribution of t, and the total α is divided between the tails. If $\alpha = .05$, then each rejection region includes a probability of $\alpha/2$, or .025. If the value of t calculated on the scores of the sample (identified as t_{obs}) falls into either rejection region, then the null hypothesis is rejected and the alternative hypothesis accepted. By locating a rejection region in each tail of the t distribution, the experimenter covers both possibilities implied by the alternative hypothesis; that is, $\overline{X}$ is greater than μ or $\overline{X}$ is less than μ. The total probability of an outcome in either of the two rejection regions is .05 if H_0 is true.

FIGURE 8–5
Two-tailed rejection regions for the t distribution for 29 df and $\alpha = .05$. A value of t_{obs} falling into either rejection region leads to rejection of H_0 and acceptance of H_1.

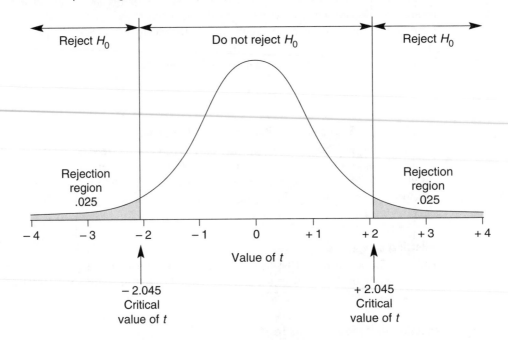

The two rejection regions for the sampling distribution of t based on 29 df are illustrated in Figure 8–5. For 29 df, if H_0 is true, then the probability that a t will be equal to or less than −2.045 is .025, and the probability that it will be equal to or larger than +2.045 is also .025. Any t_{obs} equal to or less than −2.045 or equal to or larger than +2.045 falls into a rejection region. This outcome will occur only 5 percent of the time when the null hypothesis is true. The values of −2.045 and +2.045 were obtained from a table of critical values of the sampling distribution of t. The use of this table is explained next.

Using the Table of Critical t Values
For a particular significance level, the critical t values (identified as t_{crit}) needed for locating the rejection regions depend on the df of t_{obs}. Figures of the sampling distribution of t, such as those illustrated in Figure 8–4, are useful to visualize how the shape of the t distribution varies with the degrees of freedom, but it is difficult to find exact values of t_{crit} from them. Accordingly, values of t_{crit} for the .05 and .01 significance levels have been calculated and are presented in tables.

Table 8–2 presents the two-tailed values of t_{crit} for $\alpha = .05$ and .01. Table 8–2 is part of Table A–2 in the Appendix. The first column lists degrees of freedom for t distributions. The values in any row of the $\alpha = .05$ or .01 columns are the two-tailed values of t_{crit} for the corresponding degrees of freedom for that significance level. For the example with $\alpha = .05$, the two-tailed t_{crit} value for a t_{obs} with 29 degrees of freedom

TABLE 8–2

Critical values of the *t* distribution for α = .05 and α = .01. The values provided are for a two-tailed test.

df	α = .05	α = .01
1	~~12.607~~ 12.706	63.657
2	4.303	9.925
3	3.182	5.841
4	2.776	4.604
5	2.571	4.032
6	2.447	3.707
7	2.365	3.499
8	2.306	3.355
9	2.262	3.250
10	2.228	3.169
11	2.201	3.106
12	2.179	3.055
13	2.160	3.012
14	2.145	2.977
15	2.131	2.947
16	2.120	2.921
17	2.110	2.898
18	2.101	2.878
19	2.093	2.861
20	2.086	2.845
21	2.080	2.831
22	2.074	2.819
23	2.069	2.807
24	2.064	2.797
25	2.060	2.787
26	2.056	2.779
27	2.052	2.771
28	2.048	2.763
29	2.045	2.756
30	2.042	2.750
40	2.021	2.704
60	2.000	2.660
120	1.980	2.617
∞	1.960	2.576

Reprinted with permission from Table IV.1, Percentage Points, Student's *t*-Distribution, *CRC Handbook of Tables for Probability and Statistics* (2nd ed.). Copyright 1968, CRC Press, Inc., Boca Raton, Florida.

is 2.045. Notice that this value is not preceded by a plus or minus sign. Rather, it is presented as an absolute value of *t*. For locating rejection regions, however, this value should be treated as both −2.045 and +2.045. Similarly, for α = .01, the two-tailed t_{crit} value for 29 degrees of freedom is 2.756. Notice that a significance level of .01 imposes a more stringent criterion for rejecting H_0 than does α = .05. Any observed $\overline{X} - \mu$ difference will have to be larger to reject H_0 when a .01 significance level is adopted instead of .05.

For more than 30 degrees of freedom, only selected critical values are included in the table. When the *df* for t_{obs} exceed 30, I recommend that the t_{crit} value used be based on the *df* in the table closest to but fewer than the degrees of freedom associated with the t_{obs}. For example, if *df* = 35, Table 8–2 shows t_{crit} values for 30 and 40 *df* but none between. Accordingly, for 35 *df* I use 30 *df* to determine the t_{crit} (which is 2.042 for α = .05) instead of 40 *df*. This procedure makes the actual significance level used slightly smaller than .05. If 40 *df* were used to find the t_{crit} instead, then the significance level would be slightly greater than .05. If t_{obs} falls into the rejection region for 30 *df*, then it will also fall in the rejection region for 40 *df*. Should t_{obs} (e.g., t_{obs} = 2.033) fall between the tabled values for the next lower *df* (e.g., t_{crit} = 2.045 for 30 *df*) and the next higher *df* (e.g., t_{crit} = 2.021 for 40 *df*), then a more accurate value of t_{crit} can be interpolated from the tabled values.

Locating a Rejection Region for *t*: One-tailed Test

In a two-tailed test H_0 is rejected if t_{obs} falls into a rejection region in either tail of the *t* distribution. However, when a research hypothesis predicts a directional relationship among the means (e.g., if the researcher of our example predicted that $\overline{X}$ would be less than μ) and there is no interest in an outcome opposite than predicted (e.g., if $\overline{X}$ greater than μ occurs), then some researchers use a one-tailed test. In a **one-tailed** or **directional test** a rejection region encompassing the entire value of α is located in the tail of the

FIGURE 8–6
One-tailed rejection region for the *t* distribution for 29 *df* and α = .05. A value of t_{obs} falling into the rejection region leads to rejection of H_0 and acceptance of H_1.

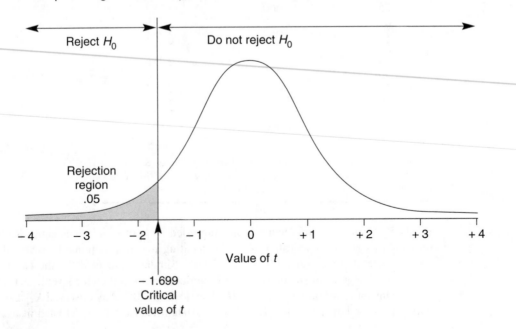

t distribution, corresponding to the direction of the outcome predicted by the research hypothesis. Values of t_{crit} for a one-tailed test at the .01 and .05 significance levels are also presented in Table A–2. For 29 df, the one-tailed t_{crit} at the .05 significance level is 1.699. A one-tailed rejection region with $t_{crit} = -1.699$ in the left tail of a t distribution is illustrated in Figure 8–6. This rejection region would be appropriate for the example if I had stated the following statistical hypotheses:

$$H_0: \ \mu \geq 95.0,$$

$$H_1: \ \mu < 95.0.$$

When Should a One-tailed Test Be Used?   The advantage of a one-tailed rejection region is that t_{crit} will be smaller because the entire rejection region lies in only one tail of the distribution. Thus it is easier to reject H_0 because a smaller difference between $\overline{X}$ and μ will result in a t_{obs} falling into the rejection region. This advantage is accompanied by a limitation, however. The decision to adopt a one-tailed or two-tailed rejection region must be made at the time the research is being planned and before the data are collected and analyzed. If a one-tailed rejection region is adopted, then the experimenter cannot reject H_0 from an obtained difference in means opposite in direction to that hypothesized, because no rejection region for such an outcome has been located. I discuss one- and two-tailed tests more fully in Chapter 9. In practice, two-tailed tests are most commonly used; thus they are used for all examples in this chapter.

Calculating t_{obs}

Calculating

$$t_{obs} = \frac{\overline{X} - \mu}{s_{\overline{X}}}$$

requires substituting values of $\overline{X}$, the hypothesized μ, and $s_{\overline{X}}$ into the formula. For the example of 30 scores of third-graders watching television, $\overline{X} = 83.0$ minutes, $s = 26.0$ minutes, and $N = 30$. The hypothesized value of μ is 95.0 minutes. The value of $s_{\overline{X}}$ is obtained from $s/\sqrt{N}$; thus

$$s_{\overline{X}} = \frac{26.0}{\sqrt{30}} = \frac{26}{5.477}$$

which equals 4.75. As a result,

$$
\begin{aligned}
t_{obs} &= \frac{83.0 - 95.0}{4.75} \\
&= \frac{-12.0}{4.75} \\
&= -2.526
\end{aligned}
$$

with $N - 1 = 29 \ df$.

Decisions about the Statistical Hypotheses

The decision rules for statistical hypotheses are the same for all statistical tests. Accordingly, for the one-sample t test:

- If t_{obs} falls into a rejection region, then H_0 is rejected and H_1 is accepted.
- If t_{obs} does not fall into a rejection region, then H_0 is not rejected, and H_1 is not accepted.

The two-tailed value of t_{crit} for 29 df and $\alpha = .05$ is 2.045. Consequently, as illustrated in Figure 8–5, a t_{obs} equal to or less than -2.045 or equal to or larger than $+2.045$ falls into a rejection region. The t_{obs} of -2.526 is more extreme than $t_{crit} = -2.045$ and therefore falls into the rejection region in the left tail of the distribution. I reject H_0: $\mu = 95.0$ minutes and accept H_1: $\mu \neq 95.0$ minutes. The difference between the sample mean and the population mean is statistically significant at the .05 level. I conclude that the sample mean of 83.0 minutes is from a population with a μ less than 95.0 minutes. The mean amount of TV viewing by the third-graders in the after-school program is significantly less than the population mean of 95.0 minutes per day.

If t_{obs} had fallen between the two critical values of -2.045 and $+2.045$ (e.g., if $\overline{X}$ had been 90.0 minutes and thus $t_{obs} = -1.053$), then I would fail to reject H_0 and not accept H_1. The observed difference between the sample mean and hypothesized population mean would be nonsignificant. In this instance there would be no evidence that H_0 is not true.

The decisions about the statistical hypotheses and the conclusions reached from either a statistically significant or a nonsignificant one-sample t test are summarized in Table 8–3.

Assumptions of the One-sample t Test

The one-sample t test makes the following assumptions of the scores in the sample:

- The scores in the sample are drawn randomly from a population of scores and each score is independent of each other score.
- The scores in the population sampled are normally distributed.

In practice, these assumptions may not be met fully by the scores in a sample, yet researchers proceed to use the t test on the data. I discuss the consequences of this action more fully in Chapter 9.

Example Problem 8–1

Using the One-sample t Test

Problem

Several psychologists have hypothesized that in competitive situations some individuals are motivated to avoid being too successful in order to minimize criticism and ostracism

TABLE 8–3
Summary of decisions and conclusions in statistical hypothesis testing using the one-sample *t* test. A .05 significance level is used.

If t_{obs} falls into a rejection region for $\alpha = .05$, then:	If t_{obs} does *not* fall into a rejection region for $\alpha = .05$, then:
Probability of t_{obs} is less than or equal to .05, or $p \le .05$.	Probability of t_{obs} is greater than .05, or $p > .05$.
H_0 is rejected.	H_0 is not rejected.
H_1 is accepted. The sample mean is from a population with a mean that is different from the hypothesized population mean.	H_1 is not accepted.
The difference between $\overline{X}$ and the hypothesized μ is statistically significant at the .05 level.	The difference between $\overline{X}$ and the hypothesized μ is nonsignificant at the .05 level.
It is decided that something other than sampling error is responsible for the difference between $\overline{X}$ and the hypothesized μ.	It is decided that sampling error is the most plausible explanation of the difference between $\overline{X}$ and the hypothesized μ.

by peers. A self-report inventory measuring this motivation to avoid success has been developed by Good and Good (1973). Suppose it is known that the population mean for female college seniors on this inventory is 8.6 for which the range of scores may be from 0, low motivation to avoid success, to 28, high motivation to avoid success. A counselor has developed a workshop dealing with responding to competitive situations. She gives the motivation-to-avoid-success scale to 33 female college seniors who have completed this workshop and obtains a mean of 8.1 with $s = 1.31$. Does this $\overline{X}$ differ significantly from a μ of 8.6 at the .05 level? Use a two-tailed test.

Statistic to Be Used: Because σ is being estimated by s, the one-sample t test is appropriate. Therefore,

$$t_{obs} = \frac{\overline{X} - \mu}{s_{\overline{X}}}.$$

Assumptions for Use:
1. The individuals measured are randomly and independently drawn from a population of female college seniors.
2. Motivation-to-avoid-success scores are normally distributed in the population sampled.

Statistical Hypotheses: H_0: $\mu = 8.6$; H_1: $\mu \ne 8.6$.

Significance Level: $\alpha = .05$.

df for t: $N - 1 = 33 - 1 = 32$.

Critical Value of t: $t_{crit} = 2.042$. A critical value of t for 32 df is not presented in Table A–2. I used t_{crit} for the next-lower df tabled, 30 df.

Rejection Regions: Values of t_{obs} equal to or less than -2.042 or equal to or greater than $+2.042$.

Calculation:

$$s_{\overline{X}} = \frac{1.31}{\sqrt{33}}$$
$$= \frac{1.31}{5.745}$$
$$= 0.228.$$

Thus

$$t_{obs} = \frac{8.1 - 8.6}{0.228}$$
$$= \frac{-0.5}{0.228}$$
$$= -2.193.$$

Decision: t_{obs} is more extreme than $t_{crit} = -2.042$ and falls into a rejection region. Thus I reject H_0 and accept H_1.

Conclusion: The mean motivation to avoid success in the sample of female college seniors who completed the workshop (i.e., $\overline{X} = 8.1$) is significantly less than the population mean of 8.6 of female college seniors.

STATISTICS IN USE 8–1

The Morinaga Misalignment Illusion: Using the One-sample t Test

Psychologists study illusions to better understand how we perceive the world. As one example, the Morinaga misalignment illusion is illustrated in Figure 8–7. The figure is an illusion because the points of each angle do not appear to be aligned on the same vertical line, although they are. The middle point appears to align with a vertical line different from the line on which the bottom and top angles align.

Day and Kasperczyk (1984) investigated whether the illusion occurs with shapes other than the angles illustrated. The 12 participants in their experiment (thus $N = 12$) were asked to adjust the center angle so that its point appeared aligned with the points of the top and bottom. The error in the adjustment was measured in millimeters (mm). If a subject aligned the points of the three angles perfectly, then he or she would have 0-mm error and there

FIGURE 8–7
Morinaga misalignment illusion.

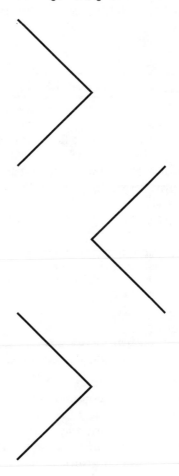

would be no illusion. On the other hand, if a subject adjusted the center angle so that it appeared aligned, but was not, then the measured error was recorded.

In one experimental condition using half-circles in place of the angles, Day and Kasperczyk found a mean error of 1.44 mm with an s of 2.07 mm. Does this measured error represent a real error in perception, that is, an illusion, or is it simply a chance difference from a 0-mm error? To answer this question, they used a one-sample t test to compare $\overline{X} = 1.44$ mm to a hypothesized μ of 0-mm error. Thus the statistical hypotheses were $H_0 : \mu = 0$ and $H_1: \mu \neq 0$. The value of $s_{\overline{X}} = 2.07/\sqrt{12}$, which equals 2.07/3.464, or 0.598. Substituting numerical values into the formula for t_{obs}, $t_{obs} = (1.44 - 0.0)/0.598 = +2.408$ with $N - 1$, or $12 - 1 = 11$ df. The value of t_{crit} for a two-tailed test with 11 df and $\alpha = .05$ is 2.201 (see Table A–2). Accordingly, the rejection regions are t_{obs} equal to or less than -2.201 or equal to or larger than $+2.201$. The t_{obs} of $+2.408$ is larger than t_{crit} of $+2.201$; thus t_{obs} falls into the rejection region. $H_0: \mu = 0$ is rejected and $H_1: \mu \neq 0$ is accepted. Hence Day and Kasperczyk concluded that the mean error of 1.44 mm differs significantly from a hypothesized μ of 0-mm error. The Morinaga misalignment illusion can be produced with circles as well as angles. This illusion is a perceptual phenomenon that is not dependent on a specific stimulus, such as an angle.

REPORTING THE RESULTS OF THE ONE-SAMPLE *t* TEST

The *Publication Manual of the American Psychological Association* (1994) requires a report of an inferential statistical test to give the symbol for the statistical test, the *df* for the test, the observed value of the statistic, the alpha level used, and the probability of obtaining the observed value of the statistic or an even more extreme value assuming that the null hypothesis is true (pp. 15–18). Relevant descriptive statistics, such as the sample mean and standard deviation, are also required. I illustrate this style with the results of the example problem of television watching by third-graders.

> The mean daily amount of time spent watching television for the 30 children was 83.0 minutes ($SD = 26.0$ minutes). For alpha equal to .05, a two-tailed one-sample *t* test indicated that the sample mean differed significantly from a hypothesized population mean of 95.0 minutes; $t(29) = -2.53$, $p < .05$.

In the report:

$\alpha = .05$ Indicates the significance level selected for the test.

$t(29)$ Identifies the test statistic as the *t*. This *t* identifies t_{obs}, although the subscript *obs* is not included. Because the *t* is identified as the one-sample *t*, we know that the test is a comparison of a sample mean against a hypothesized population mean. The degrees of freedom for t_{obs} are shown in parentheses. Thus we know that 30 scores were used in the calculation of *t* (because $df = N - 1$; thus $29 = 30 - 1$).

$= -2.53$ The value of t_{obs} (not the t_{crit} value found in Table A–2). The value of *t* should be given to at least two decimal places.

$p < .05$.   Indicates the following:
   a.   The *p* and less than sign ($p <$) indicate that the probability of t_{obs} if H_0 is true is less than (or equal to) .05. This value is the probability of t_{obs} or an even more extreme value of t_{obs} if H_0 is true; it is not necessarily the same as the value of α selected.
   b. H_0: $\mu = 95.0$ minutes was rejected.
       H_1: $\mu \neq 95.0$ minutes was accepted.
   c.   The difference between the sample mean and the hypothesized μ is statistically significant.
   d.   The sample mean is treated as being from a population with a mean less than the hypothesized $\mu = 95.0$ minutes.

e. If $p > .05$ had been reported, then the greater than sign ($>$) would indicate that H_0 was not rejected and $\overline{X}$ did not differ significantly from the hypothesized μ at the .05 significance level.

TESTING YOUR KNOWLEDGE 8-3

1. Write H_0 and H_1 for the one-sample t test for each of the following statements.
   a. The population mean for time sleeping per night is 493 minutes.
   b. The population mean on an inventory of depression proneness is 36.1.
   c. The population mean on a standardized intelligence test is 100.
2. Using Table A–2, find the values of t_{crit} for the df and value of α indicated. Use a two-tailed test.

	df	α
a.	6	.05
b.	17	.01
c.	23	.05
d.	32	.05
e.	39	.05
f.	75	.01
g.	103	.05
h.	256	.05

3. Indicate whether each of the following t_{obs} does or does not fall into a rejection region. Then indicate your decision for H_0 and H_1. Remember that you *fail to reject* or *reject* H_0, and you *do not accept* or *accept* H_1. Use $\alpha = .05$ and a two-tailed test. The df for each t_{obs} are given in parentheses.
   a. $t_{obs}(19) = +3.014$
   b. $t_{obs}(19) = -1.989$
   c. $t_{obs}(16) = -2.179$
   d. $t_{obs}(16) = +2.040$
   e. $t_{obs}(30) = -3.961$
   f. $t_{obs}(30) = +2.743$
   g. $t_{obs}(6) = -2.364$
   h. $t_{obs}(6) = +2.447$
   i. $t_{obs}(9) = -2.262$
   j. $t_{obs}(37) = +2.938$
   k. $t_{obs}(42) = -2.410$
4. Identify the assumptions underlying the use of the one-sample t test.
5. Complete the following problem and answer the questions asked. Use a two-tailed test and .05 significance level. You are interested in how well people can estimate the passage of time without the use of a watch or clock. Accordingly, you ask 11 people to tell you when they think a 7-minute interval has passed without using a watch or clock. The mean of the 11 estimates was 5.8 minutes with $s = 0.8$ minutes. Is your sample mean significantly different from a population mean of 7 minutes? In your answer, indicate the following:
   a. The statistic to be used

      b. The assumptions for its use

      c. The statistical hypotheses

      d. The significance level

      e. The critical value of the test statistic

      f. The rejection regions

      g. The value of t_{obs}

      h. Your decisions about the statistical hypotheses

      i. Your conclusion regarding the sample mean

6. This exercise presents reports of the use of the t test adapted from results of published studies. For each report, answer the following questions:

      a. What is the value of the sample mean?

      b. What is the value of the estimated population standard deviation?

      c. What t test was used in this study?

      d. What are H_0 and H_1 for this t test?

      e. How many scores were obtained in this study?

      f. What is the value of t_{obs} for this study?

      g. What are the df for this t_{obs}?

      h. What is t_{crit} for $\alpha = .05$ and a two-tailed rejection region?

      i. Do you reject or fail to reject H_0?

      j. Do you accept or not accept H_1?

      k. Do you conclude that the sample mean differs significantly from the hypothesized population mean?

Report 1: The mean weight of the male runners was 70.4 kilograms (SD = 7.6 kg). For alpha equal to .05 and a two-tailed test, a one-sample t test indicated that the sample mean did not differ significantly from a hypothesized population mean of 75 kg for 25-year-old males; $t(5) = -1.48$, $p > .05$.

Report 2: The mean hospital stay for males age 65 and over with nonterminal diseases was 10.4 days (SD = 2.3 days). For alpha equal to .05 and a two-tailed test, a one-sample t test revealed that the sample mean differed significantly from a hypothesized population mean of 8.7 days; $t(24) = +3.70$, $p < .01$.

IMPORTANT CONSIDERATIONS IN STATISTICAL HYPOTHESIS TESTING

Why We Don't Accept the Null Hypothesis

If a test statistic does not fall into a rejection region, then we do not reject the null hypothesis. This decision is often stated as "we fail to reject the null hypothesis." You may wonder why I use this awkward phrasing; typically, if we do not reject something, then we accept it. Why don't I simply accept the null hypothesis if the test statistic does not fall into a rejection region? To answer this question, I return to the example of the height of a truck seat. The seat was designed for a population of drivers with a popliteal height of 42.0 cm and σ = 3.0 cm. Suppose again that you obtained a sample of 25 drivers of your truck and found that the mean popliteal height of these drivers was 42.5 cm. The value of z_{obs} for this sample is +0.83.

$$z_{obs} = \frac{42.5 - 42.0}{3.0/\sqrt{25}} = +\frac{0.5}{0.6} = +0.83.$$

This z_{obs} does not fall into the rejection region defined by z_{crit} = plus or minus 1.96 for $\alpha = .05$ and is thus nonsignificant. I fail to reject H_0: $\mu = 42.0$ cm. But does this decision imply that the mean of the population from which the sample was drawn must be exactly 42.0 cm? Obviously, the answer is no; a sample mean of 42.5 cm does not imply that the mean of the population from which the sample was drawn must be 42.0 cm. On the other hand, $\overline{X} = 42.5$ cm also does not provide any evidence that μ may not be 42.0 cm. That is, an $\overline{X}$ of 42.5 cm does not provide evidence that I should reject H_0: $\mu = 42.0$ cm, but neither does it provide evidence that μ is exactly 42.0 cm. It indicates only that I should not reject H_0: $\mu = 42.0$ cm.

Suppose, however, that $\overline{X}$ had been 44.0 cm so that $z_{obs} = +3.33$. This z_{obs} is statistically significant at the .05 level and I reject H_0: $\mu = 42.0$ cm and accept H_1: $\mu \neq 42.0$ cm. It is appropriate to accept H_1 because H_1 states that μ is some value other than 42.0 cm, and $\overline{X} = 44.0$ cm indicates that μ indeed is some value other than 42.0 cm. In this case, the sample mean of 44.0 cm provides the best point estimate of μ for the population of drivers from which the sample was drawn.

The correct decisions about the statistical hypotheses are thus as follows:

- If the test statistic falls into a rejection region, then *reject H_0* and *accept H_1*.
- If the test statistic does not fall into a rejection region, then *fail to reject H_0* and *do not accept H_1*.

Type I and Type II Errors in Statistical Tests

Type I error: The error in statistical decision making that occurs if the null hypothesis is rejected when actually it is true of the population.

Type II error: The error in statistical decision making that occurs if H_0 is not rejected when it is false and the alternative hypothesis (H_1) is true.

Beta (β): The probability of a Type II error.

A statistical test allows a researcher to either (1) reject H_0 or (2) fail to reject H_0. The decision may be correct or incorrect depending on whether the null hypothesis is in fact true of the population. A **Type I error** occurs if the null hypothesis is rejected when actually it is true. A **Type II error** occurs if I fail to reject H_0 when it is false and the alternative hypothesis (H_1) is true. Table 8–4 illustrates these errors and the possible correct decisions that may occur with a statistical test.

Type I and Type II errors occur because statistical decision making is probabilistic. If H_0 is true, the probability of a Type I error is given by α. Thus the probability of making a correct decision and not rejecting H_0 when it is true is provided by $1 - \alpha$. The probability of a Type II error is given by β (the lowercase Greek letter **beta**). Hence the probability of correctly accepting H_1 when H_1 is true is provided by $1 - \beta$. The value $1 - \beta$ is the power of a statistical test. Therefore, the **power of a statistical test**, or

TABLE 8–4
Errors and correct decisions in statistical decision making and the probability associated with each outcome.

		Decision by the Experimenter	
		Fails to Reject H_0	Rejects H_0, Accepts H_1
	H_0 true	Correct decision: $p = 1 - \alpha$	Type I error: $p = \alpha$
True Situation in the Population			
	H_1 true	Type II error: $p = \beta$	Correct decision: $p = 1 - \beta$

Power: The probability of rejecting H_0 when H_0 is false and H_1 is true. The power of a statistical test is given by $1 - \beta$.

simply, **power**, is the probability of rejecting H_0 when H_0 is false and H_1 is true. The value of β depends on a number of factors, and I discuss these factors in Chapter 9. Each of these probabilities is identified in Table 8–4.

A Type I error can occur only when H_0 is true; hence the probability of making a Type I error depends directly on the significance level selected. Recall that the significance level indicates the probability of obtaining a value of the test statistic (e.g., either z or t) that leads to rejection of H_0 when H_0 is actually true. Accordingly, when alpha is selected for a statistical test, the risk of making a Type I error is established. With $\alpha = .05$, for example, the probability of wrongly rejecting a true H_0 is .05. Similarly, if $\alpha = .01$, then there is only a 1 in 100 chance of making a Type I error by incorrectly rejecting H_0 when it is true. Scientists typically adopt a conservative stance to assure a low probability of making a Type I error in their research. Consequently, the value of α is typically selected to be a small value such as $\alpha = .05$ or $\alpha = .01$.

Statistical and Scientific Significance

Using the word *significant* to characterize the rejection of H_0 in a statistical hypothesis test reflects an unfortunate choice of words by statisticians. The typical connotation to something significant is that it is important. But it is inappropriate to apply this meaning to a statistically significant difference. In statistical testing, significance indicates only that H_0 has been rejected. If H_0 is rejected, the statistical test neither gives a reason for this result nor indicates if the difference is scientifically important. This responsibility rests with the researcher, who must examine carefully the conditions of the study and the nature of the data obtained.

Observed values of the test statistic that do not fall into the rejection region are referred to as **nonsignificant** and not as insignificant. *Insignificant* implies that something is lacking importance or is inconsequential. Yet a nonsignificant difference may be scientifically important. For example, suppose that a program is introduced in an after-school child-care center to reduce the amount of television that the children watch. If, in comparing $\overline{X}$ to μ, a nonsignificant difference is found, the implication is that the program was ineffective in changing the children's watching of television, and this may be an important result for the researcher.

USING THE t STATISTIC TO CONSTRUCT CONFIDENCE INTERVALS FOR THE POPULATION MEAN

Confidence intervals for the population mean were defined in Chapter 7 as intervals in which we have a certain degree of confidence that the interval contains the population mean. In that chapter I constructed these intervals using $\overline{X}$, z, and $\sigma_{\overline{X}}$. For example, if $\sigma_{\overline{X}}$ is known, a 95 percent confidence interval for the population mean is given by the interval from

$$\overline{X} - 1.96\sigma_{\overline{X}} \text{ to } \overline{X} + 1.96\sigma_{\overline{X}}.$$

Often $\sigma_{\overline{X}}$ is unknown, however, and its value is estimated from $s_{\overline{X}}$. When $s_{\overline{X}}$ is used to estimate $\sigma_{\overline{X}}$, a confidence interval is constructed using the t statistic rather than z. Using t and $s_{\overline{X}}$, the 95 percent confidence interval for the population mean is given by the interval from

$$\overline{X} - (t_{.05})(s_{\overline{X}}) \text{ to } \overline{X} + (t_{.05})(s_{\overline{X}}),$$

where $\overline{X}$ = observed sample mean

$s_{\overline{X}}$ = estimated standard error of the mean obtained from $s/\sqrt{N}$

$t_{.05}$ = two-tailed value of t_{crit} at the .05 significance level with $N-1$ degrees of freedom

Similarly, a 99 percent confidence interval for the population mean is given by

$$\overline{X} - (t_{.01})(s_{\overline{X}}) \text{ to } \overline{X} + (t_{.01})(s_{\overline{X}}).$$

To illustrate, I find the 95 percent confidence interval for the 30 third-graders' television watching time scores with $\overline{X} = 83.0$ minutes and $s = 26.0$ minutes. Because $N = 30$, there are 29 df for this sample, and the two-tailed value of $t_{\text{crit}}(29)$ at the .05 level is 2.045. The standard error of the mean, $s_{\overline{X}}$, equals $26.0/\sqrt{30}$, or 4.75 minutes. Thus the 95 percent confidence interval for μ is

$$83.0 - (2.045)(4.75) \text{ to } 83.0 + (2.045)(4.75),$$

or, carrying out the mathematical operations indicated,

$$83.0 - 9.7 \text{ to } 83.0 + 9.7 \text{ minutes,}$$

which equals 73.3 to 92.7 minutes. This interval has a .95 probability of including the value of μ.

STATISTICS IN USE 8–2

Using Confidence Intervals to Analyze Premarital Cohabitation

Premarital cohabitation among couples occurs frequently in our society. To gain further understanding of this behavior, Gwartney-Gibbs (1986) studied premarital cohabitation by using archival data from marriage license applications to obtain demographic information on cohabiting and noncohabiting couples. As part of her results, she reported the mean age of marriage for males and females of couples who had either cohabited or had not cohabited prior to marriage. The mean ages were accompanied by 95 percent confidence intervals for the population mean.

As an example, Gwartney-Gibbs presents the following results for cohabiting and noncohabiting females who had not been married previously.

	Cohabiting	Noncohabiting
N	806	877
Mean age at marriage (yr)	22.8	21.7
s (yr)	4.6	4.4
95 percent confidence interval for μ	22.48 to 23.12	21.41 to 21.29

We can reconstruct these confidence intervals from the information provided. For example, the 95 percent confidence interval for the cohabiting females is provided by

$$\overline{X} - (t_{.05})(s_{\overline{X}}) \text{ to } \overline{X} + (t_{.05})(s_{\overline{X}}),$$

where $s_{\overline{X}} = s/\sqrt{N} = 4.6/\sqrt{806} = 4.6/28.39 = 0.162$. For $N = 806$, there are 805 df. From Table A–2 the value of t at the .05 significance level is 1.960. I used t_{crit} for an infinite degrees of freedom rather than for the next smaller tabled df, 120. Eight hundred five is sufficiently large to be treated as an infinite df. As a result, the 95 percent confidence interval is found by

$$22.8 - 1.96(0.162) \text{ to } 22.8 + 1.96(0.162) \text{ years,}$$

which equals $22.8 - .32$ to $22.8 + .32$ years, or from 22.48 to 23.12 years. We can be 95 percent confident that μ for age of marriage by cohabiting females falls between 22.48 to 23.12 years for the population from which Gwartney-Gibbs selected her sample. For the noncohabiting females, the 95 percent confidence interval for μ is 21.41 to 21.29 years. The two confidence intervals do not overlap; therefore, Gwartney-Gibbs concluded that cohabiting females typically married at least one-half year later in age than noncohabiting females in the population that she studied.

TESTING YOUR KNOWLEDGE 8–4

1. Explain why a researcher does not accept H_0 if t_{obs} does not fall into a rejection region.
2. Answer the following.
   a. What is a Type I error?
   b. What is the probability of making a Type I error if H_0 is true?
   c. What is the probability of making a Type I error if H_0 is false?
   d. What is a Type II error?
   e. Is it possible for an experimenter to make both Type I and Type II errors in the same statistical test? Explain your answer.
3. Distinguish between statistical significance and scientific significance.
4. An experimenter observed the amount of time that adolescents spent playing video games in an arcade. The mean playing time per day for a sample of 23 males was 97 minutes, with a standard deviation of 39 minutes. Construct a 95 percent confidence interval for the population mean for the amount of time male adolescents spent playing video games.
5. Davidson and Templin (1986) report that for a sample of 119 professional top-money-winning golfers their mean driving distance was 258 yards, with an s of 6.71 yards. Construct a 95 percent confidence interval for the population mean of driving distance.

SUMMARY

- Statistical tests may be either parametric or nonparametric.
- Statistical hypothesis testing involves the following steps:
  - Selecting a test statistic (e.g., either z or t).
  - Formulating H_0 and H_1. H_0 is used to find the sampling distribution of the test statistic.
  - Selecting a significance level. The significance level, specified by the value of α, is a probability value that provides the criterion for rejecting H_0 as being true.
  - Finding a critical value or values of the test statistic from tabled values. Critical values of the test statistic determine the boundaries of the rejection region or regions.
  - Locating a rejection region or regions. The rejection region represents values on the sampling distribution of the test statistic that have a probability equal to or less than α if H_0 is true.
  - Formulating decision rules regarding the statistical hypotheses. These rules are:
    —If the test statistic falls into a rejection region, then *reject H_0* and *accept H_1*. The difference between a sample mean and a hypothesized population mean is statistically significant.
    —If the test statistic does not fall into a rejection region, then *fail to reject H_0* and *do not accept H_1*. The difference between a sample mean and a hypothesized population mean is nonsignificant.
  - Calculating the observed value of the test statistic from the sample scores.

- Making decisions about H_0 and H_1 based on whether the observed value of the test statistic does or does not fall into the rejection region.
- The z statistic, given by $z = (\overline{X} - \mu)/\sigma_{\overline{X}}$, is used to test a sample mean against a hypothesized population mean when σ is known.
- The t statistic, given by $t = (\overline{X} - \mu)/s_{\overline{X}}$, is used to test a sample mean against a hypothesized population mean when $\sigma_{\overline{X}}$ is estimated from $s_{\overline{X}}$.
- The sampling distribution of the t statistic depends on the df of the t, where the $df = N - 1$.
- Statistical decision making is inherently probabilistic. A Type I error occurs if a true H_0 is rejected. A Type II error occurs if a false H_0 is not rejected.
- The probability of a Type I error is given by α; the probability of a Type II error is given by β.
- The power of a statistical test is the probability of rejecting H_0 when H_0 is false and H_1 is true.
- The t distribution may be used with $s_{\overline{X}}$ to find confidence intervals for the population mean.

KEY TERMS AND SYMBOLS

α

alpha level

alternative hypothesis

beta

confidence interval

critical value

degrees of freedom

df

H_0

H_1

hypothesis

nonparametric tests

null hypothesis

one-sample t

one-tailed test

parametric tests

power

rejection region

σ

$\sigma_{\overline{X}}$

$s_{\overline{X}}$

sampling distribution of t

significance level

statistical hypothesis

statistically nonsignificant difference

statistically significant difference

t_{crit}

t_{obs}

test statistic

two-tailed test

t statistic

Type I error

Type II error

z

z_{crit}

z_{obs}

REVIEW QUESTIONS

1. What are the requirements that any set of statistical hypotheses must meet?
2. What function does the null hypothesis serve in a statistical test?
3. What is a significance level?
4. What is the critical value of a test statistic?

5. What decision is made regarding H_0 and H_1 if:
    a. The observed value of a test statistic falls into a rejection region?
    b. The observed value of a test statistic does not fall into a rejection region?

6. You have been asked to test whether a sample mean of 73 differs significantly from a hypothesized population mean of 75. What will determine whether you use the z test or the one-sample t test?

7. What decision do you make about the value of a sample mean with respect to a hypothesized population mean if:
    a. z_{obs} falls into a rejection region?
    b. z_{obs} does not fall into a rejection region?

8. For each of the following values of z_{obs}, determine whether the z_{obs} falls into a two-tailed rejection region at the .01 significance level. Then indicate your decision for H_0 and H_1. Remember that you either (1) *fail to reject* or *reject* H_0, and (2) *do not accept* or *accept* H_1. (a) z_{obs} = +3.71, (b) z_{obs} = −2.60, (c) z_{obs} = +1.74, (d) z_{obs} = −3.05, (e) z_{obs} = −1.96, (f) z_{obs} = +2.58.

9. The population mean for a group intelligence scale is 100 and σ = 16. A school counselor tests seventeen 10-year-olds on this scale and obtains $\overline{X}$ = 94.1. Conduct a statistical test on these data to determine if the difference between the population mean and the sample mean is statistically significant. Use a .05 significance level and a two-tailed test.

10. Based on the outcome of a z test, there is a statistically significant difference between a sample mean and a population mean. Explain what is meant by statistical significance in this case.

11. What decision do you make about the value of a sample mean with respect to a hypothesized population mean if:
    a. t_{obs} falls into a rejection region?
    b. t_{obs} does not fall into a rejection region?

12. Indicate whether each of the following t_{obs} does or does not fall into a rejection region. Assume that α = .01 and use a two-tailed test. The *df* for each t_{obs} are given in parentheses.
    a. $t_{obs}(18)$ = +3.713
    b. $t_{obs}(7)$ = −3.015
    c. $t_{obs}(35)$ = +2.794
    d. $t_{obs}(44)$ = −3.058
    e. $t_{obs}(74)$ = −1.960
    f. $t_{obs}(15)$ = −2.368

13. Mothers with young children often complain that they do not get enough sleep. Suppose that you obtained a measure of the typical amount of sleep of nine mothers of children under 1 year of age and found the following durations (in hours): 6.4, 7.5, 6.9, 7.3, 7.6, 7.1, 6.5, 7.7, and 7.8.
    a. Does the mean amount of sleep for these mothers differ significantly from a hypothesized population mean of 7.7 hours sleep per night? Use a two-tailed test and a .05 significance level.
    b. Describe your results following the example illustrated in the Reporting the Results of the One-sample t Test section of this chapter.

   c. Could your decision about the statistical hypotheses represent the occurrence of a Type I error?
   d. Could your decision about the statistical hypotheses represent the occurrence of a Type II error?
   e. Compute the 95 percent confidence interval for the population mean of these scores. Is the hypothesized population mean of 7.7 hours per night included in this interval?

14. A medical researcher attempted to learn if a disease is accompanied by an increase in body temperature. She measured the body temperature of 12 people diagnosed as having the disease and obtained the following temperatures (in °F): 99.3, 99.1, 100.4, 98.4, 98.2, 98.9, 99.7, 100.1, 100.7, 99.0, 98.8, 99.2.
   a. Does the mean body temperature of these individuals differ from a hypothesized population mean of 98.6°F? Use a two-tailed test and a .05 significance level.
   b. Could your decision regarding the statistical hypothesis represent a Type II error? Explain your answer.

15. For each of the following statements, indicate whether the decision is correct or in error. If an error is made, indicate whether it is a Type I or Type II error.
   a. H_0 is true of the population, but on the basis of z_{obs} an experimenter rejects H_0.
   b. H_1 is true of the population, but on the basis of z_{obs} an experimenter fails to reject H_0.
   c. H_0 is true of the population, and on the basis of z_{obs} the experimenter fails to reject H_0.
   d. H_1 is true of the population, and on the basis of z_{obs} the experimenter rejects H_0.

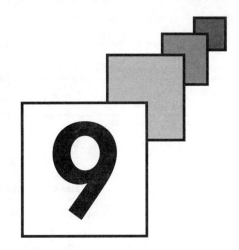

The Basics of Experimentation and Testing for a Difference Between Means

WITHIN-SUBJECTS DESIGNS AND THE *t* TEST FOR RELATED SCORES
The *t* Test for Related Scores
Constructing Confidence Intervals for the Difference between Two
Related Population Means
WHAT DOES A *t* TEST ACTUALLY TEST?
STATISTICAL AND SCIENTIFIC SIGNIFICANCE REVISITED

Chapter 8 introduced the use of statistical hypothesis testing to determine if a sample mean differs significantly from a hypothesized population mean. In this chapter I use statistical hypothesis testing to compare two sample means to determine if they differ by more than sampling error alone. One use of this type of statistical hypothesis testing is to analyze the results of experimental research. This chapter focuses on simple experiments and their statistical analysis. The initial discussion will be limited to between-subjects designs. Later in the chapter I discuss within-subjects designs.

A REVIEW OF THE RESEARCH PROCESS

All scientific research begins with asking a question that can be empirically answered. Usually, a scientist will offer a tentative answer to the question in the form of a research hypothesis. A research hypothesis is a statement of an expected or predicted relationship between two or more variables. In an experiment, a research hypothesis is a predicted relationship between an independent variable and a dependent variable. Recall that the independent variable is a variable that the experimenter plans to manipulate to find its effect on the dependent variable. The dependent variable is typically some measured behavior of a person. The form of the research hypothesis indicates to the scientist the type of research design to be used. If the research hypothesis predicts that the manipulation of an independent variable will affect a dependent variable, then an experiment is the appropriate form of research design to empirically test this research hypothesis.

A simple experiment begins by creating equivalent groups of subjects. Each group of subjects is treated identically except for being given different levels of the independent variable. After the independent variable is manipulated, scores are obtained on the dependent variable. These scores are then analyzed to find if the independent variable had an effect on the dependent variable. Consider an example of this process.

Each year, millions of prescriptions are written for tranquilizers containing the antianxiety drug diazepam. As with many drugs, diazepam has a variety of side effects, both physiological and psychological. One reported psychological effect is that diazepam alters a person's perception of the long-term passage of time (Kleinknecht & Donaldson, 1975). Unrug-Neervoort, Kaiser, and Coenen (1992) hypothesized that diazepam would have similar effects on the judgment of brief time intervals. This research hypothesis predicts that an independent variable, a drug condition, will affect a dependent variable, a person's judgment of the length of a short time interval. To test this hypothesis, Unrug-Neervoort et al. conducted a between-subjects experiment.

The experiment involved creating two equivalent groups of subjects. One group, the *placebo control group*, was given a pill containing no active ingredients. The other group, the *experimental group*, was given 15 milligrams (mg) of diazepam. Each group contained 12 subjects. The dependent variable was a person's judgment of the length of a finger-tapping task. Subjects were asked to tap a finger on a counter until told to stop. After ending the tapping, subjects were asked to estimate how long they had performed the task. Although both groups tapped for an identical length of time, the placebo control group estimated the duration to be 19.8 sec ($s = 7.6$ sec), whereas the experimental group estimated the length to be 13.6 sec ($s = 4.8$ sec). Unrug-Neervoort et al. statistically analyzed these means using the t test for independent groups and found the estimated duration of the experimental group to be significantly shorter than the estimated duration of the placebo control group. Diazepam does affect the perception of short time intervals.

Conducting an experiment requires a number of steps prior to the statistical analysis of the data. These steps are similar in all experiments and include asking a scientific question, formulating a research hypothesis, selecting a research design, selecting subjects, creating equivalent groups of subjects, controlling extraneous variables, manipulating the independent variable, and measuring the dependent variable.

Asking a Scientific Question and Formulating the Research Hypothesis

Recall that a scientific question is one that allows an answer to be found by the collection of empirical data. Our example is based on a scientific question: "What is the effect of diazepam on the perception of short intervals of time?" Clearly, this question permits systematic observation to provide an answer. The research hypothesis offers a tentative answer to this question; it states that diazepam will affect a person's judgments of the passage of short time intervals.

Selecting a Research Design

The research design is the plan used to guide the collection of data. Testing the research hypothesis of the example requires comparing one group of subjects who ingest diazepam against another group of subjects who do not ingest diazepam. In Chapter 1, I identified this design as a between-subjects design. The simplest between-subjects design is one in which only two groups of subjects are created, the research design used in the example experiment. This design requires selecting subjects to participate and then assigning those subjects to create equivalent groups.

Selecting Subjects

Random Sampling

An experiment is conducted on a sample of subjects from a population. To generalize the results of the experiment beyond the sample used, it is recommended that the sample be selected randomly from the population to which inferences are to be made. But, because of the difficulty of obtaining true random samples, random sampling is rarely achieved in actual experimentation. Often, convenience sampling is employed.

Convenience Sampling

Convenience sampling:
Obtaining subjects from among people who are accessible or convenient to the researcher.

Convenience sampling obtains subjects from among people who are accessible or convenient to the researcher. Convenience sampling clearly is not adequate if I am trying to accurately estimate a population mean, such as estimating the outcome of an election from a poll. But the purpose of an experiment is not to estimate a specific value of a population mean; rather, it is to determine if two or more groups differ because of the effect of an independent variable. If the independent variable has an effect, it should occur with any subjects, whether they are randomly selected or not. Thus, provided the groups created are equivalent, convenience sampling typically does not limit the interpretation or importance of an experiment.

Creating Equivalent Groups

Equivalent groups: Groups of subjects that are not expected to differ in any consistent or systematic way prior to receiving the independent variable of the experiment.

Equivalent groups are groups in which the subjects are not expected to differ in any systematic or consistent way prior to receiving the independent variable. Equivalent groups do not imply that subjects in each group will be exactly alike prior to administration of the independent variable; rather, it implies that an unbiased procedure was used to assign individuals to levels of the independent variable. Any differences that may then exist between the groups prior to manipulation of the independent variable will be only chance differences. As I explain later, a t test allows us to assess the probability of occurrence of such chance differences.

Random Assignment

Random assignment: A method of assigning subjects to treatment groups so that any individual selected for the experiment has an equal probability of assignment to any of the groups, and the assignment of one subject to a group does not affect the assignment of any other individual to that same group.

The typical method of creating equivalent groups is to randomly assign subjects to treatment conditions. **Random assignment** means that any individual selected for the experiment has an equal chance of being assigned to any one of the treatment groups. Specifically, random assignment satisfies two criteria:

1. The probability of assignment to any of the groups is equal for every individual.
2. The assignment of one subject to a group does not affect the assignment of any other individual to that same group.

Random assignment ensures that the effects of variables such as motivation, gender, anxiety, intelligence, and age are distributed without bias among the groups. After random assignment the groups should not differ in any systematic way before the treatments are given.

In practice, researchers may place some limits on random assignment. They may want to obtain an equal number of subjects in each group as in the example experiment, or they may want to have each group composed of an equal number of males and females. These limitations still permit the groups to be equivalent, however.

Manipulating the Independent Variable

Independent variable: A variable manipulated in an experiment to determine its effect on the dependent variable.

Level of an independent variable: One value of the independent variable. To be a variable, an independent variable must take on at least two different levels.

Factor: An alternative name for independent variable.

One-factor between-subjects design: A research design in which one independent variable is manipulated and two or more groups are created.

The **independent variable** is the variable that is manipulated and administered to subjects in the different groups in order to determine its effect on behavior. An independent variable must take on at least two different levels. A **level of an independent variable** is one value of the independent variable. An independent variable often is identified as a **factor**, such as factor A, and the levels identified as A_1 and A_2. I then indicate the number of subjects in each group by n_{A1} and n_{A2}. Notice that up to now I have used N to indicate the number of subjects in a group. Now, however, I have two groups and use n_A to indicate the number of subjects in a group. The total number of subjects in the experiment will then be indicated by N.

Each level of the independent variable is administered to one of the groups that has been formed. In the example experiment the independent variable (i.e., factor A) is the drug condition; and there are two levels: level A_1, control, the placebo drug; and level A_2, experimental, the diazepam. Thus one group of subjects (of size $n_{A1} = 12$) was given the placebo drug control, and the other group (of size $n_{A2} = 12$) was given the diazepam. This design is a **one-factor between-subjects design**, for one independent variable is manipulated, and the comparison needed to decide if the independent variable has an effect is between the two different groups of subjects.

Controlling Extraneous Variables

Extraneous variables: Any variables, other than the independent variable, that can affect the dependent variable in an experiment.

Confounded experiment: An experiment in which an extraneous variable is allowed to vary consistently with the independent variable.

To ensure that any difference created between the groups is due only to the independent variable, extraneous variables must be controlled. **Extraneous variables** are any variables, other than the independent variable, that can affect the dependent variable. They may arise from characteristics of subjects such as intelligence, anxiety level, sensitivity to drugs, or motivation; changes in the physical environment in which the experiment is conducted from one subject to another; or variations in the experimental procedure from one subject to another. To be sure that any difference found between the control and experimental groups is due only to the independent variable manipulated, extraneous variables must not vary in any systematic or consistent way with the independent variable. In a **confounded experiment** an extraneous variable is allowed to vary consistently with the independent variable. When confounding occurs, the effect of the independent variable cannot be separated from the possible effect of the confounded extraneous variable.

In the example experiment, each of the two groups was treated identically except for the administration of the independent variable. To ensure this identical treatment

Placebo control: A simulated treatment condition.

of subjects, Unrug-Neervoort et al. used a placebo control group. In research using drugs, a **placebo control** is a simulated treatment condition in which subjects are given a pill or substance that has no active ingredients. Thus both the placebo control and the experimental group were given a pill. If only the experimental group had been given a pill, then the experiment would have been confounded. People may behave differently simply because they expect a drug to affect them. Thus, when given a drug, behaviors may change for two reasons, (1) the effect of the drug itself and (2) the expectation that the drug will have an effect. By giving the placebo control group a pill with no active ingredients, Unrug-Neervoort et al. controlled for these expectations, for both groups had the same expectations about the effect of the drug. Similarly, both groups were given identical instructions and their time estimates were measured in the same way. Avoiding confounding is vital to conducting a meaningful experiment.

Measuring the Dependent Variable

Dependent variable: The variable in an experiment that depends on the independent variable.

The **dependent variable** is the variable that I expect to be affected by the independent variable. Thus, after the independent variable is manipulated, the dependent variable must be measured for each subject. This measurement results in a **score** for each subject. As we have seen in Chapters 2 to 5, the scores are summarized with a measure of central tendency and variability.

The research hypothesis of Unrug-Neervoort et al. predicted that the ingestion of diazepam alters a person's perception of time. The dependent variable was thus the perception of time, and it was measured by having subjects estimate how long they had performed a task. These estimates were summarized by presenting the mean and standard deviation of each group. Because I now have two means and two standard deviations, I will use subscripting to identify them. Thus $\overline{X}_{A1}$ is the mean of the A_1 group, s_{A1} the estimated population standard deviation of the A_1 group, $\overline{X}_{A2}$ the mean of the A_2 group, and s_{A2} the estimated population standard deviation of the A_2 group. For the example, $\overline{X}_{A1} = 19.8$ sec and $s_{A1} = 7.6$ sec for the placebo control group, and $\overline{X}_{A2} = 13.6$ sec and $s_{A2} = 4.8$ sec for the experimental group. The effect of the independent variable was found by comparing these means with a t test for independent groups. I discuss this test in the remainder of the chapter.

Figure 9–1 illustrates the various steps of designing and conducting an experiment using the example experiment. Review the steps using this figure.

TESTING YOUR KNOWLEDGE 9–1

1. Define: confounding, convenience sampling, dependent variable, equivalent groups, extraneous variable, independent variable, random assignment, random sampling.
2. What is the purpose of creating equivalent groups?
3. What is the difference between random selection of subjects and random assignment of subjects to treatment groups?
4. When does confounding occur in an experiment?
5. What difficulty does a confounded experiment pose for reaching a conclusion about the effect of an independent variable?

FIGURE 9-1
Aspects of designing and conducting an experiment using a between-subjects design. The figure illustrates the example experiment to determine the effect of diazepam on time perception.

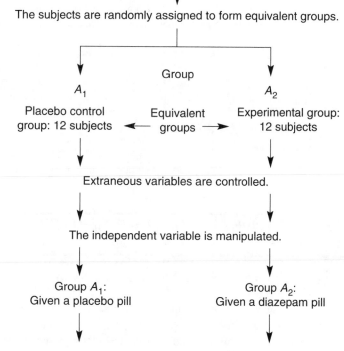

Select a sample of 24 subjects to participate in the experiment.

The subjects are randomly assigned to form equivalent groups.

Group

A_1

Placebo control
group: 12 subjects

← Equivalent groups →

A_2

Experimental group:
12 subjects

Extraneous variables are controlled.

The independent variable is manipulated.

Group A_1:
Given a placebo pill

Group A_2:
Given a diazepam pill

The dependent variable is measured:
All subjects estimate how long they performed a task.

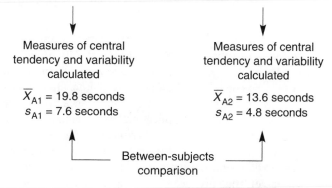

Measures of central
tendency and variability
calculated

$\overline{X}_{A1}$ = 19.8 seconds
s_{A1} = 7.6 seconds

Measures of central
tendency and variability
calculated

$\overline{X}_{A2}$ = 13.6 seconds
s_{A2} = 4.8 seconds

Between-subjects
comparison

The effect of the independent variable is determined by
comparing the measures of central tendency using a
statistical test.

6. An experimenter is investigating the effect of noise on the performance of a tracking task. The task is to keep a pointer on a spot on a rotating turntable (imagine keeping a pencil pointing to a dime on a rotating record turntable). The dependent variable is the amount of time a subject is able to keep the pointer on the spot. The experimenter hypothesized that subjects performing the task when no environmental noise is present will keep the pointer on the spot for a greater amount of time than subjects who perform the task while listening to a loud noise. Each action by the experimenter described next confounds this experiment by letting an extraneous variable vary systematically with the independent variable of noise condition. For each action, identify the extraneous variable confounding the experiment and then explain why the experiment is confounded.

   a. The experimenter assigns ten 20-year-old males to the no-noise condition and ten 60-year-old males to the noise condition.

   b. The experimenter urges the subjects in the no-noise condition to try very hard, but does not encourage the subjects in the noise condition.

   c. The experimenter assigns males to the no-noise condition and females to the noise condition.

   d. The experimenter assigns physical education majors to the no-noise condition and social science majors to the noise condition.

   e. Subjects in the no-noise condition do the experiment between 9:00 to 10:00 A.M., and subjects in the noise condition do the experiment between 4:00 to 5:00 P.M.

DID THE TREATMENT HAVE AN EFFECT? THE NEED FOR STATISTICAL TESTING

The Implications of Sampling Error for an Experiment

The steps of conducting an experiment are straightforward, yet they set the stage for the appearance of a dilemma for the experimenter. Any decision about the effect of an independent variable must be made by comparing the sample means with each other. In principle, if the sample means are equal to each other, then the treatment had no effect. On the other hand, if the sample means are not equal to each other, then it seems there is evidence that the treatment had an effect. But, because of sampling error, this decision is not made quite so simply. In Chapter 7, I defined **sampling error** as the amount a sample mean differs from the population mean (i.e., $\overline{X} - \mu$). If you were to draw two samples of subjects from the same population, measure a behavior, and calculate $\overline{X}$ for each sample, because of sampling error it would be unlikely that the two sample means would be equal to each other or to the population mean. This fact was illustrated by the empirical sampling distributions of the mean presented in Figure 7–2.

What are the implications of sampling error for reaching a decision about the effect of an independent variable in an experiment? Simply that chance differences between the means of different groups drawn from the same population are expected in any experiment, whether or not the independent variable has an effect on the dependent variable. Thus my idea of making a decision about the effect of an independent variable merely from an observed difference between sample means is too simplistic. Even if the independent variable has no effect whatsoever, the mean scores of the two treatment groups will differ from each other simply because of sampling error. How, then, does a behavioral scientist answer the following question: *How large a difference between the sample means is enough to decide that something other than sampling error is at work in the experiment?* The answer is provided by a statistical hypothesis test of the difference between two means.

An Overview of Statistical Hypothesis Testing for the Difference Between Two Means

The approach used in statistical hypothesis testing is to assume that $\overline{X}_{A1}$ represents a sample drawn from a population with μ_{A1}, and $\overline{X}_{A2}$ represents a sample drawn from a population with μ_{A2}. Then, assuming that the two population means will be equal (i.e., that $\mu_{A1} = \mu_{A2}$) if the independent variable has no effect, I can find the expected extent of sampling error between the means. The difference between the sample means observed in the experiment is then compared to the differences expected from sampling error alone. If the observed difference is large enough so that it is unlikely to occur from sampling error alone, then I decide that the difference is due not to sampling error, but to the effect of the independent variable.

I have introduced a very important point in statistical testing. To decide whether the means of two groups given different levels of an independent variable differ sufficiently to attribute the difference to the independent variable, I must first find the extent of **chance differences between the means**, differences expected from sampling error alone. If the observed difference between the sample means is among the commonly occurring chance differences, then I treat the observed difference as a chance difference. The independent variable did not affect the dependent variable. On the other hand, if the observed difference between the means is sufficiently large to be expected rarely by chance, then I decide that the sample means do not differ by chance alone; rather, the difference is due to the independent variable.

There are many different statistical tests for use with diverse types of data and research designs. Regardless of the specific test used, however, basic concepts of hypothesis testing are applicable to all statistical tests. I next introduce the *t* test for two independent groups. This *t* test allows us to statistically test the difference between two sample means when each mean is obtained from a different group of subjects.

THE *t* TEST FOR TWO INDEPENDENT GROUPS

The *t* **test for two independent treatment groups** is defined as

$$t_{\text{ind}} = \frac{(\overline{X}_{A1} - \overline{X}_{A2}) - (\mu_{A1} - \mu_{A2})}{s_{\overline{X}_{A1} - \overline{X}_{A2}}}.$$

The numerator of t_{ind} indicates how much an observed difference between two sample means (i.e., $\overline{X}_{A1} - \overline{X}_{A2}$) differs from the difference between the two population means (i.e., $\mu_{A1} - \mu_{A2}$) that the sample means are assumed to represent. In most instances, the population means are hypothesized to be equal; thus the difference between them (i.e., $\mu_{A1} - \mu_{A2}$) is zero, and the numerator of the t_{ind} simplifies to $\overline{X}_{A1} - \overline{X}_{A2}$. The denominator (i.e., $s_{\overline{X}_{A1} - \overline{X}_{A2}}$) is a measure of error variation called the *standard error of the difference between means*. The standard error of the difference between means is the standard deviation of a sampling distribution of differences between means. To understand this measure of error variation, we must develop the concept of a sampling distribution of differences between two means.

Sampling Distribution of Differences Between Means

Sampling distribution of the difference between means: The distribution of differences between sample means when all possible pairs of samples of size *n* are drawn from a population.

Consider an experiment in which two levels (A_1 and A_2) of an independent variable are manipulated. Suppose that the independent variable has no effect on the dependent variable. Because the independent variable has no effect, I can simulate this instance by sampling scores from two populations (populations A_1 and A_2) with equal means (i.e., $\mu_{A1} = \mu_{A2}$). Imagine that I conduct this experiment by drawing two samples of size 5 each (i.e., $n_{A1} = 5$, $n_{A2} = 5$), one sample from each population, A_1 and A_2, respectively. This sample size is arbitrary; any sample size would serve to illustrate the point. I calculate the mean for each sample and then subtract $\overline{X}_{A2}$ from $\overline{X}_{A1}$. Suppose that I replicated the hypothetical experiment 100 times and found 100 $\overline{X}_{A1} - \overline{X}_{A2}$ differences. Plotting a frequency distribution of $\overline{X}_{A1} - \overline{X}_{A2}$ values results in an **empirical sampling distribution of differences between means**. The sampling distribution of 100 such differences between means is portrayed in Figure 9–2. This distribution is an empirical sampling distribution of differences between means because I obtained and calculated the values of 100 differences between $\overline{X}_{A1}$ and $\overline{X}_{A2}$. In practice, however, a researcher would not calculate and construct such an empirical sampling distribution. Rather, he or she uses the theoretical sampling distribution of the difference between means as presented in Figure 9–3. A **theoretical sampling distribution of the difference between means** is the distribution of differences between sample means when all possible pairs of samples of size *n* are drawn from a population. Recall from Chapter 7 that the theoretical sampling distribution of the mean possesses important characteristics concerning its shape, mean, and standard error. A theoretical sampling distribution of the difference between means shares these characteristics.

Shape of a Sampling Distribution of Differences Between Means
Observe that the empirical sampling distribution in Figure 9–2 is relatively symmetrical and unimodal. Because of the central limit theorem, as sample size increases, a sampling distribution of the difference between means approaches a normal distribution regardless of the shape of the distributions of the underlying populations of scores. This characteristic is present in the theoretical distribution illustrated in Figure 9–3.

Mean of a Sampling Distribution of Differences Between Means
The mean of the distribution of an unlimited set of $\overline{X}_{A1} - \overline{X}_{A2}$ differences, $\overline{X}_{\overline{X}_{A1} - \overline{X}_{A2}}$, will be equal to the difference in population means $\mu_{A1} - \mu_{A2}$. Therefore, when $\mu_{A1} = \mu_{A2}$

FIGURE 9–2
Empirical sampling distribution of the difference between means $(\overline{X}_{A1} - \overline{X}_{A2})$ for 100 samples drawn from two populations with identical means $(\mu_{A1} = \mu_{A2})$.

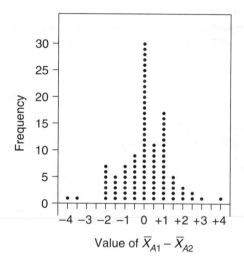

FIGURE 9–3
Theoretical sampling distribution of the difference between two means when $\mu_{A1} = \mu_{A2}$.

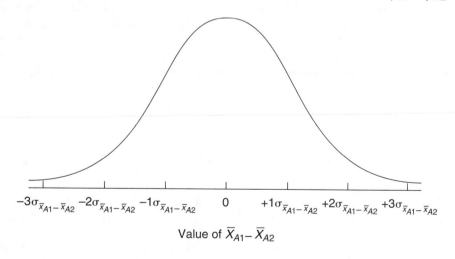

and thus $\mu_{A1} - \mu_{A2} = 0$, the mean of the observed $\overline{X}_{A1} - \overline{X}_{A2}$ values will, in the long run, equal zero, and the observed differences in sample means will be clustered around the difference of zero between the population means. This characteristic is demonstrated in the distribution shown in Figure 9–2. The mean $\overline{X}_{A1} - \overline{X}_{A2}$ difference is +0.07. Even with only 100 sets of samples, the mean of the $\overline{X}_{A1} - \overline{X}_{A2}$ difference is very close to the population difference of zero.

Standard Error of a Sampling Distribution of Differences Between Means

The standard deviation of a theoretical sampling distribution of $\overline{X}_{A1} - \overline{X}_{A2}$ values is called the **standard error of the difference between means**, or simply the **standard error of the difference**. It is symbolized as $\sigma_{\overline{X}_{A1} - \overline{X}_{A2}}$ and defined as

$$\sigma_{\overline{X}_{A1} - \overline{X}_{A2}} = \sqrt{\frac{\sigma_{A1}^2}{n_{A1}} + \frac{\sigma_{A2}^2}{n_{A2}}}.$$

Notice that the standard error is found by combining the standard error of the sampling distribution of the mean for each population. Thus its value will vary with the standard error of the mean for each distribution. In practice, however, σ^2 is not known, and the value of $\sigma_{\overline{X}_{A1} - \overline{X}_{A2}}$ is estimated from the sample variances, s_{A1}^2 and s_{A2}^2. To obtain the estimated standard error of the difference between means, a pooled or combined variance estimate, indicated by s_{pooled}^2, is first obtained from the two sample variances using the following equation:

$$s_{pooled}^2 = \frac{(n_{A1} - 1)s_{A1}^2 + (n_{A2} - 1)s_{A2}^2}{n_{A1} + n_{A2} - 2}.$$

This equation indicates that to obtain s_{pooled}^2 I multiply each sample variance by its degrees of freedom (i.e., $n_A - 1$), add the resulting values, and then divide the sum by the total of the degrees of freedom of the two groups. The next step in obtaining the estimated standard error of the difference between means is to recall from Chapter 7 that the estimated standard error of the mean, $s_{\overline{X}}$, was given by $s/\sqrt{N}$. Notice that this formula could be written as $s_{\overline{X}} = \sqrt{(s^2)(1/N)}$. The **estimated standard error of the difference between means**, identified as $s_{\overline{X}_{A1} - \overline{X}_{A2}}$ is found similarly by

$$s_{\overline{X}_{A1} - \overline{X}_{A2}} = \sqrt{s_{pooled}^2 \left[\frac{1}{n_{A1}} + \frac{1}{n_{A2}} \right]}.$$

Substituting the formula for s_{pooled}^2, I obtain

$$s_{\overline{X}_{A1} - \overline{X}_{A2}} = \sqrt{\left[\frac{(n_{A1} - 1)s_{A1}^2 + (n_{A2} - 1)s_{A2}^2}{n_{A1} + n_{A2} - 2} \right] \left[\frac{1}{n_{A1}} + \frac{1}{n_{A2}} \right]}.$$

The estimated standard error of the difference is the denominator of the t statistic. Thus the value of t indicates how many estimated standard errors away from the mean of the sampling distribution of the difference between $\overline{X}_{A1}$ and $\overline{X}_{A2}$ an observed $\overline{X}_{A1} - \overline{X}_{A2}$ difference lies. For example, suppose that an observed $\overline{X}_{A1} - \overline{X}_{A2} = 3$ and $s_{\overline{X}_{A1} - \overline{X}_{A2}} = 3$. The value of t_{obs} then equals 3/3 or 1, indicating that the observed $\overline{X}_{A1} - \overline{X}_{A2}$ difference is one standard error away from the mean of the sampling distribution of

$\overline{X}_{A1} - \overline{X}_{A2}$. If an observed $\overline{X}_{A1} - \overline{X}_{A2} = 6$ and $s_{\overline{X}_{A1} - \overline{X}_{A2}} = 3$, then t equals 6/3 or 2, indicating that the observed $\overline{X}_{A1} - \overline{X}_{A2}$ difference is two standard errors away from the mean of the sampling distribution of the difference between $\overline{X}_{A1}$ and $\overline{X}_{A2}$. Notice that, if an independent variable has no effect and sampling error alone is operating in an experiment, I expect the value of t_{obs} to be small, whereas if an independent variable has an effect and causes $\overline{X}_{A1}$ and $\overline{X}_{A2}$ to differ, then the value of t_{obs} should become larger.

TESTING YOUR KNOWLEDGE 9–2

1. Define: empirical sampling distribution of the difference between means, standard error of the difference between means, theoretical sampling distribution of the difference between means.
2. Explain why you cannot simply look at the difference between the mean scores of two groups given different treatments and decide if the difference between the means is due to the independent variable.
3. Calculate $s_{\overline{X}_{A1} - \overline{X}_{A2}}$ for each of the following sets of scores.

a.

A_1	A_2
104	99
111	107
120	105
113	110
108	115

b.

A_1	A_2
77	82
84	86
68	78
71	74
82	69
	79
	80

c.

A_1	A_2
71	85
82	80
63	73
74	76
68	70
76	67

d.

A_1	A_2
32	38
37	42
28	29
41	36
35	30
33	37
	36
	39
	34

Statistical Testing with t_{ind}

In using t_{ind} to test for a significant difference between two means, the steps for statistical hypothesis testing outlined in Chapter 8 are followed:

- A null hypothesis, H_0, and an alternative hypothesis, H_1, are formulated.
- The sampling distribution of t assuming H_0 is true is obtained. This distribution is given in Table A–2.
- A significance level is selected.
- A critical value of t, identified as t_{crit}, is found from the sampling distribution of t given in Table A–2.
- Rejection regions are located in the theoretical sampling distribution of the t statistic.
- The t statistic, identified as t_{obs}, is calculated from the sample data.
- A decision to reject or not reject H_0 is made on the basis of whether t_{obs} falls into a rejection region.

Statistical Hypotheses

For a parametric test, a statistical hypothesis is a statement about population parameters. The parameters corresponding to a statistical test of $\overline{X}_{A1}$ and $\overline{X}_{A2}$ are the population means, μ_{A1} and μ_{A2}, respectively. For t_{ind}, the statistical hypotheses are

$$H_0: \mu_{A1} = \mu_{A2} \quad \text{(null hypothesis),}$$

$$H_1: \mu_{A1} \neq \mu_{A2} \quad \text{(alternative hypothesis).}$$

For two populations of scores, one or the other of these hypotheses must be true.

Null Hypothesis.   The null hypothesis does not specify numerical values for population parameters, which, of course, are unknown. It states only that the population means are equal. Essentially, $H_0: \mu_{A1} = \mu_{A2}$ corresponds to the situation that exists if the independent variable has no effect on the dependent variable. If the independent variable has no effect, then all the subjects in the experiment are representative of the same population, and any observed difference between the two sample means is due only to sampling error. Thus H_0 establishes a situation under which the theoretical sampling distribution of the t statistic may be obtained. By knowing the sampling distribution of t, I can determine how likely or unlikely any value of t_{obs} is if sampling error alone is responsible for the difference between the sample means.

Alternative Hypothesis.   The alternative hypothesis represents the situation if $\overline{X}_{A1}$ and $\overline{X}_{A2}$ differ because the subjects in each group are from populations with different means. This situation occurs if the independent variable has an effect. And, if the independent variable has an effect and H_1 is true, then I expect $\overline{X}_{A1}$ and $\overline{X}_{A2}$ to differ by an amount greater than that expected from sampling error alone. Hence, if H_1 is true, the value of t_{obs} should typically be larger than the value of t_{obs} if H_0 is true.

Support for the research hypothesis of the experiment occurs by rejecting H_0 and accepting H_1. Rejecting H_0 and accepting H_1 are decisions that the observed difference in sample means is not due to sampling error but to the effect of the independent variable.

As an example of this reasoning, Unrug-Neervoort et al.'s research hypothesis predicted that ingestion of diazepam would change a person's time perception in comparison to ingestion of a placebo. This hypothesis is supported only if the mean time estimates for the two treatment groups represent populations with different means, the situation stated in the alternative hypothesis. Thus, rejecting H_0 and accepting H_1 provide support for the research hypothesis.

Selecting a Significance Level

The significance level is a probability value that provides the criterion for rejecting a null hypothesis in a statistical test. As you know, behavioral scientists typically choose an alpha of either .05 or .01. By doing so, they have decided that values of t occurring only 5 or fewer times in 100 occasions or only 1 or fewer times in 100 occasions if H_0 is true are statistically rare. I choose $\alpha = .05$ for the example.

Locating Rejection Regions and Finding Critical Values of t: Two-tailed Tests

A rejection region represents values of t in the sampling distribution of t that have a probability equal to or less than α if H_0 is true. Hence a rejection region defines values of t_{obs} that meet the criterion for rejecting H_0.

As discussed in Chapter 8, in a **two-tailed** or **nondirectional test**, rejection regions for t are located in either tail of the theoretical sampling distribution as illustrated in Figure 9–4. When H_0 is true, most values of t will be clustered around 0, for most values of $\overline{X}_{A1} - \overline{X}_{A2}$ will differ only slightly from zero. But some values of t will fall in either end of the distribution even when H_0 is true. These relatively large values of t occur when the numerator of the t (i.e., $\overline{X}_{A1} - \overline{X}_{A2}$) is large compared to the denominator (i.e., the standard error of the difference). These large values of t are rare occurrences, however, if H_0: $\mu_{A1} = \mu_{A2}$ is true.

If H_1 is true, however, and $\mu_{A1} \neq \mu_{A2}$, then large positive or negative values of $\overline{X}_{A1} - \overline{X}_{A2}$, and thus of t, are expected to occur more frequently. Hence the rejection regions for the t are located in each tail of the theoretical sampling distribution of t. The total probability specified by α is divided between both tails of the t distribution. If t_{obs} falls into either rejection region, then H_0 is rejected and H_1 accepted. As with the one-sample t test, the two-tailed critical values given in Table A–2 define the exact location of the rejection regions. To use this table, we must know the degrees of freedom for t_{obs}.

Degrees of Freedom for t_{ind}. Degrees of freedom represent the number of scores that are free to vary when calculating a statistic. In Chapter 8 I demonstrated that s^2 has $N - 1$ df, where N represents the number of scores on which the variance is calculated. For the t_{ind} statistic, $s_{\overline{X}_{A1} - \overline{X}_{A2}}$ is found by calculating the variances from each group, s_{A1}^2 and s_{A2}^2. Accordingly, the df for t_{ind} are based on the combined df of s_{A1}^2 and s_{A2}^2. When n_{A1} and n_{A2} represent the number of scores in groups A_1 and A_2, respectively, s_{A1}^2

FIGURE 9–4
Illustration of a two-tailed rejection region for the t distribution for 22 df and $\alpha = .05$.

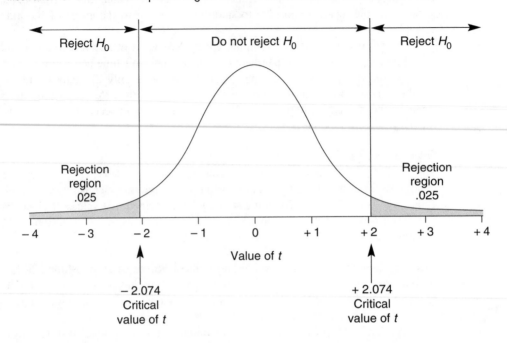

has $n_{A1} - 1$ df and s_{A2}^2 has $n_{A2} - 1$ df. Hence the combined df for t_{ind} are $(n_{A1} - 1)$ plus $(n_{A2} - 1)$. If N is used to represent the total number of scores in the two groups (i.e., $N = n_{A1} + n_{A2}$), then the df for t_{ind} are $N - 2$. Accordingly, for an experiment with 12 scores in each group (i.e., $n_{A1} = 12$, $n_{A2} = 12$, thus $N = 24$), the df for t_{ind} are $24 - 2 = 22$. From Table A–2, t_{crit} for 22 df and $\alpha = .05$ is 2.074. This value of t_{crit} is shown in Figure 9–4, locating the rejection region in each tail of the t distribution.

Locating a Rejection Region: One-tailed Tests

When a research hypothesis predicts a directional relationship between the means (e.g., that $\overline{X}_{A1}$ should be greater than $\overline{X}_{A2}$) and there is no interest in an outcome opposite than predicted (e.g., if $\overline{X}_{A1}$ less than $\overline{X}_{A2}$ occurs), then researchers may use a one-tailed or directional test. In a **one-tailed test**, a rejection region including the total value of α is located in the tail of the t distribution corresponding to the direction of the outcome predicted by the research hypothesis. Values of t_{crit} for a one-tailed test at the .01 and .05 significance levels are also presented in Table A–2. For 22 df, the one-tailed t_{crit} at the .05 significance level is 1.717. A one-tailed rejection region with $t_{\text{crit}} = +1.717$ in the right tail of a t distribution is illustrated in Figure 9–5. The null and alternative hypotheses for the use of this rejection region are

$$H_0: \mu_{A1} \leq \mu_{A2},$$
$$H_1: \mu_{A1} > \mu_{A2}.$$

FIGURE 9–5
Illustration of a one-tailed rejection region for the t distribution for 22 df and $\alpha = .05$.

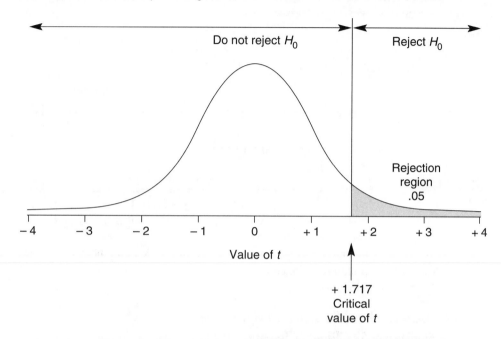

There is controversy about the use of one-tailed tests, however. The sampling distribution of t presented in Table A–2 is developed assuming H_0: $\mu_{A1} = \mu_{A2}$ is true. This sampling distribution is symmetric about 0, and positive and negative differences from 0 are expected to occur equally. For a one-tailed test, however, the statistical hypotheses are either

$$H_0: \mu_{A1} \leq \mu_{A2} \text{ and } H_1: \mu_{A1} > \mu_{A2}$$

or

$$H_0: \mu_{A1} \geq \mu_{A2} \text{ and } H_1: \mu_{A1} < \mu_{A2}.$$

But I cannot develop a sampling distribution for t under either of these null hypotheses because there are an infinite number of ways H_0: $\mu_{A1} \leq \mu_{A2}$ or $H_0 : \mu_{A1} \geq \mu_{A2}$ could be true. Thus the sampling distribution for H_0: $\mu_{A1} = \mu_{A2}$ is used to determine critical values of t for one-tailed as well as two-tailed tests. For this and other reasons, some behavioral scientists recommend against using one-tailed t tests (Gaito, 1977). Consequently, two-tailed tests are used for all examples in this chapter.

Calculating t_{ind}

The definitional formula for t_{ind} is

$$t_{\text{ind}} = \frac{(\overline{X}_{A1} - \overline{X}_{A2}) - (\mu_{A1} - \mu_{A2})}{s_{\overline{X}_{A1} - \overline{X}_{A2}}}.$$

The null hypothesis for t_{ind}, $H_0 : \mu_{A1} = \mu_{A2}$, is equivalent to $H_0: \mu_{A1} - \mu_{A2} = 0$. Thus the difference of $\mu_{A1} - \mu_{A2}$ is hypothesized to be zero, and $\mu_{A1} - \mu_{A2}$ drops from the formula, so

$$t_{ind} = \frac{\overline{X}_{A1} - \overline{X}_{A2}}{s_{\overline{X}A1 - \overline{X}A2}},$$

where $s_{\overline{X}A1 - \overline{X}A2}$ is given by

$$s_{\overline{X}A1 - \overline{X}A2} = \sqrt{\left[\frac{(n_{A1} - 1)s_{A1}^2 + (n_{A2} - 1)s_{A2}^2}{n_{A1} + n_{A2} - 2} \right] \left[\frac{1}{n_{A1}} + \frac{1}{n_{A2}} \right]}.$$

Consequently, for computational purposes,

$$t_{ind} = \frac{\overline{X}_{A1} - \overline{X}_{A2}}{\sqrt{\left[\frac{(n_{A1} - 1)s_{A1}^2 + (n_{A2} - 1)s_{A2}^2}{n_{A1} + n_{A2} - 2} \right] \left[\frac{1}{n_{A1}} + \frac{1}{n_{A2}} \right]}}.$$

To use this formula, I need know only the mean ($\overline{X}_A$), number of subjects (n_A), and estimated population variance (s_A^2) for each group. Use of this formula is illustrated in Example Problem 9–1.

Decisions about the Statistical Hypotheses

Statistically Significant Difference. If t_{obs} falls into a rejection region, then $H_0: \mu_{A1} = \mu_{A2}$ is rejected. Rejection of H_0 implies acceptance of $H_1 : \mu_{A1} \neq \mu_{A2}$. The difference between the sample means is *statistically significant*. I conclude that the two sample means involved in t_{obs} are not estimates of the same population mean, and the difference between them is due to something other than sampling error alone. If the experiment has been carefully designed and conducted, then the difference between the sample means is due to the independent variable manipulated. These decisions and conclusions are summarized in the left column of Table 9–1.

Nonsignificant Difference. If t_{obs} does not fall into a rejection region, then I fail to reject H_0. Failing to reject H_0 implies not accepting H_1. The difference between the sample means is *not statistically significant* or *nonsignificant*. I have no evidence that H_0 is not true. The two sample means are considered to be from populations with identical means, and they differ only because of sampling error. The implication for the experiment is that the independent variable had no effect, and the difference between the sample means is a chance occurrence. These decisions and conclusions are summarized in the right column of Table 9–1.

Assumptions for Use of t_{ind}
The use of t_{ind} rests on the following assumptions:

1. The scores in each sample are drawn randomly from a population of scores and the scores are independent of each other.

TABLE 9-1

Summary of decisions and conclusions in statistical hypothesis testing using the t test for two independent groups. A .05 significance level is used.

If t_{obs} falls into a rejection region for $\alpha = .05$, then:	If t_{obs} does *not* fall into a rejection region for $\alpha = .05$, then:
Probability of t_{obs} is less than or equal to .05, or $p \leq .05$.	Probability of t_{obs} is greater than .05, or $p > .05$.
H_0 is rejected.	H_0 is not rejected.
H_1 is accepted. Each sample mean is from a different population.	H_1 is not accepted.
The difference between the two sample means is statistically significant at the .05 level.	The difference between the two sample means is nonsignificant at the .05 level.
It is decided that something other than sampling error alone is responsible for the difference between the sample means. In a carefully done experiment the difference is attributed to the independent variable.	It is decided that sampling error alone is the most plausible explanation of the difference between the sample means. There is no evidence that the independent variable had an effect.

    2. The scores in the populations sampled are normally distributed.

    3. The variances of scores in the populations are equal; that is, $\sigma_{A1}^2 = \sigma_{A2}^2$.

In Chapter 8 I indicated that the assumptions of the t test are often not fully met in actual research; they are violated. Yet researchers may proceed to use the t test on the data. What are the consequences of such violations?

    The requirement of the first assumption is that each score in a group be independent of every other score in the group. That is, knowing one person's score in a group will give you no information about any other person's score in the group. This assumption requires that each individual be given only one level of the independent variable and contribute only one score in the experiment. This requirement of independence of scores cannot be violated for t_{ind}. If a person is given both levels of the independent variable and contributes two scores for analysis, then the t test for related scores, discussed later in this chapter, must be used.

    The first assumption also indicates that subjects are to be selected randomly, but, in actuality, subjects in experiments typically are obtained by convenience sampling rather than random sampling. The major impact of convenience sampling is to limit the extent to which the results can be generalized to a population.

Robustness: A term used to indicate that violating the assumptions of a statistical test has little effect on the probability of a Type I error.

    Violations of the second (the normal distribution of scores) and the third (the equality of variances, often called the *homogeneity of variances*) assumptions can change the actual probability of making a Type I error from that set by the value of α. But the t test is thought to be *robust* against violations of these assumptions. **Robustness** means that violation of the assumptions has little effect on the probability of making a Type I error. Research by Bradley (1980, 1984) has challenged this robustness notion, however. Bradley argues that there is no one set of conditions under which these assumptions may be violated and robustness of the *t* test assured. But violations of the normality and equality of variances assumptions are more likely to have minimal effects on the probability of making a Type I error when the following conditions are met:

- The number of subjects in each group is the same.
- The two distributions of scores have about the same shape, and the distributions are neither very peaked nor very flat.
- The significance level is set at .05, rather than .01.

Example Problem 9–1
Using t_{ind} to Find the Effect of Diazepam on Time Estimates

Problem
I use the problem faced by Unrug-Neervoort et al. of the effect of diazepam on time estimates to illustrate calculating t_{ind} when $\overline{X}$ and s are known. Unrug-Neervoort et al. had two treatment groups of 12 subjects each. The mean time estimate for the placebo control group (A_1) was 19.8 sec, with $s_{A1} = 7.6$ sec. For the experimental group (A_2), the mean time estimate was 13.6 sec, with $s_{A2} = 4.8$ sec. Do these mean time estimates differ significantly at the .05 level? Use a two-tailed test.

Solution   The solution requires using a statistical test to determine if the observed difference between the two sample means is one that likely results from sampling error alone or if it is too large to be attributed only to sampling error and thus indicates an effect of the independent variable.

Statistic to Be Used:

$$t_{ind} = \frac{\overline{X}_{A1} - \overline{X}_{A2}}{\sqrt{\left[\frac{(n_{A1} - 1)s_{A1}^2 + (n_{A2} - 1)s_{A2}^2}{n_{A1} + n_{A2} - 2}\right]\left[\frac{1}{n_{A1}} + \frac{1}{n_{A2}}\right]}}$$

Assumptions:
1. The subjects were sampled randomly and each subject is independent of each other subject.
2. Time estimate scores are normally distributed in the population.
3. The variances for the time estimate scores are equal in the populations for the two treatment groups.

Statistical Hypotheses: H_0: $\mu_{A1} = \mu_{A2}$,
                                      H_1: $\mu_{A1} \neq \mu_{A2}$.

Significance Level: $\alpha = .05$.

df for t: $(n_{A1} - 1) + (n_{A2} - 1) = (12 - 1) + (12 - 1) = 22$, or $N - 2 = 24 - 2 = 22$.

Critical Value of t: $t_{crit} = 2.074$ from Table A–2.

Rejection Regions: Values of t_{obs} equal to or less than -2.074 or equal to or greater than $+2.074$.

Calculation:

$$t_{obs} = \frac{19.8 - 13.6}{\sqrt{\left[\frac{(12 - 1)(7.6)^2 + (12 - 1)(4.8)^2}{12 + 12 - 2}\right]\left[\frac{1}{12} + \frac{1}{12}\right]}}.$$

$$= \frac{+6.2}{\sqrt{\left[\frac{(11)(57.76) + (11)(23.04)}{22}\right]\left[\frac{2}{12}\right]}}$$

$$= \frac{+6.2}{\sqrt{\left[\frac{635.36 + 253.44}{22}\right]\left[\frac{2}{12}\right]}}$$

$$= \frac{+6.2}{\sqrt{\left[\frac{888.80}{22}\right]\left[\frac{2}{12}\right]}}$$

$$= \frac{+6.2}{\sqrt{(40.40)(0.167)}}$$

$$= \frac{+6.2}{\sqrt{6.747}}$$

$$= \frac{+6.2}{2.597} = +2.387.$$

Decision: t_{obs} falls into the rejection region of equal to or greater than $t_{crit} = +2.074$. I reject H_0 and accept H_1.

Conclusion: The two sample means of 19.8 sec and 13.6 sec differ significantly at the .05 level. Because the treatment groups were equivalent before the treatment was administered, the difference between the mean time estimates is treated as due to the effect of the independent variable. The mean time estimates of subjects given diazepam are shorter than those of subjects given a placebo control.

Example Problem 9–2

Using t_{ind} with Raw Scores

Problem

Recent years have seen the call for improvement of education to provide the skills needed for the future. One response to this call has been to use computers to simulate laboratory experiments in science education. Geban, Askar, and Özkan (1992) investigated whether using such computer-simulated experiments in chemistry led to higher chemistry achievement in comparison to a conventional approach in which students performed actual laboratory experiments. They found significantly greater achievement for the computer-simulated teaching method. Suppose that you were interested in replicating this research using 28 high school chemistry students. You randomly assigned the students to one of two equal-sized groups, the conventional teaching group (A_1) and the computer-simulated group (A_2). At the end of the course you measured knowledge of chemistry with an achievement test on which scores could range from 0 to 100. The following scores were obtained.

Teaching Condition

Conventional (A_1)	Computer Simulated (A_2)
74	84
76	75
81	94
90	88
67	69
72	90
84	86
87	97
92	81
70	91
78	83
82	92
75	82
85	93

Do these achievement scores differ significantly at the .05 level? Use a two-tailed test.

Statistic to Be Used: t_{ind}

Assumptions:
1. The subjects were sampled randomly and each subject is independent of each other subject.
2. Chemistry achievement scores are normally distributed in the population.
3. The variances for the chemistry achievement scores are equal in the populations for the two treatment groups.

Statistical Hypotheses: H_0: $\mu_{A1} = \mu_{A2}$,

H_1: $\mu_{A1} \neq \mu_{A2}$.

Significance Level: $\alpha = .05$.

df for t: $(n_{A1} - 1) + (n_{A2} - 1) = (14 - 1) + (14 - 1) = 26$, or $N - 2 = 28 - 2 = 26$.

Critical Value of t: $t_{\text{crit}} = 2.056$ from Table A–2.

Rejection Regions: Values of t_{obs} equal to or less than -2.056 or equal to or greater than $+2.056$.

Calculation: The first step in the calculation is to find the mean and standard deviation for each group. For the conventional teaching group, $\overline{X}_{A1} = 79.50$ and $s_{A1} = 7.59$. For the computer-simulated group, $\overline{X}_{A2} = 86.07$ and $s_{A2} = 7.74$. Substituting these values into the formula for t_{obs}, I obtain

$$t_{\text{obs}} = \frac{79.50 - 86.07}{\sqrt{\left[\dfrac{(14-1)(7.59)^2 + (14-1)(7.74)^2}{14 + 14 - 2}\right]\left[\dfrac{1}{14} + \dfrac{1}{14}\right]}}$$

$$= \frac{-6.57}{\sqrt{\left[\dfrac{(13)(57.608) + (13)(59.908)}{26}\right]\left[\dfrac{2}{14}\right]}}$$

$$= \frac{-6.57}{\sqrt{\left[\dfrac{748.904 + 778.804}{26}\right]\left[\dfrac{2}{14}\right]}}$$

$$= \frac{-6.57}{\sqrt{\left[\dfrac{1527.708}{26}\right]\left[\dfrac{2}{14}\right]}}$$

$$= \frac{-6.57}{\sqrt{(58.758)(0.143)}}$$

$$= \frac{-6.57}{\sqrt{8.402}}$$

$$= \frac{-6.57}{2.899} = -2.266.$$

Decision: t_{obs} falls into the rejection region of equal to or less than $t_{\text{crit}} = -2.056$. I reject H_0 and accept H_1.

Conclusion: The two sample means of 79.50 and 86.07 differ significantly at the .05 level. The observed difference between the means is due to the effect of the teaching condition. The computer-simulated teaching method leads to higher chemistry achievement scores than does the conventional teaching method.

STATISTICS IN USE 9–1

I'll Remember Better If You Look Me in the Eye: Using t_{ind}

Nonverbal behaviors, such as eye contact, play a major role in communication between individuals. Thus Sherwood (1987) was interested in whether direct eye contact between a teacher and a learner might improve recall of material by the learner. In one experiment he formed two groups of 12 subjects each. Subjects in each group listened to a 6-minute oral presentation by an experimenter and were then given a nine-item test on the material. For a gaze condition given the first group, the experimenter maintained direct eye contact with the subject while giving the oral presentation. For a no-gaze condition given the second group, the experimenter did not maintain eye contact while making the presentation. The mean number of items answered correctly for the gaze group was 6.9 ($s = 1.0$), whereas a mean of 3.3 questions ($s = 1.5$) was answered correctly by the no-gaze group. The t_{obs} for these two means was 6.9 with 22 df, a statistically significant value at the .05 level. The subjects in the gaze condition answered more questions correctly than subjects in the no-gaze condition. If you want someone to remember your words, look them in the eye while you are speaking to them.

TESTING YOUR KNOWLEDGE 9–3

1. Define: directional test, nondirectional test, one-tailed rejection region, rejection region, t_{crit}, t_{ind}, t_{obs}, two-tailed rejection region.
2. Identify the steps in statistical testing with t_{ind}.
3. Write the statistical hypotheses for t_{ind} for a two-tailed test.
4. To what situation in an experiment does H_0 correspond?
5. To what situation in an experiment does H_1 correspond?
6. Assume that you have two groups of size n_{A1} and n_{A2}, respectively. Complete the following exercise for each set of samples given in the table by (a) finding the df for the t test on the two samples, (b) finding t_{crit} for a two-tailed test for $\alpha = .05$ (if the exact df are not tabled, then use the next lower tabled value), (c) indicating whether the t_{obs} falls into a rejection region, and (d) indicating your decisions with respect to the statistical hypotheses.

Sample Set	n_{A1}	n_{A2}	t_{obs}
1	10	10	2.341
2	8	12	1.763
3	15	15	2.120
4	16	14	3.479
5	35	35	2.912
6	19	16	2.007
7	65	64	2.002
8	75	75	2.193

7. Identify the assumptions underlying the use of t_{ind}.
8. **a.** The t test is said to be robust. What is meant by this term?
   b. Under what conditions is the t test likely to be robust?
9. For problems 1 and 2, answer the following questions. Use a two-tailed test and a .05 significance level for each problem.
   a. State the statistical hypotheses for t_{ind} for these scores.
   b. What is the value of t_{obs}?

c.   What are the *df* for this *t*?

d.   What is the value of t_{crit}?

e.   What are the rejection regions for t_{obs}?

f.   Does t_{obs} fall into a rejection region?

g.   What decisions do you make about the statistical hypotheses? Do you reject or fail to reject H_0? Accept or not accept H_1?

h.   Do you conclude that the sample means are from the same or different populations?

i.   Is the difference between the means statistically significant?

j.   Did the groups differ significantly in their estimates of the time they spent waiting? If so, what is the direction of the difference?

Problem 1: Does time seem to pass more slowly when you are expecting a delay before an event occurs? Suppose that to answer this question you randomly assigned a total of 36 subjects to either a control group or an experimental group with $n_{A1} = n_{A2}$. In both groups you told the subjects that the experiment would take only a few minutes and that they were going to fill out a questionnaire on anxiety. Subjects in the control group were told that your assistant would arrive with the questionnaires in a few minutes. Subjects in the experimental group were told that the assistant was delayed and that there would be a short delay. For both groups, however, the assistant arrived in exactly 5 minutes. When your assistant arrived, the subjects were asked to estimate how long they had waited. Suppose that you obtained the following mean time estimates and standard deviations (in minutes) for your groups:

	Group	
	Control	**Experimental**
$\overline{X}$	6.90	8.90
s	1.57	1.71

Problem 2: Suppose that you are interested in answering the same question as in problem 1: Does time seem to pass more slowly when you are expecting a delay before an event occurs? Again, you randomly assign subjects to one of two groups. Rather than an equal number in each group, however, you assign 13 subjects to the control group and 17 to the experimental group. In all other respects the experiment is identical to that described in problem 1. Suppose that you obtained the following mean estimates and standard deviations (in minutes) for your groups:

	Group	
	Control	**Experimental**
$\overline{X}$	6.60	7.80
s	1.80	1.92

REPORTING THE RESULTS OF A *t* TEST

Following the guidelines of the *Publication Manual of the American Psychological Association* (1994), the results of Example Problem 9–1 might be described in a published scientific report as follows:

With an alpha level of .05 and a two-tailed test, the mean time estimate for the placebo control group ($M = 19.8$ s, $SD = 7.6$ s) was significantly longer than the mean estimate of the experimental group ($M = 13.6$ s, $SD = 4.8$ s), $t(22) = +2.39$, $p < .05$.

In this presentation:

$\alpha = .05$ Indicates the significance level selected for the test.

$t(22)$ Identifies the test statistic as the t. This t is t_{obs}; the subscript obs is not utilized. Because two groups were identified in the description, you know the t test is the t_{ind}. The degrees of freedom for t_{obs} are shown in parentheses; thus scores were analyzed from 24 different subjects (because $df = N - 2$).

$= +2.39$ The value of t_{obs} (not the t_{crit} value found in Table A–2).

$p < .05$ Indicates the following:

     a. The probability of t_{obs} if H_0 is true is less than (or equal to) .05. This value is the probability of t_{obs} or an even more extreme value of t_{obs} if H_0 is true; it may not be the same as the value of α selected.

     b. H_0: $\mu_{A1} = \mu_{A2}$ was rejected.
         H_1: $\mu_{A1} \neq \mu_{A2}$ was accepted.

     c. The difference between the sample means is statistically significant.

     d. Something other than sampling error is responsible for the observed difference in the means. Because this was a controlled experiment, we infer that the difference was due to the drug condition given the subjects.

     e. If $p > .05$ had been reported, then the greater than sign ($>$) would indicate that H_0 was not rejected and the two sample means did not differ significantly at the .05 significance level. In this instance we would conclude that the drug condition had no effect on time estimation.

TESTING YOUR KNOWLEDGE 9–4

1. The following reports of the use of t_{ind} have been adapted from results of published studies. Answer the following questions for each report.
   a. How many levels of the independent variable were used in this experiment?
   b. How many subjects were used in this experiment?
   c. What is the value of the sample mean for each treatment condition?
   d. What is the value of the estimated population standard deviation for each treatment condition?
   e. What is the value of t_{obs}?
   f. What is the value of t_{crit} at the .05 significance level for a two-tailed rejection region?
   g. Do you reject or fail to reject H_0?
   h. Do you accept or not accept H_1?
   i. Is the difference between the means statistically significant or nonsignificant?
   j. To what do you attribute the observed difference in the sample means?

Report 1: With alpha equal to .05 and a two-tailed test, a t test indicated that subjects correctly detected a larger percentage of targets while listening to the familiar poem ($M = 79.7$, $SD = 8.57$) than while listening to the unfamiliar poem ($M = 73.0$, $SD = 5.85$), $t(60) = 3.60$, $p < .01$.

Report 2: With alpha equal to .05 and a two-tailed test, a t test revealed no difference in the number of words recalled after a retention interval of 5 minutes ($M = 22.78$, $SD = 5.23$) and a retention interval of 0.5 minutes ($M = 24.33$, $SD = 5.14$), $t(28) = -0.82$, $p > .05$.

POWER AND t_{ind}

The **power of a statistical test** was defined in Chapter 8 as the probability of rejecting H_0 when H_0 is false. Because rejecting H_0 means that the experimenter accepts H_1 and decides that the independent variable had an effect in his or her experiment, the **power of a statistical test** is the probability that an effect of an independent variable will be detected in an experiment when such an effect is present. An experimenter always wants to maximize the power of a statistical test so that he or she can detect an effect of an independent variable if it is present.

The null hypothesis is rejected when t_{obs} falls into a rejection region, and the larger that t_{obs} is, the more likely it will fall into a rejection region. There are several actions we can take to increase the value of t_{obs} and thus the power of t_{ind}. We can understand these actions by examining the formula for t_{ind},

$$t_{ind} = \frac{\overline{X}_{A1} - \overline{X}_{A2}}{s_{\overline{X}A1 - \overline{X}A2}}.$$

With this formula there are two ways to increase the value of t_{obs}: (1) increase the difference between $\overline{X}_{A1}$ and $\overline{X}_{A2}$ and (2) decrease the value of $s_{\overline{X}A1 - \overline{X}A2}$.

The first approach is to maximize the effect of the independent variable. That is, I want to manipulate the independent variable in such a way that it makes $\overline{X}_{A1}$ and $\overline{X}_{A2}$ differ as much as possible. For this reason, behavioral scientists often use widely differing levels of the independent variable.

To decrease the value of $s_{\overline{X}A1 - \overline{X}A2}$, I may do two things: increase the sample size and decrease the amount of variability in the scores of the samples. To illustrate the relationship of $s_{\overline{X}A1 - \overline{X}A2}$ to sample size, suppose that both s_{A1}^2 and $s_{A2}^2 = 36$. Consider also that these values of s^2 came from one of three sample sizes: $n_{A1} = n_{A2} = 3$, $n_{A1} = n_{A2} = 6$, or $n_{A1} = n_{A2} = 9$. Then, substituting the differing values of n_A into the formula for $s_{\overline{X}A1 - \overline{X}A2}$:

- For $n_{A1} = n_{A2} = 3$, $s_{\overline{X}A1 - \overline{X}A2} = 4.9$.
- For $n_{A1} = n_{A2} = 6$, $s_{\overline{X}A1 - \overline{X}A2} = 3.5$.
- For $n_{A1} = n_{A2} = 9$, $s_{\overline{X}A1 - \overline{X}A2} = 2.8$.

Here we see that, as the sample size increases, the standard error of the difference decreases. Thus for a given difference between $\overline{X}_{A1}$ and $\overline{X}_{A2}$, the value of t_{obs} increases as sample size becomes larger and $s_{\overline{X}A1 - \overline{X}A2}$ decreases in size. And, as t_{obs} increases, it becomes more likely that t_{obs} will fall into a rejection region and H_0 will be rejected and H_1 accepted.

In general, any treatment effect, no matter how small, may be detected if the sample size is large enough. Thus a researcher can minimize the probability of making a Type II error by maximizing sample size. But reality must intrude here, for increasing the size of a sample is often costly and time consuming. Moreover, if it takes a sample of 1000 people in each group to detect the effect of an independent variable, then I may expect this independent variable to have a very minimal effect on behavior.

A second step in decreasing $s_{\overline{X}A1 - \overline{X}A2}$ is to reduce the variability among the scores in each group. If the scores vary less within the groups, then s_A^2 will decrease for each group and consequently $s_{\overline{X}A1 - \overline{X}A2}$ will also decrease. This decrease in $s_{\overline{X}A1 - \overline{X}A2}$ will lead to an increase in t_{obs} and thus an increase in the probability that t_{obs} will fall into a rejection region. Because of this relationship, experimenters typically carefully control the conditions under which research is conducted to minimize the variability of the scores within each group in an experiment.

MEASURING THE STRENGTH OF A TREATMENT EFFECT

Strength of effect: The strength of an independent variable as measured by one of the strength of effect statistics.

A statistically significant difference indicates that an independent variable has an effect on the dependent variable of the experiment, but it does not indicate the size or strength of that effect. A number of statistics have been developed for measuring the strength of the effect of the independent variable after an experiment has been completed. These statistics are often referred to as **strength of effect measures** or **strength of association measures.** The statistic discussed next is called **eta squared** and is represented by η^2, where η is the lowercase Greek letter *eta*. Eta squared is calculated from the t_{obs} value and degrees of freedom for t by

$$\eta^2 = \frac{t_{obs}^2}{t_{obs}^2 + df}.$$

To illustrate, in Example Problem 9–2, t_{obs} for the difference between the conventional and computer-simulated teaching conditions was -2.266, with 26 df. Eta squared for this t_{obs} equals

$$\eta^2 = \frac{t_{obs}^2}{t_{obs}^2 + df}$$

$$= \frac{(-2.266)^2}{(-2.266)^2 + 26}$$

$$= \frac{5.1348}{5.1348 + 26}$$

$$= \frac{5.1348}{31.1348} = .165$$

$$= .16 \quad \text{rounded to two decimal places.}$$

Eta squared is a measure of how much knowing the level of an independent variable that a subject received reduces the error in predicting the subject's score in the sample of subjects tested. To illustrate, suppose in Example Problem 9–2 that you were asked to predict a subject's score on the achievement test, but you did not know which teaching condition the subject was given. In this instance your best prediction would be to use the grand mean of all 28 subjects, $\overline{X}_G = 82.79$, as the predicted score. Of course, this prediction will be in error, and the average error will be the standard deviation of the 28 scores around the grand mean. Here I use S rather than s because η^2 is a statistic describing only the sample; it is not an estimate of a population value. The value of S for the 28 scores around the grand mean is 8.09. This value squared [i.e., $(8.09)^2$] equals 65.448 and is the total variance of the sample of 28 scores.

Now suppose that you were asked to predict a subject's score, but you were told the teaching condition the subject received. In this instance the best prediction would be the mean of the scores of the teaching condition that the subject received, either 79.50 or 86.07. Again your prediction would be in error, but now the average error would be the standard deviation of the group that the subject was in. Again I use S; thus $S_{A1} = 7.32$ and $S_{A2} = 7.46$. Squaring each S provides the sample variance for each group: $S_{A1}^2 = 53.582$ and $S_{A2}^2 = 55.652$. The mean of these two variances is 54.617 [i.e., $(53.582 + 55.652)/2 = 109.234/2 = 54.617$]. This value is the average variance of the error when using a teaching condition mean to predict a subject's score. The difference between the variance found using the grand mean (i.e., 65.448) and the average variance using the treatment condition means as predicted scores (i.e., 54.617) is $65.448 - 54.617 = 10.831$. The reduction in variance from the total variance when treatment condition means are used to predict a score is 10.831. Dividing this reduction by the total variance yields $10.831/65.448 = .165$, or .16 rounded to two decimal places. In other words, when I know the level of an independent variable that a subject received and I use the treatment group mean rather than the grand mean to predict a subject's score, the variance of the prediction is reduced by .16, or 16 percent. This value is η^2. Thus η^2 indicates the proportion of the reduction of the total variance in the dependent variable when I know the level of the independent variable that a subject received. For this reason, η^2 often is interpreted as indicating the proportion of the variance of the dependent variable that can be "accounted for" by the independent variable.

The value of η^2 may range between .00 to 1.00. An η^2 of .00 indicates that knowing the level of an independent variable that a subject received does not reduce the error variance of the dependent variable. A prediction of the grand mean is as good a prediction of the subject's score as a prediction of the treatment group mean. There is no relation between the level of the independent variable and the score on the dependent variable. On the other hand, η^2 of 1.00 indicates that knowing the level of the independent variable that a subject received allows perfect prediction of the subject's score. There will be no error in using the treatment group mean to predict a subject's score.

In practice, an η^2 of about .10 to .15 often is treated as revealing a strong treatment effect. This interpretation finds support in published behavioral science research. For example, Haase, Waechter, and Solomon (1982) calculated η^2 on 11,044 tests of statistical significance reported in issues of the *Journal of Counseling Psychology* published between 1970 to 1979. They found a median η^2 value of 0.083. The interquartile range for the η^2 values was 0.043 to 0.268. This result gives some idea of the typical strength of association found in behavioral science research and provides a basis for evaluating a value of η^2.

The *Publication Manual of the American Psychological Association* (1994) suggests that measures of the strength of the effect of an independent variable, such as eta squared, be included in a journal report of a statistical test. A sample report is illustrated in Chapter 10.

Example Problem 9–3
Calculating η^2 in an Experiment

Problem

In Example Problem 9–1, t_{obs} for the difference in time estimates between the placebo control and the experimental groups was +2.387, with 22 df. What is the strength of effect for the independent variable of drug condition?

Solution   The strength of effect is given by η^2, where

$$\eta^2 = \frac{t_{obs}^2}{t_{obs}^2 + df}.$$

Substituting numerical values for t_{obs} and df,

$$\eta^2 = \frac{(2.387)^2}{(2.387)^2 + 22}$$
$$= \frac{5.6978}{5.6978 + 22}$$
$$= \frac{5.6978}{27.6978} = .206$$
$$= .21 \quad \text{rounded to two decimal places.}$$

Conclusion: The value of η^2 indicates that knowing the drug condition a subject received results in a 21 percent reduction in the total variance of the experiment.

USING THE *t* STATISTIC TO CONSTRUCT CONFIDENCE INTERVALS FOR THE DIFFERENCE BETWEEN TWO INDEPENDENT POPULATION MEANS

A confidence interval for a population mean was defined as an interval in which I have a certain degree of confidence that the interval contains the population mean. In this chapter we have been interested in the difference between two population means. Here I want a confidence interval for the difference between two independent population means, $\mu_{A1} - \mu_{A2}$. The approach is similar to that used in Chapter 8, except that $\overline{X}_{A1} - \overline{X}_{A2}$ is used in place of $\overline{X}$ and $s_{\overline{X}_{A1} - \overline{X}_{A2}}$ is used in place of $s_{\overline{X}}$. Accordingly, the **95 percent**

confidence interval for the difference between two independent population means is given by the interval from

$$(\overline{X}_{A1} - \overline{X}_{A2}) - t_{.05}(s_{\overline{X}_{A1} - \overline{X}_{A2}}) \text{ to } (\overline{X}_{A1} - \overline{X}_{A2}) + t_{.05}(s_{\overline{X}_{A1} - \overline{X}_{A2}}),$$

where
$\overline{X}_{A1} - \overline{X}_{A2}$ = difference between the two observed sample means

$s_{\overline{X}_{A1} - \overline{X}_{A2}}$ = estimated standard error of the difference between means

$t_{.05}$ = two-tailed value of t_{crit} at the .05 significance level with $N - 2$ degrees of freedom

The interval given by this formula has a .95 probability of including the value of $\mu_{A1} - \mu_{A2}$.

Similarly, a **99 percent confidence interval for the difference between two independent population means** is given by the interval from

$$(\overline{X}_{A1} - \overline{X}_{A2}) - t_{.01}(s_{\overline{X}_{A1} - \overline{X}_{A2}}) \text{ to } (\overline{X}_{A1} - \overline{X}_{A2}) + t_{.01}(s_{\overline{X}_{A1} - \overline{X}_{A2}}),$$

where $t_{.01}$ is the two-tailed value of t_{crit} at the .01 significance level with $N - 2$ degrees of freedom.

To illustrate the use of these formulas, I find the 95 percent confidence interval for Example Problem 9–1 comparing the time estimates of a placebo control group to a diazepam group. Here $\overline{X}_{A1} = 19.8$ seconds, $\overline{X}_{A2} = 13.6$ sec, and $s_{\overline{X}_{A1} - \overline{X}_{A2}} = 2.597$ sec. There are 22 degrees of freedom for this example (see Example Problem 9–1); thus the two-tailed value of t_{crit} at the .05 level is 2.074. The 95 percent confidence interval for $\mu_{A1} - \mu_{A2}$ is

$$(19.8 - 13.6) - (2.074)(2.597) \text{ to } (19.8 - 13.6) + (2.074)(2.597) \text{ sec,}$$

or, carrying out the mathematical operations indicated,

$$6.2 - 5.39 \text{ to } 6.2 + 5.39 \text{ sec,}$$

which equals

$$0.81 \text{ sec to } 11.59 \text{ sec.}$$

The interval of 0.81 to 11.59 sec has a .95 probability of including the value of $\mu_{A1} - \mu_{A2}$. I can be 95 percent confident that the difference between the population means of time estimates for a placebo control and a diazepam group is between 0.81 to 11.59 sec.

TESTING YOUR KNOWLEDGE 9–5

1. Define: effect size, power, strength of association, strength of effect.
2. Two sets of two samples each are obtained. For set 1, $s_{A1} = 6.3$ and $s_{A2} = 7.6$. For set 2, $s_{A1} = 11.7$ and $s_{A2} = 10.3$.
   a. Which set of scores has greater error variation?
   b. If H_1 is true, which set of scores will more likely lead to a Type II error in a statistical test?
   c. Which set of scores will lead to a more powerful statistical test?
3. Which of the following two sample sizes would be expected to lead to a smaller value of $s_{\overline{X}_{A1} - \overline{X}_{A2}}$ in a t test: $n_{A1} = n_{A2} = 12$ or $n_{A1} = n_{A2} = 20$? Why? Which sample size would lead to a more powerful statistical test?

4. Find η^2 for each of the following values of t_{obs}. The df for each t are presented in parentheses. Each t_{obs} is statistically significant at the .05 level with a two-tailed test.
   a. $t(8) = 2.413$
   b. $t(14) = 2.284$
   c. $t(20) = 2.174$
   d. $t(29) = 2.939$
   e. $t(60) = 2.306$

WITHIN-SUBJECTS DESIGNS AND THE t TEST FOR RELATED SCORES

Within-subjects design: A research design in which one group of subjects is exposed to and measured under each level of an independent variable. In a within-subjects design, each subject receives each treatment condition.

Our interest to this point has been with the analysis of between-subjects designs in which each level of the independent variable is given to a different group of subjects. A second type of research design is the **within-subjects design** in which a single group of subjects is exposed to and measured under each level of an independent variable. Thus, in a within-subjects design, each subject receives each treatment condition.

Consider the following example of a one-factor within-subjects design. When scouting college baseball pitchers for professional teams, it is common practice for the scout to measure the velocity of fastball pitches with a speed gun. Often the speed gun is used in open view of the pitcher (Weinstein, Prather, and de Man, 1987). Does the sight of the speed gun affect the pitcher's velocity? To answer this question, suppose that you measured the velocity of pitches of eight college pitchers both with the speed gun in open view of the pitcher (condition A_1) and with the gun hidden from view (condition A_2). The independent variable is the *speed gun condition*, and the two levels are *open view* (A_1) and *hidden* (A_2). Each subject is tested under each speed gun condition; thus a within-subjects design is used. Suppose that you found the mean velocities for each pitcher in each condition as given in Table 9–2. Do the mean velocities differ significantly in the two conditions? To answer this question, we use a t test for related scores to compare the means.

The t Test for Related Scores

In a within-subjects design the same subjects are measured under each treatment condition; thus the scores in each treatment condition are related. The factors that affect a subject's score in one condition will affect that subject's score in the other condition. The t_{ind} is not appropriate for this design; rather a t **test for related scores** defined as

$$t_{rel} = \frac{\overline{X}_{A1} - \overline{X}_{A2}}{s_D}$$

is used, where s_D is the standard error of the mean for the difference between each X_{A1} and X_{A2} score. The formula for s_D is

$$s_D = \sqrt{\frac{\Sigma D^2 - (\Sigma D)^2/N_{pairs}}{N_{pairs}(N_{pairs} - 1)}},$$

TABLE 9–2
Mean velocities (in mph) of eight
right-handed college baseball pitchers with
a speed gun in open view and a speed
gun hidden from view.

| | Speed Gun Condition (A) | |
| | Open View (A_1) | Hidden (A_2) |
Subject		
1	72.4	77.9
2	67.1	69.4
3	77.8	77.1
4	73.2	76.5
5	62.5	64.6
6	68.7	75.3
7	71.4	69.8
8	81.7	84.2
$\overline{X}_A$	71.85	74.35
s_A	6.03	6.13

where D represents the difference between the two scores of a subject, and N_{pairs} is the number of pairs of scores or, equivalently, the number of subjects. Substituting the formula for s_D, the computational formula for t_{rel} becomes

$$t_{rel} = \frac{\overline{X}_{A1} - \overline{X}_{A2}}{\sqrt{\dfrac{\Sigma D^2 - (\Sigma D)^2 / N_{pairs}}{N_{pairs}(N_{pairs} - 1)}}}.$$

The df are equal to $N_{pairs} - 1$, which represents the number of pairs of scores that are free to vary.

The application of this formula to the scores in Table 9–2 is illustrated in Table 9–3. The steps in this calculation are as follows:

1. Find $\overline{X}_{A1}$ and $\overline{X}_{A2}$. For the example, these values are 71.85 and 74.35 mph, respectively.
2. Find the value of D for each subject by subtracting a subject's score in condition A_2 from his or her score in condition A_1. Maintain the algebraic sign of the difference for each subject. This step is shown in the column headed by D in the table.
3. Square each value of D as shown in the column headed by D^2 of the table.
4. Find ΣD (the sum of column D; -20.0 for the example) and ΣD^2 (the sum of column D^2; 103.70 for the example).
5. Determine N_{pairs}. For the example, $N_{pairs} = 8$.

TABLE 9–3
Computation of t_{rel} on the scores of Table 9–2.

| Subject | Speed Gun Condition (A) | | D | D^2 |
	Open View (A_1)	Hidden (A_2)		
1	72.4	77.9	−5.5	30.25
2	67.1	69.4	−2.3	5.29
3	77.8	77.1	+0.7	0.49
4	73.2	76.5	−3.3	10.89
5	62.5	64.6	−2.1	4.41
6	68.7	75.3	−6.6	43.56
7	71.4	69.8	+1.6	2.56
8	81.7	84.2	−2.5	6.25
$\overline{X}_A$	71.85	74.35	$\Sigma D = -20.0$	$\Sigma D^2 = 103.70$
s_A	6.03	6.13		

$$t_{rel} = \frac{\overline{X}_{A1} - \overline{X}_{A2}}{\sqrt{\dfrac{\Sigma D^2 - (\Sigma D)^2/N_{pairs}}{N_{pairs}(N_{pairs} - 1)}}}$$

$$= \frac{71.85 - 74.35}{\sqrt{\dfrac{103.70 - (-20.00)^2/8}{(8)(7)}}}$$

$$= \frac{-2.50}{\sqrt{\dfrac{103.70 - \left(\dfrac{400}{8}\right)}{56}}}$$

$$= \frac{-2.50}{\sqrt{\dfrac{103.70 - 50}{56}}}$$

$$= \frac{-2.50}{\sqrt{\dfrac{53.7}{56}}}$$

$$= \frac{-2.50}{\sqrt{0.959}}$$

$$= \frac{-2.50}{0.979} = -2.554 \quad \text{with 7 } df.$$

6. Substitute the numerical values into the equation for t_{rel}.
7. Find the df, where $df = N_{pairs} - 1$.

The t_{obs} for the scores of Table 9–2 is −2.554. The remaining steps in using this t_{obs} are identical to those for the t_{ind}. A value of α is selected, the value of t_{crit} is found from Table A–2, and rejection regions are located on the sampling distribution of t. If the value of t_{obs} falls into a rejection region, then

$$H_0: \mu_{A1} = \mu_{A2} \text{ is rejected}$$

and

$$H_1: \mu_{A1} \neq \mu_{A2} \text{ is accepted.}$$

For 7 df and a .05 significance level, t_{crit} for a two-tailed rejection region is 2.365. The rejection region is thus composed of values of t_{obs} less than or equal to −2.365 or equal to or greater than +2.365. The t_{obs} of −2.554 is less than −2.365; hence it falls into a rejection region; H_0 is rejected and H_1 accepted. The difference between the sample means is statistically significant at the .05 level. The college pitchers in this study threw more slowly when a speed gun was in open view compared to when the speed gun was hidden from view.

Eta squared is found for this t_{rel} by

$$\eta^2 = \frac{t_{obs}^2}{t_{obs}^2 + df}.$$

Substituting numerical values for t_{obs} and df,

$$\eta^2 = \frac{(-2.554)^2}{(-2.554)^2 + 7}$$
$$= \frac{6.523}{6.523 + 7}$$
$$= \frac{6.523}{13.523} = .48.$$

This eta squared indicates that 48 percent of the variance in the dependent variable is accounted for by the speed gun condition in this experiment.

Constructing Confidence Intervals for the Difference between Two Related Population Means

The **95 percent confidence interval for the difference between two related population means** is given by the interval from

$$(\overline{X}_{A1} - \overline{X}_{A2}) - t_{.05}(s_D) \text{ to } (\overline{X}_{A1} - \overline{X}_{A2}) + t_{.05}(s_D),$$

where $\overline{X}_{A1} - \overline{X}_{A2}$ = difference between the two observed sample means

s_D = standard error of the mean for the difference between each $\overline{X}_{A1}$ and $\overline{X}_{A2}$ score

$t_{.05}$ = two-tailed value of t_{crit} at the .05 significance level with $N-1$ degrees of freedom

The interval given by this formula has a .95 probability of including the value of $\mu_{A1}-\mu_{A2}$. For the example problem, $\overline{X}_{A1} = 71.85$, $\overline{X}_{A2} = 74.35$, $N_{pairs} = 8$, $s_D = 0.979$ (from Table 9–3), and $t_{.05}$ for 7 degrees of freedom equals 2.365. To avoid obtaining a negative difference between sample means, I will subtract $\overline{X}_{A1}$ from $\overline{X}_{A2}$. Substituting numerical values, the 95 percent confidence interval for the difference between μ_{A1} and μ_{A2} is

$$(74.35 - 71.85) - (2.365)(0.979) \text{ to } (74.35 - 71.85) + (2.365)(0.979),$$

which equals an interval of 0.18 to 4.82 miles per hour. The 95 percent confidence interval for the difference between the population means of pitching speeds with and without the visual presence of a radar gun is between 0.18 to 4.82 miles per hour.

WHAT DOES A *t* TEST ACTUALLY TEST?

The *t* test provides information needed for deciding whether a research hypothesis is or is not supported by the data of the experiment. It is important to recognize, however, that a research hypothesis is not tested directly by the *t* test. The *t* test is simply a procedure for testing the statistical hypothesis H_0: $\mu_{A1} = \mu_{A2}$. Regardless of the independent and dependent variables stated in the research hypothesis, the null and alternative hypotheses for a two-tailed *t* test are always H_0: $\mu_{A1} = \mu_{A2}$ and H_1 : $\mu_{A1} \neq \mu_{A2}$, respectively. On the other hand, a research hypothesis for an experiment is a statement predicting a relationship between an independent variable and a dependent variable. As an example, the statement "it is expected that the time estimates made by subjects given diazepam will be shorter than the estimates made by a placebo control group" is a research hypothesis.

A statistically significant t_{obs} with a nondirectional alternative hypothesis (i.e., H_1: $\mu_{A1} \neq \mu_{A2}$) does not necessarily provide support for the research hypothesis. As an illustration, support for the stated research hypothesis occurs if $\overline{X}_{A1}$, the mean time estimate for the placebo control group, is significantly longer than $\overline{X}_{A2}$, the mean time estimate for the experimental group. But an $\overline{X}_{A1}$ significantly less than $\overline{X}_{A2}$ does not agree with this research hypothesis. Consequently, after obtaining a statistically significant t_{obs}, we must always examine the direction of the difference between the means to find if it agrees or disagrees with the research hypothesis.

STATISTICAL AND SCIENTIFIC SIGNIFICANCE REVISITED

In Chapter 8, I pointed out that in statistical hypothesis testing the word *significant* means only that a null hypothesis has been rejected. But a statistically significant difference between the means in an experiment is not necessarily scientifically important. The scientific importance of an experiment is determined before the data are subjected to statistical analysis. In a well-conceived and well-designed experiment, either a statistically significant or nonsignificant difference may be important scientifically. Indeed, if a particular relationship is predicted between the independent variable and the dependent variable, a failure to find that relationship empirically may have scientific importance. As an example, the drug AZT is often given to HIV-positive patients to delay the onset of AIDS symptoms. One long-term study, however, found no statistically significant difference in the delay of onset of AIDS symptoms between an experimental group of HIV-positive patients given AZT and a control group not given the drug (Kong, 1993). This lack of a difference between the two treatment conditions is clearly an important finding in the treatment of HIV-positive individuals. In a poorly designed experiment, however, in which the independent variable is confounded with an extraneous variable, even a statistically significant difference between two sample means cannot be interpreted meaningfully.

TESTING YOUR KNOWLEDGE 9–6

1. Distinguish between a research hypothesis and a statistical hypothesis.
2. Does a statistically significant difference necessarily mean that a scientifically important result has been found? Explain your answer.
3. Explain the difference between a between-subjects research design and a within-subjects research design.

SUMMARY

- An experiment requires:
  - Asking a scientific question and formulating a research hypothesis.
  - Selecting subjects.
  - Creating equivalent groups by random assignment.
  - Controlling extraneous variables.
  - Manipulating an independent variable.
  - Measuring the dependent variable.
- The t_{ind} may be used to determine if two sample means from an experiment differ significantly.
- The formula for t_{ind} is

$$t_{ind} = \frac{\overline{X}_{A1} - \overline{X}_{A2}}{s_{\overline{X}_{A1} - \overline{X}_{A2}}}$$

where $s_{\overline{X}_{A1} - \overline{X}_{A2}}$ is the standard error of the difference between means.

- Statistical hypothesis testing with t_{ind} follows the steps common to all statistical testing.
- The power of a statistical test is the probability of rejecting H_0 when H_0 is false.
- Factors affecting power of the t test include the magnitude of the effect induced by the independent variable, the amount of variability in the measure of the dependent variable, and sample size.
- Eta squared (η^2) is a measure of the strength of association in the sample measured and is calculated from t_{obs}.
- Eta squared indicates the proportion of the total variation in the dependent variable accounted for by the independent variable.
- The 95 percent confidence interval for the difference between two independent population means is given by the interval from

$$(\overline{X}_{A1} - \overline{X}_{A2}) - t_{.05}(s_{\overline{X}A1 - \overline{X}A2}) \text{ to } (\overline{X}_{A1} - \overline{X}_{A2}) + t_{.05}(s_{\overline{X}A1 - \overline{X}A2}).$$

- In a within-subjects design a single group of subjects is exposed to all levels of each independent variable.
- The t_{rel} may be used when there are two levels of an independent variable in a one-factor within-subjects design.
- The formula for t_{rel} is

$$t_{rel} = \frac{\overline{X}_{A1} - \overline{X}_{A2}}{s_D}$$

where s_D is the standard error of the mean for the difference between each X_{A1} and X_{A2} score.
- The 95 percent confidence interval for the difference between two related population means is given by the interval from

$$(\overline{X}_{A1} - \overline{X}_{A2}) - t_{.05}(s_D) \text{ to } (\overline{X}_{A1} - \overline{X}_{A2}) + t_{.05}(s_D).$$

KEY TERMS AND SYMBOLS

central limit theorem

chance difference

confidence interval for the difference between two population means

confounding

convenience sampling

dependent variable

directional test

empirical sampling distribution of the difference between means

equivalent groups

eta squared (η^2)

experiment

extraneous variable

independent variable

level of an independent variable

nondirectional test

one-tailed rejection region

one-tailed test

placebo control

power

random assignment

random sampling

rejection region

robustness

s_D

$s_{\overline{X}A1 - \overline{X}A2}$

s_{pooled}^2

standard error

standard error of the difference
   between means

strength of association

strength of effect

t_{crit}

t_{ind}

t_{obs}

t_{rel}

theoretical sampling distribution
   of the difference between
   means

two-tailed rejection region

two-tailed test

within-subjects design

REVIEW QUESTIONS

1. Suppose that you were interested in finding if noise has any effect on blood pressure. You randomly assigned 22 individuals to either a control or an experimental group ($n_{A1} = n_{A2}$). Subjects in the quiet group (A_1) relaxed in a comfortable chair in a quiet room for 30 minutes. At the end of the 30 minutes you measured their systolic blood pressure (i.e., the blood pressure during the contraction of the heart). Subjects in the noise group (A_2) also sat in the chair for 30 minutes. During the 30-minute wait, however, they listened to a recording of rush hour traffic noise from a large city. After listening to the noise for 30 minutes, the systolic blood pressure of these subjects was also recorded. Suppose that you obtained the following blood pressures in millimeters of mercury.

Group	
Quiet	Noise
106	141
117	136
124	124
129	139
115	121
131	119
121	147
115	128
128	115
136	134
127	140

a. Find the mean and standard deviation for each group. Then use a t test to answer the following question: Does noise affect systolic blood pressure? Use a two-tailed test and a .05 significance level.

b. What is the value of η^2 for this experiment? What proportion of the variance in the dependent variable can be accounted for by knowing the level of the independent variable?

c. Find the 95 percent confidence interval for the difference between the two population means.

d. Describe your results following the example illustrated in the Reporting the Results of a *t* Test section of this chapter.

2. Suppose that you obtained the blood pressures given next for question 1. Does noise affect systolic blood pressure? Use a .05 significance level and a two-tailed test.

Group

Quiet	Noise
110	116
114	111
106	120
117	119
108	123
116	108
120	122
111	115
115	117
109	101
118	116

3. Pedersen (1987) hypothesized that sex differences exist in the need for privacy among college students. The hypothesis was tested by giving the Privacy Questionnaire (Pedersen, 1979) to male and female college students. One aspect of this questionnaire measures the need for solitude. Scores on this scale may range from 6 (never need solitude) to 30 (usually need solitude). Suppose that the following scores were obtained for 13 males and 17 females.

Gender

Male (A_1)	Female (A_2)
23	16
16	29
13	11
25	14
17	17
21	19
10	18
19	21
24	9
16	15
11	17
22	20
14	14
	24
	23
	25
	24

    a. Find the mean and standard deviation for each group. Then use a t test to answer the following question: Do males and females differ in the rated need for solitude? Use a two-tailed test and a .05 significance level.

    b. Describe your results following the example illustrated in the Reporting the Results of a t Test section of this chapter.

4. Evidence exists that pressure on the carotid arteries at the neck reduces blood flow to the brain and eye. Langan and Watkins (1987) also found that, in a sample of 94 men wearing a shirt and tie, the shirt and tie were providing pressure on the neck. To find if tight neckwear affects visual functioning, Langan and Watkins measured critical flicker frequency (CFF) of men wearing a loose collar and then wearing a tight collar and tie. The CFF tests the ability to perceive when a rapidly blinking light changes from a solid light to a blinking light. The higher the frequency of the on–off blinks of the light at which this perceptual change occurs, the more sensitive is the retinal functioning. Suppose that you conducted a similar study with 12 men. Each man participated in two conditions, wearing a loose collar (A_1) and wearing a tight collar and necktie (A_2). The critical flicker frequencies (in hertz, or cycles per second) for each subject were as follows:

	Type of Neckwear (A)	
Subject	Loose (A_1)	Tight (A_2)
1	17	16
2	19	17
3	23	20
4	22	21
5	22	22
6	20	18
7	18	20
8	21	17
9	23	19
10	19	21
11	20	16
12	17	18

    a. Find the mean and standard deviation for each group. Then use a t test to answer this question: Did the type of neckwear affect the CFF scores? Use a two-tailed test and a .05 significance level.

    b. Describe your results following the example illustrated in the Reporting the Results of a t Test section of this chapter.

5. Locus of control refers to the perception a person has over the control of events that affect his or her life. A person with an external locus of control perceives that he or she has little control over these events, whereas a person with an internal locus of control perceives that he or she has a great deal of control over such events. Wiehe (1986) hypothesized that children who have been removed

from the custody of their parents might have a more external locus of control than children who live with their biological parents. To test this hypothesis, Wiehe formed two groups from among adolescents in a residential maternity home: 45 pregnant adolescents who had been removed from their biological parents and had become pregnant while in foster care and 45 pregnant adolescents who had become pregnant while living with their biological parents. Each adolescent was given a rating scale to measure locus of control, and Wiehe reported a mean locus of control score of 15.76 ($s = 4.65$) for the foster parents group and a mean score of 12.27 ($s = 5.74$) for the biological parents group. For this measure, higher scores indicate greater external locus of control.

    a. Use a t test to answer this question: Is locus of control related to the type of home of the adolescent? Use a two-tailed test and a .05 significance level.

    b. What is the value of η^2 for this study? What proportion of the variance in the dependent variable can be accounted for by knowing the level of the independent variable?

    c. Find the 95 percent confidence interval for the difference between the two population means.

    d. Describe your results following the example illustrated in the Reporting the Results of a t Test section of this chapter.

6. Hughey (1985) compared the grade point average (GPA) of college students cited for residence hall disruptions with students not involved in residence hall disruptions. The mean GPA of 1794 students involved in disruptions was 1.68 with $s = 0.34$. For 3606 students not involved in disruptions, the mean GPA was 2.19 with $s = 0.83$.

    a. Use a t test to answer this question: Do the GPAs differ significantly? Use a two-tailed test and a .05 significance level.

    b. What is the value of η^2 for this study? What proportion of the variance in the dependent variable can be accounted for by knowing the level of the independent variable?

    c. Find the 95 percent confidence interval for the difference between the two population means.

    d. Describe your results following the example illustrated in the Reporting the Results of a t Test section of this chapter.

7. Many students experience test anxiety that severely interferes with their academic performance. A college counselor hypothesized that listening to relaxing music before an examination would reduce this anxiety. To test this hypothesis, the therapist selected 34 students with severe test anxiety from a large introductory course. The students were randomly assigned to either a control or an experimental group, with an equal number of subjects in each group. Subjects in the control group spent the hour before the next exam in the course sitting in a quiet lounge where they read magazines. Subjects in the experimental group spent the hour listening to relaxing music. The mean exam grade for the control group was 73.2 ($s_{A1} = 8.4$) and the mean grade for the experimental group was 75.6 ($s_{A2} = 8.7$).

    a. Use a t test to answer this question: Did the groups differ significantly on the mean test grades? Use a two-tailed test and a .05 significance level.

    b. Describe your results following the example illustrated in the Reporting the Results of a t Test section of this chapter.

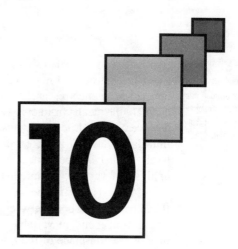

One-factor Between-subjects Analysis of Variance

The t test introduced many of the important concepts of statistical hypothesis testing in behavioral science research. But the t test possesses a major limitation; it can be used to compare the means from only two groups at a time. Many behavioral science experiments, however, are multilevel designs. A **one-factor multilevel design** (also called a **one-way multilevel design**) is an experiment with one independent variable and three or more levels of that independent variable. For these designs, a statistical technique known as **analysis of variance** (abbreviated **ANOVA**) is used as a statistical hypothesis test.

Analysis of variance is the most widely used statistical test in psychological research. It can be used for both between- and within-subjects designs and for designs in which two or more independent variables are varied. For a one-factor design, analysis of variance may be used in place of the t_{ind} test when only two levels of an independent variable are manipulated. This chapter presents the analysis of variance for the one-factor between-subjects multilevel design, the design in which one independent variable is manipulated, and each level of the independent variable is given to a different group of subjects. Its uses in other designs are presented in Chapters 11 and 12.

To develop the analysis of variance, I use an experiment concerned with the recall of visual stimuli. What aspects of a stimulus determine how well we remember it? One research hypothesis, the elaboration hypothesis, predicts that the more elaborate the memory representation of a stimulus is the better the stimulus should be remembered (Craik & Tulving, 1975). A second research hypothesis, the effort hypothesis, predicts that stimuli requiring more effort to process and remember will be recalled better than stimuli requiring less effort (Coulter, Coulter, & Glover, 1984). Suppose that we create three different types of drawings of common objects: detailed, outline, and incomplete outline drawings. The elaboration hypothesis predicts that detailed drawings should lead to the most memory elaboration and thus be best recalled, with outline and incomplete outline drawings leading to less memory elaboration and thus progressively poorer recall. The effort hypothesis, however, leads to an opposite prediction; the incomplete outline drawings require the most effort to process and remember and thus they will be best recalled. The detailed drawings require the least effort; hence they will be the most poorly recalled.

To determine which of these hypotheses best predicts memory for visual stimuli, suppose that we used a one-factor between-subjects design and manipulated the independent variable of type of drawing (factor A) over three levels: incomplete outline (A_1), outline (A_2), and detailed (A_3) drawings. The procedures discussed in Chapter 9 for designing and running an experiment were followed. Three equivalent groups were created by randomly assigning five subjects to each group. The subjects in each group were shown a set of drawings of 30 common items. For one group the drawings were detailed, for the second group the drawings were outlines, and for the third group the drawings were incomplete outlines. After viewing each of the 30 drawings for 4 seconds, each subject was asked to orally recall as many of the drawings as possible. The number of items recalled by each person, the mean and standard deviation for each group, and the grand mean for the scores are presented in Table 10–1. The **grand mean**, identified as $\overline{X}_G$, is the mean of all 15 scores in the experiment. Is the number of drawings recalled affected by the type of drawing? To answer this question, I use the one-factor between-subjects analysis of variance.

TABLE 10–1

Hypothetical scores for number of items recalled as a function of type of drawing. The mean $(\overline{X}_A)$ and standard deviation (s_A) are provided for each condition. $\overline{X}_G$ is the grand mean of the 15 scores.

	Incomplete Outline (A_1)	Outline (A_2)	Detailed (A_3)	
	19	14	15	
	13	13	10	
	16	16	11	
	17	12	12	
	20	10	12	
$\overline{X}_A$	17.0	13.0	12.0	$\overline{X}_G = 14.0$
s_A	2.74	2.24	1.87	

Type of Drawing (Factor A)

BETWEEN-GROUPS AND WITHIN-GROUPS VARIATION

Mean square: The name used for a variance in the analysis of variance.

The analysis of variance for a one-factor between-subjects design breaks down the total variation in the scores of an experiment into two parts, often called *sources*: (1) a variance that varies with both the systematic effect of an independent variable and sampling error among the group means and (2) a variance that varies only with the within-groups error variation. In the analysis of variance, however, a variance is called a *mean square*. **Mean square** (abbreviated *MS*) is another term for a variance, and it is the name used in analysis of variance.

Within-groups error variance: The variance of the scores in a group calculated about the group mean.

Figure 10–1 helps to conceptualize these variances. Panel (a) of this figure presents a frequency distribution of all 15 scores from Table 10–1. The total variation of these scores is the variance of the scores around the grand mean of 14. Panels (b), (c), and (d) present frequency distributions of the scores within each group for the incomplete outline, outline, and detailed drawing groups, respectively. Notice that, although the subjects within each group received the same treatment condition, the scores within a group vary about the group mean. The within-groups variation is given by the variance of the scores around their respective group means. In analysis of variance, this variation is called **within-groups error variance**, or simply **error variance**, and is measured by MS_{Error}. The term *error* is used to indicate that scores within a group are not all identical, even though all subjects within a group received the same treatment.

Between-groups variance: The variance calculated using the variation of the group means about the grand mean.

The variability between groups is reflected in the differences of the group means (i.e., $\overline{X}_{A1}$, $\overline{X}_{A2}$, and $\overline{X}_{A3}$) from the grand mean, $\overline{X}_G$. This variation in group means is called **between-groups variance** and is measured by MS_A.

FIGURE 10-1

(a) A frequency distribution of all 15 scores from Table 10-1. (b) A frequency distribution of the incomplete outline drawing group (A_1) scores. (c) A frequency distribution of the outline drawing group (A_2) scores. (d) A frequency distribution of the detail drawing group (A_3) scores.

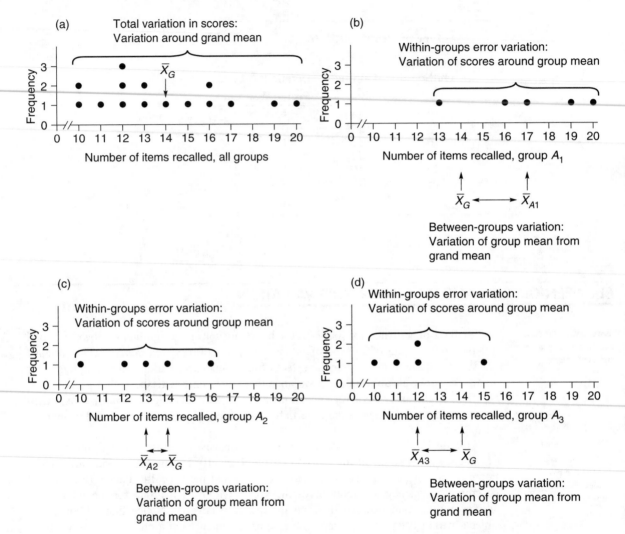

The group means in an experiment may differ from each other for two reasons: (1) the effect of an independent variable and (2) sampling error. Thus MS_A reflects systematic variation among the means of the treatment groups due to the effect of the independent variable and variation due to sampling error.

The sorting of the total variation into between-groups variance and within-groups error variance results in a test statistic called F, named after Sir Ronald A. Fisher (1890–

1962), a British statistician who developed the concepts of analysis of variance. The F statistic is a ratio of MS_A to MS_{Error} and is expressed as

$$F = \frac{MS_A}{MS_{\text{Error}}}.$$

The numerator of the F ratio, MS_A, measures the effect of the independent variable as well as sampling error among the group means. The denominator, MS_{Error}, measures only error variation of scores within treatment conditions. If the independent variable has no effect, then the variation among the treatment group means will be due only to sampling error. Consequently, MS_A and MS_{Error} will be about the same, and the F ratio will be about 1.00. But if the independent variable has an effect, it will increase the differences among sample means beyond the differences expected from sampling error alone. In this instance, the between-groups variance of the numerator, MS_A, will be greater than the within-groups variance of the denominator, MS_{Error}, and the F ratio will be larger than 1.00. Thus F increases in value as a treatment has an effect. Accordingly, the F statistic provides the basis for a statistical hypothesis test.

OBTAINING THE F RATIO

In the following section I derive the variances that enter into the F ratio in order to provide a conceptual understanding of ANOVA. If you were to perform an analysis of variance on an actual set of data, you would use the computationally easier formulas given in the supplement to this chapter or a computer data analysis program. The computational formulas give no insight into the analysis of variance, but they ease considerably the computations involved.

The F statistic requires two measures of the variability of scores, MS_A and MS_{Error}. In Chapter 5, I defined a variance, or a MS, as $SS/(n-1)$, where SS stands for sum of squares. The denominator, $n-1$, corresponds to the degrees of freedom (df) involved in obtaining the variance estimate. Thus the formula for a variance providing an unbiased estimate of the population variance is $MS = SS/df$. To obtain MS_A and MS_{Error}, we find SS_A and SS_{Error}, respectively, from the scores and then divide each sum of squares by its df. The first step, obtaining the sums of squares, begins by partitioning a score.

Partitioning a Score

The analysis of variance sorts the total variation of the scores in an experiment into between-groups and within-groups variances by assuming a simple model for a subject's score. Although the example uses only three levels of an independent variable, the model introduced here applies to the analysis of variance for any number of levels of a one-factor between-subjects design.

The scores in Table 10–1 are represented symbolically in Table 10–2. The symbols are similar to those used to this point. The independent variable is identified as factor A

with three levels, A_1, A_2, and A_3. The letter a represents the number of levels of factor A. For Tables 10–1 and 10–2, $a = 3$. A subject's score is represented by X_{ij}, where the subscript i represents a number identifying the subject within a group and the subscript j represents the number of the group, A_1, A_2, or A_3. For example, X_{52} is the fifth subject in group A_2. In Table 10–1, the score for this subject is 10, or $X_{52} = 10$. When it is not necessary to identify a specific subject, I drop the ij subscripts and simply use X. The sample means for each level of the independent variable are indicated by $\overline{X}_{A1}$, $\overline{X}_{A2}$, and $\overline{X}_{A3}$ or, generally, by $\overline{X}_A$. The grand mean is labeled $\overline{X}_G$. The number of scores in a level of the independent variable is represented by n_A, and the total number of scores in the experiment is represented by N. For Table 10–1, $n_{A1} = 5$, $n_{A2} = 5$, $n_{A3} = 5$, $N = 15$, $\overline{X}_{A1} = 17.0$, $\overline{X}_{A2} = 13.0$, $\overline{X}_{A3} = 12.0$, and $\overline{X}_G = 14.0$. Although analysis of variance does not require an equal number of scores in each treatment condition, having equal numbers simplifies the computations needed. All the examples in the chapter use an equal number of scores in each treatment condition.

The analysis of variance takes the total variation of a score, that is, the total amount by which a score (i.e., X_{ij}) differs from the grand mean of the scores (i.e., $\overline{X}_G$), and partitions, or divides, this total difference into two parts. One part, which becomes the between-groups variance (i.e., MS_A), varies with an effect of the independent variable and sampling error. The other part, which measures the error of individual scores about their group mean, becomes the within-groups error variance (i.e., MS_{Error}). This model for representing a score can be expressed as

$$
\begin{pmatrix} \text{Total variation} \\ \text{in a subject's} \\ \text{score} \end{pmatrix} = \begin{pmatrix} \text{Variation due} \\ \text{to factor } A \\ \text{plus sampling} \\ \text{error} \end{pmatrix} + \begin{pmatrix} \text{Variation due} \\ \text{to within-} \\ \text{groups error} \end{pmatrix}. \qquad (10\text{-}1)
$$

TABLE 10–2
Notational representation of scores from the hypothetical experiment in Table 10–1 with three levels of an independent variable, factor A. The means for each level of factor A are represented by $\overline{X}_A$ and the grand mean by $\overline{X}_G$.

Factor A			
A_1	A_2	A_3	
X_{11}	X_{12}	X_{13}	
X_{21}	X_{22}	X_{23}	
X_{31}	X_{32}	X_{33}	
X_{41}	X_{42}	X_{43}	
X_{51}	X_{52}	X_{53}	
$\overline{X}_{A1}$	$\overline{X}_{A2}$	$\overline{X}_{A3}$	$\overline{X}_G$

In terms of scores, this equation can be written as

$$X - \overline{X}_G \quad = \quad (\overline{X}_A - \overline{X}_G) \quad + \quad (X - \overline{X}_A). \qquad (10\text{--}2)$$

| Difference of a subject's score from the grand mean | Difference of the treatment group mean from the grand mean | Difference of the subject's score from its treatment group mean |

I examine each part of equation 10–2.

Total Variation

The difference of a score from the grand mean (i.e., $X - \overline{X}_G$) is the total variation of that score. As equation 10–2 indicates, a part of this variation is due to the effect of the independent variable and a part of it is due to error variation.

Variation due to the Effect of the Independent Variable and Sampling Error

The difference between a group mean and the grand mean (i.e., $\overline{X}_A - \overline{X}_G$) varies with the effect of an independent variable and with sampling error. Accordingly, it enters into the computation of MS_A.

Effect of the Independent Variable.   The analysis of variance uses the difference between each group mean and the grand mean to measure the effect of the independent variable. These differences will increase with an effect of the independent variable. A numerical illustration helps to clarify this important point.

Table 10–3 presents three possible outcomes of an experiment involving only three scores in each of two treatment groups. In panel (a) of this table, no treatment effect is present. Each group mean is equal to the grand mean. Furthermore, each of the two $\overline{X}_A - \overline{X}_G$ differences is equal to zero. A treatment effect of +2 is added to the scores of A_2 in panel (b); thus neither group mean is equal to the grand mean. This treatment effect of +2 is represented by a value of -1 for the $\overline{X}_{A1} - \overline{X}_G$ difference and a value of +1 for the $\overline{X}_{A2} - \overline{X}_G$ difference. Panel (c) presents a treatment effect of +6 added to the scores of A_2. In the analysis of variance this effect is broken into a -3 for the $\overline{X}_{A1} - \overline{X}_G$ difference and a value of +3 for the $\overline{X}_{A2} - \overline{X}_G$ difference. This demonstration illustrates that if a treatment has an effect it will be reflected in the value of the $\overline{X}_A - \overline{X}_G$ differences that can be calculated in an experiment.

Sampling Error.   In addition to any treatment effect, the group means also differ from each other because of sampling error. Even if the independent variable has no effect, I expect a group mean to differ from the grand mean simply because of sampling error. Thus any effect of the independent variable in an experiment occurs against a background of sampling error.

Variation due to Within-groups Error

The difference of an individual score from a treatment mean (i.e., $X - \overline{X}_A$) enters into the computation of MS_{Error}. It varies only with within-groups error variation in the

TABLE 10–3
Demonstration that $\overline{X}_A - \overline{X}_G$ responds to the effect of an independent variable in an experiment. Treatment means are represented by $\overline{X}_A$ and the grand mean for each set of scores by $\overline{X}_G$. The difference between each treatment group mean and the grand mean is shown at the bottom of each set of scores.
Panel (a) scores: No treatment effect is present.
Panel (b) scores: A treatment effect of +2 is present.
Panel (c) scores: A treatment effect of +6 is present.

	(a)		(b)		(c)	
	A_1	A_2	A_1	A_2	A_1	A_2
	11	12	11	14	11	18
	12	13	12	15	12	19
	13	11	13	13	13	17
$\overline{X}_A$	12	12	12	14	12	18
$\overline{X}_G$	12		13		15	
	$\overline{X}_{A1} - \overline{X}_G = 0$		$\overline{X}_{A1} - \overline{X}_G = -1$		$\overline{X}_{A1} - \overline{X}_G = -3$	
	$\overline{X}_{A2} - \overline{X}_G = 0$		$\overline{X}_{A2} - \overline{X}_G = +1$		$\overline{X}_{A2} - \overline{X}_G = +3$	

experiment. In fact, this difference was used in Chapter 5 as the numerator of the standard deviation and variance, measures of error variation among scores within a group. The numerical value of this difference does not vary with an effect of an independent variable. Because any effect of the independent variable is assumed to increase or decrease equally the scores of all subjects receiving a particular treatment, the treatment group mean will change by an equal amount. Thus $X - \overline{X}_A$ will remain constant regardless of the effect of an independent variable. For example, for the second person in A_2 of Table 10–3 [i.e., the score represented by $X_{22} = 13$ in panel (a)], the $X - \overline{X}_A$ difference remains a +1 over all panels of the table regardless of the absence or presence of a treatment effect. Thus the values of $X - \overline{X}_A$ reflect only error variation among the scores within a treatment condition.

Obtaining Mean Squares from Partitioned Scores

Partitioning a score into parts that measure between-groups and within-groups variation establishes the basis for obtaining the MS_A and MS_{Error} needed for the F statistic. Recall that the estimated population variance was found from

$$s^2 = \frac{\Sigma(X - \overline{X})^2}{n - 1}.$$

Notice that each term in equation 10–2 resembles the numerator of a variance. By using MS in place of s^2, *sum of squares (SS)*, to represent $\Sigma(X - \overline{X})^2$ and *df* to represent $n - 1$, this variance was expressed as

$$MS = \frac{SS}{df}.$$

This formula for the variance suggests that if each difference represented in equation 10–2 were squared for each subject and then summed over all subjects in an experiment, the result would be a sum of squared differences, or SS, the numerator of a mean square. From equation 10–2, three such SS terms can be obtained. The term $X - \overline{X}_G$ leads to SS_{Total}, which represents the total difference of scores from the grand mean. The $\overline{X}_A - \overline{X}_G$ difference leads to SS_A, which is a measure of between-group variation due to an effect of the independent variable and sampling error. Finally, $X - \overline{X}_A$ leads to SS_{Error}, which is a measure of within-group error variation in the experiment.

Obtaining the Three Sums of Squares

I illustrate how equation 10–2 may be used to find the sums of squares by partitioning the score of subject 1 of group A_1 (i.e., X_{11}) of Table 10–1, which is 19. For this score, equation 10–2 becomes

$$X_{11} - \overline{X}_G = (\overline{X}_{A1} - \overline{X}_G) + (X_{11} - \overline{X}_{A1}).$$

Substituting the appropriate numerical values for X_{11}, $\overline{X}_{A1}$, and $\overline{X}_G$ leads to

$$19.0 - 14.0 = (17.0 - 14.0) + (19.0 - 17.0),$$
$$(+5.0) \quad = \quad (+3.0) \quad + \quad (+2.0).$$

The partitioning shows that the score differs from the grand mean (i.e., $X_{11} - \overline{X}_G = +5.0$) as much as it does because of the treatment condition that the subject is in (reflected in $\overline{X}_{A1} - \overline{X}_G = +3.0$) and because of the unsystematic influences of error or chance factors (reflected in $X_{11} - \overline{X}_{A1} = +2.0$).

To obtain the SS, each subject's score is similarly partitioned as shown in Table 10–4 for the 15 scores of Table 10–1. Table 10–4 may appear intimidating; but the computations in the table require only addition, subtraction, and multiplication and proceed in a step-by-step fashion. Follow each step carefully.

Step 1.   The scores of all 15 subjects in the experiment are partitioned following equation 10–2.

Step 2.   The numerical differences are found for each score.

Step 3.   Each of the positive and negative differences found in step 2 is squared.

Step 4.   The values of the squared differences are summed over the 15 values in each of the columns. The result is three sums of squares:

$$SS_{Total} = 134.00,$$
$$SS_A = 70.00,$$
$$SS_{Error} = 64.00.$$

As shown in step 4, the SS_{Total} is represented mathematically by

$$\sum_{j=1}^{a=3} \sum_{i=1}^{n_A=5} (X - \overline{X}_G)^2.$$

TABLE 10–4

Obtaining sums of squares for a one-factor between-subjects analysis of variance. The scores used are those in Table 10–1.

Step 1: Partition scores for the 15 subjects using the following equation.

		$X - \overline{X}_G$	=	$(\overline{X}_A - \overline{X}_G)$	+	$(X - \overline{X}_A)$
Scores	X_{11}	$19 - 14$	=	$(17 - 14)$	+	$(19 - 17)$
in A_1	X_{21}	$13 - 14$	=	$(17 - 14)$	+	$(13 - 17)$
	X_{31}	$16 - 14$	=	$(17 - 14)$	+	$(16 - 17)$
	X_{41}	$17 - 14$	=	$(17 - 14)$	+	$(17 - 17)$
	X_{51}	$20 - 14$	=	$(17 - 14)$	+	$(20 - 17)$
Scores	X_{12}	$14 - 14$	=	$(13 - 14)$	+	$(14 - 13)$
in A_2	X_{22}	$13 - 14$	=	$(13 - 14)$	+	$(13 - 13)$
	X_{32}	$16 - 14$	=	$(13 - 14)$	+	$(16 - 13)$
	X_{42}	$12 - 14$	=	$(13 - 14)$	+	$(12 - 13)$
	X_{52}	$10 - 14$	=	$(13 - 14)$	+	$(10 - 13)$
Scores	X_{13}	$15 - 14$	=	$(12 - 14)$	+	$(15 - 12)$
in A_3	X_{23}	$10 - 14$	=	$(12 - 14)$	+	$(10 - 12)$
	X_{33}	$11 - 14$	=	$(12 - 14)$	+	$(11 - 12)$
	X_{43}	$12 - 14$	=	$(12 - 14)$	+	$(12 - 12)$
	X_{53}	$12 - 14$	=	$(12 - 14)$	+	$(12 - 12)$

Step 2: Perform the subtractions in step 1 to obtain numerical differences for each subject.

		$X - \overline{X}_G$	=	$(\overline{X}_A - \overline{X}_G)$	+	$(X - \overline{X}_A)$
Scores	X_{11}	$+5$	=	$+3$	+	$+2$
in A_1	X_{21}	-1	=	$+3$	+	-4
	X_{31}	$+2$	=	$+3$	+	-1
	X_{41}	$+3$	=	$+3$	+	0
	X_{51}	$+6$	=	$+3$	+	$+3$
Scores	X_{12}	0	=	-1	+	$+1$
in A_2	X_{22}	-1	=	-1	+	0
	X_{32}	$+2$	=	-1	+	$+3$
	X_{42}	-2	=	-1	+	-1
	X_{52}	-4	=	-1	+	-3
Scores	X_{13}	$+1$	=	-2	+	$+3$
in A_3	X_{23}	-4	=	-2	+	-2
	X_{33}	-3	=	-2	+	-1
	X_{43}	-2	=	-2	+	0
	X_{53}	-2	=	-2	+	0

(Continued)

TABLE 10–4
Continued

Step 3: Square each difference.

		$(X - \overline{X}_G)^2$	$(\overline{X}_A - \overline{X}_G)^2$	$(X - \overline{X}_A)^2$
Scores	X_{11}	25	9	4
in A_1	X_{21}	1	9	16
	X_{31}	4	9	1
	X_{41}	9	9	0
	X_{51}	36	9	9
Scores	X_{12}	0	1	1
in A_2	X_{22}	1	1	0
	X_{32}	4	1	9
	X_{42}	4	1	1
	X_{52}	16	1	9
Scores	X_{13}	1	4	9
in A_3	X_{23}	16	4	4
	X_{33}	9	4	1
	X_{43}	4	4	0
	X_{53}	4	4	0

Step 4: Sum the squared differences for each partition over all subjects.

$$\sum_{j=1}^{a=3} \sum_{i=1}^{n_A=5} (X - \overline{X}_G)^2 = \sum_{j=1}^{a=3} \sum_{i=1}^{n_A=5} (\overline{X}_A - \overline{X}_G)^2 + \sum_{j=1}^{a=3} \sum_{i=1}^{n_A=5} (X - \overline{X}_A)^2$$

$$134.00 = 70.00 + 64.00$$

$$SS_{Total} = SS_A + SS_{Error}$$

The double summation sign indicates that the squared differences [i.e., $(X - \overline{X}_G)^2$] are to be summed over all subjects in each treatment group (from the first subject, $i = 1$, to the last subject, n_A, in a particular group) and over all groups (from the first level of the independent variable, $j = 1$, to the last level, a). In the example there are five scores in each group ($n_A = 5$) and three groups ($a = 3$); thus the summation limits are from $i = 1$ to $n_A = 5$ and from $j = 1$ to $a = 3$, or

$$\sum_{j=1}^{3} \sum_{i=1}^{5}.$$

Because I always sum over all subjects in a group and over all groups, the double summation sign without the limits is typically used.

Similarly, to obtain SS_A, the squared differences of the treatment group mean from the grand mean are summed over all subjects in the experiment; accordingly, SS_A is represented by

$$\Sigma\Sigma(\overline{X}_A - \overline{X}_G)^2.$$

Finally, SS_{Error} is obtained by summing each squared difference of a subject's score from the mean of his or her treatment group, or

$$\Sigma\Sigma(X - \overline{X}_A)^2.$$

An important relationship exists among the sum of squares terms and is shown at the bottom of Table 10–4. The SS_{Total} is equal to the sum of SS_A and SS_{Error}, or

$$SS_{Total} = SS_A + SS_{Error}. \tag{10–3}$$

Thus the total variation in scores of an experiment, SS_{Total}, is the result of systematic variation that occurs between groups receiving different treatments, SS_A (sometimes identified as $SS_{Between-groups}$ or $SS_{Treatments}$), and error variation that occurs within groups, SS_{Error} (sometimes expressed as $SS_{Within-groups}$).

Finding Degrees of Freedom

The final step in obtaining MS_A and MS_{Error} is to divide each SS by its df. Recall that **degrees of freedom** refers to the number of scores free to vary in the computation of a statistic. The df for each sum of squares of equation 10–3 are easily determined from this definition.

Total Degrees of Freedom. To find SS_{Total}, the grand mean, $\overline{X}_G$, must be known. Because the total sum of squares is based on the difference of every score in the experiment from the grand mean (i.e., $X - \overline{X}_G$), then one less than the total number of scores are free to vary. To illustrate, the grand mean for the 15 scores in Table 10–1 is 14.0. To obtain SS_{Total}, 14.0 is subtracted from each of the 15 scores. The sum of these 15 differences must equal 0. Thus any 14 of the 15 scores are free to vary, but the fifteenth score becomes fixed if $\overline{X}_G$ is known. Accordingly, there are 14 df associated with the SS_{Total}. In general, the **total degrees of freedom**, or df_{Total}, are equal to one less than the total number of scores analyzed. In notation,

$$df_{Total} = N - 1,$$

where N is the total number of scores in the experiment.

Degrees of Freedom for SS_A. The SS_A is computed from the differences of the means of the treatment groups (e.g., $\overline{X}_{A1}$, $\overline{X}_{A2}$, and $\overline{X}_{A3}$ for the example) from $\overline{X}_G$. For a research design with three levels of the independent variable and an equal number of scores in each condition, if $\overline{X}_G$ is known, then only two treatment means are free to vary. For example, if I know that $\overline{X}_G = 14.0$, $\overline{X}_{A1} = 17.0$, and $\overline{X}_{A3} = 12.0$, as in Table 10–1, then

$\overline{X}_{A2}$ is also known; it must equal 13.0. Any other value of $\overline{X}_{A2}$ would not be consistent with $\overline{X}_G$ equal to 14.0. Accordingly, there are 2 df for SS_A in the example.

In general, the **df for SS_A**, or **df_A**, are equal to one less than the number of levels of the independent variable. In notation,

$$df_A = a - 1,$$

where a is the number of levels of the independent variable A.

Degrees of Freedom for SS_{Error}. The SS_{Error} is based on subtracting the mean of each treatment group, $\overline{X}_A$, from the scores of all subjects within that treatment group for each group in the experiment. Thus, for each level of the independent variable, after $\overline{X}_A$ is determined, only $n_A - 1$ scores are free to vary within that level. In Table 10–1, if $\overline{X}_A$ is known, only four of the five scores are free to vary within each treatment condition A_1, A_2, and A_3. Because there are three levels of the independent variable and four scores free to vary within each level, there are 12 df for SS_{Error} (4 df for A1 plus 4 df for A_2 plus 4 df for A_3 equals 12).

In general, where a is the number of levels of the independent variable and there are n_A scores within each level of the independent variable, the **df for SS_{Error}** or **df_{Error}** = **$a(n_A - 1)$**. Because $(a)(n)$ equals the total number of scores (N), the df_{Error} may also be expressed as N minus a, or

$$df_{Error} = N - a.$$

Additivity of Degrees of Freedom. The degrees of freedom are additive in the same manner as the corresponding sums of squares values. Thus

$$df_{Total} = df_A + df_{Error}. \tag{10–4}$$

This relationship holds in the example, for $df_{Total} = 14$, $df_A = 2$, and $df_{Error} = 12$.

Finding Mean Squares from SS and df

The F statistic is a ratio of two mean squares, MS_A and MS_{Error}. The two required MS values are derived from the SS obtained in equation 10–3 and the df value associated with each SS. Specifically, these mean squares are

$$MS_A = \frac{SS_A}{df_A}$$

and

$$MS_{Error} = \frac{SS_{Error}}{df_{Error}}.$$

Although it is possible to obtain a MS_{Total} by dividing the SS_{Total} by the df_{Total}, this value provides no useful information in an analysis of variance and typically it is not calculated. For the scores in Table 10–1, I have found $SS_A = 70.00$ and $SS_{Error} = 64.00$ (see Table 10–4). Furthermore, $df_A = 2$ and $df_{Error} = 12$. Consequently,

$$MS_A = \frac{SS_A}{df_A} = \frac{70.00}{2} = 35.000$$

and

$$MS_{Error} = \frac{SS_{Error}}{df_{Error}} = \frac{64.00}{12} = 5.333.$$

Computing the F Statistic

At the beginning of this chapter the F statistic was defined as

$$F = \frac{MS_A}{MS_{Error}}.$$

I now have found MS_A and MS_{Error} for the scores of Table 10–1: $MS_A = 35.000$ and $MS_{Error} = 5.333$. Thus

$$F_{obs} = \frac{35.000}{5.333} = 6.563$$

or

$$F_{obs} = 6.56 \quad \text{rounded to two decimal places,}$$

where F_{obs} is used to indicate the value of F observed from the scores analyzed. Notice that because MS_A and MS_{Error} are based on sum of squares values, which must always be positive, F, too, must always be positive. A negative value of F indicates a mistake in calculations.

The numerical values of an analysis of variance are frequently summarized in a table identifying the sources of variation; SS, df, and MS values; and the value of F_{obs}. Table 10–5 illustrates how such a summary table is organized using the numerical values obtained from the data of Table 10–1. The value of F is carried to two decimal places in a summary table, and values of the SS and MS are carried to two or more decimal places as needed to minimize rounding error. Table 10–6 summarizes the definitional formulas for the SS, df, and MS. I discuss how to interpret and use this information shortly.

TESTING YOUR KNOWLEDGE 10–1

1. Define: a, between-groups variance, df_A, df_{Error}, df_{Total}, factor A, MS_A, MS_{Error}, N, n_A, one-factor multilevel designs, SS_A, SS_{Error}, SS_{Total}, within-groups variance, $X - \overline{X}_G$, $\overline{X}_A - \overline{X}_G$, $X - \overline{X}_A$.
2. What is the limitation of a t test for analyzing the data of an experiment?
3. What is the test statistic used in analysis of variance?
4. Write the general equation for the F statistic.

TABLE 10–5
Numerical summary of the analysis of variance on the scores in Table 10–1.

Source	SS	df	MS	F[a]
Type of drawing (A)	70.00	2	35.000	6.56*
Error	64.00	12	5.333	
Total	134.00	14		

*$p < .05$.
[a]Statistically significant values of F are indicated by a probability level footnote on a summary table, i.e., *$p < .05$.

TABLE 10–6
Summary of definitional formulas for a one-factor between-subjects analysis of variance.

Source	SS	df[a]	MS	F
Factor A	$\Sigma\Sigma(\overline{X}_A - \overline{X}_G)^2$	$a - 1$	SS_A/df_A	MS_A/MS_{Error}
Error	$\Sigma\Sigma(X - \overline{X}_A)^2$	$N - a$	SS_{Error}/df_{Error}	
Total	$\Sigma\Sigma(X - \overline{X}_G)^2$	$N - 1$	Not calculated	

[a]a = number of levels of factor A, N = total number of scores.

5. Into what two sources does a one-factor between-subjects analysis of variance break down the total variation of the scores in an experiment?
6. An experimenter used a one-factor between-subjects experiment with four levels of factor A: A_1, A_2, A_3, and A_4. There were 11 different subjects in each level. What are the values of a, n_A, and N?
7. Write the general equation for partitioning scores obtained in a one-factor between-subjects experiment.
8. Explain why the value of $\overline{X}_A - \overline{X}_G$ varies with the effect of an independent variable in an experiment.
9. Explain why the value of $X - \overline{X}_A$ varies with error variation in an experiment.
10. Complete the following equations for a one-factor between-subjects analysis of variance.
    a. $\Sigma\Sigma(X - \overline{X}_G)^2 =$
    b. $SS_{Total} =$
    c. $df_A =$
    d. $df_{Error} =$
    e. $MS_A =$
    f. $MS_{Error} =$
    g. $F =$
11. What is the value of SS_{Total} if $SS_A = 50.00$ and $SS_{Error} = 100.00$?

12. What is the value of SS_A if $SS_{Total} = 75.00$ and $SS_{Error} = 50.00$?
13. What is the value of df_{Total} if $df_A = 4$ and $df_{Error} = 75$?
14. What is the value of MS_A if $SS_A = 100.00$ and $df_A = 4$?
15. What is the value of MS_{Error} if $SS_{Error} = 760.00$ and $df_{Error} = 76$?
16. A behavioral scientist used a one-factor between-subjects design with four levels of factor A. There were 11 subjects in each level. What are the values of df_A, df_{Error}, and df_{Total}?
17. You conducted an experiment with two levels of an independent variable and three subjects in each group and obtained the following scores:

Factor A

A_1	A_2
30	34
32	36
28	32

Partition these scores following the approach illustrated in Table 10–4. Find the SS_{Total}, SS_A, and SS_{Error} and the df for each SS. Then complete a numerical summary table for the analysis.

18. You conducted an experiment with three levels of an independent variable and three subjects in each group and obtained the following scores:

Factor A

A_1	A_2	A_3
30	34	37
32	36	35
28	32	33

Partition these scores following the approach illustrated in Table 10–4. Find the SS_{Total}, SS_A, and SS_{Error} and the df for each SS. Then complete a numerical summary table for the analysis.

19. The following two tables are incomplete summary tables for a one-factor between-subjects analysis of variance. Assume an equal number of subjects in each level of the independent variable. Fill in the missing values in each table by using the relationships among SS and df given in equations 10–3 and 10–4, respectively, and the formulas in Table 10–6. Then answer these questions for each table.
   a. How many levels of the independent variable were used?
   b. How many subjects were measured in each treatment group?
   c. How many subjects participated in the study?

Table 1

Source	SS	df	MS	F
Factor A	50.00	1	————	————
Error	260.00	26	————	
Total	————	————		

Table 2

Source	SS	df	MS	F
Factor A	_____	3	6.00	_____
Error	_____	76	_____	
Total	170.00	79		

STATISTICAL HYPOTHESIS TESTING WITH F_{obs}

The value of F_{obs} allows us to decide if the treatment means differ significantly. To understand how this decision is made, it is necessary to review briefly the factors influencing MS_A and MS_{Error} and the relationship of MS_A to MS_{Error}.

Factors Affecting the Value of MS_A and MS_{Error}

MS_A

The value of MS_A is given by

$$MS_A = \frac{SS_A}{df_A},$$

where

$$SS_A = \Sigma\Sigma(\overline{X}_A - \overline{X}_G)^2.$$

As I indicated in the discussion of partitioning a score, two sources of variation affect the extent of the difference between a group mean and a grand mean and thus the value of SS_A in any experiment: (1) the effect of the independent variable and (2) sampling error. Hence MS_A, too, varies with the effect of the independent variable and sampling error. Because MS_A increases with an effect of an independent variable, it is used as a measure of the systematic variance created by the independent variable.

MS_{Error}

The MS_{Error} is obtained by

$$\frac{\Sigma\Sigma(X - \overline{X}_A)^2}{df_{Error}}$$

and measures only the within-groups error variation in an experiment. It is not affected by an independent variable. As I indicated earlier, this result occurs because any systematic changes in scores due to a treatment effect will also be accompanied by a corresponding increase or decrease in the treatment group mean. Thus the difference between a subject's score and the group mean, $(X - \overline{X}_A)$, will not change with a treatment effect. Hence MS_{Error} measures only within-groups error variation in the scores of an experiment. The factors affecting each mean square are summarized in Table 10–7.

TABLE 10–7
Factors affecting MS_A and MS_{Error} in an experiment.

Mean Square	Affected by:
MS_A	The effect of the independent variable
	Sampling error
MS_{Error}	Within-groups error variation

The Relationship of MS_A and MS_{Error}

Unbiased Estimates.   Both MS_A and MS_{Error} are unbiased estimates of the population variance of scores, σ^2. They are unbiased because to obtain each MS the sum of squares is divided by degrees of freedom rather than by the actual number of scores involved in the computation of the variance. As unbiased estimates, neither MS should be systematically smaller nor larger than σ^2 when error variation alone is responsible for the variability in scores on which the estimate is based.

Independent Estimates. MS_A and MS_{Error} are also independent estimates of the population variance. **Independent estimates** mean that either mean square may change in value without affecting the value of the other, a point demonstrated in the discussion of the factors affecting SS values. These characteristics of MS_A and MS_{Error} lead to the following expectations of the value of F.

- *Expected value of F when an independent variable has no effect:* If an independent variable has no effect, then only error variation occurs in an experiment. In this circumstance I expect MS_A and MS_{Error} to estimate only error variation and thus to be about equal. Accordingly, the value of F should be equal to about 1.00.
- *Expected value of F when an independent variable has an effect:* When an independent variable does produce an effect, then MS_A responds to the systematic variation contributed by the independent variable in addition to the existing sampling error. Consequently, MS_A will be larger than MS_{Error}, and F_{obs} will be greater than 1.00. This relationship allows using F in a statistical hypothesis test.

Statistical Decision Making from the F Ratio

Statistical testing with the F follows the familiar steps:

- A null hypothesis, H_0, and an alternative hypothesis, H_1, are formulated.
- The sampling distribution of F, assuming that H_0 is true, is obtained. This distribution is given in Table A–3.
- A significance level is selected.

- A critical value of F, identified as F_{crit}, is found from the sampling distribution of F given in Table A–3.
- A rejection region is located in the sampling distribution of F.
- The F ratio, identified as F_{obs}, is calculated from the sample data.
- A decision to reject or not reject H_0 is made on the basis of whether or not F_{obs} falls into the rejection region.

Statistical Hypotheses

Null Hypothesis.   For an experiment with three levels of an independent variable, the null hypothesis tested in an analysis of variance is that the populations from which the three samples were selected have the same means and is written

$$H_0: \mu_{A1} = \mu_{A2} = \mu_{A3}.$$

This null hypothesis represents the situation that exists if the independent variable has no effect. If H_0 is true for an experiment, then any observed difference among the group means is due only to sampling error.

The number of population means identified in the null hypothesis always corresponds to the number of levels of the independent variable. If an experiment involves five levels of an independent variable, then H_0 is written

$$H_0: \mu_{A1} = \mu_{A2} = \mu_{A3} = \mu_{A4} = \mu_{A5}.$$

Alternative Hypothesis.   The alternative hypothesis, H_1, is

$$H_1: \text{The } \mu_A\text{'s are not all equal,}$$

regardless of the number of population means involved in the null hypothesis. The alternative hypothesis states a situation that exists if the independent variable has an effect.

The Sampling Distribution of F

The decision to reject or not reject H_0 depends on how rare or unlikely a value of F_{obs} would be if H_0 were true. The sampling distribution of a statistic provides the probability of values of the statistic when H_0 is true. Thus the probability of obtaining a certain value of F_{obs} if H_0 is true is determined from the sampling distribution of the F statistic. There is not just one sampling distribution of F, however, for the sampling distribution of F depends on the number of levels of the independent variable and the number of scores in each treatment group. Specifically, the sampling distribution of F varies with the degrees of freedom for the numerator (i.e., df_A) and the denominator (i.e., df_{Error}) of the F ratio.

As an illustration, the sampling distribution of F for the example experiment with 2 df for the numerator (i.e., 2 df for df_A) and 12 degrees of freedom for the denominator (i.e., 12 df for df_{Error}) is illustrated in Figure 10–2. This distribution is positively skewed and its lowest value is zero; the value of F obtained if the sample means are equal to each other and the resulting MS_A value is zero. The most probable value of F is about 1.00, for if H_0 is true, then MS_A should be about the same as MS_{Error}. There is no upper limit to the values that F may attain; F may take on any value between 0 and positive infinity. Because the probability of obtaining a value of F between 0 and positive infinity is 1.00, the area under the distribution is equal to 1.00.

Selecting a Significance Level

The significance level is a probability value that provides the criterion for rejecting H_0. As I have discussed, the significance level usually adopted in behavioral science research is either $\alpha = .05$ or $\alpha = .01$. I illustrate locating a rejection region for a .05 significance level in Figure 10–2.

Locating the Rejection Region for F

The rejection region represents values of F that have a probability equal to or less than α if H_0 is true. Thus the rejection region identifies values of F_{obs} that meet the criterion for rejecting H_0. The rejection region for F_{obs} is always in the right tail of the sampling distribution for F, as shown in Figure 10–2. We can see why the rejection region is located here by recalling how the value of F_{obs} varies with the effect of an independent variable.

If an independent variable has no effect and therefore H_0 is true, then it is expected that MS_A and MS_{Error} will be nearly equal; consequently, F_{obs} should be about 1.00. If the independent variable does have an effect and therefore H_0 is not true, then MS_A will be larger than MS_{Error}, and F_{obs} will become greater than 1.00. In order to reject the null hypothesis, then, F_{obs} must be sufficiently larger than 1.00 so that the probability

FIGURE 10–2
Theoretical sampling distribution of F for 2 and 12 degrees of freedom. The rejection region for $\alpha = .05$ is illustrated. The F_{crit} from Table A–3 is 3.88.

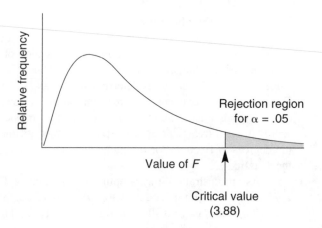

of such a value of F_{obs} occurring if H_0 were true is equal to or less than the alpha level selected. Therefore, the rejection region for F always lies among the larger values of F in the right tail of the distribution.

Critical values of F (identified as F_{crit}) identifying the lower limit of the rejection region for $\alpha = .05$ and $.01$ are presented in Appendix Table A–3. A portion of Table A–3a for the $.05$ significance level is presented in Table 10–8. This table is arranged so that the degrees of freedom for the numerator (i.e., df_A) of the F ratio appear in a row across the top of the table. The degrees of freedom for the denominator (i.e., df_{Error}) appear in the column on the left side of the table.

To locate the value of F_{crit} for the example with 2 degrees of freedom for the numerator and 12 degrees of freedom for the denominator, I find the column for 2 df and then locate the row for 12 df. This column and row intersect at the value of 3.88 (boldfaced in Table 10–8). This value is F_{crit} and locates the rejection region for F_{obs} with 2 and 12 df, as illustrated in Figure 10–2. Any value of F_{obs} with 2 and 12 df and equal to or larger than 3.88 lies in the rejection region. Values of F equal to or larger than 3.88 occur only 5 or fewer times in every 100 experiments if H_0 is true.

Decisions about the Statistical Hypotheses

The value of F_{obs} provides the basis for making decisions about the statistical hypotheses. If F_{obs} falls into the rejection region, then H_0 is rejected. And if H_0 is rejected, then H_1 must be accepted. There is a *statistically significant difference* among the sample means.

TABLE 10–8
Values of F_{crit} for $\alpha = .05$.

Degrees of Freedom for Denominator	Degrees of Freedom for Numerator				
	1	2	3	4	5
1	161.4	199.5	215.7	224.6	230.2
2	18.51	19.00	19.16	19.25	19.30
3	10.13	9.55	9.28	9.12	9.01
4	7.71	6.94	6.59	6.39	6.26
5	6.61	5.79	5.41	5.19	5.05
6	5.99	5.14	4.76	4.53	4.39
7	5.59	4.74	4.35	4.12	3.97
8	5.32	4.46	4.07	3.84	3.69
9	5.12	4.26	3.86	3.63	3.48
10	4.96	4.10	3.71	3.48	3.33
11	4.84	3.98	3.59	3.36	3.20
12	4.75	**3.88**	3.49	3.26	3.11

This table is only a portion of the complete table presented in Appendix A–3.
Reprinted with permission from Table VI.1, Percentage Points, F-Distribution, *CRC Handbook of Tables for Probability and Statistics* (2nd ed.). Copyright 1968, CRC Press, Inc., Boca Raton, Florida.

If F_{obs} does not fall into the rejection region, then I fail to reject H_0 and do not accept H_1. The differences among the sample means are *not statistically significant*, or simply *nonsignificant*.

Statistically Significant Difference.   To illustrate a statistically significant difference, I use the example experiment on the retention of drawings. In this experiment I manipulated three types of drawings to find if the type of drawing affected recall of the items depicted in the drawings. The mean number of items recalled as a function of type of drawing is given next.

	Type of Drawing (A)		
	Incomplete Outline (A_1)	Outline (A_2)	Detailed (A_3)
$\overline{X}_A$	17.0	13.0	12.0

The analysis of variance on the scores of Table 10–1 resulted in F_{obs} (2, 12) = 6.56 (see Table 10–5). For 2, 12 df, F_{crit} at the .05 level is 3.88. F_{obs} is larger than F_{crit} and thus falls into the rejection region. Accordingly, I reject the null hypothesis

$$H_0: \ \mu_{A1} = \mu_{A2} = \mu_{A3},$$

and accept the alternative

$$H_1: \text{The } \mu_A\text{'s are not all equal.}$$

We conclude that the three sample means are not all from the same population. The independent variable did affect the number of items recalled. Notice, however, that there are many ways for "H_1: The μ_A's are not all equal" to be true. The null hypothesis will be true, for example, if μ_{A1} is greater than either μ_{A2} or μ_{A3}, and μ_{A2} and μ_{A3} are equal, or if μ_{A1} is greater than μ_{A2}, and μ_{A2} is greater than μ_{A3}. Which relationship holds for the pattern of means in the example? The analysis of variance alone does not answer this question with certainty, for rejection of H_0 when there are three or more treatment groups in an experiment simply lets us conclude that there is at least one statistically significant difference among the means. A follow-up with a multiple comparison test is necessary to find the specific significant differences between the means. I discuss this test in a later section of this chapter. The decision-making procedures and corresponding conclusions for a statistically significant difference are summarized in the left column of Table 10–9.

Nonsignificant Difference.   If I fail to reject H_0 and do not accept H_1, then I have no evidence that the null hypothesis is not true. The implication for the experiment is that the independent variable had no effect. Any observed numerical differences among the means are attributed to sampling error. These decisions and conclusions are summarized in the right column of Table 10–9.

TABLE 10-9
Summary of decisions and conclusions in statistical hypothesis testing using the analysis of variance for a one-factor between-subjects design. A .05 significance level is used.

If F_{obs} falls into the rejection region for $\alpha = .05$, then:	If F_{obs} does not fall into the rejection region for $\alpha = .05$, then:
Probability of F_{obs} is less than or equal to .05, or $p \le .05$.	Probability of F_{obs} is greater than .05, or $p > .05$.
H_0 is rejected.	H_0 is not rejected.
H_1 is accepted. The sample means are not all from the same population.	H_1 is not accepted.
At least one difference between the treatment means is statistically significant at the .05 level.	There are no significant differences among the sample means at the .05 level.
It is decided that something in addition to sampling error is responsible for the differences among the sample means. In a carefully done experiment the difference is attributed to the independent variable.	It is decided that sampling error alone is the most plausible explanation for the differences among the sample means. There is no evidence that the independent variable had an effect.
Multiple comparison tests are needed if the independent variable has three or more levels.	No multiple comparison tests are needed.

Assumptions of One-factor Between-subjects Analysis of Variance

Similarly to the t test, the between-subjects analysis of variance is based on three assumptions about the scores obtained in an experiment:

1. The scores in each sample are drawn randomly from a population of scores, and each score is independent of each other score.
2. The scores in the populations sampled are normally distributed.
3. The variances of scores in the populations are equal.

These assumptions are important because the sampling distribution of F, and therefore the values of F_{crit} given in Table A–3, are generated from populations that meet these assumptions. In order for the between-subjects analysis of variance to be used, each score in the experiment must be independent of every other score. That is, every subject may be given only one level of the independent variable and contribute only one score in the experiment. If a subject is given more than one level of the independent variable and two or more scores are analyzed for a subject, then the within-subjects analysis of variance must be used. This analysis of variance is discussed in Chapter 12.

The second and third assumptions may not be met by some experiments. Violations of the second (the normal distribution of scores) and the third (the equality of variances) assumption can change the probability of obtaining a particular value of F_{obs} and thus affect the probability of making a Type I error. Violations of these assumptions are more likely to have minimal effects on the probability of making a Type I error when the following conditions are met:

- The number of subjects in each group is the same.
- The shape of the distributions of the scores for each group is about the same, and the distributions are neither very peaked nor very flat.
- The significance level is set at .05.

TESTING YOUR KNOWLEDGE 10–2

1. Define: F_{crit}, F_{obs}, rejection region.
2. What factors affect the value of MS_A in an experiment?
3. Explain why MS_A increases in value if an independent variable has an effect in an experiment.
4. What factors affect the value of MS_{Error} in an experiment?
5. Explain why the value of MS_{Error} does not change if an independent variable has an effect in an experiment.
6. What value of F_{obs} is expected if an independent variable has no effect in an experiment?
7. What is expected to happen to the value of F_{obs} if an independent variable has an effect in an experiment?
8. Write the statistical hypotheses for the F test for:
   a. Two independent groups.
   b. Four independent groups.
   c. Six independent groups.
9. To what situation in an experiment does H_0 of an analysis of variance correspond?
10. To what situation in an experiment does H_1 of an analysis of variance correspond?
11. What is the lower limit for the value of F if H_0 is true?
12. What is the upper limit for the value of F if H_0 is true?
13. This exercise provides values for df_A, df_{Error}, and F_{obs} for several hypothetical one-factor between-subjects experiments. For each set of values, obtain the value of F_{crit} for a .05 significance level from Table A–3a. Then indicate whether F_{obs} falls into the rejection region and what decision you make with respect to H_0 and H_1. If the exact df are not tabled for df_{Error}, then use the next lower tabled value.

Experiment	df_A	df_{Error}	F_{obs}
1	1	10	5.12
2	2	24	3.29
3	1	24	4.26
4	2	90	3.24
5	2	12	3.94
6	2	15	3.60
7	4	45	1.93
8	3	20	1.46
9	6	63	2.30
10	4	95	2.13

14. Identify the assumptions underlying the use of the one-factor between-subjects analysis of variance.
15. Under what conditions will violation of normality of the distribution of scores in the population have the least effect on Type I errors for a one-factor between-subjects analysis of variance?

INTERPRETING A STATISTICALLY SIGNIFICANT *F* IN A MULTILEVEL DESIGN

Multiple Comparison Tests

Multiple comparison tests: Statistical tests used to make pairwise comparisons to find which means differ significantly from one another in a one-factor multilevel design.

Earlier I indicated that rejecting H_0 when there are three or more levels of an independent variable in an experiment leads us to conclude that there is at least one statistically significant difference among the means. But the analysis does not identify specifically which means differ significantly from which other means. To decide which pairs of means differ significantly, we use multiple comparison tests. **Multiple comparison tests** are statistical tests used to make pairwise comparisons to find which means differ significantly from one another in a one-factor multilevel design.

Given the three sample means from the experiment on the effect of type of drawing on recall of details, I can make three two-mean comparisons:

$$\overline{X}_{A1} \quad \text{compared to} \quad \overline{X}_{A2},$$
$$\overline{X}_{A1} \quad \text{compared to} \quad \overline{X}_{A3},$$
$$\overline{X}_{A2} \quad \text{compared to} \quad \overline{X}_{A3}.$$

Pairwise comparisons: Statistical comparisons involving two means.

Because these comparisons each involve two means, they are called **pairwise comparisons**. By performing statistical tests on these three pairwise comparisons, I can find which pairs of means differ significantly.

One way of making pairwise comparisons would be to use t_{ind} to conduct three *t* tests, one for each comparison. From the outcome of these three tests, I could determine which means differ significantly from each other. The issue is not so easily resolved, however, because of the probability of a Type I error occurring in the comparisons to be made. Recall that a Type I error occurs when H_0 is actually true, but is rejected in the statistical hypothesis test. To keep the probability of making a Type I error low, researchers usually set the significance level at .05 or .01. For the overall analysis of variance on the example (reported in Table 10–5), the probability of a Type I error is equal to the value of α, or .05. But when conducting multiple comparisons, an investigator runs many more statistical tests, the exact number depending on the number of comparisons to be made. Consider, for example, conducting a t_{ind} on each of the three pairwise comparisons in the example experiment. For each *t*

Error rate in an experiment: The probability of making at least one Type I error in the statistical comparisons conducted in an experiment.

test the probability of a Type I error is equal to α. Hence the probability of making at least one Type I error among the three comparisons is about .14, an unacceptably high value. The **error rate in an experiment** is the probability of making at least one Type I error in the comparisons conducted. The error rate in an experiment increases very rapidly with a growing number of comparisons. As an example, consider using the t test for five pairwise comparisons with $\alpha = .05$ for each comparison. If H_0 is true, then the probability of at least one Type I error in the five comparisons is equal to about .23. This error rate is obviously too high for most researchers. To control this error rate, alternatives to the t test have been developed for making multiple comparisons. I present one specific test for making one type of multiple comparisons, post hoc comparisons.

Post hoc comparisons: Statistical tests that make all possible pairwise comparisons after a statistically significant F_{obs} has occurred for the overall analysis of variance.

Post hoc comparisons make all possible pairwise comparisons after a statistically significant F_{obs} has occurred for the overall analysis of variance. The term *post hoc* is Latin for *after this* or *after the fact*. Its use here means a comparison made after F_{obs} is statistically significant. If F_{obs} of the overall analysis of variance is nonsignificant and H_0 is not rejected, no further data analysis is needed and post hoc comparisons are not carried out. Many comparison tests have been developed for different purposes; I present only the Tukey HSD test.

The Tukey HSD Test for Post Hoc Comparisons

Critical difference (CD): The minimum numerical difference between two treatment means that is statistically significant.

The Tukey HSD test (HSD represents *honestly significant difference*) provides a **critical difference** (abbreviated **CD**) that specifies the minimum difference between two treatment means that is statistically significant at the α level chosen. The absolute value of an observed difference in a pairwise comparison of means is compared with the Tukey *CD*. If the absolute value of the observed difference between the means is equal to or larger than the *CD*, then the sample means differ significantly and are treated as representing different populations.

The *CD* for the Tukey HSD test is found from

$$CD = q\sqrt{\frac{MS_{Error}}{n_A}},$$

where

- q, the *studentized range statistic*, is a numerical value that depends on (1) the level of α selected, (2) the number of levels of the independent variable, and (3) the *df* for MS_{Error} in the analysis of variance. Values of q are given in Table A–4 for $\alpha = .01$ and $\alpha = .05$ for up to 10 levels of an independent variable.
- MS_{Error} is the error term from the overall analysis of variance.
- n_A is the number of scores in each treatment condition. The values of n_A for each treatment condition must be equal to use this formula.

Obtaining the Tukey *CD*

I illustrate calculating the Tukey HSD *CD* with the example scores given in Table 10–1 and the analysis of variance of those scores summarized in Table 10–5. The F_{obs}, 6.56, is statistically significant at the .05 level; thus I reject H_0: $\mu_{A1} = \mu_{A2} = \mu_{A3}$ and accept H_1: The μ_A's are not all equal. The overall analysis of variance indicates that there is at least one significant difference among the three means being compared. To find specifically which means differ from each other, I will calculate the Tukey HSD *CD*.

From the analysis of variance summarized in Table 10–5, $MS_{\text{Error}} = 5.333$. The number of scores in each treatment group is 5; thus $n_A = 5$. The value of q is obtained from Table A–4. This table requires knowing (1) the number of levels of the independent variable a (in the example $a = 3$) and (2) the df_{Error} from the analysis of variance (in this case, 12). At the .05 level, for $a = 3$ and 12 df_{Error}, $q = 3.77$. Substituting these values into the formula for the *CD* leads to

$$CD = q\sqrt{\frac{MS_{\text{Error}}}{n_A}}.$$

$$= 3.77\sqrt{\frac{5.333}{5}}$$

$$= 3.77\sqrt{1.067}$$

$$= (3.77)(1.033)$$

$$= 3.89$$

$$= 3.9 \quad \text{rounded to one decimal place.}$$

Interpreting the Tukey *CD*

The *CD* for the Tukey test for the example is 3.9. A difference between two treatment means in Table 10–1 equal to or larger in absolute value (i.e., the value of the difference ignoring the + or − sign) than 3.9 items recalled is statistically significant at the .05 level. The three pairwise comparisons, the absolute values of each comparison, the statistical hypothesis, and the decision for each hypothesis are shown in Table 10–10.

Notice that two pairwise comparisons are larger than 3.9 in absolute value: $\overline{X}_{A1}$ versus $\overline{X}_{A2}$ (17.0 − 13.0 = 4.0) and $\overline{X}_{A1}$ versus $\overline{X}_{A3}$ (17.0 − 12.0 = 5.0). Each of these comparisons reveals a statistically significant difference between the means compared. The absolute value of the comparison of $\overline{X}_{A2}$ versus $\overline{X}_{A3}$ (13.0 − 12.0 = 1.0) is less than 3.9. Thus the difference between outline and detailed drawings is nonsignificant. Hence the Tukey test leads to the conclusion that recall for incomplete outline drawings ($\overline{X}_{A1}$) is significantly greater than recall for outline drawings ($\overline{X}_{A2}$) or detail drawings ($\overline{X}_{A3}$), but recall for outline drawings ($\overline{X}_{A2}$) does not differ from that of detailed drawings ($\overline{X}_{A3}$).

This result provides support for the effort hypothesis of memory processing presented at the opening of this chapter. The incomplete outline drawings, requiring the most effort to process, were best recalled. The result provides no evidence to support the elaboration hypothesis, which predicted that detailed drawings would be best recalled.

TABLE 10-10
Application of the Tukey HSD *CD* to the pairwise comparisons of the example experiment.

Comparison	Absolute Value of Comparison	Statistical Hypotheses	Decision
$\overline{X}_{A1}$ vs. $\overline{X}_{A2}$ (17.0 − 13.0)	4.0	$H_0: \mu_{A1} = \mu_{A2}$ $H_1: \mu_{A1} \neq \mu_{A2}$	Reject Accept
$\overline{X}_{A1}$ vs. $\overline{X}_{A3}$ (17.0 − 12.0)	5.0	$H_0: \mu_{A1} = \mu_{A3}$ $H_1: \mu_{A1} \neq \mu_{A3}$	Reject Accept
$\overline{X}_{A2}$ vs. $\overline{X}_{A3}$ (13.0 − 12.0)	1.0	$H_0: \mu_{A2} = \mu_{A3}$ $H_1: \mu_{A2} \neq \mu_{A3}$	Fail to reject Do not accept

A_1 = incomplete outline drawing, A_2 = outline drawing, A_3 = detailed drawing.

Two Instances When a Post Hoc Test Is Not Needed

There are two instances when using a one-factor analysis of variance that post hoc tests are not needed. The first is when F_{obs} for the analysis of variance is nonsignificant. A nonsignificant F_{obs} indicates there are no significant differences between any of the means in the analysis. Consequently, no post hoc test is needed to find these differences.

The second instance is when there are only two levels of the independent variable. If F_{obs} is significant for this analysis, then $H_0: \mu_{A1} = \mu_{A2}$ is rejected and H_1: The μ_A's are not equal is accepted. Obviously, the only means that can differ significantly in this instance are $\overline{X}_{A1}$ and $\overline{X}_{A2}$. Thus no further test is needed on these means.

MEASURING THE STRENGTH OF A TREATMENT EFFECT

Similarly to the *t* test, the analysis of variance indicates whether an independent variable has an effect on the dependent variable of an experiment, but it does not indicate the size of that effect. Again, η^2 may be used as a strength-of-effect measure when a statistically significant value of F_{obs} occurs.

Calculating Eta Squared for the Analysis of Variance

For a one-factor between-subjects analysis of variance, η^2 may be obtained from two alternative formulas. If sums of squares values are known, η^2 is given by

$$\eta^2 = \frac{SS_A}{SS_{Total}}.$$

When only F_{obs} and df are known for an analysis of variance, η^2 can be obtained by

$$\eta^2 = \frac{(df_A)(F_{obs})}{(df_A)(F_{obs}) + df_{Error}}.$$

Example of Calculating η^2 for the One-factor Between-subjects Analysis of Variance

An η^2 may be calculated for the example problem either from the SS values or the F_{obs} and df values of the analysis of variance summarized in Table 10–5.

η^2 from SS Values

$$\eta^2 = \frac{SS_A}{SS_{Total}}$$

$$= \frac{70.00}{134.00}$$

$$= .52 \quad \text{rounded to two decimal places.}$$

η^2 from F_{obs} and df Values

$$\eta^2 = \frac{(df_A)(F_{obs})}{(df_A)(F_{obs}) + df_{Error}}$$

$$= \frac{(2)(6.56)}{(2)(6.56) + 12}$$

$$= \frac{13.12}{25.12} = .52 \quad \text{rounded to two decimal places.}$$

This η^2 indicates that a 52 percent reduction in the total variance of the scores occurs when the means of the levels of the independent variable are used to predict scores in comparison to using the grand mean as the predicted score. This independent variable accounts for a large proportion of the variance in the recall scores.

THE RELATIONSHIP BETWEEN t_{ind} AND F

The t_{ind} and the one-factor between-subjects analysis of variance lead to the same statistical decisions when analyzing data from an experiment with two levels of the independent variable. If I reject H_0 with a two-tailed t_{ind} at the .05 level, then I would also reject H_0 with an analysis of variance on the same data. The reason is that $t^2 = F$ or $t = \sqrt{F}$. This relation also holds for the tabled critical values of t and F for the analysis of two sample means when the same significance level is adopted. As an example, for $\alpha = .05$, F_{crit} for 1, 8 df is 5.32. The value of t_{crit} for 8 df and $\alpha = .05$ in a two-tailed test is

2.306, which is the square root of 5.32. Thus $(2.306)^2 = 5.32$, and $t^2 = F$. Because of this relationship between t and F, either test may be used for comparing two independent sample means; the tests provide identical outcomes and one is not preferred over the other. The advantage of analysis of variance appears only when three or more treatment conditions are being compared.

Example Problem 10–1

Using the One-factor Between-subjects Analysis of Variance with the Tukey HSD Test

Problem

Mood-state-dependent memory refers to the finding that recall of material is improved when one is in the same mood state at the time of recall as at the time of learning (Bower, 1981). Suppose that to study mood-state-dependent memory you create five equivalent groups of 10 subjects each. For each group you generate a mood state by having subjects read a series of statements designed to induce either a happy, sad, or neutral mood state. After the mood state is induced, the subjects learn a list of 15 common nouns. Twenty-four hours later the subjects return, and you again induce a mood state and have the subjects recall the previously learned list of nouns. At this recall session the mood state may be the same or different from the mood state induced at learning. The mood states induced at learning and recall for the five groups are as follows:

Mood State Group

	A_1	A_2	A_3	A_4	A_5
Mood induced at learning	Happy	Sad	Neutral	Happy	Sad
Mood induced at recall	Happy	Sad	Neutral	Sad	Happy

Mood-state-dependent memory predicts that the groups having congruent learning and recall states (i.e., groups A_1, A_2, and A_3) should have greater recall of the list of nouns than groups having different learning and recall mood states (i.e., groups A_4 and A_5). Suppose that you obtained the numbers of items recalled for each group as shown in Table 10–11. Which group means differ significantly from each other at the .05 level?

Solution   The design is a one-factor between-subjects design with five levels of the independent variable, mood state group. The first step in data analysis is to conduct a one-factor between-subjects analysis of variance on the scores. If F_{obs} is statistically significant, I will use the Tukey HSD test to find the statistically significant pairwise differences between the treatment means.

Statistic to Be Used: $F = MS_A/MS_{Error}$.

TABLE 10–11
Number of nouns correctly recalled as a function of mood state group.

	A_1	A_2	A_3	A_4	A_5
	8	14	9	5	6
	12	13	12	9	9
	12	6	7	6	8
	7	9	7	8	8
	10	12	11	4	5
	9	10	6	6	4
	13	8	10	10	5
	8	7	8	3	7
	14	11	13	7	7
	11	9	10	3	3
$\overline{X}_A$	10.40	9.90	9.30	6.10	6.20
s_A	2.37	2.60	2.31	2.42	1.93

Assumptions for Use:
1. The subjects were sampled randomly and independently from a population.
2. Item recall is normally distributed in the population.
3. The variances for item recall are equal in the populations sampled.

Statistical Hypotheses: H_0: $\mu_{A1} = \mu_{A2} = \mu_{A3} = \mu_{A4} = \mu_{A5}$.
H_1: The μ_A's are not all equal.

Significance Level: $\alpha = .05$.

df:
$$df_A = a - 1 = 5 - 1 = 4$$
$$df_{\text{Error}} = N - a = 50 - 5 = 45$$
$$df_{\text{Total}} = N - 1 = 50 - 1 = 49$$

Critical Value of F: $F_{\text{crit}}(4, 45) = 2.61$. A value of 45 df for the denominator is not presented in Table A–3a. I used the critical value for the next lower tabled df for df_{Error}, 40.

Rejection Region: Values of F_{obs} equal to or greater than 2.61.

Calculation: The analysis of variance may be calculated on the scores using the computational formulas given in the chapter supplement or by using a computer program. The formulas from the chapter supplement were used to obtain the following analysis of variance summary table.

Source	SS	df	MS	F
Mood state group (A)	171.880	4	42.970	7.86*
Error	245.900	45	5.464	
Total	417.780	49		

*$p < .05$.

Decision: $F_{obs} = 7.86$ falls into the rejection region, I reject H_0: $\mu_{A1} = \mu_{A2} = \mu_{A3} = \mu_{A4} = \mu_{A5}$ and accept H_1: The μ_A's are not all equal. Rejection of H_0 indicates that there is at least one statistically significant difference between the sample means. To find the statistically significant pairwise differences, I use the Tukey HSD test.

Tukey Test: The numerical values needed for this test are found as follows:

- q is obtained from Table A–4. There are five levels of the independent variable and 45 df for MS_{Error} from the analysis of variance summary table. Because 45 df is not given in Table A–4, I use 40 df, the next lower tabled df from the 45 df for MS_{Error}. Thus $q = 4.04$ for a .05 significance level.
- MS_{Error}, obtained from the analysis of variance, is 5.464.
- n_A, the number of scores in each of the means to be compared, is 10.

Substituting these numerical values into the formula,

$$CD = q\sqrt{\frac{MS_{Error}}{n_A}}$$

$$= 4.04\sqrt{\frac{5.464}{10}}$$

$$= 4.04\sqrt{0.5464}$$

$$= (4.04)(0.739)$$

$$= 2.99$$

$$= 3.0 \text{ words, } \quad \text{rounded to one decimal place.}$$

A difference between two means equal to or larger in absolute value than 3.0 words is statistically significant at the .05 level. The pairwise comparisons and their absolute values, the statistical hypotheses tested, and the decisions reached on the statistical hypotheses for each comparison are given in Table 10–12.

The absolute values of the comparisons of $\overline{X}_{A1}$ versus $\overline{X}_{A4}$ and $\overline{X}_{A5}$, $\overline{X}_{A2}$ versus $\overline{X}_{A4}$ and $\overline{X}_{A5}$, and $\overline{X}_{A3}$ versus $\overline{X}_{A4}$ and $\overline{X}_{A5}$ exceed the CD of 3.0 words. Each of these differences is statistically significant. The absolute values of the remaining comparisons, $\overline{X}_{A1}$ versus $\overline{X}_{A2}$, $\overline{X}_{A1}$ versus $\overline{X}_{A3}$, $\overline{X}_{A2}$ versus $\overline{X}_{A3}$, and $\overline{X}_{A4}$ versus $\overline{X}_{A5}$ are less than the CD. These comparisons are nonsignificant, and the observed differences between these sample means are best explained by sampling error.

TABLE 10–12
Application of the Tukey HSD CD to the pairwise comparisons of the five mood state groups.

Comparison	Absolute Value of Comparison	Statistical Hypotheses	Decision
$\overline{X}_{A1}$ vs. $\overline{X}_{A2}$ (10.40 − 9.90)	0.50	$H_0 : \mu_{A1} = \mu_{A2}$ $H_1: \mu_{A1} \neq \mu_{A2}$	Fail to reject Do not accept
$\overline{X}_{A1}$ vs. $\overline{X}_{A3}$ (10.40 − 9.30)	1.10	$H_0 : \mu_{A1} = \mu_{A3}$ $H_1: \mu_{A1} \neq \mu_{A3}$	Fail to reject Do not accept
$\overline{X}_{A1}$ vs. $\overline{X}_{A4}$ (10.40 − 6.10)	4.30	$H_0 : \mu_{A1} = \mu_{A4}$ $H_1: \mu_{A1} \neq \mu_{A4}$	Reject Accept
$\overline{X}_{A1}$ vs. $\overline{X}_{A5}$ (10.40 − 6.20)	4.20	$H_0 : \mu_{A1} = \mu_{A5}$ $H_1: \mu_{A1} \neq \mu_{A5}$	Reject Accept
$\overline{X}_{A2}$ vs. $\overline{X}_{A3}$ (9.90 − 9.30)	0.60	$H_0 : \mu_{A2} = \mu_{A3}$ $H_1: \mu_{A2} \neq \mu_{A3}$	Fail to reject Do not accept
$\overline{X}_{A2}$ vs. $\overline{X}_{A4}$ (9.90 − 6.10)	3.80	$H_0 : \mu_{A2} = \mu_{A4}$ $H_1: \mu_{A2} \neq \mu_{A4}$	Reject Accept
$\overline{X}_{A2}$ vs. $\overline{X}_{A5}$ (9.90 − 6.20)	3.70	$H_0 : \mu_{A2} = \mu_{A5}$ $H_1: \mu_{A2} \neq \mu_{A5}$	Reject Accept
$\overline{X}_{A3}$ vs. $\overline{X}_{A4}$ (9.30 − 6.10)	3.20	$H_0 : \mu_{A3} = \mu_{A4}$ $H_1: \mu_{A3} \neq \mu_{A4}$	Reject Accept
$\overline{X}_{A3}$ vs. $\overline{X}_{A5}$ (9.30 − 6.20)	3.10	$H_0 : \mu_{A3} = \mu_{A5}$ $H_1: \mu_{A3} \neq \mu_{A5}$	Reject Accept
$\overline{X}_{A4}$ vs. $\overline{X}_{A5}$ (6.10 − 6.20)	0.10	$H_0 : \mu_{A3} = \mu_{A5}$ $H_1: \mu_{A3} \neq \mu_{A5}$	Fail to reject Do not accept

A_1 = happy/happy group, A_2 = sad/sad group, A_3 = neutral/neutral group, A_4 = happy/sad group, and A_5 = sad/happy group.

Strength of Effect: $\eta^2 = 171.880/417.780 = .41$.

Conclusion: The Tukey test leads to the conclusion that mood state groups that had congruent learning and recall conditions (i.e., the happy/happy, sad/sad, and neutral/neutral groups) did not differ significantly from each other in recall. Each of these groups, however, recalled significantly more words than did either of the noncongruent mood state groups (i.e., the happy/sad and sad/happy groups). In addition, the happy/sad and sad/happy groups did not differ significantly from each other. Accordingly, the inferred relationship among the population means is

$$(\mu_{A1} = \mu_{A2} = \mu_{A3}) > (\mu_{A4} = \mu_{A5}).$$

The η^2 indicates that knowledge of mood state group reduces the total variance in prediction by 41 percent.

Example Problem 10–2

Using the One-factor Between-subjects Analysis of Variance: A Nonsignificant F_{obs}

Problem

Does drinking alcohol make a person more open to the effects of social influence? Gustafson (1987b) hypothesized that it does. To test this hypothesis, he had subjects estimate the length of a line that ranged in length from 5 to 100 centimeters. The subjects were then given written feedback about the length of the line and asked to give a second estimate of the line's length. Each subject estimated the length of 75 lines. For 60 of the 75 estimates, the written feedback indicated to the subject that the first estimate was incorrect. The number of times that each subject changed his or her second estimate was recorded as a measure of responsiveness to social influence. Three treatment groups were used. A control group was given a drink of only orange juice 15 minutes before the line-length-estimation task. The second group was a placebo control for expectations associated with a drink of alcohol. Subjects in this group were also given only orange juice 15 minutes before the line-length-estimation task, but they were led to believe that the drink contained alcohol. The subjects in the third group were given 0.8 milliliter of alcohol per kilogram of body weight in an orange juice solution 15 minutes before the task began. Gustafson hypothesized that the subjects in the alcohol and placebo groups would be more responsive to the written feedback and would thus change their second estimates more often than the control group. Suppose that the number of estimates changed for each of 13 subjects in a group were as given in Table 10–13. Does alcohol affect the number of estimates changed?

Solution   The design used is a one-factor between-subjects design with three levels of the independent variable, treatment group. The one-factor between-subjects analysis of variance is the appropriate statistical test for these data. I use a .05 significance level.

Statistic to Be Used: $F = MS_A/MS_{\text{Error}}$.

Assumptions for Use:
1. The subjects were sampled randomly and independently from a population.
2. The number of changes made in line-length estimates is normally distributed in the population.
3. The variances for the number of changes in line-length estimates are equal in the populations sampled.

Statistical Hypotheses: H_0: $\mu_{A1} = \mu_{A2} = \mu_{A3}$.
H_1: The μ_A's are not all equal.

TABLE 10–13
Number of changed estimates as a function of treatment group.

	Treatment Group (A)		
	Control (A_1)	Placebo (A_2)	Alcohol (A_3)
	18	17	31
	2	19	27
	11	26	16
	3	4	24
	26	18	41
	18	23	17
	9	31	12
	24	35	32
	17	11	16
	21	8	19
	14	29	35
	19	25	26
	33	38	17
$\overline{X}_A$	16.54	21.85	24.08
s_A	8.83	10.29	8.81

Significance Level: $\alpha = .05$.

df:

$$df_A = a - 1 = 3 - 1 = 2$$
$$df_{\text{Error}} = N - a = 39 - 3 = 36$$
$$df_{\text{Total}} = N - 1 = 39 - 1 = 38$$

Critical Value of F: $F_{\text{crit}} (2, 36) = 3.32$. The value of F_{crit} for 2, 36 df is not tabled in Table A–3a; hence I used F_{crit} for 2, 30 df.

Rejection Region: Values of F_{obs} equal to or greater than 3.32.

Calculation: The analysis of variance was calculated by using the computational formulas given in the chapter supplement. A summary of this analysis is as follows:

Source	SS	df	MS	F
Treatment group (A)	389.898	2	194.949	2.24
Error	3137.846	36	87.162	
Total	3527.744	38		

Decision: F_{obs} does not fall into the rejection region; thus I fail to reject H_0 and do not accept H_1.

Conclusion: The observed differences among the means are nonsignificant; the sample means of 16.54, 21.85, and 24.08 are treated as samples from the same population. There is no evidence for an effect of the independent variable. Subjects given an alcoholic drink do not change their line-length estimates more often than subjects given a placebo drink or only orange juice. The observed differences among the sample means are due only to sampling error. Because the F_{obs} was nonsignificant, there is no need for multiple comparison tests or a strength of association measure.

Example Problem 10–3

Using the One-factor Between-subjects Analysis of Variance with Two Levels of an Independent Variable

Problem

I introduced the Morinaga misalignment illusion in Statistics in Use 8–1. There I illustrated how Day and Kasperczyk (1984) used the one-sample t to determine if their subjects actually saw an illusion in certain stimulus conditions. In other aspects of the experiment, however, Day and Kasperczyk were interested in comparing the illusion magnitude under different stimulus conditions.

   To illustrate analysis of variance with two levels of an independent variable, suppose it is hypothesized that a greater illusion will be seen with a stimulus that forms angles in comparison with a stimulus that is circular. To test this research hypothesis, a psychologist created two equivalent groups by randomly assigning 20 people to one of two groups. The subjects in group A_1 were shown the stimulus created from angled points, and the subjects in group A_2 saw a stimulus made from partial circles, as illustrated in Figure 10–3. The error in perception of the stimulus was measured as the dependent variable for both groups. (See Statistics in Use 8–1 for a description of how perceptual error may be measured.) Suppose the error scores given in Table 10–14 were obtained. Does the amount of error perceived depend on the type of figure?

FIGURE 10–3
Morinaga misalignment illusion.
(a) Figure shown Group A_1.
(b) Figure shown Group A_2.

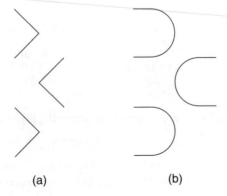

(a)   (b)

TABLE 10–14
Perceived error (in millimeters) as a function of type of figure viewed.

	Type of Figure (A)	
	Angular (A_1)	Circular (A_2)
	2.0	1.6
	1.8	1.7
	2.0	1.8
	2.1	1.6
	2.2	1.5
	1.8	1.8
	1.9	1.7
	1.8	1.8
	1.9	1.7
	1.7	1.6
$\overline{X}_A$	1.92	1.68
s_A	0.15	0.10

Solution   To find if the means differ significantly, I use the one-factor between-subjects analysis of variance. (Because only two groups are involved, a t_{ind} is also an appropriate statistical test.) I use a .05 significance level.

Statistic to Be Used: $F = MS_A/MS_{Error}$.

Assumptions for Use:
1. The subjects were sampled randomly and independently from a population.
2. The error in perceiving the illusion is normally distributed in the population.
3. The variances for the perceptual error scores are equal in the populations sampled.

Statistical Hypotheses: H_0: $\mu_{A1} = \mu_{A2}$.
  H_1: The μ_A's are not equal.

Significance Level: $\alpha = .05$.

df:
$$df_A = a - 1 = 2 - 1 = 1$$
$$df_{Error} = N - a = 20 - 2 = 18$$
$$df_{Total} = N - 1 = 20 - 1 = 19$$

Critical Value of F: $F_{crit}\ (1, 18) = 4.41$.

Rejection Region: Values of F_{obs} equal to or greater than 4.41.

Calculation: Using the computational formulas given in the chapter supplement, a summary of the analysis of variance is as follows:

Source	SS	df	MS	F
Type of figure (A)	0.288	1	0.28800	16.62
Error	0.312	18	0.01733	
Total	0.600	19		

Decision: F_{obs} falls into the rejection region; thus I reject H_0 and accept H_1.

Strength of Effect: $\eta^2 = 0.288/0.600 = .48$.

Conclusion: The means of 1.92 mm and 1.68 mm differ significantly at the .05 level; the mean of 1.92 mm is significantly larger than the mean of 1.68 mm. Because the two groups were equivalent before the independent variable was administered and extraneous variables were controlled, the observed difference between the groups is treated as due to the effect of the independent variable. Subjects see a larger illusion with angular stimuli than with circular stimuli. The Tukey HSD test is not needed because only two means are being compared. The $\eta^2 = .48$ indicates a large effect of the independent variable, accounting for 48 percent of the variance in the dependent variable. If a t_{ind} had been used in place of the analysis of variance, $t_{obs}(18) = 4.077$. This value of t_{obs} is equal to the square root of F_{obs} $(1, 18) = 16.62$. This t is statistically significant at the .05 level and leads to the same conclusion as the analysis of variance.

STATISTICS IN USE 10–1

The Effectiveness of Scrambled Answers: Using the One-factor Analysis of Variance

After taking multiple-choice examinations, students often are given feedback about the correct alternative for a question. One purpose for giving the feedback is for students to learn the correct answer and to be able to answer the question correctly in the future. What form of feedback best enhances this learning? Lhyle and Kulhavy (1987) hypothesized that the effectiveness of feedback depends on the amount of effort needed to cognitively process the correct answers. To test this hypothesis, they created three equivalent groups with 20 undergraduate students randomly assigned to each group. Each group was given a learning program on the human eye and 20 multiple-choice questions on the material in this program. After completing the multiple-choice items, the groups were given different forms of feedback on the correct answers. The control group, group A_1, was given no feedback on the correct answers. A repeated-answer group, group A_2, was given the items and the correct answers twice. A scrambled-answer group, group A_3, was given the items and the correct answers. The words in each answer were randomly ordered, however, and subjects were told to rearrange them mentally to form the correct answer. It was hypothesized that the scrambled answers would require more cognitive effort to process the feedback than would the repeated-answer condition; thus subjects in group A_3 should better remember the correct answer.

After completing the learning program and receiving the feedback on the correct alternatives, the subjects took a criterion test composed of the same 20 multiple-choice alternatives that they had just studied. The mean numbers of items correct on the criterion test were 9.00 ($s = 3.20$) for the control group, A_1, 13.55 ($s = 3.83$) for the repetition group, A_2, and 12.50 ($s = 2.84$) for the scrambled answer group, A_3. An analysis of variance summary for the scores calculated from information presented by Lhyle and Kulhavy is given next.

Source	SS	df	MS	F
Type of feedback (A)	227.08	2	113.54	10.34
Error	625.86	57	10.98	
Total	852.94	59		

F_{crit} at the .05 level for 2, 57 df is 3.23 (using the tabled value for 2, 40 df); thus F_{obs} (2, 57) = 10.34 falls into the rejection region. The null hypothesis, H_0: $\mu_{A1} = \mu_{A2} = \mu_{A3}$, was rejected and H_1: The μ_A's are not all equal was accepted. There is at least one significant difference among the three means, and a multiple comparison test is needed to make the pairwise comparisons. Using the Tukey HSD, the CD equals $CD = q(\sqrt{MS_{Error}/n_A})$, where q for 3, 40 df (the next lower df from 57 tabled in Table A–4a) is 3.44. Substituting numerical values,

$$CD = 3.44\sqrt{\frac{10.98}{20}} = 3.44\sqrt{0.549} = 3.44(0.741)$$

$$= 2.55 \text{ answers.}$$

A difference between two means equal to or larger in absolute value than 2.55 answers is statistically significant at the .05 level with the Tukey test. The pairwise comparisons and their absolute values, the statistical hypotheses tested, and the decisions reached on the statistical hypotheses for each comparison are given in Table 10–15.

TABLE 10–15
Application of the Tukey HSD CD to the pairwise comparisons of the three feedback groups.

Comparison	Absolute Value of Comparison	Statistical Hypotheses	Decision
$\overline{X}_{A1}$ vs. $\overline{X}_{A2}$ (9.00 − 13.55)	4.55	$H_0 : \mu_{A1} = \mu_{A2}$ $H_1: \mu_{A1} \neq \mu_{A2}$	Reject Accept
$\overline{X}_{A1}$ vs. $\overline{X}_{A3}$ (9.00 − 12.50)	3.50	$H_0 : \mu_{A1} = \mu_{A3}$ $H_1: \mu_{A1} \neq \mu_{A3}$	Reject Accept
$\overline{X}_{A2}$ vs. $\overline{X}_{A3}$ (12.50 − 13.55)	1.05	$H_0 : \mu_{A2} = \mu_{A3}$ $H_1: \mu_{A2} \neq \mu_{A3}$	Fail to reject Do not accept

The pairwise comparisons indicate that there was no difference between the scrambled and repeated feedback groups (A_2 and A_3), but both of these groups answered more items correctly than the control group (A_1). These results were not in agreement with the research hypotheses, which predicted that the scrambled-answers feedback, group A_3, would show the best performance on the criterion task, followed by the repeated-answers condition, group A_2, which would show better recall than the control group, group A_1. Lhyle and Kulhavy's explanation for these results was that subjects in the scrambled-answers group did not expend the necessary effort to fully unscramble the answers. To test this hypothesis, they conducted a second experiment in which greater effort was required to unscramble the answers. Here scrambled answers produced the desired improvement in criterion test performance.

TESTING YOUR KNOWLEDGE 10–3

1. In Testing Your Knowledge 9–3, problem 1 of question 9 presented an experiment dealing with the effects of an expected delay on the estimation of a time interval. Recall that subjects in the control group were not led to expect a delay in the start of an experiment, whereas subjects in the experimental group were told that the experimenter's assistant was delayed. However, the delay period was 5 minutes for both groups. After the experiment started, subjects were asked to estimate how long the delay was. Suppose that you replicated this experiment with a total of 22 subjects and obtained the following estimates of the 5-minute delay period (in minutes):

Group	
Control	Experimental
6	8
7	9
9	11
7	10
6	9
8	8
5	7
9	6
6	10
8	10
7	9

Find the mean and standard deviation for each group, then calculate an analysis of variance on these scores and answer the following questions.
  a. State the statistical hypotheses for the F test for these scores.
  b. What is the value of F_{obs}?
  c. What are the df for F_{obs}?
  d. What is F_{crit} at the .05 level?
  e. What is the rejection region for F_{obs}?
  f. Does F_{obs} fall into the rejection region?
  g. What decisions do you make about the statistical hypotheses? Do you reject or fail to reject H_0? Accept or not accept H_1?

h. Do you conclude that the group means are from the same or different populations?

i. Is the difference between the means statistically significant?

j. Did the groups differ in their estimates of the time they spent waiting? If so, what is the direction of the difference?

k. Are multiple comparison tests needed in this experiment? Give the reason for your answer.

l. What is η^2 for this experiment?

m. How much of the variance is accounted for by the independent variable in this experiment?

2. Do beards make males feel more masculine? To answer this question, Wood (1986) randomly assigned clean-shaven males to one of three treatment conditions. Subjects in group A_1 wore a theatrical beard, subjects in group A_2 wore an outlaw-style bandana around the face, and subjects in group A_3 formed a control condition where nothing was worn on the face. Each subject looked at himself in a mirror for 1 minute and then completed a self-rating of masculinity. Suppose that the following scores were obtained (lower scores indicate greater rated masculinity):

Treatment Group

Beard A_1	Bandana A_2	Control A_3
26	34	40
24	39	41
19	38	39
23	40	36
18	34	35
21	35	32
23	29	31
29	36	34

Find the mean and standard deviation for each group; then calculate an analysis of variance on these scores and answer the following questions.

a. State the statistical hypotheses for the F test for these scores.

b. What is the value of F_{obs}?

c. What are the df for F_{obs}?

d. What is F_{crit} at the .05 level?

e. What is the rejection region for F_{obs}?

f. Does F_{obs} fall into the rejection region?

g. What decisions do you make about the statistical hypotheses? Do you reject or fail to reject H_0? Accept or not accept H_1?

h. What can you conclude from the overall analysis of variance on these scores?

i. Are multiple comparison tests needed in this experiment? Give the reason for your answer.

j. What is the value of the Tukey CD?

k. Which pairwise differences are statistically significant?

l. Describe how the groups differ in rated masculinity.

m. What is η^2 for this experiment?

n. How much of the variance is accounted for by the independent variable in this experiment?

REPORTING THE RESULTS OF THE ANALYSIS OF VARIANCE

The Publication Manual of the American Psychological Association (1994) requires the report of the results of an analysis of variance to present group means, standard deviations, the value of alpha selected, the observed value of F and its degrees of freedom, the MS_{Error}, and the probability of the observed value of F if H_0 is true. I illustrate this style using the results from the example of the effect of type of drawing on item recall. The analysis of variance for this problem is summarized in Table 10–5. Although I have been using summary tables for analysis of variance, such tables may not be included in journal articles because of their expense to print. If a summary table is not included, the analysis of variance is summarized in text, as illustrated here.

> The mean number of items correctly recalled was 17.0 for the incomplete outline drawings ($SD = 2.74$), 13.0 for the outline drawings ($SD = 2.24$), and 12.0 for the detailed drawings ($SD = 1.87$). With alpha equal to .05, a one-factor between-subjects analysis of variance indicated a significant effect for the type of drawing: $F(2, 12) = 6.56$, $MSE = 5.333$, $p < .05$. Post hoc comparisons using the Tukey HSD test ($CD = 3.9$, $\alpha = .05$) indicated significantly more objects recalled for the incomplete outline drawings compared with either the outline drawings or the detailed drawings, but no significant difference in the number of objects recalled for outline drawings compared with the detailed drawings condition. Eta squared for the scores was .52.

In this presentation:

$\alpha = .05$	Indicates the significance level selected for the test.
$F(2, 12)$	Identifies the test statistic as the F; hence an analysis of variance was used to analyze the data. This F is F_{obs}; the subscript *obs* is not utilized. The *df* for the numerator (i.e., 2) and the denominator (i.e., 12) of F_{obs} are shown in parentheses. From these *df* you can determine the number of groups involved and the number of subjects used in the experiment as follows: The *df* for the numerator equal $a - 1$. In this report, $df_A = 2$; thus $a = 3$. The *df* for the denominator equal *df* $_{Error}$, which equal $N - a$. In the example, *df* $_{Error} = 12$ and $a = 3$; therefore $12 = N - 3$ and the total number of subjects in the experiment equals 15.
$= 6.56$	Gives the value of F_{obs} (not the F_{crit} value found in Table A–3). If F_{obs} is less than 1.00, it may be reported simply as $F < 1.00$.
$p < .05$	Indicates that

     a. The probability of F_{obs} if H_0 is true is less than or equal to .05. This value is the probability of F_{obs} or an even more extreme value of F_{obs} if H_0 is true; it may not be the same as the value of α selected.

     b. H_0: $\mu_{A1} = \mu_{A2} = \mu_{A3}$ was rejected.
       H_1: *The* μ_A's are not all equal   was accepted.

   c. At least one difference between group means is statistically significant.

   d. Something other than sampling error is responsible for the observed difference in sample means.

   e. If $p > .05$ had been reported, then the greater than sign would indicate that H_0 was not rejected and the sample means did not differ significantly at the .05 significance level. In this instance I conclude that the type of drawing did not affect the recall of details.

$MSE = 5.333$ Gives the value of MS_{Error} for the F_{obs}. This value is a measure of the within-group error variation in the scores.

$CD = 3.9$ Gives the critical difference for pairwise comparisons using the Tukey HSD test. The statistically significant pairwise comparisons are then described.

Eta squared   Presents the value of η^2, indicating that 52 percent of the variance
$= .52$ in the recall scores of this experiment is accounted for by the type of drawing. Sometimes a similar strength of association measure, ω^2 (omega squared), is given. The value of ω^2 will be slightly less than η^2.

TESTING YOUR KNOWLEDGE 10–4

The following exercises present sample reports of one-factor between-subjects analysis of variance. Answer the following questions for each report.

   a. How many levels of the independent variable were used in this experiment?
   b. How many subjects were used in this experiment?
   c. What is the value of F_{obs}?
   d. What is the value of F_{crit} at the .05 significance level?
   e. Do you reject or fail to reject H_0?
   f. Do you accept or not accept H_1?
   g. Is there at least one statistically significant difference between the means?
   h. Which means, if any, differ significantly?

1. The mean number of tones detected while listening to a familiar passage was 79.9 compared to a mean of 73.0 when listening to an unfamiliar poetry passage. With alpha equal to .05, a one-factor between-subjects analysis of variance indicated that the means differed significantly, $F(1, 60) = 14.15$, $MSE = 5.740$, $p < .01$.

2. With alpha equal to .05, no difference was found in the number of words recalled as a function of retention interval, $F(3, 36) = 1.13$, $MSE = 14.342$, $p > .05$.

3. The mean number of typing errors was 18.5 for the group listening to classical music, 29.9 for the group listening to hard-rock music, and 17.5 for the no-music control group. With alpha equal to .05, a one-factor between-subjects analysis of variance indicated a significant effect for the type of music, $F(2, 36) = 33.94$, $MSE = 18.261$, $p < .001$. Post hoc comparisons using the Tukey HSD test ($CD = 4.1$, $\alpha = .05$) indicated significantly more typing errors for the hard-rock music condition than for either the no-music control or the classical-music condition. The no-music and classical-music conditions did not differ significantly.

SUMMARY

- A one-factor multilevel design is an experiment with one independent variable and three or more levels of that independent variable.
- The one-factor between-subjects analysis of variance is used to analyze scores from a one-factor multilevel design.
- The F statistic is given by $F = MS_A/MS_{\text{Error}}$.
- A MS is a variance and is found by SS/df.
- MS_A varies with the effect of the independent variable and sampling error.
- MS_{Error} varies with the within-groups error variation.
- If the independent variable has no effect, then MS_A and MS_{Error} estimate only error variation in the scores, and F should be about equal to 1.00.
- When an independent variable has an effect, MS_A increases in value, but MS_{Error} is not affected. The value of F becomes larger than 1.00.
- Using the F statistic in a statistical test follows the usual steps of formulating statistical hypotheses, setting a significance level, locating a rejection region, calculating F_{obs}, and making decisions concerning the statistical hypotheses.
- A statistically significant F_{obs} when three or more levels of an independent variable are manipulated requires a multiple comparison test to follow up the analysis of variance.
- Multiple comparison tests are used to find which means differ significantly from one another in a one-factor multilevel design after a statistically significant F_{obs} has occurred for the overall analysis of variance. A comparison of two means is a pairwise comparison.
- The Tukey test is used for all possible pairwise post hoc comparisons for a set of means. The Tukey test holds the probability of a Type I error equal to or less than α for all possible pairwise comparisons.
- η^2 may be used as a measure of the strength of a treatment effect.

KEY TERMS AND SYMBOLS

a	error rate	multiple comparison test
analysis of variance	eta squared	N
ANOVA	η^2	n_A
between-groups variance	F_{crit}	one-factor multilevel design
CD	F_{obs}	pairwise comparison
critical difference	factor A	post hoc comparison
df_A	mean square	q
df_{Error}	MS_A	rejection region
df_{Total}	MS_{Error}	strength of effect

SS_A

SS_{Error}

SS_{Total}

sum of squares

Tukey HSD test

Type I error

Type II error

within-groups error variance

$X - \overline{X}_G$

$\overline{X}_A - \overline{X}_G$

$X - \overline{X}_A$

CHAPTER SUPPLEMENT: CALCULATING A ONE-FACTOR BETWEEN-SUBJECTS ANALYSIS OF VARIANCE WITH COMPUTATIONAL FORMULAS

Computational formulas for analysis of variance are based on the total of the scores in a treatment group (rather than the treatment mean) and the grand total of the scores in the experiment (rather than the grand mean). Following the notational representation introduced in Table 10–2, an experiment with three levels of an independent variable A and five subjects in each level is represented as follows:

Factor A

A_1	A_2	A_3	
X_{11}	X_{12}	X_{13}	
X_{21}	X_{22}	X_{23}	
X_{31}	X_{32}	X_{33}	
X_{41}	X_{42}	X_{43}	
X_{51}	X_{52}	X_{53}	
T_{A1}	T_{A2}	T_{A3}	G (grand total)

where X_{ij} = score of a subject

T_A = total of scores for a level of the independent variable

G = grand total of the scores

n_A = number of scores in a level of the independent variable

a = number of levels of the independent variable

N = total number of scores.

Three numerical values are found using these terms:

$[1] = \Sigma\Sigma X_{ij}^2$ the sum of all the scores squared

$[2] = \dfrac{\Sigma T_A^2}{n_A}$ the sum of each treatment group total squared, divided by the number of scores in a group

$[3] = \dfrac{G^2}{N}$ the grand total squared, divided by the total number of scores.

Using these numerical values, an analysis of variance is obtained as follows:

Source of Variance	SS	df	MS	F
Factor A	[2] − [3]	$a − 1$	$\dfrac{SS_A}{df_A}$	$\dfrac{MS_A}{MS_{Error}}$
Error	[1] − [2]	$N − a$	$\dfrac{SS_{Error}}{df_{Error}}$	
Total	[1] − [3]	$N − 1$	Not calculated	

To illustrate the computations, I use the example scores given in Table 10–1 for which an analysis of variance is summarized in Table 10–5.

Factor A

	A_1	A_2	A_3
	19	14	15
	13	13	10
	16	16	11
	17	12	12
	20	10	12
$T_A =$	85	65	60

$$G = 85 + 65 + 60 = 210$$
$$n_A = 5, \ a = 3, \text{ and } N = 15$$

The values of the numerical computational terms are

$$[1] = 19^2 + \cdots + 20^2 + 14^2 + \cdots + 10^2 + 15^2 + \cdots + 12^2 = 3074.00$$

$$[2] = \frac{85^2 + 65^2 + 60^2}{5} = \frac{15,050}{5} = 3010.00$$

$$[3] = \frac{210^2}{15} = \frac{44,100}{15} = 2940.00.$$

Then

$$SS_A = [2] - [3] = 3010.00 - 2940.00 = 70.00,$$
$$df_A = a - 1 = 3 - 1 = 2,$$
$$MS_A = \frac{70.00}{2} = 35.000.$$

$$SS_{Error} = [1] - [2] = 3074.00 - 3010.00 = 64.00,$$
$$df_{Error} = N - a = 15 - 3 = 12,$$
$$MS_{Error} = \frac{64.00}{12} = 5.333.$$

$$SS_{\text{Total}} = [1] - [3] = 3074.00 - 2940.00 = 134.00,$$

$$df_{\text{Total}} = N - 1 = 15 - 1 = 14.$$

$$F_{\text{obs}} = \frac{MS_A}{MS_{\text{Error}}} = \frac{35.000}{5.333} = 6.56.$$

The summary of the analysis of variance is as follows:

Source	SS	df	MS	F
Factor A	70.00	2	35.000	6.56*
Error	64.00	12	5.333	
Total	134.00	14		

*$p < .05$.

The values obtained by this computational approach are identical to those presented in Table 10–5 obtained from the definitional formulas of an analysis of variance.

REVIEW QUESTIONS

1. Weinstein and de Man (1987) compared 16 U.S. college students against 16 foreign college students studying in the United States on knowledge of world geography. Suppose that the following scores represent the number of countries the students could identify on a world map.

Nationality of Student

U.S. (A_1)	Foreign (A_2)
6	12
3	8
10	16
4	9
7	7
2	18
12	10
5	8
2	12
4	14
5	16
7	9
3	13
6	17
11	7
7	14

a. Find the mean and standard deviation for each group. Then analyze the scores with a one-factor between-subjects analysis of variance to answer the following question: Do U.S. and foreign students differ in their knowledge of geography? Use a .05 significance level.

b. What is the value of η^2 for this study? What proportion of the variance in the dependent variable can be accounted for by knowing the level of the independent variable?

c. Describe the results of this experiment following the style illustrated in the Reporting the Results of the Analysis of Variance section of this chapter.

2. Elementary school teachers must have many talents, among them the ability to teach children the physical skills needed for certain sports and other skilled activities. To determine how well elementary education majors could learn the necessary skills from instructional videotapes, Morrison and Reeve (1986) created three equivalent groups of subjects and varied the instructional videotape shown them. Group A_1 was a control group and saw no videotape. Group A_2 saw a videotape on soccer kicks, and group A_3 saw a videotape on throwing, catching, and striking skills. After viewing the instructional videotape, or no tape for group A_1, all subjects were shown a second videotape on throwing, catching, and striking and asked to identify correct performances displayed on the tape. Suppose the following scores were obtained for nine subjects in each instructional condition.

Instructional Condition

No Videotape (A_1)	Soccer Videotape (A_2)	Throwing, Catching Videotape (A_3)
50	53	61
46	48	58
39	37	49
52	49	56
44	46	45
51	48	66
41	37	58
36	41	64
48	40	57

a. Find the mean and standard deviation for each group. Then analyze the scores with a one-factor between-subjects analysis to answer the following question: Did the instructional condition affect a subject's skill to correctly identify throwing, catching, and striking performance? Use a .05 significance level. If needed, use the Tukey HSD test for multiple comparisons.

    b. What is the value of η^2 for this experiment? What proportion of the variance in the dependent variable can be accounted for by knowing the level of the independent variable?

    c. Describe the results of this experiment following the style illustrated in the Reporting the Results of the Analysis of Variance section of this chapter.

3. Problem 1 of the Chapter 9 Review Questions dealt with the physiological effects of noise. In the experiment described, subjects either sat in a quiet room for 30 minutes or listened to a recording of traffic noise for 30 minutes. At the end of 30 minutes, their systolic blood pressures were measured and the following scores obtained (in millimeters of mercury).

Group	
Quiet	Noise
106	141
117	136
124	124
129	139
115	121
131	119
121	147
115	128
128	115
136	134
127	140

    a. Find the mean and standard deviation for each group. Then analyze the scores with a one-factor between-subjects analysis to answer the following question: Does noise affect systolic blood pressure? Use a .05 significance level.

    b. Compare the value of F_{obs} to the value of t_{obs} for Problem 1 of the Chapter 9 Review Questions. Do you find the expected relationship between t and F?

4. An experimenter used a one-factor between-subjects design with six levels of the independent variable, A_1, A_2, A_3, A_4, A_5, and A_6, and seven subjects in each level.

    a. What are the values of a, n_A, and N for this experiment?

    b. What are the values of df_A, df_{Error}, and df_{Total} for the analysis of variance for this experiment?

5. The following tables are incomplete summary tables for an analysis of variance. Assume an equal number of subjects in each level of the independent variable. By using the relationships among SS, df, and MS, provide the missing values in each table. Then answer the following questions for each table.

    a. How many levels of the independent variable were manipulated?

    b. How many subjects were tested in each treatment condition?

c. What was the total number of subjects in the experiment?
d. Is the value of F_{obs} statistically significant at the .05 level?
e. What decision do you make for H_0 and H_1 for each analysis?

TABLE 1

Source	SS	df	MS	F
Factor A	50.0	2	_____	_____
Error	270.0	27	_____	
Total	_____	_____		

TABLE 2

Source	SS	df	MS	F
Factor A	60.0	_____	12.0	_____
Error	_____	72	_____	
Total	276.0	77		

TABLE 3

Source	SS	df	MS	F
Factor A	_____	_____	_____	3.00
Error	320.0	_____	5.0	
Total	365.0	67		

6. Does rejection of H_0 and acceptance of H_1 in an analysis of variance necessarily provide support for a research hypothesis? Explain your answer.

7. You conducted a t_{ind} on two groups and $t_{obs}(18) = 2.000$. If you had analyzed the scores with an analysis of variance, what value of F_{obs} would you have found? Indicate the df for F_{obs}.

8. You conducted an analysis of variance on two independent groups and F_{obs} $(1, 22) = 9.00$. If you had analyzed the scores with a t_{ind}, what value of t_{obs} would you have found? Indicate the df for t_{obs}.

9. Explain why a statistical test cannot identify the reason for two groups differing significantly.

10. A psychologist was interested in comparing four treatments for a smoking-cessation program. She created four groups of 17 subjects each by random assignment and gave each group a different treatment. The dependent variable measured was the mean time between smoking cigarettes after 5 weeks of treatment. The treatment groups and the mean time between cigarettes (in minutes)

are given in Table 1, and an analysis of variance for these data is presented in Table 2.

TABLE 1
Treatment conditions and mean times between smoking cigarettes (in minutes).

	Treatment Condition	Mean Time
A_1	Control group; no treatment given	24.0
A_2	Behavior modification	38.0
A_3	Cigarettes anonymous club	34.0
A_4	Smoke-Stop gum	28.0

TABLE 2
Analysis of variance summary table for mean time between smoking cigarettes in Table 1.

Source	SS	df	MS	F
Treatment condition	1972.00	3	657.333	21.64*
Error	1944.00	64	30.375	
Total	3916.00	67		

*$p < .01$.

A Tukey HSD gave a $CD = 5.0$ minutes at the .05 significance level.
   a. What is the effect of the treatment conditions on the amount of time between smoking cigarettes?
   b. Describe the results of this experiment following the style illustrated in the Reporting the Results of the Analysis of Variance section of this chapter.

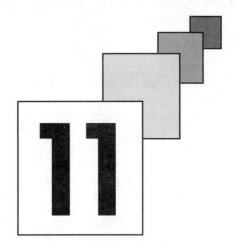

Two-factor Between-subjects Designs and Analysis of Variance

Many behaviors are determined by two or more independent variables functioning simultaneously. For example, the effect of noise (one independent variable) on reading comprehension (the dependent variable) differs for introverted and extroverted personality types (a second independent variable) (Standing, Lynn, & Moxness, 1990). Or, as another example, memory for a list of noun pairs (the dependent variable) depends on the imagery ability of the person learning the list (one independent variable), the type of image provided to the learner (a second independent variable), and the length of the retention interval (a third independent variable) (O'Brien & Wolford, 1982). One-factor designs do not permit the manipulation of more than one independent variable at a time; thus, to study the influence of two or more independent variables in combination, factorial designs are used.

Factorial design: A research design in which two or more independent variables are varied simultaneously.

Factorial designs are research designs in which two or more independent variables are simultaneously varied. In the simplest factorial design, two independent variables are varied and each independent variable assumes two levels. This design often is called a 2×2 ("two-by-two") design. The first 2 of the 2×2 indicates that there are two levels of the first independent variable (identified as factor A), and the second 2 indicates the number of levels of the second independent variable (identified as factor B). A $2 \times 2 \times 2$ design is a three-factor design with factors A, B, and C, and each independent variable varies over two levels. There are many possible factorial designs, such as a 2×4 design (two levels of factor A, four levels of factor B), a $3 \times 3 \times 2$ design (three levels of factors A and B, two levels of factor C), and a $2 \times 2 \times 2 \times 2$ design (four factors, A, B, C, and D, with two levels of each). Factorial designs may also be totally between subjects, totally within subjects, or a combination of the two, resulting in a mixed design. In this text I discuss only the two-factor (also called a *two-way*) between-subjects design.

THE 2 × 2 BETWEEN-SUBJECTS DESIGN

Cell or treatment condition: A combination formed from one level of each independent variable in a factorial design.

The 2×2 between-subjects design is convenient for introducing the statistical data analysis of factorial designs. Table 11–1 illustrates two independent variables or factors identified as A and B, each taking on two levels: factor A with levels A_1 and A_2 and factor B with levels B_1 and B_2. Generally, there are a levels of factor A and b levels of factor B. In the example, $a = 2$ and $b = 2$. The combination of the two independent variables creates four treatment conditions, called **cells**, in the table. Each **cell** or **treatment condition** represents a combination formed from one level of each independent variable, for example, the A_1B_1, A_1B_2, A_2B_1, and A_2B_2 cells. An equal number of subjects typically is randomly assigned to each of the treatment conditions. Thus, if 20 subjects are used in a 2×2 between-subjects design, five subjects are assigned to each treatment condition or cell. Each subject experiences only one treatment condition.

An Example 2 × 2 Between-subjects Design

People generally don't like to give other people bad news. This phenomenon is called the *MUM effect*. Several hypotheses have been proposed to explain this effect. The personal discomfort hypothesis states that the bearer of bad news feels personal discomfort

TABLE 11-1

Plan of a 2 × 2 between-subjects design. The combination of a level of factor A with a level of factor B forms a treatment condition or cell.

		Factor A	
		A_1	A_2
Factor B	B_1	A_1B_1 treatment condition (A_1B_1 cell)	A_2B_1 treatment condition (A_2B_1 cell)
	B_2	A_1B_2 treatment condition (A_1B_2 cell)	A_2B_2 treatment condition (A_2B_2 cell)

when delivering the bad news and avoids this discomfort by not delivering the news. A second hypothesis, the self-presentational hypothesis, suggests that individuals do not feel discomfort when delivering the bad news; rather, failing to deliver the bad news is a public display to maintain a positive social image. After all, who wants to be known as the bearer of bad news? To test these hypotheses, Bond and Anderson (1987) used a 2×2 between-subjects design. The two independent variables were the visibility of the subject to the person to whom the bad news was to be delivered (subject visibility, factor A) and the type of news to be delivered (type of news, factor B). Each independent variable was manipulated over two levels. For subject visibility, the subject was either not visible (level A_1) or visible (level A_2) to the person to whom the news was to be delivered. The type of news was either good (level B_1) or bad (level B_2). The experimental procedure was as follows. A subject was to administer a multiple-choice intelligence test to another person who, unknown to the subject, was a confederate of the experimenter. The subject and the confederate were in separate rooms joined by a one-way mirror. In the subject-not-visible condition (level A_1), the subject was told that the confederate could not see through the mirror. For the subject-visible condition (level A_2), the subject was told that the confederate could see him or her through the mirror. The type of news was manipulated by the confederate's success on the test. In the good news condition (level B_1), the subject informed the confederate that her performance was in the top 20 percent of the scores on the test. In the bad news condition (level B_2), the subject informed the confederate that her performance was in the bottom 20 percent of the scores on the test. The dependent variable was the latency of feedback of the test score from the subject to the confederate. This latency was the length of time from the completion of the test to the subject's telling the confederate what her score was.

Two different outcomes for the experiment were predicted from the two hypotheses concerning the MUM effect. If the MUM effect occurs because subjects experience personal discomfort, then it should take longer to deliver the bad news than the good news, regardless of whether the subject is or is not visible to the confederate. In other words, the difference between the good (level B_1) and bad (level B_2) news conditions should not depend on whether the subject is visible or not to the confederate. On the other hand, if the MUM effect is simply a public display, then the latency to deliver the bad news should depend on whether the subject is or is not visible to the confederate. That is, an interaction of the independent variables should occur. When good news is delivered, there should be no difference in the latencies of the not visible and visible conditions. When bad news is delivered, however, the latency of the visible condition should be significantly longer than the latency of the not visible condition. Correspondingly, for the not visible condition, there should be no difference between the latencies of the good and bad news conditions. For the visible condition, however, the latency of the bad news condition should be significantly longer than the good news condition.

Suppose five male subjects were randomly assigned to each cell and the latency scores (in seconds) presented in Table 11–2 were obtained. Which prediction, if either, do the results agree with, those of the personal discomfort hypothesis or those of the public display hypothesis?

INFORMATION OBTAINED FROM A FACTORIAL DESIGN

The scores in Table 11–2 are represented notationally in Table 11–3. A score for a subject is represented by X_{ijk}, where the subscripts provide the following information:

i = number identifying the subject within a treatment condition
j = level of the A variable that the subject receives
k = level of the B variable that the subject receives

For example, X_{311} is the score of the third subject in the A_1B_1 treatment condition (80.0 seconds in Table 11–2), X_{421} is the score of the fourth subject in the A_2B_1 treat-

TABLE 11–2

Hypothetical response latencies (in seconds) as a function of subject visibility and type of news for 20 subjects in the example 2 × 2 between-subjects experiment.

		Subject Visibility Condition (Factor A)	
		Not Visible (A_1)	Visible (A_2)
	Good (B_1)	97.0	70.0
		90.0	87.0
		80.0	81.0
		107.0	95.0
		80.0	90.0
Type of News (Factor B)			
	Bad (B_2)	68.0	114.0
		87.0	96.0
		92.0	127.0
		80.0	110.0
		84.0	115.0

TABLE 11–3

Notational representation of scores in a 2×2 between-subjects design with two levels of each independent variable and five subjects per cell.

		Factor A	
		A_1	A_2
		X_{111}	X_{121}
		X_{211}	X_{221}
	B_1	X_{311}	X_{321}
		X_{411}	X_{421}
		X_{511}	X_{521}
Factor B			
		X_{112}	X_{122}
		X_{212}	X_{222}
	B_2	X_{312}	X_{322}
		X_{412}	X_{422}
		X_{512}	X_{522}

ment condition (95.0 seconds), X_{212} is the score of the second subject in the A_1B_2 treatment condition (87 seconds), X_{522} is the score of the fifth subject in the A_2B_2 treatment condition (115 seconds), and so on. When it is not necessary to identify a specific subject, I drop the *ijk* subscripts and simply use X. For each cell there are n_{AB} subjects with a total of N subjects in the experiment. For the example, $n_{AB} = 5$ and $N = 20$. The first step in data analysis begins with computing measures of central tendency, the sample means. Table 11–4 illustrates the cell and main effect means that may be calculated from the example scores.

Cell Means

Cell mean: The mean of the n_{AB} scores for a treatment combination in a factorial design.

The **cell means**, symbolized by $\overline{X}_{A1B1}$, $\overline{X}_{A1B2}$, $\overline{X}_{A2B1}$, and $\overline{X}_{A2B2}$, or, in general, by $\overline{X}_{AB}$, are the means of the n_{AB} scores for a treatment combination (see Table 11–4a). A cell mean indicates the typical performance of subjects in a treatment condition. The numerical value of the cell means for the scores of Table 11–2 are presented in Table 11–5. The standard deviations for the scores in each cell of Table 11–2 are presented in parentheses in Table 11–5. In a factorial design the standard deviation typically is calculated only for the cell means.

Main Effect Means

Main effect mean: The mean of all subjects given one level of an independent variable, ignoring the classification by the other independent variable in a factorial design.

A **main effect mean** indicates the typical performance of all subjects given one level of an independent variable, ignoring the classification by the other independent variable. Thus there are two sets of main effect means, those for factor A and those for factor B.

TABLE 11–4
Cell and main effect means in a 2 × 2 between-subjects design.

(a) Cell means

		Factor A	
		A_1	A_2
	B_1	$\overline{X}_{A1B1}$	$\overline{X}_{A2B1}$
Factor B			
	B_2	$\overline{X}_{A1B2}$	$\overline{X}_{A2B2}$

(b) Main effect means for factor A, $\overline{X}_{A1}$ and $\overline{X}_{A2}$

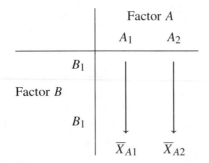

Ignore classification of scores by factor B to obtain main effect means for factor A. The difference between $\overline{X}_{A1}$ and $\overline{X}_{A2}$ is the main effect of factor A.

(c) Main effect means for factor B, $\overline{X}_{B1}$ and $\overline{X}_{B2}$

		Factor A		
		A_1	A_2	
	B_1	⟶		$\overline{X}_{B1}$
Factor B				
	B_2	⟶		$\overline{X}_{B2}$

Ignore classification of scores by factor A to obtain main effect means for factor B. The difference between $\overline{X}_{B1}$ and $\overline{X}_{B2}$ is the main effect of factor B.

Main effect of factor A:
The difference between $\overline{X}_{A1}$ and $\overline{X}_{A2}$, symbolized by $\overline{X}_{A1} - \overline{X}_{A2}$.

Factor A

The **main effect means for factor** A are symbolized by $\overline{X}_{A1}$ and $\overline{X}_{A2}$. These means, sometimes called **column means**, are found for all subjects within either level A_1 or A_2, while disregarding the level of factor B that they received. Collapsing the data over levels of factor B to obtain main effect means for factor A is shown in Table 11–4b. As an example, the main effect means for factor A, subject visibility in Table 11–2, are based on the 10 scores of subjects either not visible or visible to the confederate. Type of news (factor B) is ignored when finding the main effect means of factor A. The numerical

TABLE 11-5
Cell and main effect means for the data of Table 11–2. The numerical values are response latency in seconds. Standard deviations of cell means are given in parentheses.

| | | Subject Visibility (Factor A) | | Main Effect Means |
		Not Visible (A_1)	Visible (A_2)	for Type of News ($\overline{X}_B$)
Type of News (Factor B)	Good (B_1)	90.8 (11.56)	84.6 (9.61)	87.7
	Bad (B_2)	82.2 (9.07)	112.4 (11.15)	97.3
	Main Effect Means for Subject Visibility ($\overline{X}_A$)	86.5	98.5	Grand mean 92.5

values of $\overline{X}_{A1}$ and $\overline{X}_{A2}$ are presented in Table 11–5. The **main effect of factor A** is the difference between $\overline{X}_{A1}$ and $\overline{X}_{A2}$. If factor A has an effect on the dependent variable, then $\overline{X}_{A1}$ and $\overline{X}_{A2}$ will differ from each other, and the value of $\overline{X}_{A1} - \overline{X}_{A2}$ will become larger.

Factor B

Main effect of factor B: The difference between $\overline{X}_{B1}$ and $\overline{X}_{B2}$, symbolized by $\overline{X}_{B1} - \overline{X}_{B2}$.

A similar logic applies to finding the main effect for independent variable B. The **main effect means for factor B** (sometimes called **row means**), symbolized as $\overline{X}_{B1}$ and $\overline{X}_{B2}$, are obtained by collapsing over factor A as shown in Table 11–4c. To find the main effect means for factor B in the example, type of news, the categorization by subject visibility (factor A) is ignored. The numerical values of $\overline{X}_{B1}$ and $\overline{X}_{B2}$ also are presented in Table 11–5. The **main effect of factor B** is the difference $\overline{X}_{B1} - \overline{X}_{B2}$. If factor B has an effect on the dependent variable, then $\overline{X}_{B1}$ and $\overline{X}_{B2}$ will differ from each other, and the value of $\overline{X}_{B1} - \overline{X}_{B2}$ will become larger.

Grand Mean

The grand mean, symbolized as $\overline{X}_G$, is the mean of all the scores in the table. For the data in Table 11–2, the grand mean of 92.5 seconds is the mean of all 20 scores. The grand mean typically is not presented as a descriptive statistic, but it is needed in this chapter for developing an analysis of variance for this design.

Interaction of the Independent Variables

Interaction: A situation in a factorial design when the effect of one independent variable depends on the level of the other independent variable with which it is combined.

An **interaction** occurs in a factorial design when the effect of one independent variable (e.g., factor A) depends on the level of the other independent variable (e.g., either B_1 or B_2) with which it is combined. For example, if an interaction occurs in a 2×2 design, then the effect of factor A, the difference in behavior between treatments A_1 and A_2, depends on the level of factor B. Similarly, if an interaction occurs, the effect of factor B, the difference in behavior between treatments B_1 and B_2, depends on the level of factor A. An interaction often is symbolized as $A \times B$, which is read as "A by B" or the "A by B interaction."

The public display hypothesis predicted an interaction for the example experiment. This hypothesis predicted no difference in the response latency between the not visible and visible conditions for good news (i.e., no difference between the A_1B_1 and A_2B_1 cell means). For bad news, however, the hypothesis predicted significantly longer latencies for the visible condition (the A_2B_2 cell mean) compared to the not visible condition (the A_1B_2 cell mean). Notice that the occurrence of an interaction is analyzed by comparing differences among the cell means rather than among the main effect means. I discuss these comparisons more fully later in the chapter.

TESTING YOUR KNOWLEDGE 11–1

1. Define: cell, cell mean, column mean, factor, factorial design, grand mean, interaction, level of an independent variable, main effect for factor A, main effect for factor B, main effect mean, row mean, treatment condition, $\overline{X}_{AB}, \overline{X}_A, \overline{X}_B, \overline{X}_G$.
2. For each of the following factorial designs, identify how many independent variables are varied and indicate the number of levels for each factor. Then, assuming that the design is a between-subjects design, indicate how many subjects would be needed if 10 subjects were to be tested in each treatment combination.
   Type of design: (a) 3×3, (b) 3×2, (c) 2×3, (d) 6×2, (e) 4×4, (f) $2\times2\times2$, (g) $2\times4\times3$, (h) $3\times3\times2$.
3. Find cell means, main effect means, and the grand mean for the scores in each of the following tables:

TABLE 1

		A₁	A₂
		10	17
		13	23
		8	17
	B_1	17	21
		12	19
		20	24
		19	27
		13	21
		10	16
	B_1	20	19
		22	30
		17	24

Factor A across top; Factor B at side.

TABLE 2

		A₁	A₂
		23	41
		13	22
		28	27
	B_1	11	32
		19	26
		20	24
		18	39
		29	28
		33	31
		18	26
	B_1	29	34
		36	39
		47	44
		27	35

ANALYSIS OF VARIANCE OF A TWO-FACTOR BETWEEN-SUBJECTS DESIGN

The statistical analysis of a factorial design involves hypothesis testing to determine if the main effect means differ significantly from each other for each independent variable and to determine if the interaction of the independent variables is statistically significant. Again, this testing is done with an analysis of variance that partitions the total variation of scores into sources of variation that are independent of each other. The one-factor between-subjects analysis of variance (discussed in Chapter 10) partitions the total variation into two independent sources: that due to the effect of the independent variable (i.e., factor A) and that due to within-groups error variation. In a two-factor between-subjects design, the total variation of scores is partitioned into three between-groups sources and one within-group source. The between-groups sources of variation are the following:

The variation due to the effect of factor A
The variation due to the effect of factor B
The variation due to the interaction of factors A and B, symbolized as $A \times B$

The within-groups source is the within-cells error variation.

The analysis of variance then uses these partitioned scores to generate four mean squares:

1. MS_A, which varies with the effect of factor A
2. MS_B, which varies with the effect of factor B
3. $MS_{A \times B}$, which varies with an interaction of factors A and B
4. MS_{Error}, which varies with the within-cells variation of the scores

Following this step, three separate F ratios are generated, one for each independent variable and one for interaction, as follows:

Source of Variation	F Ratio
Factor A	MS_A / MS_{Error}
Factor B	MS_B / MS_{Error}
Interaction of $A \times B$	$MS_{A \times B} / MS_{Error}$

Each of the three F ratios is used in a statistical hypothesis test to find if the source of variation that the F ratio corresponds to is statistically significant.

To provide a conceptual understanding of a factorial analysis of variance, the next section derives the mean squares that enter into these F ratios. If you were to perform a factorial analysis of variance on an actual set of data, however, you would use the computationally easier formulas given in the computational formulas supplement to this chapter or a computer data analysis program.

Partitioning a Score

The analysis of variance finds the mean squares for the three F ratios by partitioning the total variation of the scores in an experiment into parts varying with factor A (between groups), factor B (between groups), the $A \times B$ interaction (between groups), and error variation (within groups). This model for representing a score in a two-factor between-subjects design can be expressed as follows:

$$\begin{pmatrix} \text{Total} \\ \text{variation} \\ \text{in a} \\ \text{subject's} \\ \text{score} \end{pmatrix} = \begin{pmatrix} \text{Variation} \\ \text{due to the} \\ \text{effect of} \\ \text{factor } A \text{ plus} \\ \text{sampling error} \end{pmatrix} + \begin{pmatrix} \text{Variation} \\ \text{due to the} \\ \text{effect of} \\ \text{factor } B \text{ plus} \\ \text{sampling error} \end{pmatrix} + \begin{pmatrix} \text{Variation due} \\ \text{to interaction} \\ \text{of factors } A \\ \text{and } B \text{ plus} \\ \text{sampling error} \end{pmatrix} + \begin{pmatrix} \text{Variation} \\ \text{due to} \\ \text{within-} \\ \text{cells} \\ \text{error} \end{pmatrix}. \quad (11\text{--}1)$$

In terms of scores, this equation can be written as

$$(X - \overline{X}_G) = (\overline{X}_A - \overline{X}_G) + (\overline{X}_B - \overline{X}_G) + (\overline{X}_{AB} - \overline{X}_A - \overline{X}_B + \overline{X}_G) + (X - \overline{X}_{AB}). \quad (11\text{--}2)$$

| Difference of a subject's score from the grand mean | Difference of factor A main effect mean from the grand mean | Difference of factor B main effect mean from the grand mean | Interaction: Difference of a cell mean from the grand mean after the main effects of factors A and B have been removed | Difference of the subject's score from its cell mean |

I examine each part of equation 11–2.

Total Variation

The difference of a score from the grand mean (i.e., $X - \overline{X}_G$) represents the total variation of that score. As equation 11–2 indicates, a part of this variation is due to the effect of each independent variable and the interaction of the independent variables, and a part of it is due to error variation.

Variation due to the Effect of Factor A and Sampling Error

The difference between a main effect mean of factor A and the grand mean (i.e., $\overline{X}_A - \overline{X}_G$) varies with the effect of factor A and with sampling error among the main effect means of factor A. Its use in a two-factor design is identical to its use in the one-factor between-subjects design to measure the effect of the independent variable. Any effect of factor A is expected to affect all subjects within a level of this factor equally. Thus an effect of factor A changes the value of the main effect means for factor A. These main effect means will then differ from the grand mean. Hence the difference $\overline{X}_A - \overline{X}_G$ reflects any effect of factor A (the treatment effect for factor A in equation 11–1). In addition to any treatment effect, the main effect means for factor A will also differ from each other because of sampling error. Therefore, the value of any $\overline{X}_A - \overline{X}_G$ difference reflects both a treatment effect of factor A and sampling error affecting the values of $\overline{X}_A$. Accordingly, it enters into the computation of MS_A.

Variation due to the Effect of Factor *B* and Sampling Error

The difference between a main effect mean of factor B and the grand mean (i.e., $\overline{X}_B - \overline{X}_G$) varies with the effect of factor B and sampling error among the main effect means of factor B. As with factor A, any effect of factor B is expected to affect all individuals within a level of this factor equally and thus change the value of the main effect means for factor B, which will then differ from the grand mean. Therefore, the difference $\overline{X}_B - \overline{X}_G$ reflects any effect of factor B (the treatment effect for factor B in equation 11–1). In addition, the main effect means for factor B will differ from each other because of sampling error. Hence the difference $\overline{X}_B - \overline{X}_G$ reflects both a treatment effect of factor B and sampling error affecting the values of $\overline{X}_B$ and thus enters into the computation of MS_B.

Variation due to the Interaction of Factors *A* and *B*

The interaction of factors A and B is the remaining difference of the cell means from the grand mean after the main effect of each independent variable has been removed. Symbolically, this statement may be represented as follows:

$$A \times B \quad = \quad (\overline{X}_{AB} - \overline{X}_G) \quad - \quad (\overline{X}_A - \overline{X}_G) \quad - \quad (\overline{X}_B - \overline{X}_G),$$

$$\begin{pmatrix} \text{Interaction} \\ \text{of } A \text{ and } B \end{pmatrix} = \begin{pmatrix} \text{Difference of} \\ \text{cell mean from} \\ \text{grand mean} \end{pmatrix} - \begin{pmatrix} \text{Main effect} \\ \text{of factor } A \end{pmatrix} - \begin{pmatrix} \text{Main effect} \\ \text{of factor } B \end{pmatrix}.$$

The equation indicates that the interaction represents the variation in cell means after the main effect of each independent variable has been removed. This remaining variation in the cell means is due to the interaction of the independent variables and any sampling error among the cell means.

Carrying out the subtractions indicated in the equation results in a simplified expression of the interaction:

$$\overline{X}_{AB} - \overline{X}_A - \overline{X}_B + \overline{X}_G.$$

The interaction is expressed in this form in equation 11–2. This part of the equation enters into the computation of $MS_{A \times B}$.

Variation due to Within-cells Error

The difference of a score from its cell mean (i.e., $X - \overline{X}_{AB}$) reflects only within-cells error variation in the experiment. This error is what is left over in the score after the main effects of both factors and their interaction have been taken into account. As in a one-factor analysis of variance, the error reflects the uniqueness of a person's score in a group of individuals all of whom receive the same treatment. It enters into the computation of MS_{Error}.

Obtaining Mean Squares from Partitioned Scores

As discussed in Chapter 10, the partitioning equation provides the basis for obtaining the SS and df that produce the mean squares for the F ratio. The first step is to obtain the SS from the subjects' scores.

Obtaining Sums of Squares

Sums of squares (SS) are obtained by partitioning each score in the form of equation 11–2. To illustrate this partitioning, I use the score for the first subject in the not visible/good news treatment condition (i.e., X_{111}) of Table 11–2, which is 97.0. For this score, equation 11–2 becomes

$$X_{111} - \overline{X}_G = (\overline{X}_{A1} - \overline{X}_G) + (\overline{X}_{B1} - \overline{X}_G) + (\overline{X}_{A1B1} - \overline{X}_{A1} - \overline{X}_{B1} + \overline{X}_G) + (X_{111} - \overline{X}_{A1B1}).$$

Substituting numerical values, I obtain

$$97.0 - 92.5 = (86.5 - 92.5) + (87.7 - 92.5) + (90.8 - 86.5 - 87.7 + 92.5) + (97.0 - 90.8)$$

or, carrying out the arithmetic functions indicated,

$$+4.5 = (-6.0) + (-4.8) + (+9.1) + (+6.2).$$

This partitioning shows that this score differs from the grand mean as much as it does because of the systematic effect of the level of factor A received (reflected in $\overline{X}_{A1} - \overline{X}_G = -6.0$), the systematic effect of the level of factor B received (reflected in $\overline{X}_{B1} - \overline{X}_G = -4.8$), the interaction of factors A and B (reflected in $\overline{X}_{A1B1} - \overline{X}_{A1} - \overline{X}_{B1} + \overline{X}_G = +9.1$), and because of the unsystematic influences of within-cells error variation (reflected in $X_{111} - \overline{X}_{A1B1} = +6.2$). A similar partitioning for each of the other scores in Table 11–2 is shown in step 1 of Table 11–6. The remaining steps in the table obtain sums of squares from these partitioned scores. Follow each of these steps carefully.

Step 1. The scores of all 20 subjects in the experiment are partitioned following equation 11–2.

Step 2. The numerical differences are found for each score.

Step 3. Each positive and negative difference found in step 2 is squared.

Step 4. The values of the squared differences are summed over all scores in the experiment. This summing is achieved by adding the 20 values in each of the columns. The result is five sums of squares:

$$SS_{Total} = 4567.000,$$
$$SS_A = 720.000,$$
$$SS_B = 460.800,$$
$$SS_{A \times B} = 1656.200,$$
$$SS_{Error} = 1730.000.$$

TABLE 11–6
Obtaining sums of squares for a two-factor analysis of variance based on the scores of Table 11–2.

Step 1: Partition the scores for the 20 subjects using the following equation:

$$X - \overline{X}_G = (\overline{X}_A - \overline{X}_G) + (\overline{X}_B - \overline{X}_G) + (\overline{X}_{AB} - \overline{X}_A - \overline{X}_B + \overline{X}_G) + (X - \overline{X}_{AB})$$

	$97.0 - 92.5$ = $(86.5 - 92.5)$ + $(87.7 - 92.5)$ + $(90.8 - 86.5 - 87.7 + 92.5)$ + $(97.0 - 90.8)$
Scores	$90.0 - 92.5$ = $(86.5 - 92.5)$ + $(87.7 - 92.5)$ + $(90.8 - 86.5 - 87.7 + 92.5)$ + $(90.0 - 90.8)$
in A_1B_1	$80.0 - 92.5$ = $(86.5 - 92.5)$ + $(87.7 - 92.5)$ + $(90.8 - 86.5 - 87.7 + 92.5)$ + $(80.0 - 90.8)$
	$107.0 - 92.5$ = $(86.5 - 92.5)$ + $(87.7 - 92.5)$ + $(90.8 - 86.5 - 87.7 + 92.5)$ + $(107.0 - 90.8)$
	$80.0 - 92.5$ = $(86.5 - 92.5)$ + $(87.7 - 92.5)$ + $(90.8 - 86.5 - 87.7 + 92.5)$ + $(80.0 - 90.8)$

	$70.0 - 92.5$ = $(98.5 - 92.5)$ + $(87.7 - 92.5)$ + $(84.6 - 98.5 - 87.7 + 92.5)$ + $(70.0 - 84.6)$
Scores	$87.0 - 92.5$ = $(98.5 - 92.5)$ + $(87.7 - 92.5)$ + $(84.6 - 98.5 - 87.7 + 92.5)$ + $(87.0 - 84.6)$
in A_2B_1	$81.0 - 92.5$ = $(98.5 - 92.5)$ + $(87.7 - 92.5)$ + $(84.6 - 98.5 - 87.7 + 92.5)$ + $(81.0 - 84.6)$
	$95.0 - 92.5$ = $(98.5 - 92.5)$ + $(87.7 - 92.5)$ + $(84.6 - 98.5 - 87.7 + 92.5)$ + $(95.0 - 84.6)$
	$90.0 - 92.5$ = $(98.5 - 92.5)$ + $(87.7 - 92.5)$ + $(84.6 - 98.5 - 87.7 + 92.5)$ + $(90.0 - 84.6)$

	$68.0 - 92.5$ = $(86.5 - 92.5)$ + $(97.3 - 92.5)$ + $(82.2 - 86.5 - 97.3 + 92.5)$ + $(68.0 - 82.2)$
Scores	$87.0 - 92.5$ = $(86.5 - 92.5)$ + $(97.3 - 92.5)$ + $(82.2 - 86.5 - 97.3 + 92.5)$ + $(87.0 - 82.2)$
in A_1B_2	$92.0 - 92.5$ = $(86.5 - 92.5)$ + $(97.3 - 92.5)$ + $(82.2 - 86.5 - 97.3 + 92.5)$ + $(92.0 - 82.2)$
	$80.0 - 92.5$ = $(86.5 - 92.5)$ + $(97.3 - 92.5)$ + $(82.2 - 86.5 - 97.3 + 92.5)$ + $(80.0 - 82.2)$
	$84.0 - 92.5$ = $(86.5 - 92.5)$ + $(97.3 - 92.5)$ + $(82.2 - 86.5 - 97.3 + 92.5)$ + $(84.0 - 82.2)$

	$114.0 - 92.5$ = $(98.5 - 92.5)$ + $(97.3 - 92.5)$ + $(112.4 - 98.5 - 97.3 + 92.5)$ + $(114.0 - 112.4)$
Scores	$96.0 - 92.5$ = $(98.5 - 92.5)$ + $(97.3 - 92.5)$ + $(112.4 - 98.5 - 97.3 + 92.5)$ + $(96.0 - 112.4)$
in A_2B_2	$127.0 - 92.5$ = $(98.5 - 92.5)$ + $(97.3 - 92.5)$ + $(112.4 - 98.5 - 97.3 + 92.5)$ + $(127.0 - 112.4)$
	$110.0 - 92.5$ = $(98.5 - 92.5)$ + $(97.3 - 92.5)$ + $(112.4 - 98.5 - 97.3 + 92.5)$ + $(110.0 - 112.4)$
	$115.0 - 92.5$ = $(98.5 - 92.5)$ + $(97.3 - 92.5)$ + $(112.4 - 98.5 - 97.3 + 92.5)$ + $(115.0 - 112.4)$

Step 2: Perform the subtractions in step 1 to obtain numerical differences for each subject.

	$+4.5$	=	-6.0	+	-4.8	+	$+9.1$	+	$+6.2$
Scores	-2.5	=	-6.0	+	-4.8	+	$+9.1$	+	-0.8
in A_1B_1	-12.5	=	-6.0	+	-4.8	+	$+9.1$	+	-10.8
	$+14.5$	=	-6.0	+	-4.8	+	$+9.1$	+	$+16.2$
	-12.5	=	-6.0	+	-4.8	+	$+9.1$	+	-10.8

	-22.5	=	$+6.0$	+	-4.8	+	-9.1	+	-14.6
Scores	-5.5	=	$+6.0$	+	-4.8	+	-9.1	+	$+2.4$
in A_2B_1	-11.5	=	$+6.0$	+	-4.8	+	-9.1	+	-3.6
	$+2.5$	=	$+6.0$	+	-4.8	+	-9.1	+	$+10.4$
	-2.5	=	$+6.0$	+	-4.8	+	-9.1	+	$+5.4$

	-24.5	=	-6.0	+	$+4.8$	+	-9.1	+	-14.2
Scores	-5.5	=	-6.0	+	$+4.8$	+	-9.1	+	$+4.8$
in A_1B_2	-0.5	=	-6.0	+	$+4.8$	+	-9.1	+	$+9.8$
	-12.5	=	-6.0	+	$+4.8$	+	-9.1	+	-2.2
	-8.5	=	-6.0	+	$+4.8$	+	-9.1	+	$+1.8$

	$+21.5$	=	$+6.0$	+	$+4.8$	+	$+9.1$	+	$+1.6$
Scores	$+3.5$	=	$+6.0$	+	$+4.8$	+	$+9.1$	+	-16.4
in A_2B_2	$+34.5$	=	$+6.0$	+	$+4.8$	+	$+9.1$	+	$+14.6$
	$+17.5$	=	$+6.0$	+	$+4.8$	+	$+9.1$	+	-2.4
	$+22.5$	=	$+6.0$	+	$+4.8$	+	$+9.1$	+	$+2.6$

Continued

TABLE 11–6
continued

Step 3: Square each difference.

	$(X-\overline{X}_G)^2$	$(\overline{X}_A-\overline{X}_G)^2$	$(\overline{X}_B-\overline{X}_G)^2$	$(\overline{X}_{AB}-\overline{X}_A-\overline{X}_B+\overline{X}_G)^2$	$(X-\overline{X}_{AB})^2$
	20.25	36.00	23.04	82.81	38.44
Scores	6.25	36.00	23.04	82.81	0.64
in A_1B_1	156.25	36.00	23.04	82.81	116.64
	210.25	36.00	23.04	82.81	262.44
	156.25	36.00	23.04	82.81	116.64
	506.25	36.00	23.04	82.81	213.16
Scores	30.25	36.00	23.04	82.81	5.76
in A_2B_1	132.25	36.00	23.04	82.81	12.96
	6.25	36.00	23.04	82.81	108.16
	6.25	36.00	23.04	82.81	29.16
	600.25	36.00	23.04	82.81	201.64
Scores	30.25	36.00	23.04	82.81	23.04
in A_1B_2	0.25	36.00	23.04	82.81	96.04
	156.25	36.00	23.04	82.81	4.84
	72.25	36.00	23.04	82.81	3.24
	462.25	36.00	23.04	82.81	2.56
Scores	12.25	36.00	23.04	82.81	268.96
in A_2B_2	1190.25	36.00	23.04	82.81	213.16
	306.25	36.00	23.04	82.81	5.76
	506.25	36.00	23.04	82.81	6.76

Step 4: Sum the squared differences for each partition over all subjects.

4567.000	= 720.000	+ 460.800	+ 1656.200	+ 1730.000
SS_{Total}	= SS_A	+ SS_B	+ $SS_{A \times B}$	+ SS_{Error}

The steps illustrated in Table 11–6 and the sums of squares resulting from those steps are expressed in mathematical notation as follows:

$$SS_{\text{Total}} = \sum_{k=1}^{b}\sum_{j=1}^{a}\sum_{i=1}^{n_{AB}}(X-\overline{X}_G)^2,$$

$$SS_A = \sum_{k=1}^{b}\sum_{j=1}^{a}\sum_{i=1}^{n_{AB}}(\overline{X}_A-\overline{X}_G)^2,$$

$$SS_B = \sum_{k=1}^{b}\sum_{j=1}^{a}\sum_{i=1}^{n_{AB}}(\overline{X}_B-\overline{X}_G)^2,$$

$$SS_{A\times B} = \sum_{k=1}^{b}\sum_{j=1}^{a}\sum_{i=1}^{n_{AB}}(\overline{X}_{AB}-\overline{X}_A-\overline{X}_B+\overline{X}_G)^2,$$

$$SS_{\text{Error}} = \sum_{k=1}^{b}\sum_{j=1}^{a}\sum_{i=1}^{n_{AB}}(X-\overline{X}_{AB})^2.$$

The summing notation $\sum_{k=1}^{b}$, $\sum_{j=1}^{a}$, and $\sum_{i=1}^{n_{AB}}$ indicates that each squared difference is first summed over all n_{AB} subjects within a cell (from the first subject, $i = 1$, to the last subject, n_{AB}, in a cell), then summed over all a levels of factor A (from the first level, $j = 1$, to the last level, a), and finally over all b levels of factor B (from the first level, $k = 1$, to the last level, b). In the example, because there are five scores in each treatment condition ($n_{AB} = 5$) and two levels of each independent variable ($a = 2$, $b = 2$), the summation limits are from $i = 1$ to $n_{AB} = 5$, from $j = 1$ to $a = 2$, and from $k = 1$ to $b = 2$. Because I always sum over all subjects in a cell and over all cells, I typically use the summation signs without including the limits.

The SS_{Total} is the sum of its components; thus

$$SS_{Total} = SS_A + SS_B + SS_{A \times B} + SS_{Error}. \tag{11-3}$$

This equation indicates that the total variation of the scores in the experiment (SS_{Total}) is the result of variation that occurs from four independent sources: factor A, factor B, the interaction of factors A and B, and the within-cells error.

Finding Degrees of Freedom

Mean squares (MS) are obtained by dividing each SS by its degrees of freedom. Recall that degrees of freedom are defined as the number of scores that are free to vary in the computation of a statistic. I use this definition to calculate the df for each SS of equation 11–3.

Total Degrees of Freedom. To find the SS_{Total}, the grand mean $\overline{X}_G$ must be known. Because the total sum of squares is based on the difference of every score in the experiment from the grand mean (i.e., $X - \overline{X}_G$), then one less than the total number of scores are free to vary when calculating SS_{Total}. In notation,

$$df_{Total} = N - 1,$$

where N is the total number of scores in the experiment. With $N = 20$, $df_{Total} = 20 - 1 = 19$.

Degrees of Freedom for SS_A. The SS_A is computed from the differences of the main effect means of factor A (i.e., $\overline{X}_{A1}$ and $\overline{X}_{A2}$ for the example) from $\overline{X}_G$. For a factorial design with two levels of factor A, if $\overline{X}_G$ is known, then only one main effect mean for factor A is free to vary. In general, the df for SS_A are equal to one less than the number of levels of factor A, or

$$df_A = a - 1,$$

where a is the number of levels of independent variable A. For the example, $a = 2$; thus $df_A = 2 - 1 = 1$.

Degrees of Freedom for SS_B. The SS_B is computed from the differences of the main effect means of factor B (i.e., $\overline{X}_{B1}$ and $\overline{X}_{B2}$ in the example) from $\overline{X}_G$. For a factorial design with two levels of factor B, if $\overline{X}_G$ is known, then only one main effect mean for factor B is free to vary. Thus the df for SS_B are equal to one less than the number of levels of factor B, or

$$df_B = b - 1,$$

where b is the number of levels of independent variable B. For the example, $b = 2$; thus $df_B = 2 - 1 = 1$.

Degrees of Freedom for $SS_{A \times B}$.   The $SS_{A \times B}$ is found by subtracting the appropriate main effect means from each cell mean. For a 2×2 design, if each main effect mean is known, then only one cell mean is free to vary. Given one cell mean and knowing the main effect means for factors A and B, you can find the other three cell means. In general,

$$df_{A \times B} = (a - 1)(b - 1).$$

In the 2×2 design, $a = 2$ and $b = 2$; thus

$$df_{A \times B} = (2 - 1)(2 - 1) = 1.$$

Degrees of Freedom for SS_{Error}.   The SS_{Error} is found by subtracting each $\overline{X}_{AB}$ from all the scores within that cell, for all the cells in the experiment. Thus, for each treatment condition, after $\overline{X}_{AB}$ is found, only $n_{AB} - 1$ scores are free to vary within that cell. For example, in Table 11–2 only four of the five scores are free to vary within each cell if each $\overline{X}_{AB}$ is known. Because there are four cells and four scores free to vary within each cell, there are 16 df for the SS_{Error}. In general, where a is the number of levels of factor A, b the levels of factor B, and n_{AB} the number of scores within each cell,

$$df_{Error} = ab(n_{AB} - 1).$$

Additivity of Degrees of Freedom.   The degrees of freedom for a factorial analysis are additive in the same manner as they are for the one-factor analysis of variance. Thus

$$df_{Total} = df_A + df_B + df_{A \times B} + df_{Error}. \tag{11--4}$$

This relationship holds in the example, for $df_{Total} = 19$, $df_A = 1$, $df_B = 1$, $df_{A \times B} = 1$, and $df_{Error} = 16$.

Obtaining MS from SS and df

Dividing each SS in equation 11–3 by its corresponding df produces the four mean squares needed for the two-factor between-subjects analysis of variance:

$$MS_A = \frac{SS_A}{df_A}$$

$$MS_B = \frac{SS_B}{df_B}$$

$$MS_{A \times B} = \frac{SS_{A \times B}}{df_{A \times B}},$$

$$MS_{Error} = \frac{SS_{Error}}{df_{Error}}.$$

I do not obtain MS_{Total} because it is not used for any F ratios in this analysis.

For the scores in Table 11–2, I have found $SS_A = 720.000$, $SS_B = 460.800$, $SS_{A \times B} = 1656.200$, and $SS_{Error} = 1730.000$. Furthermore, $df_A = 1$, $df_B = 1$, $df_{A \times B} = 1$, and $df_{Error} = 16$. Consequently,

$$MS_A = \frac{720.000}{1} = 720.000,$$

$$MS_B = \frac{460.800}{1} = 460.800,$$

$$MS_{A \times B} = \frac{1656.200}{1} = 1656.200,$$

$$MS_{Error} = \frac{1730.000}{16} = 108.125.$$

Computing the F Statistics

An F statistic is formed by the ratio of two mean squares, one MS varying with the effect of an independent variable, as well with sampling error, and the other MS varying only with error variation in the experiment. In the two-factor between-subjects analysis of variance, MS_A varies with factor A, MS_B varies with factor B, $MS_{A \times B}$ varies with the interaction of factors A and B, and MS_{Error} varies only with the within-cells error variation. Thus three F ratios are formed, one for each systematic source of variation in the experiment:

Source of Variation	F Ratio
Factor A	$\dfrac{MS_A}{MS_{Error}}$
Factor B	$\dfrac{MS_B}{MS_{Error}}$
Interaction of $A \times B$	$\dfrac{MS_{A \times B}}{MS_{Error}}$

Substituting numerical values for the mean squares, I obtain the following F ratios:

Source of Variation	F Ratio
Factor A	$\dfrac{720.000}{108.125} = 6.66$
Factor B	$\dfrac{460.800}{108.125} = 4.26$
Interaction of $A \times B$	$\dfrac{1656.200}{108.125} = 15.32$

I discuss how to use and interpret each ratio shortly.

Table 11–7 provides a summary of the sources of variance in a two-factor between-subjects analysis of variance and the definitional formulas for each SS, df, MS, and F

TABLE 11–7
Summary of definitional formulas for a two-factor between-subjects analysis of variance.

Source	SS	df [a]	MS	F
Factor A	$\sum\sum\sum(\overline{X}_A - \overline{X}_G)^2$	$a - 1$	$\dfrac{SS_A}{df_A}$	$\dfrac{MS_A}{MS_{\text{Error}}}$
Factor B	$\sum\sum\sum(\overline{X}_B - \overline{X}_G)^2$	$b - 1$	$\dfrac{SS_B}{df_B}$	$\dfrac{MS_B}{MS_{\text{Error}}}$
Interaction of A and B	$\sum\sum\sum(\overline{X}_{AB} - \overline{X}_A - \overline{X}_B + \overline{X}_G)^2$	$(a-1)(b-1)$	$\dfrac{SS_{A \times B}}{df_{A \times B}}$	$\dfrac{MS_{A \times B}}{MS_{\text{Error}}}$
Error	$\sum\sum\sum(X - \overline{X}_{AB})^2$	$ab(n_{AB} - 1)$	$\dfrac{SS_{\text{Error}}}{df_{\text{Error}}}$	
Total	$\sum\sum\sum(X - \overline{X}_G)^2$	$N - 1$	Not calculated	

[a] a = number of levels of factor a; b = number of levels of factor B; n_{AB} = number of scores in each cell; N = total number of scores.

TABLE 11–8
Numerical summary of the analysis of variance on the hypothetical scores of Table 11–2.

Source	SS	df	MS	F
Subject visibility (A)	720.000	1	720.000	6.66*
Type of news (B)	460.800	1	460.800	4.26
$A \times B$	1656.200	1	1656.200	15.32**
Error	1730.000	16	108.125	
Total	4567.000	19		

*$p < .05$.
**$p < .01$.

ratio. A numerical summary of the analysis of variance on the data of Table 11–2 is presented in Table 11–8.

TESTING YOUR KNOWLEDGE 11-2

1. Identify the sources of variation in scores from a two-factor between-subjects design.
2. Write the equation to partition a score for the two-factor between-subjects analysis of variance.
3. Explain why the value of $\overline{X}_A - \overline{X}_G$ varies with the effect of factor A in a factorial experiment.
4. Explain why the value of $\overline{X}_B - \overline{X}_G$ varies with the effect of factor B in a factorial experiment.

5. Explain why the value of $\overline{X}_{AB} - \overline{X}_A - \overline{X}_B + \overline{X}_G$ varies with the effect of the interaction of factors A and B in a factorial experiment.

6. Explain why the value of $X - \overline{X}_{AB}$ varies only with within-cells error variation in a factorial experiment.

7. Complete the following equations for a two-factor between-subjects analysis of variance.
    a. $SS_{Total} =$
    b. $SS_A =$
    c. $SS_B =$
    d. $SS_{A \times B} =$
    e. $SS_{Error} =$
    f. $df_A =$
    g. $df_B =$
    h. $df_{A \times B} =$
    i. $df_{Error} =$
    j. $df_{Total} =$
    k. $MS_A =$
    l. $MS_B =$
    m. $MS_{A \times B} =$
    n. $MS_{Error} =$

8. What is the value of SS_{Total} if $SS_A = 40.00$, $SS_B = 70.00$, $SS_{A \times B} = 30.00$, and $SS_{Error} = 100.00$?

9. What is the value of SS_A if $SS_{Total} = 224.00$, $SS_B = 14.00$, $SS_{A \times B} = 64.00$, and $SS_{Error} = 101.00$?

10. What is the value of $SS_{A \times B}$ if $SS_{Total} = 302.00$, $SS_A = 75.00$, $SS_B = 19.00$, and $SS_{Error} = 153.00$?

11. What is the value of SS_{Error} if $SS_{Total} = 98.00$, $SS_A = 14.00$, $SS_B = 7.00$, and $SS_{A \times B} = 17.00$?

12. Find df_A, df_B, $df_{A \times B}$, df_{Error}, and df_{Total} for a 2×3 between-subjects analysis of variance with six subjects in each cell.

13. Find df_A, df_B, $df_{A \times B}$, df_{Error}, and df_{Total} for a 3×2 between-subjects analysis of variance with 13 subjects in each treatment condition.

14. What is the value of df_{Total} if $df_A = 3$, $df_B = 1$, $df_{A \times B} = 3$, and $df_{Error} = 72$?

15. Find the numerical values of mean squares for the following SS and df: $SS_A = 14.00$, $SS_B = 26.00$, $SS_{A \times B} = 44.00$, $SS_{Error} = 480.00$, $df_A = 1$, $df_B = 2$, $df_{A \times B} = 2$, and $df_{Error} = 60$.

16. Suppose that you conducted a 2×2 factorial experiment with three subjects in each cell and obtained the following scores:

		Factor A	
		A_1	A_2
	B_1	30	34
		32	36
		28	32
Factor B			
	B_2	28	38
		30	34
		26	36

   a. Partition these scores following the approach illustrated in Table 11–6. Obtain the
       SS_{Total}, SS_A, SS_B, $SS_{A \times B}$, SS_{Error}, and the corresponding degrees of freedom for
       each partition. Then complete a numerical summary table with values of MS and F.
   b. Why is SS_B equal to zero in this example?
17. Tables 1 and 2 are incomplete summary tables for a factorial between-subjects analysis
     of variance. Assume an equal number of scores in each cell. Fill in the missing values
     in each table by using the relationships among SS and df given in equations 11–3 and
     11–4, respectively. Then answer these questions for each table.
   a. How many levels of factor A were used?
   b. How many levels of factor B were used?
   c. How many subjects were measured in each cell?
   d. How many subjects participated in the study?

TABLE 1

Source	SS	df	MS	F
Factor A	_____	2	16.00	_____
Factor B	24.00	1	_____	3.00
$A \times B$	_____	_____	12.00	_____
Error	_____	_____	_____	
Total	560.00	65		

TABLE 2

Source	SS	df	MS	F
Factor A	_____	2	_____	4.50
Factor B	24.00	4	_____	1.50
$A \times B$	160.00	_____	_____	5.00
Error	_____	_____	4.00	
Total	_____	224		

STATISTICAL HYPOTHESIS TESTING WITH THE TWO-FACTOR BETWEEN-SUBJECTS ANALYSIS OF VARIANCE

To understand statistical hypothesis testing using the F statistics obtained from a factorial
analysis of variance, we must know what affects MS_A, MS_B, $MS_{A \times B}$, and MS_{Error} in an
experiment.

Factors Affecting the Value of Mean Squares in a Factorial Analysis of Variance

Each MS in a factorial analysis is affected by a different source of variation in the
experiment. If neither of the independent variables has an effect on the dependent variable
and there is no interaction of the independent variables, then each MS estimates only error

variation. Under these circumstances, all four mean squares should be approximately equal in value and reflect only the effects of sampling error. But if either or both of the independent variables have a main effect or if they interact, then the effect increases the value of the corresponding MS. For example, if factor A produces a main effect, then MS_A will increase relative to MS_{Error}, but MS_B, $MS_{A \times B}$, and MS_{Error} will not be affected by this main effect. A similar situation holds if factor B has a main effect. If factor B produces a main effect, then MS_B will increase relative to MS_{Error}, but MS_A, $MS_{A \times B}$, and MS_{Error} will not be affected by this main effect. If the independent variables interact, then $MS_{A \times B}$ increases, but MS_A, MS_B, and MS_{Error} will not be affected. The MS_{Error} is not affected by either main effects or interaction of the independent variables. It reflects only within-cells error variance in the experiment. Thus the value of each MS is independent of the value of the other mean squares.

The four mean squares and the sources of variation affecting them may be summarized as follows:

Mean Square	Affected by:
MS_A	**Systematic variance due to factor A** **Sampling error**
MS_B	**Systematic variance due to factor B** **Sampling error**
$MS_{A \times B}$	**Systematic variance due to the interaction of factors A and B** **Sampling error**
MS_{Error}	**Within-cell error variance**

To relate this understanding of the factors affecting each MS to the three F ratios of Table 11–8, notice that each F ratio uses MS_{Error} as the denominator and the appropriate MS for the independent variable or the interaction as the numerator. If the independent variable affecting the MS in the numerator of a particular F ratio does not have an effect, then that F ratio should equal about 1.00, for both the numerator and denominator MS will measure only error variation in the experiment. But if the independent variable does have an effect, then the value of the MS for that variable increases, and the value of F for that factor becomes greater than 1.0. This reasoning is identical to that expressed in Chapter 10 for the one-factor analysis of variance.

Statistical Decision Making from the F Ratios

With this understanding of the factors affecting each value of F, we are ready to use each F in a statistical hypothesis test. The steps followed are identical to those discussed in Chapter 10.

- A null hypothesis, H_0, and an alternative hypothesis, H_1, are formulated for each F ratio.

- The sampling distribution of F, assuming that H_0 is true, is obtained for each F ratio. This distribution is given in Table A–3.
- A significance level is selected.
- A critical value of F, identified as F_{crit}, is found for each of the F ratios from the sampling distribution of F given in Table A–3.
- A rejection region is located in the sampling distribution of F for each F ratio.
- The three F ratios, identified as F_{obs}, are calculated from the sample data.
- A decision to reject or not reject H_0 for each F_{obs} is made on the basis of whether or not F_{obs} falls into the rejection region.

Statistical Hypotheses

For a two-factor between-subjects analysis of variance, three different null hypotheses are tested, one for each F_{obs}. For a 2×2 factorial analysis of variance, the null (H_0) and alternative hypotheses (H_1) for each F ratio are as follows:

F Ratio for:	Statistical Hypotheses
Factor A	H_0: $\mu_{A1} = \mu_{A2}$ H_1: The μ_A's are not equal
Factor B	H_0: $\mu_{B1} = \mu_{B2}$ H_1: The μ_B's are not equal
$A \times B$	H_0: All $(\mu_{AB} - \mu_A - \mu_B + \mu_G) = 0$ H_1: Not all $(\mu_{AB} - \mu_A - \mu_B + \mu_G) = 0$

Main Effects.   The null and alternative hypotheses for the main effects of factors A and B are identical in form to the statistical hypotheses for a one-factor analysis. For the main effect of an independent variable, the factorial analysis of variance is treating the data as if they were obtained from a one-factor design as illustrated in Table 11–4. The number of population means identified in H_0 for either factor A or B corresponds to the number of levels of that factor in the experiment. For example, if an experiment involves three levels of factor A, then H_0 for factor A is written as

$$H_0: \mu_{A1} = \mu_{A2} = \mu_{A3}$$

and H_1 as

$$H_1: \text{The } \mu_A\text{'s are not all equal.}$$

The null hypothesis for each factor represents the situation that exists if the independent variable has no effect. If the null hypothesis is true, then any observed difference between the corresponding main effect means is due only to sampling error.

The alternative hypothesis states that the population means are not equal to each other, a situation that exists if the independent variable does have an effect.

Interaction. The null hypothesis for the interaction states that in the population, if no interaction occurs, then the difference of a cell mean, μ_{AB}, from the grand mean, μ_G, will be equal to zero after the main effects of each independent variable [i.e., $(\mu_A - \mu_G)$ and $(\mu_B - \mu_G)$] have been subtracted from it. In other words, this H_0 states that with no interaction of the independent variables the value of each cell mean may be exactly predicted from the main effects of the independent variables. The alternative hypothesis states that this relation is not the case and that the variation in cell means is not predictable from the main effects alone.

Decision Making from the F Ratio

Making decisions about each of the three sets of hypotheses from the values of F_{obs} is identical to the process followed in a one-factor analysis of variance. A value of α defining the size of the rejection region is chosen prior to conducting the analysis. The sampling distribution of F under H_0 is then determined for each of the three F ratios, and a rejection region is located in each sampling distribution. This step requires looking up three values of F_{crit} with the appropriate numerator and denominator df in Table A–3a or b, depending on the value of α selected. Then, for each F_{obs}, if F_{obs} is equal to or larger than its corresponding F_{crit} value, the H_0 for that F_{obs} is rejected and H_1 accepted. The difference between the means entering into that value of F_{obs} is statistically significant. If F_{obs} is less than its F_{crit} value, then the decision is to fail to reject H_0 and to not accept H_1 for that source of variance. The difference between the means entering into that value of F_{obs} is nonsignificant. The two sets of decisions for each F_{obs} in a two-factor analysis of variance are summarized in Table 11–9.

I illustrate decision making with the analysis of variance on the example data of Table 11–2, summarized in Table 11–8. In this table, each F_{obs} has 1 df for its numerator

TABLE 11–9
Summary of statistical decisions in a two-factor analysis of variance.

F Ratio for:	Value of F_{obs}	Statistical Decision	
Factor A	Less than F_{crit}	Fail to reject H_0 Do not accept H_1	The main effect of factor A is nonsignificant.
	Equal to or greater than F_{crit}	Reject H_0 Accept H_1	The main effect of factor A is statistically significant.
Factor B	Less than F_{crit}	Fail to reject H_0 Do not accept H_1	The main effect of factor B is nonsignificant.
	Equal to or greater than F_{crit}	Reject H_0 Accept H_1	The main effect of factor B is statistically significant.
$A \times B$	Less than F_{crit}	Fail to reject H_0 Do not accept H_1	The interaction of factors A and B is nonsignificant.
	Equal to or greater than F_{crit}	Reject H_0 Accept H_1	The interaction of factors A and B is statistically significant.

and 16 *df* for its denominator. Hence each F_{obs} has the same value of F_{crit} and thus the same rejection region. This relationship is not necessarily the case in all factorial analyses of variance. Depending on the number of levels of each independent variable, it is possible for each F_{obs} to have a different *df* for the numerator and thus a different rejection region.

     For $\alpha = .05$, F_{crit} with 1, 16 *df* is 4.49 (obtained from Table A–3a). Hence, for each F_{obs} in Table 11–8, the rejection region consists of values of F_{obs} equal to or larger than 4.49. Accordingly, I make the following decisions from this analysis of variance:

F Ratio for:	F_{obs}	Falls into Rejection Region	Statistical Decision	
Factor *A*	6.66	Yes	Reject H_0 Accept H_1	The main effect of factor *A* is statistically significant.
Factor *B*	4.26	No	Fail to reject H_0 Do not accept H_1	The main effect of factor *B* is nonsignificant.
$A \times B$	15.32	Yes	Reject H_0 Accept H_1	The interaction of *A* and *B* is statistically significant.

Assumptions of Factorial Between-subjects Analysis of Variance

     The factorial between-subjects analysis of variance is based on the same three assumptions about the scores obtained in an experiment as is the one-factor between-subjects analysis.

1. The scores in each sample are drawn randomly from a population of scores, and each score is independent of each other score.
2. The scores in the populations sampled are normally distributed.
3. The variances of scores in the populations are equal.

     As I pointed out with a one-factor analysis, the first assumption of independence of scores must be met for a between-subjects analysis of variance to be used. Each subject may contribute only one score in the experiment. The second and third assumptions, however, may not always be met by the data of an experiment. Again, violations of the normality and equality of variance assumptions are more likely to have minimal effects on the probability of making a Type I error when the following conditions are met:

- The number of subjects in each cell is the same.
- The shape of the distributions of the scores for each treatment condition is about the same and the distributions are neither very peaked nor very flat.
- The significance level is set at .05.

TESTING YOUR KNOWLEDGE 11-3

1. Identify the factors affecting the value of each MS in a between-subjects factorial analysis of variance.
2. Explain why MS_A increases in value if factor A has an effect in a factorial experiment.
3. Explain why MS_B increases in value if factor B has an effect in a factorial experiment.
4. Explain why $MS_{A \times B}$ increases in value if factors A and B interact in a factorial experiment.
5. Explain why the value of MS_{Error} is not affected by either factors A or B or their interaction in a factorial experiment.
6. What is expected to happen to the value of F_{obs} for factor A if factor A has an effect in an experiment?
7. What is expected to happen to the value of F_{obs} for $A \times B$ if the independent variables interact in an experiment?
8. Identify the steps in statistical testing with a factorial analysis of variance.
9. Write the statistical hypotheses for the following:
   a. A 2×4 between-subjects analysis of variance
   b. A 3×2 between-subjects analysis of variance
   c. A 3×3 between-subjects analysis of variance
10. This exercise provides incomplete analysis of variance summary tables for several two-factor between-subjects designs. For each F_{obs}, find F_{crit} for a .05 significance level from Table A–3a and indicate whether F_{obs} falls into the rejection region. Then indicate your decision with respect to H_0 and H_1. If the exact df are not tabled for df_{Error}, use the next lower tabled value.

TABLE 1

Source	df	F_{obs}
Factor A	1	4.63
Factor B	3	2.11
$A \times B$	3	3.97
Error	56	
Total	63	

TABLE 2

Source	df	F_{obs}
Factor A	3	1.42
Factor B	2	3.51
$A \times B$	6	2.37
Error	144	
Total	155	

TABLE 3

Source	df	F_{obs}
Factor A	2	4.12
Factor B	4	2.83
$A \times B$	8	1.87
Error	150	
Total	164	

11. Identify the assumptions underlying the use of the factorial between-subjects analysis of variance.

INTERPRETING A 2×2 FACTORIAL ANALYSIS OF VARIANCE

I begin discussion of the interpretation of the results of a factorial design with the steps needed to interpret a statistically significant interaction. I then turn to the interpretation of statistically significant main effects.

The Simple Effect of an Independent Variable

Simple effect of an independent variable: The effect of one independent variable at only one level of the other independent variable in a factorial design.

An **interaction of two independent variables** occurs when the effect of one independent variable depends on the level of the other independent variable with which it is combined. Consequently, a statistically significant interaction in the analysis of variance is interpreted by comparing differences among the cell means in the experiment. The differences between the cell means reveal the simple effects of the independent variables. The **simple effect of an independent variable** (sometimes called a **simple main effect**) in a factorial design is the effect of that independent variable at only one level of the other independent variable. Table 11–10 illustrates the four simple effects as well as the two main effects in a 2 × 2 design. The simple effects for each independent variable are identified in the rectangular boxes between cells. In a 2 × 2 design there are only two simple effects for each independent variable.

TABLE 11–10
Simple and main effects in a 2 × 2 between-subjects analysis of variance.

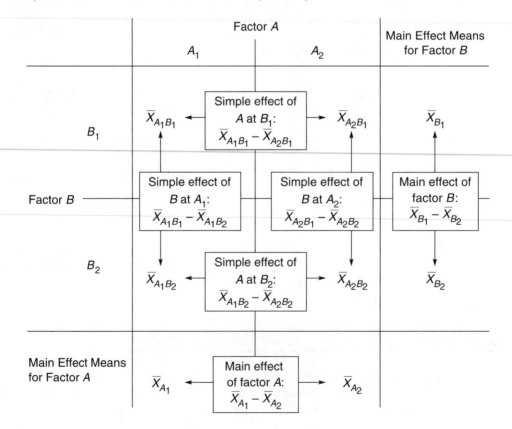

Simple Effects of Factor A

The simple effect of factor A at level B_1 of factor B is given by the difference between the $\overline{X}_{A1B1}$ and $\overline{X}_{A2B1}$ cell means (i.e., $\overline{X}_{A1B1} - \overline{X}_{A2B1}$). This difference reveals the effect of factor A at level B_1 of factor B. Similarly, the simple effect of factor A at level B_2 of factor B is given by the difference between the $\overline{X}_{A1B2}$ and $\overline{X}_{A2B2}$ cell means (i.e., $\overline{X}_{A1B2} - \overline{X}_{A2B2}$). This difference reveals the effect of factor A at level B_2. In finding the numerical values of the simple effects, it is important to maintain a consistency of direction in the comparisons and to retain the sign (+ or −) of the effect.

Simple Effects of Factor B

The simple effect of factor B at level A_1 of factor A is given by the difference between the $\overline{X}_{A1B1}$ and $\overline{X}_{A1B2}$ cell means (i.e., $\overline{X}_{A1B1} - \overline{X}_{A1B2}$), and the simple effect of factor B at level A_2 of factor A is given by the difference between the $\overline{X}_{A2B1}$ and $\overline{X}_{A2B2}$ cell means (i.e., $\overline{X}_{A2B1} - \overline{X}_{A2B2}$). Each simple effect indicates the effect of factor B at only one level of factor A.

A Numerical Example of Simple and Main Effects.   The numerical values of the simple and main effect differences from the means of Table 11–5 are presented in Table 11–11. The main effect and simple effect differences between means are shown in the rectangular boxes. For example, the simple effect of subject visibility for good news (the simple effect of factor A at B_1) is $\overline{X}_{A1B1} - \overline{X}_{A2B1}$, which equals 90.8 − 84.6, or +6.2 seconds. Likewise, the simple effect of type of news for the subject-not-visible condition (the simple effect of B at A_1) is $\overline{X}_{A1B1} - \overline{X}_{A1B2}$, which equals 90.8 − 82.2, or +8.6 seconds.

Interpreting Simple Effects When a Statistically Significant Interaction Occurs

If a statistically significant interaction of the independent variables occurs in an analysis of variance, then the two simple effects for a factor are not equal to each other or to the main effect for that factor. Thus, if there is a statistically significant interaction, the simple effect of factor A at level B_1, $\overline{X}_{A1B1} - \overline{X}_{A2B1}$, is not equal to the simple effect of factor A at level B_2, $\overline{X}_{A1B2} - \overline{X}_{A2B2}$. In addition, neither simple effect of factor A is equal to the main effect of factor A given by $\overline{X}_{A1} - \overline{X}_{A2}$.

Applying this relationship to the example results in Table 11–11, I find that the simple effect of subject visibility for good news (an effect of +6.2 seconds) is not equal to the simple effect of subject visibility for bad news (an effect of −30.2 seconds), and neither simple effect is equal to the main effect for subject visibility (an effect of −12.0 seconds).

A similar relationship applies to the simple effects of factor B. If a statistically significant interaction occurs, then the simple effect of factor B at level A_1, $\overline{X}_{A1B1} - \overline{X}_{A1B2}$, is not equal to the simple effect of B at level A_2, $\overline{X}_{A2B1} - \overline{X}_{A2B2}$. And neither simple effect equals the main effect of factor B given by $\overline{X}_{B1} - \overline{X}_{B2}$.

Applying this relationship to the example results in Table 11–11 indicates that the simple effect of type of news for the subject-not-visible condition (an effect of +8.6 seconds) is not equal to the simple effect of type of news for the subject-visible condition

TABLE 11-11
Main effect and simple effect differences of latency of response (in seconds) for subject visibility and type of news in the example experiment.

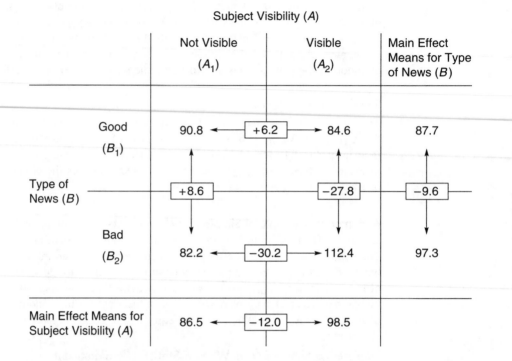

(an effect of −27.8 seconds), and neither simple effect is equal to the main effect for type of news (an effect of −9.6 seconds).

Multiple Comparison Tests for a Statistically Significant Interaction.   Each simple effect comparison in Tables 11-10 and 11-11 is a pairwise comparison; two cell means are compared with each other. To determine if the two cell means differ significantly from each other, a multiple comparison test is used to find a critical difference (CD) for the simple effect. If the observed value of the simple effect is equal to or exceeds the CD, then the difference between the cell means is statistically significant.

Again, the Tukey HSD test is frequently used for post hoc comparisons of simple effects. The CD for this test is given by

$$CD = q\sqrt{\frac{MS_{\text{Error}}}{n_{AB}}}.$$

The value of q is found from Table A-4 and depends on the number of simple effect comparisons to be made and df_{Error}. Because Table A-4 was constructed for a one-factor design, we use the following conversion to enter the table:

Type of Design	Use q from Table A–4 found in the column for ___ levels of the independent variable:
2 × 2	3
2 × 3	5
3 × 2	5
3 × 3	7
3 × 4	8
4 × 3	8
4 × 4	10

The MS_{Error} is the value of MS_{Error} calculated in the factorial analysis of variance, and n_{AB} is the number of scores in each cell.

To illustrate this computation for the 2×2 experiment on the effects of subject visibility and type of news, I use the column for $a = 3$ in Table A–4 to find q. With 16 df for MS_{Error} (from Table 11–8) and $\alpha = .05$, the value of q (3, 16) is 3.65. $MS_{Error} = 108.125$ from Table 11–8, and n_{AB}, the number of scores entering into each cell mean, is 5. Hence the numerical value of the Tukey CD is

$$CD = 3.65 \sqrt{\frac{108.125}{5}} = 3.65\sqrt{21.625}$$

$$= (3.65)(4.65) = 17.0 \quad \text{rounded to one decimal place.}$$

Any simple effect in Table 11–11 equal to or greater than 17.0 seconds in absolute value is statistically significant at the .05 level. The simple effects of subject visibility for bad news (i.e., $82.2 - 112.4 = -30.2$ seconds) and for type of news for the visible condition (i.e., $84.6 - 112.4 = -27.8$ seconds) are greater in absolute value than the CD of 17.0 seconds. These simple effects reveal statistically significant differences between the cell means involved. The simple effects for subject visibility for good news (i.e., $90.8 - 84.6 = +6.2$ seconds) and for type of news in the not visible condition (i.e., $90.8 - 82.2 = +8.6$ seconds) are less in absolute value than the CD of 17.0 seconds. These simple effects are nonsignificant, and the cell means involved differ only because of sampling error.

Interpreting Main Effects When an Interaction Occurs

When a statistically significant interaction occurs, the main effects for the independent variables may not lend themselves to meaningful interpretation. This condition happens because the main effect of an independent variable is the mean of the simple effects for that variable. For example, with an equal number of subjects in each cell, the main effect for subject visibility (-12.0 seconds) in Table 11–11 is the mean of the simple effects for subject visibility for good and bad news (i.e., $[(+6.2) + (-30.2)]/2 = -12.0$ seconds). A similar relationship holds for the main effect for type of news, -9.6 seconds.

Artifactual main effect: A main effect that does not give meaningful information about the effect of an independent variable in a factorial design.

It is the mean of the simple effects for type of news for the subject-not-visible condition, +8.6 seconds, and the subject-visible condition, −27.8 seconds. Accordingly, when an interaction occurs so that the simple effects of an independent variable are not equal to each other, the main effect of that independent variable may not accurately represent the effect of the variable. Such main effects are **artifacts of the interaction** and do not provide meaningful information about the results of the experiment. An **artifactual main effect**, then, is a main effect that does not give meaningful information about the effect of an independent variable, for it occurs only because of the specific pattern of interaction observed. It is an artificial result of the pattern of simple effects for that variable. Consequently, an important note of caution about interpreting main effects in a factorial design is in order:

- If a statistically significant interaction occurs in a factorial design, then main effects for either factor A or factor B may be artifactual and may not present meaningful results about the effect of that independent variable.
- If the interaction in a factorial design is nonsignificant, then main effects for either factor A or factor B will present meaningful results about the outcome of that independent variable.

A statistically significant interaction in an analysis of variance does not ensure that the main effects will be artifactual, but it is a warning to examine any significant main effect to find whether it provides meaningful results about the effect of the independent variable. Table 11–12a summarizes these relationships among simple and main effects when a statistically significant interaction occurs.

Interpreting Simple and Main Effects When No Statistically Significant Interaction Occurs

If no statistically significant interaction of the independent variables occurs, then the effect of one independent variable does not depend on the level of the other independent variable. Thus, if no interaction occurs, the simple effect of factor A at level B_1 will be equivalent to the simple effect of factor A at level B_2. Any observed difference between these simple effects is due only to sampling error. Furthermore, if the simple effects of factor A are equivalent to each other, they are also equivalent to the main effect of factor A, and the main effect of factor A provides the best description of the effect of this independent variable.

A similar relationship holds for the simple effects of factor B. If no interaction occurs, then the simple effect of factor B at level A_1 will be equivalent to the simple effect of factor B at level A_2. Any observed difference between these simple effects is due only to sampling error. The simple effects of factor B also are equivalent to the main effect of factor B, and the main effect of factor B provides the best description of the effect of this independent variable. These relationships are summarized in part (b) of Table 11–12.

TABLE 11–12
Interaction and interpretation of simple effects and main effects in a 2 × 2 factorial analysis of variance.

(a) If F_{obs} for the $A \times B$ interaction falls into the rejection region, then:
  - The F ratio for interaction is statistically significant.
  - The effect of one independent variable depends on the level of the other independent variable.
  - The simple effect of factor A at B_1 (i.e., $\overline{X}_{A1B1} - \overline{X}_{A2B1}$) is not equal to the simple effect of factor A at B_2 (i.e., $\overline{X}_{A1B2} - \overline{X}_{A2B2}$). The observed difference between the two simple effects for factor A is due to the interaction of the independent variables and not simply to sampling error.
  - The simple effect of factor B at A_1 (i.e., $\overline{X}_{A1B1} - \overline{X}_{A1B2}$) is not equal to the simple effect of factor B at A_2 (i.e., $\overline{X}_{A2B1} - \overline{X}_{A2B2}$). The observed difference between the two simple effects for factor B is due to the interaction of the independent variables and not simply to sampling error.
  - The simple effects of factor A are not equal to the main effect of factor A.
  - The simple effects of factor B are not equal to the main effect of factor B.
  - Each simple effect should be compared to a Tukey CD to find which cell means differ significantly from each other.
  - The main effects for either factor A or factor B may be artifactual and may not present meaningful results about the effect of the independent variable.

(b) If F_{obs} for the $A \times B$ interaction does not fall into the rejection region, then:
  - The F ratio for interaction is nonsignificant.
  - The effect of one independent variable does not depend on the level of the other independent variable.
  - The main effects for factor A and factor B will present meaningful results about the outcome of the experiment.
  - The simple effect of factor A at B_1 (i.e., $\overline{X}_{A1B1} - \overline{X}_{A2B1}$) does not differ significantly from the simple effect of factor A at B_2 (i.e., $\overline{X}_{A1B2} - X_{A2B2}$). The observed difference between the two simple effects for factor A is due to sampling error.
  - The simple effect of factor B at A_1 (i.e., $\overline{X}_{A1B1} - \overline{X}_{A1B2}$) does not differ significantly from the simple effect of factor B at A_2 (i.e., $\overline{X}_{A2B1} - \overline{X}_{A2B2}$). The observed difference between the two simple effects for factor B is due to sampling error.
  - The simple effects of factor A do not differ from the main effect of factor A. The main effect of factor A provides the best description of the effect of factor A.
  - The simple effects of factor B do not differ from the main effect of factor B. The main effect of factor B provides the best description of the effect of factor B.
  - There is no need to analyze the simple effects with a multiple comparison test.

Putting It All Together: Interpreting the Analysis of Variance on the Example Experiment

Understanding the results of a factorial experiment requires looking at each main effect and the interaction and interpreting them with respect to the decisions made in the analysis of variance. Whenever a statistically significant interaction occurs, as in the example experiment (see Table 11–8), I begin interpretation with the interaction.

Interpreting the Interaction of Subject Visibility and Type of News

The value of F_{obs} for interaction = 15.32 in Table 11–8 is greater than the F_{crit} value of 4.49 and thus falls into the rejection region. Consequently, H_0 for the interaction of factors A and B,

$$H_0: \text{All } (\mu_{AB} - \mu_A - \mu_B + \mu_G) = 0,$$

is rejected and

$$H_1: \text{Not all } (\mu_{AB} - \mu_A - \mu_B + \mu_G) = 0$$

is accepted. To interpret this interaction, I first apply the Tukey HSD critical difference to the simple effects in Table 11–11. The Tukey CD is 17.0 seconds; thus any simple effect in Table 11–11 equal to or larger than 17.0 seconds in absolute value is statistically significant at the .05 level.

Turning to Table 11–11, I first examine the simple effects of factor A, subject visibility. The simple effect of factor A at B_1, a difference of +6.2 seconds, is less than the CD of 17.0 seconds; this simple effect is nonsignificant. Subject visibility does not have an effect when good news is delivered. The difference between the not visible and visible cell means for good news (90.8 and 84.6 seconds, respectively) is due only to sampling error. The simple effect of factor A at B_2, a difference of −30.2 seconds, however, is larger in absolute value than the CD of 17.0 seconds. This simple effect is statistically significant. Bad news is delivered significantly more slowly when the subject is visible (at 112.4 seconds) than when the subject is not visible (at 82.2 seconds).

I now turn to the simple effects of factor B, type of news. The simple effect of factor B at A_1, a difference of +8.6 seconds, is less in absolute value than the CD of 17.0 seconds; this simple effect is nonsignificant. When the subject is not visible, good and bad news are delivered with equal rapidity. The difference between the good and bad news cell means for the not visible subjects (90.8 and 82.2 seconds, respectively) is due only to sampling error. The simple effect of factor B at A_2, a difference of −27.8 seconds, is larger in absolute value than the CD of 17.0 seconds; thus this simple effect is a significant difference. When the subject is visible, bad news is delivered significantly more slowly (at 112.4 seconds) than good news (at 84.6 seconds).

This analysis leads to the following summary of the outcome of this interaction of subject visibility with type of news.

- The effect of subject visibility depends on the type of news delivered.
    - a. For good news, there was no significant difference in response latency between visible and not visible subjects (90.8 and 84.6 seconds, respectively).
    - b. For bad news, the response latency of visible subjects (112.4 seconds) was significantly longer than the latency of the not visible subjects (82.2 seconds).
- The effect of type of news depends on the subject's visibility.

    a. For not visible subjects, there was no significant difference between good and bad news; not visible subjects delivered good and bad news with equivalent latencies (90.8 and 82.2 seconds, respectively).

    b. Visible subjects took significantly longer to deliver bad news compared to good news, 112.4 seconds versus 84.6 seconds, respectively.

These outcomes are in clear agreement with the predictions offered by the self-presentational hypothesis that the MUM effect is simply a public display to maintain a positive social image.

Graphic Presentation of the Results of the Example Experiment.   In published results of factorial designs, cell means frequently are presented graphically in a figure, rather than in a table such as Table 11–5, for a figure often provides a clearer portrayal of an interaction.

    The cell means from Table 11–5 are plotted in Figure 11–1. Each cell mean is identified in this figure, but in published articles the cell means are represented only by a symbol such as filled or open circles, which are labeled in a legend on the figure. When plotting a figure, one of the independent variables is placed on the abscissa (i.e., horizontal axis), and the second independent variable is represented as a function on the figure. The measure of the dependent variable is represented on the ordinate (i.e., vertical axis). Which of the two independent variables is placed on the abscissa? The rule generally followed is that the independent variable that is more quantitative in nature or with a more continuous underlying dimension is plotted on the abscissa. In the example experiment, this variable is factor B, the type of news, for type of news may vary over the good–bad dimension in a continuous manner; some news may be very good, other news may be very bad, and some news is between these two extremes. Thus the type of news variable was placed on the abscissa. The second independent variable, subject visibility, varies in a less continuous manner; there is not a continuous gradation from not visible to visible. Accordingly, this independent variable is represented by the two functions within the figure. The filled circles connected by the solid line represent the subject-not-visible condition (A_1) and the open circles connected by the dashed line indicate the subject visible condition (A_2). The dependent variable is represented on the ordinate. Because the shortest latency is 82.2 seconds, the axis is broken (by the $\doteq$) and the first labeled value begins at 80 seconds.

    Figure 11–1 portrays the differing simple effects for each of the two independent variables. When a statistically significant interaction occurs, the effect of one independent variable depends on the level of the other independent variable with which it is combined. This "it depends" nature of an interaction becomes clear from this figure. If you were asked, "What is the effect of subject visibility on response latency?", your answer would be, "It depends on the type of news delivered. For good news there is a nonsignificant difference between the subject-visible and subject-not-visible conditions, but for bad news the subject-visible condition results in a significantly longer response latency than the subject-not-visible condition." Likewise, if you were asked, "What is the effect of type

FIGURE 11-1

Latency of response (in seconds) in the example experiment as a function of the type of news (good versus bad) and subject visibility (not visible versus visible). This figure plots the cell means of Table 11-5.

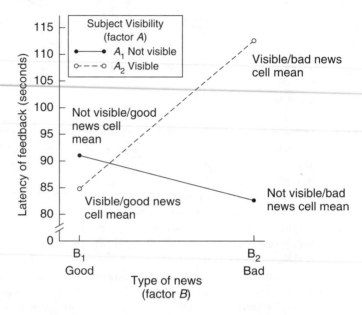

of news on response latency?", your answer would take the form, "It depends on the subject visibility condition. For the subject-not-visible condition there is a nonsignificant difference in the latency of delivery of good and bad news. For the subject-visible condition, however, there is a significantly longer latency for the bad news condition compared to the good news condition."

The lines connecting data points in Figure 11-1 are nonparallel, a distinguishing characteristic of a figure of a statistically significant interaction. Because an interaction indicates that the simple effects of an independent variable are not equal to its main effect, the plot of a statistically significant interaction must show nonparallel lines. But the lines need not cross as they do in Figure 11-1; they will only do so when the simple effects for an independent variable have opposite signs, as in this example.

In practice, it is rare for any two lines in a figure to be exactly parallel. Because of sampling error, the lines will not be precisely parallel, even when there is no statistically significant interaction. Thus visual inspection alone is not adequate to determine whether an interaction has occurred. An interaction is present in data *only* if a statistically significant F_{obs} is found for the interaction term in an analysis of variance.

Interpreting the Main Effect for Independent Variable A: Subject Visibility

The value of $F_{obs}(1, 16) = 6.66$ for the main effect of factor A in Table 11-8 is greater than $F_{crit}(1, 16) = 4.49$. This F_{obs} falls into the rejection region and "H_0: $\mu_{A1} = \mu_{A2}$" for subject visibility is rejected, and "H_1: The μ_A's are not equal" is accepted. This decision implies that the main effect for subject visibility (the difference of -12.0 seconds between the main effect means of 86.5 and 98.5 seconds for subject not visible and subject visible, respectively) is statistically significant. This main effect indicates that news is delivered more rapidly in the subject-not-visible condition than it is in the subject-visible condition. But this main effect is artifactual, and the relationship it implies does not hold for both good and bad news. As our examination of the interaction revealed, the subject-visible condition leads to a significantly longer latency only when bad news is delivered. For good news, the latencies under the subject-not-visible and subject-visible conditions do not differ significantly. Thus, although the main effect for subject visibility indicates a longer latency for the subject-visible condition, analysis of the simple effects indicates that this relationship holds only when bad news is delivered; it does not hold for good news. Thus the main effect for subject visibility does not convey meaningful information about the results of the experiment; it is artifactual.

Interpreting the Main Effect for Independent Variable B: Type of News

The value of F_{obs} for factor B, the type of news, is 4.26. This value of F_{obs} is less than F_{crit} of 4.49 and hence "H_0: $\mu_{B1} = \mu_{B2}$" is not rejected and "H_1: The μ_B's are not equal" is not accepted. This decision implies that the main effect for type of news (the difference of -9.6 seconds between 87.7 and 97.3 seconds for good and bad news, respectively) is nonsignificant. From this nonsignificant main effect alone, I would conclude that type of news does not affect the response latency of a subject; the 9.6-second main effect difference between the good and bad news conditions is due to sampling error. But does this conclusion accurately describe the effect of type of news? Again, examination of the simple effects indicates that it does not; type of news does have an effect, but the effect depends on the visibility of the subject. When the subject is not visible to the confederate, there is no significant difference in the response latency between good and bad news (i.e., the difference between 90.8 and 82.2 seconds is due to sampling error); but when the subject is visible to the confederate, the bad news ($\overline{X}_{A2B2} = 112.4$ seconds) is delivered significantly more slowly than the good news ($\overline{X}_{A2B1} = 84.6$ seconds). The statistically significant interaction has made it inappropriate to interpret the nonsignificant main effect for type of news. The personal discomfort hypothesis predicted a statistically significant and meaningful main effect for type of news. It should take longer to deliver bad news than good news, regardless of whether the subject is or is not visible to the confederate. The result of the main effect for type of news in this example is clearly not in agreement with the prediction of the personal discomfort hypothesis.

Patterns of Interaction

The relationship among the cell means in the example experiment is only one of many that may result in a statistically significant interaction. A statistically significant interaction in the analysis of variance indicates only that the simple effect and main effect differences for an independent variable will not be equal. It alone does not provide any further information about the numerous ways in which this result may occur. The exact nature of the interaction can be determined only by carefully analyzing the relationships among the cell means, as I have done for the example experiment.

Measuring the Strength of a Treatment Effect in a Factorial Analysis of Variance

As with the one-factor analysis of variance, the strength of a statistically significant effect in a factorial design may be measured by η^2. Because there are tests for two main effects and the interaction, I obtain three different values of η^2 as follows:

$$\eta^2 = \frac{SS_A}{SS_{Total}} \quad \text{for a statistically significant main effect of factor } A.$$

$$\eta^2 = \frac{SS_B}{SS_{Total}} \quad \text{for a statistically significant main effect of factor } B.$$

$$\eta^2 = \frac{SS_{A \times B}}{SS_{Total}} \quad \text{for a statistically significant interaction of factors } A \text{ and } B.$$

To illustrate the use of η^2 for the example, the interaction provided the only meaningful information in the experiment; thus η^2 for the interaction based on the SS values from Table 11–8 is

$$\eta^2 = \frac{SS_{A \times B}}{SS_{Total}} = \frac{1656.200}{4567.000} = .36.$$

This value indicates that 36 percent of the variance in the response latencies is accounted for by the interaction of subject visibility and type of news.

TESTING YOUR KNOWLEDGE 11–4

1. Define: artifactual main effect, main effect, simple effect.
2. Each of the following tables and Figures 11–2 and 11–3 present cell means obtained in an experiment. A summarized analysis of variance is included for each set of means. In the summarized analysis, a statistically significant F_{obs} is indicated by $p < .05$. A nonsignificant F_{obs} is indicated by $p > .05$. When a significant interaction occurs, the Tukey HSD CD for the simple effects is given at the bottom of the analysis of variance summary. Assume that factor A is teaching method with two levels, computer-assisted (A_1) and noncomputer-assisted teaching (A_2). Factor B is type of material to be learned, mathematical (B_1) or social studies (B_2). The dependent variable is test score. Interpret each set of means by finding the simple and main effects for each independent variable and relating these effects to the summarized analysis of variance. Then answer these questions for each example:
   a. Do the main effect means of factor A differ significantly from each other?
   b. Do the main effect means of factor B differ significantly from each other?
   c. Is there a statistically significant interaction of factors A and B?
   d. What is the effect of teaching method (factor A) on test scores?
   e. What is the effect of type of material (factor B) on test scores?
   f. Do the main effects provide useful information about the results of the experiment?

FIGURE 11–2

Outcome of an experiment involving manipulation of factors A and B.

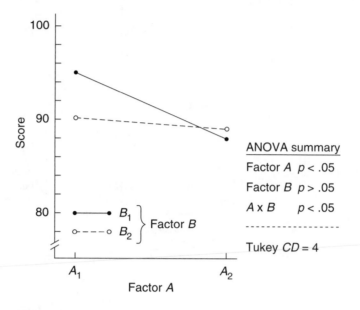

ANOVA summary

Factor A $p < .05$

Factor B $p > .05$

$A \times B$ $p < .05$

- - - - - - - - - - - - - - - - -

Tukey $CD = 4$

FIGURE 11–3

Outcome of an experiment involving manipulation of factors A and B.

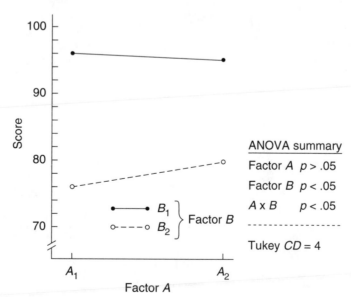

ANOVA summary

Factor A $p > .05$

Factor B $p < .05$

$A \times B$ $p < .05$

- - - - - - - - - - - - - - - - -

Tukey $CD = 4$

TABLE 1

		Factor A		ANOVA Summary	
		A_1	A_2		
Factor B	B_1	91	85	Factor A	$p < .05$
				Factor B	$p > .05$
	B_2	92	87	$A \times B$	$p > .05$

TABLE 2

		Factor A		ANOVA Summary	
		A_1	A_2		
Factor B	B_1	89	90	Factor A	$p > .05$
				Factor B	$p < .05$
	B_2	81	80	$A \times B$	$p > .05$

TABLE 3

		Factor A		ANOVA Summary	
		A_1	A_2		
Factor B	B_1	85	94	Factor A	$p < .05$
				Factor B	$p < .05$
	B_2	78	86	$A \times B$	$p > .05$

TABLE 4

		Factor A		ANOVA Summary	
		A_1	A_2		
Factor B	B_1	88	75	Factor A	$p > .05$
				Factor B	$p > .05$
	B_2	76	90	$A \times B$	$p < .05$
				Tukey $CD = 4$	

TABLE 5

		Factor A		ANOVA Summary	
		A_1	A_2		
Factor B	B_1	87	88	Factor A	$p < .05$
				Factor B	$p < .05$
	B_2	74	80	$A \times B$	$p < .05$
				Tukey $CD = 4$	

TABLE 6

		Factor A		ANOVA Summary	
		A_1	A_2		
	B_1	90	80	Factor A	$p < .05$
Factor B				Factor B	$p < .05$
	B_2	81	82	$A \times B$	$p < .05$
				Tukey $CD = 4$	

Example Problem 11–1

Analyzing a 2 × 2 Design with a Statistically Significant Interaction and Nonsignificant Main Effects

Problem

Vision and hearing are two independent senses, yet, there may be a common dimension of experience across them. Visual stimuli are sometimes described as loud and sounds as bright. Thus Lindner and Hynan (1987) hypothesized that the type of music a person listened to would affect the perception of an abstract painting. To test this hypothesis, they varied the type of music a subject listened to, either unstructured avant-garde or structured minimalistic music (factor A), and the gender of the subject, male or female (factor B), in a 2×2 between-subjects design. While listening to the music, each subject viewed eight abstract paintings. After viewing the paintings, the subject rated the paintings on several 7-point rating scales. One rating scale was composed of the adjective pairs *constrained* (1) to *free* (7), *rigid* (1) to *flexible* (2), and *constricted* (1) to *expanded* (7). Suppose that scores were obtained by summing over the three sets of adjective pairs so that a rating could range from 3 to 21. Assume that the following hypothetical scores were obtained from 24 subjects.

	Type of Music (A)	
	Avant-garde (A_1)	Minimalistic (A_2)
Male (B_1)	4	16
	5	14
	7	17
	6	19
	10	16
	4	20
Gender of Subject (B)		
Female (B_2)	12	5
	15	9
	18	7
	13	6
	16	10
	16	5

Is there an effect of type of music on the ratings of pictures, do males and females differ in the ratings given, and is there an interaction of type of music with gender of the subjects?

Solution   The design used is a 2×2 between-subjects design. The first step is to perform a two-factor between-subjects analysis of variance on the scores to determine if either statistically significant main effects or a statistically significant interaction exists. I use a .05 significance level.

Assumptions for Use:
1. The subjects were sampled randomly and independently from a population.
2. The error in ratings is normally distributed in the population.
3. The variances for the rating scores are equal in the populations sampled.

Statistical Hypotheses:

Factor A H_0: $\mu_{A1} = \mu_{A2}$.
                 H_1: The μ_A's are not equal.

Factor B H_0: $\mu_{B1} = \mu_{B2}$.
                 H_1: The μ_B's are not equal.

$A \times B$ H_0: All $(\mu_{AB} - \mu_A - \mu_B + \mu_G) = 0$.
                 H_1: Not all $(\mu_{AB} - \mu_A - \mu_B + \mu_G) = 0$.

Significance Level: $\alpha = .05$.

df:

$$df_A = a - 1 = 2 - 1 = 1$$
$$df_B = b - 1 = 2 - 1 = 1$$
$$df_{A \times B} = (a - 1)(b - 1) = (2 - 1)(2 - 1) = 1$$
$$df_{\text{Error}} = ab(n_{AB} - 1) = (2)(2)(6 - 1) = 20$$
$$df_{\text{Total}} = N - 1 = 24 - 1 = 23$$

Critical Value of F: Each F_{obs} has 1 df for the numerator and 20 df for the denominator; thus $F_{\text{crit}}(1, 20) = 4.35$ from Table A–3a.

Rejection Region: Values of F_{obs} equal to or greater than 4.35.

Calculation: The analysis of variance may be calculated on the scores using the computational formulas given in the chapter supplement or by using a computer program. I used the formulas from the chapter supplement to obtain the following summary table.

Source	df	SS	MS	F
Music (A)	1	13.50	13.50	2.81
Gender (B)	1	1.50	1.50	0.31
A × B	1	541.50	541.50	112.81*
Error	20	96.00	4.80	
Total	23	652.50		

$^*p < .01.$

Decisions: Three decisions must be made for the statistical hypotheses of this analysis, one for each F_{obs}.

- Type of music (factor A): $F_{obs} = 2.81$. This F_{obs} does not fall into the rejection region; I fail to reject H_0 and do not accept H_1.
- Gender (factor B): $F_{obs} = 0.31$. This F_{obs} does not fall into the rejection region; I fail to reject H_0 and do not accept H_1.
- Type of music by gender (A×B): $F_{obs} = 112.81$. This F_{obs} falls into the rejection region; I reject H_0 and accept H_1.

Strength of Effect: η^2 for the statistically significant interaction equals $SS_{A \times B}/SS_{Total}$ = 541.50/652.50 =.83.

Interpretation and Conclusions: To interpret the statistically significant interaction, I find the Tukey HSD CD for the simple effects and then compare the simple effects to this CD. The numerical values needed for this test are found as follows:

- q is obtained from Table A–4. Using the conversion chart for a 2×2 design given with this table, the value of q is obtained for $a = 3$ and 20 df for MS_{Error}. This value is 3.58 for $\alpha = .05$.
- MS_{Error}, obtained from the analysis of variance, is 4.80.
- n_{AB}, the number of scores in each cell, is 6.

Substituting these numerical values into the formula,

$$CD = q \sqrt{\frac{MS_{Error}}{n_{AB}}}$$

$$= 3.58 \sqrt{\frac{4.80}{6}}$$

$$= 3.58 \sqrt{0.8}$$

$$= (3.58)(0.89)$$

$$= 3.2 \quad \text{rating points.}$$

Any simple effect equal to or larger than 3.2 rating points in absolute value is statistically significant at the .05 level.

Table 11–13 presents the cell and main effect means and the simple and main effects for the scores. Each simple effect in this table is larger in absolute value than the $CD = 3.2$ and thus is statistically significant. Notice, however, that for each independent variable the simple effects are opposite in sign. The effect of type of music clearly depends on the gender of the subject. Males hearing avant-garde music typically rate the paintings as 6.0 (constrained, rigid, and constricted), but males hearing minimalistic music rate the paintings significantly higher at 17.0 (free, flexible, and expanded). This rating pattern is reversed for females. When listening to avant-garde music, females rate the paintings as 15.0, whereas when listening to minimalistic music they give a significantly lower rating of 7.0. The simple effects for type of music (−11.0 for males, +8.0 for females) are not equal to each other, nor are they equal to the nonsignificant main effect of −1.5 for music.

Similarly, the difference between males and females in rating the paintings depends on the type of music. Females listening to avant-garde music ($\overline{X}_{A1B2} = 15.0$) rate the paintings as significantly more free, flexible, and expanded than do males

TABLE 11–13
Main effect and simple effect differences in ratings of paintings as function of type of music and gender of subject.

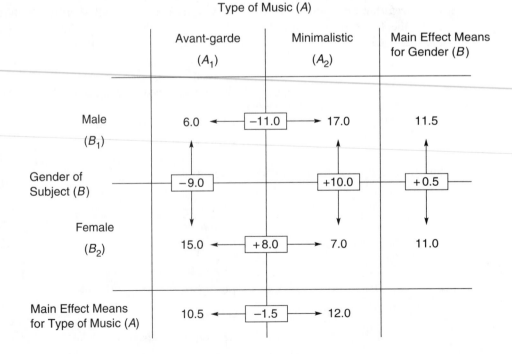

$(\overline{X}_{A1B1} = 6.0)$ listening to avant-garde music. But males listening to the minimalistic music $(\overline{X}_{A2B1} = 17.0)$ rate the paintings as significantly higher in this dimension than do females $(\overline{X}_{A2B2} = 7.0)$. Thus the simple effects for gender (-9.0 for avant-garde music, $+10.0$ for minimalistic music) are not equal to each other or to the nonsignificant main effect of $+0.5$ for gender of the subjects.

The main effects do not provide useful information about the results of this experiment. From the main effects alone, I would conclude that there is no effect for type of music and that males and females do not differ on their ratings. The analysis of the interaction, however, indicates that type of music does have an effect on the ratings given, but the direction of the effect depends on gender. Furthermore, males and females differ in their ratings, but the difference depends on the type of music. The η^2 indicates that 83 percent of the variance in the ratings is determined by the interaction. Predicting scores from the cell means rather than the grand mean reduces the total variance by 83 percent in this sample.

Example Problem 11–2

Analyzing a 2 × 2 Design with a Statistically Significant Interaction and Main Effects

Problem

The keyword method is a memory-enhancement technique in which a person uses a visual image to form an association between two items. One use of this method is in helping to learn the vocabulary of a second language. Suppose that you are asked to learn a list of unfamiliar French words and their English equivalents, such as the French word *boue* and its English equivalent *mud*. Here the keyword might be *boot*, an English word that sounds like the French *boue*. To use the technique, when you hear *boue*, you think of *boot* and then form an image of a person wearing boots and walking through *mud*. A number of studies have shown that the keyword technique enhances learning and immediate recall of a second language vocabulary (Wang, Thomas, & Ouellette, 1992). How long this improved recall lasts, however, is open to question. Wang et al. (1992) found that, although the keyword technique enhanced immediate retention in comparison to rote learning by simple repetition of the words, the keyword subjects also forgot at a greater rate over a one-week retention interval.

Suppose that you are interested in finding if this relationship holds for adult learners as well as for the college students tested by Wang et al. Accordingly, you use a 2 × 2 between-subjects design with learning method, either rote or keyword as factor *A*, and retention interval, either immediate or delayed for one week, as factor *B*. You randomly assigned eight adult learners unfamiliar with French to each treatment condition. Subjects in the rote learning method were told to simply repeat the French words and their English equivalents over and over in order to remember them. In the keyword method, subjects were taught the keyword method and given a keyword for each French–English pair. For the immediate-retention condition, recall of the English equivalents was tested 5 minutes after the list was learned. For the delayed-retention groups, subjects were tested for recall of the English equivalents one week after they had learned the list. The list of words was 25 items long, so a subject's recall score could vary from 0 (no recall) to 25 (perfect recall). Assume that the accompanying hypothetical recall scores were given by the 32 subjects. Analyze and describe the results of this experiment.

	Learning Condition (A)	
	Rote (A_1)	Keyword (A_2)
Immediate (B_1)	12	25
	9	22
	11	19
	19	23
	16	17
	14	24
	13	20
	15	21
Retention Interval (B)		
Delayed (B_2)	6	9
	7	4
	3	7
	11	11
	5	5
	10	8
	5	12
	8	6

Solution   A two-factor between-subjects analysis of variance is needed to statistically analyze this experiment. I use a .05 significance level.

Assumptions for Use:
1. The subjects were sampled randomly and independently from a population.
2. Recall scores are normally distributed in the population.
3. The variances for the recall scores are equal in the populations sampled.

Statistical Hypotheses:

Factor A H_0: $\mu_{A1} = \mu_{A2}$.
H_1: The μ_A's are not equal.

Factor B H_0: $\mu_{B1} = \mu_{B2}$.
H_1: The μ_B's are not equal.

$A \times B$ H_0: All $(\mu_{AB} - \mu_A - \mu_B + \mu_G) = 0$.
H_1: Not all $(\mu_{AB} - \mu_A - \mu_B + \mu_G) = 0$.

Significance Level: $\alpha = .05$.

df:
$$df_A = a - 1 = 2 - 1 = 1$$
$$df_B = b - 1 = 2 - 1 = 1$$
$$df_{A \times B} = (a - 1)(b - 1) = (2 - 1)(2 - 1) = 1$$
$$df_{\text{Error}} = ab(n_{AB} - 1) = (2)(2)(8 - 1) = 28$$
$$df_{\text{Total}} = N - 1 = 32 - 1 = 31$$

Critical Value of F: $F_{\text{crit}}(1, 28) = 4.20$ for each value of F_{obs}.

Rejection Region: Values of F_{obs} equal to or greater than 4.20.

Calculation: The formulas from the chapter supplement were used to obtain the following summary table.

Source	SS	df	MS	F^*
Learning condition (A)	148.781	1	148.781	18.59*
Retention interval (B)	830.281	1	830.281	103.73*
$A \times B$	94.531	1	94.531	11.81*
Error	224.125	28	8.004	
Total	1297.718	31		

$^*p < .01.$

Decisions:
- Learning condition (factor A): $F_{\text{obs}} = 18.59$. This F_{obs} falls into the rejection region; I reject H_0 and accept H_1.
- Retention interval (factor B): $F_{\text{obs}} = 103.73$. This F_{obs} falls into the rejection region; I reject H_0 and accept H_1.
- Learning condition by retention interval ($A \times B$): $F_{\text{obs}} = 11.81$. This F_{obs} falls into the rejection region; I reject H_0 and accept H_1.

Strength of Effect:

Learning condition: $\eta^2 = SS_A / SS_{\text{Total}}$
$$= 148.781/1297.718 = .11.$$

Retention interval: $\eta^2 = SS_B / SS_{\text{Total}}$
$$= 830.281/1297.718 = .64.$$

Learning condition $\times$ retention interval:
$$\eta^2 = SS_{A \times B} / SS_{\text{Total}}$$
$$= 94.531/1297.718 = .07.$$

Interpretation and Conclusions: I first interpret the interaction by finding the Tukey HSD CD for the simple effects and then comparing the simple effects to this CD. The numerical values needed for this test are found as follows:

- q is obtained from Table A–4 for $a = 3$ and 28 df for MS_{Error}. Because 28 df are not tabled for MS_{Error}, q for the next lower tabled df, 24 was used. This value is 3.53 for $\alpha = .05$.
- MS_{Error} is 8.004.
- n_{AB} is 8.

Substituting these numerical values into the formula,

$$CD = q \sqrt{\frac{MS_{Error}}{n_{AB}}}$$

$$= 3.53 \sqrt{\frac{8.004}{8}}$$

$$= 3.53\sqrt{1.000}$$

$$= 3.5 \text{ words,} \quad \text{rounded to one decimal place.}$$

Any simple effect equal to or larger than 3.5 words in absolute value is statistically significant at the .05 level. Table 11–14 presents the cell and main effect means and the simple and main effects for the scores. I first interpret the interaction for each independent variable and then the main effect of that variable.

Learning Condition: The simple effect of learning condition for immediate recall, -7.8, is greater in absolute value than the CD of 3.5 and is statistically significant. The keyword condition ($\overline{X}_{A2B1} = 21.4$ words) results in significantly greater recall than does rote learning for immediate retention ($\overline{X}_{A1B1} = 13.6$ words). For delayed retention, however, the simple effect of learning condition, -0.9, is smaller in absolute value than the CD of 3.5. This simple effect is nonsignificant. Thus, for delayed retention, rote ($\overline{X}_{A1B2} = 6.9$ words) and keyword ($\overline{X}_{A2B2} = 7.8$ words) conditions do not differ significantly. Learning condition has no effect on recall for delayed retention. The $F_{obs}(1, 28) = 18.59$ for the main effect of learning condition is statistically significant, indicating that the main effect means for learning condition ($\overline{X}_{A1} = 10.2$ and $\overline{X}_{A2} = 14.6$) differ significantly. But this significant main effect does not provide meaningful information about the outcome of the experiment. This main effect indicates that subjects recall more words with the keyword condition, but the analysis of the simple effects for learning condition revealed that this relationship holds only for the immediate-recall interval; it does not hold for the delayed-retention interval. Hence the main effect of learning condition does not provide a correct description of the effect of learning condition. I thus ignore it in the description of the results of the experiment.

Retention Interval: The significant interaction indicates also that the effect of retention interval depends on learning condition. For both levels of learning condition, the simple effects of retention interval ($+6.7$ for rote learning, $+13.6$ for keyword learning) are larger

TABLE 11–14
Main effect and simple effect differences in number of words correctly recalled as a function of learning condition and retention interval.

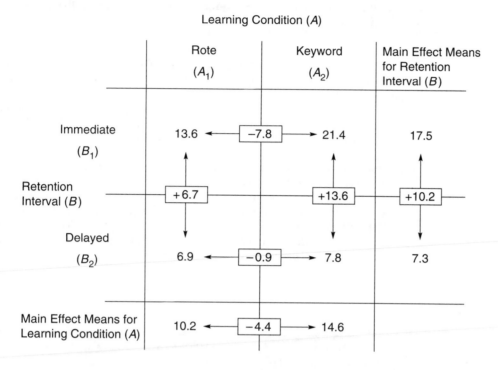

Learning Condition (A)

	Rote (A_1)	Keyword (A_2)	Main Effect Means for Retention Interval (B)
Immediate (B_1)	13.6 ◄— −7.8 —► 21.4		17.5
Retention Interval (B)	+6.7	+13.6	+10.2
Delayed (B_2)	6.9 ◄— −0.9 —► 7.8		7.3
Main Effect Means for Learning Condition (A)	10.2 ◄— −4.4 —► 14.6		

in absolute value than the *CD* of 3.5. These statistically significant simple effects indicate that, for both rote and keyword learning, delayed recall results in significantly less recall than does immediate recall. Examination of the simple effects, however, reveals that the decrease in retention from immediate to delayed recall is greater for the keyword condition (13.6 words) than it is for the rote condition (6.7 words). The statistically significant main effect of retention interval [i.e., $F_{obs}(1, 28) = 103.73$, $p < .05$] indicates that the main effect means for retention interval ($\overline{X}_{B1} = 17.5$ and $\overline{X}_{B2} = 7.3$) differ significantly. From this significant main effect alone, I conclude that immediate recall leads to greater retention than does delayed retention. This conclusion is correct, for the relationship holds for both rote and keyword conditions. Hence the main effect for retention interval is meaningful and provides useful information about the results of the experiment. The interpretation of this main effect must be qualified, however, by recognizing that the interaction indicates that the extent of the difference between immediate and delayed recall depends on learning condition.

The η^2 for the main effect of retention interval, .64, indicates that the retention interval accounts for a large proportion of the variance in recall scores. The η^2 for the interaction, .07, indicates that the interaction accounts for a smaller portion of the variance in the recall scores. Because the main effect of learning condition is artifactual, I do not utilize the eta squared for this factor.

STATISTICS IN USE 11–1

Do Token Rewards Increase Intelligence Test Scores? Using the Two-factor Analysis of Variance

Schoolchildren are frequently given individual intelligence tests, and it is assumed that when taking these tests the children are motivated highly and will perform to the best of their abilities. To ensure the highest level of motivation, examiners are trained to provide praise for a child's efforts on the test. But does this praise necessarily lead to the highest level of performance for a child? What if a child were given a token for a correct answer and then allowed to trade tokens for a toy after completing the test? Bradley-Johnson, Graham, and Johnson (1986) hypothesized that this use of token rewards would improve performance over the standard testing conditions. To test this hypothesis, they used a 2×2 between-subjects design and varied administration of the *Wechsler Intelligence Scale for Children—Revised* (WISC—R) (factor A) over two conditions: standard administration (identified as the control condition A_1) and tokens given for correct answers (identified as the token reward condition A_2). Two different grade levels of children (factor B) were used: 20 first- and second-graders (B_1) and 20 fourth- and fifth-graders (B_2). Ten students from each grade level were tested under each administration condition. The mean WISC—R verbal score for each condition is shown in Figure 11–4.

A summary table of a 2×2 between-subjects analysis of variance on the intelligence test scores is given next.

Source	SS	df	MS	F
Administration (A)	313.600	1	313.600	5.66*
Grade level (B)	577.600	1	577.600	10.42*
$A \times B$	25.600	1	25.600	0.46
Error	1995.270	36	55.424	
Total	2912.070	39		

*$p < .05$.

The analysis of variance revealed that the main effects of both independent variables were statistically significant, but the interaction was nonsignificant. The use of tokens led to significantly higher verbal intelligence scores for both grade levels. In addition, first- and second-graders obtained higher scores than fourth- and fifth-graders in both administration conditions. Because there is no statistically significant interaction, the effect of the token did not depend on the grade level of the child. Thus no analysis of the simple effects using the Tukey HSD test is required. The two lines in the figure are considered parallel. The slight observable lack of parallelness is treated as due to sampling error. The results of the experiment are completely described by the main effects of administration condition and grade level. Eta squared is .11 for factor A and .20 for factor B, indicating that both the type of administration and the grade level account for a considerable portion of the variance on the test scores.

FIGURE 11–4
Mean WISC—R scores as a function of type
of administration conditions and grade level.
(Adapted with permission of publisher and
authors from Table 1 of "Token reinforcement on
WISC—R performance for white, low-socioeconomic, upper and lower elementary-school-
age students." Sharon Bradley-Johnson, Dixie
Payne Graham, and C. Merle Johnson, *Journal
of School Psychology* 1986, *24*, 73–79.)

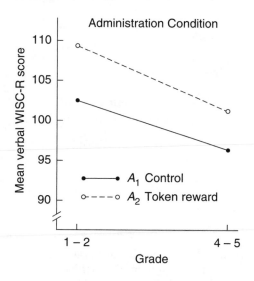

These results indicate that standard testing conditions do not lead necessarily to maximal performance on an intelligence test. Bradley-Johnson et al. thus suggest that additional research is necessary to understand conditions that improve performance on these tests.

TESTING YOUR KNOWLEDGE 11–5

Complete these problems using a two-factor between-subjects analysis of variance following the format illustrated in the example problems. Use a .05 significance level for each problem.

1. A psychologist hypothesized that the effect of type of instructions on a person's performance on an anagram solution task would depend on that individual's perceived locus of control. To evaluate this hypothesis, she obtained 12 females who scored low on a locus of control scale (thus indicating an internal locus of control) and 12 females who scored high on the scale (thus indicating an external locus of control). Half the females in each group were randomly assigned to one of two instructional conditions, skill or chance instructions. In the skill-instructions condition, subjects were told that their performance on an anagram solution

task depended on their verbal ability and was under their control. The chance instructions indicated that performance on this task does not depend on verbal ability and is beyond a person's control. The subjects then solved a series of anagrams, and the amount of time devoted to the task was recorded. Suppose that the following amounts of time (in seconds) that each subject worked on solving the anagrams were obtained:

		Locus of Control (A)	
		Internal (A_1)	External (A_2)
	Skill (B_1)	175	115
		202	106
		193	87
		186	93
		150	99
		212	157
Instructions (B)			
	Chance (B_1)	125	218
		100	202
		77	196
		101	244
		131	237
		152	180

a. Calculate the cell and main effect means. Then analyze the scores to determine (1) if there is a main effect for either independent variable and (2) if there is an interaction of the independent variables.

b. Describe the effect of type of instructions. If needed, use the Tukey HSD test to determine the statistically significant simple effects.

c. Are you able to meaningfully interpret any statistically significant main effects or are they artifactual?

d. What proportion of the variance in the dependent variable can be accounted for by the interaction of the independent variables?

2. In many jurisdictions, potential jurors are shown a film to acquaint them with the legal process and the nature of the jury system. Suppose that a lawyer was interested in finding out whether the film alters a juror's behavior in comparison to standard oral instructions. Furthermore, the lawyer wanted to know if any effect of the film may depend on the type of crime the juror is to evaluate. To answer these questions, the lawyer conducted a 2×2 between-subjects factorial experiment with nine subjects in each treatment condition serving as mock jurors. Factor A was the type of instruction given to jurors: A_1, normal oral instructions by a court officer, and A_2, filmed instructions. Factor B was the type of crime that the subject was asked to evaluate; this variable was manipulated by having the subjects read a description of an auto theft case (level B_1) or of an aggravated assault case (level B_2). Each subject was then asked to assign a prison term to the defendant described in the case. The prison terms assigned (in months) are given in the accompanying table.

		Type of Instruction (A)	
		Normal (A_1)	Filmed (A_2)
Type of Crime (B)	Auto Theft (B_1)	15	13
		10	16
		10	9
		14	11
		17	14
		9	8
		8	10
		12	10
		10	12
	Aggravated Assault (B_2)	25	30
		20	33
		23	26
		20	25
		19	30
		17	35
		18	30
		22	28
		20	32

a. Calculate the cell and main effect means. Then analyze the scores to determine (1) if there is a main effect for either independent variable and (2) if there is an interaction of the independent variables.

b. Describe the effect of type of instructions.

c. Describe the effect of type of crime.

d. Are you able to meaningfully interpret any statistically significant main effects or are they artifactual?

e. What proportion of the variance in the dependent variable can be accounted for by the type of crime and the interaction of the independent variables?

REPORTING THE RESULTS OF A FACTORIAL ANALYSIS OF VARIANCE

The style of reporting the results of a factorial experiment follows that used for the one-factor design in Chapter 10. I illustrate using the results of the example problem on the effects of subject visibility (subject visible or subject not visible) and type of news (good or bad) on the latency to deliver the news. Cell means for this experiment are presented in Table 11–5 and the analysis of variance summarized in Table 11–8. Because of the expense of printing tables, the results of an experiment, including cell means and the statistical analysis, are often reported in text format as illustrated here.

An alpha level of .05 was used for all statistical tests. There was a significant interaction of subject visibility with the type of news to be delivered, $F(1, 16) = 15.32$, $MSE = 108.125$, $p < .01$. The Tukey HSD test (critical difference = 17.0 s with $\alpha = .05$) was used for testing the statistical significance of the simple effects. When good news was delivered, the effect of subject visibility was nonsignificant ($M = 90.8$ s, $SD = 11.56$ s for subject not visible, and $M = 84.6$ s, $SD = 9.61$ s for subject visible). For the delivery of bad news, however, the latency of the subject-visible condition ($M = 112.4$ s, $SD = 11.15$ s) was significantly longer than for the subject-not-visible condition ($M = 82.2$ s, $SD = 9.07$ s). The difference in latency between the good and bad news for the subject-not-visible condition was non-significant. For the subject-visible condition, however, the latency of the delivery of bad news was significantly longer than the latency for the delivery of good news. Eta squared for the interaction was .36. The main effect of subject visibility was statistically significant, $F(1, 16) = 6.66$, $p < .05$, but was not meaningful. The main effect for type of news was nonsignificant, $F(1, 16) = 4.26$, $p > .05$.

In this presentation:

$\alpha = .05$	Indicates the significance level selected for the statistical tests.
$F(1, 16)$	Identifies the test statistic as the F. The df for the numerator and denominator of each F_{obs} reported are shown in parentheses. Three values of F_{obs} are reported, one for each independent variable and one for the interaction of the independent variables. The order in which F_{obs} is reported is not necessarily factor A, factor B, and $A \times B$. Often an experimenter has more interest in the interaction and will present this F_{obs} value first in the description of the results, as illustrated in the example.
$= 15.32$	Gives the value of F_{obs} (not the F_{crit} value found in Table A–3). In some instances, only two of the three F_{obs} obtained in the analysis of variance may be reported. In this case you may assume that the unreported value of F_{obs} was nonsignificant.
$p < .01$	Indicates that

    a. The probability of F_{obs} if H_0 is true is less than or equal to .01. This value is the probability of F_{obs} or an even more extreme value of F_{obs} if H_0 is true; it may not be the same as the value of α selected.

    b. H_0 was rejected and H_1 was accepted.

    c. The F_{obs} was for the interaction term of the analysis of variance; thus it indicates that the interaction of factors A and B is statistically significant.

    d. Something other than sampling error is responsible for the interaction of factors A and B.

$MSE = 108.125$	Gives the MS_{Error} for the F_{obs}. This value is a measure of the within-cells error variation in the scores.
$CD = 17.0$	Gives the critical difference for simple effect comparisons using the Tukey HSD test. The statistically significant simple effects are then described.

$\eta^2 = .36$ Indicates that 36 percent of the variance in the response latencies in this experiment is accounted for by the interaction of factors A and B. In this example, the interaction provides the only meaningful information about the outcome of the experiment; thus η^2 is given only for this source of variance.

TESTING YOUR KNOWLEDGE 11-6

The following exercises present sample reports of two-factor between-subjects analyses of variance. Answer the following questions for each report.

    a. How many levels of factor A were varied in this experiment?
    b. How many levels of factor B were varied in this experiment?
    c. How many subjects were used in the experiment?
    d. What is the value of F_{crit} at the .05 significance level for each F_{obs} reported?
    e. Is the value of F_{obs} for factor A statistically significant?
    f. Is the value of F_{obs} for factor B statistically significant?
    g. Is the value of F_{obs} for $A \times B$ statistically significant?

1. An alpha level of .05 was used for all statistical tests. The main effect of drug level (factor A) was statistically significant, $F(2, 36) = 9.43$, $p < .01$, $MSE = 17.814$. There was also a main effect for retention interval (factor B), $F(1, 36) = 5.60$, $p < .05$. The interaction was nonsignificant, $F(2, 36) = 2.46$, $p > .05$.

2. An alpha level of .05 was used for all statistical tests. There was a significant gender of athlete (factor A) by type of sport (factor B) interaction on self-esteem ratings, $F(3, 88) = 3.28$, $p < .05$, $MSE = 42.163$. In addition, males gave higher-rated self-esteem than females, $F(1, 88) = 4.82$, $p < .05$. There were no main effect differences among sport types, $F(3, 88) = 1.65$, $p > .05$.

3. An alpha level of .05 was used for all statistical tests. There was a significant interaction of noise condition with personality type $F(1, 56) = 5.33$, $p < .05$, $MSE = 26.718$. Neither the main effect for noise condition, $F(1, 56) < 1.0$, nor personality type $F(1, 56) = 1.43$, $p > .05$, was significant.

SUMMARY

- Factorial designs are research designs in which two or more independent variables are varied simultaneously.
- Each cell or treatment condition of a factorial design represents a combination formed from one level of each independent variable.
- Main effect means indicate the typical performance of all individuals given one level of an independent variable, while ignoring the classification by the other independent variable.
- An interaction occurs in a factorial design when the effect of one independent variable depends on the level of the other independent variable with which it is combined.

- Three F ratios are obtained in the two-factor between-subjects analysis of variance.

Source of Variation	F Ratio
Factor A	MS_A/MS_{Error}
Factor B	MS_B/MS_{Error}
Interaction of $A \times B$	$MS_{A \times B}/MS_{\text{Error}}$

- The steps in statistical testing with these F ratios are identical to those discussed in Chapter 10.
- The simple effect of an independent variable in a factorial design is the effect of that independent variable at only one level of the other independent variable.
- If a statistically significant interaction of the independent variables occurs, then the two simple effects for a factor are not equal to each other or to the main effect for that factor.
- An artifactual main effect is a main effect that cannot be meaningfully interpreted; it occurs only because of the specific pattern of interaction obtained.
- Follow-up tests are needed to statistically analyze the simple effects if a significant interaction is obtained. The Tukey HSD test is used for post hoc comparisons.
- η^2 is used as a measure of the strength of a treatment effect for statistically significant main effects and interaction.

KEY TERMS AND SYMBOLS

$A \times B$ interaction
artifactual main effect
cell
cell mean
column mean
critical difference
CD
df_A
df_B
$df_{A \times B}$
df_{Error}
df_{Total}
eta squared (η^2)
factor

factor A
factor B
factorial design
grand mean
interaction
level of an independent variable
main effect for factor A
main effect for factor B
main effect mean
MS_A
MS_B
$MS_{A \times B}$
MS_{Error}
n_{AB}

row mean
simple effect
strength of effect
SS_A
SS_B
$SS_{A \times B}$
SS_{Error}
SS_{Total}
treatment condition
Tukey HSD test
$\overline{X}_{AB}$
$\overline{X}_A$
$\overline{X}_B$
$\overline{X}_G$

CHAPTER SUPPLEMENT: CALCULATING A TWO-FACTOR BETWEEN-SUBJECTS ANALYSIS OF VARIANCE WITH COMPUTATIONAL FORMULAS

This supplement provides the computational formulas for a two-factor between-subjects analysis of variance with an equal number of subjects in each cell. The notational representation with two levels of each factor and five scores per cell is as follows:

Factor A

		A_1		A_2		
	B_1	X_{111} X_{211} X_{311} X_{411} X_{511}	T_{A1B1}	X_{121} X_{221} X_{321} X_{421} X_{521}	T_{A2B1}	T_{B1}
Factor B	B_2	X_{112} X_{212} X_{312} X_{412} X_{512}	T_{A1B2}	X_{122} X_{222} X_{322} X_{422} X_{522}	T_{A2B2}	T_{B2}
		T_{A1}		T_{A2}		G

where
X_{ijk} = score of a subject
T_A = total of scores for a level of factor A
T_B = total of scores for a level of factor B
T_{AB} = total of scores in a cell
G = grand total of scores
n_{AB} = number of scores in a cell
a = number of levels of factor A
b = number of levels of factor B
N = total number of scores

Five numerical values are found using these terms:

$$[1] = \Sigma\Sigma\Sigma X_{ijk}^2 \qquad \text{the sum of all the scores squared,}$$

$$[2] = \frac{\Sigma\Sigma T_{AB}^2}{n_{AB}} \qquad \text{the sum of each cell total squared divided by the number of scores in a cell,}$$

$$[3] = \frac{\Sigma T_A^2}{bn_{AB}}$$
the sum of each level total for factor A squared divided by the number of scores entering into each total,

$$[4] = \frac{\Sigma T_B^2}{an_{AB}}$$
the sum of each level total for factor B squared divided by the number of scores entering into each total,

$$[5] = \frac{G^2}{N}$$
the grand total squared divided by the total number of scores.

Using these numerical values, an analysis of variance is obtained as follows:

Source of Variance	SS	df	MS	F
Factor A	$[3] - [5]$	$a - 1$	$\dfrac{SS_A}{df_A}$	$\dfrac{MS_A}{MS_{\text{Error}}}$
Factor B	$[4] - [5]$	$b - 1$	$\dfrac{SS_B}{df_B}$	$\dfrac{MS_B}{MS_{\text{Error}}}$
$A \times B$	$[2] - [3] - [4] + [5]$	$(a - 1)(b - 1)$	$\dfrac{SS_{A \times B}}{df_{A \times B}}$	$\dfrac{MS_{A \times B}}{MS_{\text{Error}}}$
Error	$[1] - [2]$	$ab(n_{AB} - 1)$	$\dfrac{SS_{\text{Error}}}{df_{\text{Error}}}$	
Total	$[1] - [5]$	$N - 1$	Not calculated	

To illustrate the computations, I use the example scores given in Table 11–2 for which an analysis of variance is summarized in Table 11–8.

		Factor A				
		A_1		A_2		
Factor B	B_1	97 90 80 107 80	$T_{A1B1} = 454$	70 87 81 95 90	$T_{A2B1} = 423$	$T_{B1} = 877$
	B_2	68 87 92 80 84	$T_{A1B2} = 411$	114 96 127 110 115	$T_{A2B2} = 562$	$T_{B2} = 973$
		$T_{A1} = 865$		$T_{A2} = 985$		$G = 1850$

and $n_{AB} = 5$, $a = 2$, $b = 2$, and $N = 20$.

The values of the numerical computational terms are

$$[1] = 97^2 + \cdots + 80^2 + 70^2 + \cdots + 90^2 + 68^2 + \cdots + 84^2 + 114^2 + \cdots + 115^2$$

$$= 175{,}692.000$$

$$[2] = \frac{(454)^2 + (423)^2 + (411)^2 + (562)^2}{5} = \frac{869{,}810.00}{5} = 173{,}962.000$$

$$[3] = \frac{(865)^2 + (985)^2}{(2)(5)} = \frac{1{,}718{,}450.00}{10} = 171{,}845.000$$

$$[4] = \frac{(877)^2 + (973)^2}{(2)(5)} = \frac{1{,}715{,}858.00}{10} = 171{,}585.800$$

$$[5] = \frac{1850^2}{20} = \frac{3{,}422{,}500.00}{20} = 171{,}125.000$$

Then

$$SS_A = [3] - [5] = 171{,}845.000 - 171{,}125.000 = 720.000$$

$$df_A = a - 1 = 2 - 1 = 1$$

$$MS_A = \frac{720.000}{1} = 720.00$$

$$SS_B = [4] - [5] = 171{,}585.800 - 171{,}125.000 = 460.800$$

$$df_B = b - 1 = 2 - 1 = 1$$

$$MS_B = \frac{460.800}{1} = 460.800$$

$$SS_{A \times B} = [2] - [3] - [4] + [5]$$

$$= 173{,}962.000 - 171{,}845.000 - 171{,}585.800 + 171{,}125.000 = 1656.200$$

$$df_{A \times B} = (a - 1)(b - 1) = (2 - 1)(2 - 1) = 1$$

$$MS_{A \times B} = \frac{1656.200}{1} = 1656.200$$

$$SS_{\text{Error}} = [1] - [2] = 175{,}692.000 - 173{,}962.000 = 1730.000$$

$$df_{\text{Error}} = ab(n_{AB} - 1) = (2)(2)(5 - 1) = 16$$

$$MS_{\text{Error}} = \frac{1730.000}{16} = 108.125$$

$$SS_{\text{Total}} = [1] - [5] = 175{,}692.000 - 171{,}125.000 = 4567.000$$

$$df_{\text{Total}} = N - 1 = 20 - 1 = 19$$

Values of F_{obs} are thus

Factor A: $F_{obs} = \dfrac{MS_A}{MS_{Error}} = \dfrac{720.000}{108.125} = 6.66$

Factor B: $F_{obs} = \dfrac{MS_B}{MS_{Error}} = \dfrac{460.800}{108.125} = 4.26$

Interaction of factors A and B: $F_{obs} = MS_{A \times B}/MS_{Error}$

$$F_{obs} = \dfrac{1656.200}{108.125} = 15.32.$$

The summary of the analysis of variance is

Source	SS	df	MS	F
Subject visibility (A)	720.000	1	720.000	6.66*
Type of news (B)	460.800	1	460.800	4.26
$A \times B$	1656.200	1	1656.200	15.32**
Error	1730.000	16	108.125	
Total	4567.000	19		

$^*p < .05.$ $^{**}p < .01.$

The values obtained by this computational approach are identical to those presented in Table 11–8 obtained from the definitional formulas of an analysis of variance.

REVIEW QUESTIONS

Answer questions 1 to 3 by performing a two-factor between-subjects analysis of variance on the scores given.

1. How does level of physiological arousal change when we engage in social exchange with others? To partially answer this question, Wellens (1987) used a 2×2 between-subjects design in which subjects were interviewed by an experimenter. One independent variable (factor A) was eye contact of the experimenter with the subject during the interview. Two levels were manipulated: no eye contact (A_1) and eye contact (A_2) made. The second independent variable (factor B) was a manipulation of affect with two levels: positive (B_1) and negative (B_2). In the positive-affect condition, subjects were given a written "first impression" of them by the interviewer that was very favorable. For the negative-affect condition, they were given a written first impression of them by the interviewer that was very unfavorable. The dependent variable was the subject's heart rate in beats per minute recorded while the interview was being conducted. Suppose that

you replicated this experiment with eight subjects per cell and obtained the following heart rates.

	Eye-contact Condition (A)	
	No Eye Contact (A_1)	Eye Contact (A_2)
Positive (B_1)	75	61
	77	68
	68	71
	72	59
	83	74
	78	66
	70	67
	65	57
Negative (B_2)	79	84
	82	79
	75	88
	77	90
	84	75
	72	75
	78	77
	69	85

Affect Condition (B)

a. Does the effect of eye contact depend on the level of affect? If so, use the Tukey HSD test for the simple effect comparisons. Describe the relationship that you found.
b. Does the effect of the affect condition depend on the eye-contact condition? If so, use the Tukey HSD test for the simple effect comparisons. Describe the relationship that you found.
c. Are you able to meaningfully interpret any main effects or are they artifactual?
d. What proportion of the variance in the dependent variable can be accounted for by the interaction of the independent variables?
e. Describe the results of this experiment following the style illustrated in the Reporting the Results of a Factorial Analysis of Variance section of this chapter.

2. Bellizzi and Hite (1987) hypothesized that the headline size and position of an advertisement convey an impression of the magnitude of a sale. To test this hypothesis, they used a 2×2 between-subjects design. Subjects in the experiment were shown an advertisement and asked to judge the magnitude of the sale by estimating the percentage off the regular price that they would expect in the sale. One independent variable (factor A) was the size of the word *sale* in the ad. The small size (A_1) was 0.5 inch and the large size (A_2) was 2.0 inches. The second independent variable (factor B) was the placement of the word *sale* on the ad. One placement (B_1) was horizontal and the second (B_2) was diagonal across the page.

Suppose that you conducted a similar experiment with 12 subjects per cell and obtained the following estimates of the percentage reduction in prices.

	Word-size Condition	
	Small (A_1)	Large (A_2)
Horizontal (B_1)	7	15
	9	10
	13	17
	5	12
	6	10
	8	16
	9	11
	11	14
	10	15
	10	15
	5	9
	16	20
Diagonal (B_2)	10	15
	6	17
	8	20
	8	11
	14	11
	5	10
	5	14
	5	13
	11	15
	9	17
	7	16
	7	13

Word-placement Condition (B)

a. Does word size affect the perceived magnitude of the sale? If so, describe the effect.

b. Does word placement affect the perceived magnitude of the sale? If so, describe the effect.

c. Does the effect of word size depend on the level of word placement? Does the effect of word placement depend on the word size?

d. Are you able to meaningfully interpret any main effects or are they artifactual?

e. Find the values of η^2 for any meaningful effects.

f. Describe the results of this experiment following the style illustrated in the Reporting the Results of a Factorial Analysis of Variance section of this chapter.

3. One aspect of teaching children to read is to have them learn to process information from the material read. A strategy proposed to enhance this processing is to ask the reader to answer questions after reading each page of a story. To test if this strategy does indeed increase reading

comprehension, Seretny and Dean (1986) divided a sample of second-graders into three reading-level ability groups (factor A): below average (A_1), average (A_2), and above average (A_3). Half the subjects in each group were given reading instruction (factor B) in which the children read orally and the teacher did not ask questions each time the child finished reading a page (the control group, level B_1). The other half of the subjects (the questions group, level B_2) were given reading instruction in which they too read orally, but the teacher asked questions each time a page was completed. After eight weeks of instruction the children were tested on reading comprehension. Suppose that the following comprehension scores were obtained for nine children in each cell (larger scores indicate higher levels of reading comprehension).

		Reading Ability Level (A)	
	Below Average (A_1)	Average (A_2)	Above Average (A_3)
Control (B_1)	10	16	21
	14	17	24
	16	23	23
	12	19	20
	14	20	23
	13	15	25
	15	19	21
	11	18	26
	13	21	22
Type of Instruction (B)			
Questions (B_2)	15	18	21
	18	24	19
	22	19	20
	18	22	23
	21	21	24
	17	20	24
	18	20	22
	16	22	25
	16	23	20

a. Does the effect of type of instruction depend on the level of reading ability? If so, use the Tukey HSD test for the simple effects. Describe the relationship between type of instruction and reading-level ability that you found.
b. What is η^2 for the interaction?
c. Are you able to meaningfully interpret any main effects or are they artifactual?
d. Describe the results of this experiment following the style illustrated in the Reporting the Results of a Factorial Analysis of Variance section of this chapter.

4. A psychologist used a 2×3 between-subjects design with eight subjects in each cell.
   a. What are the values of a, b, n_{AB}, and N for this design?
   b. What are the values of df_A, df_B, $df_{A \times B}$, df_{Error}, and df_{Total} for this design?

5. The following tables are incomplete summary tables for between-subjects factorial analyses of variance. Assume an equal number of subjects in each cell. Use the relationships among SS, df, and MS to provide the missing values in each table. Then answer the following questions for each table.
   a. How many levels of factor A were varied?
   b. How many levels of factor B were varied?
   c. How many subjects were used in each cell?
   d. What was the total number of subjects in the experiment?
   e. Which values of F_{obs} are statistically significant at the .05 level?
   f. What decision do you make for each null and alternative hypothesis for this analysis?

TABLE 1

Source	SS	df	MS	F
Type of task (A)	_____	3	5.00	_____
Noise level (B)	16.00	_____	_____	_____
A × B	36.00	6	_____	_____
Error	_____	60	2.00	
Total	_____	_____		

TABLE 2

Source	SS	df	MS	F
Training length (A)	40.00	_____	10.00	_____
Skill level (B)	_____	3	40.00	_____
A × B	960.00	_____	80.00	_____
Error	3200.00	160	_____	
Total	_____	179		

TABLE 3

Source	SS	df	MS	F
Type of feedback (A)	200.00	_____	50.00	_____
Task difficulty (B)	_____	_____	_____	_____
A × B	_____	8	30.00	_____
Error	_____	_____	20.00	
Total	3300.00	149		

6. Suppose that you had subjects learn a series of sentences and then recall the nouns in the sentences. You manipulated two levels of type of imagery (factor A), ordinary imagery and bizarre imagery, and two levels of the amount of elaboration (factor B), low and high elaboration, of the sentences. Each subject had 30 sentences to learn; thus a maximum of 30 nouns could be recalled. The cell means for number of nouns correctly recalled are shown in Table 1. An analysis of variance for these data is presented in Table 2. Assume a between-subjects design with five subjects per cell.

TABLE 1
Mean number of nouns correctly recalled as a function of type of imagery and amount of elaboration.

		Type of imagery (A)	
		Ordinary (A_1)	Bizarre (A_2)
Amount of Elaboration	Low (B_1)	21.4	4.8
	High (B_2)	10.4	18.8

TABLE 2
Analysis of variance summary table for mean number of nouns recalled in Table 1.

Source	SS	df	MS	F
Type of imagery A)	84.050	1	84.050	4.91*
Amount of elaboration (B)	11.250	1	11.250	0.66
$A \times B$	781.250	1	781.250	45.62**
Error	274.000	16	17.125	
Total	1150.550	19		

*$p < .05$.   **$p < .01$.

A Tukey HSD yielded a $CD = 6.8$ words for the simple effects.
   a. What is the effect of type of imagery on the recall of nouns?
   b. What is the effect of amount of elaboration on the recall of nouns?
7. A human factors psychologist was interested in the ability of pilots to read aircraft instruments after a period of sleep deprivation. She used two different types of gauges for the pilots to read, analog and digital, as illustrated in Figure 11–5.
   The psychologist obtained a sample of pilots, and half were assigned to read the analog gauge and the other half, the digital gauge. For each group, half the pilots were tested after a normal night's sleep and the other half after they had been deprived of sleep for 24 hours. Thus a 2×2 between-subjects design was used with type of gauge, analog or digital,

FIGURE 11–5
Illustration of an analog and a digital gauge.

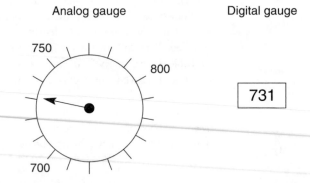

Analog gauge   Digital gauge

as one independent variable, and amount of sleep deprivation, none or 24 hours, as the second independent variable. The dependent variable was the number of correct readings out of 100 trials. The cell means for the number of correct readings are given in Table 1. An analysis of variance for these data is presented in Table 2.

TABLE 1
Mean number of correct gauge readings as a function of type of gauge and amount of sleep deprivation.

	Type of Gauge (A)	
	Analog (A_1)	Digital (A_2)
None (B_1)	89.0	91.0
Amount of sleep deprivation (B)		
24 hours (B_2)	72.0	81.0

TABLE 2
Analysis of variance summary for mean correct gauge readings in Table 1.

Source	SS	df	MS	F
Type of gauge (A)	211.750	1	211.750	11.71**
Amount of sleep deprivation (B)	1275.750	1	1275.750	70.56**
$A \times B$	85.750	1	85.750	4.74*
Error	433.920	24	18.080	
Total	2007.170	27		

*$p < .05$.   **$p < .01$.

The *CD* for simple effects using a Tukey HSD test is 5.7 correct readings.

    a. What is the effect of type of gauge on the number of correct readings?

    b. What is the effect of amount of sleep deprivation on the number of correct readings?

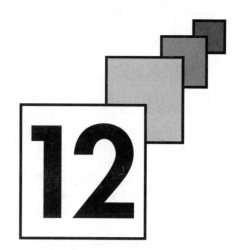

One-factor Within-subjects Designs and Analysis of Variance

ONE-FACTOR WITHIN-SUBJECTS DESIGNS

Chapter 9 introduced within-subjects designs and the t test for related scores. This chapter expands the discussion of within-subjects designs and introduces the analysis of variance for these designs.

Within-subjects design: A research design in which one group of subjects is exposed to and measured under each level of the independent variable.

In a **one-factor within-subjects design** a single group of subjects is exposed to and measured under each level of the independent variable. Because subjects are measured repeatedly in a within-subjects design, it also is called a **repeated measures design** or a **treatments-by-subjects design**, a reminder that each subject is tested under all levels of the independent variable.

Table 12–1 presents the notation for the scores of a one-factor within-subjects design with four levels of an independent variable and five subjects. The independent variable is identified as factor A with levels A_1, A_2, A_3, and A_4. The number of levels of factor A is represented by a; for Table 12–1, $a = 4$. A score for a subject is represented by X_{ij}, where the subscript i represents a number identifying the subject (e.g., X_{1j}, X_{2j},..., X_{5j}) and the subscript j represents a number identifying the level of the independent variable. Thus X_{34} represents the score of subject 3 in level 4 of factor A. When it is not necessary to identify a specific subject, I drop the ij subscripts and simply use X. The means for each level of the independent variable are indicated by $\overline{X}_{A1}$, $\overline{X}_{A2}$, $\overline{X}_{A3}$, and $\overline{X}_{A4}$, or generally by $\overline{X}_A$. The number of scores in a level of the independent variable is represented by n_A. Notice that n_A is also the number of subjects in a within-subjects design. The total number of scores in the experiment is represented by N. For Table 12–1, $n_A = 5$ and $N = 20$. The mean for a subject over all levels of factor A is represented by $\overline{X}_S$. This mean represents the typical performance of a subject over all levels of the independent variable.

TABLE 12–1
Notational representation of scores from a one-factor within-subjects design with four levels of the independent variable and five subjects.

Subject	Factor A				Means for Subject
	A_1	A_2	A_3	A_4	
S_1	X_{11}	X_{12}	X_{13}	X_{14}	$\overline{X}_{S1}$
S_2	X_{21}	X_{22}	X_{23}	X_{24}	$\overline{X}_{S2}$
S_3	X_{31}	X_{32}	X_{33}	X_{34}	$\overline{X}_{S3}$
S_4	X_{41}	X_{42}	X_{43}	X_{44}	$\overline{X}_{S4}$
S_5	X_{51}	X_{52}	X_{53}	X_{54}	$\overline{X}_{S5}$
Means for Factor A	$\overline{X}_{A1}$	$\overline{X}_{A2}$	$\overline{X}_{A3}$	$\overline{X}_{A4}$	$\overline{X}_G$

An Example One-factor Within-subjects Experiment

Look at Figure 12–1. Although there are only partially filled circles present, it appears that there are edges forming a triangle between the dots. These edges are called *subjective contours*, for they do not exist in the stimulus itself. Is it possible to use subjective contours to induce an illusion in perception? Suppose that we decide to investigate this question by using several forms of the Ponzo illusion, as did Meyer (1986). Figure 12–2a illustrates the standard Ponzo illusion. This figure is an illusion because the two horizontal lines are physically equal in length, although they do not appear to be equal. The top line appears longer than the bottom line. Figure 12–2b presents a subjective contours version of this illusion. The version in Figure 12–2c provides orientation information, but the solid dots do not introduce a subjective contour. Finally, Figure 12–2d presents a control condition in which no illusion should occur. Suppose that a subject is asked to adjust the length of the bottom horizontal line so that it appears equal in length to the top horizontal line, and suppose further that the length of the top line is 14.0 centimeters (cm). If no illusion appears, then the bottom line also should be adjusted to 14.0 cm. If, however, an illusion appears, then the top line should appear to be longer than it really is (i.e., it should appear to be longer than 14.0 cm), and the bottom line should be adjusted to match its perceived length.

A one-factor within-subjects experiment with four levels of type of illusion (factor *A*) and five subjects is used to test the effect of illusion condition on the perceived magnitude of the illusion. Each subject views each of the four stimuli shown in Figure 12–2 and adjusts the bottom horizontal line to look equal in length to the top horizontal line. The adjusted length of the bottom horizontal line, in centimeters, is the dependent variable. Suppose that the scores obtained are those presented in Table 12–2. Is the magnitude of the perceived illusion affected by the illusion condition?

As with between-subjects designs, the analysis of the data in Table 12–2 begins with calculation of descriptive statistics. Thus treatment means and standard deviations are shown at the bottom of each column in the table. If the independent variable does affect the perception of the illusion, then the treatment means should differ from each other. But, as we know, any differences observed between treatment means must always be viewed against a background of error variation. How much might the means differ

FIGURE 12–1
Subjective contours form-
ing a triangle.

FIGURE 12–2
Four versions of the Ponzo illusion: (a) standard, (b) subjective contours, (c) solid dots, and (d) control (no illusion).

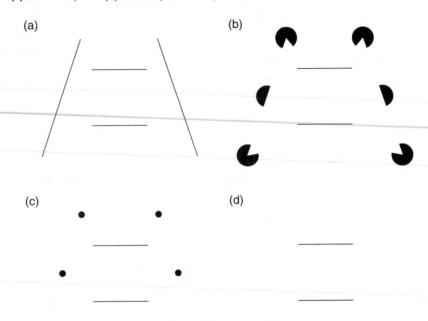

TABLE 12–2
Perceived equal line lengths (in cm) from five subjects viewing four versions of the Ponzo illusion.

	Illusion Condition (A)				
Subject	Standard (A_1)	Subjective Contours (A_2)	Solid Dots (A_3)	Control (A_4)	Subject Means
1	16.6	15.8	14.7	14.4	15.38
2	16.9	15.6	15.1	13.8	15.35
3	17.1	16.1	14.8	13.9	15.48
4	17.2	16.3	15.2	14.1	15.70
5	16.8	15.7	15.3	14.3	15.53
$\overline{X}_A$	16.92	15.90	15.02	14.10	
s_A	0.24	0.29	0.26	0.25	

by sampling error alone? A simple visual inspection of the means does not permit an answer to this question. As I have done for between-subjects designs, I resolve this decision-making problem by using a statistical test, the one-factor within-subjects analysis of variance.

ONE-FACTOR WITHIN-SUBJECTS ANALYSIS OF VARIANCE

The one-factor within-subjects analysis of variance is used to analyze one-factor multilevel within-subjects designs. If only two levels of an independent variable are manipulated, the one-factor within-subjects analysis of variance may be used in place of t_{rel}. This analysis partitions the total variation of scores in an experiment into three sources:

1. The effect of the independent variable (**factor** A)
2. The effect of individual differences among subjects (**factor** S)
3. The interaction of the treatments with the subjects ($A \times S$)

These three partitions are used to obtain three mean squares:

1. MS_A, which varies with the effect of the independent variable and error variation
2. MS_S, which varies with differences among subjects
3. $MS_{A \times S}$, which varies with the interaction of treatments with subjects and provides a measure of the error variation in the experiment

The F ratio used in the statistical hypothesis test is

$$F = \frac{MS_A}{MS_{A \times S}}.$$

Partitioning a Score and Obtaining Sums of Squares

In this section I discuss the partitioning of scores and obtaining sums of squares for a within-subjects design. Because the approach followed is very similar to that for the between-subjects design, the presentation of the partitioning will be brief.

To understand how sources of variance from a within-subjects design are partitioned, it is useful to think of the within-subjects design as a two-factor design with the independent variable as one factor (factor A) and the subjects being tested as the second factor (factor S, where S represents the subject). Because each subject is tested under each level of the independent variable, a one-factor within-subjects design can be regarded as an $A \times S$ factorial design with a levels of factor A and n_A levels of factor S. Thus there are $a \times n_A$ conditions, or cells, and each cell represents one level of the independent variable combined with a particular subject. In Table 12–2, there are four levels of factor A and five subjects; therefore, the experiment can be viewed as a 4 (levels of illusion condition) $\times$ 5 (number of subjects) factorial design, producing a total of 20 different treatment-by-subject ($A \times S$) conditions. But only one score is obtained for each $A \times S$ condition.

Thinking of the one-factor within-subjects analysis of variance as a two-factor analysis of variance allows obtaining "main effect" means for factors A and S. Notice in Table 12–2 that means are given for each subject, as well as for each level of the independent variable. Each subject mean is the mean of the scores of a single subject over all the illusion conditions. These means reflect individual differences in the perception of illusions among the subjects in the experiment. Although the subject means are relevant to the analysis of variance, these means typically are not reported as descriptive statistics for experiments using a within-subjects design.

Conceptualizing a one-factor within-subjects analysis of variance as a two-factor analysis does not change the nature of the experiment; only one independent variable is manipulated and its effect analyzed. Thinking of the analysis as a two-factor design, however, helps to understand the introduction of the $A \times S$ interaction as the error term for the F ratio.

To obtain the F ratio, the analysis of variance for a within-subjects design takes the total amount by which a score differs from the grand mean and partitions this difference into three components, as follows:

$$\begin{pmatrix} \text{Total} \\ \text{variation} \\ \text{in a} \\ \text{subject's} \\ \text{score} \end{pmatrix} = \begin{pmatrix} \text{Variation due} \\ \text{to factor } A \\ \text{plus error due} \\ \text{to the interaction} \\ \text{of factors } A \\ \text{and } S \end{pmatrix} + \begin{pmatrix} \text{Variation due} \\ \text{to individual} \\ \text{differences} \\ \text{among} \\ \text{subjects} \\ \text{(factor } S\text{)} \end{pmatrix} + \begin{pmatrix} \text{Variation} \\ \text{due to} \\ \text{interaction} \\ \text{of factors} \\ A \text{ and } S \end{pmatrix} . \quad (12\text{--}1)$$

Following the basic approach of analysis of variance, the components of the partitioned scores are squared and summed over subjects and treatment conditions to obtain the sum of squares:

$$SS_{\text{Total}} = SS_A + SS_S + SS_{A \times S}. \quad (12\text{--}2)$$

These sums of squares indicate that the total variation of the scores in the experiment (given by SS_{Total}) is the result of variation that occurs from factor A (given by SS_A), factor S (given by SS_S), and the interaction of factors A and S (given by $SS_{A \times S}$). For the scores in Table 12–2, this process leads to the numerical values

$$SS_{\text{Total}} = 22.926,$$
$$SS_A = 21.830,$$
$$SS_S = 0.314,$$
$$SS_{A \times S} = 0.782.$$

I examine each sum of squares of equation 12–2.

SS_{Total}

The SS_{Total} represents the total variation of the scores in the experiment. As equation 12–2 indicates, a part of this variation is due to the effect of the independent variable, part is due to individual differences among subjects, and part is due to the treatments-by-subjects interaction.

SS_A

The SS_A varies with the effect of an independent variable and with treatments-by-subjects interaction. As with the one-factor between-subjects design, an effect of an independent variable increases the value of SS_A. In addition, the SS_A responds to any treatments-by-subjects interaction. In a within-subjects design, the treatments-by-subjects interaction is considered to be error variation.

SS_S

The SS_S varies with individual differences among the subjects in the experiment. I refer to these differences among subjects as factor S. Notice from Table 12–2 that subject 4 tends to see the largest amount of an illusion over all levels of the independent variable ($\overline{X}_{S4} = 15.70$ cm), whereas subject 2 perceives the least illusion ($\overline{X}_{S2} = 15.35$ cm). The more the subject means differ from each other in an experiment, the larger SS_S becomes.

$SS_{A \times S}$

Treatments-by-subjects interaction: A situation in a one-factor within-subjects design where the effect of the independent variable depends on the subject.

The interaction of the treatment with the subjects is the remaining variation in a score and affects $SS_{A \times S}$. This **treatments-by-subjects interaction** can be seen in Figure 12–3, which depicts the hypothetical data of Table 12–2. The four types of illusion figures are represented on the abscissa. The functions within the figure depict the four scores obtained from each of the five subjects. The perceived equal line length is longest for all subjects at the standard illusion condition. Thus there is an apparent effect-of-illusion condition on perceived line length. Because the five functions are not parallel, however, a treatments-by-subjects interaction is present, too. The difference in perceived line length between the illusion conditions is not the same for all subjects. For example, for subject 1, the difference in the standard condition and subjective contour condition scores is $16.6 - 15.8 = 0.8$ cm, but for subject 2 the difference is $16.9 - 15.6 = 1.3$ cm. Thus the effect-of-illusion condition on perceived line length depends on the subjects. The $SS_{A \times S}$ provides a measure of the extent of the treatments-by-subjects interaction in a within-subjects experiment. But, because only one score is obtained from each subject in each treatment condition, the treatments-by-subjects interaction cannot be separated from any error that may be affecting the score. Accordingly, $SS_{A \times S}$ is considered to be a measure of the error variation in a one-factor within-subjects design and is the basis for the error term of the F ratio for this analysis.

Finding Degrees of Freedom

To obtain the mean squares needed for the F ratio, each SS is divided by its corresponding degrees of freedom. The process of finding degrees of freedom is very similar to that for the between-subjects design.

Total Degrees of Freedom

$$df_{\text{Total}} = N - 1,$$

where N is the total number of scores in the experiment. For the example, $N = 20$; thus $df_{\text{Total}} = 20 - 1 = 19$.

FIGURE 12–3

Perceived equal line lengths (in centimeters) for each subject as a function of type of illusion.

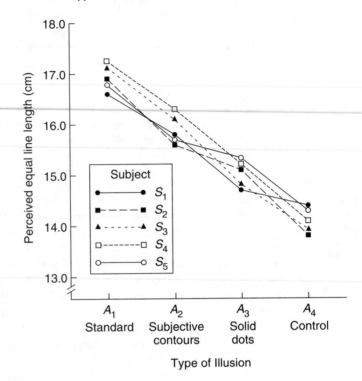

Degrees of Freedom for SS_A

$$df_A = a - 1,$$

where a is the number of levels of the independent variable A. For the four levels of factor A in the example, $a = 4$; hence $df_A = 4 - 1 = 3$.

Degrees of Freedom for SS_S

$$df_S = n_A - 1.$$

There are five subjects in the example experiment; accordingly, $n_A = 5$ and $df_S = 5 - 1 = 4$.

Degrees of Freedom for $SS_{A \times S}$

$$df_{A \times S} = (a - 1)(n_A - 1).$$

In the example, $a = 4$ and $n_A = 5$; therefore,

$$df_{A \times S} = (4 - 1)(5 - 1) = 12.$$

Additivity of Degrees of Freedom

The degrees of freedom are additive, so

$$df_{Total} = df_A + df_S + df_{A \times S}.$$

This relationship holds for the example; for

$$df_{Total} = 19, \ df_A = 3, \ df_S = 4, \ \text{and} \ df_{A \times S} = 12.$$

Finding Mean Squares and the F Ratio

Three mean squares are obtained from the SS in equation 12–2 by dividing each SS by its df:

$$MS_A = \frac{SS_A}{df_A},$$

$$MS_S = \frac{SS_S}{df_S},$$

$$MS_{A \times S} = \frac{SS_{A \times S}}{df_{A \times S}}.$$

MS_{Total} is not calculated because it is not used in the analysis of variance. For the scores in Table 12–1,

$$SS_A = 21.830,$$

$$SS_S = 0.314,$$

$$SS_{A \times S} = 0.782.$$

The degrees of freedom for these sums of squares are

$$df_A = 3,$$

$$df_S = 4,$$

$$df_{A \times S} = 12.$$

Therefore,

$$MS_A = \frac{21.830}{3} = 7.277,$$

$$MS_S = \frac{0.314}{4} = 0.078,$$

$$MS_{A \times S} = \frac{0.782}{12} = 0.065.$$

The F ratio for the one-factor within-subjects analysis of variance is given by

$$F = \frac{MS_A}{MS_{A \times S}}.$$

Thus, for the scores of Table 12–1,

$$F_{\text{obs}} = \frac{7.277}{0.065} = 111.95.$$

This F_{obs} is the only F to be computed in this analysis; no F is found for factor S. A numerical summary of the analysis of variance on the scores of Table 12–2 is presented in Table 12–3. Computational formulas for this analysis are given in the chapter supplement. Table 12–4 summarizes the sources of variance in a one-factor within-subjects analysis of variance, the SS, df, MS, and F ratio.

TABLE 12–3
Analysis of variance summary table for hypothetical perceived equal line length scores of Table 12–2.

Source	SS	df	MS	F
Type of illusion (A)	21.830	3	7.277	111.95*
Subjects (S)	0.314	4	0.078	
$A \times S$	0.782	12	0.065	
Total	22.926	19		

*$p < .01$.

TABLE 12–4
Summary of formulas for a one-factor within-subjects analysis of variance.

Source	SS	df [a]	MS	F
Factor A	SS_A	$a - 1$	$\dfrac{SS_A}{df_A}$	$\dfrac{MS_A}{MS_{A \times S}}$
Factor S	SS_S	$n_A - 1$	$\dfrac{SS_S}{df_S}$	
$A \times S$	$SS_{A \times S}$	$(a-1)(n_A-1)$	$\dfrac{SS_{A \times S}}{df_{A \times S}}$	
Total	SS_{Total}	$N - 1$	Not calculated	

[a] a = number of levels of factor A; n_A = number of scores in a treatment condition or, equivalently, the number of subjects; N = total number of scores.

TESTING YOUR KNOWLEDGE 12–1

1. Define: $A \times S$ interaction, df_A, $df_{A \times S}$, df_S, df_{Total}, factor A, factor S, MS_A, $MS_{A \times S}$, MS_S, MS_{Total}, n_A, one-factor within-subjects design, repeated measures design, SS_A, $SS_{A \times S}$, SS_S, SS_{Total}, treatments-by-subjects design.

2. Identify the sources of variation in scores from a one-factor within-subjects design.

3. Complete the following equations for a one-factor within-subjects analysis of variance:
    a. $SS_{Total} =$
    b. $df_A =$
    c. $df_S =$
    d. $df_{A \times S} =$
    e. $MS_A =$
    f. $MS_S =$
    g. $MS_{A \times S} =$
    h. $F =$

4. What is the value of SS_{Total} if $SS_A = 74.00$, $SS_S = 29.00$, and $SS_{A \times S} = 96.00$?

5. What is the value of SS_A if $SS_{Total} = 426.00$, $SS_S = 92.00$, and $SS_{A \times S} = 301.00$?

6. What is the value of SS_S if $SS_{Total} = 96.00$, $SS_A = 15.00$, and $SS_{A \times S} = 56.00$?

7. What is the value of $SS_{A \times S}$ if $SS_{Total} = 173.00$, $SS_A = 41.00$, and $SS_S = 36.00$?

8. A psychologist used a one-factor within-subjects analysis of variance with five levels of factor A and 13 subjects. What are the values of df_A, df_S, $df_{A \times S}$, and df_{Total}?

9. What is the value of df_{Total} in a one-factor within-subjects analysis of variance if $df_A = 2$ and $df_S = 19$?

10. Find the numerical values of mean squares for the following SS and df: $SS_A = 22.00$, $SS_S = 18.00$, $SS_{A \times S} = 36.00$, $df_A = 2$, $df_S = 9$, and $df_{A \times S} = 18$.

11. Tables 1 and 2 are incomplete summary tables for a one-factor within-subjects analysis of variance. Fill in the missing values in each table by using the relationships among SS and df given in Table 12–4. Then answer these questions for each table.
    a. How many levels of the independent variable were manipulated?
    b. How many scores were obtained in each treatment condition?
    c. How many subjects participated in the study?

TABLE 1

Source	SS	df	MS	F
Factor A	48.00	4	_____	_____
Factor S	27.00	9	_____	
$A \times S$	72.00	_____	_____	
Total	_____	_____		

TABLE 2

Source	SS	df	MS	F
Factor A	6.00	_____	_____	_____
Factor S	36.00	12	3.00	
$A \times S$	_____	24	_____	
Total	78.00	_____		

STATISTICAL HYPOTHESIS TESTING WITH F_{obs}

$F_{obs} = MS_A/MS_{A \times S}$ is used to decide if the treatment condition means differ significantly. As the discussion of $SS_{A \times S}$ indicated, the denominator of F, $MS_{A \times S}$, represents the error variation in this analysis. The numerator of F, MS_A, varies with the systematic effect of the independent variable and with any treatments-by-subjects interaction. If the independent variable has no effect and variation in the treatment means is due only to treatments-by-subjects interaction, then the value of MS_A should be about the same as $MS_{A \times S}$, and F_{obs} should be approximately 1.00. If factor A has an effect, however, and the treatment means differ because of both this effect and the treatments-by-subjects interaction, then MS_A will have a value larger than $MS_{A \times S}$, and F_{obs} becomes greater than 1.00.

No F ratio is constructed involving MS_S for individual differences. Although MS_S varies with the extent of the differences among the subjects in the experiment, there is no MS calculated in this analysis that provides an estimate of the chance variation expected among individuals. Therefore, the value of MS_S often is not included in a summary table.

The three mean squares and the sources of variation affecting them may be summarized as follows:

Mean Square	Affected by
MS_A	The effect of the independent variable
	Treatments-by-subjects interaction (i.e., error variation)
MS_S	Individual differences
$MS_{A \times S}$	Treatments-by-subjects interaction (i.e., error variation)

Statistical testing with F follows the now familiar procedure:

- A null hypothesis, H_0, and an alternative hypothesis, H_1, are formulated.
- The sampling distribution of F, assuming that H_0 is true, is obtained. This distribution is given in Table A–3.
- A significance level is selected.
- A critical value of F, identified as F_{crit}, is found from the sampling distribution of F given in Table A–3.
- A rejection region is located in the sampling distribution of F.
- The F ratio, identified as F_{obs}, is calculated from the sample data.
- A decision to reject or not reject H_0 is made on the basis of whether or not F_{obs} falls into the rejection region.

Statistical Hypotheses

Null Hypothesis.   The null hypothesis for a within-subjects design with four levels of factor A is expressed as

$$H_0: \mu_{A1} = \mu_{A2} = \mu_{A3} = \mu_{A4}.$$

This null hypothesis represents the situation that exists if the independent variable has no effect. If H_0 is true, then any observed differences among the treatment means are due simply to error variation. As with the between-subjects design, the number of population means identified in the null hypothesis always corresponds to the number of levels of the independent variable.

Alternative Hypothesis.   The alternative hypothesis is

$$H_1: \text{The } \mu_A\text{'s are not all equal,}$$

regardless of the number of population means involved in the null hypothesis. The alternative hypothesis states a situation that exists if the independent variable has an effect.

Decision Making from the F Ratio

The statistical decision-making process in a one-factor within-subjects design is identical to that followed in the one-factor between-subjects analysis of variance. A value of α defining the size of the rejection region for F_{obs} is selected prior to conducting the analysis. The value of F_{crit} with the appropriate numerator and denominator df is then found from Table A–3a or b. If F_{obs} is equal to or larger than F_{crit}, then F_{obs} falls into the rejection region. The null hypothesis is rejected and the alternative hypothesis accepted. There is at least one statistically significant difference among the treatment means. If F_{obs} is less than F_{crit}, then F_{obs} does not fall into the rejection region; the null hypothesis is not rejected and the alternative hypothesis is not accepted. The treatment means do not differ significantly; the observed differences among the means are due to error variation. I conclude that the independent variable did not have an effect. The decisions from F_{obs} and the conclusions that follow are summarized in Table 12–5.

To illustrate the decision process, I use the analysis summarized in Table 12–3 on the example scores of Table 12–2. In this analysis, F_{obs} has 3 (numerator) and 12 (denominator) df. Thus, for $\alpha = .05$, $F_{crit} = 3.49$ (obtained from Table A–3a). The $F_{obs} = 111.95$ is larger than F_{crit} and falls into the rejection region. I reject

$$H_0: \mu_{A1} = \mu_{A2} = \mu_{A3} = \mu_{A4}$$

and accept

$$H_1: \text{The } \mu_A\text{'s are not all equal.}$$

This decision indicates that there is at least one statistically significant difference among the four means of Table 12–2, but it does not indicate specifically which means differ from each other. To find which pairwise comparisons differ significantly, multiple comparison tests are conducted.

Multiple Comparison Tests for Within-subjects Analysis of Variance

The problems and issues of multiple comparison tests for the within-subjects analysis of variance are the same as those discussed in Chapter 10 for the between-subjects analysis

TABLE 12–5
Summary of decisions and conclusions in statistical hypothesis testing using the analysis of variance for a one-factor within-subjects design. A .05 significance level is illustrated.

If F_{obs} falls into the rejection region for $\alpha = .05$, then:	If F_{obs} does not fall into the rejection region for $\alpha = .05$, then:
Probability of F_{obs} is less than or equal to .05, or $p \leq .05$.	Probability of F_{obs} is greater than .05, or $p > .05$.
H_0 is rejected.	H_0 is not rejected.
H_1 is accepted. The sample means are not all from the same population.	H_1 is not accepted.
At least one difference between the treatment means is statistically significant at the .05 level.	The difference among the sample means is nonsignificant at the .05 level.
It is decided that something in addition to sampling error is responsible for the differences among the sample means. In a carefully done experiment the difference is attributed to the independent variable.	It is decided that sampling error alone is the most plausible explanation for the differences among the sample means. There is no evidence that the independent variable had an effect.
Multiple comparison tests are needed if the independent variable has three or more levels.	No multiple comparison tests are needed.

of variance. For post hoc comparisons, the **Tukey HSD test** with a critical difference of

$$CD = q\sqrt{\frac{MS_{A \times S}}{n_A}}$$

may be used. Applying this test to the example experiment:

- $MS_{A \times S} = 0.065$ (obtained from Table 12–3).
- $n_A = 5$.
- q at the .05 level for four levels of the independent variable and 12 df for $MS_{A \times S}$ is 4.20 (obtained from Table A–4).

Substituting these values, I obtain

$$CD = 4.20\sqrt{\frac{0.065}{5}}$$

$$= 4.20\sqrt{0.013}$$

$$= (4.20)(0.114)$$

$$= 0.48 \text{ cm.}$$

For each pairwise comparison a difference between the treatment means larger in absolute value than 0.48 cm is a statistically significant difference at the .05 level. The six pairwise comparisons, the absolute values of each comparison, the statistical hypothesis, and the decision for each hypothesis are shown in Table 12–6 (where A_1 = standard illusion, A_2 = subjective contours illusion, A_3 = solid dots illusion, A_4 = control condition).

The absolute value of each difference is larger than the CD of 0.48; thus each comparison is statistically significant at the .05 level. The standard illusion creates the greatest illusion of the four conditions, the subjective contours create a significantly lesser amount of illusion, the solid dots significantly less illusion, and the control condition the least illusion.

Measuring the Strength of a Treatment Effect

Eta squared may be used as a strength of effect measure for a one-factor within-subjects design. The formula used is modified slightly from that for a between-subjects design,

$$\eta^2 = \frac{SS_A}{SS_A + SS_{A \times S}}.$$

Notice that with this formula, the variability due to individual differences, given by SS_S, is not included in the total variation of the experiment.

TABLE 12–6
Application of the Tukey HSD CD to the pairwise comparisons of the example experiment.

Comparison	Absolute Value of Comparison	Statistical Hypotheses	Decision
$\overline{X}_{A1}$ vs. $\overline{X}_{A2}$		H_0: $\mu_{A1} = \mu_{A2}$	Reject
(16.92 − 15.90)	1.02	H_1: $\mu_{A1} \neq \mu_{A2}$	Accept
$\overline{X}_{A1}$ vs. $\overline{X}_{A3}$		H_0: $\mu_{A1} = \mu_{A3}$	Reject
(16.92 − 15.02)	1.90	H_1: $\mu_{A1} \neq \mu_{A3}$	Accept
$\overline{X}_{A1}$ vs. $\overline{X}_{A4}$		H_0: $\mu_{A1} = \mu_{A4}$	Reject
(16.92 − 14.10)	2.82	H_1: $\mu_{A1} \neq \mu_{A4}$	Accept
$\overline{X}_{A2}$ vs. $\overline{X}_{A3}$		H_0: $\mu_{A2} = \mu_{A3}$	Reject
(15.90 − 15.02)	0.88	H_1: $\mu_{A2} \neq \mu_{A3}$	Accept
$\overline{X}_{A2}$ vs. $\overline{X}_{A4}$		H_0: $\mu_{A2} = \mu_{A4}$	Reject
(15.90 − 14.10)	1.80	H_1: $\mu_{A2} \neq \mu_{A4}$	Accept
$\overline{X}_{A3}$ vs. $\overline{X}_{A4}$		H_0: $\mu_{A3} = \mu_{A4}$	Reject
(15.02 − 14.10)	0.92	H_1: $\mu_{A3} \neq \mu_{A4}$	Accept

For the example, $SS_A = 21.830$ and $SS_{A \times S} = 0.782$. Thus,

$$\eta^2 = \frac{21.830}{21.830 + 0.782}$$
$$= \frac{21.830}{22.612}$$
$$= .97.$$

Ninety-seven percent of the variance in the length of line measures is accounted for by the illusion condition after the variability due to individual differences is removed, a very strong effect of the independent variable.

Assumptions of a Within-subjects Analysis of Variance

The assumptions for the appropriate use of a one-factor within-subjects analysis are as follows:

1. Each subject is tested under each level of the independent variable.
2. The scores in the sample are drawn randomly from a population.
3. The populations of scores for the different treatment conditions are normally distributed.
4. The population variances of scores for the different treatment conditions are equal.
5. The contribution of the individual differences of a subject remains the same for his or her scores over all treatment conditions.

The first assumption is necessary for the within-subjects analysis of variance to be the appropriate statistical test for the data; it cannot be violated. The second, third, and fourth assumptions are identical to assumptions for a between-subjects analysis of variance. They are sometimes violated in experiments, but the analysis of variance maintains some robustness toward such violations. The fifth assumption states that the person's behavior, independent of the treatment effect, remains stable over all levels of the independent variable. It is likely that this assumption is violated in many cases of behavioral research. The effect of such a violation is to increase the probability of making a Type I error above the value set by the significance level.

Several approaches have been offered for dealing with this increased error rate. The Geisser–Greenhouse correction changes the df used to obtain F_{crit} so that a larger F_{crit} will be used to evaluate F_{obs}. With this correction, F_{crit} is found using 1 df for the numerator and $(n_A - 1)$ df for the denominator in place of the $a - 1$, $(a - 1)(n_A - 1)$ df normally used. Applying the Geisser–Greenhouse correction to the example, $F_{crit}(1, 4) = 7.71$. The $F_{obs}(3, 12) = 111.95$ still is larger than F_{crit} and H_0 is rejected, the same decision made using F_{crit} with 3, 12 df. This approach and others for reducing the error rate if assumption 5 is violated are discussed in Keppel (1991).

An alternative approach is to use the nonparametric Wilcoxon signed ranks test or the Friedman analysis of variance in place of the within-subjects analysis of variance. The Wilcoxon test is presented in Chapter 13.

TESTING YOUR KNOWLEDGE 12-2

1. Identify the factors affecting the value of each MS in a one-factor within-subjects analysis of variance.
2. Explain why MS_A increases in value if factor A has an effect in a one-factor within-subjects experiment.
3. Write the statistical hypotheses for a one-factor within-subjects analysis of variance with five levels of the independent variable.
4. Identify the assumptions underlying the use of the one-factor within-subjects analysis of variance.

Example Problem 12-1

Analyzing a One-factor Within-subjects Design with Four Levels of an Independent Variable

Problem
Many tasks require people to be vigilant over a long period, such as an air traffic controller monitoring a radar screen to maintain the proper distance between planes. Thus psychologists have studied various factors affecting vigilance. As an example, Pfendler and Widdel (1986) had subjects monitor a simulated display of the dials in the control room of a ship for a $2^1/_2$-hour period. As time progressed, their subjects took longer to detect changes in the readings of the controls. Suppose that a similar study was conducted requiring subjects to monitor a set of dials for a 4-hour period. The subject's task was to indicate whenever a dial changed its displayed value. The dependent variable measured was the amount of time it took the subject to detect the change. The mean detection times (in seconds) for each of the four 1-hour periods for 13 subjects are shown in Table 12–7. Did the detection times increase significantly over time periods?

Solution   The design is a one-factor within-subjects design with four levels of the independent variable, time period. The first step in data analysis is to conduct a one-factor within-subjects analysis of variance on the scores. If F_{obs} is statistically significant, I will use the Tukey HSD test to find the statistically significant pairwise differences between the treatment means. I use a .05 significance level.

Statistic to Be Used: $F = MS_A/MS_{A \times S}$.

Assumptions for Use:
1. Each subject is tested under each time period.
2. The scores in the sample are drawn randomly from a population.
3. The populations of detection times for the different time periods are normally distributed.

TABLE 12–7
Mean number of seconds to detect a change in a dial over a four-hour time period for 13 subjects.

Subject	Time Period (in hours) (A)			
	1 (A_1)	2 (A_2)	3 (A_3)	4 (A_4)
1	6.2	6.7	7.4	7.8
2	5.9	4.8	6.1	6.9
3	8.4	8.7	9.9	10.3
4	7.6	7.8	8.7	8.9
5	4.1	4.7	5.4	6.6
6	5.4	5.3	5.9	7.1
7	6.6	6.7	7.2	7.5
8	6.1	5.8	6.4	6.7
9	4.9	5.1	5.2	6.8
10	8.2	8.6	9.3	10.4
11	5.7	5.7	6.5	7.2
12	5.9	6.4	6.9	7.6
13	6.9	6.6	7.1	7.5
$\overline{X}_A$	6.30	6.38	7.08	7.79
s_A	1.24	1.34	1.45	1.28

4. The population variances of detection times for the different time periods are equal.
5. The contribution of the individual differences of a subject remains the same for his or her scores over all time periods.

Statistical Hypotheses: H_0: $\mu_{A1} = \mu_{A2} = \mu_{A3} = \mu_{A4}$.
   H_1: The μ_A's are not all equal.

Significance Level: $\alpha = .05$.

df:

$$df_A = a - 1 = 4 - 1 = 3$$
$$df_S = n_A - 1 = 13 - 1 = 12$$
$$df_{A \times S} = (a - 1)(n_A - 1)$$
$$= (4 - 1)(13 - 1) = 36$$
$$df_{Total} = N - 1 = 52 - 1 = 51$$

Critical value of F: F_{crit} (3, 36) = 2.92. A value of 36 df for the denominator is not presented in Table A–3a. I used the critical value for the next lower tabled df for df_{Error}, 30.

Rejection Region: Values of F_{obs} equal to or greater than 2.92.

Calculation: I calculated the analysis of variance using the formulas given in the chapter supplement to obtain the following analysis of variance summary table.

Source	SS	df	MS	F
Time period (A)	18.985	3	6.328	60.85*
Subjects (S)	81.188	12	6.766	
$A \times S$	3.727	36	0.104	
Total	103.900	51		

$*p < .05.$

Decision: $F_{obs} = 60.85$ falls into the rejection region; I reject H_0: $\mu_{A1} = \mu_{A2} = \mu_{A3} = \mu_{A4}$ and accept H_1: The μ_A's are not all equal. Rejecting H_0 indicates that there is at least one statistically significant difference between the treatment condition means. To find the statistically significant pairwise differences, I use the Tukey HSD test.

Tukey Test: The numerical values needed for this test are found as follows:

- q is obtained from Table A–4. There are four levels of the independent variable and 36 df for $MS_{A \times S}$. Because 36 df is not given in Table A–4, I use 30 df, the next lower tabled df from the 36 df for $MS_{A \times S}$. Thus $q = 3.85$ for a .05 significance level.
- $MS_{A \times S}$, obtained from the analysis of variance, is 0.104.
- n_A, the number of scores in each of the means to be compared, is 13.

Substituting these numerical values into the formula,

$$CD = q\sqrt{\frac{MS_{A \times S}}{n_A}}$$

$$= 3.85\sqrt{\frac{0.104}{13}}$$

$$= 3.85\sqrt{0.008}$$

$$= (3.85)(0.089)$$

$$= 0.34 \text{ second.}$$

Any difference equal to or larger in absolute value than 0.34 second is statistically significant at the .05 level. The pairwise comparisons, their absolute values, the statistical hypothesis tested, and the decision reached on the statistical hypothesis for each comparison are shown in Table 12–8 (where $A_1 = 1$ hour, $A_2 = 2$ hours, $A_3 = 3$ hours, and $A_4 = 4$ hours).

Strength of Effect:
$$\eta^2 = \frac{SS_A}{SS_A + SS_{A \times S}}$$

$$= \frac{18.985}{18.985 + 3.727}$$

$$= \frac{18.985}{22.712} = .84.$$

TABLE 12-8
Application of the Tukey HSD *CD* to the pairwise comparisons of the four time periods.

Comparison	Absolute Value of Comparison	Statistical Hypotheses	Decision
$\overline{X}_{A1}$ vs. $\overline{X}_{A2}$ (6.30 − 6.38)	0.08	H_0: $\mu_{A1} = \mu_{A2}$ H_1: $\mu_{A1} \neq \mu_{A2}$	Fail to reject Do not accept
$\overline{X}_{A1}$ vs. $\overline{X}_{A3}$ (6.30 − 7.08)	0.78	H_0: $\mu_{A1} = \mu_{A3}$ H_1: $\mu_{A1} \neq \mu_{A3}$	Reject Accept
$\overline{X}_{A1}$ vs. $\overline{X}_{A4}$ (6.30 − 7.79)	1.49	H_0: $\mu_{A1} = \mu_{A4}$ H_1: $\mu_{A1} \neq \mu_{A4}$	Reject Accept
$\overline{X}_{A2}$ vs. $\overline{X}_{A3}$ (6.38 − 7.08)	0.70	H_0: $\mu_{A2} = \mu_{A3}$ H_1: $\mu_{A2} \neq \mu_{A3}$	Reject Accept
$\overline{X}_{A2}$ vs. $\overline{X}_{A4}$ (6.38 − 7.79)	1.41	H_0: $\mu_{A2} = \mu_{A4}$ H_1: $\mu_{A2} \neq \mu_{A4}$	Reject Accept
$\overline{X}_{A3}$ vs. $\overline{X}_{A4}$ (7.08 − 7.79)	0.71	H_0: $\mu_{A3} = \mu_{A4}$ H_1: $\mu_{A3} \neq \mu_{A4}$	Reject Accept

Conclusion: The only comparison smaller than the $CD = 0.34$ second is between the first and second hours. This difference is nonsignificant; all other differences are statistically significant. Thus the comparisons reveal that there is no increase in the detection times between the first and second hours of the task, but a statistically significant increase occurs between hours 2 and 3, and between hours 3 and 4. The strength of effect, $\eta^2 = .84$ indicates that the time period accounts for a large proportion of the variance in the detection times after individual differences variability has been removed from the experiment.

Example Problem 12-2

Using the One-factor Within-subjects Analysis of Variance with Two Levels of an Independent Variable

Problem
The yawn of a student during class often is interpreted by an instructor as a sign of boredom. But is yawning actually such a sign? To explore this hypothesis, Provine and Hamernik (1986) designed an experiment to test if studying uninteresting material actually increases the frequency of yawning. In this experiment, subjects saw 30 minutes of rock music videos (A_1, the interesting stimulus) and 30 minutes of a color-bar test pattern without sound (A_2, the uninteresting stimulus) in two different sessions. The number of times a subject yawned during the two sessions was observed and recorded. Suppose I replicated this experiment using 11 subjects and observed the number of yawns for each

TABLE 12–9
Number of yawns observed as a function of type of video viewed for 11 subjects.

| Subject | Type of Video (A) | |
	Interesting (A_1)	Uninteresting (A_2)
1	5	7
2	2	1
3	4	7
4	3	8
5	0	2
6	4	5
7	7	6
8	6	9
9	3	3
10	1	4
11	8	9
$\overline{X}_A$	3.9	5.5
s	2.47	2.77

session given in Table 12–9. Does the type of video affect the amount of yawning that occurs?

Solution   A statistical test is needed to determine if the means of the two video conditions differ significantly. Because the subjects were tested under both types of videos, a within-subjects design was used. Thus a one-factor within-subjects analysis of variance is an appropriate statistical test for these data. Because only two treatment conditions are involved, a t_{rel} also would be an appropriate statistical test. I use a .05 significance level.

Statistic to Be Used: $F = MS_A / MS_{A \times S}$.

Assumptions for Use:
1. Each subject is tested under each type of video condition.
2. The scores in the sample are drawn randomly from a population.
3. The populations of yawning scores for the different treatment conditions are normally distributed.
4. The population variances of yawning scores for the different treatment conditions are equal.
5. The contribution of the individual differences of a subject remains the same for his or her scores over both video conditions.

Statistical Hypotheses:

$$H_0: \mu_{A1} = \mu_{A2}.$$

$$H_1: \text{The } \mu_A\text{'s are not equal.}$$

Significance Level: $\alpha = .05$.

df:

$$df_A = a - 1 = 2 - 1 = 1$$
$$df_S = n_A - 1 = 11 - 1 = 10$$
$$df_{A \times S} = (a - 1)(n_A - 1)$$
$$= (2 - 1)(11 - 1) = 10$$
$$df_{Total} = N - 1 = 22 - 1 = 21$$

Critical Value of F: $F_{crit}\ (1, 10) = 4.96$.

Rejection Region: Values of F_{obs} equal to or greater than 4.96.

Calculation: Using the formulas given in the chapter supplement, the summary of this analysis is as follows:

Source	SS	df	MS	F
Type of video (A)	14.728	1	14.728	8.53*
Subjects (S)	120.364	10	12.036	
A × S	17.272	10	1.727	
Total	152.364	21		

$^*p < .05$.

Decision: F_{obs} falls into the rejection region; thus I reject H_0 and accept H_1.

Strength of Effect:

$$\eta^2 = \frac{14.728}{14.728 + 17.272}$$
$$= \frac{14.728}{32.000} = .46.$$

Conclusion: The difference between the two treatment means of 3.9 and 5.5 yawns is statistically significant. When viewing the interesting video, individuals yawned less often than when watching the uninteresting video. Because only two means are involved, no multiple comparison test is necessary. The η^2 indicates that 46 percent of the variance in the dependent variable is accounted for by the type of video after SS_S has been removed from the experiment.

STATISTICS IN USE 12–1

Strength and Time of Day Using a One-factor Within-subjects Design

Does physical strength vary with time of day? No doubt many people feel more tired later in the day, but does this subjective feeling correspond to actual decreases in physical strength? To investigate this problem, Ishee and Titlow (1986) used a one-factor within-subjects design and measured subject's handgrip strength at different times of the day: 9:00 A.M., 12:00

noon, and 3:00 P.M. Eighteen subjects were used, and each subject was tested for handgrip strength at each of the three times. To avoid confounding by repeated tests on the same day, the test for each time was conducted on a separate day. In addition, three different orders of the time sequence were used (e.g., sequence 1: 9:00 A.M., 12:00 noon, 3:00 P.M.; sequence 2: 12:00 noon, 3:00 P.M., 9:00 A.M.; sequence 3: 3:00 P.M., 9:00 A.M., 12:00 noon) with six subjects in each sequence.

Mean handgrip strength was 44.3 kilograms (kg) for 9:00 A.M. ($s = 16.2$), 44.2 kg for 12:00 noon ($s = 14.0$), and 42.7 kg for 3:00 P.M. ($s = 15.0$). A one-factor analysis of variance indicated that the observed differences among the means were nonsignificant, $F_{obs}(2, 34) = 0.78$, $p > .05$. Although we may feel more tired in the afternoon, there was no change in handgrip strength over the three times tested in this experiment.

REPORTING THE RESULTS OF THE ANALYSIS OF VARIANCE

A description of the results of the analysis of the example experiment on illusion condition and perceived line length (see Tables 12–2 and 12–3) following the style of *The Publication Manual of the American Psychological Association* (1994) might be written for the results section of an article as follows:

> The mean perceived equal line lengths for the standard, subjective contours, solid dots, and control illusion conditions were 16.92 ($SD = 0.24$), 15.90 ($SD = 0.29$), 15.02 ($SD = 0.26$), and 14.10 ($SD = 0.25$) cm, respectively. With an alpha level of .05, a one-factor within-subjects analysis of variance indicated that the means differed significantly, $F(3, 12) = 111.95$, $MSE = 0.065$, $p < .01$. A Tukey test on the pairwise comparisons revealed that each illusion condition differed significantly from each other illusion condition, $p < .05$ ($CD = 0.48$ cm). Eta squared for the scores was .97.

Much of the information in this report is similar to that of a between-subjects design. I review this presentation briefly.

Sample means	The obtained values of the sample means and standard deviations are presented in the first sentence. Because only four means were obtained, they are presented in a sentence rather than in a table or a figure.
$\alpha = .05$	Indicates the significance level selected for the test.
$F(3, 12)$	Identifies the name of the test statistic as the F. The numbers shown in parentheses indicate the *df* for the numerator (i.e., 3) and the denominator (i.e., 12) of F_{obs}, respectively.
$= 111.95$	Gives the value of F_{obs}.
$p < .01$.	Indicates that: **a.** The probability of F_{obs} if H_0 is true is less than or equal to .01. This value is the probability of F_{obs} or an even more extreme value of F_{obs} if H_0 is true.

b. H_0: $\mu_{A1} = \mu_{A2} = \mu_{A3} = \mu_{A4}$ was rejected.

H_1: The u_A's are not all equal was accepted.

c.   There is at least one statistically significant difference among the treatment means.

d.   Something other than sampling error alone is responsible for a difference in the treatment means.

$MSE = 0.065$	Gives the value of the $MS_{A \times S}$ for F_{obs}. This MS is the error term for the F ratio; it also may be identified as $MS_{A \times S}$.
$CD = 0.48$ cm	Gives the critical difference for pairwise comparisons using the Tukey HSD test. The statistically significant pairwise comparisons are then described.
$\eta^2 = .97$	Indicates that 97 percent of the variance in the perceived equal line lengths in this experiment is accounted for by the illusion condition after variability due to individual differences has been removed.

TESTING YOUR KNOWLEDGE 12–3

1.   Emling and Yankell (1985) evaluated a mouthrinse containing sodium benzoate for its ability to remove and loosen tooth plaque. In one study subjects were measured under three treatment conditions: a baseline control condition (A_1), after using an experimental mouthrinse (A_2), and after using a nonactive placebo mouthrinse (A_3). For each treatment condition the amount of plaque on the teeth was rated on a 0 (no plaque) to 5 (plaque covering two-thirds or more of the crown) scale. Suppose the ratings shown in Table 12–10 were obtained for 14 subjects.

   Find the mean and standard deviation for each treatment condition. Then perform a one-factor within-subjects analysis of variance on these scores to determine if the experimental mouthrinse reduced plaque compared to the control or placebo conditions and answer the following questions.

   a.   State the statistical hypotheses for the F test for these scores.

   b.   What is the value of F_{obs}?

   c.   What are the df for F_{obs}?

   d.   What is F_{crit} at the .05 level?

   e.   What is the rejection region for F_{obs}?

   f.   Does F_{obs} fall into the rejection region?

   g.   What decisions do you make about the statistical hypotheses? Do you reject or fail to reject H_0? Accept or not accept H_1?

   h.   Do you conclude that the means are from the same or different populations?

   i.   Is there a statistically significant difference between at least one pair of means?

   j.   Are multiple comparison tests needed in this experiment? Give the reason for your answer.

   k.   What is the value of the Tukey CD?

   l.   Which pairwise differences are statistically significant?

   m.   What is η^2 for this experiment?

   n.   Describe the results of this experiment following the style illustrated in the Reporting the Results of an Analysis of Variance section of this chapter.

TABLE 12–10
Ratings of amount of plaque as a function of treatment
condition for 14 subjects.

Subject	Control (A_1)	Experimental (A_2)	Placebo (A_3)
1	6	5	6
2	5	5	5
3	4	3	5
4	6	4	5
5	3	4	4
6	3	1	2
7	6	3	5
8	4	4	6
9	4	5	4
10	6	5	6
11	5	2	6
12	2	2	3
13	5	4	3
14	4	1	3

Exercises 2 and 3 present sample reports of one-factor within-subjects analysis of variance. Answer the following questions for each exercise.
  a. How many levels of the independent variable were used in this experiment?
  b. How many subjects were used in this experiment?
  c. What is the value of F_{obs}?
  d. What is the value of F_{crit} at the .05 significance level?
  e. Do you reject or fail to reject H_0?
  f. Do you accept or not accept H_1?
  g. Is there at least one statistically significant difference between the means?
  h. Which treatment conditions, if any, differ significantly?

2. The mean reaction time for the simple stimulus condition was 396 milliseconds (ms), whereas the mean for the complex stimulus condition was 412 ms. With alpha equal to .05, a one-factor within-subjects analysis of variance revealed a significant difference between the means, $F(1, 18) = 4.76$, $MSE = 510.924$, $p < .05$.

3. The mean number of faces correctly recognized was 13.9 on trial 1, 14.6 on trial 2, and 14.1 on trial 3. With alpha equal to .05, a one-factor within-subjects analysis of variance indicated no difference in the number of correct recognitions over trials, $F(2, 22) = 2.81$, $MSE = 0.555$, $p > .05$.

CHOICE OF RESEARCH DESIGN: BETWEEN SUBJECTS OR WITHIN SUBJECTS

How does a behavioral scientist decide whether to use a between-subjects or within-subjects research design to evaluate a research hypothesis? Each type of design has its advantages and limitations. In general, there are three concerns when making this decision: (1) the number of subjects needed, (2) the anticipated effectiveness of the independent variable, and (3) the possibility of multiple treatment effects occurring.

Number of Subjects Needed

A subject in a within-subjects design is measured under each treatment condition; thus fewer subjects are needed than would be required for a corresponding between-subjects design. In the example shown in Table 12–2, five scores are obtained under each of the four levels of illusion condition for a total of 20 scores. But only five subjects are required to obtain these 20 scores. For a corresponding between-subjects design, 20 different subjects would be needed to obtain the 20 scores. Thus, when subjects are difficult to obtain or where obtaining and instructing subjects requires considerably more time than actually performing the experimental task, the within-subjects design may be advantageous in comparison to a between-subjects design with respect to utilization of subjects.

Effectiveness of the Independent Variable

How easily the effect of an independent variable can be detected in an experiment depends partially on the strength of effect of that variable. A within-subjects design is often more sensitive to detecting the effect of an independent variable than is a between-subjects design. Therefore, a within-subjects design may be preferred when the anticipated effect of the independent variable is weak. The increased sensitivity of the within-subjects design occurs because each subject receives each level of the independent variable and is exposed to all treatment conditions. The within-subjects analysis of variance partitions out the variability due to individual differences among subjects (i.e., the variability due to factor S, MS_S) so that it does not contribute to the error term for the F ratio (i.e., $MS_{A \times S}$). In a between-subjects design, this variation is included in the MS_{Error}. Thus the error term in a within-subjects design (i.e., $MS_{A \times S}$) will be smaller than the error term in a between-subjects design (i.e., MS_{Error}). A smaller error term leads to a larger value of F_{obs}, which is more likely to result in the rejection of H_0. Thus, in an experiment where there are large individual differences among subjects and the effect of the independent variable is not expected to be strong, a within-subjects design is more likely to detect the effect of the independent variable than is a between-subjects design.

Multiple Treatment Effects

In a within-subjects design a subject is given each level of the independent variable over a period of time. This sequence of treatments opens the within-subjects design

Multiple treatment effects:
Changes in subjects' performance in a within-subjects design that are due to being tested in each level of the independent variable.

Practice effect: A multiple treatment effect that occurs because subjects may become more practiced or fatigued on the experimental task.

Treatment carry-over effect: A multiple treatment effect that occurs when the effect of one level of the independent variable carries over to affect performance in the next level of the independent variable.

to the possibility of **multiple treatment effects** occurring; the effect of a level of the independent variable may depend on the levels preceding it. Multiple treatment effects include both practice effects and treatment carry-over effects.

Practice effects are changes in performance due simply to repeated practice in the experimental task. These changes may result either in improved or impaired performance as the experiment progresses. For instance, in the example experiment measuring the extent of an illusion in four different illusion conditions, subjects may become bored with the experiment as it progresses, or they may become more accurate with their estimates as they make more of them. In either case, the subject's performance may change whether or not the illusion condition affects behavior.

Treatment carry-over effects are specific effects from one level of an independent variable that may carry over to affect performance on a subsequent level of the independent variable. For example, in the problem of the perception of illusions as a function of the illusion condition, if subjects always saw the control condition last, they may perceive an illusion because they had seen conditions creating illusions prior to the control condition. They have an expectation of seeing an illusion that carries over to the control condition. If they had seen the control condition first without the expectation of seeing an illusion, they would not have perceived it as an illusion.

Practice effects and treatment carry-over effects are important, because if they occur and are not controlled for they confound an experiment. Control for these effects is usually obtained by giving each subject the treatments in a different order.

Each of the issues discussed, the number of subjects needed, the anticipated effectiveness of the independent variable, and the possibility of multiple treatment effects occurring must be considered when choosing a research design. The effective use of subjects and the greater sensitivity to detecting the effect of an independent variable are advantages of the within-subjects design. The potential for multiple treatment effects occurring, however, is a disadvantage of this design. Multiple treatment effects cannot occur in a between-subjects design, for each subject experiences only one level of the independent variable. Thus, when multiple treatment effects are likely to occur in an experiment and cannot be easily controlled through the ordering of treatments, a between-subjects design will likely be used. Because multiple treatment effects occur with many independent variables and cannot be easily controlled in a within-subjects design, behavioral scientists often choose to use between-subjects designs.

SUMMARY

- In a one-factor within-subjects design a single group of subjects is given each level of the independent variable.
- The one-factor within-subjects analysis of variance is used to analyze scores from a one-factor multilevel within-subjects design.
- Three mean squares are generated in a one-factor within-subjects analysis of variance: MS_A, which varies with the effect of the independent variable and

treatments by subjects interaction, MS_S, which varies with differences among subjects, and $MS_{A \times S}$, which varies with the interaction of treatments with subjects and provides a measure of the error variation in the experiment.

- The F ratio used in the one-factor within-subjects analysis of variance is $F = MS_A/MS_{A \times S}$.

- Using the F statistic follows the usual steps of formulating statistical hypotheses, setting a significance level, locating a rejection region, calculating F_{obs}, and making decisions concerning the statistical hypotheses.

- A statistically significant F when three or more levels of an independent variable are manipulated requires a multiple comparison test to find the statistically significant pairwise differences.

- The Tukey test is used for all possible pairwise post hoc comparisons.

- η^2 may be used as a measure of the strength of a treatment effect.

- Choosing between a between-subjects or a within-subjects design requires considering the number of subjects needed, the anticipated effectiveness of the independent variable, and the possibility of occurrence of multiple treatment effects.

KEY TERMS AND SYMBOLS

$A \times S$ interaction	F_{obs}	repeated measures design
critical difference	factor A	SS_A
CD	factor S	SS_S
df_A	MS_A	$SS_{A \times S}$
df_S	MS_S	SS_{Total}
$df_{A \times S}$	$MS_{A \times S}$	treatment carry-over effect
df_{Total}	multiple treatment effects	treatments-by-subjects design
eta squared (η^2)	n_A	within-subjects design
F_{crit}	practice effect	

CHAPTER SUPPLEMENT: CALCULATING A ONE-FACTOR WITHIN-SUBJECTS ANALYSIS OF VARIANCE WITH COMPUTATIONAL FORMULAS

This supplement provides the computational format for a one-factor within-subjects analysis of variance. An experiment with four levels of an independent variable A and five subjects in each level is represented as follows:

	Factor A				
Subject	A_1	A_2	A_3	A_4	
S_1	X_{11}	X_{12}	X_{13}	X_{14}	T_{S1}
S_2	X_{21}	X_{22}	X_{23}	X_{24}	T_{S2}
S_3	X_{31}	X_{32}	X_{33}	X_{34}	T_{S3}
S_4	X_{41}	X_{42}	X_{43}	X_{44}	T_{S4}
S_5	X_{51}	X_{52}	X_{53}	X_{54}	T_{S5}
	T_{A1}	T_{A2}	T_{A3}	T_{A4}	G

where

X_{ij} = score of a subject

T_A = total of scores for a level of the independent variable

T_S = total of scores for a subject

G = grand total of the scores

n_A = number of scores in a level of the independent variable

a = number of levels of the independent variable

N = total number of scores

Four numerical values are found using these terms:

$[1] = \sum\sum X_{ij}^2$ the sum of all the scores squared

$[2] = \dfrac{\sum T_A^2}{n_A}$ the sum of each level of the independent variable total squared, divided by the number of subjects

$[3] = \dfrac{\sum T_S^2}{a}$ the sum of each subject's scores squared, divided by the number of levels of factor A

$[4] = \dfrac{G^2}{N}$ the grand total squared, divided by the total number of scores.

Using these numerical values, an analysis of variance is obtained as follows:

Source of Variance	SS	df	MS	F
Factor A	$[2] - [4]$	$a - 1$	$\dfrac{SS_A}{df_A}$	$\dfrac{MS_A}{MS_{A \times S}}$
Subjects (S)	$[3] - [4]$	$n_A - 1$	$\dfrac{SS_S}{df_S}$	
$A \times S$	$[1] - [2] - [3] + [4]$	$(a-1)(n_A-1)$	$\dfrac{SS_{A \times S}}{df_{A \times S}}$	
Total	$[1] - [4]$	$N - 1$	Not calculated	

To illustrate the computations, I use the example scores given in Table 12–2 for which an analysis of variance is summarized in Table 12–3.

Subject	Illusion Condition (A)				Subject Totals
	Standard A_1	Subjective Contours A_2	Solid Dots A_3	Control A_4	
1	16.6	15.8	14.7	14.4	$T_{S1} = 61.50$
2	16.9	15.6	15.1	13.8	$T_{S2} = 61.40$
3	17.1	16.1	14.8	13.9	$T_{S3} = 61.90$
4	17.2	16.3	15.2	14.1	$T_{S4} = 62.80$
5	16.8	15.7	15.3	14.3	$T_{S5} = 62.10$
$T_A =$	84.60	79.50	75.10	70.50	$G = 309.70$

$n_A = 5$, $a = 4$, and $N = 20$.

The values of the numerical computational terms are:

$$[1] = [(16.6)^2 + \cdots + (16.8)^2 + (15.8)^2 + \cdots + (15.7)^2 + (14.7)^2 + \cdots + (15.3)^2 + (14.4)^2$$
$$+ \cdots + (14.3)^2] = 4818.630$$

$$[2] = \frac{(84.60)^2 + (79.50)^2 + (75.10)^2 + (70.50)^2}{5} = 4817.534$$

$$[3] = \frac{(61.50)^2 + (61.40)^2 + (61.90)^2 + (62.80)^2 + (62.10)^2}{4} = 4796.018$$

$$[4] = \frac{(309.70)^2}{20} = 4795.704$$

Then

$$SS_A = [2] - [4] = 4817.534 - 4795.704 = 21.830$$
$$df_A = a - 1 = 4 - 1 = 3$$
$$MS_A = \frac{21.830}{3} = 7.277$$

$$SS_S = [3] - [4] = 4796.018 - 4795.704 = 0.314$$
$$df_S = n_A - 1 = 5 - 1 = 4$$
$$MS_S = \frac{0.314}{4} = 0.078$$

$$SS_{A \times S} = [1] - [2] - [3] + [4]$$
$$= 4818.630 - 4817.534 - 4796.018 + 4795.704 = 0.782$$
$$df_{A \times S} = (a - 1)(n_A - 1) = (4 - 1)(5 - 1) = 12$$
$$MS_{A \times S} = \frac{0.782}{12} = 0.065$$

$$SS_{Total} = [1] - [4] = 4818.630 - 4795.704 = 22.926$$

$$df_{Total} = N - 1 = 20 - 1 = 19$$

$$F_{obs} = \frac{MS_A}{MS_{A \times S}} = \frac{7.277}{0.065} = 111.95$$

The summary of the analysis of variance is as follows:

Source	SS	df	MS	F
Factor A	21.830	3	7.277	111.95*
Subjects	0.314	4	0.078	
$A \times S$	0.782	12	0.065	
Total	22.926	19		

*$p < .01.$

The values obtained by this computational approach are identical to those presented in Table 12–3 from the definitional formulas of an analysis of variance.

REVIEW QUESTIONS

1. Suppose that you are interested in whether the type of mood reflected by a word (happy, neutral, or sad) affects how well the word is remembered from a list. You construct a list composed of six happy words (e.g., joyful, bright), six neutral words (e.g., derive, convey) and six sad words (e.g., gloomy, lonely). Each of eight subjects then learns the list to a criterion of two complete correct recitations. One week later each subject attempts to recall the list. The number of items correctly recalled as a function of the type of word was as follows:

	Type of Word		
Subject	Happy	Neutral	Sad
1	5	4	3
2	6	3	4
3	4	5	2
4	5	3	1
5	3	1	2
6	6	3	4
7	2	2	3
8	5	3	1

a. Find the mean and standard deviation for each type of word condition. Then analyze the scores with a one-factor within-subjects analysis to answer the following question: Does the type of word affect recall? Use a .05 significance level. If needed, use the Tukey HSD test for multiple comparisons.

b. What is the strength of effect of the independent variable of type of word?

c. Describe the results following the style illustrated in the Reporting the Results of the Analysis of Variance section of this chapter.

2. Review Question 4 of Chapter 9 presented research based on that of Langan and Watkins (1987) on the effect of pressure on the carotid arteries from neckwear on critical flicker frequency (CFF). In the study described, the CFF of 12 men was measured with the men wearing a loose collar and then wearing a tight collar and tie. The critical flicker frequencies (in hertz, or cycles per second) for each subject were as follows:

| | Type of Neckwear | |
Subject	Loose	Tight
1	17	16
2	19	17
3	23	20
4	22	21
5	22	22
6	20	18
7	18	20
8	21	17
9	23	19
10	19	21
11	20	16
12	17	18

a. Find the mean and standard deviation for each type of word condition. Then analyze the scores with a one-factor within-subjects analysis to answer the following question: Did the type of neckwear affect the CFF scores? Use a .05 significance level.

b. Compare F_{obs} to t_{obs} for Chapter 9 Review Question 4. Does $\sqrt{F_{obs}} = t_{obs}$?

c. Do you reach the same or different conclusions about the effect of the independent variable from the analysis of variance and the t_{rel} test?

d. Describe the results of this experiment following the style illustrated in the Reporting the Results of the Analysis of Variance section of this chapter.

3. Assume that you plan to conduct a one-factor within-subjects experiment with five levels of the independent variable and 12 subjects.

a. Write the statistical hypothesis tested by the analysis of variance on the scores that you would obtain.

b. Find the df for the analysis of variance of this design.

c. What is the value of F_{crit} at the .05 significance level for the analysis of variance of this design?

d. Suppose that the value of F_{obs} was larger than F_{crit}. What decision would you make about H_0 and H_1?

e. Suppose that you reject H_0 and accept H_1 for this experiment. What inference would you make about the treatment means from these decisions?

4. The following tables are incomplete summary tables for an analysis of variance. By using the relationships among SS, df, and MS, provide the missing values in each table. Then answer the following questions for each table.

a. How many levels of the independent variable were manipulated?

b. How many scores were obtained in each level of the independent variable?

c. How many subjects participated in the study?

d. Is the value of F_{obs} statistically significant at the .05 level?

e. What decision do you make for H_0 and H_1 for each analysis?

TABLE 1

Source	SS	df	MS	F
Factor A	_____	_____	11.00	_____
Factor S	138.00	23	6.00	
$A \times S$	253.00	46	_____	
Total	_____	71		

TABLE 2

Source	SS	df	MS	F
Factor A	60.00	_____	_____	_____
Factor S	133.00	19	7.00	
$A \times S$	_____	95	_____	
Total	573.00	_____		

5. Several experimenters recently investigated an infant's interest in unfamiliar faces in comparison to familiar faces. Each of 14 infants viewed photographs of familiar faces (e.g., photographs of the mother and father), unfamiliar faces (e.g., photographs of males and females unknown to the infant), and a blank oval the same size as a face. The experimenters recorded the amount of time each infant fixated on the face. The stimulus conditions and the mean duration of time fixated on the stimulus for each condition are presented in Table 1. An analysis of variance on these data is presented in Table 2.

TABLE 1

Mean fixation time (in seconds)
as a function of stimulus condition.

Stimulus Condition		
Familiar Face (A_1)	Unfamiliar Face (A_2)	Blank Oval (A_3)
34.2	26.8	18.5

TABLE 2

Analysis of variance summary for mean
fixation times presented in Table 1.

Source	SS	df	MS	F
Stimulus condition (A)	1727.32	2	863.66	15.99*
Subjects (S)	2047.37	13	157.49	
$A \times S$	1404.52	26	54.02	
Total	5179.21	41		

*$p < .01$.

A Tukey HSD gave a $CD = 6.9$ minutes at the .05 significance level.

    a. What is the effect of the stimulus conditions on fixation time?

    b. Describe the results of this experiment following the style illustrated in the Reporting the Results of the Analysis of Variance section of this chapter.

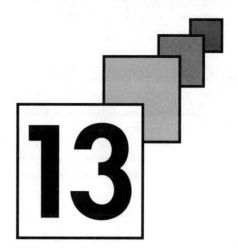

Nonparametric Statistical Tests

Nonparametric statistical test: A statistical test involving hypotheses that do not state a relationship about a population parameter.

I have developed statistical hypothesis testing emphasizing the *t* test and the analysis of variance. Both tests are **parametric tests**, for they use sample statistics (e.g., $\overline{X}$) to make inferences about population parameters (μ). **Nonparametric statistical methods** test hypotheses that do not involve population parameters. They also make fewer assumptions about the shapes of populations than do parametric tests. For this reason, nonparametric tests are sometimes called **distribution-free tests**.

Recall that parametric tests assume the following:

- The scores in the populations sampled are normally distributed.
- The variances of scores in the populations are equal.

In practice the data collected may not meet these assumptions. Yet, because parametric tests are thought to be robust, researchers may use the *t* test or analysis of variance on the data even if the assumptions are not fully met.

In some instances, however, these assumptions are not met sufficiently to allow using a parametric test. For example, in measuring the reaction time of an individual, most reaction times are likely to be short (e.g., perhaps about 500 milliseconds or less). No reaction time can be less than 0 seconds; but there is no upper limit on the maximum time that may be measured. A few individuals may have very long reaction times compared to other people. Thus a frequency distribution of reaction-time measures is likely to be positively skewed; most reaction times are very short, and a few may be much longer. Such a distribution clearly is not an approximately normal distribution.

Parametric tests also assume that it makes sense to compute a mean (i.e., $\overline{X}$) on the scores obtained. This requirement implies that the scores should achieve either an interval or ratio scale of measurement. But often behaviors cannot be measured at these levels. An experimenter simply may count the number of people displaying a certain behavior, thus obtaining frequencies of occurrence of the behavior, a nominal measurement. Or the scores obtained may represent an ordinal scale, such as rank ordering individuals on a certain personality trait. Because parametric tests require $\overline{X}$ to be calculated, they are not appropriate for use if the scores represent nominal or ordinal measurements. Thus nonparametric tests are used when:

- The assumptions of parametric tests are not met, or
- Scores are at either the nominal or ordinal level of measurement.

Table 13–1 presents parametric tests and corresponding nonparametric tests for one-factor designs. I discuss the chi-square, Mann–Whitney U, and the Wilcoxon signed-ranks tests in this chapter. A nonparametric test of correlation, the Spearman rank-order correlation coefficient, is presented in Chapter 14.

ANALYSIS OF FREQUENCY DATA: THE CHI-SQUARE TEST

Many studies lead to scores that indicate only whether a behavior occurred or not. For example, when observing animals in the wild, a scientist may record only whether an

TABLE 13-1

Parametric and nonparametric tests for one-factor designs as a function of type of design and scale of measurement.

		Type of Design			
		Between Subjects		**Within Subjects**	
	Scale of Measure of Data	**Two Levels**	**Three or More Levels**	**Two Levels**	**Three or More Levels**
Parametric tests	Ratio or interval	t_{ind} or between-subjects ANOVA	Between-subjects ANOVA	t_{rel} or within-subjects ANOVA	Within-subjects ANOVA
Nonparametric tests	Ordinal	Mann–Whitney U	Kruskal–Wallis ANOVA by ranks	Wilcoxon signed ranks	Friedman ANOVA by ranks
	Nominal	Chi square	Chi square		

Chi-square test: A statistical test used to analyze nominal level of measurement scores where frequencies of occurrence of the various categories are obtained.

animal does or does not behave in a certain way. These scores achieve nominal measurement; they simply represent the occurrence of mutually exclusive categories of behavior. The frequency of occurrence of responses in the various categories may be obtained, but an individual score indicates only whether a behavior occurred or not; it conveys no numerical information about the response. A nonparametric test, the **chi-square test** (pronounced "ky square") provides an appropriate test for these scores when a between-subjects design is used and the scores are nominal measures representing only the frequency of occurrence of a response. I discuss two forms of the chi-square test, the chi-square test of independence and the chi-square test for goodness of fit.

The Chi-square Test of Independence

Chi-square test of independence: The chi square used when a score is categorized on two independent dimensions.

The **chi-square test of independence** (also called a **two-way chi square**) is used when a score is categorized on two independent dimensions. Consider an example. The *walker problem* is used to study people's knowledge of the physics of falling objects (McCloskey, Washburn, & Felch, 1983). In this problem, a subject is shown a side view of a man walking at a constant speed. The walker is holding his arm straight out from the shoulder and has a small metal ball in his hand. As he is walking, the man drops the ball. The task of a subject is to indicate on the picture where he or she believes the ball will fall. The correct answer is that the ball, because it is moving at the same forward speed as the walker, will fall in a forward arc and land even with the walker. Many people, however, indicate that the ball will fall straight down or in a backward arc.

Suppose you hypothesized that students who have had training in physics will give correct answers more frequently than students who have not had training in physics. To test this hypothesis, you presented the problem to 40 physics-trained and 40 physics-untrained students and obtained the frequencies of correct responses shown in Table 13–2. The values in this table designated by *O* (for *observed frequency*) represent the frequency of correct and incorrect answers given by the subjects. A subject's response is categorized on two dimensions in this table: (1) whether the response is correct or

TABLE 13–2

Hypothetical data for responses of physics-trained and physics-untrained students on the walker problem. The values given for O are the observed frequencies, and the values given for E are the expected frequencies obtained from the marginal frequencies.

		Type of Student		
		Physics-trained	**Physics-untrained**	**(Marginal)**
Response	Correct	$O = 26$ $E = 17$	$O = 8$ $E = 17$	34
	Incorrect	$O = 14$ $E = 23$	$O = 32$ $E = 23$	46
	(Marginal)	40	40	(Total) 80

incorrect and (2) whether it came from a physics-trained or a physics-untrained subject. Notice that each subject contributes only one response to the table, the subject is either physics-trained or physics-untrained, and his or her response is either correct or incorrect.

Contingency Tables

Contingency table: A rows-by-columns table presenting the frequency of each category formed by the intersection of the row and column variables in the table.

Marginal frequencies: The row totals and the column totals of the observed frequencies in a contingency table.

Table 13–2 is called a **rows (r) by columns (c) contingency table** or a **two-way frequency table**. The columns (symbolized by c) of the table represent one categorization into which subjects may be placed. The rows (symbolized by r) provide a second categorization for the response. Table 13–2 is thus a 2 rows (r = two categories of the response, correct or incorrect) by 2 columns (c = two categories of the type of subject, physics-trained or physics-untrained) contingency table. It is called a contingency table because we are trying to find if the subject's response, correct or incorrect, is contingent on, or depends on, the type of training experienced. The **marginal frequencies** shown in the table are the row totals (i.e., the **row marginals**) and the column totals (i.e., the **column marginals**) of the obtained frequencies.

Expected Frequencies

Expected frequencies: The frequencies in a contingency table obtained assuming that the two dimensions of the table are independent.

Correct responses were given by 34 subjects and incorrect responses by 46 subjects in Table 13–2. If correctness of response is not related to the type of student, then I expect that one-half of the 34 correct responses (i.e., 17) would be given by physics-trained students and one-half by physics-untrained students. A similar expectation holds for the incorrect responses if there is no relation between type of student and correctness of response; 23 incorrect responses should be given by each type of student group. These values are called **expected frequencies**, the frequencies of response expected if correctness of response is not related to type of student. Expected frequencies are indicated by the value of E (for **expected frequency**) in each cell of the table. Expected frequencies, then, are obtained assuming that there is no relationship of the two dimensions on which the subject is categorized. In this example, the expected frequencies assume that the type of subject and the correctness of a response are independent of each other.

The chi-square test uses expected and observed frequencies to develop a test statistic. If there is no relation between the two dimensions in the population sampled, then the observed frequencies should be about the same as the expected frequencies. Large differences of the observed from the expected frequencies should occur only rarely by chance if the column and row variables are not associated. But if the column and row variables are related in the population sampled, then the observed frequencies should differ from the expected frequencies by larger amounts. For example, if the frequency of correct and incorrect responses is related to the type of student, then it is likely that the physics-trained students will produce more correct and fewer incorrect responses than the 17 expected by chance and that the physics-untrained students will produce more incorrect and fewer correct answers than the 23 expected by chance.

The χ^2 Statistic

The chi-square test measures the difference of the obtained frequencies from the expected frequencies with the test statistic:

$$\chi^2 = \sum_{r=1}^{r} \sum_{c=1}^{c} \frac{(O_{rc} - E_{rc})^2}{E_{rc}},$$

where χ (pronounced "ky") is *chi*, the twenty-second letter of the Greek alphabet. In this formula

O_{rc} = observed frequency in the *rc* cell, where *r* represents the row number and *c* the column number,

E_{rc} = expected frequency of the *rc* cell,

r   = number of categories of the row variable (*r* = 2, correctness of response in this example),

c   = number of levels of the columns variable (*c* = 2, type of student in this example).

Statistical Hypothesis Testing with χ^2

Using χ^2 to determine whether the correctness of response is related to type of student in the example requires statistical hypothesis testing following the familiar steps:

- A null hypothesis, H_0, and an alternative hypothesis, H_1, are formulated. The null hypothesis provides the sampling distribution of the χ^2 statistic.
- A significance level is selected.
- A critical value of χ^2, identified as χ^2_{crit}, is found from the sampling distribution of χ^2 in Table A–5.
- Using the value of χ^2_{crit}, a rejection region is located in the sampling distribution of χ^2.
- χ^2_{obs} is calculated from the scores in the study.
- A decision to reject or not reject H_0 is made on the basis of whether χ^2_{obs} falls into the rejection region.

Statistical Hypotheses

Null Hypothesis.   The null hypothesis under which the sampling distribution of χ^2 is developed and under which expected frequencies for each cell are found is

> H_0: The row variable and the column variable are independent in the population.

For the example study, H_0 may be stated specifically as

> H_0: The correctness of the response is independent of the type of student.

Alternative Hypothesis.   The alternative hypothesis is

> H_1: The row and column variables are related in the population.

For the example study, H_1 may be stated specifically as

> H_1: The correctness of the response is related to the type of student.

Selecting a Significance Level

The process of selecting a significance level is identical to that discussed in earlier chapters. In line with common practice, I choose $\alpha = .05$.

Finding χ^2_{crit} and Locating a Rejection Region

Degrees of Freedom of χ^2.   The specific sampling distribution of χ^2 and thus the value of χ^2_{crit} depends on the degrees of freedom of the statistic. The *df* for χ^2 are given by

$$(r-1)(c-1)$$

where r represents the number of rows and c represents the number of columns in the contingency table. For the example, $r = 2$ and $c = 2$; thus $df = (2-1)(2-1)$, which equals 1. Values of χ^2_{crit} for $\alpha = .05$ and .01 from the sampling distribution of χ^2 at various *df* are given in Appendix Table A–5. The critical value of χ^2 for 1 *df* and $\alpha = .05$ from Table A–5 is 3.84.

Locating a Rejection Region.   If the null hypothesis is true and correctness of the response is independent of the type of student, then χ^2_{obs} should be relatively small; the expected and observed frequencies for each cell of the contingency table should be much alike. On the other hand, if H_1 is true and the row variable is related to the column variable, then χ^2_{obs} should become larger because the expected and observed frequencies will differ from each other. Consequently, relatively large values of χ^2_{obs} should be rare if the null hypothesis is true, but common if the alternative hypothesis is true. Thus a value of χ^2_{obs} equal to or greater than χ^2_{crit} is statistically significant at the value of α

selected. Accordingly, for the example, if χ^2_{obs} is equal to or greater than 3.84, it falls into the rejection region and will lead to rejection of H_0 and acceptance of H_1.

Calculating χ^2_{obs}

Calculating χ^2_{obs} requires knowing both the observed and expected frequencies of responses. The expected frequencies for each cell of a contingency table are obtained from the marginal frequencies by

$$\begin{pmatrix} \textbf{Expected} \\ \textbf{frequency} \\ \textbf{of a cell} \end{pmatrix} = \frac{\textbf{(Row marginal for cell)(Column marginal for cell)}}{\textbf{Total number of responses}}.$$

For example, the expected frequency for the physics-trained/correct response cell (row 1, column 1) is found by

$$E_{11} = \frac{(\text{row 1 marginal})(\text{column 1 marginal})}{\text{total}},$$

or

$$E_{11} = \frac{(34)(40)}{80} = \frac{1360}{80} = 17.$$

This expected frequency is the E in the physics-trained correct response cell of Table 13–2.

After expected frequencies for each cell are obtained, χ^2_{obs} is found as follows:

- Subtract the expected frequency (E) from the observed frequency (O) for each cell.
- Square each $O - E$ difference.
- Divide each squared $O - E$ difference by the expected frequency of the cell.
- Sum the resulting $(O-E)^2/E$ values over all cells in the contingency table to obtain χ^2_{obs}.

The numerical value of χ^2_{obs} for the frequencies shown in Table 13–2 is calculated as follows:

$$\chi^2_{obs} = \frac{(26-17)^2}{17} + \frac{(8-17)^2}{17} + \frac{(14-23)^2}{23} + \frac{(32-23)^2}{23},$$

$$= \frac{9^2}{17} + \frac{-9^2}{17} + \frac{-9^2}{23} + \frac{9^2}{23},$$

$$= \frac{81}{17} + \frac{81}{17} + \frac{81}{23} + \frac{81}{23},$$

$$= 4.765 + 4.765 + 3.522 + 3.522,$$

$$= 16.57.$$

Decisions about the Statistical Hypotheses

The χ^2_{obs} of 16.57 is larger than χ^2_{crit} of 3.84 and thus falls into the rejection region. Accordingly, H_0 is rejected and H_1 is accepted. There is a statistically significant relationship between the row and column variables.

Conclusion from the Test

The rejection of H_0 indicates that the type of student and correctness of response are related. The nature of the relationship is seen by examining Table 13–2: A greater than chance frequency of a correct response is associated with a physics-trained student and a greater than chance frequency of an incorrect response is associated with a physics-untrained student. Physics-trained students are more likely to give correct responses, and physics-untrained students are more likely to give incorrect responses on this problem.

Assumptions for the Use of the Chi-square Test

A chi-square test of independence may be used on a contingency table of any size (e.g., 2×3, 3×4, or 4×4). Several assumptions apply to its use, however.

- Each subject may contribute only one response to the contingency table.
- The number of responses obtained should be large enough so that no expected frequency is less than 10 in a 2×2 contingency table or less than 5 in a contingency table larger than 2×2. If this condition is not met, then either more responses should be collected or an alternative test such as the Fisher exact test should be used.

Further details of the use of chi-square and alternative tests for frequency data may be found in most advanced statistics texts.

Example Problem 13–1

Using the Chi-square Test with a 3 × 2 Contingency Table

Problem

Being a firstborn often appears to confer certain advantages to a child. Several studies have indicated that firstborn children typically perform better on academic-type measures than do later-born children, and Eisenman (1987) found a relationship between birth order and creativity among college males. Firstborn males' scores were more frequently above the median on creativity, and later-born males' creativity scores were more frequently below the median in his sample. Suppose that you extend this research by testing 100 firstborn and 100 later-born adult males by asking them for creative uses of common objects. You categorize their responses as being either in the top, middle, or bottom one-third of the scores for creativity. The categorization by birth order and creativity test score resulted in the following observed frequencies.

		Birth Order	
		Firstborn	**Later Born**
Creativity test score	Top one-third	47	29
	Middle one-third	29	35
	Bottom one-third	24	36

Is there a relationship between birth order and creativity in males? Use a .05 significance level.

Solution   One categorization of a subject in this study is birth order with two levels, firstborn and later born. The second categorization was based on the creativity test score being in the top, middle, or bottom one-third of scores for a college population. Each subject contributes only one score or count to the frequency; hence the chi-square test is an appropriate statistical test for these data.

Statistic to Be Used: χ^2.

Assumptions for Use:
   1. Each subject contributes only one response to the contingency table.
   2. No expected frequency will be less than 5. This minimum expected frequency applies because the contingency table, a 3×2, is greater than a 2×2.

Statistical Hypotheses:
   H_0:   Birth order and creativity are independent in the male population sampled.
   H_1:   Birth order and creativity are related in the male population sampled.

Significance Level: $\alpha = .05$.

df: $df = (r - 1)(c - 1) = (3 - 1)(2 - 1) = 2$.

Critical Value: $\chi^2_{crit}(2) = 5.99$ from Table A–5.

Rejection Region: Values of χ^2_{obs} equal to or greater than 5.99.

Calculation: The formula for χ^2_{obs} requires finding expected frequencies; to do so I must find the marginal frequencies. The observed frequencies (indicated by O), the expected frequencies (indicated by E), and the marginal frequencies are provided in the following contingency table:

		Birth Order		
		Firstborn	**Later Born**	**(Row Marginals)**
	Top one-third	$O = 47$ $E = 38$	$O = 29$ $E = 38$	76
Creativity Test Score	Middle one-third	$O = 29$ $E = 32$	$O = 35$ $E = 32$	64
	Bottom one-third	$O = 24$ $E = 30$	$O = 36$ $E = 30$	60
	(Column marginals)	100	100	(Total) 200

Column marginals are obtained by summing the observed frequencies in each column. Row marginals are obtained analogously by summing the observed frequencies in each row. Given the marginal frequencies, expected frequencies are found using

$$\binom{\text{Expected}}{\text{frequency of a cell}} = \frac{(\text{Row marginal for cell})(\text{Column marginal for cell})}{\text{Total number of responses}}.$$

Expected frequencies for each cell of the table are then as follows:

$$\text{Firstborn–top } \tfrac{1}{3} \text{ cell:} \quad E_{11} = \frac{(76)(100)}{200} = \frac{7600}{200} = 38,$$

$$\text{Later born–top } \tfrac{1}{3} \text{ cell:} \quad E_{12} = \frac{(76)(100)}{200} = \frac{7600}{200} = 38,$$

$$\text{Firstborn–middle } \tfrac{1}{3} \text{ cell:} \quad E_{21} = \frac{(64)(100)}{200} = \frac{6400}{200} = 32,$$

$$\text{Later born–middle } \tfrac{1}{3} \text{ cell:} \quad E_{22} = \frac{(64)(100)}{200} = \frac{6400}{200} = 32,$$

$$\text{Firstborn–bottom } \tfrac{1}{3} \text{ cell:} \quad E_{31} = \frac{(60)(100)}{200} = \frac{6000}{200} = 30,$$

$$\text{Later born–bottom } \tfrac{1}{3} \text{ cell:} \quad E_{32} = \frac{(60)(100)}{200} = \frac{6000}{200} = 30.$$

The value of χ^2_{obs} is found by

$$\chi^2_{obs} = \sum_{r=1}^{3} \sum_{c=1}^{2} \frac{(O_{rc} - E_{rc})^2}{E_{rc}}.$$

Substituting numerical values,

$$\chi^2_{obs} = \frac{(47-38)^2}{38} + \frac{(29-38)^2}{38} + \frac{(29-32)^2}{32} + \frac{(35-32)^2}{32} + \frac{(24-30)^2}{30} + \frac{(36-30)^2}{30},$$

$$= 2.13 + 2.13 + 0.28 + 0.28 + 1.20 + 1.20,$$

$$= 7.22.$$

Decision: The χ^2_{obs} = 7.22 is greater than χ^2_{crit} = 5.99; thus it falls into the rejection region. I reject H_0 and accept H_1.

Conclusion: Birth order and creativity are related in the male population sampled. By examining the table of observed and expected frequencies, we see that firstborn males' scores occur more frequently and later-born males' scores occur less frequently in the top one-third of the scores than expected by chance. We notice also that firstborn males' scores occur less frequently and later-born males' more frequently in the bottom one-third of scores than a chance hypothesis predicts.

THE χ^2 TEST FOR GOODNESS OF FIT

Chi-square test of goodness of fit: The chi square used when a score is categorized on only one dimension.

In the chi-square test of independence, scores were categorized on two different dimensions, for example, whether a score was from a physics-trained or a physics-untrained student and whether the score was correct or incorrect. With the **chi-square test of goodness of fit**, scores are categorized on only one dimension or variable. Consider an example.

Many people believe that abnormal behavior is more likely to occur during a full moon. As a test for empirical evidence to support this belief, suppose that you categorized the admission of new clients into a mental health unit over a one-year period by lunar phases and found the following distribution of admissions.

Lunar Phase

Full Moon	New Moon	First Quarter	Third Quarter
62	50	60	56

Do admissions vary with the phase of the moon? The chi-square goodness of fit test may be used to answer this question.

The given frequencies categorize behavior only by lunar phase. To use a chi-square test, I need to find expected frequencies of admissions for each lunar phase. Because I do not have row and column marginals to obtain expected frequencies, I must have some other basis for predicting expected frequencies. For this example, I use the following reasoning to obtain the expected frequencies. If admission into the mental health unit is unrelated to phase of the moon, then the frequency of new admissions should be equal in each phase, with any observed differences reflecting only sampling error. This reasoning may be expressed in the null hypothesis:

H_0: New admissions to the mental health unit and phase of the moon are
   independent in the population sampled.

The alternative hypothesis, then, is

> H_1: New admissions to the mental health unit and phase of the moon are related in the population sampled.

If this alternative hypothesis is true, then new admissions should not be equal among the lunar phases. But if H_0 is true, then about one-fourth of the new admissions should occur in each lunar phase. Hence expected frequencies of admissions incidents may be obtained by dividing the total frequency of admissions by 4, the number of lunar phases. Applying this reasoning to our example, there are 228 total new admissions, so the expected frequency for each phase is $\frac{228}{4}$ or 57. The observed and expected frequencies for each lunar phase are then as follows:

	Lunar Phase		
Full Moon	**New Moon**	**First Quarter**	**Third Quarter**
$O = 62$	$O = 50$	$O = 60$	$O = 56$
$E = 57$	$E = 57$	$E = 57$	$E = 57$

Chi square may be obtained from these data by

$$\chi^2 = \sum_{c=1}^{c} \frac{(O_c - E_c)^2}{E_c}.$$

The degrees of freedom for this χ^2_{obs} are $c-1$, where c represents the number of categories used. For the example, $c = 4$; thus $df = 4 - 1 = 3$. Accordingly,

$$
\begin{aligned}
\chi^2_{obs} &= \frac{(62-57)^2}{57} + \frac{(50-57)^2}{57} + \frac{(60-57)^2}{57} + \frac{(56-57)^2}{57}, \\
&= \frac{(5)^2}{57} + \frac{(-7)^2}{57} + \frac{(3)^2}{57} + \frac{(-1)^2}{57}, \\
&= \frac{25}{57} + \frac{49}{57} + \frac{9}{57} + \frac{1}{57}, \\
&= \frac{84}{57} = 1.47.
\end{aligned}
$$

The critical value of χ^2 for 3 df and $\alpha = .05$ is given in Table A–5; $\chi^2_{crit}(3) = 7.81$. $\chi^2_{obs} = 1.47$ is less than χ^2_{crit} and does not fall into the rejection region. I fail to reject the null hypothesis. There is no evidence that the frequency of new admissions to the mental health unit is related to phases of the moon in the population sampled.

The assumptions for the chi-square goodness of fit test are similar to those for the chi-square test of independence; each subject must contribute only one observation to the data, and the expected frequencies should not be less than 10 if there are only two categories or not less than 5 if there are three or more categories.

STATISTICS IN USE 13-1

A Portrait of Women on Television: Analysis with the Chi Square

In Chapter 1, I indicated that in the typical U.S. household a television set is on for over 7 hours a day. There is no question that much of what people know and believe about the world arises from what they see on television. Because of its informational capabilities, behavioral scientists are concerned that television may present an inaccurate portrait of society. As an example, Davis (1990) examined the demographics of women on television. He categorized 894 TV characters from 64 different shows on a variety of dimensions and analyzed the frequencies of occurrence of the various categories with a chi square. His findings reveal interesting differences in the characterization of men and women on television. Females slightly outnumber males in the population, but on television, about 65 percent of the characters are males and only 35 percent females. This difference from the population distribution of males and females was statistically significant, χ^2 (2, $N = 894) = 23.86$, $p < .01$. And those females typically were in the 18- to 34-year-old range compared to males being most frequently in the 35- to 49-year-old range. Over 35 percent of the female characters had blonde hair, a frequency much higher than the 15 to 18 percent of blondes in the general population. Grey hair was an unusual occurrence for a female (2.1 percent), whereas it was relatively common for males (13.9 percent). Although in the population men and women's hair colors are about equally distributed (for example, the proportion of men and women having grey hair is about equal), such is not the case on television; men and women differed significantly on hair colors, χ^2 (5, $N = 894) = 157.24$, $p < .01$. Finally, women were also much more likely to be dressed provocatively than males: about 7 percent of the male characters were shown wearing provocative dress, whereas such dress was worn by over 24 percent of the female characters, χ^2 (6, $N = 894) = 30.62$, $p < .01$.

Davis notes that these characteristics of females and males on television have changed little from similar studies done in the 1950s and 1970s. The female on TV seems to be valued for her youth and sex appeal.

REPORTING THE RESULTS OF THE CHI-SQUARE TEST

The Publication Manual of the American Psychological Association (1994) requires that a report of the chi-square test include the *df* and the sample size on which χ^2_{obs} is based. To illustrate, I use the example of the chi-square test for independence on the walker problem.

Table 1 presents the observed frequencies for type of student and response correctness. With alpha equal to .05, a chi-square test on these frequencies was statistically significant, χ^2 (1, $N = 80) = 16.57$, $p < .01$. Physics-trained students are more likely to give a correct answer, whereas physics-untrained students are more likely to give an incorrect answer.

TABLE 1
Hypothetical data for correctness of responses
by physics-trained and physics-untrained
students on the walker problem.

	Type of Student	
	Physics Trained	Physics Untrained
Correct Response	26	8
Incorrect	14	32

In this report:

Table 1	Provides the observed frequencies of the responses.
$\alpha = .05$	Indicates the significance level selected for the test.
$\chi^2 (1, N = 80)$	Identifies the test statistic as the chi square. The 1 in parentheses indicates the test was based on 1 df and the $N = 80$ gives the total sample size.
$= 16.57$	Gives the value of χ^2_{obs} (not the χ^2_{crit} value of Table A–5).
$p < .01$	Indicates that

a.   the probability of χ^2_{obs} if H_0 is true is less than or equal to .01. This value is the probability of χ^2_{obs} or an even more extreme value of χ^2_{obs} if H_0 is true; it may not be the same as the value of α selected.

b.   "H_0 : The correctness of the response is independent of the type of student" was rejected.
"H_1: The correctness of the response is related to the type of student" was accepted.

TESTING YOUR KNOWLEDGE 13–1

1.   Define: c, chi-square test, expected frequencies, marginal frequencies, nonparametric test, observed frequencies, parametric test, r, rows-by-columns contingency table, two-way frequency table.
2.   Under what circumstances is a nonparametric test used to analyze data from an experiment?
3.   Identify the appropriate statistical test for each of the following one-factor designs with two levels of the independent variable and the level of measurement of the scores indicated.
   a.   Within-subjects, ratio measurement.
   b.   Between-subjects, nominal measurement.
   c.   Between-subjects, ratio measurement.
   d.   Between-subjects, ordinal measurement.
   e.   Within-subjects, ordinal measurement.

4. What form of data is suitable for analysis by the chi-square test?
5. What is represented by the columns of a rows-by-columns contingency table?
6. What is represented by the rows of a rows-by-columns contingency table?
7. The following are values of χ^2_{obs} for various degrees of freedom (given in parentheses).

$$\chi^2_{obs}(2) = 7.26 \qquad \chi^2_{obs}(4) = 8.33$$
$$\chi^2_{obs}(7) = 14.19 \qquad \chi^2_{obs}(20) = 26.94$$

For each value of χ^2_{obs} and df, find the value of χ^2_{crit} at the .05 level. Then indicate whether χ^2_{obs} falls into the rejection region and the decisions you make concerning H_0 and H_1.

8. For each of the following contingency tables, calculate expected frequencies; then find χ^2_{obs} and indicate whether it is statistically significant at the .05 level. The values in each cell represent observed frequencies.

a.

		Column	
		1	2
Row	1	12	32
	2	16	38

b.

		Column	
		1	2
Row	1	27	22
	2	17	46

c.

		Column	
		1	2
Row	1	33	66
	2	27	14

9. Complete the following problem using the chi-square test following the format illustrated in the example problem. Use a .05 significance level. Have you ever run a traffic stop sign while driving? Perhaps not, but no doubt you have seen others do so. How frequently do drivers fail to stop for stop signs, and does the frequency of occurrence of such behaviors depend on the time of day or day of the week? Suppose that a researcher investigated this problem by observing the number of vehicles not stopping for a stop sign at an intersection. He observed traffic from 10:00 A.M. to 11:00 A.M. and from 2:00 P.M. to 3:00 P.M. on Tuesday, Wednesday, and Thursday of one week. Car licenses were

noted and each car was counted only on its first trip through the intersection for the week. Suppose that the investigator reported the following frequency of vehicles ignoring the stop sign during the two times on each of the days of the week observed.

| | | Day of Week | | |
		Tuesday	Wednesday	Thursday
	10:00 to 11:00 A.M.	38	46	58
Time				
	2:00 to 3:00 P.M.	46	54	63

Is there a relationship between day of the week and time of day with respect to drivers ignoring stop signs?

10. Complete the following problem using the chi-square test following the format illustrated in the example problem. Use a .05 significance level. Psychologists have hypothesized that one cause for eating disorders among females is the many cues that stress thinness as desirable for females. Smith, Waldorf, and Trembath (1990) investigated one form of cue, the personal ad, to see if these ads indicated weight as an important characteristic of a desired partner. They hypothesized that ads placed by males seeking females would more likely indicate a weight requirement than would an ad placed by a female seeking a male. To test this hypothesis, they examined a set of personal ads and categorized them by gender of the person placing the ad and whether or not the ad expressed a weight preference. The following hypothetical frequencies typify the outcome of their study. Does the hypothesized relationship exist in these scores?

| | Preference for Weight Indicated | |
	Yes	No
Ad placed by male	89	186
Ad placed by female	6	219

MANN–WHITNEY U TEST

Mann–Whitney U test: A nonparametric test for a between-subjects design using two levels of an independent variable with scores representing at least ordinal measurement.

The **Mann–Whitney U test** is a nonparametric test for a between-subjects design using two levels of an independent variable with scores representing at least ordinal measurement. I develop the Mann–Whitney U test using an example of research on perceiving ambiguous figures (Reisberg, 1983).

Ambiguous figures are stimuli involving two or more possible perceptual organizations. For example, Figure 13–1 illustrates the Schroeder staircase. This figure has two possible perceptual organizations: In one, a set of stairs appears normal; in the other, the stairs seem upside down. The stairs will reverse perceptually if you view them for a while. If attention and memory are required to reverse the perception from one organization to the other, then an additional task that occupies attention and memory should lengthen the time needed to reverse the perception. To test this hypothesis, two equivalent

FIGURE 13–1
The Schroeder staircase, an ambiguous figure.

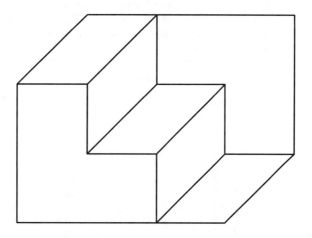

groups of subjects were created. Both groups viewed the Schroeder staircase and reported when they had seen both organizations of the stimulus. The independent variable was the type of interfering task. Subjects in the control group (A_1) simply viewed the figure and reported the reversal. Subjects in the experimental group (A_2) counted backward by threes from a three-digit number, a task requiring both attention and memory, while they viewed the stimulus. If perceiving reversal of the figure also requires attention and memory, then counting backward should interfere with perception of the figure and delay the reports of a reversal. The experimenter timed how long it took the subject to make the report of a reversal. If a subject did not report a reversal at the end of 2 minutes, the test was stopped and the subject assigned an "infinite" (∞) latency.

Table 13–3 presents hypothetical data for this experiment, with nine subjects in each of the two groups. The scores are shown in order of increasing latency in each group, although they would not occur in this order as they actually were recorded from subjects. Notice that for the experimental group one subject did not report a reversal within 2 minutes. This subject was assigned an infinite latency without a numerical value. Because both the t test and the analysis of variance require numerical values from each subject, they cannot be used to analyze these data. The Mann–Whitney U test, however, only requires that scores be ranked, and an infinite latency can be ranked. Thus the scores are analyzed with the Mann–Whitney U test.

Statistical Hypothesis Testing with the Mann–Whitney U

I first present a conceptual overview of the U test and then a computational format. Both approaches require ranking scores to develop a test statistic and a sampling distribution of that statistic. This ranking is done even if the scores represent an interval or ratio measurement; the scores are converted to ordinal measurement by ranking them.

TABLE 13–3

Hypothetical perceptual reversal latencies (in seconds) of the Schroeder staircase figure. Subjects in the control group simply viewed the figure. Subjects in the experimental group counted backward by threes while viewing the figure.

Group	
Control (A_1)	Experimental (A_2)
2	4
5	10
6	11
8	12
9	14
13	17
15	85
21	98
42	∞[a]

For ease of discussion, the scores are presented in order of increasing latency in each treatment group.

[a]This score represents an "infinite" reversal latency; this subject did not see the reversal within the 2-minute time limit.

Ranking Scores

The first step in ranking the scores is to combine the scores of both groups (for a total of N scores) and then place the scores in order of increasing magnitude from smallest to largest. This procedure is shown in step 1 of Table 13–4 for the data of Table 13–3. In performing the ranking, the group identity of the scores is maintained (see step 2 of Table 13–4). Then the ranks from 1 to N are assigned to the scores, giving the smallest score the rank of 1 and the largest score the rank of N. This ranking is shown in step 3 of Table 13–4.

The U Statistic

The U statistic is the number of times that the rank of a score in one group precedes the rank of a score in the other group. This calculation is illustrated in steps 4 and 5 of Table 13–4. For example, the score of 2 (shown in step 1) from the A_1 group (identified in step 2) precedes all the A_2 scores in rank (given in step 3). Thus this score precedes nine of the A_2 scores in rank. Scores of 5, 6, 8, and 9 from the A_1 group each precede eight of the scores in the A_2 group in rank. Step 4 of Table 13–4 presents the number of times that an A_1 score precedes an A_2 score in rank. Examine the numerical values in this step and understand how they were obtained. The total number of times that an A_1 score precedes an A_2 score in rank is 56, the total of the values in step 4 (i.e.,

TABLE 13–4
Rank ordering scores of Table 13–3.

1. Latency scores ordered from smallest to largest	2	4	5	6	8	9	10	11	12	13	14	15	17	21	42	85	98	∞
2. Group identity[a]	1	2	1	1	1	1	2	2	2	1	2	1	2	1	1	2	2	2
3. Rank	1	2	3	4	5	6	7	8	9	10	11	12	13	14	15	16	17	18
4. Number of times an A_1 score precedes A_2 scores	9		8	8	8	8				5		4		3	3			
5. Number of times an A_2 score precedes A_1 scores		8					4	4	4		3		2					

[a] A 1 indicates the score is from group A_1, control; 2 indicates the score is from group A_2, experimental.

$9 + 8 + 8 + 8 + 8 + 5 + 4 + 3 + 3 = 56$). Thus the value of $U_{A1\,\text{obs}}$ (for the U observed on group A_1) is 56.

There is also a value of U for the A_2 group. This value represents the number of times that the rank of an A_2 score precedes the rank of an A_1 score. Step 5 of Table 13–4 indicates the number of times that an A_2 score precedes an A_1 score in rank. The sum of the values in this step (i.e., $8 + 4 + 4 + 4 + 3 + 2 = 25$) provides $U_{A2\,\text{obs}} = 25$.

Characteristics of the U Statistic
If a treatment has no effect, then it is expected that, when the scores are combined and ordered as they are in Table 13–4, scores from each group will be approximately equally distributed over the rankings. I do not expect the scores from one group to be represented exclusively among the lower ranks and the scores of the other condition to be exclusively among the higher ranks. Consequently, the value of $U_{A1\,\text{obs}}$ should be about equal to $U_{A2\,\text{obs}}$. For example, if the treatment had no effect in the example, then $U_{A1\,\text{obs}}$ and $U_{A2\,\text{obs}}$ would each equal about 40. If the treatment had an exceptionally strong effect, however, and all the A_1 scores had lower ranks than the A_2 scores, then $U_{A1\,\text{obs}}$ would be 81 and $U_{A2\,\text{obs}}$ would be equal to 0. The values of $U_{A1\,\text{obs}}$ and $U_{A2\,\text{obs}}$ are perfectly inversely related. As $U_{A1\,\text{obs}}$ increases, $U_{A2\,\text{obs}}$ decreases by an equal amount. Hence only one value of U, the smaller value, is used in a statistical test. I can easily determine if the smaller value has been calculated by using the relation

$$U_{A2\,\text{obs}} = n_{A1}n_{A2} - U_{A1\,\text{obs}},$$

where n_{A1} is the number of scores in group A_1 and n_{A2} is the number of scores in group A_2. In the example, $U_{A2\,\text{obs}}$ is found from $U_{A1\,\text{obs}}$ by

$$U_{A2\,\text{obs}} = (9)(9) - 56 = 81 - 56 = 25,$$

and 25 is the smaller of the two values of U for the data of Table 13–3. Thus $U_{\text{obs}} = 25$.

The U statistic is used in a statistical hypothesis test by following the steps of statistical hypothesis testing.

Statistical Hypotheses

Null Hypothesis.   The null hypothesis under which the sampling distribution of U is developed is

H_0: The population distribution of A_1 scores is identical to the population distribution of A_2 scores.

If H_0 is true, then the value of $U_{A1\,\text{obs}}$ should be about the same as $U_{A2\,\text{obs}}$.

Alternative Hypothesis.   The alternative hypothesis for the U test is

H_1: The population distribution of A_1 scores is not identical to the population distribution of A_2 scores.

If H_1 is true, then $U_{A1\,\text{obs}}$ and $U_{A2\,\text{obs}}$ should differ from each other.

Sampling Distributions and Critical Values of U

The sampling distribution of U varies with n_{A1} and n_{A2}. To simplify the use of the U statistic, tables of its sampling distribution and critical values of U at the .01 and .05 levels have been developed for various sizes of n_{A1} and n_{A2}. Because the maximum value of U is determined by n_{A1} and n_{A2}, tables of the sampling distribution of U present only the smaller of the two values of U that may be obtained from a study. The sampling distribution for the smaller value of U for groups ranging in size from 1 to 20 for $\alpha = .01$ and $\alpha = .05$ is presented in Appendix Table A–6. The values in this table present the critical value of U, identified as U_{crit}, for the smaller U_{obs}. Values of the smaller U_{obs} **less than or equal to U_{crit}** are statistically significant for the value of α selected. Notice, in contrast to the t, F, and χ^2 statistics, that the rejection region for U_{obs} consists of values of the smaller U_{obs} that are *less than or equal to* U_{crit}. For the example data, $n_{A1} = 9$ and $n_{A2} = 9$; thus $U_{\text{crit}} = 17$ at the .05 significance level.

Decisions about the Statistical Hypotheses

Decisions about the statistical hypotheses are made using the smaller of the two values of U_{obs}, as follows:

Value of Smaller U_{obs}	Statistical Decision
Less than or equal to U_{crit}	Reject H_0 Accept H_1
Greater than U_{crit}	Do not reject H_0 Do not accept H_1

For our example of the reversal latency scores of Table 13–3, $U_{A1\,\text{obs}} = 56$ and $U_{A2\,\text{obs}} = 25$. $U_{A2\,\text{obs}}$ is the smaller of the two values, and this value is used as U_{obs} for the statistical hypothesis test. $U_{obs} = 25$ is larger than $U_{crit} = 17$. Accordingly, the value of U_{obs} does not fall into the rejection region; I fail to reject H_0 and I do not accept H_1.

Conclusion from the Test

Failing to reject H_0 leads to the conclusion that there is no evidence to indicate that the population distribution of the control group scores differs from the population distribution of experimental group scores in the example. Counting backward did not change the latency of a reversal in comparison to the control condition.

Assumptions of the Mann–Whitney U Test

The assumptions applying to the U test are the following:

- Each subject contributes only one score to the data.
- Scores are at least ordinal measurement and represent a continuous variable. In many instances, as in the example problem, scores will be either interval or ratio measurements, and these measures will be converted to ranks for application of the U test.

Computational Formulas for U

The approach taken in Table 13–4 to obtain U_{A1} and U_{A2} is cumbersome, but it illustrates what U_{A1} and U_{A2} represent. For computational purposes, however, simplified formulas have been developed.

$U_{A1\,obs}$

The value of $U_{A1\,obs}$ is found from the formula

$$U_{A1\,obs} = n_{A1}n_{A2} + \frac{n_{A1}(n_{A1} + 1)}{2} - \sum R_{A1},$$

where n_{A1} = number of scores in group A_1
n_{A2} = number of scores in the A_2 group
$\sum R_{A1}$ = sum of the ranks assigned to scores in group A_1

The $\sum R_{A1}$ is obtained by adding the ranks assigned to the A_1 scores in step 3 of Table 13–4. For the example, the ranks of the scores in the A_1 group are 1, 3, 4, 5, 6, 10, 12, 14, and 15. The sum of these ranks is 70; thus $\sum R_{A1} = 70$. Substituting values into the equation for U_{A1} provides

$$U_{A1\,obs} = (9)(9) + \frac{9(9 + 1)}{2} - 70 = 56.$$

$U_{A2\,obs}$

The value of $U_{A2\,obs}$ is obtained from the formula

$$U_{A2\,obs} = n_{A1}n_{A2} + \frac{n_{A2}(n_{A2} + 1)}{2} - \sum R_{A2},$$

where $\sum R_{A2}$ is the sum of the ranks assigned to scores in A_2. For the example, the ranks of the scores in the A_2 group are 2, 7, 8, 9, 11, 13, 16, 17, and 18 (see step 3 in Table 13–4). The sum of these ranks is 101; thus $\sum R_{A2} = 101$. Substituting into the formula,

$$U_{A2\,obs} = (9)(9) + \frac{9(9 + 1)}{2} - 101 = 25.$$

Table 13–5 summarizes the U test using these computational formulas. This table also includes the procedure to be followed if ranks are tied. Example Problem 13–2 illustrates the steps in this table.

Example Problem 13–2

Using the Mann–Whitney U Test

Problem

At many colleges and universities the major drug-use problem of students is alcohol abuse. Suppose that a counselor developed an alcohol education program for students. At the beginning of an academic year the counselor randomly selected 8 first-year males and

TABLE 13–5

Using the Mann–Whitney U test with computational formulas.

Step 1.	Rank order the combined scores of both groups from the smallest score (rank $= 1$) to the largest score (rank $= N$). Maintain the group designation (A_1 or A_2) of each score. Assign tied scores the mean of the ranks they would have been assigned if they were not tied.
Step 2.	Find $\sum R_{A1}$ and $\sum R_{A2}$.
Step 3.	Compute $U_{A1\,obs}$.

$$U_{A1\,obs} = n_{A1}n_{A2} + \frac{n_{A1}(n_{A1} + 1)}{2} - \sum R_{A1}.$$

Step 4.	Compute $U_{A2\,obs}$.

$$U_{A2\,obs} = n_{A1}n_{A2} + \frac{n_{A2}(n_{A2} + 1)}{2} - \sum R_{A2}$$

or

$$U_{A2\,obs} = n_{A1}n_{A2} - U_{A1}.$$

Step 5.	Choose the smaller of the two values of U_{obs}. This U_{obs} is compared with the U_{crit}.

presented the educational program to them. Six weeks after presenting the program, she gave the students a questionnaire on their alcohol consumption. At the same time she randomly chose 10 other first-year males who had not been given the alcohol education program and also gave them the questionnaire. The estimated daily alcohol consumption of the two groups in ounces of pure alcohol was as follows:

Educational Program Condition

Program Given (A_1)	No Program Given (A_2)
0.31	0.41
0.53	0.63
0.58	1.14
0.14	0.21
0.16	0.89
0.52	0.55
0.53	0.89
0.02	0.91
	0.08
	0.59

Because these scores are estimates of a behavior, the counselor believed that they do not meet the requirements of interval measurement. Consequently, she treated them as presenting ordered information only. Did the educational program condition affect the estimated alcohol consumption of those students exposed to it? Use a .05 significance level.

Solution   The research design is a between-subjects design with two levels of the independent variable, educational program condition. The dependent variable, estimated alcohol consumption, is considered an ordinal measure. Accordingly, the Mann–Whitney U test is an appropriate statistical test for these data.

Statistic to Be Used: Smaller U_{obs}.

Assumptions for Use:
1. Each subject is measured in only one treatment condition.
2. The dependent variable is at least ordinal measurement and represents a continuous variable.

Statistical Hypotheses:
H_0: The population distribution of the educational-program-given (A_1) scores is identical to the population distribution of the no-educational-program-given (A_2) scores.
H_1: The population distribution of the educational-program-given (A_1) scores is not identical to the population distribution of the no-educational-program-given (A_2) scores.

Significance Level: $\alpha = .05$.

Critical Value of U: For $n_{A1} = 8$, $n_{A2} = 10$, and $\alpha = .05$, $U_{\text{crit}} = 17$ from Table A–6.

Rejection Region: Values of the smaller U_{obs} equal to or less than 17.

Calculation: The steps of Table 13–5 are followed to calculate U_{obs}.
Step 1: Rank order the combined scores of both groups from smallest to largest.

Ordered scores:	0.02	0.08	0.14	0.16	0.21	0.31	0.41	0.52	0.53	0.53	0.55	0.58	0.59	0.63	0.89	0.89	0.91	1.14
Group identity:	1	2	1	1	2	1	2	1	1	1	2	1	2	2	2	2	2	2
Rank:	1	2	3	4	5	6	7	8	9.5	9.5	11	12	13	14	15.5	15.5	17	18

Two sets of scores are tied, 0.53 and 0.89. For 0.53, the scores occupy the ranks of 9 and 10; hence each score was assigned the mean (i.e., 9.5) of the two ranks. Similarly, the two scores of 0.89 occupy the ranks of 15 and 16; thus each score was assigned the mean (i.e., 15.5) of the two ranks.
Step 2: Obtain the sum of the ranks for each group.

$$\sum R_{A1} = 1 + 3 + 4 + 6 + 8 + 9.5 + 9.5 + 12 = 53.$$

$$\sum R_{A2} = 2 + 5 + 7 + 11 + 13 + 14 + 15.5 + 15.5 + 17 + 18 = 118.$$

Step 3: Compute $U_{A1\,\text{obs}}$.

$$U_{A1\,\text{obs}} = (8)(10) + \frac{8(8+1)}{2} - 53$$

$$= 80 + (72/2) - 53$$

$$= 80 + 36 - 53 = 63.$$

Step 4: Compute $U_{A2\,\text{obs}}$.

$$U_{A2\,\text{obs}} = (8)(10) + \frac{10(10+1)}{2} - 118$$

$$= 80 + (110/2) - 118$$

$$= 80 + 55 - 118 = 17.$$

Step 5: Choose the smaller U_{obs}.

$$U_{A2\,\text{obs}} = 17 \text{ is the smaller } U_{\text{obs}}.$$

Decision: $U_{\text{obs}} = 17$ is equal to $U_{\text{crit}} = 17$. Thus it falls into the rejection region; H_0 is rejected and H_1 is accepted.

Conclusion: Rejection of H_0 indicates that the distribution of estimates from the educational program group is different from the distribution of estimates of the no educational program group. The alcohol education program reduced the amount of alcohol consumed as measured by students' estimates of daily alcohol consumption.

STATISTICS IN USE 13–2

What Is the Effect of a Stott? Analyzing Data with the Mann–Whitney U Test

When approached by a predator, Thomson's gazelles often leap straight up with all four feet simultaneously off the ground. This behavior, known as stotting, appears to be costly to the animal, for it delays beginning flight from the predator. To learn more about the function of stotting, Caro (1986) studied gazelles in Serengeti National Park, Tanzania. One behavior measured was the estimated distance the gazelle traveled when fleeing from a predator, such as a cheetah. Caro also timed the length of flight so that he was able to obtain a speed measure by dividing the distance traveled by the length of time taken to travel the distance. Because the distance was estimated rather than actually measured, Caro treated this measure as an ordinal measurement. Correspondingly, flight speed also was treated as an ordinal measurement.

One question of interest was whether flight speed differed if the flight was or was not preceded by a stott. Thus Caro compared the flight speed for flights with and without initial stotts. One comparison on neonate gazelles (less than 2 weeks old) involved 16 neonates that did not stott before fleeing and 15 neonates that did. A Mann–Whitney U test comparing the two distributions of flight speed revealed the smaller $U_{obs} = 119.5$. From Table A–6, U_{crit} for group sizes of 16 and 15 is 70 for $\alpha = .05$. Thus the rejection region consists of values of U_{obs} equal to or less than 70. The $U_{obs} = 119.5$ does not fall into the rejection region and the null hypothesis is not rejected. There is no evidence that the distributions of flight speeds either preceded or not preceded by a stott differ in this population. A similar result occurred when comparing flight speeds of fawns (2 weeks to 4 months in age) preceded or not by a stott. Accordingly, Caro concluded that, for neonates and fawn gazelles, stotting did not affect the distribution of flight speeds observed.

REPORTING THE RESULTS OF THE MANN–WHITNEY U TEST

The journal presentation of the U test follows the general guidelines for statistical presentations. I illustrate using the example problem on the effect of counting backward on the perception of reversals in the Schroeder staircase figure.

A Mann–Whitney U test was used to compare the distributions of the reversal latencies of the control ($n = 9$) and experimental groups ($n = 9$). With an alpha level of .05, the distributions did not differ significantly, $U = 25$, $p > .05$.

This presentation provides the typical information about the test used. The value of $U = 25$ is the smaller U_{obs}, and the $p > .05$ indicates that this U is nonsignificant at the

.05 level. The group size information ($n_{A1} = n_{A2} = 9$) provides the information needed to look up U_{crit} in Table A–6.

TESTING YOUR KNOWLEDGE 13–2

1. Combine the following scores of groups A_1 and A_2 and rank order from 1 to N. Maintain the group identity of each score. Then find $U_{A1 \, obs}$, the number of times an A_1 score precedes an A_2 score, and $U_{A2 \, obs}$, the number of times an A_2 score precedes an A_1 score.

Group	
A_1	A_2
15	7
23	26
10	14
19	16

    a. Which value of U_{obs} is the smaller value?

    b. Is the smaller U_{obs} statistically significant at the .05 level?

2. Find $U_{A1 \, obs}$ and $U_{A2 \, obs}$ for the scores of question 1 using the computational formulas for U.

    a. Do the values of $U_{A1 \, obs}$ and $U_{A2 \, obs}$ obtained with the computational formulas agree with those obtained in question 1?

3. Write the statistical hypotheses for the Mann–Whitney U test.

4. If H_0 is true, then what should be the relation of $U_{A1 \, obs}$ to $U_{A2 \, obs}$?

5. If H_1 is true, then what should be the relation of $U_{A1 \, obs}$ to $U_{A2 \, obs}$?

6. Given in the following table are the smaller values of U_{obs} for various group sizes. For each set of U_{obs} and group sizes, find the value of U_{crit} at the .01 level. Then indicate whether U_{obs} falls into the rejection region and the decisions you make concerning H_0 and H_1.

	U_{obs}	n_{A1}	n_{A2}
a.	3	6	4
b.	12	10	10
c.	28	16	9
d.	21	7	19
e.	4	13	19
f.	126	18	19

7. Complete the following problem using the Mann–Whitney U test following the format illustrated in the example problem. Use a .05 significance level. The use of music to induce relaxation in dental patients is becoming more widespread. Suppose that a dentist tested the effectiveness of music in relaxing patients by randomly assigning patients to one of two groups. Thirteen patients in a music condition listened to music while dental procedures were performed; 12 patients in a no music condition did not listen to music

while similar dental procedures were performed. Midway through the appointment, each patient was asked to estimate his or her anxiety on a scale of 1 (not at all anxious) to 100 (extremely anxious). The anxiety estimates obtained were as follows:

Music Condition	
No Music	Music
52	44
75	21
66	66
33	54
17	37
78	84
94	30
89	29
27	54
49	49
53	33
78	10
	78

Do the groups differ in their distributions of anxiety estimates?

THE WILCOXON SIGNED-RANKS TEST

Wilcoxon signed-ranks test: A nonparametric test for within-subjects designs with two levels of an independent variable.

The **Wilcoxon signed-ranks test** is a nonparametric test for within-subjects designs with two levels of an independent variable. Thus it is a nonparametric analog of the t_{rel}. The Wilcoxon test assumes only that the underlying dimension of behavior measured is continuous and that scores may be placed in rank order.

To illustrate the Wilcoxon signed-ranks test, I introduce an experiment on the expression of emotion in voice patterns (Cosmides, 1983). Suppose a psychologist hypothesized that vocal frequencies will change with different emotional states. To test this hypothesis, she uses a one-factor within-subjects design with two levels of an independent variable, the type of script a subject is to read, either a script reflecting a happy scene (A_1) or a script reflecting a sad scene (A_2). The purpose of the script is to induce either a happy or sad emotion in the subject. In each condition the subject's task is to read the script silently and, on a signal from the experimenter, say aloud the words "I'm still reading." The frequency span of the vocal expression of "I'm still reading" is the dependent variable for each subject and is measured in cycles per second (cps, or hertz). Thus a score is the range of the highest vocal frequency minus the lowest vocal frequency in a subject's expression of the three words.

Suppose that the frequency spans for 10 subjects tested under both script conditions are those presented in Table 13–6. The means, standard deviations, and variances for these scores are also shown here. Notice that not only do the mean frequency ranges appear to

TABLE 13–6
Hypothetical scores for vocal-frequency span (in hertz) as a function of type of script read.

Subject	Type of Script	
	Happy (A_1)	Sad (A_2)
1	305	214
2	275	385
3	360	519
4	299	307
5	317	483
6	326	454
7	284	501
8	347	463
9	331	382
10	314	297
X_A	315.80	400.50
s_A	26.54	101.40
s^2	704.37	10,281.96

differ, but there is a large difference in the variability of the two conditions. Recall that t_{rel} requires the variances of the two populations to be equal. In this example, however, the two variances differ considerably (704.37 and 10,281.96 for the happy and sad scripts, respectively). Thus one of the assumptions of t_{rel} is violated by these data. The Wilcoxon signed-ranks test does not make assumptions about the variances; accordingly, it is an appropriate test for these scores.

Statistical Hypothesis Testing with the Wilcoxon Signed-ranks Test

The *T* Statistic
The Wilcoxon test uses ranked scores to obtain a test statistic called the T, which is the smaller sum of the ranks from the two treatment conditions.

Statistical Hypotheses
Null Hypothesis.   The null hypothesis tested with the T is

H_0: The population distributions of the related A_1 and A_2 scores are identical.

Alternative Hypothesis.   The alternative hypothesis is

H_1: The population distributions of the related A_1 and A_2 scores are not identical.

Sampling Distribution and Critical Values of T

Values of T_{crit} for $\alpha = .05$ and $\alpha = .01$ are presented in Appendix Table A–7 for samples from 6 to 50. This table is entered with the value of N_{pairs}, the number of pairs of scores or, equivalently, the number of subjects. Values of T_{obs} *equal to or less than* T_{crit} fall into the rejection region and are statistically significant for the value of α selected. In the example with $N_{pairs} = 10$ and $\alpha = .05$, $T_{crit} = 8$. The rejection region is thus defined by values of T_{obs} equal to or less than 8.

Calculating T

The computations for obtaining T_{obs} involve the following steps. The result of each step is shown in Table 13–7 using the example vocal-frequency-span scores.

Step 1. Find $d = X_{A1} - X_{A2}$, the difference between the A_1 and A_2 scores for each subject as shown in column a of Table 13–7. Maintain the + or − sign of the difference.

Step 2. Find the absolute value of each difference ($|d|$, the value without regard to sign) as shown in column b.

Step 3. Rank the absolute differences from smallest (rank = 1) to largest (rank = N) as shown in column c. Differences of zero are not ranked, and the value of N used to find T_{crit} is reduced by the number of zero differences occurring. Tied values of d are assigned the mean of the ranks that would have been assigned had no tie occurred.

Step 4. Give each rank in column c the sign of the difference in column a. The signed ranks are shown in column d.

Step 5. Sum the ranks of like sign (i.e., the sum of the positive-signed ranks and the sum of the negative-signed ranks) in column d. For example, the sum

TABLE 13–7
Computation of the Wilcoxon T on the scores of Table 13–6.

Subject	Type of Script Happy (A_1)	Sad (A_2)	(a) d	(b) $|d|$	(c) Ranked $|d|$	(d) Signed Rank
1	305	214	+91	91	4	+4
2	275	385	−110	110	5	−5
3	360	519	−159	159	8	−8
4	299	307	−8	8	1	−1
5	317	483	−166	166	9	−9
6	326	454	−128	128	7	−7
7	284	501	−217	217	10	−10
8	347	463	−116	116	6	−6
9	331	382	−51	51	3	−3
10	314	297	+17	17	2	+2

of the positive-signed ranks in column d equals 6 [i.e., (+4) + (+2)] and the sum of the negative-signed ranks equals −49 [i.e., (−5) + (−8) + (−1) + (−9) + (−7) + (−10) + (−6) + (−3)].

Step 6.   Find the absolute value of each sum of the ranks. Then choose the smaller of the two sums of the ranks. In this case it is 6, the sum of the positive ranks. This sum is T_{obs}; thus $T_{obs} = 6$.

Decisions about the Statistical Hypotheses

The $T_{obs} = 6$ is less than $T_{crit} = 8$; accordingly, T_{obs} falls into the rejection region. I reject H_0 and accept H_1.

Conclusion from the Test

Rejection of H_0 and acceptance of H_1 lead to the conclusion that the two distributions of scores differ; the type of script produced differences in the vocal-frequency span. The vocal-frequency span for a sad script is larger than for a happy script.

Example Problem 13–3

Using the Wilcoxon Signed-ranks Test

Problem

It has been hypothesized that music tempo affects the speed of behaviors, with fast-tempo music increasing the speed with which a behavior may occur (McElrea & Standing, 1992; Roballey et al., 1985). To investigate this hypothesis, suppose a researcher conducted the following study. Eleven cafeteria patrons were observed eating on two different days with two different background music conditions, slow music on day 1 (A_1) and fast music on day 2 (A_2). The same subjects were observed unobtrusively on both days. The number of bites per minute taken by each subject under each music condition was recorded. Suppose that the following median bites per minute were observed for each subject under the two music tempo conditions.

| | Music Tempo | |
Subject	Slow (A_1)	Fast (A_2)
1	3	4
2	4	6
3	2	3
4	3	3
5	3	8
6	4	2
7	1	4
8	5	4
9	3	6
10	5	9
11	2	8

The experimenter considered the scores to achieve ordinal measurement. Does music tempo affect biting rate? Use a .05 significance level.

Solution   The research design is a one-factor within-subjects design with two levels of the independent variable, music tempo. The dependent variable is measured at least at the ordinal level; thus the Wilcoxon signed-ranks test is an appropriate statistical test for these data.

Statistic to Be Used: T, the smaller sum of the ranks.

Assumptions for Use:
   1. Each subject is measured on both levels of the independent variable.
   2. The dependent variable is measured at least at the ordinal level.

Statistical Hypotheses:
   H_0: The population distributions of the related A_1 and A_2 scores are identical.
   H_1: The population distributions of the related A_1 and A_2 scores are not identical.

Significance Level: $\alpha = .05$.

Critical Value of T: For $N_{pairs} = 11$ and $\alpha = .05$, $T_{crit} = 11$. In the calculation of T, however, subject 4 shows a zero change between the music conditions. This subject is dropped from the analysis. Accordingly, N_{pairs} becomes 10 and T_{crit} for $N = 10$ is 8 from Table A–7.

Rejection Region: Values of T_{obs} equal to or less than 8.

Calculation
   Step 1.   The value of $d = X_{A1} - X_{A2}$ is found for each subject (column a of Table 13–8).
   Step 2.   Absolute values of d are obtained (column b of Table 13–8).
   Step 3.   The absolute values of d are ranked from 1 to 10; $d = 0$ is not included in the ranking (column c). Notice the ranking of the several sets of tied d values. Tied scores are given the mean of the ranks that they occupy. For example, there are three differences of $|d| = 1$ in column b. These values occupy the ranks 1, 2, and 3. The mean of these ranks is 2; thus each value of $|d| = 1$ is assigned a rank of 2.
   Step 4.   The sign of each d (from column a) is attached to the rank of d (column d).
   Step 5.   Like-signed ranks are summed. The absolute value of the sum of the positive-signed ranks = 6.5 [i.e., $(+4.5) + (+2) = 6.5$]. The absolute value of the sum of the negative-signed ranks = 48.5 [i.e., $(-2)+(-4.5)+(-2)+ (-9) + (-6.5) + (-6.5) + (-8) + (-10) = 48.5$].

TABLE 13–8
Computation of the Wilcoxon T on the number of bites taken as a function of music tempo.

Subject	Music Tempo Slow (A_1)	Music Tempo Fast (A_2)	(a) d	(b) $\lvert d \rvert$	(c) Ranked $\lvert d \rvert$	(d) Signed Rank
1	3	4	−1	1	2	−2
2	4	6	−2	2	4.5	−4.5
3	2	3	−1	1	2	−2
4	3	3	0	0	—	—
5	3	8	−5	5	9	−9
6	4	2	+2	2	4.5	+4.5
7	1	4	−3	3	6.5	−6.5
8	5	4	+1	1	2	+2
9	3	6	−3	3	6.5	−6.5
10	5	9	−4	4	8	−8
11	2	8	−6	6	10	−10

Step 6.   The absolute value of the sum of the positive-signed ranks is the smaller sum of the ranks; hence $T_{obs} = 6.5$.

Decision: $T_{obs} = 6.5$ is less than $T_{crit} = 8$ and falls into the rejection region; H_0 is rejected and H_1 accepted.

Conclusion: The distributions of the number of bites taken per minute differ significantly under the two music tempos; more bites are taken per minute under a fast tempo than under a slow tempo.

STATISTICS IN USE 13–3

Agonistic Behavior in Preschoolers: Data Analysis Using the Wilcoxon Signed-ranks Test

Agonistic behavior is defensive or aggressive interaction between individuals. Anyone who has observed children knows that such behavior often occurs in their social interactions. Addison (1986) was interested in the occurrence of such behavior in preschool children and the sex of the recipient of the behavior. He observed preschool children and recorded several types of agonistic behavior, including threats to other children and displacement, where one child caused another child to move away from a location. For each child observed, the behaviors were categorized according to the sex of the recipient: same-sex or opposite-sex of the initiator. Addison analyzed the number of occurrences of each type of behavior using the Wilcoxon signed-ranks test. For nine children who displayed displacement behavior, the smaller sum of the ranks was 3, which is statistically significant at the .05 level. The percentage of same-sex displacements was significantly greater than the percentage of opposite-sex displacements. The difference between same-sex and opposite-sex threats was nonsignificant, however. For 14 children displaying threat behaviors, the smaller sum of the ranks was 22.5, larger than the T_{crit} of 21 at the .05 level.

The results indicate that certain forms of agonistic behavior in preschoolers most frequently occur between members of the same sex. Addison suggests that this finding may be related to the development of dominance relationships among children. He suggests also that the results may reflect the reinforcement of sex-appropriate interactions among children by adults.

REPORTING THE RESULTS OF THE WILCOXON SIGNED-RANKS TEST

I illustrate the reporting of the Wilcoxon signed-ranks test using the example manipulating the type of script and measuring the vocal-frequency span of subjects.

A Wilcoxon signed-ranks test was used to compare the vocal-frequency spans of the happy and sad script conditions. With an alpha level of .05, the script conditions differed significantly, $T = 6$ ($N = 10$), $p < .05$. There was a significantly greater range of frequencies in the sad-script condition compared to the happy-script condition.

Again, this presentation provides the information needed to interpret the value of T_{obs}. Knowing the value of N_{pairs}, I can look up the value of T_{crit} if necessary.

TESTING YOUR KNOWLEDGE 13–3

1. For what type of research design is the Wilcoxon test appropriate?
2. What is the test statistic used by the Wilcoxon signed-ranks test?
3. Write the statistical hypotheses for the Wilcoxon signed-ranks test.
4. Given next are the smaller absolute values of the sum of the signed ranks for experiments of different group sizes. For each smaller rank and value of N_{pairs}, identify the value of T_{obs}. Then find T_{crit} for the .05 significance level and indicate whether T_{obs} falls into the rejection region. Finally, identify the decisions you make concerning H_0 and H_1.

	Smaller Rank	N_{pairs}
a.	2	8
b.	9	10
c.	17	13
d.	40	19
e.	98	25

5. Complete the following problem using the Wilcoxon signed-ranks test following the format illustrated in the example problem. Use a .05 significance level.

Sport psychologists are interested in the relationship of anxiety to performance in sports competition. For example, Maynard and Howe (1987) measured anxiety of rugby players before games 1 and 2 of a playoff series. Suppose that you attempted a similar study and found the following anxiety scores. The range of possible scores is from 12 (very low reported anxiety) to 84 (very high reported anxiety).

	Game	
Player	1 (A_1)	2 (A_2)
1	68	72
2	56	65
3	78	77
4	49	54
5	66	64
6	43	53
7	77	70
8	68	78
9	28	29
10	69	75
11	75	78
12	80	72
13	75	75
14	65	76
15	71	70

It is likely that the population distribution of anxiety of scores is negatively skewed (most players reporting very high anxiety, a few reporting very low anxiety levels); thus you plan to use a nonparametric statistical analysis for these scores. Do the distributions of anxiety scores differ from game 1 to game 2?

USING NONPARAMETRIC TESTS

As we have seen, nonparametric tests do not make assumptions about the population distribution of scores for a sample. Furthermore, they usually require only that we be able to rank order the scores obtained. Parametric tests, such as the t or analysis of variance, require stronger assumptions about the nature of scores in an experiment, assumptions that sometimes may be questionable for the scores collected in a study. Nevertheless, nonparametric statistical tests are less widely used in behavioral science research than are parametric statistical tests. Why?

There are several answers to this question. In general, if the assumptions for a parametric test are met by the scores being analyzed, then a nonparametric test is less likely to detect an effect of the independent variable than its corresponding parametric test. That is, nonparametric tests typically are less powerful and thus more likely to lead to Type II errors than parametric tests when the assumptions for parametric tests are met by the data. Because most parametric tests are considered robust with respect to violation of assumptions, many researchers routinely analyze their data with parametric tests.

Nonparametric tests also provide different information than do parametric tests. For example, the t_{ind} leads to conclusions about the equality or inequality of the population means, but conclusions with the U test concern the equality or inequality of the population distributions. In addition, for more complex designs, such as the factorial designs discussed in Chapter 11, there are no nonparametric tests that provide as much information as the parametric factorial analysis of variance.

As I have suggested, there are no hard and fast rules about when a nonparametric test should be used. The perception of reversals in the Schroeder staircase example presented to introduce the U test in this chapter provides an unusually clear-cut instance when a nonparametric statistical test is necessary. One of the scores in this experiment was an infinite value. With such a value, a mean or standard deviation of scores cannot be computed. Obviously, then, a parametric test cannot be used on these data.

Other instances are often not so straightforward. For example, how much must the underlying distribution of a population of scores differ from a normal distribution before the use of a parametric test is inappropriate? When are the variances of two or more populations considered to be unequal? Behavioral scientists are not in agreement on the answers to these questions; consequently, they may not agree on whether a parametric or nonparametric test should be used to analyze a set of scores.

SUMMARY

- The chi-square test is used for scores that represent the frequency of occurrence of a response.
- The chi-square test of independence is used to test for a relationship between categories on two independent dimensions.
- The chi-square test of independence is obtained by

$$\chi^2_{obs} = \sum_{r=1}^{r} \sum_{c=1}^{c} \frac{(O_{rc} - E_{rc})^2}{E_{rc}}.$$

- The chi-square goodness of fit test is used to determine how well scores categorized on one dimension agree with theoretically derived expected frequencies for those categories.
- The chi-square test for goodness of fit is obtained by

$$\chi^2_{obs} = \sum_{c=1}^{c} \frac{(O_c - E_c)^2}{E_c}.$$

- The Mann–Whitney U test is a nonparametric test for a between-subjects design using two levels of an independent variable and scores at least at an ordinal level.
- The U statistic is the number of times that the rank of a score in one group precedes the rank of a score in the other group.

- The value of $U_{A1\,\text{obs}}$ is found from

$$U_{A1\,\text{obs}} = n_{A1}n_{A2} + \frac{n_{A1}(n_{A1}+1)}{2} - \sum R_{A1}$$

and the value of $U_{A2\,\text{obs}}$ from

$$U_{A2\,\text{obs}} = n_{A1}n_{A2} + \frac{n_{A2}(n_{A2}+1)}{2} - \sum R_{A2}.$$

The smaller U_{obs} is used as the test statistic.
- The Wilcoxon signed-ranks test is a parametric test for within-subjects designs with two levels of an independent variable.
- The test statistic used in the Wilcoxon signed-ranks test is the T, the smaller sum of the ranks from the two treatment conditions.
- When the assumptions for a parametric test are met by the data being analyzed, a parametric test is more powerful than its corresponding nonparametric test.

KEY TERMS AND SYMBOLS

chi-square test for goodness of fit	expected frequencies	$\sum R_A$
chi-square test of independence	goodness of fit test	T
χ^2	Mann–Whitney U test	T_{crit}
χ^2_{crit}	marginal frequencies	T_{obs}
χ^2_{obs}	nonparametric test	two-way frequency table
contingency table	observed frequencies	U
	parametric test	U_{crit}
distribution-free test	rows-by-columns contingency table	U_{obs}
		Wilcoxon signed-ranks test

REVIEW QUESTIONS

1. Many individuals in psychotherapy terminate the therapy before its scheduled completion. These people (known as psychotherapy dropouts) appear to comprise a substantial minority of those in psychotherapy (Stahler & Eisenman, 1987). Suppose that to gain more knowledge of this problem you obtain the records of several community mental health centers and categorize dropouts and nondropouts by gender and severity of the problem that they exhibit.

   a. You obtained the following frequencies of dropouts and nondropouts for males and females.

Gender

	Male	Female
Nondropout	99	130
Dropout	75	78

Is the dropout frequency related to gender at the .05 significance level? If so, what is the relationship?

b. The subjects were then categorized by the severity of their psychological problem: mild, moderate, and severe. The following frequencies were obtained:

Severity of Psychological Problem

	Mild	Moderate	Severe
Nondropout	51	66	112
Dropout	64	54	35

Is the dropout rate related to severity of the psychological problem at the .05 significance level? If so, what is the relationship?

2. Example Problem 12–2 introduced a study testing whether yawning is a sign of boredom. Using a one-factor within-subjects design, subjects saw a 30-minute rock music video (A_1, the interesting stimulus) and 30 minutes of a color-bar test pattern without sound (A_2, the uninteresting stimulus). The number of times a subject yawned during the two sessions was observed and recorded. Suppose that we replicated this experiment using 11 subjects and observed the following number of yawns for each session:

Type of Video (A)

Subject	Interesting (A_1)	Uninteresting (A_2)
1	5	7
2	2	1
3	4	7
4	3	8
5	0	2
6	4	5
7	7	6
8	6	23
9	3	3
10	1	4
11	8	9

a. Use the Wilcoxon signed-ranks test and a .05 significance level to find if the type of task affects the amount of yawning that occurs.

b. Why might the Wilcoxon signed-ranks test be more appropriate for these data than t_{rel}? (*Hint:* Examine the distribution of the scores.)

c. What conclusions do you reach from the Wilcoxon test?

3. Chapter 9, Review Question 1, presented a study to determine the effect of noise on blood pressure. Two groups of subjects were formed. Subjects in the quiet group relaxed in a comfortable chair for 30 minutes, and at the end of the 30 minutes their systolic blood pressure was measured. Subjects in the noise group also sat in the same chair for 30 minutes. During the 30-minute wait, however, they listened to a recording of traffic noise from a large city during rush hour. After listening to the noise for 30 minutes, the systolic blood pressure of these individuals was also recorded. Suppose that the following blood pressure measures (in millimeters of mercury) were obtained:

Group	
Quiet	Noise
106	141
117	136
124	124
129	139
115	121
147	119
121	147
115	128
128	115
136	134
127	140

Use the U test and a .05 significance level to find if the distributions differ. Describe your conclusions.

4. To find if sex differences exist in trait anxiety, a researcher gave an anxiety inventory to 9 females and 13 males. The scores on the inventory may range from 20 (low anxiety) to 80 (high anxiety). Suppose that the following scores were obtained.

Gender	
Female	Male
36	54
25	70
47	34
39	53
55	41
41	56
29	32
59	44
38	40
	61
	50
	30
	37

Use the Mann–Whitney U test and a .05 significance level to find if the distribution of female anxiety scores differs from that of the males. Describe your conclusions.

5. In Chapter 9, I presented a problem dealing with the pitching speed of college baseball pitchers. In that study, the velocity of pitches of eight college pitchers was measured both with a speed gun in open view of the pitcher and with the gun hidden from view. The following speeds were obtained.

	Speed Gun Condition	
Subject	Open View	Hidden
1	72.4	77.9
2	67.1	69.4
3	77.8	77.1
4	73.2	76.5
5	62.5	64.6
6	68.7	75.3
7	71.4	69.8
8	81.7	84.2

Analyze the scores with the Wilcoxon signed-ranks test to find if the distributions differ at the .05 level.

Correlation

Chapters 9 through 12 dealt with the use of statistics in experiments where an independent variable is manipulated and a dependent variable measured. In many studies, however, a researcher is interested only in finding whether two variables are related. **Correlational research** involves studies in which two or more variables are measured to find the direction and degree to which they are related. Neither variable is manipulated; thus there is no independent or dependent variable in these studies. As an example, in Chapter 1, I discussed a study that obtained both loneliness and depression scores on a group of college undergraduates (Ouellet & Joshi, 1986). Each student provided two scores: a loneliness score and a depression score. A statistical analysis of these scores indicated that they were related; lonely people also tend to be depressed. In this chapter I introduce concepts of correlation needed to understand such research and a statistic called the correlation coefficient. Using correlated scores to predict one score from another is introduced in Chapter 15.

The simplest instance of a correlational study involves obtaining measures on two different variables from each of a number of subjects. The paired measures then are statistically analyzed to determine if any relationship exists between them. Consider the following example.

Loneliness is a psychological state that all of us experience at one time or another. For many, loneliness appears to be a long-lasting state and may be related to mental health problems (Roberts, Lewinsohn, & Seeley, 1993). Suppose that we are interested in exploring the relationship between loneliness and depression as were Ouellet and Joshi (1986). I obtain a sample of 10 subjects and measure both their loneliness and depression levels. Loneliness is measured by asking the subject to respond to 10 statements similar to

"I feel left out of activities with others"

with Never (0), Rarely (1), Sometimes (2), or Often (3). The numbers in parentheses indicate the numerical weight assigned to the response. A subject who answers with "never" to all 10 statements will receive a zero for loneliness, whereas a subject who responds with "often" for all 10 statements will receive a 30 for loneliness. Depression is measured similarly with 10 statements, such as "I feel sad." Again the subject responds with Never (1), Rarely (2), Sometimes (3), or Often (4). Notice, however, in this scale that the numerical values assigned to the responses differ from those assigned for the loneliness scale. The lowest score is 10, obtained by a subject who answers "never" to all 10 statements and the highest is 40, obtained by a subject who answers "often" to all 10 statements. Thus, for each subject two scores were obtained, one a score on loneliness and the other a score on depression.

Suppose that the loneliness scores (designated variable X) and the depression scores (designated variable Y) obtained are those presented in Table 14–1. The designation of a variable as either X or Y is arbitrary. In general, however, a researcher asks the question, What is the level of Y as a function of X? By identifying the loneliness score as the X variable, we are asking what is the depression score for a certain loneliness score? If depression were designated the X variable, then the question would be, What is the level of loneliness for a certain depression score? The paired scores in Table 14–1 represent a **bivariate distribution** of scores. The prefix *bi* means two; thus these scores are bivariate in that two scores are obtained from each subject.

TABLE 14-1

Hypothetical scores for 10 subjects on loneliness and depression.

Subject	Loneliness Score: X	Depression Score: Y
1	4	16
2	27	37
3	18	33
4	7	23
5	30	34
6	12	32
7	18	24
8	23	29
9	19	26
10	12	26

Are these scores related? Perhaps higher loneliness scores are associated with higher depression scores, and lower loneliness scores are related to lower scores on depression? Or perhaps the relationship is the inverse: higher loneliness scores are associated with lower depression scores, and lower scores on loneliness are related to higher scores on depression. It is also possible that the scores do not covary, that loneliness and depression scores are independent of each other. To find if the scores are related, I first construct a graph of the scores, called a scatterplot; then I calculate a Pearson correlation coefficient on the scores.

SCATTERPLOTS

Scatterplot: A graph of a bivariate distribution in which the X variable is plotted on the horizontal axis and the Y variable is plotted on the vertical axis.

A scatterplot of the scores of Table 14–1 is presented in Figure 14–1. In a **scatterplot** (sometimes called a **scattergram** or a **scatter diagram**), the variable labeled X (in the example, the loneliness score) is plotted on the horizontal axis (the abscissa), and the Y variable (in the example, the depression score) is plotted on the vertical axis (the ordinate). The score of a subject on each of the two measures is indicated by one point on the scatterplot. For example, in Figure 14–1 the scores for subject 1 are plotted at the point that intersects a value of 4 on the loneliness score and 16 on the depression scale. To illustrate how the scatterplot was constructed, I have identified each subject by placing the number of the subject from Table 14–1 next to the point that represents his or her scores on the scatterplot. Typically, however, subjects are not identified by name or number on a scatterplot.

Positive Relationships

Covary: Two variables covary when a change in one variable is related to a consistent change in the other variable.

The scatterplot indicates that scores tend to covary: higher depression scores tend to be related to higher loneliness scores, and lower depression scores tend to be related to lower loneliness scores. Scores **covary** when a change in one score is accompanied by a consistent change in the other score. The relationship among the scores in Figure 14–1

FIGURE 14-1
Scatterplot of loneliness and depression scores for 10 subjects. The numbers next to the plotted scores identify the subjects. The scores are from Table 14-1.

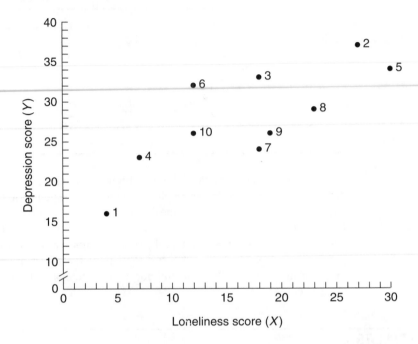

is also positive. In a **positive relationship** (also called a **direct relationship**), as the value of variable X increases, the value of variable Y tends to increase also. Thus, in Figure 14-1, as the loneliness scores increase, the depression scores also tend to increase. Because both variables are measured, and not manipulated, it is equally appropriate to state that as the depression scores increase the loneliness scores tend to increase also. But in Figure 14-1 the positive relationship is not perfect. Subject 9, for example, has a higher loneliness score than subject 10, but both have a depression score of 26. Similarly, subjects 6 and 10 both have loneliness scores of 12, but depression scores of 32 and 26, respectively.

A perfect positive relationship between depression and loneliness scores is illustrated in Figure 14-2. In this instance the scatterplot results in a straight line. Relationships between two variables that can be described by a straight line are called **linear relationships**. In a perfect positive relationship, such as that illustrated in Figure 14-2, for every value of X, there is only one corresponding value of Y. Thus, knowing the value of one score permits us to know or predict perfectly the score on the second variable. For example, a subject who obtained a loneliness score of 8 scored 18 on the depression measurement. Or a subject who scored 24 on depression obtained a 14 on loneliness. There is no error in predicting one score from the other in a perfect relationship. Perfect positive relationships seldom, if ever, occur between scores obtained in actual research, however.

Positive relationship: A relationship between two variables in which, as the value of one variable increases, the value of the other variable tends to increase also.

Linear relationship: A relationship between two variables that can be described by a straight line.

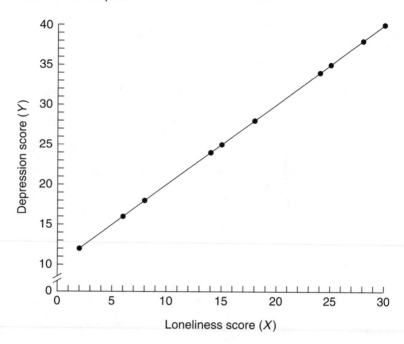

FIGURE 14-2
A perfect positive relationship between loneliness scores and depression scores for ten subjects.

Negative Relationships

Negative relationship: A relationship between two variables in which, as the value of one variable increases, the value of the other variable tends to decrease.

Suppose that the relationship obtained between the loneliness and depression scores was that shown in Figure 14–3. This figure illustrates a **negative relationship** between the two variables: as the value of variable X increases, the value of variable Y tends to decrease. In Figure 14–3 you can see that low scores on loneliness tend to be associated with high depression scores, and high loneliness scores are associated with low depression scores. Negative relationships sometimes are identified as **inverse relationships**, for the variables are oppositely related: low values on X are related to high values on Y, and high values on X are related to low values on Y.

The negative relationship illustrated in Figure 14–3 is not a perfect relationship between loneliness and depression scores. For example, two subjects have loneliness scores of 20, but depression scores of 17 and 24, respectively. Similarly, two subjects have depression scores of 32, but one has a loneliness score of 5 and the other a loneliness score of 12.

A perfect negative relationship between depression and loneliness scores is illustrated in Figure 14–4. In this instance the scatterplot again creates a straight line, and knowing one score allows a perfect prediction of the other score. For example, if I know that a subject obtained 8 on loneliness, I know also that his or her depression

FIGURE 14-3

A negative relationship between loneliness scores and depression scores for ten subjects.

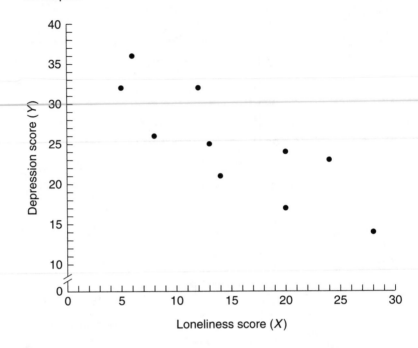

score was 32. Similarly, if I know a subject obtained a depression score of 22, then his or her loneliness score was 18. As with perfect positive relationships, perfect negative relationships rarely occur with actual scores. Notice that *positive* or *negative* applied to a scatterplot indicates only the direction, not the strength, of a relationship. For predicting one score from another, positive and negative relationships are equally useful.

TESTING YOUR KNOWLEDGE 14-1

1. Define: bivariate distribution of scores, correlational study, covary, direct relationship, inverse relationship, linear relationship, negative relationship, positive relationship, scatterplot.

2. For Tables 1 and 2, construct a scatterplot of the scores on a sheet of graph paper; then answer the following questions for each table.

   a. Does the relationship between the scores appear to be positive or negative, or is there no relationship between the scores?

FIGURE 14–4
A perfect negative relationship between loneliness scores and depression scores for ten subjects.

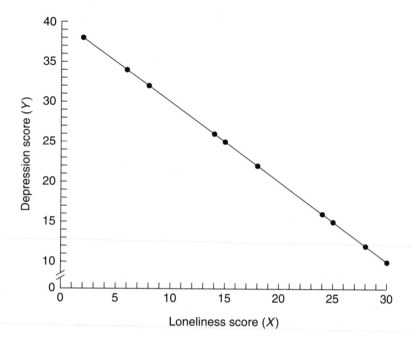

b. Is the relationship between the scores perfect or less than perfect?
c. Would knowing the loneliness score of a subject increase the accuracy of predicting the depression score for that subject?

TABLE 1

Subject	Loneliness	Depression
1	4	19
2	12	20
3	28	33
4	18	32
5	14	26
6	6	19
7	22	28
8	23	36
9	15	30
10	18	27

TABLE 2

Subject	Loneliness	Depression
1	5	29
2	11	31
3	23	23
4	17	17
5	28	16
6	13	21
7	12	26
8	4	28
9	21	14
10	16	25

3. The following scores represent the body weight in pounds and self-esteem scores from a sample of 10 subjects.

Subject	Body Weight	Self-esteem
1	100	39
2	111	47
3	117	54
4	124	23
5	136	35
6	139	30
7	143	48
8	151	20
9	155	28
10	164	46

   a. Plot a scatterplot of the scores on a sheet of graph paper. Does the relationship between the scores appear to be positive or negative, or is there no relationship between the scores?
   b. Is the relationship between the scores perfect or less than perfect?
   c. Would knowing the body weight of a subject increase the accuracy of predicting the self-esteem score for that subject?

THE PEARSON CORRELATION COEFFICIENT

An inspection of a scatterplot gives an impression of whether two variables are related and the direction of their relationship. But it alone is not sufficient to determine whether there is an association between two variables. The relationship depicted in the scatterplot needs to be described quantitatively. Descriptive statistics that express the degree of relation between two variables are called *correlation coefficients*. A commonly used correlation coefficient for scores at the interval or ratio level of measurement is

Pearson correlation coefficient: A statistic, symbolized by r, that indicates the degree of linear relationship between two variables measured at the interval or ratio level.

the **Pearson correlation coefficient**, symbolized as **r**. The **Pearson correlation coefficient** is defined as

$$r = \frac{\sum (X - \overline{X})(Y - \overline{Y})}{\sqrt{\left[\sum (X - \overline{X})^2\right]\left[\sum (Y - \overline{Y})^2\right]}}$$

where X = score of a subject on the X variable
$\overline{X}$ = mean of all scores on the X variable
Y = score of a subject on the Y variable
$\overline{Y}$ = mean of all scores on the Y variable

This formula may be written using simpler notation as

$$r = \frac{CP_{XY}}{\sqrt{(SS_X)(SS_Y)}},$$

where $CP_{XY} = \sum (X - \overline{X})(Y - \overline{Y})$, the cross products of X and Y (the subscripts X and Y indicate that the cross products are calculated on variables identified as X and Y)
SS_X = sum of squares for the X scores [i.e., $\sum (X - \overline{X})^2$]
SS_Y = sum of squares for the Y scores [i.e., $\sum (Y - \overline{Y})^2$].

The definitional formula is not usually used to actually calculate r. Instead either a standard score formula or a computational formula given later in this chapter is used. But the definitional formula illustrates what the correlation coefficient is measuring. I will work through this formula and then present the standard score and computational formulas.

Obtaining a Measure of Covariation: Cross Products

To see how r provides a measure of how much two variables covary, return to the scores of Table 14–1. The scatterplot of these scores (see Figure 14–1) indicated that the scores tend to be positively related: low scores on loneliness are related to low depression scores, and higher scores on loneliness are related to higher depression scores. I develop a statistic that indicates how much the two variables covary by using a difference score: how much a score differs from the mean of the scores, either $X - \overline{X}$ or $Y - \overline{Y}$. For example, the mean of the loneliness scores in Table 14–1 is 17. Subject 2 obtained a loneliness score of 27. If I find $X_2 - \overline{X}$, or $27 - 17 = +10$, we see that subject 2 obtained a loneliness score 10 points above the mean of the loneliness scores. Similarly, subject 4 obtained a loneliness score of 7. This subject's loneliness score could also be expressed as $X_4 - \overline{X}$; in this case, $7 - 17 = -10$, or 10 points below the mean loneliness score. Converting a score into a difference from the mean of the scores indicates both whether the score is above or below the mean and how far below or above it is.

The Y scores could be indexed similarly with respect to their mean, $\overline{Y}$. For example, the mean of the depression scores is 28. Subject 2 obtained a depression score of 37. Converting this score to a difference from the mean, I obtain $Y_2 - \overline{Y} = 37 - 28 = +9$. On the other hand, subject 4 obtained a depression score of 23. Expressed as a difference from the mean, this score is $Y_4 - \overline{Y} = 23 - 28 = -5$, or 5 points below the mean depression score.

From these difference scores we see that subject 2 was above the mean on both loneliness and depression, whereas subject 4 was below the mean on both scores. Suppose that I obtain difference scores for both loneliness and depression for all the subjects as shown in columns b and d, respectively, of Table 14–2. Notice that four of the six subjects who are above the mean on loneliness (column b, subjects 2, 3, 5, and 8) are also above the mean on depression (column d). Likewise, three of the four subjects below the mean on loneliness (column b, subjects 1, 4, and 10) are also below the mean on depression (column d).

A measure of how much the scores covary can be obtained by multiplying each subject's difference from the mean on the X variable by his or her difference from the mean on the Y variable and then summing the product of each multiplication over all the subjects. This process is illustrated in column e of Table 14–2. For example, for subject 4, $(X - \overline{X})(Y - \overline{Y}) = (-10)(-5) = +50$. The sum of the products in this column is +367.

The $\sum(X - \overline{X})(Y - \overline{Y})$ is called the **cross products of X and Y**, symbolized as CP_{XY}, and it forms the numerator of the formula for r. The CP_{XY} reflect the amount and direction of a relationship between two sets of scores. If the scores are positively related as in Table 14–2, the cross products take on a positive value; the more strongly the X and Y scores covary, the larger the CP_{XY} becomes. For negatively related scores, the CP_{XY} is negative and becomes larger as the negative relationship becomes stronger. The value of the CP_{XY} for a negative relationship of X and Y is illustrated in Table 14–3a with the scores of the negative relationship in Figure 14–3. The CP_{XY} is −399 for these scores.

When the X and Y scores are not related, the CP_{XY} will be closer to zero. The CP_{XY} for an instance when X and Y are not related are presented in Table 14–3b. Figure 14–5 is a scatterplot of these scores. Notice that the X and Y scores do not

Cross products of X and Y: The value of $\sum(X - \overline{X})(Y - \overline{Y})$ for variables X and Y.

TABLE 14–2

Calculation of the cross products of X and Y. Scores in columns a and c are the loneliness scores and depression scores of Table 14–1, respectively.

	(a)	(b)	(c)	(d)	(e)
	Loneliness		Depression		
Subject	X	$X - \overline{X}$	Y	$Y - \overline{Y}$	$(X - \overline{X})(Y - \overline{Y})$
1	4	−13	16	−12	+156
2	27	+10	37	+9	+90
3	18	+1	33	+5	+5
4	7	−10	23	−5	+50
5	30	+13	34	+6	+78
6	12	−5	32	+4	−20
7	18	+1	24	−4	−4
8	23	+6	29	+1	+6
9	19	+2	26	−2	−4
10	12	−5	26	−2	+10
$\overline{X}$	17		$\overline{Y}$ 28	Sum	+367

TABLE 14–3
(a) Cross products of X and Y for a negative relationship between loneliness and depression scores.

Subject	Loneliness		Depression		
	X	$X - \overline{X}$	Y	$Y - \overline{Y}$	$(X - \overline{X})(Y - \overline{Y})$
1	5	−10	32	+7	−70
2	24	+9	23	−2	−18
3	20	+5	17	−8	−40
4	12	−3	32	+7	−21
5	14	−1	21	−4	+4
6	20	+5	24	−1	−5
7	28	+13	14	−11	−143
8	13	−2	25	0	0
9	6	−9	36	+11	−99
10	8	−7	26	+1	−7
$\overline{X}$	15		$\overline{Y}$ 25		Sum − 399

(b) Cross products of X and Y for no relationship between loneliness and depression scores.

Subject	Loneliness		Depression		
	X	$X - \overline{X}$	Y	$Y - \overline{Y}$	$(X - \overline{X})(Y - \overline{Y})$
1	24	+7	14	−12	−84
2	16	−1	36	+10	−10
3	4	−13	24	−2	+26
4	12	−5	16	−10	+50
5	22	+5	28	+2	+10
6	30	+13	26	0	0
7	10	−7	34	+8	−56
8	28	+11	30	+4	+44
9	14	−3	28	+2	−6
10	10	−7	24	−2	+14
$\overline{X}$	17		$\overline{Y}$ 26		Sum − 12

covary: high scores on X are not related consistently to either high or low scores on Y. Similarly, low scores on X are not related consistently to either high or low scores on Y. The $CP_{XY} = -12$ calculated in Table 14–3b corresponds to this lack of relationship.

r: Comparing the CP_{XY} with a Measure of the Total Variation in Scores

The CP_{XY} indicates the direction of a relationship between two variables, but the numerical value of the CP_{XY} depends on the units of measurement of X and Y and the number of scores obtained. Two different sets of scores may have the same degree of relationship, but different values of CP_{XY}, because the scores measure different units or

FIGURE 14–5

No relationship between loneliness scores and depression scores for ten subjects. The scores are from Table 14–3b.

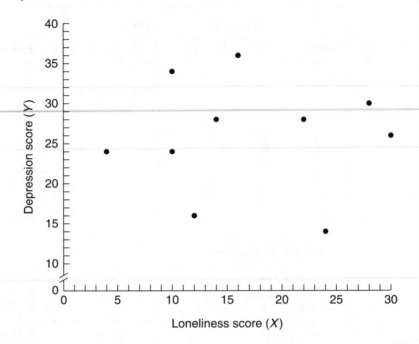

because one set of scores involves a larger sample than the other. To be useful as a measure of the covariation of X and Y, CP_{XY} must be put into a form that will take on a common range of values regardless of the unit of measurement used or the number of scores obtained.

The cross products take on a common range of values when they are compared to a measure of the total variation in each set of scores. One measure of variation we commonly have used is the sum of squares (SS). For scores identified as the X variable, $SS_X = \sum(X - \overline{X})^2$, and for the scores identified as the Y variable, $SS_Y = \sum(Y - \overline{Y})^2$. To put the SS into the same units as the cross products, I take the square root of each SS. Then, by multiplying the square root of SS_X by the square root of SS_Y, I obtain a measure of the total variation in the two sets of scores, $\sqrt{(SS_X)(SS_Y)}$. The Pearson correlation coefficient, r, is a ratio of the CP_{XY} to this measure of the total variation. Accordingly, we see that the two formulas

$$r = \frac{\sum(X - \overline{X})(Y - \overline{Y})}{\sqrt{[\sum(X - \overline{X})^2][\sum(Y - \overline{Y})^2]}}$$

and

$$r = \frac{CP_{XY}}{\sqrt{(SS_X)(SS_Y)}},$$

use identical numerical values to obtain r.

Notice that because the denominator of the formula for r involves squared differences it always takes on positive values. Hence the sign of the correlation coefficient, either positive (+) or negative (−), is determined by the sign of the numerator. The computation of r on the 10 scores of Table 14–1 using the definitional formula is illustrated in Table 14–4. For each subject,

- Column a is the loneliness score.
- Column b is the difference between the subject's loneliness score and the mean of the loneliness scores (i.e., $X - \overline{X}$).
- Column c is the squared value of column b.
- Column d is the depression score, Y.
- Column e is the difference between the depression score and the mean of the depression scores (i.e., $Y - \overline{Y}$).
- Column f is the squared value of column e.
- Column g presents column b multiplied by column e [i.e., $(X - \overline{X})(Y - \overline{Y})$], or the CP_{XY}.

The SS_X is obtained by summing the values of column c, the SS_Y by summing the values of column f, and the CP_{XY} by summing the values of column g. These sums are then substituted into the formula to obtain a numerical value of r, identified as r_{obs} (see step 2 of Table 14–4). For the scores of Table 14–1, $r_{obs} = +.78$. Before I discuss the interpretation of r_{obs}, however, I present two alternative formulas frequently used to calculate the correlation coefficient.

ALTERNATIVE FORMULAS FOR THE PEARSON CORRELATION

Standard Scores Formula for r

The definitional formula for r may be rewritten separating the denominator into its two separate sums of squares as follows:

$$r = \frac{\sum(X - \overline{X})(Y - \overline{Y})}{\sqrt{[\sum(X - \overline{X})^2]}\sqrt{[\sum(Y - \overline{Y})^2]}}$$

or

$$r = \frac{\sum(X - \overline{X})(Y - \overline{Y})}{(\sqrt{SS_X})(\sqrt{SS_Y})}.$$

Notice that $(X - \overline{X})/\sqrt{SS_X}$ appears very similar to a standard score, $z = (X - \overline{X})/S$, introduced in Chapter 6. All that is needed to make this expression a standard score is to divide the SS_X by N, the number of scores entering into SS_X, to obtain S_X, the sample standard deviation of the X scores. A similar argument follows for $(Y - \overline{Y})/\sqrt{SS_Y}$. Accordingly, r may also be found from standard scores by

$$r = \frac{\sum(z_X z_Y)}{N_{pairs}},$$

TABLE 14–4
Calculating r on the loneliness and depression scores of Table 14–1 using the definitional formula.

Step 1. Finding $SS_X = \sum(X - \overline{X})^2$, $SS_Y = \sum(Y - \overline{Y})^2$, $CP_{XY} = \sum(X - \overline{X})(Y - \overline{Y})$

	(a)	(b)	(c)	(d)	(e)	(f)	(g)
	Loneliness			Depression			
Subject	X	$X - \overline{X}$	$(X - \overline{X})^2$	Y	$Y - \overline{Y}$	$(Y - \overline{Y})^2$	$(X - \overline{X})(Y - \overline{Y})$
1	4	−13	169	16	−12	144	+156
2	27	+10	100	37	+9	81	+ 90
3	18	+1	1	33	+5	25	+ 5
4	7	−10	100	23	−5	25	+ 50
5	30	+13	169	34	+6	36	+ 78
6	12	−5	25	32	+4	16	− 20
7	18	+1	1	24	−4	16	− 4
8	23	+6	36	29	+1	1	+ 6
9	19	+2	4	26	−2	4	− 4
10	12	−5	25	26	−2	4	+ 10
	$\overline{X}$ 17.0		SS_X 630.0	$\overline{Y}$ 28.0		SS_Y 352.0	CP_{XY} +367.0

Step 2. Calculating r:

$$\sum(X - \overline{X})^2 = SS_X = 630.0,$$

$$\sum(Y - \overline{Y})^2 = SS_Y = 352.0,$$

$$\sum(X - \overline{X})(Y - \overline{Y}) = CP_{XY} = +367.0,$$

and

$$r = \frac{\sum(X - \overline{X})(Y - \overline{Y})}{\sqrt{[\sum(X - \overline{X})^2][\sum(Y - \overline{Y})^2]}}$$

or

$$r = \frac{CP_{XY}}{\sqrt{(SS_X)(SS_Y)}}.$$

Substituting numerical values,

$$r_{obs} = \frac{+367.0}{\sqrt{(630.0)(352.0)}}$$

$$= \frac{+367.0}{\sqrt{221,760.0}}$$

$$= \frac{+367.0}{470.914}$$

$$= +.779 = +.78.$$

where $\quad z_X = (X - \overline{X})/S_X$
$\qquad z_Y = (Y - \overline{Y})/S_Y$
$\qquad N_{\text{pairs}}$ = number of pairs of scores

The sample standard deviation for the X scores, S_X, is found by

$$S_X = \sqrt{\frac{\sum (X - \overline{X})^2}{N}}$$

and S_Y, the sample standard deviation for the Y scores, by

$$S_Y = \sqrt{\frac{\sum (Y - \overline{Y})^2}{N}}.$$

Table 14–5 illustrates the use of this formula for finding r_{obs} on the scores of Table 14–1. The first step is to obtain S_X and S_Y needed to find the z scores. The values of $\sum(X - \overline{X})^2 = 630.0$ and $\sum(Y - \overline{Y})^2 = 352.0$ in this step were obtained from Table 14–4. From these calculations we find that to convert X scores into standard scores $z_X = (X - 17.0)/7.937$. Similarly, for the Y scores $z_Y = (Y - 28.0)/5.933$ (see step 2 of the table).

The third step is to convert each raw score into a standard score using the z formulas. Column a of step 3 in Table 14–5 presents the X score for each subject. Column b presents the $X - \overline{X}$ differences for each subject and column c the z score for each X. Similarly, column d presents the Y score for each subject. Column e presents the $Y - \overline{Y}$ differences for each subject, and column f the z score for each Y. The z_X and z_Y scores of each subject are multiplied in column g, and the sum of this column, +7.794, provides the value of $\sum(z_X z_Y)$ needed for the numerator of the formula for r.

Step 4 of the table illustrates substituting $\sum(z_X z_Y)$ and N_{pairs} into the formula. The $r_{\text{obs}} = +.78$, the same value obtained using the definitional formula in Table 14–4. I recommend the standard score method when you have data expressed as standard scores. If scores are not standard scores, then I recommend you use the computational formula that follows.

Computational Formula for r

The value of r using a computational formula is given by

$$r = \frac{(N_{\text{pairs}})\left(\sum XY\right) - \left(\sum X\right)\left(\sum Y\right)}{\sqrt{\left[(N_{\text{pairs}})\left(\sum X^2\right) - \left(\sum X\right)^2\right]\left[(N_{\text{pairs}})\left(\sum Y^2\right) - \left(\sum Y\right)^2\right]}}.$$

This formula works directly with the raw scores and does not require finding the difference between a score and the mean of the scores. Table 14–6 illustrates using this formula

TABLE 14-5
Calculating r on the loneliness and depression scores of Table 14-1 using the standard score formula.

Step 1. Obtaining S_X and S_Y

$$S_X = \sqrt{\frac{\sum(X-\overline{X})^2}{N_{pairs}}}, \qquad S_Y = \sqrt{\frac{\sum(Y-\overline{Y})^2}{N_{pairs}}}.$$

From Column c of Table 14-4	From Column f of Table 14-4
$\sum(X-\overline{X})^2 = 630.0$	$\sum(Y-\overline{Y})^2 = 352.0$
$N_{pairs} = 10$	$N_{pairs} = 10$
$S_X = \sqrt{\dfrac{630.0}{10}}$	$S_Y = \sqrt{\dfrac{352.0}{10}}$
$S_X = \sqrt{63.0}$	$S_Y = \sqrt{35.2}$
$S_X = 7.937$	$S_Y = 5.933$

Step 2. Finding z_X, z_Y, and $\sum z_X z_Y$:

To convert X scores to standard scores

$\overline{X} = 17.0, \qquad S_X = 7.937.$

Thus

$$z_X = \frac{X-17.0}{7.937}.$$

To convert Y scores to standard scores:

$\overline{Y} = 28.0, \qquad S_Y = 5.933.$

Thus

$$z_Y = \frac{Y-28.0}{5.933}.$$

Step 3. Converting raw scores to z scores:

	(a)	(b)	(c)	(d)	(e)	(f)	(g)
	Loneliness			Depression			
Subject	X	$X-\overline{X}$	z_X	Y	$Y-\overline{Y}$	z_Y	$z_X z_Y$
1	4	−13.0	−1.638	16	−12.0	−2.023	+3.314
2	27	+10.0	+1.260	37	+9.0	+1.517	+1.911
3	18	+1.0	+0.126	33	+5.0	+0.843	+0.106
4	7	−10.0	−1.260	23	−5.0	−0.843	+1.062
5	30	+13.0	+1.638	34	+6.0	+1.011	+1.656
6	12	−5.0	−0.630	32	+4.0	+0.674	−0.425
7	18	+1.0	+0.126	24	−4.0	−0.674	−0.085
8	23	+6.0	+0.756	29	+1.0	+0.169	+0.128
9	19	+2.0	+0.252	26	−2.0	−0.337	−0.085
10	12	−5.0	−0.630	26	−2.0	−0.337	+0.212
$\overline{X}$	17.0			$\overline{Y}$ 28.0		Sum	+7.794

Step 4. Calculating r:

$\sum(z_X z_Y) = +7.794$ (see column g),
$N_{pairs} = 10,$
$$r = \frac{\sum(z_X z_Y)}{N_{pairs}}.$$

Substituting numerical values,

$$r_{obs} = \frac{+7.794}{10}$$
$$= +.779$$
$$= +.78.$$

TABLE 14-6

Calculating r on the loneliness and depression scores of Table 14–1 using the computational formula.

Step 1. Finding $\sum X, \sum Y, \sum X^2, \sum Y^2, \sum XY$:

Subject	(a) X	(b) Y	(c) X^2	(d) Y^2	(e) XY
1	4	16	16	256	64
2	27	37	729	1369	999
3	18	33	324	1089	594
4	7	23	49	529	161
5	30	34	900	1156	1020
6	12	32	144	1024	384
7	18	24	324	576	432
8	23	29	529	841	667
9	19	26	361	676	494
10	12	26	144	676	312
Sums	170.0	280.0	3520.0	8192.0	5127.0

Step 2. Calculating r:

$$\sum X = 170.0 \qquad\qquad \sum Y = 280.0$$

$$(\sum X)^2 = (170.0)^2 = 28{,}900.0 \qquad (\sum Y)^2 = (280.0)^2 = 78{,}400.0$$

$$\sum X^2 = 3520.0 \qquad\qquad \sum Y^2 = 8192.0$$

$$\sum XY = 5127.0$$

$$N_{\text{pairs}} = 10$$

$$r = \frac{(N_{\text{pairs}})\,(\sum XY) - (\sum X)\,(\sum Y)}{\sqrt{\left[(N_{\text{pairs}})\,(\sum X^2) - (\sum X)^2\right]\left[(N_{\text{pairs}})\,(\sum Y^2) - (\sum Y)^2\right]}}$$

Substituting numerical values, we obtain

$$r_{\text{obs}} = \frac{(10)(5127.0) - (170.0)(280.0)}{\sqrt{[(10)(3520.0) - 28{,}900.0][(10)(8192.0) - 78{,}400.0]}}$$

$$= \frac{51{,}270.0 - 47{,}600.0}{\sqrt{(35{,}200.0 - 28{,}900.0)(81{,}920.0 - 78{,}400.0)}}$$

$$= \frac{+3670.0}{\sqrt{(6300.0)(3520.0)}}$$

$$= \frac{+3670.0}{\sqrt{22{,}176{,}000.0}}$$

$$= \frac{+3670.0}{4709.14}$$

$$= +.779 = +.78$$

on the scores of Table 14–1. Columns a and b of Table 14–6 present the loneliness (X) and depression (Y) scores, respectively. The sums of these columns, $\sum X = 170.0$ and $\sum Y = 280.0$, provide the $\sum X$ and $\sum Y$ needed in the formula. Column c shows each X^2, and the sum of this column, 3520.0, provides the value of $\sum X^2$. Column d obtains each Y^2, and the sum of this column, 8192.0, is the value of $\sum Y^2$. Column e obtains the value of XY for each subject, and the sum of this column, 5127.0, provides the value of $\sum XY$.

Step 2 of Table 14–6 illustrates substituting numerical values into the formula for r. The $r_{obs} = +.78$. Notice that, regardless of the formula used (definitional, z score, or computational), $r_{obs} = +.78$ for the scores of Table 14–1.

SUMMARY OF FORMULAS FOR r

The four different formulas for r are summarized in Table 14–7. All the formulas produce the same value of r_{obs} when applied to a set of scores.

TABLE 14–7
Summary of formulas for r.

Definitional formula:

$$r = \frac{\sum(X - \overline{X})(Y - \overline{Y})}{\sqrt{\left[\sum(X - \overline{X})^2\right]\left[\sum(Y - \overline{Y})^2\right]}}$$

Definitional formula expressed as CP_{XY} and SS_X, SS_Y:

$$r = \frac{CP_{XY}}{\sqrt{(SS_X)(SS_Y)}}$$

Standard scores formula:

$$r = \frac{\sum(z_X z_Y)}{N_{pairs}}$$

Computational formula:

$$r = \frac{(N_{pairs})(\sum XY) - (\sum X)(\sum Y)}{\sqrt{\left[(N_{pairs})(\sum X^2) - (\sum X)^2\right]\left[(N_{pairs})(\sum Y^2) - (\sum Y)^2\right]}}$$

1. Define: cross product, CP_{XY}, r, SS_X, SS_Y.
2. Explain why the cross products provide a measure of the covariation of two sets of scores.
3. Given the following scores:

Subject	Loneliness	Depression
1	4	19
2	12	20
3	28	33
4	18	32
5	14	26
6	6	19
7	22	28
8	23	36
9	15	30
10	18	27

   a. Use the definitional formula to find r_{obs} for these scores.
   b. The scores for this question were drawn from Testing Your Knowledge 14–1, question 2, Table 1. Compare r_{obs} to the scatterplot of the scores constructed for that question. Use this comparison to visualize the relationship a value of r_{obs} describes.
4. Given the following scores:

Subject	Loneliness	Depression
1	5	29
2	11	31
3	23	23
4	17	17
5	28	16
6	13	21
7	12	26
8	4	28
9	21	14
10	16	25

   a. Use the standard score formula to find r_{obs} for these scores.
   b. The scores for this question were drawn from Testing Your Knowledge 14–1, question 2, Table 2. Compare r_{obs} to the scatterplot of the scores constructed for that question. Use this comparison to visualize the relationship a value of r_{obs} describes.
5. Given the following scores:

Subject	Body Weight	Self-esteem
1	100	39
2	111	47
3	117	54
4	124	23
5	136	35
6	139	30
7	143	48
8	151	20
9	155	28
10	164	46

a. Use the computational formula to find r_{obs} for these scores.

b. The scores for this question were drawn from Testing Your Knowledge 14–1, question 3. Compare r_{obs} to the scatterplot of the scores constructed for that question. Use this comparison to visualize the relationship a value of r_{obs} describes.

CHARACTERISTICS OF r

The correlation coefficient reveals both the direction and the degree of linear relationship between two variables. The direction of the relationship is indicated by the positive or negative sign of the correlation coefficient. The degree to which the points on the scatterplot lie on a straight line is given by the absolute value of r, a value that may vary from .00 to 1.00. Combining the sign (+ or −) with the numerical values of r allows r to vary from −1.00 through .00 to +1.00.

Direction of Relationship

Earlier I discussed positive and negative relationships among the scores in a scatterplot. The correlation coefficient indicates the direction of the relationship by the plus or minus sign of the coefficient. A positive r (e.g., r_{obs} = +.86) indicates that there is a positive relationship between variables X and Y; as the scores on variable X increase, the scores on variable Y tend to increase also. The scores in Figures 14–1 and 14–2 illustrate positive relationships; r_{obs} = +.78 for Figure 14–1 and r_{obs} = +1.00 for Figure 14–2.

A negative r (e.g., r_{obs} = −.86) indicates an inverse relationship between the variables; as scores increase on variable X, they tend to decrease on variable Y. A negative relation is illustrated in Figures 14–3 and 14–4. Here r_{obs} = −.83 for Figure 14–3 and −1.00 for Figure 14–4.

Degree of Relationship

The numerical value of r indicates how well the relationship between variables X and Y is described by a straight line. An r of 1.00 means that the relationship is perfectly linear; all points in the scatterplot lie in a straight line. Figure 14–2 portrays a scatterplot showing a perfect positive correlation, $r_{obs} = +1.00$, for loneliness and depression scores. A perfect negative correlation, $r_{obs} = -1.00$, is illustrated in Figure 14–4. When r equals either plus or minus 1.00, for every value of X there is only one corresponding value of Y. You can see this relationship in either Figure 14–2 or 14–4. For every loneliness score there is only one depression score. This relation allows us to predict perfectly the Y from the X scores. In either Figure 14–2 or 14–4, if you are given a loneliness score, then you can predict perfectly the depression score associated with that loneliness score.

At the other extreme, if the variables are unrelated, then the value of the correlation coefficient approaches zero. When r is about zero, a value of one score is not systematically associated with a value of the other score. Such an instance is shown in Figure 14–5, where $r_{obs} = -.02$.

Values of the correlation coefficient between .00 and 1.00 indicate that there is some, but not a perfect, relationship between X and Y. To illustrate, we notice in Figure 14–1, for which $r = +.78$, that the X and Y variables are not perfectly related. As the loneliness scores increase, the depression scores tend to increase, but knowing a loneliness score does not allow perfect prediction of the depression score. For example, two subjects obtained a loneliness score of 12, but one subject had a depression score of 32 and the other a depression score of 26.

An analogous negative correlation is demonstrated in Figure 14–3, for which $r_{obs} = -.83$. Here, as loneliness scores increase, depression tends to decrease. But again the relationship is not perfect; knowing the loneliness score does not allow us to perfectly predict the associated depression score. As an example, notice that two subjects obtained a score of 20 on loneliness, but one subject had a 17 on depression, the other a 24.

It is often difficult to visualize what a value of r might look like if the scores were placed on a scatterplot. This ability is gained only by comparing values of r to a scatterplot of the scores that produced the correlation. Figure 14–6 presents several scatterplots exhibiting different values of r. Panels (a) to (e) of this figure illustrate correlations decreasing from 1.00 to .00. Notice that as r decreases the linear relationship between X and Y becomes less strong, until $r_{obs} = .00$ and there is no relationship remaining.

The Pearson r is a measure of the linear or straight-line relationship between variables X and Y. Figure 14–6f presents a nonlinear, U-shaped relationship between the X and Y variables. In this relation, low values of X are associated with high values of Y. As X increases, Y decreases to a point; then further increases in X are associated with increases in Y. This relationship between X and Y cannot be represented by a straight line, and r cannot be used to describe such a relationship.

Restriction of Range and the Value of r

The value of r is sensitive to the range of values that either the X or Y variable may take on. As the range of values for one or both of the variables becomes smaller, the value of

FIGURE 14-6

Scatterplots illustrating various correlations between scores on variable X and variable Y for 10 scores. The value of the Pearson correlation coefficient between the sets of scores is given by r_{obs}.

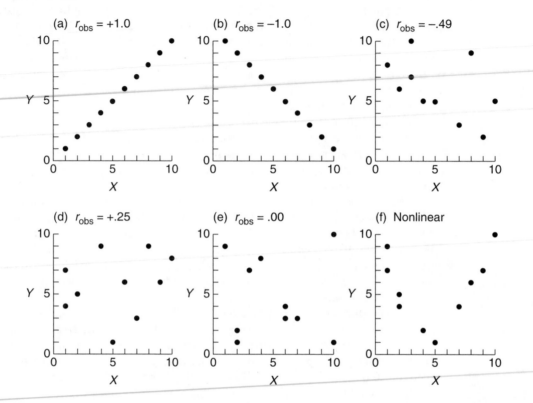

r also becomes smaller. To illustrate this relationship, consider the scores in Figure 14–1 with $r_{obs} = +.78$. Suppose that I want to examine the relationship of loneliness and depression on only the six subjects highest on loneliness. These are loneliness scores that range from 18 to 30 (i.e., loneliness scores from subjects 2, 3, 5, 7, 8, and 9). The range of depression scores for these six subjects is from 24 to 37. In comparison to the range of loneliness and depression scores for the full 10 subjects, the range of both the loneliness and depression scores for the top 6 subjects has become restricted or truncated (i.e., shortened). The r_{obs} of these six scores is +.69, less than the r_{obs} of +.78 on the full set of scores.

The implication of this illustration is clear. Correlation coefficients calculated on scores that have a restricted range may lead us to believe that there is no relationship between two variables, when, had a larger range of scores been employed, a relationship would have been found. Accordingly, before calculating a correlation coefficient, carefully examine the scores obtained to determine if they represent a restricted range.

Coefficient of Determination

Coefficient of determination: The value of r^2 indicating the common variance of variables X and Y.

In Chapter 9, I introduced eta squared as a measure of the strength of the effect of an independent variable on a dependent variable in an experiment. In correlational studies, the **coefficient of determination,** r^2 (the squared value of r), provides an analogous measure of the strength of association between X and Y.

The interpretation of r^2 is similar to that of η^2. That is, r^2 indicates the proportion of variance in one set of scores that is related to the variance in the other set of scores. To illustrate, for the scores of Table 14–1, $r_{obs} = +.78$; thus r_{obs}^2 is equal to $(+.78)^2$, or .61. This value means that these pairs of scores have 61 percent of their variance in common. In other words, 61 percent of the variance in scores for loneliness is associated with the variance in depression scores.

Correlation and Causality

Many variables are highly correlated, but the existence of a correlation between variables X and Y does not imply that one causes the other. If variables X and Y are correlated, then at least three possibilities exist with respect to a causal relation between the variables:

- X causes Y.
- Y causes X.
- Neither X nor Y causally affect each other, but both are caused by a third variable, Z.

Consider the example problem of the correlation between loneliness (variable X) and depression (variable Y). Ouellet and Joshi (1986) found a correlation of +.41 between loneliness and depression. People who are more lonely tend also to be more depressed. Which variable, if either, causally affects the other? Does being lonely cause depression? Or does being depressed cause loneliness? Or does neither of these relationships apply, and a third variable, Z, such as lack of social skills appropriate for forming friendships, cause a person to be both lonely and depressed? These three possible causal relationships are illustrated in Table 14–8. A correlation between two variables indicates only that they are linearly related; it does not provide any information about what causes them to be related.

A correlation between variables often leads to misinterpretations in the popular media. Newspaper articles, for example, have reported studies showing a negative correlation between moderate levels of alcohol consumption and the probability of having a heart attack. One report was headlined, "Drinking Beer Can Cut Your Chances of a Heart Attack in Half." This statement implies that drinking beer produces a healthier heart. But can you reach this causal relationship from a study that correlated the amount of beer drunk (i.e., variable X) and heart-attack rates (i.e., variable Y)? Perhaps a third variable, a person's underlying health (i.e., variable Z), produces the observed correlation between beer consumption and heart-attack rate. Individuals who are not very healthy may avoid drinking beer and also possess a higher probability of having a heart attack,

TABLE 14–8

Possible causal relationships from an observed correlation of two variables, loneliness (X) and depression (Y).

A. *The observed correlation:*

Positive correlation obtained
between variables X and Y

Individuals high in loneliness (X) are high in depression (Y)	Individuals low in loneliness (X) are low in depression (Y)

B. *Possible causal relationships that may explain the observed relationship:*

Possibility 1

       variable X causes   variable Y

Loneliness (X) causes a person to be depressed (Y).

Possibility 2

       variable Y causes   variable X

Being depressed (Y) causes a person to be lonely (X).

Possibility 3

       variable Z causes   both variables X and Y

The lack of appropriate social skills (variable Z) causes a person to be both lonely (X) and depressed (Y).

whereas healthy individuals possess a lower probability of heart attack and also drink moderate amounts of beer.

Another study reported a negative correlation between the reported amount of sleep per night and energy levels during the day; people who sleep less also report higher daytime energy levels. Should you conclude from this relationship that if you lack energy during the day then you should sleep less during the night? The answer is no, for a correlational relationship does not allow such a causal conclusion. Probably a third variable, such as a physiological condition that affects both daytime energy level and the amount of sleep needed, accounts for the observed relationship.

A curious positive correlation between the use of cellophane tape and diet margarine has also been reported in a study conducted by an advertising research firm ("You Are," 1976). People who use more cellophane tape also use more diet margarine. It is unlikely that you will fall into the causality trap with this relationship; it is doubtful you would believe that eating diet margarine causes one to use more cellophane tape, or vice versa.

Obviously, a third variable underlies this reported relationship. I let you speculate about what it may be.

1. What does the plus or minus sign of r tell you about the relationship of variables X and Y?
2. What does the numerical value of r tell you about the relationship of variables X and Y?
3. What effect may restricting the range of scores on either the X or Y variable have on the value of r?
4. Calculate the coefficient of determination for the following values of r_{obs} =

a. +.12   **b.** −.74   **c.** −.59

d. −.36   **e.** +.23   **f.** +.19
5. You observe a correlation between variables X and Y. Identify the three possible causal relationships that may explain the correlation.
6. Various researchers have reported the following correlations. Identify a third variable that may be responsible for the observed correlation.

a. A negative correlation between income and blood pressure.

b. A positive correlation between coffee drinking and cigarette smoking.

c. A positive correlation between exposure to violence on television and aggressive behavior in children.

TESTING THE STATISTICAL SIGNIFICANCE OF THE PEARSON r

The Population Correlation, ρ

The Pearson r describes the linear relationship between the X and Y scores of a sample. As with any set of scores, the sample is drawn from a larger population of scores, and I may wish to test if a correlation exists among the X and Y scores in the population. In a population, a linear correlation between X and Y scores is represented by the parameter ρ (the seventeenth letter of the Greek alphabet, *rho*, pronounced "row"). In the example problem of the correlation between loneliness and depression, r_{obs} = +.78 provides an estimate of ρ. Because of sampling error, however, r_{obs} will not be equal to ρ. As with any statistic, r_{obs}, because it is obtained from a sample, will vary from sample to sample, even though the samples are from the same population. Accordingly, I may test a statistical hypothesis that r_{obs} represents a sample from a population with a specific ρ. Although it is possible to test hypotheses concerning any value of ρ, the most commonly tested hypothesis is that ρ equals zero in the population sampled.

Testing for a Nonzero Correlation in the Population

The statistical test to determine if r is a chance difference from a zero correlation in the population is straightforward. The familiar steps of statistical hypothesis testing are followed:

- A null hypothesis, H_0, and an alternative hypothesis, H_1, are formulated.
- The sampling distribution of r, assuming that H_0 is true, is obtained. This distribution is given in Table A–8.
- A significance level is selected.
- A critical value of r, identified as r_{crit}, is found from the sampling distribution of r given in Table A–8.
- A rejection region is located in the sampling distribution of r.
- The correlation coefficient, identified as r_{obs}, is calculated from the sample data.
- A decision to reject or not reject H_0 is made on the basis of whether or not r_{obs} falls into the rejection region.

Statistical Hypotheses

Null Hypothesis.   The null hypothesis is

$$H_0: \rho = 0.$$

This hypothesis states that the correlation between the X and Y variables is zero in the population.

Alternative Hypothesis.   The alternative hypothesis is

$$H_1: \rho \neq 0.$$

This hypothesis states that the correlation between the X and Y variables is not zero in the population.

Sampling Distribution of r and Critical Values

Because r may take on values only between .00 to 1.00, its sampling distribution under $H_0 : \rho = 0$ may be determined readily. As is the case with most other statistical tests, however, the sampling distribution of r depends on its degrees of freedom. The *df* for r are equal to $N_{pairs} - 2$, where N_{pairs} is the number of pairs of scores from which r is calculated. Critical values of r, identified as r_{crit}, from sampling distributions of r with *df* ranging from 1 to 100 are presented in Appendix Table A–8 for $\alpha = .05$ and .01.

Locating a Rejection Region

If H_1 is true, I expect to obtain values of r greater than zero. Accordingly, the rejection region for r_{obs} is a value of r equal to or greater than r_{crit}. An r_{obs} equal to or larger in absolute value (that is, ignoring the + or − sign of r_{obs}) than r_{crit} falls into the rejection region. The probability of such an r_{obs} is equal to or less than the value of alpha if H_0 is true.

Decision Rules

The decision rules for the statistical hypotheses follow the common pattern:

- If r_{obs} falls into the rejection region, then:
   Reject $H_0 : \rho = 0$.
   Accept $H_1 : \rho \neq 0$.
- If r_{obs} does not fall into the rejection region, then:
   Do not reject H_0.
   Do not accept H_1.

I illustrate this process in the example problems that follow. Table 14–9 summarizes the decisions and conclusions reached from a statistical test on r.

Assumptions of the Test for Statistical Significance of r

Bivariate normal distribution: A distribution of X and Y variables in which (1) the X scores are normally distributed in the population sampled, (2) the Y scores are normally distributed in the population sampled, (3) for each X score the distribution of Y scores in the population is normal, and (4) for each Y score the distribution of X scores in the population is normal.

The test for statistical significance of r assumes that X and Y form a bivariate normal distribution in the population. A **bivariate normal distribution** possesses the following characteristics:

- The X scores, loneliness scores in the example, are normally distributed in the population sampled.
- The Y scores, depression scores in the example, are normally distributed in the population sampled.
- For each X score, the distribution of Y scores in the population is normal. Using the example, this assumption means that for each loneliness score in the population there is a normal distribution of depression scores.

TABLE 14–9

Summary of decisions and conclusions in statistical hypothesis testing with r. A .05 significance level is illustrated.

If r_{obs} falls into the rejection region for $\alpha = .05$, then:	If r_{obs} does not fall into the rejection region for $\alpha = .05$, then:
Probability of r_{obs} is less than or equal to .05, or $p \leq .05$.	Probability of r_{obs} is greater than .05, or $p > .05$.
$H_0 : \rho = 0$ is rejected.	H_0 is not rejected.
$H_1: \rho \neq 0$ is accepted. The r_{obs} estimates a population ρ different from zero.	H_1 is not accepted.
r_{obs} is statistically significant at the .05 level.	r_{obs} is not statistically significant at the .05 level.
It is decided that the X and Y variables are correlated in the population from which the sample was selected.	It is decided that the X and Y variables are not correlated in the population from which the sample was selected.

- For each Y score, the distribution of X scores in the population is normal. This assumption is similar to the previous assumption, except now for each depression score in the population there is a normal distribution of loneliness scores.

For many paired measures of behavior, we may assume that they form a bivariate normal distribution in the population and thus test for a nonzero correlation of the scores in the population.

Example Problem 14–1

Testing the Statistical Significance of r_{obs} between Loneliness and Depression

Problem
The Pearson correlation for the loneliness and depression scores of Table 14–1 was found to be $r_{obs} = +.78$. Does this sample value indicate the presence of a nonzero correlation between loneliness and depression scores in the population from which the subjects were sampled? Use a .05 significance level.

Solution   The problem requires that I test the statistical hypothesis that the population correlation, ρ, for loneliness and depression scores is zero.

Statistic to Be Used: $r_{obs} = +.78$.

Assumptions for Use: Loneliness and depression scores possess a bivariate normal distribution in the population from which the scores were sampled.

Statistical Hypotheses: H_0: $\rho = 0$
H_1: $\rho \neq 0$

Significance Level: $\alpha = .05$.

df: $df = N_{pairs} - 2 = 10 - 2 = 8$.

Critical Value of *r*: r_{crit} (8) $= .632$ from Table A–8.

Rejection Regions: Values of r_{obs} equal to or less than $-.632$ or equal to or greater than $+.632$.

Decision: The $r_{obs} = +.78$ is greater than $r_{crit} = +.632$. Accordingly, it falls into the rejection region. Therefore, we

$$\text{Reject } H_0 : \rho = 0,$$
$$\text{Accept } H_1 : \rho \neq 0.$$

Conclusion: Loneliness and depression scores are correlated in the population; the $r_{obs} = +.78$ is not simply a chance difference from a true population correlation of zero. The best estimate I have of the population correlation is provided by $r_{obs} = +.78$. Lonely people tend to be depressed. The coefficient of determination $r_{obs}^2 = (+.78)^2 = .61$, indicating that loneliness and depression have 61 percent of their variance in common.

Example Problem 14–2

Is a Sense of Humor Related to Physical Health?

Problem

One characteristic often noted about others is their sense of humor. Carroll and Shmidt (1992) hypothesized that having a good sense of humor may be related to good physical health, for those who can deal with anxiety-evoking situations with humor may be able to control the stresses of life more easily. Suppose that you test this hypothesis by measuring 16 subjects on their sense of humor and their physical health. Sense of humor is measured using the Situation Humor Response Questionnaire (Martin & Lefcourt, 1984). This questionnaire presents descriptions of 18 situations and asks a subject to rate each situation on a scale from 1 to 5 on how amusing they would find the situation. Accordingly, scores on this questionnaire may range from 18 to 90, with higher scores indicating more use of humor in dealing with situations. Physical health is measured by having subjects complete a 20-item self-report inventory on health problems. Scores on this inventory may range from zero (no reported health problems) to 20 (20 reported health problems). You obtain the following scores on these two measures.

Subject	Humor Questionnaire: X	Physical Health: Y
1	36	9
2	68	3
3	61	12
4	47	12
5	35	15
6	48	17
7	42	10
8	30	17
9	56	11
10	39	17
11	51	14
12	54	8
13	60	3
14	29	13
15	65	7
16	47	8

Is the humor questionnaire score related to the number of reported health problems? Use a .05 significance level.

Solution   The problem requires testing a statistical hypothesis that the population correlation, ρ, for humor questionnaire and health problems scores is zero.

Statistic to Be Used: r.

Assumption for Use: The humor questionnaire and health problems scores possess bivariate normal distributions in the populations from which the scores were sampled.

Statistical Hypotheses: H_0: $\rho = 0$
$\qquad\qquad\qquad\qquad\qquad\qquad H_1$: $\rho \neq 0$

Significance Level: $\alpha = .05$.

df: $df = N_{pairs} - 2 = 16 - 2 = 14$.

Critical Value of r: r_{crit} (14) = .497 from Table A–8.

Rejection Regions: Values of r_{obs} equal to or less than $-.497$ or equal to or greater than $+.497$.

Calculation: The computational formula

$$r = \frac{(N_{pairs})\left(\sum XY\right) - \left(\sum X\right)\left(\sum Y\right)}{\sqrt{\left[(N_{pairs})\left(\sum X^2\right) - \left(\sum X\right)^2\right]\left[(N_{pairs})\left(\sum Y^2\right) - \left(\sum Y\right)^2\right]}}$$

will be used to obtain r_{obs}. The numerical values needed for this formula are

$$N_{pairs} = 16$$
$$\sum XY = 7908$$
$$\sum X = 768$$
$$\sum Y = 176$$
$$\sum X^2 = 39,092$$
$$\sum Y^2 = 2242$$
$$\left(\sum X\right)^2 = 589,824$$
$$\left(\sum Y\right)^2 = 30,976.$$

Substituting values into the formula,

$$r_{obs} = \frac{16(7908) - (768)(176)}{\sqrt{[16(39,092) - 589,824][16(2242) - 30,976]}}$$

$$= \frac{126,528 - 135,168}{\sqrt{(625,472 - 589,824)(35,872 - 30,976)}}$$

$$= \frac{-8640}{\sqrt{(35,648)(4896)}}$$

$$= \frac{-8640}{\sqrt{174,532,608}}$$

$$= \frac{-8640}{13,211.079}$$

$$= -.65$$

$$r_{obs}^2 = (-.65)^2 = .42.$$

Decision: The value of $r_{obs} = -.65$ is larger than $r_{crit} = -.497$ and thus falls into a rejection region. The decisions with respect to H_0 and H_1 are

$$\text{Reject } H_0 : \rho = 0,$$

$$\text{Accept } H_1 : \rho \neq 0.$$

Conclusion: There is a significant negative correlation between humor questionnaire scores and self-reported health problems in the population sampled. Subjects who scored higher on the humor questionnaire reported fewer physical health problems than did subjects who obtained lower humor questionnaire scores. The coefficient of determination indicates that the humor questionnaire and health scores have 42 percent of their variance in common.

STATISTICS IN USE 14–1

Talkativeness and Leadership Ratings: Analyzing Scores with r

We often use a person's speech to make attributions about characteristics of that person. To define some of the relationships between talkativeness and aptitudes, Ruback and Dabbs (1986) measured a subject's talkativeness in a group. Small groups of subjects were formed and asked to talk about a topic. The amount that each subject talked was recorded and scored in the form of a vocalization score. The vocalization score was the percentage of time during the discussion period that a subject actually emitted speech sounds. Other measures also were obtained from the participants in the study, including the Scholastic Aptitude Test (SAT) verbal aptitude score and a leadership rating of each subject in the group made by the other members of the group. Thus, for each of 59 subjects in one sample, three scores were obtained: a vocalization score, the subject's SAT verbal aptitude score, and a rated leadership score.

To find if the scores were related, Ruback and Dabbs calculated two separate correlations: the correlation between the vocalization score (i.e., X) and the SAT verbal aptitude score (i.e., Y) and the correlation between the vocalization score (i.e., X) and rated leadership (i.e., Y). For 59 pairs of scores, there are 57 degrees of freedom; thus r_{crit} at the .05 level is .273 (the critical value for 50 df). The r_{obs} for the vocalization and SAT scores was +.14, a nonsignificant value. The r_{obs} for vocalization and rated leadership scores was +.69, which is statistically significant at the .05 level. Accordingly, Ruback and Dabbs concluded that the SAT verbal aptitude score is not related to talkativeness. People who are high on verbal aptitude, at least as measured by the SAT, do not talk any more or less in a group than people of lower verbal aptitude. On the other hand, rated leadership in a group is related to the amount of talking a person does: the more talking, the greater the rated leadership.

REPORTING THE RESULTS OF A CORRELATIONAL STUDY

The report of a correlational study should include the value of r_{obs}, the df for r_{obs}, the significance level used, and whether or not r_{obs} was statistically significant. Often, the mean and standard deviation for each set of scores are included in the report. To illustrate, I use the example of the correlation between loneliness and depression.

With an alpha level of .05, there was a significant correlation between the loneliness ($M = 17.0$, $SD = 8.4$) and depression scores ($M = 28.0$, $SD = 6.3$), $r(8) = +.78$, $p < .01$. The loneliness and depression scores were significantly positively related.

TESTING YOUR KNOWLEDGE 14–4

1. Define: bivariate normal distribution, ρ.
2. Identify the statistical hypotheses needed to test if r_{obs} differs significantly from zero.
3. For each of the following values of N_{pairs}, determine the df and then find the r_{crit} for $\alpha = .05$ and $\alpha = .01$ from Table A–8. $N_{pairs} =$

   a. 8   **b.** 15   **c.** 20
   d. 32   **e.** 43   **f.** 75

4. For each of the following r_{obs} and N_{pairs}, identify the statistical null and alternative hypotheses; then find r_{crit} at the .05 significance level. Indicate whether the r_{obs} falls into a rejection region and then indicate your decisions with respect to the statistical hypotheses.

	r_{obs}	N_{pairs}
a.	+.580	12
b.	−.346	12
c.	−.682	20
d.	+.204	24
e.	+.249	80
f.	−.731	9

5. College professors often believe that class attendance and course grades are correlated. Suppose that a professor maintained attendance records and found the following number of absences from class and examination averages for 12 students:

Student	Absences	Exam Average
1	22	72
2	6	88
3	1	99
4	8	78
5	6	66
6	11	77
7	10	52
8	6	78
9	10	76
10	0	96
11	5	91
12	10	86

a. Find the value of r_{obs} for these scores using the computational formula.
b. Test to determine if r_{obs} differs significantly from a population correlation of zero.
c. What do you conclude about the relationship of absences and exam averages?

THE SPEARMAN RANK-ORDER CORRELATION COEFFICIENT

Spearman rank-order correlation coefficient (r_s): A correlation coefficient used with ordinal measurements.

The Pearson r is appropriate when scores on the variables to be correlated are interval or ratio measures. Sometimes, however, measures represent rank ordering on both the X and Y variables. When ranked scores are obtained, the **Spearman rank-order correlation coefficient**, symbolized by r_s, is commonly used to quantify the relationship between the two sets of scores. The Spearman rank-order correlation coefficient is found from the formula

$$r_s = 1 - \left[\frac{6 \sum D^2}{(N_{pairs})(N_{pairs}^2 - 1)} \right],$$

where

D = difference in a pair of ranked scores for a subject

N_{pairs} = number of pairs of ranks in the study

As with the Pearson r, values of r_s may be positive or negative and range from -1.00 through .00 to $+1.00$.

An Example of the Use of r_s

We have all observed that animals within a species behave differently from each other. To study differences in animal behaviors, Feaver, Mendl, and Bateson (1986) developed a method of measuring behaviors such as playing, chasing, fleeing, crouching, and so forth. Suppose that an investigator using this technique hypothesizes that playing (X) and chasing (Y) behaviors are related in cats. Ten cats are observed for a period of time in the same environment and ranked separately on playing and chasing behaviors. The most playful cat receives a rank of 1 and the least playful a rank of 10. Similarly, the cat that chases most is ranked 1 and the cat that chases least is ranked 10.

Ranks of the 10 cats on playing and chasing behaviors are presented in columns a and b of Table 14–10. Cats 1 and 10 were judged to be equal in chasing behavior. Therefore, both cats were assigned the same rank, 6.5, which is the average of the two ranks, 6 and 7, that would be assigned to them if they were not tied.

The procedures involved in calculating r_s are illustrated in the remainder of Table 14–10. The first step is to find the difference, D, in each pair of ranks by subtracting one rank from the other. This step is shown in column c, where the chasing rank (Y) is subtracted from the playing rank (X) for each cat. Then each D is squared, as shown in column d. The sum of this column, 80.50, provides the value of $\sum D^2$. The $\sum D^2$ and N_{pairs} are substituted into the formula, and r_s is calculated; $r_{s\ obs} = +.51$.

Statistical Significance of the Spearman Rank-order Correlation

The test for the statistical significance of r_s is similar to that for the Pearson r. The null hypothesis is that the rank-order correlation in the population, symbolized by ρ_s, is zero, or $H_0 : \rho_s = 0$. The alternative hypothesis is that the population correlation is not zero, or $H_1 : \rho_s \neq 0$. Critical values of r_s for the .05 and .01 levels are presented in Appendix Table A–9. The critical values are based on N_{pairs} rather than degrees of freedom. If $r_{s\ obs}$ is equal to or larger than the critical value, then the decision is to reject H_0 and accept H_1.

For the example, the critical value of r_s for $N_{pairs} = 10$ and $\alpha = .05$ is .648. Because $r_{s\ obs} = +.51$ is smaller than the critical value, the null hypothesis is not rejected at the .05 level. The relationship between the ranks on playing and chasing is not statistically significant; playing and chasing behaviors were not related in the sample observed.

Characteristics of r_s

The Spearman correlation coefficient shows the agreement of the ranks of two variables. If variables X and Y are ranked identically, then r_s will be +1.00. If the variables are ranked oppositely, so that a rank of 1 on variable X corresponds to the lowest rank on variable Y, and the lowest rank on variable X corresponds to a rank of 1 on variable Y, then r_s will be −1.00. If there is no agreement on the rankings, then r_s will be about zero. When there is some, but not perfect, agreement on the ranks, then r_s will take on a value between .00 and 1.00. The direction of the relationship is indicated by the plus or minus sign of the correlation.

TABLE 14–10
Calculating the Spearman rank-order correlation coefficient (r_s) on playing and chasing behavior of ten cats. Columns a and b present ranks of each cat on chasing and playing behavior, respectively.

Cat	(a) Playing: X	(b) Chasing: Y	(c) $D = (X - Y)$	(d) $D^2 = (X - Y)^2$
1	2	6.5	−4.5	20.25
2	6	8	−2	4.00
3	8	4	4	16.00
4	4	1	3	9.00
5	7	5	2	4.00
6	5	9	−4	16.00
7	10	10	0	0.00
8	3	2	1	1.00
9	1	3	−2	4.00
10	9	6.5	2.5	6.25
			Sum	80.50

The formula for r_s is

$$r_{s\,obs} = 1 - \left[\frac{6 \sum D^2}{(N_{pairs})(N_{pairs}^2 - 1)} \right]$$

Substituting the values of $\sum D^2 = 80.50$ and $N_{pairs} = 10$,

$$r_{s\,obs} = 1 - \left[\frac{(6)(80.50)}{(10)(10^2 - 1)} \right]$$

$$= 1 - \left[\frac{483.00}{(10)(99)} \right]$$

$$= 1 - \left[\frac{483.00}{990} \right]$$

$$= 1 - 0.488$$

$$= +.512$$

$$= +.51, \text{ rounded to two decimal places}$$

SUMMARY

- Correlational studies attempt to find the extent to which two or more variables are related.
- In a scatterplot, one of the two scores (variable X) is represented on the horizontal axis (the abscissa) and the other measure (variable Y) is plotted on the vertical axis (the ordinate). The score of a subject on each of the two variables is represented by one point on the scatterplot.

- In a positive or direct relationship, as the value of variable X increases, the value of variable Y also increases.
- In a negative or inverse relationship, as the value of variable X increases, the value of variable Y decreases.
- The Pearson correlation coefficient is defined as

$$r = \frac{\sum(X - \overline{X})(Y - \overline{Y})}{\sqrt{[\sum(X - \overline{X})^2][\sum(Y - \overline{Y})^2]}}.$$

- The $\sum(X - \overline{X})(Y - \overline{Y})$ is the cross product of X and Y and is symbolized as CP_{XY}. Thus the correlation coefficient also may be expressed as

$$r = \frac{CP_{XY}}{\sqrt{(SS_X)(SS_Y)}}.$$

- The value of r using standard scores is given by

$$r = \frac{\sum(z_X z_Y)}{N_{pairs}}.$$

- The value of r using a computational formula is given by

$$r = \frac{(N_{pairs})(\sum XY) - (\sum X)(\sum Y)}{\sqrt{\left[(N_{pairs})(\sum X^2) - (\sum X)^2\right]\left[(N_{pairs})(\sum Y^2) - (\sum Y)^2\right]}}.$$

- The direction of a relationship is indicated by the positive or negative sign of r.
- The degree to which the points on the scatterplot lie on a straight line is given by the absolute value of r, a value that may vary from .00 to 1.00.
- A linear correlation between variables X and Y is represented in a population by ρ.
- The statistical significance of r is tested using Table A–8.
- The coefficient of determination, r^2, indicates the proportion of variance in the X variable that is related to the variance in the Y variable.
- If variables X and Y are correlated, then at least three possibilities exist with respect to the causal relations among the variables:
  - X causally affects Y.
  - Y causally affects X.
  - Neither X nor Y causally affect each other, but both are causally affected by a third variable, Z.
- The Spearman rank-order correlation coefficient is found by

$$r_s = 1 - \left[\frac{6\sum D^2}{(N_{pairs})(N_{pairs}^2 - 1)}\right].$$

- The statistical significance of r_s is tested using Table A–9.

KEY TERMS AND SYMBOLS

bivariate distribution of scores	inverse relationship	r_s
bivariate normal distribution	linear relationship	r^2
coefficient of determination	negative relationship	scatterplot
correlation coefficient	Pearson correlation coefficient	Spearman rank-order correlation
correlational study	positive relationship	coefficient
covary	restriction of range	SS_X
CP_{XY}	ρ	SS_Y
cross products	ρ_s	third variable problem
direct relationship	r	

REVIEW QUESTIONS

1. Crews et al. (1986) were interested in variables associated with successful performance of professional women golfers. For one sample of female golfers, they found r_{obs} between percentage of body fat (variable X) and average golf score (variable Y) to be +.64. Suppose that you replicated this study with 12 different professional female golfers and obtained the following values of percentage of body fat and average golf scores (in strokes).

Golfer	Body Fat: X	Golf Score: Y
1	20.1	70
2	28.9	77
3	25.4	75
4	19.6	67
5	36.3	79
6	22.9	73
7	26.5	74
8	30.7	72
9	29.8	83
10	33.2	75
11	24.1	68
12	27.3	75

    a. Construct a scatterplot of the percentage of body fat (on the abscissa) and average golf score (on the ordinate).

    b. Does the relationship between the scores on the scatterplot appear to be positive or negative, or is no relationship apparent?

    c. Calculate r_{obs} using the computational formula and test to find if it differs significantly from a correlation of zero in the population at the .05 significance level.

d. What conclusion do you reach about the relationship of percentage of body fat to golfing scores in the sample?

e. Calculate r^2. What proportion of the variation in percentage body fat and average golf score is common to the two measures?

f. Identify a potential third variable that may explain the correlation found between percentage body fat and average golf score.

g. Report the results of your study following the example in the Reporting the Results of a Correlational Study section of this chapter.

2. Our reaction to others is often based on their physical appearance. For males, at least, tallness frequently seems to evoke positive reactions from others. As the old adage says, "Tall, dark, and handsome." Following this line of thinking, Villimez, Eisenberg, and Carroll (1986) were interested in finding if any relationships exist between physical size and academic performance for primary school children. They obtained a number of measures of childrens' size and related them to test scores and report card grades. Holding age constant to control for height differences related to age, they found an r_{obs} of $-.12$ between height and report card grades for 53 third-grade girls and an r_{obs} of $+.32$ for 42 third-grade boys.

a. Test each correlation coefficient to find if it differs significantly at the .05 level from a correlation of zero in the population sampled.

b. Calculate the coefficient of determination for each value of r_{obs}.

c. What conclusion do you reach concerning the relationship between height and report card grades in primary school children?

3. Students are often interested in predicting their final examination grade from the grade received on a midterm examination. To make such predictions, grades on the midterm and final exam must be correlated. Suppose that for an elementary statistics class the following grades were obtained for 10 students on a midterm and final examination.

Student	Examination	
	Midterm: X	Final: Y
1	87	84
2	89	91
3	97	96
4	80	87
5	73	66
6	85	90
7	81	79
8	74	80
9	80	89
10	89	86

a. Plot a scatterplot of the midterm exam (on the abscissa) and final exam (on the ordinate).

b. Does the relationship between the scores on the scatterplot appear to be positive or negative, or is no relationship apparent?

     c. Calculate r_{obs} using the computational formula and test to find if it differs significantly from a correlation of zero in the population at the .05 significance level.

     d. What conclusion do you reach about the relationship of midterm exam grades and final exam grades in the sample?

4. Krantz (1987) found that physical attractiveness and popularity are positively correlated for kindergarten girls, but not for kindergarten boys. Suppose that you conducted a similar study and had an observer rank kindergarten children on physical attractiveness and popularity. Twelve girls and 14 boys were ranked, and you found the following rankings.

Girls

Physical Attractiveness: X	Popularity: Y
3	1
6	7
2	3
9	10
12	11
1	3
7	8
8	7
4	5
10	9
5	6
11	12

Boys

Physical Attractiveness: X	Popularity: Y
5	9
11	1
3	10
9	4
4	6
8	12
12	5
1	13
14	8
10	14
6	2
13	11
2	7
7	3

a. Calculate $r_{s\,obs}$ on the scores of the girls and test to find if it differs significantly from a correlation of zero in the population at the .05 significance level.

b. What conclusion do you reach about the relationship of physical attractiveness and popularity rankings for the girls?

c. Calculate $r_{s\,obs}$ on the scores of the boys and test to find if it differs significantly from a correlation of zero in the population at the .05 significance level.

d. What conclusion do you reach about the relationship of physical attractiveness and popularity rankings for the boys?

5. A study by Wong (1993) measured 76 college students with the Wechsler Adult Intelligence Scale—Revised and correlated the resulting IQ scores with the students' grade-point averages. The range of IQ scores was from 83 to 133. The r_{obs} between IQ score and grade-point average was +.18, which is nonsignificant at the .05 level. Identify one reason why there may be no correlation between the two variables in this study.

6. As computers become more ubiquitous in the workplace and home, there is increasing interest in the possible effects of prolonged viewing of a computer screen on perceptual abilities. A study by Weiss, Kimmel, and Stein (1993) correlated a measure of depth perception to the number of hours a subject had spent working on a computer immediately prior to the test of depth perception. They measured the number of hours a subject had been working on a computer and the amount of error (in centimeters) in aligning two vertical rods in a depth-perception test. If the subject had perfect depth perception, the error score would be zero centimeters. If a subject was unable to align the two rods perfectly, there would be an error; the larger the error, the poorer the depth perception. Suppose that you measured 13 subjects on the number of hours they had worked on a computer and on a test of depth perception immediately after they had finished on the computer and obtained the following scores.

Subject	Hours of Computer Use: X	Depth-perception Error (cm): Y
1	0.5	4.3
2	1.7	3.1
3	4.2	2.1
4	6.0	0.4
5	2.8	6.3
6	5.3	3.7
7	0.9	1.6
8	3.4	1.2
9	1.4	2.4
10	5.1	5.2
11	1.9	0.6
12	4.8	4.1
13	2.6	5.4

a. Construct a scatterplot of the hours of computer use (on the abscissa) and depth-perception error (on the ordinate).

b. Does the relationship between the scores on the scatterplot appear to be positive or negative, or is no relationship apparent?

c. Calculate r_{obs} using the computational formula and test to find if it differs significantly from a correlation of zero in the population at the .05 significance level.

d. What conclusion do you reach about the relationship of the hours of computer use and depth-perception error in the sample?

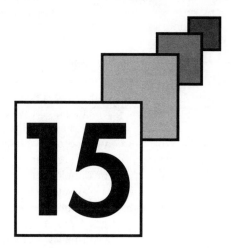

Regression and Prediction

The discussion of correlation in Chapter 14 indicated that if two variables were correlated perfectly, such as the scores in Figures 14–2 and 14–4, then knowing the value of the X variable permits a perfect prediction of the value of the Y variable. But even if variables X and Y are not correlated perfectly, I still may use the score on one variable to predict the score on the second when a statistically significant correlation exists between the two variables. There are many reasons why we want to predict one variable from another. Suppose, for example, that you want to know what your first examination score in a course might indicate about your final grade. Here you want to predict your final course grade from the first examination grade. College admission officers want to predict grade-point averages from standardized achievement tests. Personnel managers may predict employee performance from employment test scores. And your doctor may predict your risk of developing a certain disease from the results of a medical test. Other examples are given later in the chapter.

This chapter deals with predicting one variable from another when the two variables are related linearly. The approach I take is to fit a straight line, called a *linear regression line*, to a scatterplot of the two variables and use this regression line to predict one score from the other. Two variables may be related in a nonlinear way also, but the following discussion is limited only to straight-line relationships. I begin with several simple examples of linear relationships; then I introduce an example of predicting depression scores from responses to a questionnaire on loneliness.

LINEAR RELATIONS

Definition of a Linear Relation

Linear relation: A relation between two variables such that each time that variable X changes by 1 unit variable Y changes by a constant amount.

A linear relationship between two variables is a straight-line relationship between the variables. Figure 15–1 illustrates two variables, X and Y, that are perfectly positively linearly related. This figure permits us to more completely define a linear relation. In a **linear relation**, each time one variable changes by one unit there is a constant change in the second variable. In Figure 15–1, for each 1-unit increase in X, Y increases by 0.5 unit. For example, as X increases from 2 to 3 (1 unit on the X measurement), Y increases from 1.0 to 1.5 (0.5 unit on the Y measurement). Similarly, as X increases from 4 to 5 (1 unit on the X measurement), Y increases from 2.0 to 2.5 (0.5 unit on the Y measurement). In this illustration, then, a change in X of 1 unit of its measurement results in a constant change of 0.5 unit on the Y measure.

The requirement of a linear relationship that a change of 1 unit in the X variable be accompanied by a constant amount of change in the Y variable applies whether the relationship is positive or negative. Figure 15–2 illustrates a perfect negative linear relationship between X and Y. Each time X changes by 1 unit, Y also changes by a constant amount. For example, as X changes 1 unit from 2 to 3, Y changes from 9.4 to 8.6, a change of -0.8 on the Y measurement. Similarly, a change of X from 8 to 9 results in a change of Y from 4.6 to 3.8, again a change of -0.8 on the Y measurement.

FIGURE 15-1

A perfect positive linear relationship between variable X and variable Y with a slope of +0.5.

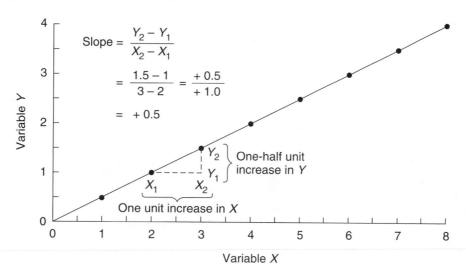

Variable X

For the linear relationship in Figure 15–2, every change in X of 1 unit is accompanied by a corresponding and constant change of Y of -0.8 unit.

General equation of a straight line:
$Y = bX + a.$

The **general equation of a straight line** is given by

$$Y = bX + a,$$

where Y = score on the Y variable
   X = score on the X variable
   b = slope of the line
   a = constant called the Y-intercept

Slope of a Line

Slope of a straight line:
The slope of a straight line is given by
$b = \dfrac{\text{change in value of } Y}{\text{change in value of } X}.$

In Figures 15–1 and 15–2, every change in X by 1 unit of its measure is accompanied by a corresponding and constant change in the Y variable. The relationship of the change in the Y variable corresponding to a change in the X variable is the slope of the straight line relating the two variables. Specifically, the **slope of a line relating variables X and Y** is symbolized by b and defined as

$$b = \frac{\textbf{Change in value of } Y}{\textbf{Change in value of } X}$$

FIGURE 15–2
A perfect negative linear relationship between variable X and variable Y with a slope of -0.8 and a Y-intercept of $+11$.

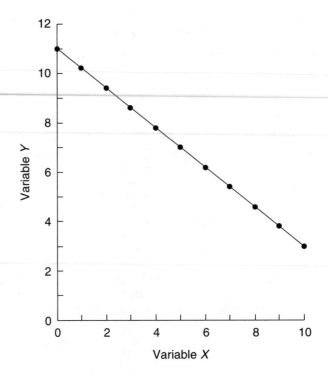

This relationship is expressed as

$$b = \frac{Y_2 - Y_1}{X_2 - X_1},$$

where X_1 and X_2 = two values of X
    Y_1 and Y_2 = values of Y corresponding to X_1 and X_2, respectively

The numerical values presented in Figure 15–1 allow us to find the slope of the line relating X and Y using the values of $X_1 = 2$ and $X_2 = 3$. The values of Y corresponding to these X values are $Y_1 = 1$ and $Y_2 = 1.5$, respectively. Thus

$$
\begin{aligned}
b &= \frac{Y_2 - Y_1}{X_2 - X_1} \\
&= \frac{1.5 - 1}{3 - 2} \\
&= \frac{+0.5}{+1} = +0.5.
\end{aligned}
$$

The slope of this straight line is +0.5; for every increase of 1 unit in X, Y increases by 0.5 unit. The slope of a straight line is constant over its length. Thus, regardless of the values of X used, b will be +0.5 for this example. For instance, suppose I use $X_1 = 3$ and $X_2 = 5$. For these values of X, the corresponding Y values are $Y_1 = 1.5$ and $Y_2 = 2.5$. Hence

$$b = \frac{2.5 - 1.5}{5 - 3} = \frac{+1}{+2} = +0.5.$$

Knowing the slope of the line in Figure 15–1, I can write an equation relating the value of Y to X for this line. This equation is

$$Y = +0.5X.$$

For each value of X, this equation provides the corresponding value of Y, and I can solve $Y = +0.5X$ for different values of X as follows:

If X = _____ ,	Then Y = _____
0	0
1	0.5
2	1.0
3	1.5
4	2.0
5	2.5
6	3.0
7	3.5
8	4.0

Compare these values of Y with the values of Y plotted in Figure 15–1 for each X value. Notice that $Y = +0.5X$ provides the equation describing the linear relationship plotted in Figure 15–1. Thus, if I knew only this equation and the X score for a subject, I could predict the Y score perfectly.

The equation $Y = bX$ provides part of the general equation for a straight line and describes any linear relationship between X and Y provided that $Y = 0$ when $X = 0$. But what if Y does not equal zero when $X = 0$? I turn to this problem next.

The Y-intercept of a Line

Look at the relationship between variables X and Y presented in Figure 15–3. The slope of this line is also +0.5, for every change of 1 unit in X, Y changes by +0.5 unit. But this line cannot be described by the equation $Y = +0.5X$, for this equation indicates that Y should equal zero when $X = 0$. But, looking at Figure 15–3, we see that $Y = 3$ when $X = 0$. Let us substitute another value for X, say $X = 10$, into the equation $Y = +0.5X$. Doing so, I find that Y should be 5 when $X = 10$. From Figure 15–3, however, we see that $Y = 8$ when $X = 10$. By comparing Y found from the equation $Y = +0.5X$ with the values of Y plotted in Figure 15–3, we find that the equation $Y = +0.5X$ gives a value

FIGURE 15–3
A linear relationship between X and Y with a slope of +0.5 and a
Y-intercept of +3.

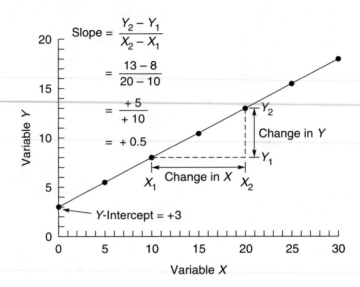

of Y that is 3 units less than the Y plotted on the figure. Suppose, then, that I use the equation $Y = +0.5X$ and add 3 to each value of Y obtained from it. Then the equation is

$$Y = +0.5X + 3.$$

This equation now describes the relationship between X and Y in Figure 15–3. To demonstrate, solving $Y = +0.5X + 3$ for different values of X, I obtain the following:

If $X =$ _____ ,	Then $Y =$ _____
0	3.0
2	4.0
4	5.0
10	8.0
13	9.5
19	12.5
24	15.0
26	16.0
30	18.0

These values of Y for each value of X correspond perfectly with the values of Y plotted on Figure 15–3. Thus $Y = 0.5X + 3$ is the equation describing the line shown in Figure 15–3.

This example provides a specific instance of the equation for a linear relationship between X and Y. To express the general equation for a straight line, I substitute the

Y-intercept: The value of Y when $X = 0$ in the equation $Y = bX + a$. letter b for the slope of $+0.5$ and the letter a for the constant of 3 in the equation $Y = +0.5X + 3$. Doing so, I obtain $Y = bX + a$, the general equation of a straight line with slope b, and Y-intercept, a. The **Y-intercept** is the value of Y when $X = 0$. When $X = 0$, the line intercepts, or intersects, the Y axis, and the value of Y at this point is the Y-intercept. In Figure 15–3 the Y-intercept is $+3$, whereas in Figure 15–1 the Y-intercept is 0.

Example Linear Relations and Their Equations

To gain familiarity with linear relationships and the equations describing them, Figure 15–4 provides examples of both positive and negative linear relationships between X and Y. The equation of the straight line with the slope and Y-intercept is given for each relationship illustrated. For example, panel (b) presents the linear relationship used in Figure 15–2 to illustrate a negative relationship between X and Y. The equation for this relationship is $Y = -0.8X + 11$. Here we see that the slope is -0.8; the minus sign indicates the relationship is negative. For every increase of 1 unit in X, Y decreases by 0.8 unit. When X is zero, the line intercepts the Y axis at a value of $+11$; thus the Y-intercept for this equation is $+11$. Study each example and ensure that you can obtain the value of b and a for each relationship presented.

TESTING YOUR KNOWLEDGE 15–1

1. Define: a, b, linear relation, slope of a straight line, Y-intercept.
2. Write the general equation for a straight line.
3. Write the equation for the slope of a straight line.
4. For each of the graphs in Figure 15–5, find the slope and Y-intercept. Then write the equation for each line.

   a.   b.

   c.   d.

FINDING A LINEAR REGRESSION LINE

An Example Problem

The previous examples involved variables identified simply as X and Y. To introduce how we find the equation that describes the linear relationship of two sets of scores, I return to the problem introduced in Chapter 14, the relationship between loneliness and depression scores.

FIGURE 15–4

Various linear relationships between variables X and Y: (a) $Y = +1.2X + 2$; (b) $Y = -0.8X + 11$; (c) $Y = -1.0X + 30$; (d) $Y = +0.2X + 25$; (e) $Y = +1.5X - 2$; (f) $Y = -1.4X + 100$.

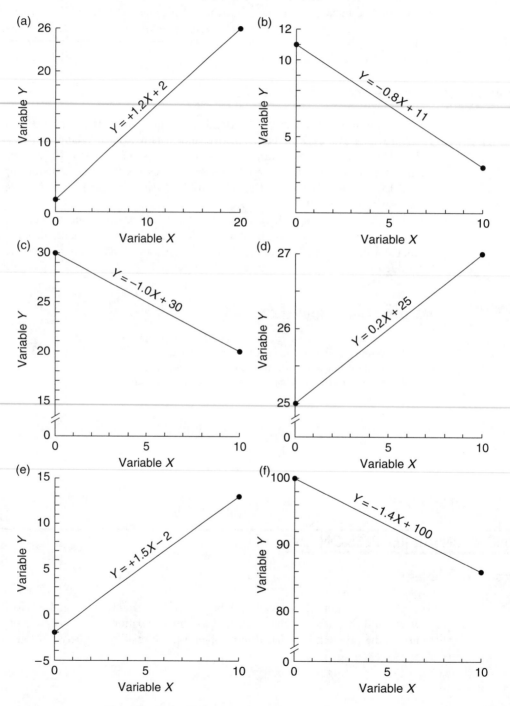

FIGURE 15–5
Linear relationships between variables X and Y.

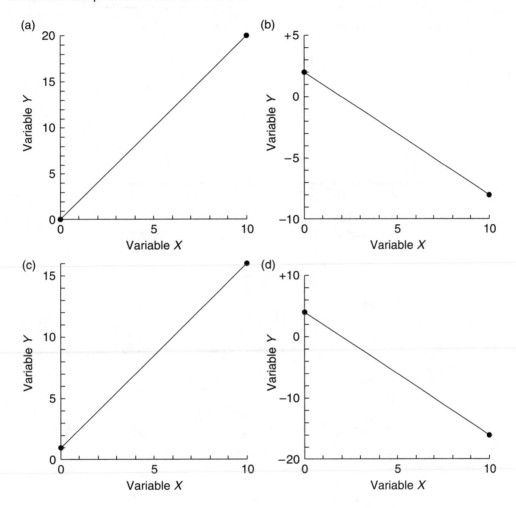

Suppose, for a moment, that the scores in Table 15–1 were obtained from 10 subjects. These scores are perfectly positively related, $r_{obs} = +1.00$. Consequently, I expect a scatterplot to reveal that the scores fall on a straight line, as Figure 15–6 illustrates. I obtain the equation for the linear relationship between loneliness and depression scores by finding the slope and Y-intercept of the line. Both values were found on the figure: $b = +1$ and $a = +10$. Thus the equation relating the depression scores (Y) to the loneliness scores (X) is

$$Y = 1X + 10$$

or

$$\text{Depression score} = (+1)(\text{loneliness score}) + 10.$$

TABLE 15-1

Hypothetical scores for 10 subjects on loneliness and depression.

Subject	Loneliness Score: X	Depression Score: Y
1	6	16
2	15	25
3	28	38
4	2	12
5	24	34
6	8	18
7	25	35
8	30	40
9	14	24
10	18	28

FIGURE 15-6

Scatterplot of the loneliness and depression scores given in Table 15-1.

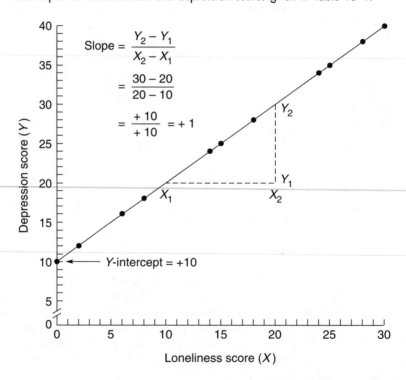

Because the correlation of the scores is +1.00, I can use this equation to predict perfectly each subject's depression score knowing only his or her loneliness score. The predicted depression scores are given in column b of Table 15-2. For example, subject 1 has a loneliness score of 6. Applying the equation,

TABLE 15–2

Depression scores predicted from loneliness scores using the equation

Depression score = (+1.0)(loneliness score) + 10.

Column a identifies the obtained loneliness score, column b the
depression score predicted from the equation, and column c the actual
depression score from Table 15–1.

Subject	(a) Loneliness Score: X	(b) Predicted Depression: Y'	(c) Actual Depression: Y
1	6	16	16
2	15	25	25
3	28	38	38
4	2	12	12
5	24	34	34
6	8	18	18
7	25	35	35
8	30	40	40
9	14	24	24
10	18	28	28

$$\text{Predicted depression score} = (+1)(\text{loneliness score}) + 10,$$

we find

$$\text{Predicted depression score} = (+1)(6) + 10$$

$$= 6 + 10 = 16.$$

The depression score predicted from the loneliness score of 6 is 16. The depression scores
predicted from the other loneliness scores are presented in column b of Table 15–2. These
predicted scores are identified with the letter Y' (read as "Y prime" or "Y predicted") to
indicate that they have been predicted from the X score of loneliness using the equation

$$Y' = 1X + 10.$$

The actual depression score obtained by each subject (symbolized by Y) is presented in
column c. Notice that the predicted and actual depression scores are identical. Because
$r_{obs} = +1.00$, Y' and Y are the same and there is no error in predicting depression scores
from loneliness scores.

A More Realistic Example Problem

From an applied perspective, the scores in Table 15–1 are unusual. Rarely, if ever, are
two variables perfectly correlated as they are in Table 15–1. More realistically, scores

on two variables will exhibit a less-than-perfect correlation, such as the scores presented in Table 15–3. These scores were used in Chapter 14 to present the Pearson correlation coefficient (see Table 14–1). The r_{obs} for these scores is +.78, which is statistically significant at the .05 level.

The scores of Table 15–3 are presented in a scatterplot in Figure 15–7. As r_{obs} = +.78 indicates, these scores are positively related; higher depression scores are associated with higher scores on loneliness, and lower depression scores are related to lower loneliness scores. Although the relationship between the loneliness and depression scores in Figure 15–7 is not perfect, it does appear to be linear. But what would be the best straight line to describe these scores? Obviously, a number of straight lines could be drawn on the scatterplot. For example, I have drawn two different straight lines labeled A and B on the figure. The lines were drawn arbitrarily, except that each line passes through $\overline{X}$ = 17 and $\overline{Y}$ = 28. Does line A appear to "fit" or describe the scores better or worse than line B? To answer this question, I need a criterion to decide how well a particular straight line fits a set of correlated scores.

The Least-squares Criterion

Each line, A and B, in Figure 15–7 allows predicting a value of Y (that is, a Y') for each value of X. For example, for a loneliness score of 7, line A predicts a Y' of 24.0, and for a loneliness score of 27, a Y' equal to 32.0. On the other hand, line B predicts Y' equal to 20.0 for an X of 7 and Y' equal to 36.0 for a loneliness score of 27. These predicted Y scores are presented in column c of Table 15–4 for line A

TABLE 15–3
Hypothetical scores for 10 subjects on loneliness and depression. The mean and estimated population standard deviation are given for each set of scores.

Subject	Loneliness Score: X	Depression Score: Y
1	4	16
2	27	37
3	18	33
4	7	23
5	30	34
6	12	32
7	18	24
8	23	29
9	19	26
10	12	26
$\overline{X}$	17.0	$\overline{Y}$ 28.0
s_X	8.37	s_Y 6.25

FIGURE 15–7

Scatterplot of the loneliness and depression scores given in Table 15–3. Lines A and B were drawn arbitrarily on the scatterplot.

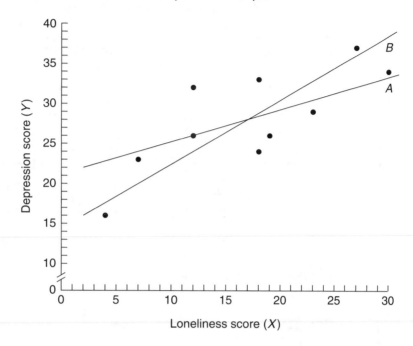

and in column f for line B. Each Y' score is in error in comparison with the Y score actually obtained, and the difference $Y - Y'$ is a measure of the error in prediction of the Y score from the X score. Table 15–4 illustrates the errors in prediction of each Y score from the X scores using either line A (see column d) or line B (see column g) of Figure 15–7.

Each line leads to errors in prediction. But does one line lead to smaller errors in prediction than the other? I might try to answer this question by adding up the errors in columns e and h, respectively, of Table 15–4. But if I sum the columns, as I have done in Table 15–4, I find that the sum of the errors, $\sum(Y - Y')$, is zero for each line. Thus the sum of the errors cannot be used as a criterion to determine the fit of a straight line to the points in a scatterplot; it will always be equal to zero. A similar problem occurred in Chapter 5 when attempting to find a measure of the variation of scores about the mean of a distribution. In that instance we found that $\sum(X - \overline{X})$ was always equal to zero. The problem was resolved by squaring each $X - \overline{X}$ before the differences were summed. Then I used $\sum(X - \overline{X})^2$ to develop a measure of error variation in the scores.

The current problem may be resolved similarly by squaring each $Y - Y'$ difference and summing the squared $Y - Y'$ differences. Then I will use $\sum(Y - Y')^2$ to determine which line best fits the scatterplot. Table 15–4 illustrates obtaining $\sum(Y - Y')^2$ for each line, A and B in columns e and h, respectively. The $\sum(Y - Y')^2$ for line

TABLE 15–4
Error of prediction of Y scores from the X scores of Figure 15–7 using either line A or line B. The error is given by the difference between the obtained Y score and the Y score predicted from X, or Y − Y'. Columns a and b identify the obtained X and Y scores, respectively, column c the Y predicted from line A, columns d and e the error and squared error of the predicted score from line A, respectively, column f the Y predicted from line B, and columns g and h the error and squared error of the predicted score from line B, respectively.

	(a)	(b)	(c)	(d)	(e)	(f)	(g)	(h)
	Obtained Scores		**Predicted from Line A**			**Predicted from Line B**		
			Scores	**Error**		**Scores**	**Error**	
Subject	X	Y	Y'	Y − Y'	(Y − Y')²	Y'	Y − Y'	(Y − Y')²
1	4	16	22.8	−6.8	46.24	17.6	−1.6	2.56
2	27	37	32.0	+5.0	25.00	36.0	+1.0	1.00
3	18	33	28.4	+4.6	21.16	28.8	+4.2	17.64
4	7	23	24.0	−1.0	1.00	20.0	+3.0	9.00
5	30	34	33.2	+0.8	0.64	38.4	−4.4	19.36
6	12	32	26.0	+6.0	36.00	24.0	+8.0	64.00
7	18	24	28.4	−4.4	19.36	28.8	−4.8	23.04
8	23	29	30.4	−1.4	1.96	32.8	−3.8	14.44
9	19	26	28.8	−2.8	7.84	29.6	−3.6	12.96
10	12	26	26.0	0.0	0.00	24.0	+2.0	4.00
			Sum	0.0	159.20		0.0	168.00

A is 159.20 (see column e), whereas for line B it is 168.00 (see column h). Based on $\sum(Y - Y')^2$ as a measure of error in prediction, line A produces less error than line B.

Least-squares regression line: A straight line that minimizes the value of $\sum(Y - Y')^2$.

A straight line that minimizes the value of $\sum(Y - Y')^2$ is called a **least-squares regression line**, for it minimizes the value of the sum of the squared differences of every predicted Y' score from the obtained Y score. That is, it minimizes $\sum(Y - Y')^2$. Figure 15–8 illustrates a least-squares regression line fitted to the scatterplot of the scores in Table 15–3. The equation for this line is $Y' = +0.583X + 18.1$. This line possesses the characteristic that $\sum(Y - Y')^2$ is a minimum; no other straight line fitted to the scores of Table 15–3 will produce a smaller value of $\sum(Y - Y')^2$. I now explain how to find the slope and Y-intercept for a least-squares regression line.

The Slope and Y-intercept of a Least-squares Regression Line for Predicting Y from X

To find a least-squares regression line to predict variable Y from variable X, I must determine the slope (b) and Y-intercept (a) of a straight line that minimizes the value of $\sum(Y - Y')^2$.

FIGURE 15–8
The least-squares regression line for the loneliness and depression scores of Table 15–3.

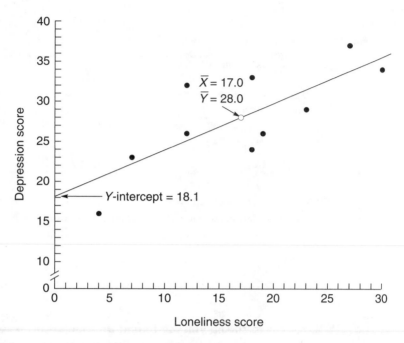

Slope of a Least-squares Regression Line

There are several alternative formulas for finding the slope of a least-squares regression line; each formula produces the same value for b.

Deviational and Cross-products Formula.   The slope of the least-squares regression line for two variables using deviations of scores from their mean is given by

$$b = \frac{\sum (X - \overline{X})(Y - \overline{Y})}{\sum (X - \overline{X})^2}.$$

Recall that the numerator of this formula, $\sum (X - \overline{X})(Y - \overline{Y})$, is the cross product of X and Y and is symbolized as CP_{XY}. The denominator of the formula,

$$\sum (X - \overline{X})^2,$$

is the sum of squares for X, or SS_X. Thus I may also write an equation for b in cross-products and sum-of-squares form as

$$b = \frac{CP_{XY}}{SS_X}.$$

Computational Formula.   A formula that provides easier computations is

$$b = \frac{(N_{\text{pairs}})\left(\sum XY\right) - \left(\sum X\right)\left(\sum Y\right)}{(N_{\text{pairs}})\left(\sum X^2\right) - \left(\sum X\right)^2},$$

where N_{pairs} is the number of pairs of scores.

Correlation Formula.   The value of b may also be obtained from r by using the equation

$$b = r\left(\frac{s_Y}{s_X}\right),$$

where $r = r_{\text{obs}}$ between two sets of scores

s_Y = estimated population standard deviation for the Y scores

s_X = estimated population standard deviation for the X scores

I illustrate the use of this equation in Example Problem 15–1.

Which formula should you use to find b?

Table 15–5 presents each of the preceding formulas for the slope. Each formula provides the same value of b when applied to a set of scores. Which formula should you choose to calculate b from a set of scores? In general, the computations needed for the computational formula are easier to perform and less likely to lead to an error than those needed for the deviational or cross-products formulas. Consequently, the computational formula is the approach you would most likely use to obtain b from a set of scores, and I illustrate its use next. If, however, you have already found the value of r_{obs} on the scores, then the correlation formula would be easiest, for it requires only that you find s_X and s_Y in addition to the value of r_{obs}.

Finding b Using the Computational Formula

Table 15–6 illustrates using the computational formula to find the slope of the least-squares regression line shown in Figure 15–8 fitted to the loneliness and depression scores of Table 15–3. Columns a and b of Table 15–6 present the X and Y scores, respectively. The sums of these columns provide the $\sum X$ and $\sum Y$ needed: $\sum X = 170$ and $\sum Y = 280$. Column c obtains each X^2, and the sum of this column, 3520, provides $\sum X^2$. Column d gives the value of each XY (i.e., each X score multiplied by its corresponding Y score), and the sum of this column, 5127, provides the $\sum XY$.

Step 2 of Table 15–6 illustrates substituting values of $\sum X, \sum Y, \sum XY$, and $\sum X^2$ into the equation. The value of b obtained for the scores of Table 15–3 is +0.583. The plus sign indicates that the slope is positive.

TABLE 15-5
Formulas for the slope of a least-squares
regression line.

Deviational formula

$$b = \frac{\sum (X - \overline{X})(Y - \overline{Y})}{\sum (X - \overline{X})^2}$$

Cross-products and sum-of-squares formula

$$b = \frac{CP_{XY}}{SS_X}$$

Computational formula

$$b = \frac{(N_{\text{pairs}})\left(\sum XY\right) - \left(\sum X\right)\left(\sum Y\right)}{(N_{\text{pairs}})\left(\sum X^2\right) - \left(\sum X\right)^2}$$

N_{pairs} is the number of pairs of scores

Correlation formula

$$b = r\left(\frac{s_Y}{s_X}\right)$$

Y-intercept of a Least-squares Regression Line

The Y-intercept of a least-squares regression line is calculated from the value of b by the formula

$$a = \overline{Y} - b\overline{X},$$

where
$\overline{Y}$ = mean of the Y scores
$\overline{X}$ = mean of the X scores
b = slope of the least-squares regression line obtained by using one of the formulas given in the previous section

To illustrate the use of this formula for the scores of Table 15–3, $\overline{Y} = 28.0$, $\overline{X} = 17.0$, and $b = +0.583$. Thus

$$a = 28 - (+0.583)(17.0) = 28.0 - 9.911 = 18.089 = 18.1$$

rounded to one decimal place. The least-squares regression line for these scores intersects the Y axis at a value of $Y = 18.1$.

TABLE 15-6
Calculating b using the computational formula. The loneliness scores (X) in column a and depression scores (Y) in column b are from Table 15-3.

Step 1. Finding $\sum X, \sum Y, \sum X^2, \sum XY$:

Subject	(a) X	(b) Y	(c) X^2	(d) XY
1	4	16	16	64
2	27	37	729	999
3	18	33	324	594
4	7	23	49	161
5	30	34	900	1020
6	12	32	144	384
7	18	24	324	432
8	23	29	529	667
9	19	26	361	494
10	12	26	144	312
Sums	170	280	3520	5127

Step 2. Calculating b:

$$\sum X = 170,$$
$$(\sum X)^2 = 170^2 = 28{,}900,$$
$$\sum Y = 280,$$
$$\sum X^2 = 3520,$$
$$\sum XY = 5127,$$
$$N_{\text{pairs}} = 10,$$

and

$$b = \frac{(N_{\text{pairs}})(\sum XY) - (\sum X)(\sum Y)}{(N_{\text{pairs}})(\sum X^2) - (\sum X)^2}.$$

Substituting numerical values,

$$b = \frac{(10)(5127) - (170)(280)}{(10)(3520) - 28{,}900}$$

$$= \frac{51{,}270 - 47{,}600}{35{,}200 - 28{,}900}$$

$$= \frac{+3670}{6300}$$

$$= +0.583.$$

Equation for the Least-squares Regression Line

When the values of b and a are substituted into the equation for a straight line,

$$Y' = bX + a,$$

we find

$$Y' = +0.583X + 18.1.$$

Hence the least-squares regression line for the scores of Table 15–3 is described by the equation $Y' = +0.583X + 18.1$. To obtain predicted values of Y, a value of X is entered into the equation and the equation solved for Y'. Predicted values of Y for the scores of Table 15–3 are as follows:

Subject	If $X =$ _____ ,	Then $Y' =$ _____
1	4	20.4
2	27	33.8
3	18	28.6
4	7	22.2
5	30	35.6
6	12	25.1
7	18	28.6
8	23	31.5
9	19	29.2
10	12	25.1

The Y' values lie on the regression line illustrated in Figure 15–8.

Fitting a Least-squares Regression Line to Scores

I now illustrate how the least-squares regression line given by $Y' = +0.583X + 18.1$ is fitted to the scores plotted in Figure 15–8. If any two points on a straight line are known, then we have sufficient information to plot the line on a figure. For the regression line, one point on the line is the Y-intercept, the value of Y' when $X = 0$. For the example, the Y-intercept is 18.1. Thus one point on the line has the coordinates $X = 0$, $Y = 18.1$.

A second point may be obtained by substituting a different value of X and solving for Y'. Although I may substitute any value for X, I use the value of $\overline{X}$, where $\overline{X} = 17.0$ for the example. Substituting $\overline{X} = 17.0$ into the equation, I obtain

$$Y' = +0.583(17.0) + 18.1$$

$$= 9.91 + 18.1 = 28.011$$

$$Y' = 28.0 \quad \text{rounded to one decimal place}$$

Consequently, when $\overline{X} = 17.0$, $Y' = 28.0$. The predicted value of Y, $Y' = 28.0$, is the value of $\overline{Y}$. For any least-squares regression line, when the value of X is the mean of the X scores, Y' will be equal to the mean of the obtained Y scores. Therefore, a second point on the regression line will always be a point with coordinates of $\overline{X}$, $\overline{Y}$. For the scores in Figure 15–8, $\overline{X} = 17.0$, $\overline{Y} = 28.0$, and the regression line on Figure 15–8 passes through these coordinates.

By examining Figure 15–8 you can see why the line given by

$$Y' = +0.583X + 18.1$$

is called the **regression line of Y on X**. One meaning of the word *regression* is to move toward or approach a mean. Notice that for extreme values of Y (e.g., depression scores of 16 or 37) the Y' values are closer to the value of $\overline{Y} = 28.0$ than the obtained Y values. Thus the Y' values for Y values in the tails of the distribution tend to move or regress toward the mean of Y. For this reason, the line is called a regression line.

ERROR IN PREDICTION

Residuals: A Measure of the Error in Prediction

Residual: The value of $Y - Y'$.

As we saw from Figure 15–8, using variable X to predict variable Y leads to some error in prediction, unless, of course, X and Y are perfectly correlated. The difference between a score and its predicted value, $Y - Y'$, is a measure of this error and is called the **residual**. The residual is used as the basis for a measure of the accuracy of prediction called the *standard error of estimate*. To develop the standard error of estimate, I turn to Table 15–7.

Table 15–7 presents the loneliness and depression scores of Table 15–3 in columns a and b, respectively. Predicted depression scores (i.e., Y') obtained from the regression equation $Y' = +0.583X + 18.1$ are shown in column c. For example, Y' for subject 6 with a loneliness score of 12 is

$$Y'_6 = (+0.583)(12) + 18.1 = 25.10.$$

To minimize rounding error in later calculations the predicted values in column c were carried to two decimal places. You should calculate the remaining Y' values in column c to ensure that you are able to work with the regression equation for these scores.

The residual, $Y - Y'$, is shown in column d for each subject. The sum of these residuals is equal to zero (within the limits of rounding error), so I cannot use this sum as a measure of error in prediction. Therefore, to develop a measure of error in

TABLE 15–7

Calculating the residual for the predicted depression scores (Y', column c) from the loneliness scores (X, column a) of Table 15–3 using the regression equation $Y' = +0.583X + 18.1$. The residual, or error in prediction, is presented in column d, and the squared value of the residual is presented in column e.

Subject	(a) X	(b) Y	(c) Y'	(d) $Y - Y'$	(e) $(Y - Y')^2$
1	4	16	20.43	−4.43	19.6249
2	27	37	33.84	+3.16	9.9856
3	18	33	28.59	+4.41	19.4481
4	7	23	22.18	+0.82	0.6724
5	30	34	35.59	−1.59	2.5281
6	12	32	25.10	+6.90	47.6100
7	18	24	28.59	−4.59	21.0681
8	23	29	31.51	−2.51	6.3001
9	19	26	29.18	−3.18	10.1124
10	12	26	25.10	+0.90	0.8100
					138.1597 Sum

$SS_{Residual}$: The value of $\sum (Y - Y')^2$.

prediction, I square the residuals as shown in column e. Summing the squared values of $Y - Y'$ in column e results in a sum of squares called the $SS_{Residual}$, the sum of squared residuals. The $SS_{Residual}$ is equal to $\sum(Y - Y')^2$, or 138.1597 for the example.

The Standard Error of Estimate

Standard error of estimate ($s_{Y \cdot X}$): The value of $\sqrt{\dfrac{\sum (Y - Y')^2}{(N_{pairs} - 2)}}$.

In Chapter 5 I developed a measure of error variation for a set of scores, the standard deviation, s, by dividing the SS for a set of scores by its degrees of freedom and then taking the square root of the obtained value. I obtain a similar measure of error variation in the prediction of Y from X, the *standard error of estimate*, by finding the square root of the quotient of the $SS_{Residual}$ divided by its degrees of freedom. The df for $SS_{Residual}$ are $N_{pairs} - 2$, where N_{pairs} is the number of pairs of scores. Accordingly, the **standard error of estimate**, symbolized as $s_{Y \cdot X}$ to indicate that Y is predicted from X, is defined as

$$s_{Y \cdot X} = \sqrt{\frac{SS_{Residual}}{N_{pairs} - 2}},$$

or, equivalently,

$$s_{Y \cdot X} = \sqrt{\frac{\sum (Y - Y')^2}{N_{pairs} - 2}}.$$

In the example, $SS_{Residual} = 138.1597$, and $N_{pairs} = 10$; thus the standard error of estimate of predicting depression scores from loneliness scores is

$$s_{Y \cdot X} = \sqrt{\frac{138.1597}{10 - 2}}$$

$$= \sqrt{\frac{138.1597}{8}}$$

$$= \sqrt{17.2700}$$

$$= 4.16 \quad \text{rounded to two decimal places.}$$

The definition of $s_{Y \cdot X}$ as

$$s_{Y \cdot X} = \sqrt{\frac{\sum (Y - Y')^2}{N_{pairs} - 2}}$$

illustrates that it is a measure of error variation of the predicted scores compared with the actual scores. Because this formula requires finding $Y - Y'$ differences, however, it is both time consuming and open to computational error. Thus two alternative formulas have been developed, one a computational formula that can be applied to scores without obtaining $Y - Y'$ differences and the other a formula using r.

Computational Formula for Calculating $s_{Y \cdot X}$

A computational formula for calculating $s_{Y \cdot X}$ directly from the scores without finding residuals is

$$s_{Y \cdot X} = \sqrt{\left[\frac{1}{N_{pairs}(N_{pairs} - 2)}\right]\left[N_{pairs} \sum Y^2 - \left(\sum Y\right)^2 - \frac{[N_{pairs}\left(\sum XY\right) - \left(\sum X\right)\left(\sum Y\right)]^2}{N_{pairs} \sum X^2 - \left(\sum X\right)^2}\right]},$$

where N_{pairs} is the number of pairs of scores.

This equation is not as difficult to use as it may first appear. The computations using this equation to find $s_{Y \cdot X}$ for the example loneliness and depression scores are illustrated in Table 15–8. Step 1 of the table obtains the numerical values needed to solve the formula. For each subject:

- Column a presents the loneliness score, X.
- Column b is the depression score, Y.
- Column c is the loneliness score squared (X^2).
- Column d is the depression score squared (Y^2).
- Column e is the loneliness score multiplied by the depression score (XY).

TABLE 15–8

Calculating $s_{Y \cdot X}$ using the computational formula. The loneliness scores (X, column a) and depression scores (Y, column b) are from Table 15–3.

Step 1. Finding $\sum X, \sum Y, \sum X^2, \sum Y^2,$ and $\sum XY$:

	(a)	(b)	(c)	(d)	(e)
Subject	X	Y	X^2	Y^2	XY
1	4	16	16	256	64
2	27	37	729	1369	999
3	18	33	324	1089	594
4	7	23	49	529	161
5	30	34	900	1156	1020
6	12	32	144	1024	384
7	18	24	324	576	432
8	23	29	529	841	667
9	19	26	361	676	494
10	12	26	144	676	312
Sums	170	280	3520	8192	5127

Step 2. Calculating $s_{Y \cdot X}$:

$$\sum X = 170 \qquad\qquad \sum Y = 280$$

$$(\sum X)^2 = 170^2 = 28,900 \qquad\qquad (\sum Y)^2 = 280^2 = 78,400$$

$$\sum X^2 = 3520 \qquad\qquad \sum Y^2 = 8192$$

$$\sum XY = 5127$$

$$N_{\text{pairs}} = 10$$

and

$$s_{Y \cdot X} = \sqrt{\left[\frac{1}{N_{\text{pairs}}(N_{\text{pairs}} - 2)} \right] \left[N_{\text{pairs}} \sum Y^2 - (\sum Y)^2 - \frac{[N_{\text{pairs}} (\sum XY) - (\sum X)(\sum Y)]^2}{N_{\text{pairs}} \sum X^2 - (\sum X)^2} \right]}$$

$$= \sqrt{\left[\frac{1}{10(8)} \right] \left[10(8192) - 78,400 - \frac{[10(5127) - (170)(280)]^2}{10(3520) - 28,900} \right]}$$

$$= \sqrt{\left[\frac{1}{80} \right] \left[81,920 - 78,400 - \frac{(51,270 - 47,600)^2}{35,200 - 28,900} \right]}$$

$$= \sqrt{\left[\frac{1}{80} \right] \left[3520 - \frac{(3670)^2}{6300} \right]} = \sqrt{\left[\frac{1}{80} \right] \left[3520 - \frac{13,468,900}{6300} \right]}$$

$$= \sqrt{\left(\frac{1}{80} \right)(3520 - 2137.921)} = \sqrt{\left(\frac{1}{80} \right) 1382.079}$$

$$= \sqrt{17.2760} = 4.156$$

$$= 4.16 \quad \text{rounded to two decimal places.}$$

The $\sum X$ is the sum of column a, $\sum Y$ is the sum of column b, $\sum X^2$ is the sum of column c, $\sum Y^2$ is the sum of column d, and $\sum XY$ is the sum of column e. Step 2 illustrates substituting these values into the formula. The obtained value of $s_{Y \cdot X}$ is 4.16, the same as found using the definitional formula.

Calculating $s_{Y \cdot X}$ from r

The standard error of estimate also may be calculated from the r and the standard deviation of the Y variable with the formula

$$s_{Y \cdot X} = s_Y \sqrt{\left[\frac{N_{\text{pairs}} - 1}{N_{\text{pairs}} - 2}\right](1 - r_{\text{obs}}^2)}.$$

For the scores of Table 15–3,

$$s_Y = 6.25,$$
$$r_{\text{obs}} = +.78,$$
$$N_{\text{pairs}} = 10.$$

Thus

$$s_{Y \cdot X} = (6.25)\sqrt{\left[\frac{10 - 1}{10 - 2}\right][1 - (+.78)^2]}$$

$$= (6.25)\sqrt{\left(\frac{9}{8}\right)(1 - .6084)}$$

$$= (6.25)\sqrt{(1.125)(.3916)}$$

$$= (6.25)\sqrt{0.4406}$$

$$= (6.25)(0.6638)$$

$$= 4.15,$$

which, within the limits of rounding error, is the same as the value found by either the definitional or computational formulas.

When N_{pairs} is large, the ratio of $N_{\text{pairs}} - 1$ to $N_{\text{pairs}} - 2$ approaches 1.0 and the formula is often written as

$$s_{Y \cdot X} = s_Y \sqrt{1 - r_{\text{obs}}^2}.$$

Information Provided by the Standard Error of Estimate

To understand what information the standard error of estimate provides, I return briefly to a consideration of the standard deviation, s. The standard deviation for a set of scores provides a measure of error variation for those scores. If I know nothing about the scores other than the mean, then the best prediction I can make for any score is the mean. Of course, this prediction will likely be in error; and, on the average, the error will be the value of the standard deviation. For example, suppose that you are told that the mean depression score for Table 15–3 is 28.0. If you are asked to predict an individual score knowing nothing other than $\overline{Y} = 28.0$, your best prediction is 28.0. But for any score in Table 15–3 this prediction is in error; no subject obtained a depression score of 28.0. The average error in this prediction is the value of the standard deviation, $s_Y = 6.25$, for this set of scores.

Suppose now you are told that there is a linear relation between the loneliness and depression scores given by

$$Y' = +0.583X + 18.1.$$

Further suppose that you are told that subject 1 has a loneliness score of 4. Using this score and applying the regression equation, you predict this person's Y score to be 20.43. Although this prediction, too, is in error (the subject's actual score was 16), the prediction of 20.43 is closer to the actual score than is the prediction of 28.0 made from $\overline{Y}$. The standard error of estimate is the standard deviation of the error in the predicted scores. Thus $s_{Y \cdot X}$ indicates the average error in predictions from the linear regression line. Notice in the example that $s_{Y \cdot X} = 4.16$ is smaller than $s_Y = 6.25$. Accordingly, if I predict Y from X, the error in prediction typically will be less than if I simply used $\overline{Y}$ as a predictor for all the Y values. Table 15–9 presents the relationship between s_Y and $s_{Y \cdot X}$ as a function of the correlation between variables X and Y. The table was constructed by substituting values of r_{obs} into the formula

$$s_{Y \cdot X} = s_Y \sqrt{1 - r_{XY}^2}{}_{obs}.$$

Notice that when r_{obs} is zero, $s_{Y \cdot X} = s_Y$, and knowing the loneliness score for a subject does not improve the accuracy of prediction of the subject's depression score. For small values of r (e.g., $r = .1, .2,$ or $.3$), knowing the X variable score does little to improve

TABLE 15–9
Relationship between $s_{Y \cdot X}$ and s_Y as a function of r.

If r_{obs} = _____ ,	Then $s_{Y \cdot X}$ = _____ s_Y.
0	1.000
.1	.995
.2	.980
.3	.954
.4	.917
.5	.866
.6	.800
.7	.714
.8	.600
.9	.436
1.0	.000

the accuracy of prediction of the Y variable score. On the other hand, large values of r (e.g., $r = .7$, .8, or .9) improve the accuracy considerably. For example, if the correlation between X and Y is .8, then $s_{Y \cdot X}$ is only .6 of s_Y. When r is 1.00, then $s_{Y \cdot X} = 0$; prediction of the Y score from the X score is perfect and there is no error of prediction.

Using a Linear Regression Line

Two conditions are required for appropriate use of linear regression. First, r for the scores must be statistically significant. If the scores are not correlated, then the best prediction for a Y score is to use the mean of the Y scores. If the X and Y scores are not correlated, then if you are given an X score and asked to predict a Y score, the best prediction of Y is simply $\overline{Y}$. The knowledge of X does not give you any information about the value of Y.

A second requirement is that the relationship between the X and Y scores must be linear. The least-squares regression line is a straight line. If the X and Y scores are not linearly related, then it is inappropriate to fit a least-squares regression line to them. For example, if X and Y are related in a U-shaped or an inverted U-shaped (i.e., ∩) fashion, then constructing a least-squares regression line for the scores will not lead to accurate predictions, for the scores are not linearly related.

We must be cautious also not to predict beyond the range of scores encompassed in the sample from which the prediction equation was developed. The relationship may be nonlinear for values outside the range in the sample.

TESTING YOUR KNOWLEDGE 15–2

1. Define: least-squares regression line, residual, $SS_{Residual}$, standard error of estimate, $s_{Y \cdot X}$, $Y - Y'$, Y'.
2. Write the general equation for predicting a value of Y from X with a straight line.
3. Why is $\sum(Y - Y')$ not used as a measure of error for predicting Y from X?
4. Why may $\sum(Y - Y')^2$ be used as a measure of error for predicting Y from X?
5. Give the definitional formula for the standard error of estimate.
6. The slope and Y-intercept for the regression of Test 2 on Test 1 grades are $b = +0.8$ and $a = 9$.
   a. Write the equation for the regression line of Test 2 on Test 1 grades.
   b. Find values of predicted Test 2 grades (i.e., Y') for the following Test 1 scores (i.e., X): 60, 65, 80, 85, 90.
   c. Plot the regression line on a sheet of graph paper. The value of $\overline{X} = 76$.
7. The slope and Y-intercept for the regression of Task 2 on Task 1 scores are $b = -1.4$ and $a = 23$.
   a. Write the equation for the regression line of Task 2 on Task 1 scores.
   b. Find values of predicted Task 2 scores (i.e., Y') for the following Task 1 scores (i.e., X): 5, 8, 11, 14, 17.
   c. Plot the regression line on a sheet of graph paper. The value of $\overline{X} = 11$.

Example Problem 15–1
Finding a Regression Line from the Correlation Coefficient

Problem
One avenue of research into the problem of eating disorders, such as anorexia and bulimia, has been to investigate the relationship of a person's body image to other attributes of the individual, such as sex role, perceived attractiveness, or self-esteem. Mintz and Betz (1986), for example, measured body satisfaction and depression proneness in college students using self-report rating scales. Body satisfaction scores could range from 1 (indicating strong positive feelings toward one's body) to 7 (indicating strong negative feelings toward one's body). Depression proneness scores also ranged from 1 (indicating strong resistance to depression) to 7 (indicating proneness to depression). For a group of 23 slightly underweight females, Mintz and Betz found a statistically significant correlation of body satisfaction ratings (variable X) with depression proneness ratings (variable Y) of $r_{obs} = +.44$. Suppose that I replicated this study for a group of 15 slightly underweight females and found r_{obs} between body satisfaction and depression proneness of +.58. For 13 df, $r_{crit} = .514$; thus r_{obs} is statistically significant. The mean of the body satisfaction scores was $\overline{X} = 3.7$ with a standard deviation of 1.8. For depression proneness, $\overline{Y} = 3.8$ and $s_Y = 1.9$. Find (a) the least-squares regression line of depression proneness on body satisfaction, (b) predicted depression proneness scores as a function of body satisfaction scores, and (c) the standard error of estimate.

Solution   The problem requires finding values for the slope and Y-intercept of the regression line. Because r_{obs} is given, I find the slope using the correlational formula shown in Table 15–5.

Finding the Slope: The slope, b, of the regression line is found from r by

$$b = r\left(\frac{s_Y}{s_X}\right).$$

Substituting values of r_{obs}, s_X, and s_Y, I obtain

$$b = +.58\left(\frac{1.9}{1.8}\right) = +0.61.$$

Finding the Y-intercept: The Y-intercept is found from

$$a = \overline{Y} - b\overline{X}$$
$$= 3.8 - (+0.61)(3.7) = 1.54.$$

Obtaining the Regression Equation: The regression equation of depression proneness (Y) on body satisfaction (X) is given by

$$Y' = +0.61X + 1.54.$$

Obtaining Predicted Depression Proneness Scores (Y'): Depression proneness scores (Y') predicted from body satisfaction scores (X) are obtained by solving the regression equation for a value of X. For example, for a body satisfaction rating score of 1, the regression equation becomes

$$Y' = +0.61(1) + 1.54 = 2.15.$$

The depression proneness rating predicted from a body satisfaction rating of 1 is 2.15 or, rounding to one decimal place, 2.2.

Plotting the Regression Line: The regression line given by

$$Y' = +0.61X + 1.54$$

is plotted in Figure 15–9. Values of the predictor variable, body satisfaction (X), are placed on the abscissa, and values of the predicted variable, depression proneness score (Y'), are placed on the ordinate. The regression line is located on the graph by identifying the Y-intercept (1.54) and the coordinates of $\overline{X}, \overline{Y}$ (3.7 and 3.8, respectively) and drawing a straight line connecting these two points. The predicted depression proneness scores for each value of X are identified by the dots on the line.

Finding the Standard Error of Estimate: The $s_{Y \cdot X}$ is found by

$$s_{Y \cdot X} = s_Y \sqrt{\left[\frac{N_{\text{pairs}} - 1}{N_{\text{pairs}} - 2} \right] (1 - r_{\text{obs}}^2)}.$$

Substituting $s_Y = 1.9$, $N_{\text{pairs}} = 15$, and $r_{\text{obs}} = +.58$, I obtain

$$s_{Y \cdot X} = (1.9) \sqrt{\left[\frac{15 - 1}{15 - 2} \right] [1 - (+.58)^2]}$$

$$= (1.9) \sqrt{\left(\frac{14}{13} \right) (1 - .3364)}$$

$$= (1.9) \sqrt{(1.077)(.6636)}$$

$$= (1.9) \sqrt{0.7147}$$

$$= (1.9)(0.845)$$

$$= 1.6 \quad \text{rounded to one decimal place.}$$

FIGURE 15-9
The least-squares regression line for body image and depression proneness ratings. Predicted values of depression proneness for each body image rating are indicated by the dots on the regression line.

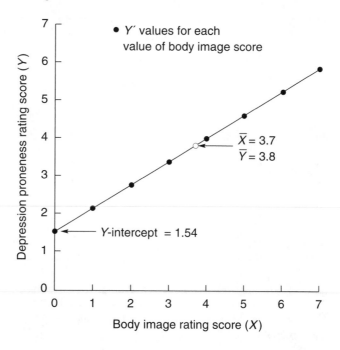

This $s_{Y \cdot X}$ is less than $s_Y = 1.9$. Knowing a person's body satisfaction score increases the accuracy of predicting depression proneness in comparison to using $\overline{Y} = 3.8$ as a predicted value for all subjects.

Example Problem 15-2

Finding a Regression Line and the Standard Error of Estimate with the Computational Formula

Problem
Example Problem 15–1 introduced the research of Mintz and Betz (1986) on the relationship of body satisfaction and depression proneness scores. They also obtained self-ratings of social self-esteem from their subjects. The self-esteem rating scales gave scores ranging from 20 (indicating low self-esteem) to 100 (indicating high self-esteem). Body satisfaction scores could range from 1 (indicating strong positive feelings toward one's body) to 7 (indicating strong negative feelings toward one's body). For slightly underweight females,

Mintz and Betz obtained a statistically significant correlation between body satisfaction (X) scores and social self-esteem (Y) scores of $r_{obs} = -.60$. Suppose in a replication of this study with 15 subjects that I obtained the following body satisfaction and social self-esteem scores:

Subject	Body Satisfaction: X	Self-esteem: Y
1	2	76
2	4	48
3	6	27
4	1	70
5	3	41
6	5	38
7	6	37
8	3	61
9	7	33
10	1	91
11	4	36
12	2	55
13	3	49
14	5	51
15	4	52

We want to find: (a) the least-squares regression line of social self-esteem scores on body satisfaction scores, (b) predicted self-esteem scores as a function of body satisfaction, (c) the value of $s_{Y \cdot X}$ from the residuals $Y - Y'$, and (d) the value of $s_{Y \cdot X}$ using the computational formula.

Solution   Table 15–10 provides the values necessary to find the information requested. In this table, the following values are given:

	Column
a	Body satisfaction scores (X) and the $\sum X$
b	Self-esteem scores (Y) and the $\sum Y$
c	Body satisfaction scores squared (X^2) and the $\sum X^2$
d	Self-esteem scores squared (Y^2) and the $\sum Y^2$
e	Cross products of the body satisfaction and self-esteem scores and the $\sum XY$
f	Values of Y' predicted from the regression line found
g	Residual for each self-esteem score

TABLE 15–10
Calculating the least-squares regression line, predicted scores, and residuals for self-esteem scores from body image scores.

	(a)	(b)	(c)	(d)	(e)	(f)	(g)
Subject	X	Y	X^2	Y^2	XY	Y'	$Y - Y'$
1	2	76	4	5,776	152	64.859	+11.141
2	4	48	16	2,304	192	48.837	−0.837
3	6	27	36	729	162	32.815	−5.815
4	1	70	1	4,900	70	72.870	−2.870
5	3	41	9	1,681	123	56.848	−15.848
6	5	38	25	1,444	190	40.826	−2.826
7	6	37	36	1,369	222	32.815	+4.185
8	3	61	9	3,721	183	56.848	+4.152
9	7	33	49	1,089	231	24.804	+8.196
10	1	91	1	8,281	91	72.870	+18.130
11	4	36	16	1,296	144	48.837	−12.837
12	2	55	4	3,025	110	64.859	−9.859
13	3	49	9	2,401	147	56.848	−7.848
14	5	51	25	2,601	255	40.826	+10.174
15	4	52	16	2,704	208	48.837	+3.163
Sums	56	765	256	43,321	2480		
Mean	3.73	51.00					
s	1.83	17.54					

Finding the Regression Line:

Calculating b:

$$\sum X = 56,$$

$$(\sum X)^2 = 56^2 = 3136,$$

$$\sum X^2 = 256,$$

$$\sum Y = 765,$$

$$\sum XY = 2480,$$

$$N_{\text{pairs}} = 15,$$

and

$$b = \frac{(N_{\text{pairs}})(\sum XY) - (\sum X)(\sum Y)}{(N_{\text{pairs}})(\sum X^2) - (\sum X)^2}.$$

Substituting numerical values,

$$b = \frac{(15)(2480) - (56)(765)}{(15)(256) - 3136}$$
$$= \frac{37,200 - 42,840}{3840 - 3136}$$
$$= \frac{-5640}{704}$$
$$= -8.011.$$

Calculating a: $\overline{X} = 3.73$ and $\overline{Y} = 51.00$. Substituting these values into $a = \overline{Y} - b\overline{X}$, I obtain

$$a = 51.00 - (-8.011)(3.73)$$
$$= 51.00 - (-29.881)$$
$$= 51.00 + 29.881$$
$$= 80.881.$$

Regression line: The regression line is given by

$$Y' = -8.011X + 80.881.$$

Predicted Self-esteem Scores: Predicted self-esteem scores from the regression equation are given in column f of the table. To minimize rounding error in finding $s_{Y \cdot X}$ from the residuals, the Y' values were carried to three decimal places.

$s_{Y \cdot X}$ **from the Residuals:** The residual values are presented in column g of the table. The value of $s_{Y \cdot X}$ is obtained from these residuals by

$$s_{Y \cdot X} = \sqrt{\frac{\sum (Y - Y')^2}{N_{\text{pairs}} - 2}}.$$

To obtain $\sum (Y - Y')^2$, each residual in column g is squared and the 15 squared values are summed. The $\sum (Y - Y')^2 = 1293.7380$. $N_{\text{pairs}} - 2 = 15 - 2 = 13$.
Substituting numerical values,

$$s_{Y \cdot X} = \sqrt{\frac{1293.7380}{13}}$$
$$= \sqrt{99.5183}$$
$$= 9.98.$$

$s_{Y \cdot X}$ **from the Computational Formula:** The computational formula is

$$s_{Y \cdot X} = \sqrt{\left[\frac{1}{N_{\text{pairs}}(N_{\text{pairs}} - 2)} \right] \left[N_{\text{pairs}} \sum Y^2 - \left(\sum Y \right)^2 - \frac{\left[N_{\text{pairs}} \left(\sum XY \right) - \left(\sum X \right) \left(\sum Y \right) \right]^2}{N_{\text{pairs}} \sum X^2 - \left(\sum X \right)^2} \right]}.$$

Substituting numerical values

$$s_{Y \cdot X} = \sqrt{\left[\frac{1}{(15)(13)}\right]\left[15(43{,}321) - (765)^2 - \frac{[(15)(2480) - (56)(765)]^2}{(15)(256) - (56)^2}\right]}$$

$$= \sqrt{\left[\frac{1}{195}\right]\left[649{,}815 - 585{,}225 - \frac{(37{,}200 - 42{,}840)^2}{3840 - 3136}\right]}$$

$$= \sqrt{\left[\frac{1}{195}\right]\left[64{,}590 - \frac{(-5640)^2}{704}\right]}$$

$$= \sqrt{\left(\frac{1}{195}\right)(64{,}590 - 45{,}184.091)}$$

$$= \sqrt{\left(\frac{1}{195}\right)19{,}405.909}$$

$$= \sqrt{99.517}$$

$$= 9.98.$$

The value of $s_{Y \cdot X}$ from this formula is the same as the value obtained using the definitional formula and residuals.

Conclusion: The regression equation

$$Y' = -8.011X + 80.881$$

allows prediction of self-esteem scores from body satisfaction scores with considerable reduction in the error of prediction. The value of $s_{Y \cdot X} = 9.98$, the average error associated with a predicted self-esteem score from the regression equation, is smaller than $s_Y = 17.54$, the average amount of error that is associated with using $\overline{Y}$ (i.e., 51.0) as the predicted value of self-esteem for all individuals.

Example Problem 15–3

Predicting Job Performance with a Regression Equation

Problem
A major aspect of industrial psychology is predicting the work success of applicants to business and governmental organizations. Regression analysis is often used to make these predictions. Applicants may take a work-related test, and scores from the test are used to predict potential success on the job. Consider a simple example. Suppose that a business gives job applicants a work-sample test. A work-sample test is a miniature version of

the job. Performance on the work-sample test (variable X) is used to predict actual job proficiency (Y') with the regression equation

$$Y' = +0.76X + 55.$$

The business runs a help-wanted ad and 12 applicants are given the work-sample test. They obtain the following scores.

Applicant	Work-sample Test Score: X
1	12
2	37
3	27
4	34
5	17
6	39
7	24
8	40
9	47
10	15
11	31
12	21

The company will not hire anyone whose predicted job proficiency is less than 75. Which applicants are eligible for hiring based on their work-sample test scores?

Solution   The solution requires applying the regression equation to each applicant's work-sample test score to obtain a predicted job-proficiency score. The predicted job-proficiency score for each applicant is shown next.

Applicant	Predicted Job-proficiency Score: Y'
1	64.1
2	83.1
3	75.5
4	80.8
5	67.9
6	84.6
7	73.2
8	85.4
9	90.7
10	66.4
11	78.6
12	71.0

The predicted scores of applicants 1, 5, 7, 10, and 12 are below the required predicted score of 75; hence these applicants would not be eligible for hiring. The scores of all other applicants are 75 or above; thus these applicants are eligible for hiring. The regression line for $Y' = +0.76X + 55$ is illustrated in Figure 15–10. Notice that a

FIGURE 15–10

The regression line $Y' = +0.76X + 55$ used to predict job proficiency (Y') from a work-sample test (X). Predicted values of job proficiency for work-sample scores are indicated by dots on the regression line.

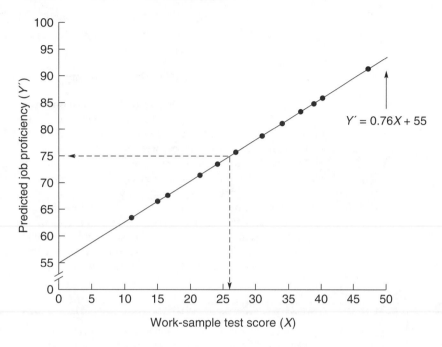

predicted job-proficiency score of 75 corresponds to a work-sample score of 26.3. Any work-sample test score below 26.3 leads to a predicted job-proficiency score of less than 75. Accordingly, applicants with work-sample test scores less than 26.3 would not be hired.

STATISTICS IN USE 15–1

Using a Regression Analysis to Describe the Relationship between Preference for Sexual Relations and Number of Children

One well-established finding in the study of marital relations is that the frequency of sexual relations declines as the length of a marriage increases. Indeed, Doddridge, Schumm, and Bergen (1987) cite a press clipping titled "Marriage Council Says Tying the Knot Can Ruin Sex Life" (p. 395). To investigate this phenomenon more fully, Doddridge et al. asked each partner of 30 married couples to indicate their preferred frequency of sexual relations on a weekly basis. They related this measure (the Y variable) to a variety of other measures such as the number of children in the marriage and the length of the marriage, among others. They found a significant negative correlation between number of children (the X variable) and preferred frequency of relations (the Y variable): r_{obs} for husbands equal to $-.37$ and r_{obs} for wives equal to $-.39$.

A linear regression analysis yielded an equation for preferred frequency of sexual relations (Y') as a function of number of children (X) as

$$Y' = -0.50X + 3.5$$

for husbands and

$$Y' = -0.39X + 2.7$$

for wives. Using these equations, we find that for husbands with no children the preferred frequency is 3.5 instances per week. With two children, however, the preferred frequency drops to 2.5 instances per week. Similar values for wives are 2.7 instances per week with no children and 1.9 instances per week with two children.

Doddridge et al. caution against wide generalization of these specific values because their sample of couples was not randomly selected from a population. Nevertheless, their research illustrates how linear regression analysis can be used to describe functional relationships between variables. We must be cautious, however, not to attribute causality to the relationships found. The regression equation simply describes the relationship between preferred frequency of sexual relations and number of children in the marriage. The limitations in reaching causal relationships that exist in correlational studies apply equally to linear regression analysis using two measured variables.

TESTING YOUR KNOWLEDGE 15-3

1. Personality attributes and performance of specific tasks are often related. For example, Gormly and Gormly (1986) correlated ratings of social introversion to performance on a block design test measuring spatial abilities. They found a statistically significant positive correlation: more socially introverted individuals created the required block designs more quickly. Suppose that you replicated this study rating subjects on a 9-point social introversion scale, where 1 indicates highly socially introverted and 9 indicates not at all socially introverted. The amount of time in seconds each subject took to create a particular design with nine colored blocks was recorded. The scores obtained for 12 subjects were as follows:

Subject	Introversion: (X)	Block Design Times: (Y)
1	6	217
2	3	230
3	9	315
4	1	224
5	4	271
6	2	198
7	3	256
8	5	263
9	8	321
10	7	289
11	8	265
12	6	291

The mean block design time was 261.67 seconds, with $sy = 38.82$ seconds. The r_{obs} for these scores is statistically significant at the .05 level. Using the computational formula for b, construct the regression line of block design on introversion scores.

    a. What is the slope of the regression line?

    b. What is the Y-intercept of the regression line?

    c. Write the equation for the regression line.

    d. Plot a scatterplot of the introversion and block design scores. Place the regression line on this plot.

    e. What is the predicted block design score (Y') for each introversion score?

    f. Use the Y' given to find the residual for each subject.

    g. Find the $SS_{Residual}$.

    h. Find $s_{Y \cdot X}$ using the $SS_{Residual}$.

    i. Compare $s_{Y \cdot X}$ to the s_Y, 38.82, for these scores. Does the use of the regression equation to predict block design scores from introversion scores reduce the error of prediction in comparison to using the mean block design score (i.e., 261.7 seconds) as the predicted value for all block design scores?

2. Bird watchers notice that many species spend a great deal of time scanning the environment. Elgar, McKay, and Woon (1986) observed house sparrows to find the relationship between amount of scanning and feeding rate. They found a statistically significant negative correlation between the two variables. Suppose that you replicated this study observing 15 house sparrows. You recorded the number of scans of the environment each bird made per minute (variable X) and the number of pecks at food each bird made per minute (variable Y) and found the mean scan rate $(\overline{X})$ was 26.2 scans per minute with $s_X = 8.7$. The mean pecks per minute $(\overline{Y})$ was 13.3 with $s_Y = 4.5$. The r_{obs} between the two variables was $-.84$. Using the correlational formula to find b, construct the regression line of pecking rate (Y) on scans per minute (X).

    a. What is the slope of the regression line?

    b. What is the Y-intercept of the regression line?

    c. Write the equation for the regression line.

    d. What is the predicted pecking rate for a scan rate of 41 scans per minute? For 18 scans per minute?

Multiple Regression

Regression analysis is widely used in the behavioral sciences and in an array of practical settings. While almost all our problems have presented both X and Y variables, in practice, only the X variable and a regression equation for predicting Y from this X may be known, the regression equation having been developed from previous instances where both X and Y were known. For example, a heating fuel dealer may predict how much fuel oil she needs to order for a subsequent week (variable Y) based on the mean daily temperature of the previous week (variable X). Or a retailer may attempt to predict sales volume (variable Y) from the amount of money spent on advertising (variable X). Each of our examples used only one X variable to predict the Y variable. In practice, however, regression equations typically are more complex than those that I introduced and use several X variables to predict Y. This

Multiple regression:
Predicting the value of Y scores using several X variables.

approach is called **multiple regression** because multiple predictors are used. For example, an employer may want to predict potential employee performance as a function of an aptitude test score, a score on a standardized interview, and a score on a work-sample test. The general regression equation for representing this approach is

$$Y' = b_1X_1 + b_2X_2 + b_3X_3 + a,$$

where Y' is the predicted job performance; X_1, X_2, and X_3 are predictor variables (in this example, X_1 is the score on the aptitude test, X_2 is the score on the standardized interview, and X_3 is the score on the work-sample test); b_1, b_2, and b_3 are regression coefficients for X_1, X_2, and X_3, respectively; and a is the Y-intercept.

The regression coefficients weight each X variable in the prediction of Y. For example, if $b_1 = +0.18$, $b_2 = +0.10$, $b_3 = +0.34$, and $a = 30.3$, then the equation becomes

$$Y' = +0.18X_1 + 0.10X_2 + 0.34X_3 + 30.3.$$

If an applicant obtains an aptitude test score of 75, an interview score of 20, and a work-sample test score of 90, then

$$Y' = (0.18)(75) + (0.10)(20) + (0.34)(90) + 30.3$$
$$= 13.5 + 2.0 + 30.6 + 30.3 = 76.4.$$

Multiple regression equations are widely used for prediction in the behavioral sciences. Friedman et al. (1993), for example, used seven dimensions of childhood personality—sociability, physical energy, cheerfulness, conscientiousness, motivation, permanency of mood, and intelligence—to predict longevity. And health psychologists predict the risk of cardiovascular disease from a person's gender, smoking behavior, measures of life-style, and dietary habits. Obtaining the regression coefficients for these complex equations, however, requires knowledge beyond the scope of this introductory chapter.

SUMMARY

- In a linear relation, each time that variable X changes by 1 unit there is a constant change in variable Y.
- The general equation of a straight line is given by $Y = bX + a$.
- The slope, b, is defined as

$$b = \frac{\text{change in value of } Y}{\text{change in value of } X}.$$

- The Y-intercept, a, is the value of Y when $X = 0$.
- The general equation of a straight line may be used to predict Y scores from known X scores: $Y' = bX + a$. Y' represents the predicted value of Y.
- The residual, $Y - Y'$, is the difference between an obtained Y score and Y' predicted from X.
- A least-squares regression line minimizes the value of the sum of the squared residuals.
- The standard error of estimate is found by

$$s_{Y \cdot X} = \sqrt{\frac{SS_{\text{Residual}}}{N_{\text{pairs}} - 2}}$$

or

$$s_{Y \cdot X} = \sqrt{\frac{\sum (Y - Y')^2}{N_{\text{pairs}} - 2}}.$$

- The standard error of estimate indicates the average amount of error when predicting Y scores from X.
- Multiple regression involves using several X variables to predict variable Y.

KEY TERMS AND SYMBOLS

a	regression coefficient	SS_{Residual}
b	regression line	standard error of estimate
least-squares regression line	residual	Y-intercept
linear relation	$s_{Y \cdot X}$	Y'
multiple regression	slope of a line	$Y - Y'$

REVIEW QUESTIONS

1. Jamie received her midterm grade in her statistics class. Her instructor said that for a previous semester the following midterm and final examination grades were obtained by 10 students in the class.

	Examination	
Student	Midterm: X	Final: Y
1	87	84
2	89	91
3	97	96
4	80	87
5	73	66
6	85	90
7	81	79
8	74	80
9	80	89
10	89	86

   a. Find the slope of the least-squares regression line for predicting final exam grades from midterm grades using the computational formula.

   b. The r_{obs} for these scores is $+.781$, $s_X = 7.37$, and $s_Y = 8.34$. Find b using the correlational formula.

   c. Find the equation of the least-squares regression line for predicting Y from X for these scores.

   d. Jamie received a 77 on her midterm examination. Based on the regression line found in part c, what is her predicted final examination score?

   e. What is the value of $s_{Y \cdot X}$ for this regression line?

2. An investigator observed 12 students on the amount of time playing video games per week (variable X) and correlated this time with their semester grade-point averages (variable Y). For a range of 0 to 15 hours per week of video-game playing, r_{obs} was $-.632$ ($p < .05$). The $s_X = 4.10$ hours and $s_Y = 0.75$. The Y-intercept of the regression line was 3.23.

   a. Find the least-squares regression line for predicting grade-point average from video-game playing time.

   b. Brian plays video games about 3 hours per week. What is his predicted grade-point average?

   c. The mean video-game playing time in the sample observed was 5.1 hours per week. What is the mean grade-point average for the sample?

3. One study found a linear relationship between amount of smoking by a pregnant woman and the amount of weight loss of the neonate ("Birth Weight," 1986). For each cigarette smoked per day during pregnancy by the mother the baby's birth weight is reduced by 4.3 ounces. Thus, if a mother smoked an average of two cigarettes per day during pregnancy, the baby's birth weight would be reduced by 8.6 ounces. Assume that if the pregnant mother does not smoke the average weight of the neonate is 128 ounces.

a. Write the equation for the linear relationship for these data. (*Hint:* Both the slope and the Y-intercept are given.)

b. Plot the linear regression line on a sheet of graph paper. Place the number of cigarettes smoked (X) on the abscissa.

c. What is the predicted birth weight of a baby whose mother smoked the following number of cigarettes per day during pregnancy?

$$0 \quad 1 \quad 5 \quad 8 \quad 10 \quad 13 \quad 20$$

4. In Chapter 14, Review Question 1, I gave the following values of percentage of body fat and average golf scores (in strokes) for 12 professional female golfers.

Golfer	Body Fat: X	Golf Score: Y
1	20.1	70
2	28.9	77
3	25.4	75
4	19.6	67
5	36.3	79
6	22.9	73
7	26.5	74
8	30.7	72
9	29.8	83
10	33.2	75
11	24.1	68
12	27.3	75

a. Find the equation for the regression of golf score (Y) on percentage of body fat (X) for these scores.

b. What is the predicted golf score for each player as a function of percentage of body fat?

c. Plot a scatterplot of the percentage of body fat (on the abscissa) and average golf score (on the ordinate). Place the regression line on this plot also.

d. Compare each predicted score with the obtained score. Do the predicted scores demonstrate regression to the mean? Explain your answer.

5. Exercise 2 of Testing Your Knowledge 15–3 presented a study on the relationship of the number of scans per minute (X) and number of pecks per minute (Y) for 15 house sparrows. Suppose you made similar observations with 13 wrens and obtained the following scores.

Bird	Scans: X	Pecks: Y
1	29	12
2	34	8
3	24	14
4	14	20
5	37	11
6	22	13
7	11	23
8	33	9
9	24	11
10	30	14
11	36	9
12	20	23
13	32	7

a. What is the slope of the regression line?

b. What is the Y-intercept of the regression line?

c. Write the equation for the regression line.

d. Plot a scatterplot of the scans and pecks scores. Place the regression line on this plot.

e. Use the computational formula to find $s_{Y \cdot X}$ for this set of scores.

f. Compare $s_{Y \cdot X}$ to $s_Y = 5.41$ for these scores. Does use of the regression equation to predict pecks from scans reduce the error of prediction in comparison to using the mean number of scans (i.e., 13.4) as the predicted value for all scan scores?

6. A company uses a score on a standardized interview to predict work performance of job applicants. The regression equation used is $Y' = +1.2X + 18$, where Y' is the predicted job performance and X is the job applicant's score on the standardized interview. The company will hire only applicants whose predicted job performance is 60 or better. The standardized interview scores of eight applicants are as follows. Which of the applicants will the company hire?

Applicant	Standardized Interview Score: X
Dianne	31
Rodrigo	36
Colin	30
Maria	41
Ruben	39
Luke	29
Holly	27
Blythe	44

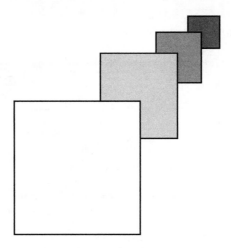

Appendixes

Appendix A
Statistical Tables

TABLE A-1

Proportions of area under the standard normal distribution.

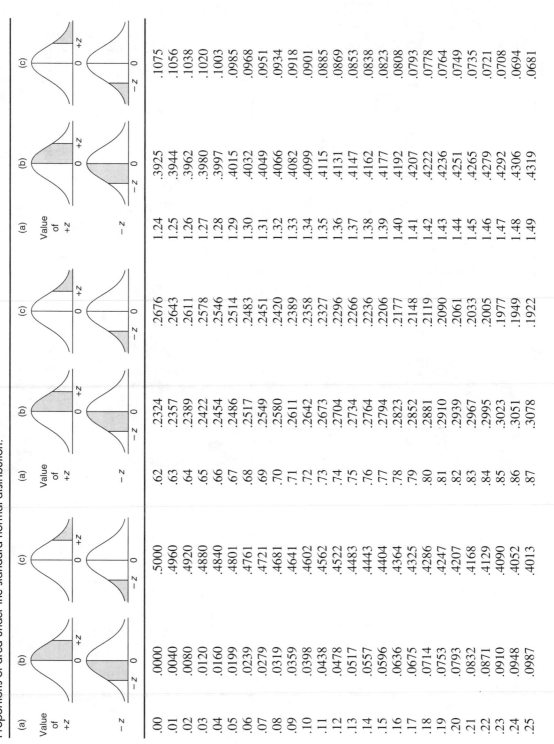

(a) Value of +z / −z	(b)	(c)	(a) Value of +z / −z	(b)	(c)	(a) Value of +z / −z	(b)	(c)
.00	.0000	.5000	.62	.2324	.2676	1.24	.3925	.1075
.01	.0040	.4960	.63	.2357	.2643	1.25	.3944	.1056
.02	.0080	.4920	.64	.2389	.2611	1.26	.3962	.1038
.03	.0120	.4880	.65	.2422	.2578	1.27	.3980	.1020
.04	.0160	.4840	.66	.2454	.2546	1.28	.3997	.1003
.05	.0199	.4801	.67	.2486	.2514	1.29	.4015	.0985
.06	.0239	.4761	.68	.2517	.2483	1.30	.4032	.0968
.07	.0279	.4721	.69	.2549	.2451	1.31	.4049	.0951
.08	.0319	.4681	.70	.2580	.2420	1.32	.4066	.0934
.09	.0359	.4641	.71	.2611	.2389	1.33	.4082	.0918
.10	.0398	.4602	.72	.2642	.2358	1.34	.4099	.0901
.11	.0438	.4562	.73	.2673	.2327	1.35	.4115	.0885
.12	.0478	.4522	.74	.2704	.2296	1.36	.4131	.0869
.13	.0517	.4483	.75	.2734	.2266	1.37	.4147	.0853
.14	.0557	.4443	.76	.2764	.2236	1.38	.4162	.0838
.15	.0596	.4404	.77	.2794	.2206	1.39	.4177	.0823
.16	.0636	.4364	.78	.2823	.2177	1.40	.4192	.0808
.17	.0675	.4325	.79	.2852	.2148	1.41	.4207	.0793
.18	.0714	.4286	.80	.2881	.2119	1.42	.4222	.0778
.19	.0753	.4247	.81	.2910	.2090	1.43	.4236	.0764
.20	.0793	.4207	.82	.2939	.2061	1.44	.4251	.0749
.21	.0832	.4168	.83	.2967	.2033	1.45	.4265	.0735
.22	.0871	.4129	.84	.2995	.2005	1.46	.4279	.0721
.23	.0910	.4090	.85	.3023	.1977	1.47	.4292	.0708
.24	.0948	.4052	.86	.3051	.1949	1.48	.4306	.0694
.25	.0987	.4013	.87	.3078	.1922	1.49	.4319	.0681

TABLE A 1 continued

(a) Value of +z / −z	(b)	(c)	(a) Value of +z / −z	(b)	(c)	(a) Value of +z / −z	(b)	(c)
.26	.1026	.3974	.88	.3106	.1894	1.50	.4332	.0668
.27	.1064	.3936	.89	.3133	.1867	1.51	.4345	.0655
.28	.1103	.3897	.90	.3159	.1841	1.52	.4357	.0643
.29	.1141	.3859	.91	.3186	.1814	1.53	.4370	.0630
.30	.1179	.3821	.92	.3212	.1788	1.54	.4382	.0618
.31	.1217	.3783	.93	.3238	.1762	1.55	.4394	.0606
.32	.1255	.3745	.94	.3264	.1736	1.56	.4406	.0594
.33	.1293	.3707	.95	.3289	.1711	1.57	.4418	.0582
.34	.1331	.3669	.96	.3315	.1685	1.58	.4429	.0571
.35	.1368	.3632	.97	.3340	.1660	1.59	.4441	.0559
.36	.1406	.3594	.98	.3365	.1635	1.60	.4452	.0548
.37	.1443	.3557	.99	.3389	.1611	1.61	.4463	.0537
.38	.1480	.3520	1.00	.3413	.1587	1.62	.4474	.0526
.39	.1517	.3483	1.01	.3438	.1562	1.63	.4484	.0516
.40	.1554	.3446	1.02	.3461	.1539	1.64	.4495	.0505
.41	.1591	.3409	1.03	.3485	.1515	1.65	.4505	.0495
.42	.1628	.3372	1.04	.3508	.1492	1.66	.4515	.0485
.43	.1664	.3336	1.05	.3531	.1469	1.67	.4525	.0475
.44	.1700	.3300	1.06	.3554	.1446	1.68	.4535	.0465
.45	.1736	.3264	1.07	.3577	.1423	1.69	.4545	.0455
.46	.1772	.3228	1.08	.3599	.1401	1.70	.4554	.0446
.47	.1808	.3192	1.09	.3621	.1379	1.71	.4564	.0436
.48	.1844	.3156	1.10	.3643	.1357	1.72	.4573	.0427
.49	.1879	.3121	1.11	.3665	.1335	1.73	.4582	.0418
.50	.1915	.3085	1.12	.3686	.1314	1.74	.4591	.0409
.51	.1950	.3050	1.13	.3708	.1292	1.75	.4599	.0401
.52	.1985	.3015	1.14	.3729	.1271	1.76	.4608	.0392
.53	.2019	.2981	1.15	.3749	.1251	1.77	.4616	.0384
.54	.2054	.2946	1.16	.3770	.1230	1.78	.4625	.0375

55	.2088	.2912	1.17	.3790	.1210	1.79	.4633	.0367
.56	.2123	.2877	1.18	.3810	.1190	1.80	.4641	.0359
.57	.2157	.2843	1.19	.3830	.1170	1.81	.4649	.0351
.58	.2190	.2810	1.20	.3849	.1151	1.82	.4656	.0344
.59	.2224	.2776	1.21	.3869	.1131	1.83	.4664	.0336
.60	.2257	.2743	1.22	.3888	.1112	1.84	.4671	.0329
.61	.2291	.2709	1.23	.3907	.1093	1.85	.4678	.0322
1.86	.4686	.0314	2.48	.4934	.0066	3.10	.4990	.0010
1.87	.4693	.0307	2.49	.4936	.0064	3.11	.4991	.0009
1.88	.4699	.0301	2.50	.4938	.0062	3.12	.4991	.0009
1.89	.4706	.0294	2.51	.4940	.0060	3.13	.4991	.0009
1.90	.4713	.0287	2.52	.4941	.0059	3.14	.4992	.0008
1.91	.4719	.0281	2.53	.4943	.0057	3.15	.4992	.0008
1.92	.4726	.0274	2.54	.4945	.0055	3.16	.4992	.0008
1.93	.4732	.0268	2.55	.4946	.0054	3.17	.4992	.0008
1.94	.4738	.0262	2.56	.4948	.0052	3.18	.4993	.0007
1.95	.4744	.0256	2.57	.4949	.0051	3.19	.4993	.0007
1.96	.4750	.0250	2.58	.4951	.0049	3.20	.4993	.0007
1.97	.4756	.0244	2.59	.4952	.0048	3.21	.4993	.0007
1.98	.4761	.0239	2.60	.4953	.0047	3.22	.4994	.0006
1.99	.4767	.0233	2.61	.4955	.0045	3.23	.4994	.0006
2.00	.4772	.0228	2.62	.4956	.0044	3.24	.4994	.0006
2.01	.4778	.0222	2.63	.4957	.0043	3.25	.4994	.0006
2.02	.4783	.0217	2.64	.4959	.0041	3.26	.4994	.0006
2.03	.4788	.0212	2.65	.4960	.0040	3.27	.4995	.0005
2.04	.4793	.0207	2.66	.4961	.0039	3.28	.4995	.0005
2.05	.4798	.0202	2.67	.4962	.0038	3.29	.4995	.0005
2.06	.4803	.0197	2.68	.4963	.0037	3.30	.4995	.0005
2.07	.4808	.0192	2.69	.4964	.0036	3.31	.4995	.0005
2.08	.4812	.0188	2.70	.4965	.0035	3.32	.4995	.0005
2.09	.4817	.0183	2.71	.4966	.0034	3.33	.4996	.0004
2.10	.4821	.0179	2.72	.4967	.0033	3.34	.4996	.0004
2.11	.4826	.0174	2.73	.4968	.0032	3.35	.4996	.0004
2.12	.4830	.0170	2.74	.4969	.0031	3.36	.4996	.0004
2.13	.4834	.0166	2.75	.4970	.0030	3.37	.4996	.0004
2.14	.4838	.0162	2.76	.4971	.0029	3.38	.4996	.0004

z	ordinate	area	z	area	ordinate	z	area	ordinate
2.15	.0158	.4842	2.77	.4972	.0028	3.39	.4997	.0003
2.16	.0154	.4846	2.78	.4973	.0027	3.40	.4997	.0003
2.17	.0150	.4850	2.79	.4974	.0026	3.41	.4997	.0003
2.18	.0146	.4854	2.80	.4974	.0026	3.42	.4997	.0003
2.19	.0143	.4857	2.81	.4975	.0025	3.43	.4997	.0003
2.20	.0139	.4861	2.82	.4976	.0024	3.44	.4997	.0003
2.21	.0136	.4864	2.83	.4977	.0023	3.45	.4997	.0003
2.22	.0132	.4868	2.84	.4977	.0023	3.46	.4997	.0003
2.23	.0129	.4871	2.85	.4978	.0022	3.47	.4997	.0003
2.24	.0125	.4875	2.86	.4979	.0021	3.48	.4997	.0003
2.25	.0122	.4878	2.87	.4979	.0021	3.49	.4998	.0002
2.26	.0119	.4881	2.88	.4980	.0020	3.50	.4998	.0002
2.27	.0116	.4884	2.89	.4981	.0019	3.51	.4998	.0002
2.28	.0113	.4887	2.90	.4981	.0019	3.52	.4998	.0002
2.29	.0110	.4890	2.91	.4982	.0018	3.53	.4998	.0002
2.30	.0107	.4893	2.92	.4982	.0018	3.54	.4998	.0002
2.31	.0104	.4896	2.93	.4983	.0017	3.55	.4998	.0002
2.32	.0102	.4898	2.94	.4984	.0016	3.56	.4998	.0002
2.33	.0099	.4901	2.95	.4984	.0016	3.57	.4998	.0002
2.34	.0096	.4904	2.96	.4985	.0015	3.58	.4998	.0002
2.35	.0094	.4906	2.97	.4985	.0015	3.59	.4998	.0002
2.36	.0091	.4909	2.98	.4986	.0014	3.60	.4998	.0002
2.37	.0089	.4911	2.99	.4986	.0014	3.61	.4998	.0002
2.38	.0087	.4913	3.00	.4987	.0013	3.62	.4999	.0001
2.39	.0084	.4916	3.01	.4987	.0013	3.63	.4999	.0001
2.40	.0082	.4918	3.02	.4987	.0013	3.64	.4999	.0001
2.41	.0080	.4920	3.03	.4988	.0012	3.65	.4999	.0001
2.42	.0078	.4922	3.04	.4988	.0012	3.66	.4999	.0001
2.43	.0075	.4925	3.05	.4989	.0011	3.67	.4999	.0001
2.44	.0073	.4927	3.06	.4989	.0011	3.68	.4999	.0001
2.45	.0071	.4929	3.07	.4989	.0011	3.69	.4999	.0001
2.46	.0069	.4931	3.08	.4990	.0010	3.70	.4999	.0001
2.47	.0068	.4932	3.09	.4990	.0010			

Excerpted and adapted from Table II.1, The Normal Probability Function and Related Functions. *CRC Handbook of Tables for Probability and Statistics* (2nd ed.). Copyright 1968, CRC Press, Inc., Boca Raton, Florida. Used by permission.

TABLE A–2

Critical values of the t distribution for $\alpha = .05$ and $\alpha = .01$. A value of $t_{obs}(df)$ equal to or greater than the tabled value is statistically significant at the α level selected.

	Two-tailed Test	
df	$\alpha = .05$	$\alpha = .01$
1	12.706	63.657
2	4.303	9.925
3	3.182	5.841
4	2.776	4.604
5	2.571	4.032
6	2.447	3.707
7	2.365	3.499
8	2.306	3.355
9	2.262	3.250
10	2.228	3.169
11	2.201	3.106
12	2.179	3.055
13	2.160	3.012
14	2.145	2.977
15	2.131	2.947
16	2.120	2.921
17	2.110	2.898
18	2.101	2.878
19	2.093	2.861
20	2.086	2.845
21	2.080	2.831
22	2.074	2.819
23	2.069	2.807
24	2.064	2.797
25	2.060	2.787
26	2.056	2.779
27	2.052	2.771
28	2.048	2.763
29	2.045	2.756
30	2.042	2.750
40	2.021	2.704
60	2.000	2.660
120	1.980	2.617
∞	1.960	2.576

	One-tailed Test	
df	α = .05	α = .01
1	6.314	31.821
2	2.920	6.965
3	2.353	4.541
4	2.132	3.747
5	2.015	3.365
6	1.943	3.143
7	1.895	2.998
8	1.860	2.896
9	1.833	2.821
10	1.812	2.764
11	1.796	2.718
12	1.782	2.681
13	1.771	2.650
14	1.761	2.624
15	1.753	2.602
16	1.746	2.583
17	1.740	2.567
18	1.734	2.552
19	1.729	2.539
20	1.725	2.528
21	1.721	2.518
22	1.717	2.508
23	1.714	2.500
24	1.711	2.492
25	1.708	2.485
26	1.706	2.479
27	1.703	2.473
28	1.701	2.467
29	1.699	2.462
30	1.697	2.457
40	1.684	2.423
60	1.671	2.390
120	1.658	2.358
∞	1.645	2.326

Reprinted with permission from Table IV.1, Percentage Points, Student's *t*-Distribution, *CRC Handbook of Tables for Probability and Statistics* (2nd ed.). Copyright 1968, CRC Press, Inc., Boca Raton, Florida.

TABLE A–3a

Critical values of the F distribution for a = .05. A value of F_{obs} ($df_{numerator}$, $df_{denominator}$) equal to or greater than the tabled value is statistically significant at the .05 significance level.

Degrees of Freedom for the Denominator	Degrees of Freedom for the Numerator																		
	1	2	3	4	5	6	7	8	9	10	12	15	20	24	30	40	60	120	∞
1	161.4	199.5	215.7	224.6	230.2	234.0	236.8	238.9	240.5	241.9	243.9	245.9	248.0	249.1	250.1	251.1	252.2	253.3	254.3
2	18.51	19.00	19.16	19.25	19.30	19.33	19.35	19.37	19.38	19.40	19.41	19.43	19.45	19.45	19.46	19.47	19.48	19.49	19.50
3	10.13	9.55	9.28	9.12	9.01	8.94	8.89	8.85	8.81	8.79	8.74	8.70	8.66	8.64	8.62	8.59	8.57	8.55	8.53
4	7.71	6.94	6.59	6.39	6.26	6.16	6.09	6.04	6.00	5.96	5.91	5.86	5.80	5.77	5.75	5.72	5.69	5.66	5.63
5	6.61	5.79	5.41	5.19	5.05	4.95	4.88	4.82	4.77	4.74	4.68	4.62	4.56	4.53	4.50	4.46	4.43	4.40	4.36
6	5.99	5.14	4.76	4.53	4.39	4.28	4.21	4.15	4.10	4.06	4.00	3.94	3.87	3.84	3.81	3.77	3.74	3.70	3.67
7	5.59	4.74	4.35	4.12	3.97	3.87	3.79	3.73	3.68	3.64	3.57	3.51	3.44	3.41	3.38	3.34	3.30	3.27	3.23
8	5.32	4.46	4.07	3.84	3.69	3.58	3.50	3.44	3.39	3.35	3.28	3.22	3.15	3.12	3.08	3.04	3.01	2.97	2.93
9	5.12	4.26	3.86	3.63	3.48	3.37	3.29	3.23	3.18	3.14	3.07	3.01	2.94	2.90	2.86	2.83	2.79	2.75	2.71
10	4.96	4.10	3.71	3.48	3.33	3.22	3.14	3.07	3.02	2.98	2.91	2.85	2.77	2.74	2.70	2.66	2.62	2.58	2.54
11	4.84	3.98	3.59	3.36	3.20	3.09	3.01	2.95	2.90	2.85	2.79	2.72	2.65	2.61	2.57	2.53	2.49	2.45	2.40
12	4.75	3.88	3.49	3.26	3.11	3.00	2.91	2.85	2.80	2.75	2.69	2.62	2.54	2.51	2.47	2.43	2.38	2.34	2.30
13	4.67	3.81	3.41	3.18	3.03	2.92	2.83	2.77	2.71	2.67	2.60	2.53	2.46	2.42	2.38	2.34	2.30	2.25	2.21
14	4.60	3.74	3.34	3.11	2.96	2.85	2.76	2.70	2.65	2.60	2.53	2.46	2.39	2.35	2.31	2.27	2.22	2.18	2.13
15	4.54	3.68	3.29	3.06	2.90	2.79	2.71	2.64	2.59	2.54	2.48	2.40	2.33	2.29	2.25	2.20	2.16	2.11	2.07
16	4.49	3.63	3.24	3.01	2.85	2.74	2.66	2.59	2.54	2.49	2.42	2.35	2.28	2.24	2.19	2.15	2.11	2.06	2.01
17	4.45	3.59	3.20	2.96	2.81	2.70	2.61	2.55	2.49	2.45	2.38	2.31	2.23	2.19	2.15	2.10	2.06	2.01	1.96
18	4.41	3.55	3.16	2.93	2.77	2.66	2.58	2.51	2.46	2.41	2.34	2.27	2.19	2.15	2.11	2.06	2.02	1.97	1.92
19	4.38	3.52	3.13	2.90	2.74	2.63	2.54	2.48	2.42	2.38	2.31	2.23	2.16	2.11	2.07	2.03	1.98	1.93	1.88
20	4.35	3.49	3.10	2.87	2.71	2.60	2.51	2.45	2.39	2.35	2.28	2.20	2.12	2.08	2.04	1.99	1.95	1.90	1.84
21	4.32	3.47	3.07	2.84	2.68	2.57	2.49	2.42	2.37	2.32	2.25	2.18	2.10	2.05	2.01	1.96	1.92	1.87	1.81
22	4.30	3.44	3.05	2.82	2.66	2.55	2.46	2.40	2.34	2.30	2.23	2.15	2.07	2.03	1.98	1.94	1.89	1.84	1.78
23	4.28	3.42	3.03	2.80	2.64	2.53	2.44	2.37	2.32	2.27	2.20	2.13	2.05	2.01	1.96	1.91	1.86	1.81	1.76
24	4.26	3.40	3.01	2.78	2.62	2.51	2.42	2.36	2.30	2.25	2.18	2.11	2.03	1.98	1.94	1.89	1.84	1.79	1.73
25	4.24	3.39	2.99	2.76	2.60	2.49	2.40	2.34	2.28	2.24	2.16	2.09	2.01	1.96	1.92	1.87	1.82	1.77	1.71
26	4.23	3.37	2.98	2.74	2.59	2.47	2.39	2.32	2.27	2.22	2.15	2.07	1.99	1.95	1.90	1.85	1.80	1.75	1.69
27	4.21	3.35	2.96	2.73	2.57	2.46	2.37	2.31	2.25	2.20	2.13	2.06	1.97	1.93	1.88	1.84	1.79	1.73	1.67
28	4.20	3.34	2.95	2.71	2.56	2.45	2.36	2.29	2.24	2.19	2.12	2.04	1.96	1.91	1.87	1.82	1.77	1.71	1.65
29	4.18	3.33	2.93	2.70	2.55	2.43	2.35	2.28	2.22	2.18	2.10	2.03	1.94	1.90	1.85	1.81	1.75	1.70	1.64
30	4.17	3.32	2.92	2.69	2.53	2.42	2.33	2.27	2.21	2.16	2.09	2.01	1.93	1.89	1.84	1.79	1.74	1.68	1.62
40	4.08	3.23	2.84	2.61	2.45	2.34	2.25	2.18	2.12	2.08	2.00	1.92	1.84	1.79	1.74	1.69	1.64	1.58	1.51
60	4.00	3.15	2.76	2.53	2.37	2.25	2.17	2.10	2.04	1.99	1.92	1.84	1.75	1.70	1.65	1.59	1.53	1.47	1.39
120	3.92	3.07	2.68	2.45	2.29	2.17	2.09	2.02	1.96	1.91	1.83	1.75	1.66	1.61	1.55	1.50	1.43	1.35	1.25
∞	3.84	3.00	2.60	2.37	2.21	2.10	2.01	1.94	1.88	1.83	1.75	1.67	1.57	1.52	1.46	1.39	1.32	1.22	1.00

Reprinted with permission from Table VI.1, Percentage Points, F-Distribution, *CRC Handbook of Tables for Probability and Statistics* (2nd ed.). Copyright 1968, CRC Press, Inc., Boca Raton, Florida.

TABLE A–3b

Critical values of the *F* distribution for a = .01. A value of F_{obs} ($df_{numerator}$, $df_{denominator}$) equal to or greater than the tabled value is statistically significant at the .01 significance level.

Degrees of Freedom for the Denominator	Degrees of Freedom for the Numerator																		
	1	*2*	*3*	*4*	*5*	*6*	*7*	*8*	*9*	*10*	*12*	*15*	*20*	*24*	*30*	*40*	*60*	*120*	¥
1	4052	4999.5	5403	5625	5764	5859	5928	5982	6022	6056	6106	6157	6209	6235	6261	6287	6313	6339	6366
2	98.50	99.00	99.17	99.25	99.30	99.33	99.36	99.37	99.39	99.40	99.42	99.43	99.45	99.46	99.47	99.47	99.48	99.49	99.50
3	34.12	30.82	29.46	28.71	28.24	27.91	27.67	27.49	27.35	27.23	27.05	26.87	26.69	26.60	26.50	26.41	26.32	26.22	26.13
4	21.20	18.00	16.69	15.98	15.52	15.21	14.98	14.80	14.66	14.55	14.37	14.20	14.02	13.93	13.84	13.75	13.65	13.56	13.46
5	16.26	13.27	12.06	11.39	10.97	10.67	10.46	10.29	10.16	10.05	9.89	9.72	9.55	9.47	9.38	9.29	9.20	9.11	9.02
6	13.75	10.92	9.78	9.15	8.75	8.47	8.26	8.10	7.98	7.87	7.72	7.56	7.40	7.31	7.23	7.14	7.06	6.97	6.88
7	12.25	9.55	8.45	7.85	7.46	7.19	6.99	6.84	6.72	6.62	6.47	6.31	6.16	6.07	5.99	5.91	5.82	5.74	5.65
8	11.26	8.65	7.59	7.01	6.63	6.37	6.18	6.03	5.91	5.81	5.67	5.52	5.36	5.28	5.20	5.12	5.03	4.95	4.86
9	10.56	8.02	6.99	6.42	6.06	5.80	5.61	5.47	5.35	5.26	5.11	4.96	4.81	4.73	4.65	4.57	4.48	4.40	4.31
10	10.04	7.56	6.55	5.99	5.64	5.39	5.20	5.06	4.94	4.85	4.71	4.56	4.41	4.33	4.25	4.17	4.08	4.00	3.91
11	9.65	7.21	6.22	5.67	5.32	5.07	4.89	4.74	4.63	4.54	4.40	4.25	4.10	4.02	3.94	3.86	3.78	3.69	3.60
12	9.33	6.93	5.95	5.41	5.06	4.82	4.64	4.50	4.39	4.30	4.16	4.01	3.86	3.78	3.70	3.62	3.54	3.45	3.36
13	9.07	6.70	5.74	5.21	4.86	4.62	4.44	4.30	4.19	4.10	3.96	3.82	3.66	3.59	3.51	3.43	3.34	3.25	3.17
14	8.86	6.51	5.56	5.04	4.69	4.46	4.28	4.14	4.03	3.94	3.80	3.66	3.51	3.43	3.35	3.27	3.18	3.09	3.00
15	8.68	6.36	5.42	4.89	4.56	4.32	4.14	4.00	3.89	3.80	3.67	3.52	3.37	3.29	3.21	3.13	3.05	2.96	2.87
16	8.53	6.23	5.29	4.77	4.44	4.20	4.03	3.89	3.78	3.69	3.55	3.41	3.26	3.18	3.10	3.02	2.93	2.84	2.75
17	8.40	6.11	5.18	4.67	4.34	4.10	3.93	3.79	3.68	3.59	3.46	3.31	3.16	3.08	3.00	2.92	2.83	2.75	2.65
18	8.29	6.01	5.09	4.58	4.25	4.01	3.84	3.71	3.60	3.51	3.37	3.23	3.08	3.00	2.92	2.84	2.75	2.66	2.57
19	8.18	5.93	5.01	4.50	4.17	3.94	3.77	3.63	3.52	3.43	3.30	3.15	3.00	2.92	2.84	2.76	2.67	2.58	2.49
20	8.10	5.85	4.94	4.43	4.10	3.87	3.70	3.56	3.46	3.37	3.23	3.09	2.94	2.86	2.78	2.69	2.61	2.52	2.42
21	8.02	5.78	4.87	4.37	4.04	3.81	3.64	3.51	3.40	3.31	3.17	3.03	2.88	2.80	2.72	2.64	2.55	2.46	2.36
22	7.95	5.72	4.82	4.31	3.99	3.76	3.59	3.45	3.35	3.26	3.12	2.98	2.83	2.75	2.67	2.58	2.50	2.40	2.31
23	7.88	5.66	4.76	4.26	3.94	3.71	3.54	3.41	3.30	3.21	3.07	2.93	2.78	2.70	2.62	2.54	2.45	2.35	2.26
24	7.82	5.61	4.72	4.22	3.90	3.67	3.50	3.36	3.26	3.17	3.03	2.89	2.74	2.66	2.58	2.49	2.40	2.31	2.21
25	7.77	5.57	4.68	4.18	3.85	3.63	3.46	3.32	3.22	3.13	2.99	2.85	2.70	2.62	2.54	2.45	2.36	2.27	2.17
26	7.72	5.53	4.64	4.14	3.82	3.59	3.42	3.29	3.18	3.09	2.96	2.81	2.66	2.58	2.50	2.42	2.33	2.23	2.13
27	7.68	5.49	4.60	4.11	3.78	3.56	3.39	3.26	3.15	3.06	2.93	2.78	2.63	2.55	2.47	2.38	2.29	2.20	2.10
28	7.64	5.45	4.57	4.07	3.75	3.53	3.36	3.23	3.12	3.03	2.90	2.75	2.60	2.52	2.44	2.35	2.26	2.17	2.06
29	7.60	5.42	4.54	4.04	3.73	3.50	3.33	3.20	3.09	3.00	2.87	2.73	2.57	2.49	2.41	2.33	2.23	2.14	2.03
30	7.56	5.39	4.51	4.02	3.70	3.47	3.30	3.17	3.07	2.98	2.84	2.70	2.55	2.47	2.39	2.30	2.21	2.11	2.01
40	7.31	5.18	4.31	3.83	3.51	3.29	3.12	2.99	2.89	2.80	2.66	2.52	2.37	2.29	2.20	2.11	2.02	1.92	1.80
60	7.08	4.98	4.13	3.65	3.34	3.12	2.95	2.82	2.72	2.63	2.50	2.35	2.20	2.12	2.03	1.94	1.84	1.73	1.60
120	6.85	4.79	3.95	3.48	3.17	2.96	2.79	2.66	2.56	2.47	2.34	2.19	2.03	1.95	1.86	1.76	1.66	1.53	1.38
∞	6.63	4.61	3.78	3.32	3.02	2.80	2.64	2.51	2.41	2.32	2.18	2.04	1.88	1.79	1.70	1.59	1.47	1.32	1.00

Reprinted with permission from Table VI.1, Percentage Points, *F*-Distribution, *CRC Handbook of Tables for Probability and Statistics* (2nd ed.). Copyright 1968, CRC Press, Inc., Boca Raton, Florida.

TABLE A-4a

Values of the studentized range statistic, q, for $\alpha = .05$.

| | | \multicolumn{9}{c}{**Number of Means Being Compared**} | | | | | | | | |
		2	**3**	**4**	**5**	**6**	**7**	**8**	**9**	**10**
	1	17.97	26.98	32.82	37.08	40.41	43.12	45.40	47.36	49.07
	2	6.08	8.33	9.80	10.88	11.74	12.44	13.03	13.54	13.99
	3	4.50	5.91	6.82	7.50	8.04	8.48	8.85	9.18	9.46
	4	3.93	5.04	5.76	6.29	6.71	7.05	7.35	7.60	7.83
	5	3.64	4.60	5.22	5.67	6.03	6.33	6.58	6.80	6.99
	6	3.46	4.34	4.90	5.30	5.63	5.90	6.12	6.32	6.49
	7	3.34	4.16	4.68	5.06	5.36	5.61	5.82	6.00	6.16
Degrees	8	3.26	4.04	4.53	4.89	5.17	5.40	5.60	5.77	5.92
of	9	3.20	3.95	4.41	4.76	5.02	5.24	5.43	5.59	5.74
Freedom	10	3.15	3.88	4.33	4.65	4.91	5.12	5.30	5.46	5.60
for										
MS_{Error}	11	3.11	3.82	4.26	4.57	4.82	5.03	5.20	5.35	5.49
	12	3.08	3.77	4.20	4.51	4.75	4.95	5.12	5.27	5.39
	13	3.06	3.73	4.15	4.45	4.69	4.88	5.05	5.19	5.32
	14	3.03	3.70	4.11	4.41	4.64	4.83	4.99	5.13	5.25
	15	3.01	3.67	4.08	4.37	4.59	4.78	4.94	5.08	5.20
	16	3.00	3.65	4.05	4.33	4.56	4.74	4.90	5.03	5.15
	17	2.98	3.63	4.02	4.30	4.52	4.70	4.86	4.99	5.11
	18	2.97	3.61	4.00	4.28	4.49	4.67	4.82	4.96	5.07
	19	2.96	3.59	3.98	4.25	4.47	4.65	4.79	4.92	5.04
	20	2.95	3.58	3.96	4.23	4.45	4.62	4.77	4.90	5.01
	24	2.92	3.53	3.90	4.17	4.37	4.54	4.68	4.81	4.92
	30	2.89	3.49	3.85	4.10	4.30	4.46	4.60	4.72	4.82
	40	2.86	3.44	3.79	4.04	4.23	4.39	4.52	4.63	4.73
	60	2.83	3.40	3.74	3.98	4.16	4.31	4.44	4.55	4.65
	120	2.80	3.36	3.68	3.92	4.10	4.24	4.36	4.47	4.56
	∞	2.77	3.31	3.63	3.86	4.03	4.17	4.29	4.39	4.47

Reprinted with permission from Table VIII.3, Percentage Points, Studentized Range, *CRC Handbook of Tables for Probability and Statistics* (2nd ed.). Copyright 1968, CRC Press, Inc., Boca Raton, Florida.

TABLE A–4b
Values of the studentized range statistic, q, for $\alpha = .01$.

		Number of Means Being Compared								
		2	**3**	**4**	**5**	**6**	**7**	**8**	**9**	**10**
	1	90.03	135.0	164.3	185.6	202.2	215.8	227.2	237.0	245.6
	2	14.04	19.02	22.29	24.72	26.63	28.20	29.53	30.68	31.69
	3	8.26	10.62	12.17	13.33	14.24	15.00	15.64	16.20	16.69
	4	6.51	8.12	9.17	9.96	10.58	11.10	11.55	11.93	12.27
	5	5.70	6.98	7.80	8.42	8.91	9.32	9.67	9.97	10.24
	6	5.24	6.33	7.03	7.56	7.97	8.32	8.61	8.87	9.10
	7	4.95	5.92	6.54	7.01	7.37	7.68	7.94	8.17	8.37
Degrees	8	4.75	5.64	6.20	6.62	6.96	7.24	7.47	7.68	7.86
of	9	4.60	5.43	5.96	6.35	6.66	6.91	7.13	7.33	7.49
Freedom	10	4.48	5.27	5.77	6.14	6.43	6.67	6.87	7.05	7.21
for										
MS_{Error}	11	4.39	5.15	5.62	5.97	6.25	6.48	6.67	6.84	6.99
	12	4.32	5.05	5.50	5.84	6.10	6.32	6.51	6.67	6.81
	13	4.26	4.96	5.40	5.73	5.98	6.19	6.37	6.53	6.67
	14	4.21	4.89	5.32	5.63	5.88	6.08	6.26	6.41	6.54
	15	4.17	4.84	5.25	5.56	5.80	5.99	6.16	6.31	6.44
	16	4.13	4.79	5.19	5.49	5.72	5.92	6.08	6.22	6.35
	17	4.10	4.74	5.14	5.43	5.66	5.85	6.01	6.15	6.27
	18	4.07	4.70	5.09	5.38	5.60	5.79	5.94	6.08	6.20
	19	4.05	4.67	5.05	5.33	5.55	5.73	5.89	6.02	6.14
	20	4.02	4.64	5.02	5.29	5.51	5.69	5.84	5.97	6.09
	24	3.96	4.55	4.91	5.17	5.37	5.54	5.69	5.81	5.92
	30	3.89	4.45	4.80	5.05	5.24	5.40	5.54	5.65	5.76
	40	3.82	4.37	4.70	4.93	5.11	5.26	5.39	5.50	5.60
	60	3.76	4.28	4.59	4.82	4.99	5.13	5.25	5.36	5.45
	120	3.70	4.20	4.50	4.71	4.87	5.01	5.12	5.21	5.30
	∞	3.64	4.12	4.40	4.60	4.76	4.88	4.99	5.08	5.16

Reprinted with permission from Table VIII.3, Percentage Points, Studentized Range, *CRC Handbook of Tables for Probability and Statistics* (2nd ed.). Copyright 1968, CRC Press, Inc., Boca Raton, Florida.

If Appendix A–4 is used to find q for the *CD* of a test of simple effects in a factorial design, use the following conversion to find the column to be used.

Type of Design	Use q from Table A–4 Found in the Column for Levels of the Independent Variable
2 × 2	3
2 × 3	5
3 × 2	5
3 × 3	7
3 × 4	8
4 × 3	8
4 × 4	10

TABLE A–5

Critical values of the chi-square distribution for $\alpha = .05$ and $\alpha = .01$. A value of $\chi^2_{obs}(df)$ equal to or greater than the tabled value is statistically significant at the α level selected.

df	$\alpha = .05$	$\alpha = .01$
1	3.84	6.63
2	5.99	9.21
3	7.81	11.3
4	9.49	13.3
5	11.1	15.1
6	12.6	16.8
7	14.1	18.5
8	15.5	20.1
9	16.9	21.7
10	18.3	23.2
11	19.7	24.7
12	21.0	26.2
13	22.4	27.7
14	23.7	29.1
15	25.0	30.6
16	26.3	32.0
17	27.6	33.4
18	28.9	34.8
19	30.1	36.2
20	31.4	37.6
21	32.7	38.9
22	33.9	40.3
23	35.2	41.6
24	36.4	43.0
25	37.7	44.3
26	38.9	45.6
27	40.1	47.0
28	41.3	48.3
29	42.6	49.6
30	43.8	50.9

Reprinted with permission from Table V.1, Percentage Points, Chi-square Distribution, *CRC Handbook of Tables for Probability and Statistics* (2nd ed.). Copyright 1968, CRC Press, Inc., Boca Raton, Florida.

TABLE A–6a

Critical values of U in the Mann–Whitney U test for $\alpha = .05$ (two-tailed test). If the group sizes are unequal, n_1 is the smaller group. A value of U_{obs} equal to or less than the tabled value is statistically significant at the .05 significance level.

		n_2																		
n_1	1	2	3	4	5	6	7	8	9	10	11	12	13	14	15	16	17	18	19	20
1																				
2								0	0	0	0	1	1	1	1	1	2	2	2	2
3					0	1	1	2	2	3	3	4	4	5	5	6	6	7	7	8
4				0	1	2	3	4	4	5	6	7	8	9	10	11	11	12	13	13
5			0	1	2	3	5	6	7	8	9	11	12	13	14	15	17	18	19	20
6			1	2	3	5	6	8	10	11	13	14	16	17	19	21	22	24	25	27
7			1	3	5	6	8	10	12	14	16	18	20	22	24	26	28	30	32	34
8		0	2	4	6	8	10	13	15	17	19	22	24	26	29	31	34	36	38	41
9		0	2	4	7	10	12	15	17	20	23	26	28	31	34	37	39	42	45	48
10		0	3	5	8	11	14	17	20	23	26	29	33	36	39	42	45	48	52	55
11		0	3	6	9	13	16	19	23	26	30	33	37	40	44	47	51	55	58	62
12		1	4	7	11	14	18	22	26	29	33	37	41	45	49	53	57	61	65	69
13		1	4	8	12	16	20	24	28	33	37	41	45	50	54	59	63	67	72	76
14		1	5	9	13	17	22	26	31	36	40	45	50	55	59	64	67	74	78	83
15		1	5	10	14	19	24	29	34	39	44	49	54	59	64	70	75	80	85	90
16		1	6	11	15	21	26	31	37	42	47	53	59	64	70	75	81	86	92	98
17		2	6	11	17	22	28	34	39	45	51	57	63	67	75	81	87	93	99	105
18		2	7	12	18	24	30	36	42	48	55	61	67	74	80	86	93	99	106	112
19		2	7	13	19	25	32	38	45	52	58	65	72	78	85	92	99	106	113	119
20		2	8	13	20	27	34	41	48	55	62	69	76	83	90	98	105	112	119	127

Reprinted with permission from Table X.4, Critical Values of U in the Wilcoxon (Mann–Whitney) Two-sample Statistic, *CRC Handbook of Tables for Probability and Statistics* (2nd ed.). Copyright 1968, CRC Press, Inc., Boca Raton, Florida.

TABLE A–6b

Critical values of U in the Mann–Whitney U test for $\alpha = .01$ (two-tailed test). If the group sizes are unequal, n_1 is the smaller group. A value of U_{obs} equal to or less than the tabled value is statistically significant at the .01 significance level.

											n_2									
n_1	1	2	3	4	5	6	7	8	9	10	11	12	13	14	15	16	17	18	19	20
1																				
2																			0	0
3									0	0	0	1	1	1	2	2	2	2	3	3
4						0	0	1	1	2	2	3	3	4	5	5	6	6	7	8
5					0	1	1	2	3	4	5	6	7	7	8	9	10	11	12	13
6				0	1	2	3	4	5	6	7	9	10	11	12	13	15	16	17	18
7				0	1	3	4	6	7	9	10	12	13	15	16	18	19	21	22	24
8				1	2	4	6	7	9	11	13	15	17	18	20	22	24	26	28	30
9			0	1	3	5	7	9	11	13	16	18	20	22	24	27	29	31	33	36
10			0	2	4	6	9	11	13	16	18	21	24	26	29	31	34	37	39	42
11			0	2	5	7	10	13	16	18	21	24	27	30	33	36	39	42	45	48
12			1	3	6	9	12	15	18	21	24	27	31	34	37	41	44	47	51	54
13			1	3	7	10	13	17	20	24	27	31	34	38	42	45	49	53	56	60
14			1	4	7	11	15	18	22	26	30	34	38	42	46	50	54	58	63	67
15			2	5	8	12	16	20	24	29	33	37	42	46	51	55	60	64	69	73
16			2	5	9	13	18	22	27	31	36	41	45	50	55	60	65	70	74	79
17			2	6	10	15	19	24	29	34	39	44	49	54	60	65	70	75	81	86
18			2	6	11	16	21	26	31	37	42	47	53	58	64	70	75	81	87	92
19		0	3	7	12	17	22	28	33	39	45	51	56	63	69	74	81	87	93	99
20		0	3	8	13	18	24	30	36	42	48	54	60	67	73	79	86	92	99	105

Reprinted with permission from Table X.4, Critical Values of U in the Wilcoxon (Mann–Whitney) Two-sample Statistic, *CRC Handbook of Tables for Probability and Statistics* (2nd ed.). Copyright 1968, CRC Press, Inc., Boca Raton, Florida.

TABLE A-7

Critical values of T in the Wilcoxon test for $\alpha = .05$ and $\alpha = .01$ (two-tailed test). A value of T_{obs} equal to or less than the tabled value is statistically significant at the α level selected. Dashes indicate that statistical significance cannot be attained at this level for this group size.

N_{pairs}	$\alpha = .05$	$\alpha = .01$	N_{pairs}	$\alpha = .05$	$\alpha = .01$
6	1	—	29	127	100
7	2	—	30	137	109
8	4	0	31	148	118
9	6	2	32	159	128
10	8	3	33	171	138
11	11	5	34	183	149
12	14	7	35	195	160
13	17	10	36	208	171
14	21	13	37	222	183
15	25	16	38	235	195
16	30	19	39	250	208
17	35	23	40	264	221
18	40	28	41	279	234
19	46	32	42	295	248
20	52	37	43	311	262
21	59	43	44	327	277
22	66	49	45	344	292
23	73	55	46	361	307
24	81	61	47	379	323
25	90	68	48	397	339
26	98	76	49	415	356
27	107	84	50	434	373
28	117	92			

Excerpted and adapted from Table X.2, Critical Values of T in the Wilcoxon Matched-pairs Signed-ranks Test, *CRC Handbook of Tables for Probability and Statistics* (2nd ed.). Copyright 1968, CRC Press, Inc., Boca Raton, Florida. Used by permission.

TABLE A–8

Critical values of r for $\alpha = .05$ and $\alpha = .01$ (two-tailed test). A value of r_{obs} equal to or greater than the tabled value is statistically significant at the α level selected.

df [a]	$\alpha = .05$	$\alpha = .01$
1	.99692	.999877
2	.9500	.99000
3	.878	.9587
4	.811	.9172
5	.754	.875
6	.707	.834
7	.666	.798
8	.632	.765
9	.602	.735
10	.576	.708
11	.553	.684
12	.532	.661
13	.514	.641
14	.497	.623
15	.482	.606
16	.468	.590
17	.456	.575
18	.444	.561
19	.433	.549
20	.423	.537
25	.381	.487
30	.349	.449
35	.325	.418
40	.304	.393
45	.288	.372
50	.273	.354
60	.250	.325
70	.232	.302
80	.217	.283
90	.205	.267
100	.195	.254

[a]df are equal to $N_{pairs} - 2$ where N_{pairs} is the number of paired observations.

Reprinted with permission from Table IX.1, Percentage Points, Distribution of the Correlation Coefficient, When $\rho = 0$, *CRC Handbook of Tables for Probability and Statistics* (2nd ed.). Copyright 1968, CRC Press, Inc., Boca Raton, Florida.

TABLE A-9

Critical values of r_s for $\alpha = .05$ and $\alpha = .01$ (two-tailed test). A value of $r_{s\,obs}$ equal to or greater than the tabled value is statistically significant at the α level selected.

N_{pairs}	$\alpha = .05$	$\alpha = .01$
5	—	—
6	.886	—
7	.786	.929
8	.738	.881
9	.700	.833
10	.648	.794
11	.618	.818
12	.591	.780
13	.566	.745
14	.545	.716
15	.525	.689
16	.507	.666
17	.490	.645
18	.476	.625
19	.462	.608
20	.450	.591
21	.438	.576
22	.428	.562
23	.418	.549
24	.409	.537
25	.400	.526
26	.392	.515
27	.385	.505
28	.377	.496
29	.370	.487
30	.364	.478

Reprinted with permission from Table X.12, Critical Values of Spearman's Rank Correlation Coefficient, *CRC Handbook of Tables for Probability and Statistics* (2nd ed.). Copyright 1968, CRC Press, Inc., Boca Raton, Florida.

Appendix B
Mathematics Review

This review briefly covers the mathematics needed to understand the statistics presented in this text.

STATISTICAL SYMBOLS

A **symbol**, sometimes called a **sign**, is a letter or character used to represent something. The following table presents the common symbols used in statistics.

Symbol and Example	Description
X or X_i	X is used to represent a score or a measurement obtained from a subject. The subscript i, when used, indicates the score of a particular subject. For example, X_1 represents the score of subject number 1.
$=$	Equals sign.
$X_1 = 3$	The score of subject 1 equals 3.
$X_5 = 27$	The score of subject 5 equals 27.
$a = 2$	The value of a equals 2.
$\neq$	Does not equal sign.
$6 \neq 3$	6 is not equal to 3.
$+$	Plus sign. This sign indicates that the numbers joined by the $+$ should be added. The result of addition is called the *sum*. A statement such as "The sum of 5 and 1" indicates that the numbers are to be added together.
$5 + 1 = 6$	The sum of 5 plus 1 equals 6.
$5 + 1 + 6 = 12$	The sum of 5 plus 1 plus 6 equals 12.
$a + b$	a plus b: The value of b is to be added to the value of a.
$-$	Minus sign. This sign indicates that the number that follows the $-$ should be subtracted from the number preceding the $-$ sign. The result of subtraction is called the *difference*. A statement such as

"The difference of 5 and 1" indicates that one number is to be subtracted from the other.

$5 - 1 = 4$ The difference of 5 minus 1 is 4.

$a - b$ a minus b: The value of b is to be subtracted from the value of a.

$(\ )(\ )$ or $\times$ Multiplication or times sign. The values in parentheses or separated by the $\times$ are multiplied. The result of multiplication is called a *product*.

$(2)(3) = 6$ The product of 2 multiplied by 3 is 6.

$2 \times 3 = 6$ The product of 2 multiplied by 3 is 6.

$(a)(b)$ or $a \times b$ a times b: The value of a is to be multiplied by the value of b.

Exception to the rule: In a factorial design the interaction of factors A and B is indicated by $A \times B$. In this instance, the term should be read as "the A by B interaction." It does not mean that A is multiplied by B.

$\div$ or $/$ or $-$ Division sign. The number preceding the $\div$ or the $/$ or the number above the $-$ (the *numerator*) is divided by the number following the $\div$ or the $/$ or the number below the $-$ (the *denominator*), respectively. The result of division is called the *quotient*.

$6 \div 2 = 3$ The quotient of 6 divided by 2 is 3.

$6/2 = 3$ The quotient of 6 divided by 2 is 3.

$\frac{6}{2} = 3$ The quotient of 6 divided by 2 is 3.

$a \div b$, or a/b, or $\frac{a}{b}$ The quotient of a divided by b.

$<$ Less than symbol. The number preceding the $<$ is less than the number following the $<$.

$2 < 3$ 2 is less than 3.

$a < b$ The value of a is less than the value of b.

$X_3 < 10$ The score of subject 3 is less than 10.

$>$ Greater than symbol. The number preceding the $>$ is greater than the number following the $>$.

$3 > 2$ 3 is greater than 2.

$a > b$ The value of a is greater than the value of b.

$X_3 > 10$ The score of subject 3 is greater than 10.

$\leq$ Less than or equal to symbol. The number preceding the $\leq$ is less than or equal to the number following the $\leq$.

$2 \leq 3$ 2 is less than or equal to 3.

$4 \leq 4$	4 is less than or equal to 4.
$a \leq b$	The value of a is less than or equal to the value of b.
$X_3 \leq 10$	The score of subject 3 is less than or equal to 10.
$\geq$	Equal to or greater than symbol. The number preceding the $\geq$ is equal to or greater than the number following the $\geq$.
$3 \geq 2$	3 is equal to or greater than 2.
$4 \geq 4$	4 is equal to or greater than 4.
$a \geq b$	The value of a is equal to or greater than the value of b.
$X_3 \geq 10$	The score of subject 3 is equal to or greater than 10.
$5 < X_1 < 10$	The greater than and less than symbols may be placed in one term as illustrated. This term is read as "The score of subject 1 is greater than 5 and less than 10."
$5 \leq X_1 \leq 10$	The equal to or greater than and less than or equal to symbols may also be placed in one term as illustrated. This term is read as "The score of subject 1 is equal to or greater than 5 and equal to or less than 10."
$\mid \ \mid$	Absolute value symbol. This symbol indicates that we ignore the $+$ or $-$ sign attached to a number.
$\mid -6 \mid = 6$	The absolute value of minus 6 is 6.
$\mid +6 \mid = 6$	The absolute value of plus 6 is 6.
$(\ )^2$	The number enclosed in parentheses is squared, or multiplied by itself. Sometimes the parentheses are not used, and the square indicator, ^{2}, simply follows the number to be squared.
$(5)^2 = 25$	5 squared, which is 5×5, equals 25.
$5^2 = 25$	5 squared equals 25.
$\sqrt{\ }$	Square root symbol. The $\sqrt{\ }$ indicates finding the number that, when multiplied by itself (i.e., when squared), equals the number under the $\sqrt{\ }$ symbol.
$\sqrt{25} = 5$	The square root of 25 equals 5, for 5 multiplied by itself (i.e., 5×5) equals 25.
$\sqrt{36} = 6$	The square root of 36 equals 6, for 6 multiplied by itself (i.e., 6×6) equals 36.
$\sum$	Summation symbol. The numbers following the $\sum$ should be added together.
$\sum(3+2) = 5$	The sum of 3 plus 2 is 5.
$\sum(3+2+4) = 9$	The sum of 3 plus 2 plus 4 is 9.

$\sum X$ or $\sum X_i$ — The sum of X. Add all the scores that are represented by X. For example, if the scores of three subjects are $X_1 = 3$, $X_2 = 6$, and $X_3 = 4$, then $\sum X = 3 + 6 + 4 = 13$. Sometimes limits are placed on the summation sign, such as $\sum_{i=1}^{3} X_i$. These limits indicate to add the scores of subjects 1 to 3. If limits are not used, then $\sum X$ means to add all the scores designated by X.

MATHEMATICAL OPERATIONS

Negative Numbers

A negative number may occur as a result of subtraction, such as $6 - 8 = -2$. The 8, which is larger than the 6 by 2, results in a difference of -2 when it is subtracted from the 6. Negative numbers occur often in statistics and then are used in basic mathematical operations. If a number is not preceded by a minus sign, it is assumed to be positive.

Adding Negative Numbers

$6 + (-4) = 2$ — Adding a negative number to a positive number is equivalent to subtracting the negative number from the positive number. Thus $6 + (-4) = 6 - 4 = 2$.

$(-6) + (-4) = -10$ — In this instance, the -4 is subtracted from the -6, or $(-6) + (-4) = -6 - 4 = -10$.

Subtracting Negative Numbers

$6 - (-4) = 10$ — Subtracting a negative number is equivalent to adding the absolute value of the negative number. Thus $6 - (-4) = 6 + |-4| = 6 + 4 = 10$.

Multiplying Negative Numbers

$(-6)(-4) = 24$ — If both numbers to be multiplied are negative, then the product is positive.

$(6)(-4) = -24$
$(-6)(4) = -24$ — If only one of the two numbers is negative, then the product is negative.

Dividing Negative Numbers

$-10 \div 5 = -2$
$10 \div -5 = -2$ — If either the numerator or the denominator is negative, then the quotient is negative.

$-10 \div -5 = 2$ — If both the numerator and the denominator are negative, then the quotient is positive.

Fractions

The easiest approach to working with fractions is to convert the fraction to a decimal by dividing the numerator by the denominator, for example, $\frac{1}{4} = 0.25$, $2/4 = 0.50$, and $\frac{3}{4} = 0.75$. If the decimal is to be involved in further calculations, then it should be carried to at least four decimal places (e.g., $\frac{4}{11} = 0.3636$). Thus $\frac{2}{5} + \frac{1}{8} + \frac{1}{3}$ equals $0.4000 + 0.1250 + 0.3333 = 0.8583$.

Proportions and Percents

Proportion
A proportion is a part of a whole. As an example, if 100 people answer a questionnaire and 45 of them are males, then the proportion of male respondents is $\frac{45}{100}$ or .45. The proportion of female respondents is $\frac{55}{100}$ or .55.

Percent
A percent is formed when a proportion is multiplied by 100. Thus a proportion of .45 male respondents equals .45 × 100 or 45 percent male respondents. The percentage of female respondents is .55 × 100 = 55 percent.

Order of Mathematical Operations

The following examples illustrate the order in which mathematical operations are performed with common statistical terms.

Term	Order of Mathematical Operations
$\sum(X - \overline{X})$	1. The mean is subtracted from each score in a set of scores.
	2. The differences are summed.
$\sum(X - \overline{X})^2$	1. The mean is subtracted from each score in a set of scores.
	2. Each difference is squared.
	3. The squared differences are summed.
$\sum X^2$	1. Each X value is squared.
	2. The squared X values are summed.
$(\sum X)^2$	1. The X values are summed.
	2. The sum of the X values (i.e., $\sum X$) is squared.
$\sum XY$	1. The corresponding X and Y values are multiplied for the set of scores.

2. The multiplied XY values are summed for the set of scores.

$(\sum X)(\sum Y)$

1. The X values are summed to obtain $\sum X$.

2. The Y values are summed to obtain $\sum Y$.

3. The sum of the X values (i.e., $\sum X$) is multiplied by the sum of the Y variables (i.e., $\sum Y$).

Appendix C
Glossary

Alpha or α: The value of the significance level stated as a probability.

Archival records: Research using existing records.

Artifactual main effect: A main effect that does not give meaningful information about the effect of an independent variable in a factorial design.

Beta (β): The probability of a Type II error.

Between-groups variance: The variance calculated using the variation of the group means about the grand mean.

Between-subjects design: An experiment in which two or more groups are created.

Bimodal: A distribution with two modes.

Bivariate distribution: A distribution in which two scores are obtained from each subject.

Bivariate normal distribution: A distribution of X and Y variables in which (1) the X scores are normally distributed in the population sampled, (2) the Y scores are normally distributed in the population sampled, (3) for each X score the distribution of Y scores in the population is normal, and (4) for each Y score the distribution of X scores in the population is normal.

Cell mean: The mean of the n_{AB} scores for a treatment combination in a factorial design.

Cell or treatment condition: A combination formed from one level of each independent variable in a factorial design.

Central limit theorem: A mathematical theorem stating that, as sample size increases, the sampling distribution of the mean approaches a normal distribution.

Chance difference: A difference between equivalent groups occurring for no predictable reason or for no discernible cause.

Chi-square test: A statistical test used to analyze nominal level of measurement scores where frequencies of occurrence of the various categories are obtained.

Chi-square test of goodness of fit: The chi square used when a score is categorized on only one dimension.

Chi-square test of independence: The chi square used when a score may be categorized on two independent dimensions.

Class interval: The width of the interval used in a grouped frequency distribution.

Coefficient of determination: The value of r^2 indicating the common variance of variables X and Y.

Confidence interval: A range of score values expected to contain the value of mu with a certain level of confidence.

Confidence limits: The lower and upper scores defining the confidence interval.

Confounded experiment: An experiment in which an extraneous variable is allowed to vary consistently with the independent variable.

Consistent estimator: A statistic for which the probability that the statistic has a value closer to the parameter increases as the sample size increases.

Contingency table: A rows-by-columns table presenting the frequency of each category formed by the intersection of the row and column variables in the table.

Continuous variable: A variable that can take on an infinite set of values between any two levels of the variable.

Convenience sampling: Obtaining subjects from among people who are accessible or convenient to the researcher.

Correlation coefficient: A statistic that provides a numerical description of the extent of the relatedness of two sets of scores and the direction of the relationship.

Correlational studies: Studies in which two or more variables are measured to find the direction and degree to which they covary.

Covary: Two variables covary when a change in one variable is related to a consistent change in the other variable.

Critical difference: The minimum numerical difference between two treatment means that is statistically significant.

Critical value: The specific numerical values that define the boundaries of the rejection region.

Cross products of X and Y: The value of $\sum(X - \overline{X})(Y - \overline{Y})$ for variables X and Y.

Cumulative frequency of a class interval: The frequency of occurrence of scores in that interval plus the sum of the frequencies of scores of lower class intervals.

Cumulative frequency of a score: The frequency of occurrence of that score plus the sum of the frequencies of all the scores of lower value.

Cumulative grouped percentage frequency of a class interval: The percentage frequency of the scores in that interval plus the sum of the percentage frequencies of all the class intervals of lower value.

Cumulative grouped relative frequency of a class interval: The relative frequency of the scores in that interval plus the sum of the relative frequencies of class intervals of lower value.

Data: The scores or numerical measurements of behavior or characteristics obtained from observations of a sample of people or animals.

Degrees of freedom: The number of scores free to vary when calculating a statistic.

Dependent variable: The variable in an experiment that depends on the independent variable. In most instances the dependent variable is some measure of a behavior.

Descriptive statistics: Statistical procedures used to summarize and describe the data from a sample.

Discrete variable: A variable that can take on only a finite or potentially countable set of values.

Empirical data: Scores or measurements based on observation and sensory experience.

Equivalent groups: Groups of subjects that are not expected to differ in any consistent or systematic way prior to receiving the independent variable of the experiment.

Error rate in an experiment: The probability of making at least one Type I error in the statistical comparisons conducted in an experiment.

Estimated population standard deviation (s): The square root of the estimated population variance.

Estimated population variance (s^2): A measure of variability obtained by subtracting the mean of a distribution from each score in the distribution, squaring each difference, summing the differences, and then dividing the sum by the number of scores minus 1.

Estimated standard error of the mean: The standard error of the mean obtained by using s to estimate σ.

Expected frequencies: The frequencies in a contingency table obtained assuming that the two dimensions of the table are independent.

Experiment: A controlled situation in which one or more independent variables are manipulated to observe the effect on the dependent variable.

Extraneous variables: Any variables, other than the independent variable, that can affect the dependent variable in an experiment.

Factor: An alternative name for an independent variable.

Factorial design: A research design in which two or more independent variables are varied simultaneously.

Frequency distribution: A table showing each score in a set of scores and how frequently each score occurred.

Frequency polygon: A graph constructed by placing the midpoints of each class interval of a frequency distribution on the abscissa and indicating the frequency of a class interval by placing a dot at the appropriate frequency above the midpoint. The dots are connected with straight lines.

General equation of a straight line: $Y = bX + a$.

Grand mean: The mean of all scores in an experiment.

Grouped frequency distribution: A frequency distribution in which scores are grouped together in class intervals and the frequency of scores occurring within each class is tabulated.

Grouped percentage distribution: A grouped frequency distribution obtained by multiplying the relative frequency values by 100 to obtain percentages.

Grouped relative frequency distribution: A grouped frequency distribution obtained by dividing the frequency of scores in an interval by the total number of scores in the distribution.

Histogram: A form of bar graph in which the frequency of occurrence of scores in a class interval is given by the height of the bar and the size of each class interval is represented by the width of the bar on the abscissa.

Independent variable: A variable manipulated in an experiment to determine its effect on the dependent variable.

Interaction: A situation in a factorial design when the effect of one independent variable depends on the level of the other independent variable with which it is combined.

Interquartile range: The range of values for the middle 50 percent of the scores in a distribution.

Interval measurement: The amount of a variable is ordered along a dimension and the differences between the assigned numbers represent equal amounts in the magnitude of the variable measured. The zero point of an interval scale is an arbitrary starting point.

Least-squares regression line: A straight line that minimizes the value of $\sum(Y - Y')^2$.

Level of an independent variable: One value of the independent variable. To be a variable, an independent variable must take on at least two different levels.

Linear relation: A relation between two variables such that each time variable X changes by 1 unit, variable Y changes by a constant amount.

Linear relationship: A relationship between two variables that can be described by a straight line.

Main effect of factor A: The difference between $\overline{X}_{A1}$ and $\overline{X}_{A2}$ in a factorial design, symbolized by $\overline{X}_{A1} - \overline{X}_{A2}$.

Main effect of factor B: The difference between $\overline{X}_{B1}$ and $\overline{X}_{B2}$ in a factorial design, symbolized by $\overline{X}_{B1} - \overline{X}_{B2}$.

Main effect mean: The mean of all subjects given one level of an independent variable, ignoring the classification by the other independent variable in a factorial design.

Mann–Whitney U test: A nonparametric test for a between-subjects design using two levels of an independent variable with the scores representing at least ordinal measurement.

Marginal frequencies: The row totals and the column totals of the observed frequencies in a contingency table.

Mean square: The name used for a variance in the analysis of variance.

Measurement: Assigning numbers to variables following a set of rules.

Measures of central tendency: Numbers that represent the average or typical score obtained from measurements of a sample.

Median: A score value in the distribution with an equal number of scores above and below it. The median is the 50th percentile in a distribution.

Midpoint of a class interval: The point midway between the real limits of the class interval.

Mode: The most frequently occurring score in a distribution of scores.

Multimodal: A distribution with more than two modes.

Multiple comparison tests: Statistical tests used to make pairwise comparisons to find which means differ significantly from one another in a one-factor multilevel design.

Multiple regression: Predicting the value of Y scores using several X variables.

Multiple treatment effects: Changes in subjects' performance in a within-subjects design that are due to being tested in each level of the independent variable.

Naturalistic observation: Research involving the observation of behaviors occurring in natural settings.

Negative relationship: A relationship between two variables in which as the value of one variable increases the value of the other variable tends to decrease.

Nominal measurement: A classification of the measured variable into different categories.

Nonparametric test: A statistical test involving hypotheses that do not state a relationship about a population parameter.

Nonsignificant difference: The observed value of the test statistic does not fall into a rejection region and the null hypothesis is not rejected.

Normal distribution: A theoretical mathematical distribution that specifies the relative frequency of a set of scores in a population.

One-factor between-subjects design: A research design in which one independent variable is manipulated and two or more groups are created.

One-factor multilevel design: An experiment with one independent variable and three or more levels of that independent variable.

One-sample t test: A t test used to test the difference between a sample mean and an hypothesized population mean for statistical significance when $\sigma_{\overline{X}}$ is estimated by $s_{\overline{X}}$.

One-tailed test: A statistical test employing a rejection region in only one tail of the sampling distribution of the test statistic.

Operational definition: A specification of the operations used to make observations, to manipulate an independent variable, or to measure the dependent variable.

Ordinal measurement: The amount of a variable is placed in order of magnitude along a dimension.

Pairwise comparisons: Statistical comparisons involving two means.

Parameter: A number that describes a characteristic of a population.

Parametric test: A statistical test involving hypotheses that state a relationship about a population parameter.

Pearson correlation coefficient: A statistic, symbolized by r, that indicates the degree of linear relationship between two variables measured at the interval or ratio level.

Percentage frequency distribution: The frequency of occurrence of a score expressed as a percentage of the total number of scores obtained.

Percentile: The score at or below which a specified percentage of scores in a distribution fall.

Percentile rank of a score: The percentage of scores in the distribution that are equal to or less than that score.

Placebo control: A simulated treatment condition.

Point estimation: Estimating the value of a parameter as a single point from the value of a statistic.

Population: A complete set of people, animals, objects, or events that share a common characteristic.

Positive relationship: A relationship between two variables in which as the value of one variable increases the value of the other variable tends to increase also.

Post hoc comparisons: Statistical tests that make all possible pairwise comparisons after a statistically significant F_{obs} has occurred for the overall analysis of variance.

Power: The probability of rejecting H_0 when H_0 is false and H_1 is true. The power of a statistical test is given by $1 - \beta$.

Practice effect: A multiple treatment effect that occurs because subjects may become more practiced or fatigued on the experimental task.

Probability of a discrete event:

$$p(\text{event}) = \frac{\text{Number of occurrences of the event in a population}}{\text{Total number of possible events in a population}}.$$

Qualitative data: Data obtained from nominal measurement indicating that variables differ in quality.

Quantitative data: Data obtained from ordinal, interval, or ratio measurements indicating how much of a variable exists.

Random assignment: A method of assigning subjects to treatment groups so that any individual selected for the experiment has an equal probability of assignment to any of the groups and the assignment of one subject to a group does not affect the assignment of any other individual to that same group.

Random sample: A sample in which individuals are selected so that each member of the population has an equal chance of being selected for the sample, and the selection of one member is independent of the selection of any other member of the population.

Range: The numerical difference between the lowest and highest score in a distribution.

Ratio measurement: The amount of a variable is ordered along a dimension, the differences between the assigned numbers represent equal amounts in the magnitude of the variable measured, and a true zero point exists, which represents the absence of the characteristic measured.

Raw data: The scores obtained from all the subjects before the scores have been analyzed statistically.

Real limit of a class interval: The point midway between the stated limit of a class interval and the stated limit of the next lower or upper class interval.

Real limits of a number: The points midway between the number and the next lower and the next higher numbers on the scale used to make the measurements.

Regression analysis: The use of statistical methods to predict one set of scores from a second set of scores.

Rejection region: Values on the sampling distribution of the test statistic that have a probability equal to or less than α if H_0 is true. If the test statistic falls into the rejection region, H_0 is rejected.

Relative frequency: The frequency of a score divided by the total number of scores obtained.

Research hypothesis: A statement of an expected, or predicted, relationship between two or more variables. In an experiment, a research hypothesis is a predicted relationship between an independent variable and a dependent variable.

Research method: An approach used to collect data.

Residual: The value of $Y - Y'$.

Robustness: A term used to indicate that violating the assumptions of a statistical test has little effect on the probability of a Type I error.

Sample: A subset, or subgroup, selected from a population.

Sample mean: The sum of a set of scores divided by the number of scores summed.

Sample standard deviation (S): The square root of the sample variance.

Sample variance (S^2): A measure of variability obtained by subtracting the mean of a distribution from each score in the distribution, squaring each difference, summing the differences, and then dividing the sum by the number of scores in the distribution.

Sampling distribution: A theoretical probability distribution of values of a statistic resulting from drawing all possible samples of size n from a population.

Sampling distribution of the difference between means: The distribution of differences between sample means when all possible pairs of samples of size n are drawn from a population.

Sampling distribution of the mean: The distribution of $\overline{X}$ values when all possible samples of size n are drawn from a population.

Sampling error: The amount by which a sample mean differs from the population mean.

Scatterplot: A plot of a bivariate distribution in which the X variable is plotted on the horizontal axis and the Y variable is plotted on the vertical axis.

Score: The measurement obtained on the subject's performance of a task.

Semi-interquartile range: One-half of the interquartile range.

Significance level: A probability value that provides the criterion for rejecting a null hypothesis in a statistical test.

Simple effect of an independent variable: The effect of one independent variable at only one level of the other independent variable in a factorial design.

Simple random sampling: Selecting members from a population such that each member of the population has an equal chance of being selected for the sample, and the selection of one member is independent of the selection of any other member of the population.

Skewed distribution: A frequency distribution in which scores are clustered at one end of the distribution with scores occurring infrequently at the other end of the distribution.

Slope of a straight line: The slope of a straight line is given by

$$b = \frac{\text{Change in value of } Y}{\text{Change in value of } X}.$$

Spearman rank-order correlation coefficient: A correlation coefficient used with ordinal measures.

Standard error of estimate: The value of

$$\sqrt{\frac{\sum (Y - Y')^2}{N_{\text{pairs}} - 2}}.$$

Standard error of the difference between means, or the standard error of the difference: The standard deviation of a theoretical sampling distribution of $\overline{X}_{A1} - \overline{X}_{A2}$ values.

Standard error of the mean: The standard deviation of the sampling distribution of the mean found by dividing σ by the square root of the size of the sample.

Standard normal deviate: The value of z_{obs} when a score is transformed into a score on the standard normal distribution.

Standard normal distribution: A normal distribution with $\mu = 0$ and $\sigma = 1$.

Standard score: A score obtained by using the transformation $z = (X - \overline{X})/S$.

Stated limits of a class interval: The highest and lowest scores that could fall into that class interval.

Statistic: A single number used to describe a set of data from a sample or to analyze those data more fully.

Statistical alternative hypothesis: A statement of what must be true if the null hypothesis is false.

Statistical hypothesis: A statement about a population parameter (for a parametric test).

Statistical inference: Estimating population values from statistics obtained from a sample.

Statistical null hypothesis: A statement of a condition that a scientist tentatively holds to be true about a population; it is the hypothesis that is tested by a statistical test.

Statistically significant difference: The observed value of the test statistic falls into a rejection region and H_0 is rejected.

Statistics: The methods or procedures used to summarize, analyze, and draw inferences from data.

Stem-and-leaf display: A display of data in which the first (or second) digit of a score is the stem and the second (or last) digit is the leaf.

Stratified random sampling: A sampling method in which members of a population are categorized into homogeneous subgroupings called strata. Members of the population are randomly sampled from the strata in the proportion to which the strata occur in the population.

Strength of effect: The strength of an independent variable as measured by one of the strength of effect statistics.

Subject: The person who participates in an experiment.

Sum of squares: A numerical value obtained by subtracting the mean of a distribution from each score in the distribution, squaring each difference, and then summing the differences.

Sum of squares residual: The value of $\sum(Y-Y')^2$.

Survey research: Research involving obtaining data from either oral or written interviews with people.

Symmetrical frequency distribution: A frequency distribution that when folded in half about a midpoint produces two halves identical in shape.

Test statistic: A number calculated from the scores of the sample that allows testing a statistical null hypothesis.

Treatment carry-over effect: A multiple treatment effect that occurs when the effect of one level of the independent variable carries over to affect performance in the next level of the independent variable.

Treatments-by-subject interaction: A situation in a one-factor within-subjects design where the effect of the independent variable depends on the subject.

Two-tailed test: A statistical test using rejection regions in both tails of the sampling distribution of the test statistic.

Type I error: The error in statistical decision making that occurs if the null hypothesis is rejected when actually it is true of the population.

Type II error: The error in statistical decision making that occurs if H_0 is not rejected when it is false and the alternative hypothesis (H_1) is true.

Unbiased estimator: A statistic with a mean value over an infinite number of random samples equal to the parameter it estimates.

Ungrouped frequency distribution: A frequency distribution constructed by listing all possible score values between the lowest and highest scores obtained and then placing a tally mark ($/$) beside a score each time it occurs.

Unimodal: A distribution with one mode.

Variable: Any environmental condition or event, stimulus, personal characteristic or attribute, or behavior that can take on different values at different times or with different people.

Variability: How much scores differ from each other and the measure of central tendency in a distribution.

Wilcoxon signed-ranks test: A nonparametric test for within-subjects designs with two levels of an independent variable.

Within-groups error variance: The variance of the scores in a group calculated about the group mean.

Within-subjects design: A research design in which one group of subjects is exposed to and measured under each level of an independent variable. In a within-subjects design, each subject receives each treatment condition.

Y-intercept: The value of Y when $X = 0$ in the equation $Y = bX + a$.

Appendix D
Statistical Symbols

A	Factor A, the independent variable in an experiment.
A_1, A_2, A_3	Levels of factor A in either a one-factor or a factorial design.
α	Alpha, the probability of a Type I error.
$A \times B$	The representation of the interaction of factors A and B in a factorial design.
a	(1) Number of levels of factor A. (2) Y-intercept of an equation for a straight line in a regression analysis.
B	Factor B, the second independent variable in a factorial design.
B_1, B_2, B_3	Levels of factor B in a factorial design.
b	(1) Number of levels of factor B. (2) Slope of a straight line in a regression analysis.
β	Beta, the probability of a Type II error.
χ^2	Chi-squared statistic.
χ^2_{crit}	Critical value of χ^2.
χ^2_{obs}	Value of χ^2 statistic obtained from data.
CD	Critical difference in a multiple comparison test.
CP_{XY}	Cross products of X and Y in a correlational study.
$cum\ f$ or cf	Cumulative frequency of a score.
cf_L	Cumulative frequency of scores up to the lower real limit of an interval in a grouped frequency distribution.
$cum\ rf$ or crf	Cumulative relative frequency of a score.
$cum\ \%f$ or $c\%f$	Cumulative percentage frequency of a score.
D	(1) Difference in a pair of ranked scores for an individual; used in Spearman rank-order correlation coefficient.

	(2) Difference between two scores obtained from a subject in a within-subjects design.
df	Degrees of freedom. In an analysis of variance, the df are usually subscripted, such as df_A, df_B, $df_{A \times B}$, df_{Error}, or df_{Total}, to indicate which source of variance they correspond to.
η^2	Eta squared.
E_{rc}	Expected frequency of a score in row r, column c of a chi-square test contingency table.
f	Frequency of a score.
f_i	Frequency of scores in an interval of a grouped frequency distribution.
F	The F statistic in the analysis of variance.
F_{crit}	Critical value of F.
F_{obs}	Value of F obtained from data.
H_0	Statistical null hypothesis.
H_1	Statistical alternative hypothesis.
IQR	Interquartile range.
i	Size or width of the class interval in a grouped frequency distribution.
M	Sample mean. The symbol used in publications following the editorial style of the *Publication Manual of the American Psychological Association* (1994).
Mdn	Median.
MS	Mean square, a variance estimate in the analysis of variance. Mean squares typically are subscripted, such as MS_A, MS_B, $MS_{A \times B}$, or MS_{Error}, to indicate which source of variance they represent.
MSE	Mean square error. The symbol used to identify the MS_{Error} for an analysis

of variance in publications following the editorial style of the *Publication Manual of the American Psychological Association* (1994).

μ — Mu, the population mean.

$\mu_{\overline{X}}$ — Mean of the theoretical sampling distribution of the mean.

N — Total number of scores in a sample or the total number of scores in an experiment.

N_{Pairs} — Number of pairs of scores.

n — Number of scores in a subgroup of a larger sample.

n_A — Number of scores in a level of a one-factor design.

n_{AB} — Number of scores in a cell of a two-factor design.

O_{rc} — Observed frequency of a score in row r, column c of a chi-square test contingency table.

$\%f$ — Percentage frequency of a score.

P — A percentile point expressed as a proportion. Used to obtain the score at a specified percentile point.

P_X — Percentile rank of score of X.

p — Probability.

q — Studentized range statistic used in the Tukey HSD test.

r — Pearson correlation coefficient for a sample.

r_{crit} — Critical value of Pearson correlation coefficient.

r_{obs} — Observed value of a Pearson correlation between variables X and Y.

rf — Relative frequency of a score.

ρ — Rho, the population correlation coefficient.

ρ_S — Population Spearman rank-order correlation coefficient.

r_S — Spearman rank-order correlation coefficient.

r^2 — Coefficient of determination.

σ — Sigma, the population standard deviation.

σ^2 — Population variance.

$\sigma_{\overline{X}}$ — Population standard error of the mean.

$\sigma_{\overline{X}A1-\overline{X}A2}$ — Standard error of the difference between means.

$\sum_{i=1}^{N}$ — Summation notation from $i = 1$ to N.

S — Sample standard deviation.

s — Estimated population standard deviation.

SD — Standard deviation. The symbol used in publications following the editorial style of the *Publication Manual of the American Psychological Association* (1994).

S^2 — Sample variance.

s^2 — Estimated population variance.

s^2_{pooled} — Pooled variance estimate for the difference between two population means.

$s_{\overline{X}}$ — Estimated standard error of the mean.

SE — Standard error of the mean. The symbol used in publications following the editorial style of the *Publication Manual of the American Psychological Association* (1994).

$s_{\overline{X}A1-\overline{X}A2}$ — Estimated standard error of the difference between means.

$s_{Y \cdot X}$ — Standard error of estimate when predicting Y from X.

$SIQR$ — Semi-interquartile range.

$\sum R$ — Sum of ranks.

SS — Sum of squares. In an analysis of variance a SS is usually subscripted such as SS_A, SS_B, $SS_{A \times B}$, SS_{Error}, or SS_{Total} to indicate which source of variation it represents.

SS_X — Sum of squares of the X variable in a correlation.

SS_Y — Sum of squares of the Y variable in a correlation.

t — t statistic in the t test.

t_{crit} — Critical value of t.

t_{ind} — t statistic obtained in the t test for independent groups.

t_{obs} — Value of t obtained from data.

t_{rel} — t statistic obtained in the t test for related measures.

T — Wilcoxon T statistic.

T_{crit}	Critical value of T.
T_{obs}	Value of T obtained from data.
U	Mann–Whitney U statistic.
U_{crit}	Critical value of U.
U_{obs}	The smaller value of U obtained from data.
X	A subject's score on the variable identified as the X variable. Depending on the design used, a score may be represented by X_i, X_{ij}, or X_{ijk}.
$X_{Highest}$	The highest score in a distribution of scores.
X_{Lowest}	The lowest score in a distribution of scores.
X_L	Lower real limit of an interval containing the score X in a frequency distribution.
X_P	Score at the P percentile point in a distribution.
X_{25}	Score corresponding to the 25th percentile of a distribution.
X_{50}	Score corresponding to the median of a distribution.

X_{75}	Score corresponding to the 75th percentile of a distribution.
$\overline{X}$	X bar, the sample mean.
$\overline{X}_{A1}, \overline{X}_{A2}, \overline{X}_{A3}$	Main effect means for levels of factor A.
$\overline{X}_{B1}, \overline{X}_{B2}, \overline{X}_{B3}$	Main effect means for levels of factor B.
$\overline{X}_{AB}$	Cell mean in a two-factor design.
$\overline{X}_G$	Grand mean.
$\overline{X}_S$	Subject mean in a within-subjects design.
$\overline{X}_{\overline{X}}$	Mean of the empirical sampling distribution of the mean.
$\overline{X}_{\overline{X}A1-\overline{X}A2}$	Mean of an empirical sampling distribution of the difference between means.
Y	A subject's score on the variable identified as the Y variable.
$\overline{Y}$	Y bar. The sample mean for scores identified as the Y variable.
Y'	Predicted value of Y from a linear regression line.
z	Value of a score obtained from using the z transformation.

Appendix E
Answers for Computational Problems

Solutions are given for most of the numerical problems in the Testing Your Knowledge and Chapter Review Questions sections. For formulas and explanations, see the relevant sections of the text.

CHAPTER 1

Testing Your Knowledge 1–1

2. **b.** From a sample statistic of 52% to a population parameter of 52%.

Testing Your Knowledge 1–2

2. **a.** Type of feedback given.
   b. Duration of foot pronation.
   c. The study involved the creation of two equivalent groups in a between-subjects design and the manipulation of an independent variable.
   d. To determine if the pronation durations differed more than expected by chance.

Testing Your Knowledge 1–3

2. **a.** To find if belief in paranormal phenomena and number of science courses taken are related.
   b. Belief in paranormal phenomena; number of science courses taken.

Review Questions

3. **a.** Correlation and regression.
   b. To find if golf score is related to percentage of body fat.
   c. Percentage of body fat; average golf score.
4. **a.** Description and statistical hypothesis testing.
   b. Type of treatment given a child.
   c. Child's body temperature.
   d. The study involved the creation of two equivalent groups in a between-subjects design and the manipulation of an independent variable.
   e. To find if body temperatures in the two groups differed by more than chance.
5. **a.** Description.   **c.** Percentage.
6. **a.** Raw data.   **d.** Raw data.
   b. Inference.   **e.** Inference.
   c. Statistic.   **f.** Statistic.

CHAPTER 2

Testing Your Knowledge 2–1

2. **a.** Survey research.
   b. Experiment.
   c. Archival records.
   d. Naturalistic observation.
3. By the subject's answer on the 10-point rating scale.

Testing Your Knowledge 2–2

3. People are assigned to the same category although they do not possess the same amount of the variable being measured.
5. **b.** No.

Testing Your Knowledge 2–3

2. **a.** Yes, the scale is interval.
   b. No.   **c.** No.
3. **a.** Yes, the scale is ratio.
   b. Yes.   **c.** Yes.

Testing Your Knowledge 2–4

2. **a.** Continuous.   **e.** Continuous.
   b. Continuous.   **f.** Discrete.
   c. Discrete.   **g.** Discrete.
   d. Continuous.   **h.** Discrete.
3. **a.** 152.35 to 152.45 cm.
   b. 17.25 to 17.35 sec.
   c. 3.5 to 4.5.
   d. 0.4365 to 0.4375 sec.
   e. 6.85 to 6.95 mm.
   f. 67.805 to 67.815 lb.
4. **a.** 27.44.   **d.** 1263.7592.
   b. 119.028.   **e.** 0.35.
   c. 1.44.   **f.** 13.27.

Review Questions

1. **a.** Survey research.
   b. Archival records.
   c. Experiment.
   d. Naturalistic observation.
3. **a.** Career orientation.
   b. Ordinal.
4. **a.** Body weight.
   b. Ratio.
   c. 134.55 to 134.65 lb.
   d. 127.6 or 127.65 lb. depending on the convention followed.
5. **a.** Emotional stability.
   b. Rating scale: gray area between ordinal and interval scale.
   c. 7.5 to 8.5.

d. No, it should be rounded to 5.8 or 5.83 depending on the convention followed.
6. **a.** Ratio.
   b. 96.5 to 97.5 minutes.
   c. 82.7 or 82.67 minutes depending on the convention followed.
7. Ordinal.
8. Nominal.
9. **a.** Discrete.   **c.** Discrete.
   b. Continuous.   **d.** Continuous.
10. **a.** 141.25 to 141.35 lb.
    b. 33.5 to 34.5 minutes.
    c. 175.55 to 175.65 yards.
    d. 98.15 to 98.25°F.
    e. 108.5 to 109.5 mm of mercury.
11. **a.** 42.26.   **e.** 13.90.
    b. 1.16.   **f.** 24.62.
    c. 163.65.   **g.** 19.28.
    d. 27.43.
12. The scale used is a rating scale. See Statistics in Use 2–3 for a discussion of rating scales.
13. **a.** Ordinal.   **b.** Ratio.

CHAPTER 3

Testing Your Knowledge 3–1

2. **a.**

Score	Tally	f	rf	$\%f$
19	/	1	.05	5
18		0	.00	0
17		0	.00	0
16		0	.00	0
15	/	1	.05	5
14	/	1	.05	5
13	/	1	.05	5
12	/	1	.05	5
11	/	1	.05	5
10	/	1	.05	5
9	//	2	.10	10
8	////	4	.20	20
7		0	.00	0
6	//	2	.10	10
5	//	2	.10	10
4	//	2	.10	10
3	/	1	.05	5
2		0	.00	0

  b. Lowest = 3; highest = 19.
  c. 8.

Testing Your Knowledge 3–2

2.   10 to 20.

3.   5.   4.   11.

7.   a.   i = 10.

6.   a.   123, 125.   d.   128.5 to 131.5.
     b.   129, 131.   e.   121.
     c.   122.5, 125.5.   f.   3.

Class Interval	Real Limits Lower	Real Limits Upper	Midpoint of Class	Tally	f	rf	$\%f$	cf	crf	$c\%f$
200–209	199.5	209.5	204.5	/	1	.02	2	50	1.00	100
190–199	189.5	199.5	194.5	/	1	.02	2	49	.98	98
180–189	179.5	189.5	184.5		0	.00	0	48	.96	96
170–179	169.5	179.5	174.5		0	.00	0	48	.96	96
160–169	159.5	169.5	164.5		0	.00	0	48	.96	96
150–159	149.5	159.5	154.5	/	1	.02	2	48	.96	96
140–149	139.5	149.5	144.5	/	1	.02	2	47	.94	94
130–139	129.5	139.5	134.5		0	.00	0	46	.92	92
120–129	119.5	129.5	124.5		0	.00	0	46	.92	92
110–119	109.5	119.5	114.5		0	.00	0	46	.92	92
100–109	99.5	109.5	104.5		0	.00	0	46	.92	92
90–99	89.5	99.5	94.5	//	2	.04	4	46	.92	92
80–89	79.5	89.5	84.5	///	3	.06	6	44	.88	88
70–79	69.5	79.5	74.5	//////	6	.12	12	41	.82	82
60–69	59.5	69.5	64.5	///////////	11	.22	22	35	.70	70
50–59	49.5	59.5	54.5	////////	8	.16	16	24	.48	48
40–49	39.5	49.5	44.5	//////	6	.12	12	16	.32	32
30–39	29.5	39.5	34.5	////////	7	.14	14	10	.20	20
20–29	19.5	29.5	24.5	//	2	.04	4	3	.06	6
10–19	9.5	19.5	14.5	/	1	.02	2	1	.02	2

b.   The large majority of stotting distances were 99 meters or less. Distances in the interval of 60 to 69 meters occurred most frequently. No distance was less than 10 meters or greater than 209 meters.

c. $P_{68} = 67$.

d. $X_{50} = 60.4$ meters.

Testing Your Knowledge 3–3

1.   a.   See Figures E3–1 and E3–2.

b.   The distributions are similar to those in Figures E3–1 and E3–2 except that relative frequencies are portrayed on the ordinate.

c.   The majority of stotting distances were less than 104.5 meters.   The most frequently occurring distances were in the interval with a midpoint of 64.5 meters. No distance was less than 9.5 meters or greater than 209.5 meters.

2.

Stem	Leaf
20	5
19	0
18	
17	
16	
15	4
14	0
13	
12	
11	
10	
9	11
8	133
7	022256
6	11234666778
5	04456789
4	237899
3	1377889
2	59
1	8

a.   18 meters.

b.   205 meters. c.   66 and 72 meters.

FIGURE E3–1
Histogram of stotting distances.

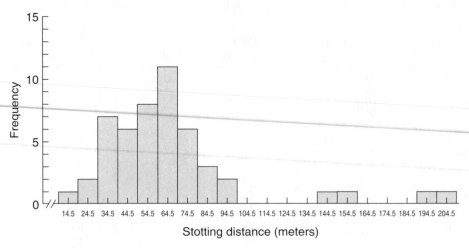

FIGURE E3–2
Frequency polygon of stotting distances.

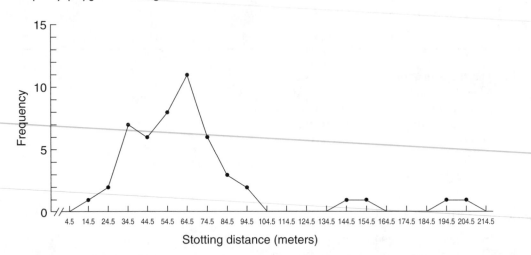

Testing Your Knowledge 3–4

2. a. Symmetrical, unimodal.
    b. Asymmetrical, positively skewed, unimodal.
    c. Asymmetrical, positively skewed, bimodal.
    d. Asymmetrical, negatively skewed, unimodal.

Review Questions

1. a. Size of class interval = 20; class intervals start at stated limit of 220; first midpoint at 229.5; upper stated limit of last class interval = 499.
    b. 400 to 419; midpoint = 409.5; no, it is shorter.
    c. Value will be in interval 340 to 359.

d. $X_{50} = 356.2$.

e. $P_{431} = 89$.

2. a. Size of class interval = 5; class intervals start at stated limit of 0; first midpoint at 2.0; upper stated limit of last class interval = 64.

b. 0 to 4.

c. $X_{50} = 6.2$.

d. $P_{24} = 86$.

e.

Stem	Leaf
*	
6 .	3
*	8
5 .	1
*	67
4 .	
*	7
3 .	
*	66
2 .	114
*	5778
1 .	0124
*	5555566666678899
0 .	000000001111223333444444

Lowest score = 0; highest score = 63. Most frequently occurring score = 0.

4. a.

Number of Days Absent	Reward-policy School	No-reward-policy School
More than 25	.02	.03
24–25	.00	.03
22–23	.02	.005
20–21	.00	.04
18–19	.01	.00
16–17	.00	.02
14–15	.02	.11
12–13	.00	.05
10–11	.03	.09
8–9	.08	.10
6–7	.04	.015
4–5	.13	.07
2–3	.23	.17
0–1	.42	.27

b. $X_{50} =$ 2.2   5.2

c. $P_4 =$ 68   46

d. For the reward-policy school, 78% of the students are absent 5 days or less with a median absence of 2.2 days. For the no-reward-policy school, only 51% of the students are absent 5 days or less, and the median number of absences is 5.2 days.

CHAPTER 4

Testing Your Knowledge 4–1

3. a. 49.   **b.** Unimodal.

4. a. 27.   **b.** Unimodal.

5. a. 24, 27, 49. **b.** Multimodal.

7. 46.

8. 42.

9. 46.

Testing Your Knowledge 4–2

2. $\overline{X} = 88.0$. **b.** 262.

3. a. 41.7.   **b.** 39.5.

   c. 37.7.

Testing Your Knowledge 4–3

1. a. Median.   **c.** Mode.

   b. Mean.   **d.** Mean.

2. Smaller than median.

3. Positively skewed.

Review Questions

1. Possibly negatively skewed because the mean is less than the median.

2. Positively skewed because the mean is considerably larger than the median.

3. Positively skewed because the mean is considerably larger than the median.
4. *Set 1*
   b. Mode = 38, *Mdn* = 38, $\overline{X}$ = 38.6.
   c. Approximately symmetrical; all measures of central tendency are about the same.
   Set 2
   b. Mode = 28, *Mdn* = 29, $\overline{X}$ = 33.5.
   c. Positively skewed; mean is larger than the median.
   Set 3
   b. Mode = 52, *Mdn* = 50, $\overline{X}$ = 46.7.
   c. Negatively skewed; mean is less than the median.
   Set 4
   b. Mode = bimodal, 26, 52; *Mdn* = 40; $\overline{X}$ = 38.6.
   c. Approximately symmetrical, bimodal.
   d. Because the distribution is bimodal, neither the *Mdn* nor the $\overline{X}$ represents the typical score of a subject very well.

5.

	$\overline{X}$	*Mdn*	Mode	
Roberto	64	65	90	Mode
Dimitrios	58	65	None	Median
Karen	71	67	56	Mean

6. a. It is likely that some subjects estimated very high numbers of drinks consumed each week, thus positively skewing the distribution.
   b. Median number of drinks per week.
7. a. Mode or median.
   b. Mode = 793, *Mdn* = 832.

CHAPTER 5

Testing Your Knowledge 5-1

2. Range = 44, *IQR* = 18, *SIQR* = 9.
3. a. Range = 287 ms, *IQR* = 85 ms, *SIQR* = 42.5 ms.

Testing Your Knowledge 5-2

2. a and b.

	Read by Themselves	Read by Teacher
$\overline{X}$	59.0	57.0
s	5.54	10.23
s^2	30.69	104.65

   c. Read by teacher group.
   d. 10.23.
3. a.

	Male	Female
$\overline{X}$	15.55	7.05
s	7.41	2.59
s^2	54.91	6.71

   b. Males.
   c. 7.41 minutes.
   d. Females; the *s* is smaller for females than for males.

Testing Your Knowledge 5-3

1. a. *Mdn*, *SIQR*.   e. $\overline{X}$, *s*.
   b. *Mdn*, *SIQR*.   f. *Mdn*, *SIQR*.
   c. $\overline{X}$, *s*.   g. *Mdn*, *SIQR*.
   d. *Mdn*, *SIQR*.

Review Questions

1. a. *Mdn* = 50, $\overline{X}$ = 49.60, *IQR* = 10, *s* = 7.26.
   b. Both are equally good.
2. a. *Mdn* = 50, $\overline{X}$ = 49.45, *IQR* = 10, *s* = 11.56.
   b. Both are equally good.
   c. The *IQR* is not affected by scores in the tails of the distribution.

3. a. Range.   g. Range.
    b. *IQR*.   h. S^2.
    c. *SIQR*.   i. s^2.
    d. s^2.   j. *S*.
    e. *s*.   k. *s*.
    f. *IQR*.   l. *SIQR*.
4. a. 15.4 drinks per week.
    b. Large.
    c. The large standard deviations indicate that the distributions were positively skewed. Some subjects estimated a very large number of drinks per week and inflated the value of *s*. This result indicates that the median would be a better measure of central tendency for the scores.
5. The *IQR* or *SIQR* because they do not require knowing the numerical value of the score assigned to the ninth patient.

CHAPTER 6

Testing Your Knowledge 6–1

4. a. .3413.   g. .8400.
    b. .4772.   h. .9544.
    c. .4987.   i. .9974.
    d. .3413.   j. .1359.
    e. .4772.   k. .1574.
    f. .4987.   l. .0215.

Testing Your Knowledge 6–2

2.

	z	Area 0 to z	Area beyond z
a.	+1.90	.4713	.0287
b.	−0.52	.1985	.3015
c.	+0.77	.2794	.2206
d.	−1.83	.4664	.0336
e.	+1.75	.4599	.0401
f.	−1.26	.3962	.1038

3. a. .0401.

b. .1465.
c. .3345.
d. Approximately 58.8 to 85.2 using $z =$ + or − 1.65.

Testing Your Knowledge 6–3

3. .0014.
4. .19.

5.

	z	p
a.	+1.90	.0287
b.	−0.52	.3015
c.	+0.77	.2206
d.	−1.83	.0336
e.	+1.75	.0401
f.	−1.26	.1038

6. a. .0668.   c. .2426.
    b. .1865.

Review Questions

3. a. .1587.   d. .4082.
    b. .0228.   e. .4525.
    c. .0038.
    f. Approximately 80.8 to 119.2 using $z =$ + or − 1.28.
    g. .6568.   i. .0475.
    h. .0918.   j. .0038.
4. a. .016.   b. .018.
5. a. .00033.   c. .00022.
    b. .00019.
6. a. .0968.   c. .8064.
    b. .0968.
7. a. .0668.   d. .8664.
    b. .0401.   e. .2266.
    c. .9544.   f. .3085.

8.   a.

	Video Games	GPA
$\overline{X}$	8.0	2.7
S	5.86	0.87
Alex	−0.34	−0.23
Lauren	0.00	−0.80
Yvonne	−1.37	+1.38
Laval	+1.19	+0.80
Bonnie	−0.85	+0.46
Jason	+1.37	−1.61

b. That she is at the mean of the group for video-game playing.
c. That she is 1.38 standard deviations above the mean GPA of the group.
d. That the person's GPA is below the mean of the group.
e. That the person's video-game playing time is above the mean of the group.

9.

English Literature	World History
$z = +0.83$	$z = +1.00$

World history, where your score is one standard deviation above the class mean.

CHAPTER 7

Testing Your Knowledge 7–1

2.

	(a) Proportion	(b) Number
Generalized anxiety disorder	.27	27
Agoraphobia	.23	23
Simple phobia	.19	19
Panic disorder	.22	22
Obsessive-compulsive	.09	9

Testing Your Knowledge 7–2

2. Biased; underestimates.

3. Unbiased.
4. Biased; slightly underestimates.
7.   a. .6826.   **d.** .0475.
      b. .1587.   **e.** .4525.
      c. .0228.

Testing Your Knowledge 7–3

1.   a. 9 seconds.
      b. 6 seconds.
      c. 3 seconds.
      d. As N increases, $s_{\overline{X}}$ decreases.
2.   a. $s = 10, s_{\overline{X}} = 2$.
          $s = 15, s_{\overline{X}} = 3$.
          $s = 20, s_{\overline{X}} = 4$.
      b. As s increases, $s_{\overline{X}}$ also increases.
3. Population A_2 because it has a larger value of σ.

Testing Your Knowledge 7–4

2.   a. 73.0.
      b. 69.1 to 76.9.
      c. 67.8 to 78.2.
      d. 73.0.
      e. 71.0 to 75.0.
      f. 70.4 to 75.6.
      g. The value of $\sigma_{\overline{X}}$ becomes smaller as N increases.

Review Questions

1.   a. σ.   **c.** σ^2.
      b. μ.   **d.** $\sigma_{\overline{X}}$.
2. $N = 24$, because $\overline{X}$ is a consistent estimator.
3. Stratified; see text for explanation.
5.   a. 9.0 cigarettes per day.
      b. 7.5 to 10.5 cigarettes per day.
6.   a. 0.3.   **c.** .1587.
      b. .0013.   **d.** .9544.

8.

Sample	a.	b.	d.
A	2.00	.1587	.3413
B	1.33	.0668	.4332
C	1.00	.0228	.4772
D	0.80	.0062	.4938
E	0.40	< .0001	> .4999

9. **a.** .0228.   **b.** .1151.

CHAPTER 8

Testing Your Knowledge 8–1

3. **a.** $H_0: \mu = 100$.
       $H_1: \mu \neq 100$.
    b. $H_0: \mu = 8.3$.
       $H_1: \mu \neq 8.3$.
    c. $H_0: \mu = 423.0$.
       $H_1: \mu \neq 423.0$.

4.

	z_{obs}	
a.	−2.13	Falls into rejection region; reject H_0, accept H_1.
b.	−1.20	Does not fall into rejection region; do not reject H_0, do not accept H_1.
c.	+2.25	Falls into rejection region; reject H_0, accept H_1.
d.	+1.72	Does not fall into rejection region; do not reject H_0, do not accept H_1.

5. **a.** $z = (\overline{X} - \mu)/\sigma_{\overline{X}}$.
    b. $H_0: \mu = 100$; $H_1: \mu \neq 100$.
    c. $\alpha = .05$.
    d. $z_{crit} = 1.96$.
    e. Values of z_{obs} more extreme than $z = -1.96$ or $+1.96$.
    f. $z_{obs} = +2.50$.
    g. Reject H_0; accept H_1.
    h. The sample mean differs significantly from the population mean.

Testing Your Knowledge 8–2

3. **a.** 7.   **c.** 6.
    b. 6.

4. **a.** 9.   **d.** 53.
    b. 15.   **e.** 119.
    c. 6.   **f.** 29.

5. The distribution with 13 df.
6. When the $df = \infty$.

Testing Your Knowledge 8–3

1. **a.** $H_0: \mu = 493$; $H_1: \mu \neq 493$.
    b. $H_0: \mu = 36.1$; $H_1: \mu \neq 36.1$.
    c. $H_0: \mu = 100$; $H_1: \mu \neq 100$.

2. **a.** 2.447.   **e.** 2.042.
    b. 2.898.   **f.** 2.660.
    c. 2.069.   **g.** 2.000.
    d. 2.042.   **h.** 1.980.

3.

	Falls into Rejection Region	Decision
a.	Yes	Reject H_0 Accept H_1
b.	No	Fail to reject H_0 Do not accept H_1
c.	Yes	Reject H_0 Accept H_1
d.	No	Fail to reject H_0 Do not accept H_1
e.	Yes	Reject H_0 Accept H_1
f.	Yes	Reject H_0 Accept H_1
g.	No	Fail to reject H_0 Do not accept H_1
h.	Yes	Reject H_0 Accept H_1
i.	Yes	Reject H_0 Accept H_1
j.	Yes	Reject H_0 Accept H_1
k.	Yes	Reject H_0 Accept H_1

5. a. $t = (\overline{X} - \mu)/s_{\overline{X}}$.
    b. See text.
    c. H_0: $\mu = 7.0$; H_1: $\mu \neq 7.0$.
    d. $\alpha = .05$.
    e. $t_{crit}(10) = 2.228$.
    f. Values of t_{obs} more extreme than -2.228 or $+2.228$.
    g. $t_{obs} = -4.979$.
    h. Reject H_0; accept H_1.
    i. The sample mean of 5.8 minutes differs significantly from the population mean of 7.0 minutes.

6. *Report 1*
    a. 70.4 kg.
    b. 7.6 kg.
    c. One-sample t.
    d. H_0: $\mu = 75$ kg; H_1: $\mu \neq 75$ kg.
    e. 6.
    f. -1.48.
    g. 5.
    h. 2.571.
    i. Fail to reject H_0.
    j. Do not accept H_1.
    k. The sample mean does not differ significantly from the population mean.
    Report 2
    a. 10.4 days.
    b. 2.3 days.
    c. One-sample t.
    d. H_0: $\mu = 8.7$ days; H_1: $\mu \neq 8.7$ days.
    e. 25.
    f. $+3.70$.
    g. 24.
    h. 2.064.
    i. Reject H_0.
    j. Accept H_1.
    k. The sample mean differs significantly from the population mean; 10.4 days is significantly longer than the hypothesized mean of 8.7 days.

Testing Your Knowledge 8–4

2. b. $p = \alpha$.
    c. A Type I error cannot occur if H_0 is false.
    e. No.
4. 80.1 to 113.9 minutes.
5. 256.8 to 259.2 yards.

Chapter Review

5. a. Reject H_0; accept H_1.
    b. Fail to reject H_0; do not accept H_1.
7. a. The sample mean differs significantly from the hypothesized population mean.
    b. The sample mean does not differ significantly from the hypothesized population mean.
8. Rejection region consists of values of z_{obs} more extreme than $z = -2.58$ or $+2.58$.

z_{obs}	Falls into Rejection Region	Decision
$+3.71$	Yes	Reject H_0 Accept H_1
-2.60	Yes	Reject H_0 Accept H_1
$+1.74$	No	Fail to reject H_0 Do not accept H_1
-3.05	Yes	Reject H_0 Accept H_1
-1.96	No	Fail to reject H_0 Do not accept H_1
$+2.58$	Yes	Reject H_0 Accept H_1

9. $z_{obs} = -1.52$; nonsignificant; fail to reject H_0.
11. a. The sample mean differs significantly from the hypothesized population mean.
    b. The sample mean does not differ significantly from the hypothesized population mean.

12.

	Falls into Rejection Region	Decision
a.	Yes	Reject H_0 Accept H_1
b.	No	Fail to reject H_0 Do not accept H_1
c.	Yes	Reject H_0 Accept H_1
d.	Yes	Reject H_0 Accept H_1
e.	No	Fail to reject H_0 Do not accept H_1
f.	No	Fail to reject H_0 Do not accept H_1

13. **a.** $t_{obs}(8) = -2.924$; significant at the .05 level; reject H_0, accept H_1.
   c. Yes.
   d. No.
   e. 6.81 to 7.59 hours; $\mu = 7.7$ is not included in this interval.
14. **a.** $t_{obs}(11) = +3.139$; significant at the .05 level; reject H_0, accept H_1.
   b. No.
15. **a.** Type I error.
   b. Type II error.
   c. Correct decision.
   d. Correct decision.

CHAPTER 9

Testing Your Knowledge 9–1

6. **a.** Extraneous variable = age; groups differ systematically in average age as well as noise condition.
   b. Extraneous variable = experimenter's encouragement; groups differ systematically in encouragement as well as noise condition.
   c. Extraneous variable = gender; groups differ systematically in gender as well as noise condition.
   d. Extraneous variable = college major; groups differ systematically in college major as well as noise condition.
   e. Extraneous variable = time of day when the experiment was conducted; groups differ systematically in time of day as well as noise condition.

Testing Your Knowledge 9–2

3. **a.** 3.77.   **c.** 3.81.
   b. 3.56.   **d.** 2.25.

Testing Your Knowledge 9–3

6.

Sample Set	df	t_{crit}	Falls into Rejection Region	Decision
1.	18	2.101	Yes	Reject H_0 Accept H_1
2.	18	2.101	No	Fail to reject H_0 Do not accept H_1
3.	28	2.048	Yes	Reject H_0 Accept H_1
4.	28	2.048	Yes	Reject H_0 Accept H_1
5.	68	2.000	Yes	Reject H_0 Accept H_1
6.	33	2.042	No	Fail to reject H_0 Do not accept H_1
7.	127	1.980	Yes	Reject H_0 Accept H_1
8.	148	1.980	Yes	Reject H_0 Accept H_1

9. *Problem 1*
   a. H_0: $\mu_{A1} = \mu_{A2}$; H_1: $\mu_{A1} \neq \mu_{A2}$.
   b. $t_{obs}(34) = -3.656$.
   c. 34.
   d. 2.042.
   e. Values of t_{obs} more extreme than -2.042 or $+2.042$.
   f. Yes.
   g. Reject H_0; accept H_1.
   h. Different populations.

i. Yes.

j. Yes; the control group estimated a statistically significant shorter time interval than the experimental group.

Problem 2

a. H_0: $\mu_{A1} = \mu_{A2}$; H_1: $\mu_{A1} \neq \mu_{A2}$.

b. $t_{obs}(28) = -1.742$.

c. 28.

d. 2.048.

e. Values of t_{obs} more extreme than -2.048 or $+2.048$.

f. No.

g. Fail to reject H_0; do not accept H_1.

h. There is no evidence that they are not from the same population.

i. No; it is nonsignificant.

j. No; the difference between the group means is treated as a chance difference.

Testing Your Knowledge 9–4

1. *Report 1*
   a. 2.
   b. 62.
   c. 79.7; 73.0.
   d. 8.57; 5.85.
   e. 3.60.
   f. 2.000.
   g. Reject H_0.
   h. Accept H_1.
   i. Statistically significant.
   j. The effect of the treatment.

2. *Report 2*
   a. 2.
   b. 30.
   c. 22.78; 24.33.
   d. 5.23; 5.14.
   e. −0.82.
   f. 2.048.
   g. Fail to reject H_0.
   h. Do not accept H_1.
   i. Nonsignificant.
   j. Sampling error.

Testing Your Knowledge 9–5

2. a. Set 2.   c. Set 1.
   b. Set 2.

3. $n_{A1} = n_{A2} = 20$ expected to have a smaller $s_{\overline{X}A1-\overline{X}A2}$ and lead to a more powerful statistical test.

4. a. .42.   d. .23.
   b. .27.   e. .08.
   c. .19.

Review Questions

1.

	Group	
	Quiet	**Noise**
$\overline{X}$	122.64	131.27
s	8.76	10.45

a. $t_{obs}(20) = -2.099$, $p < .05$. The mean blood pressure of the quiet group is significantly lower than that of the noise group.

b. $\eta^2 = .18$; 18% of the variance in the dependent variable.

c. 0.05 to 17.21.

2.

	Group	
	Quiet	**Noise**
$\overline{X}$	113.09	115.27
s	4.55	6.48

$t_{obs}(20) = -0.913$, $p > .05$. The mean blood pressures of the two groups do not differ significantly.

3.

	Gender	
	Male	**Female**
$\overline{X}$	17.77	18.59
s	4.99	5.32

$t_{obs}(28) = -0.429$, $p > .05$. Males and females do not differ significantly on the rated need for solitude.

4.

Type of Neckwear		
	Loose	**Tight**
$\overline{X}$	20.08	18.75
s	2.15	2.05

$t_{obs}(11) = +2.072$, $p > .05$. t_{obs} is nonsignificant at the .05 level.   There is no evidence that neckwear affected flicker fusion frequency.

5. **a.** $t_{obs}(88) = +3.170$, $p < .01$. The mean locus of control score for the foster parents group was significantly higher than the mean locus of control score for the biological parents group.
  b. $\eta^2 = .10$.
  c. 1.29 to 5.69.

6. **a.** $t_{obs}(5398) = -25.003$, $p < .001$; the GPAs of the two groups differ significantly. The GPA of students involved in residence hall disruptions is significantly lower than the GPA of students not involved in disruptions.
  b. $\eta^2 = .10$.
  c. 0.47 to 0.55.

7. $t_{obs}(32) = -0.818$, $p > .05$. The nonsignificant t indicates that the group means do not differ significantly at the .05 level.

CHAPTER 10

Testing Your Knowledge 10–1

6. $a = 4$, $n_A = 11$, $N = 44$.
11. 150.00.
12. 25.00.
13. 79.
14. 25.00.
15. 10.00.
16. $df_A = 3$, $df_{Error} = 40$, $df_{Total} = 43$.

17.

Source	SS	df	MS	F
Factor A	24.00	1	24.00	6.00
Error	16.00	4	4.00	
Total	40.00	5		

18.

Source	SS	df	MS	F
Factor A	42.00	2	21.00	5.25
Error	24.00	6	4.00	
Total	66.00	8		

19. *Table 1*

Source	SS	df	MS	F
Factor A	50.00	1	50.00	5.00
Error	260.00	26	10.00	
Total	310.00	27		

  a. 2.   **c.** 28.
  b. 14.

Table 2

Source	SS	df	MS	F
Factor A	18.00	3	6.00	3.00
Error	152.00	76	2.00	
Total	170.00	79		

  a. 4.   **c.** 80.
  b. 20.

Testing Your Knowledge 10–2

6. Approximately 1.00.
7. It becomes greater than 1.00.
8. **a.** H_0: $\mu_{A1} = \mu_{A2}$;
        H_1: The μ_A's are not equal.
  b. H_0: $\mu_{A1} = \mu_{A2} = \mu_{A3} = \mu_{A4}$;
        H_1: The μ_A's are not all equal.
  c. H_0: $\mu_{A1} = \mu_{A2} = \mu_{A3} = \mu_{A4} = \mu_{A5} = \mu_{A6}$;
        H_1: The μ_A's are not all equal.
9. The independent variable has no effect.
10. The independent variable has an effect.
11. Zero.
12. No upper limit.

13.

Experiment	F_{crit}	Falls into Rejection Region	Decision
1.	4.96	Yes	Reject H_0 Accept H_1
2.	3.40	No	Fail to reject H_0 Do not accept H_1
3.	4.26	Yes	Reject H_0 Accept H_1
4.	3.15	Yes	Reject H_0 Accept H_1
5.	3.88	Yes	Reject H_0 Accept H_1
6.	3.68	No	Fail to reject H_0 Do not accept H_1
7.	2.61	No	Fail to reject H_0 Do not accept H_1
8.	3.10	No	Fail to reject H_0 Do not accept H_1
9.	2.25	Yes	Reject H_0 Accept H_1
10.	2.53	No	Fail to reject H_0 Do not accept H_1

Testing Your Knowledge 10–3

1.

	Group	
	Control	Experimental
$\overline{X}$	7.09	8.82
s	1.30	1.47

  a. H_0: $\mu_{A1} = \mu_{A2}$;
  H_1: The μ_A's are not equal.
  b. $F_{obs}(1, 20) = 8.51$.
  c. $df_A = 1$, $df_{Error} = 20$.
  d. $F_{crit}(1, 20) = 4.35$.
  e. Values of $F_{obs} \geq 4.35$.
  f. Yes.
  g. Reject H_0; accept H_1.
  h. Different populations.
  i. Yes.
  j. They differ; the control group estimated a shorter time interval.
  k. No, because only two levels of the independent variable were manipulated.

  l. $\eta^2 = .30$.
  m. 30 percent.

2.

	Treatment Group		
	Beard	Bandana	Control
$\overline{X}$	22.88	35.63	36.00
s	3.60	3.50	3.70

  a. H_0: $\mu_{A1} = \mu_{A2} = \mu_{A3}$;
  H_1: The μ_A's are not all equal.
  b. $F_{obs}(2, 21) = 34.39$.
  c. $df_A = 2$, $df_{Error} = 21$.
  d. $F_{crit}(2, 21) = 3.47$.
  e. Values of $F_{obs} \geq 3.47$.
  f. Yes.
  g. Reject H_0; accept H_1.
  h. There is at least one significant difference among the means.
  i. Yes; because F_{obs} is statistically significant and there are three means being compared in the experiment.
  j. $CD = 4.6$.
  k. The beard versus bandana groups and beard versus control groups differences are larger than the CD.
  l. The theatrical beard group had significantly lower ratings (thus higher-rated masculinity) than either the bandana or control group. The bandana and control groups did not differ significantly on their ratings.
  m. $\eta^2 = .77$.
  n. 77 percent.

Testing Your Knowledge 10–4

1.
  a. 2.
  b. 62.
  c. 14.15.
  d. 4.00.
  e. Reject H_0.
  f. Accept H_1.
  g. Yes.
  h. The familiar and unfamiliar poetry passage group means.

2.
  a. 4.
  b. 40.
  c. 1.13.
  d. 2.92.

e. Fail to reject H_0.
f. Do not accept H_1.
g. No.
h. There are no significant differences among the means.

3. a. 3.   e. Reject H_0.
   b. 39.   f. Accept H_1.
   c. 33.94. g. Yes.
   d. 3.32.
   h. The Tukey CD indicates that the mean for the hard rock music (29.9) was significantly higher than the mean for either classical music (18.5) or the mean for the no-music control group (17.5). The classical and no-music control group means did not differ significantly.

Review Questions

1. a.

	Nationality of Student	
	U.S.	Foreign
$\overline{X}$	5.88	11.88
s	3.05	3.70

F_{obs} (1, 30) = 25.01, p < .01. The U.S. mean is significantly lower than the foreign mean.

b. η^2 = .45.

2. a.

	Instructional Condition		
	No Videotape	Soccer Videotape	Throwing, Catching Videotape
$\overline{X}$	45.22	44.33	57.11
s	5.63	5.74	6.68

F_{obs} (2, 24) = 12.57, p < .01. Tukey CD = 7.1. The throwing, catching videotape mean differs significantly from both the no videotape and the soccer videotape means. The no videotape and soccer videotape means do not differ significantly.

b. η^2 = .51.

3. a.

	Group	
	Quiet	Noise
$\overline{X}$	122.64	131.27
s	8.76	10.45

F_{obs} (1, 20) = 4.41, p < .05. The mean for the quiet group is significantly lower than the mean for the noise group.

b. Yes, $t = \sqrt{F} = \sqrt{4.41} = 2.10$.

4. a. $a = 6$, $n_A = 7$, $N = 42$.
   b. $df_A = 5$, $df_{Error} = 36$, $df_{Total} = 41$.

5. *Table 1*

Source	SS	df	MS	F
Factor A	50.00	2	25.00	2.50
Error	270.00	27	10.00	
Total	320.00	29		

a. 3.
b. 10.
c. 30.
d. F_{crit} (2, 27) = 3.35; F_{obs} is nonsignificant.
e. Fail to reject H_0; do not accept H_1.

Table 2

Source	SS	df	MS	F
Factor A	60.00	5	12.00	4.00
Error	216.00	72	3.00	
Total	276.00	77		

a. 6.
b. 13.
c. 78.
d. F_{crit} (5, 72) = 2.37; F_{obs} is statistically significant.
e. Reject H_0; accept H_1.

Table 3

Source	SS	df	MS	F
Factor A	45.00	3	15.00	3.00
Error	320.00	64	5.00	
Total	365.00	67		

a. 4.
b. 17.
c. 68.
d. F_{crit} (3, 64) = 2.76; F_{obs} is statistically significant.
e. Reject H_0; accept H_1.

7. F_{obs} (1, 18) = 4.00.

8. t_{obs} (22) = 3.00.

10. The statistically significant F_{obs} (3, 64) = 21.64 indicates that there is at least one significant difference between the groups. Applying the CD = 5.0 minutes to the pairwise comparisons reveals that the Behavior Modification and Cigarettes Anonymous Club have significantly longer mean times between smoking cigarettes than either the Control group or the Smoke-Stop Gum group. The Behavior Modification and Cigarettes Anonymous means do not differ significantly from each other, and the Control group and Smoke-Stop Gum group means also do not differ significantly from each other.

CHAPTER 11

Testing Your Knowledge 11–1

2.

	Number of Independent Variables	Levels	Number of Subjects Needed
a.	2	$A = 3; B = 3$	90
b.	2	$A = 3; B = 2$	60
c.	2	$A = 2; B = 3$	60
d.	2	$A = 6; B = 2$	120
e.	2	$A = 4; B = 4$	160
f.	3	$A = 2; B = 2$ $C = 2$	80
g.	3	$A = 2; B = 4$ $C = 3$	240
h.	3	$A = 3; B = 3$ $C = 2$	180

3. *Table 1*

		Factor A		Main Effect Means for Factor B
		A_1	A_2	
Factor B	B_1	13.3	20.2	16.8
	B_2	16.8	22.8	19.8
Main Effect Means for Factor A		15.1	21.5	$\overline{X}_G = 18.3$

Table 2

		Factor A		Main Effect Means for Factor B
		A_1	A_2	
Factor B	B_1	18.9	30.1	24.5
	B_2	31.3	33.9	32.6
Main Effect Means for Factor A		25.1	32.0	$\overline{X}_G = 28.6$

Testing Your Knowledge 11–2

8. 240.00.   **10.** 55.00.

9. 45.00.   **11.** 60.00.

12. $df_A = 1$, $df_B = 2$, $df_{A \times B} = 2$, $df_{Error} = 30$, $df_{Total} = 35$.

13. $df_A = 2$, $df_B = 1$, $df_{A \times B} = 2$, $df_{Error} = 72$, $df_{Total} = 77$.

14. 79.

15. $MS_A = 14.00/1 = 14.00$; $MS_B = 26.00/2 = 13.00$; $MS_{A \times B} = 44.00/2 = 22.00$; $MS_{Error} = 480.00/60 = 8.00$.

16. **a.**

Source	SS	df	MS	F
Factor A	108.00	1	108.00	27.00
Factor B	0.00	1	0.00	0.00
A × B	12.00	1	12.00	3.00
Error	32.00	8	4.00	
Total	152.00	11		

b. Both main effect means for factor B are equal to 32.0.

17. *Table 1*

Source	SS	df	MS	F
Factor A	32.00	2	16.00	2.00
Factor B	24.00	1	24.00	3.00
A × B	24.00	2	12.00	1.50
Error	480.00	60	8.00	
Total	560.00	65		

a. 3.

b. 2.

c. 11.

d. 66.

Table 2

Source	SS	df	MS	F
Factor A	36.00	2	18.00	4.50
Factor B	24.00	4	6.00	1.50
$A \times B$	160.00	8	20.00	5.00
Error	840.00	210	4.00	
Total	1060.00	224		

a. 3.
b. 5.
c. 15.
d. 225.

Testing Your Knowledge 11-3

6. F_{obs} becomes greater than 1.00.
7. F_{obs} becomes greater than 1.00.

9. a.

F Ratio for:	Statistical Hypotheses
Factor A	H_0: $\mu_{A1} = \mu_{A2}$; H_1: The μ_A's are not equal.
Factor B	H_0: $\mu_{B1} = \mu_{B2} = \mu_{B3} = \mu_{B4}$; H_1: The μ_B's are not all equal.
$A \times B$	H_0: All $(\mu_{AB} - \mu_A - \mu_B + \mu_G) = 0$; H_1: Not all $(\mu_{AB} - \mu_A - \mu_B + \mu_G) = 0$.

b.

F Ratio for:	Statistical Hypotheses
Factor A	H_0: $\mu_{A1} = \mu_{A2} = \mu_{A3}$; H_1: The μ_A's are not equal.
Factor B	H_0: $\mu_{B1} = \mu_{B2}$; H_1: The μ_B's are not equal.
$A \times B$	H_0: All $(\mu_{AB} - \mu_A - \mu_B + \mu_G) = 0$; H_1: Not all $(\mu_{AB} - \mu_A - \mu_B + \mu_G) = 0$.

c.

F Ratio for:	Statistical Hypotheses
Factor A	H_0: $\mu_{A1} = \mu_{A2} = \mu_{A3}$; H_1: The μ_A's are not all equal.
Factor B	H_0: $\mu_{B1} = \mu_{B2} = \mu_{B3}$; H_1: The μ_B's are not all equal.
$A \times B$	H_0: All $(\mu_{AB} - \mu_A - \mu_B + \mu_G) = 0$; H_1: Not all $(\mu_{AB} - \mu_A - \mu_B + \mu_G) = 0$.

10. *Table 1*

Source	df	F_{obs}	F_{crit}	F_{obs} Falls into Rejection Region	Decision
Factor A	1	4.63	4.08	Yes	Reject H_0 Accept H_1
Factor B	3	2.11	2.84	No	Fail to reject H_0 Do not accept H_1
$A \times B$	3	3.97	2.84	Yes	Reject H_0 Accept H_1

Table 2

Source	df	F_{obs}	F_{crit}	F_{obs} Falls into Rejection Region	Decision
Factor A	3	1.42	2.68	No	Fail to reject H_0 Do not accept H_1
Factor B	2	3.51	3.07	Yes	Reject H_0 Accept H_1
$A \times B$	6	2.37	2.17	Yes	Reject H_0 Accept H_1

Table 3

Source	df	F_{obs}	F_{crit}	F_{obs} Falls into Rejection Region	Decision
Factor A	2	4.12	3.07	Yes	Reject H_0 Accept H_1
Factor B	4	2.83	2.45	Yes	Reject H_0 Accept H_1
$A \times B$	8	1.87	2.02	No	Fail to reject H_0 Do not accept H_1

Testing Your Knowledge 11-4

Figure 11-2
a. Yes.
b. No.
c. Yes.
d. Because of the statistically significant interaction, the effect of the type of teaching method depends on the type of material, factor B. For mathematical material (B_1), computer-assisted teaching (A_1) leads to significantly higher test

scores than does noncomputer-assisted teaching (A_2). For social studies material (B_2), however, the teaching methods do not differ from each other.

e. The statistically significant interaction indicates that the effect of type of material depends on the type of teaching, factor A. For computer-assisted teaching (A_1), mathematical material (B_1) leads to significantly higher test scores compared to social studies material (B_2). For noncomputer-assisted teaching (A_2), there is no difference between the types of materials.

f. No; the main effect for factor A indicates an overall superiority for computer-assisted teaching, but computer-assisted teaching leads to significantly higher test scores only with mathematical material. Thus the main effect for factor A is an artifact of the interaction; it conveys no meaningful information about the effect of factor A on test scores.

Figure 11–3

a. No.

b. Yes.

c. Yes.

d. The statistically significant interaction indicates that the effect of type of teaching depends on the type of material, factor B. For mathematical material (B_1), the teaching methods do not differ significantly. For social studies material (B_2), noncomputer-assisted teaching (A_2) leads to significantly higher test scores than does computer-assisted teaching (A_1).

e. The statistically significant interaction indicates that the effect of type of material depends on the type of teaching, factor A. Both types of teaching lead to higher test scores for mathematical material, but the difference between mathematical and social studies material is larger for computer-assisted teaching than it is for noncomputer-assisted teaching.

f. Yes; the main effect for factor B indicates an overall superiority for mathematical material, and mathematical material leads to significantly higher test scores for both types of teaching. The interaction, however, indicates that the difference between mathematical and social studies material depends on the type of teaching method.

2. *Table 1*

a. Yes.

b. No.

c. No.

d. Computer-assisted teaching (A_1) leads to significantly higher test scores than does noncomputer-assisted teaching (A_2).

e. No effect.

f. Yes; there is no interaction of A and B.

Table 2

a. No.

b. Yes.

c. No.

d. No effect.

e. Mathematical material (B_1) leads to significantly higher test scores than does social studies material (B_2).

f. Yes; there is no interaction of A and B.

Table 3

a. Yes.

b. Yes.

c. No.

d. Noncomputer-assisted teaching (A_2) leads to significantly higher test scores than does computer-assisted teaching (A_1).

e. Mathematical material (B_1) leads to significantly higher test scores than does social studies material (B_2).

f. Yes; there is no interaction of A and B.

Table 4

a. No.

b. No.

c. Yes.

d. Because of the statistically significant interaction, the effect of teaching method depends on the type of material, factor B. For mathematical material (B_1), computer-assisted teaching (A_1) leads to significantly higher test scores than does noncomputer-assisted teaching (A_2). For social studies material (B_2), however, noncomputer-assisted teaching (A_2) leads to significantly higher test scores than does computer-assisted teaching (A_1).

e. Because of the statistically significant interaction, the effect of the type of material depends on the type of teaching, factor A. For computer-assisted teaching (A_1), mathematical material (B_1) leads to significantly higher test scores than social studies material. For noncomputer-assisted teaching (A_2), social studies material (B_2) leads to significantly higher test scores than mathematical material.

f. No; the main effect for each independent variable indicates no overall effect of the independent variable. However, each independent variable does have an effect, but the effect of each independent variable depends on the level of the other independent variable.

Table 5

a. Yes.

b. Yes.

c. Yes.

d. Because of the statistically significant interaction, the effect of the type of teaching method depends on the type of material. For mathematical material (B_1), the difference between computer-assisted (A_1) and noncomputer-assisted (A_2) teaching is nonsignificant. For social studies material, however, noncomputer-assisted teaching (A_2) leads to significantly higher test scores compared to computer-assisted teaching (A_1).

e. Because of the statistically significant interaction, the effect of the type of material depends on the type of teaching. For both computer-assisted (A_1) and noncomputer-assisted (A_2) teaching,

mathematical material (B_1) leads to significantly higher test scores than does social studies material (B_2). However, the difference between mathematical and social studies scores is greater for computer-assisted teaching (A_1) than it is for noncomputer-assisted teaching (A_2).

f. The main effect of factor A, teaching method, is artifactual because it indicates an overall superiority for noncomputer-assisted teaching. But noncomputer-assisted teaching leads to significantly higher performance only with social studies material. The main effect of factor B, type of material, is meaningful; mathematical material leads to significantly higher performance for both computer-assisted and noncomputer-assisted teaching.

Table 6

a. Yes.

b. Yes.

c. Yes.

d. Because of the statistically significant interaction, the effect of the type of teaching method depends on the type of material. For mathematical material (B_1), computer-assisted teaching (A_1) leads to significantly higher test scores compared to noncomputer-assisted teaching (A_2). For social studies material, however, there is no effect of teaching method.

e. The effect of type of material depends on the type of teaching. For computer-assisted teaching (A_1), mathematical material (B_1) leads to significantly higher test scores than does social studies material (B_2). For noncomputer-assisted teaching (A_2), the difference between mathematical material (B_1) and social studies material (B_2) scores is nonsignificant.

f. The main effects for both factor A, teaching method, and factor B, type of material, are artifactual.

Testing Your Knowledge 11-5

1. Analysis of variance summary.

Source	SS	df	MS	F
Locus of control (A)	704.167	1	704.167	1.15
Instructions (B)	1,472.667	1	1,472.667	2.41
$A \times B$	46,112.666	1	46,112.666	75.39*
Error	12,233.000	20	611.650	
Total	60,522.500	23		

*$p < .01$.

a. (1) No significant main effect for either independent variable.
(2) Significant interaction.

b. ($CD = 36.15$) The statistically significant interaction indicates that the effect of instructions depends on the locus of control. For internal locus of control subjects, skill instructions led to significantly more time spent on the task than did chance instructions. For external locus of control subjects, however, chance instructions led to significantly more time spent on the task than did skill instructions.

c. Because of the interaction, the nonsignificant main effects do not provide useful information for interpreting the outcome.

d. $\eta^2 = .76$ for the interaction of factors A and B.

2. Analysis of variance summary.

Source	SS	df	MS	F
Instruction (A)	191.361	1	191.361	23.61*
Crime (B)	1667.361	1	1667.361	205.75*
$A \times B$	210.250	1	210.250	25.94*
Error	259.333	32	8.104	
Total	2328.305	35		

*$p < .01$.

a. (1) Significant main effects for both factors A and B.
(2) Significant interaction.

b. ($CD = 3.31$) The statistically significant interaction indicates that the effect of type of instructions depends on the type of crime; the difference between the filmed and normal instructions for auto theft is nonsignificant, but a significantly longer term is assigned with filmed instruction compared to normal instructions for aggravated assault.

c. The statistically significant interaction indicates that the effect of type of crime depends on the type of instructions. For both types of instructions, aggravated assault leads to significantly longer prison terms than does auto theft. However, the difference between the prison terms for auto theft and aggravated assault is larger for filmed instructions than it is for normal instructions.

d. The statistically significant main effect for type of crime is meaningful; significantly longer terms are assigned for aggravated assault under both normal and filmed instructions. The main effect for type of instruction is artifactual; there is no difference between the filmed and normal instructions for auto theft, but a significantly longer term is assigned with filmed instruction for aggravated assault.

e. $\eta^2 = .72$ for type of crime.
$\eta^2 = .09$ for the interaction of factors A and B.

Testing Your Knowledge 11-6

1. a. 3.
   b. 2.
   c. 42.
   d.

	F_{crit}
A	3.32
B	4.17
$A \times B$	3.32

e. Yes.
f. Yes.
g. No.
2. a. 2.
b. 4.
c. 96.
d.

	F_{crit}
A	4.00
B	2.76
$A \times B$	2.76

e. Yes.
f. No.
g. Yes.
3. a. 2.
b. 2.
c. 60.
d.

	F_{crit}
A	4.08
B	4.08
$A \times B$	4.08

e. No.
f. No.
g. Yes.

Review Questions

1. Analysis of variance summary.

Source	SS	df	MS	F
Eye contact (A)	24.500	1	24.500	0.76
Affect (B)	780.125	1	780.125	24.17*
$A \times B$	325.125	1	325.125	10.07*
Error	903.750	28	32.277	
Total	2033.500	31		

*$p < .01$.

a. Yes; there is a significant interaction of factors A and B (Tukey $CD = 7.1$). For positive affect conditions, the no-eye-contact mean is significantly higher than the eye-contact mean. For negative affect conditions, the eye-contact condition means do not differ significantly.

b. For the no-eye-contact condition, there is no significant difference between positive and negative affect conditions. For the eye-contact condition, however, negative affect leads to a significantly higher heart rate than does positive affect.

c. The statistically significant main effect for affect condition is artifactual; there is no significant difference between the affect conditions in the no-eye-contact condition, but in the eye-contact condition, the negative affect cell mean is significantly higher than the positive affect cell mean.

d. $\eta^2 = .16$ for the interaction of factors A and B.

2. Analysis of variance summary.

Source	SS	df	MS	F
Word size (A)	363.000	1	363.000	38.47*
Placement (B)	0.750	1	0.750	0.08
$A \times B$	10.083	1	10.083	1.07
Error	415.167	44	9.436	
Total	789.000	47		

*$p < .01$.

a. The main effect for word size is statistically significant; the estimated percentage off the regular price was greater for large word size than for small. Because there is no statistically significant interaction, the effect of word size does not depend on word placement. Thus the main effect of word size best describes the effect of this variable.

b. The main effect for word placement is nonsignificant. The main effect means for word placement do not differ significantly.

c. No; there is no significant interaction.

d. The main effect for word size is meaningful. For both horizontal and diagonal placement, the large size leads to significantly greater percentage reduction estimates.

e. $\eta^2 = .46$ for word size.

3. Analysis of variance summary.

Source	SS	df	MS	F*
Reading ability (A)	436.594	2	218.297	47.78*
Instruction (B)	60.168	1	60.168	13.17*
A × B	69.777	2	34.888	7.64*
Error	219.332	48	4.569	
Total	785.871	53		

*$p < .01$.

a. There is a statistically significant interaction; thus the effect of type of instruction depends on the level of reading ability. For below-average readers the control condition mean was significantly less than the questions instruction condition mean ($CD = 2.9$). However, there was no significant difference between the control and questions instruction conditions for either the above-average or average readers. In addition, the differences between levels of reading ability depend on the type of instruction. For the control instruction condition, each reading ability group differed significantly from the others; the above-average readers obtained the highest test score, the average readers the next highest score, and the below-average readers the lowest score. For the questions instruction condition, the below-average readers score was significantly less than either the average or above-average readers. The average and above-average readers did not differ significantly, however.

b. $\eta^2 = .09$ for the interaction of factors A and B.

c. Both main effects are artifactual.

4. $a = 2$, $b = 3$, $n_{AB} = 8$, $N = 48$, $df_A = 1$, $df_B = 2$, $df_{A \times B} = 2$, $df_{Error} = 42$, $df_{Total} = 47$.

5. *Table 1*

Source	SS	df	MS	F
Type of task (A)	15.00	3	5.00	2.50
Noise level (B)	16.00	2	8.00	4.00*
A × B	36.00	6	6.00	3.00*
Error	120.00	60	2.00	
Total	187.00	71		

*$p < .05$.

a. 4.
b. 3.
c. 6.
d. 72.
e. F_{obs} for factor B and the $A \times B$ interaction are statistically significant.
f. Factor A: Fail to reject H_0
                     Do not accept H_1
     Factor B: Reject H_0
                     Accept H_1
     $A \times B$: Reject H_0
                     Accept H_1

Table 2

Source	SS	df	MS	F
Training length (A)	40.00	4	10.00	0.50
Skill level (B)	120.00	3	40.00	2.00
A × B	960.00	12	80.00	4.00*
Error	3200.00	160	20.00	
Total	4320.00	179		

*$p < .01$.

a. 5.
b. 4.
c. 9.
d. 180.
e. F_{obs} for the $A \times B$ interaction is statistically significant.
f. Factor A: Fail to reject H_0
                     Do not accept H_1
     Factor B: Fail to reject H_0
                     Do not accept H_1
     $A \times B$: Reject H_0
                     Accept H_1

Table 3

Source	SS	df	MS	F
Type of feedback (A)	200.00	4	50.00	2.50*
Task difficulty (B)	160.00	2	80.00	4.00*
A × B	240.00	8	30.00	1.50
Error	2700.00	135	20.00	
Total	3300.00	149		

*$p < .05$.

   a. 5.
   b. 3.
   c. 10.
   d. 150.
   e. F_{obs} for factor A and factor B are statistically significant.
   f. Factor A: Reject H_0
                Accept H_1
       Factor B: Reject H_0
                Accept H_1
       $A \times B$:   Fail to reject H_0
                Do not accept H_1

6. **a.** Because of the statistically significant interaction, the effect of type of imagery depends on the amount of elaboration. For low elaboration, ordinary imagery leads to significantly greater recall than does bizarre imagery. For high elaboration, however, ordinary imagery leads to significantly less recall than does bizarre imagery. The main effect of type of imagery is artifactual.

   b. Again, because of the statistically significant interaction, the effect of amount of elaboration depends on the type of imagery. For ordinary imagery, low elaboration leads to significantly higher recall than does high elaboration. For bizarre imagery, an opposite relation holds; low elaboration leads to significantly lower recall than does high elaboration.

7. **a.** The statistically significant interaction indicates that the effect of type of gauge depends on the amount of sleep deprivation. For no sleep deprivation, the difference between the number of correct readings for analog and digital gauges is nonsignificant. For 24 hours of sleep deprivation, digital gauges result in significantly more correct readings than do analog gauges. The main effect of type of gauge is artifactual.

   b. Again, the statistically significant interaction indicates that the effect of amount of sleep deprivation depends on the type of gauge. For both analog and digital gauges, 24 hours of sleep deprivation results in significantly fewer correct readings than does no sleep deprivation. However, the difference between the number of correct readings for no and 24 hours of sleep deprivation is greater for analog gauges than it is for digital gauges. Because 24 hours of sleep deprivation results in fewer correct readings for both analog and digital gauges, the main effect of amount of sleep deprivation is meaningful.

CHAPTER 12

Testing Your Knowledge 12–1

   4. 199.00.
   5. 33.00.
   6. 25.00.
   7. 96.00.
   8. $df_A = 4$, $df_S = 12$, $df_{A \times S} = 48$, $df_{Total} = 64$.
   9. 59.
  10. $MS_A = 11.00$, $MS_S = 2.00$, $MS_{A \times S} = 2.00$.
  11. *Table 1*

Source	SS	df	MS	F
Factor A	48.00	4	12.00	6.00
Factor S	27.00	9	3.00	
A × S	72.00	36	2.00	
Total	147.00	49		

   a. 5.
   b. 10.
   c. 10.

Table 2

Source	SS	df	MS	F
Factor A	6.00	2	3.00	2.00
Factor S	36.00	12	3.00	
$A \times S$	36.00	24	1.50	
Total	78.00	38		

a. 3.
b. 13.
c. 13.

Testing Your Knowledge 12–2

3. H_0: $\mu_{A1} = \mu_{A2} = \mu_{A3} = \mu_{A4} = \mu_{A5}$;
H_1: The μ_A's are not all equal.

Testing Your Knowledge 12–3

1.

	Treatment Condition (A)		
	Control	Experimental	Placebo
$\overline{X}$	4.50	3.43	4.50
s	1.29	1.45	1.34

a. H_0: $\mu_{A1} = \mu_{A2} = \mu_{A3}$;
   H_1: The μ_A's are not all equal.

b.

Source	SS	df	MS	F
Mouthrinse (A)	10.714	2	5.357	6.54*
Subjects (S)	51.143	13	3.934	
$A \times S$	21.286	26	0.819	
Total	83.143	41		

*$p < .01$.

c. 2, 26.
d. F_{crit} (2, 26) = 3.37.
e. Values of $F_{obs} \geq 3.37$.
f. Yes.
g. Reject H_0; accept H_1.
h. Different populations.
i. Yes.
j. Yes, because the F_{obs} is statistically significant and three levels of the independent variable are varied.

k. Tukey $CD = 0.85$.
l. The experimental mouthrinse group had significantly lower plaque ratings than either the control or placebo groups. The control and placebo groups did not differ significantly in their ratings.
m. $\eta^2 = .33$.

2. a. 2.
b. 19.
c. 4.76.
d. 4.41.
e. Reject H_0.
f. Accept H_1.
g. Yes.
h. The simple and complex stimulus conditions.

3. a. 3.
b. 12.
c. 2.81.
d. 3.44.
e. Fail to reject H_0.
f. Do not accept H_1.
g. No.
h. No treatment conditions differ significantly.

Review Questions

1. a.

	Type of Word		
	Happy	Neutral	Sad
$\overline{X}$	4.5	3.0	2.5
s	1.41	1.20	1.20

Source	SS	df	MS	F
Type word (A)	17.333	2	8.666	7.00*
Subjects (S)	16.667	7	2.381	
$A \times S$	17.333	14	1.238	
Total	51.333	23		

*$p < .05$.

Tukey $CD = 1.5$. The mean for happy words is significantly greater than the mean for either neutral or sad words. The neutral and sad words means do not differ significantly.

b. $\eta^2 = .50$.

2. a.

	Type of Neckwear	
	Loose	Tight
$\overline{X}$	20.1	18.8
s	2.15	2.05

Source	SS	df	MS	F
Neckwear (A)	10.668	1	10.668	4.29
Subjects (B)	69.834	11	6.349	
$A \times S$	27.332	11	2.485	
Total	107.834	23		

F_{obs} is nonsignificant at the .05 level. There is no evidence that neckwear affected flicker fusion frequency.

b. t_{obs} (11) = 2.07. $\sqrt{F} = \sqrt{4.29} = 2.07$.

c. Same conclusions.

3. **a.** H_0: $\mu_{A1} = \mu_{A2} = \mu_{A3} = \mu_{A4} = \mu_{A5}$.
H_1: The μ_A's are not all equal.

b. $df_A = 4$, $df_S = 11$, $df_{A \times S} = 44$, $df_{Total} = 59$.

c. F_{crit} (4, 44) = 2.61.

d. Reject H_0; accept H_1.

e. There is at least one significant difference among the means. A Tukey HSD test is necessary to locate the specific significant differences.

4. *Table 1*

Source	SS	df	MS	F
Factor A	22.00	2	11.00	2.00
Factor S	138.00	23	6.00	
$A \times S$	253.00	46	5.50	
Total	413.00	71		

a. 3.   **c.** 24.
b. 24.   **d.** No.
e. Fail to reject H_0; do not accept H_1.

Table 2

Source	SS	df	MS	F
Factor A	60.00	5	12.0	3.00
Factor S	133.00	19	7.0	
$A \times S$	380.00	95	4.0	
Total	573.00	119		

a. 6.   **c.** 20.
b. 20.   **d.** Yes.
e. Reject H_0; accept H_1.

5. The statistically significant F_{obs} (2, 26) = 15.99 indicates that there is at least one significant difference among the means. Pairwise comparisons with the Tukey *CD* indicate that each mean differs significantly from each other mean. Consequently, infants fixated on the familiar face for the longest duration. The duration of fixation on the unfamiliar face was significantly less than the fixation on the familiar face, and the duration of fixation on the blank oval was significantly less than the fixation on either the familiar or unfamiliar face.

CHAPTER 13

Testing Your Knowledge 13–1

3. **a.** t_{rel} or a one-factor within-subjects analysis of variance.

b. Chi-square test.

c. t_{ind} or a one-factor between-subjects analysis of variance.

d. Mann–Whitney U test.

e. Wilcoxon signed-ranks test.

7.

χ^2_{obs}	df	χ^2_{crit}	Falls into Rejection Region	Decisions
7.26	2	5.99	Yes	H_0: Reject H_1: Accept
8.33	4	9.49	No	H_0: Fail to reject H_1: Do not accept
14.19	7	14.1	Yes	H_0: Reject H_1: Accept
26.94	20	31.4	No	H_0: Fail to reject H_1: Do not accept

8. The values in each cell are expected frequencies.

a.

		Column	
		1	2
Row	1	12.6	31.4
	2	15.4	38.6

$\chi^2_{obs}(1) = 0.073$, $p > .05$; nonsignificant.

b.

	Column	
	1	2
Row 1	19.2	29.8
Row 2	24.8	38.2

$\chi^2_{obs}(1) = 9.256$, $p < .01$; statistically significant.

c.

	Column	
	1	2
Row 1	42.4	56.6
Row 2	17.6	23.4

$\chi^2_{obs}(1) = 12.442$, $p < .01$; statistically significant.

9. $\chi^2_{obs}(2) = 0.168$. This χ^2_{obs} is nonsignificant; there is no relationship between day of the week and time of day for cars passing stop signs in this example.

10. $\chi^2_{obs}(1) = 70.914$, $p < .01$; the hypothesized relationship exists.

Testing Your Knowledge 13–2

1.

Scores ordered from smallest to largest	7	10	14	15	16	19	23	26
Group identity	2	1	2	1	2	1	1	2
Rank	1	2	3	4	5	6	7	8
Number of times an A_1 score precedes A_2 scores			3		2		1	1
Number of times an A_2 score precedes A_1 scores	4	3		2				

$U_{A1} = 7$; $U_{A2} = 9$.

a. U_{A1}.   **b.** No.

2. $U_{A1} = 7$; $U_{A2} = 9$.
   a. Yes.
4. U_{A1} should be about equal to U_{A2}.
5. They should differ considerably.

6.

	U_{crit}	Falls into Rejection Region	Decision
a.	0	No	H_0: Fail to reject / H_1: Do not accept
b.	16	Yes	H_0: Reject / H_1: Accept
c.	27	No	H_0: Fail to reject / H_1: Do not accept
d.	22	Yes	H_0: Reject / H_1: Accept
e.	56	Yes	H_0: Reject / H_1: Accept
f.	87	No	H_0: Fail to reject / H_1: Do not accept

7. Smaller $U = U_{A1} = 54.5$; $U_{crit} = 41$; U_{A1} does not fall into the rejection region. There is no evidence that the groups differ in their anxiety estimates.

Testing Your Knowledge 13–3

4.

	T_{crit}	Falls into Rejection Region	Decision
a.	4	Yes	H_0: Reject / H_1: Accept
b.	8	No	H_0: Fail to reject / H_1: Do not accept
c.	17	Yes	H_0: Reject / H_1: Accept
d.	46	Yes	H_0: Reject / H_1: Accept
e.	90	No	H_0: Fail to reject / H_1: Do not accept

5. $T_{obs}(14) = 27$; $T_{crit}(14) = 21$; T_{obs} is not statistically significant. The anxiety level did not change from game 1 to game 2 in this sample.

Review Questions

1. **a.** $\chi^2_{obs}(1) = 1.235$, $p > .05$. The frequency of dropout is not related to gender.
    b. $\chi^2_{obs}(2) = 28.990$, $p < .01$. The frequency of dropout is related to the severity of the problem. A larger than expected number of individuals with mild problems drop out; fewer than expected individuals with severe problems drop out.
2. $\sum(-R) = 50$, $\sum(+R) = 5$; therefore, $T_{obs}(11) = 5$, $p < .01$. Reject H_0; the type of task affects yawning.
    a. The uninteresting video condition scores are positively skewed.
    b. The distributions of the number of yawns differ. More yawns occur with an uninteresting stimulus than with an interesting stimulus.
3. $U_{A2} = 38.5$, $p > .05$. The distributions do not differ significantly.
4. $U_{A2} = 44.5$, $p > .05$. The distributions do not differ significantly.
5. $T_{obs} = 3$, $p < .05$. The distributions differ significantly.

CHAPTER 14

Testing Your Knowledge 14–1

2. *Table 1*
    a. Positive relationship.
    b. Less than perfect.
    c. Yes. Knowing the loneliness score allows better prediction of depression than can be achieved without knowing it.
    Table 2
    a. Negative relationship.
    b. Less than perfect.
    c. Yes.
3. **a.** Weak negative relationship.
    b. Less than perfect.
    c. No, it would do little to increase the accuracy of the prediction.

Testing Your Knowledge 14–2

3. **a.** $r_{obs} = +.870$.
4. **a.** $r_{obs} = -.764$.
5. **a.** $r_{obs} = -.277$.

Testing Your Knowledge 14–3

4.

	r^2
a.	.0144
b.	.5476
c.	.3481
d.	.1296
e.	.0529
f.	.0361

Testing Your Knowledge 14–4

2. H_0: $\rho = 0$; H_1: $\rho \neq 0$.

3.

		Critical Value	
	df	.05	.01
a.	6	.707	.834
b.	13	.514	.641
c.	18	.444	.561
d.	30	.349	.449
e.	41	.304	.393
f.	73	.232	.302

4.

	Statistical Hypotheses	Critical Value	Falls into Rejection Region?	Decision
a.	H_0: $\rho = 0$ H_1: $\rho \neq 0$	.576	Yes	H_0: Reject H_1: Accept
b.	H_0: $\rho = 0$ H_1: $\rho \neq 0$	.576	No	H_0: Fail to reject H_1: Do not accept
c.	H_0: $\rho = 0$ H_1: $\rho \neq 0$	.444	Yes	H_0: Reject H_1: Accept
d.	H_0: $\rho = 0$ H_1: $\rho \neq 0$	.423	No	H_0: Fail to reject H_1: Do not accept
e.	H_0: $\rho = 0$ H_1: $\rho \neq 0$	.232	Yes	H_0: Reject H_1: Accept
f.	H_0: $\rho = 0$ H_1: $\rho \neq 0$	.666	Yes	H_0: Reject H_1: Accept

5. **a.** $r_{obs} = -.550$.

b. $r_{crit}(10) = .576$; r_{obs} is nonsignificant.

c. There is no evidence for a relationship between absences and test scores for the population from which these scores were sampled.

Review Questions

1. **b.** Positive.

c. $r_{obs} = +.701$; $r_{crit}(10) = .576$; r_{obs} is statistically significant.

d. There is a positive relationship between golf score and percentage of body fat. The higher the percentage of body fat, the higher the golf score.

e. $r^2 = .49$.

2. **a.** $r_{obs} = -.12$ for girls; $r_{crit}(51) = .273$; r_{obs} is nonsignificant. $r_{obs} = +.32$ for boys; $r_{crit}(40) = .304$; r_{obs} is statistically significant.

b. $r^2 = .01$ for girls. $r^2 = .10$ for boys.

c. There is no relationship for girls. For boys, the relationship is positive; taller boys tend to obtain higher report card grades.

3. **b.** Positive.

c. $r_{obs} = +.781$; $r_{crit}(8) = .632$; r_{obs} is statistically significant.

d. They are positively related; the higher the midterm grade, the higher the final exam grade tends to be.

4. **a.** $r_{s\ obs} = +.937$; $r_{crit}(12) = .591$; $r_{s\ obs}$ is statistically significant.

b. Popularity and physical attractiveness are positively related in the population of girls from which the sample was drawn.

c. $r_{s\ obs} = -.134$; $r_{crit}(14) = .545$; $r_{s\ obs}$ is nonsignificant.

d. There is no relationship between popularity and physical attractiveness of boys in the population from which the sample was drawn.

5. The IQ of college students involves a restricted range of that variable. Very low and very high IQ scores were not included in the sample. It is also possible that the grade-point averages are similarly restricted in range.

6. **b.** No relationship.

c. $r_{obs} = -.001$; $r_{crit}(11) = .553$; r_{obs} is nonsignificant.

d. The number of hours of computer use and depth perception error are not related in the sample measured.

CHAPTER 15

Testing Your Knowledge 15–1

4. **a.** $b = +2$; $a = 0$; $Y = +2X$.

b. $b = -1$; $a = +2$; $Y = -1X + 2$.

c. $b = +1.5$; $a = +1$; $Y = +1.5X + 1$.

d. $b = -2$; $a = +4$; $Y = -2X + 4$.

Testing Your Knowledge 15–2

6. **a.** $Y' = +0.8X + 9$.

b.

X	Y'
60	57
65	61
80	73
85	77
90	81

c. $\overline{Y} = 69.8$. The regression line passes through the points $X = 0$, $Y = 9$; $\overline{X} = 76$, $\overline{Y} = 69.8$.

7. **a.** $Y' = -1.4X + 23$.

b.

X	Y'
5	16.0
8	11.8
11	7.6
14	3.4
17	−0.8

c. $\overline{Y} = 7.6$. The regression line passes through the points $X = 0$, $Y = 23$; $\overline{X} = 11$, $\overline{Y} = 7.6$.

Testing Your Knowledge 15–3

1. a. +11.507.
    b. 202.215.
    c. $Y' = +11.507X + 202.215$.
    d. The regression line passes through the points $X = 0$, $Y = 202.215$; $\overline{X} = 5.17$, $\overline{Y} = 261.7$.
    e.
X	Y'
6	271.3
3	236.7
9	305.8
1	213.7
4	248.2
2	225.2
3	236.7
5	259.8
8	294.3
7	282.8
8	294.3
6	271.3

    f.
Subject	Residual (Y − Y')
1	−54.3
2	−6.7
3	+9.2
4	+10.3
5	+22.8
6	−27.2
7	+19.3
8	+3.2
9	+26.7
10	+6.2
11	−29.3
12	+19.7

    g. 6824.43.
    h. 26.12.
    i. Yes; $s_{Y \cdot X}$ is smaller than s_Y.
2. a. $b = -0.43$.
    b. $a = 24.6$.
    c. $Y' = -0.43X + 24.6$.
    d. 41 scans, $Y' = 7.0$.
    e. 18 scans, $Y' = 16.9$.

Review Questions

1. a. +0.884.
    b. +0.884.
    c. $Y' = +0.884X + 10.96$.
    d. 79.0.
    e. 5.52.
2. a. $Y' = -0.116X + 3.23$.
    b. 2.88.
    c. 2.64.
3. a. $Y' = -4.3X + 128$, where X = number of cigarettes smoked per day.
    c.
Cigarettes per Day	Predicted Birth Weight (oz)
0	128.0
1	123.7
5	106.5
8	93.6
10	85.0
13	72.1
20	42.0
4. a. $Y' = +0.627X + 57.04$.
    b.
Golfer	Predicted Score
1	69.6
2	75.2
3	73.0
4	69.3
5	79.8
6	71.4
7	73.7
8	76.3
9	75.7
10	77.9
11	72.2
12	74.2
    d. Yes, the mean golf score, $\overline{Y}$, is 74.0. Notice that the predicted values for the extreme golf scores (e.g., 67, 68, 83) are closer to the mean than the actual scores. These predicted scores have regressed toward the mean.
5. a. −0.562.
    b. 28.33.
    c. $Y' = -0.562X + 28.33$.
    e. 2.90.

6.

Applicant	Predicted Job Performance: Y'
Dianne	55.2
Rodrigo	61.2
Colin	54.0
Maria	67.2
Ruben	64.8
Luke	52.8
Holly	50.4
Blythe	70.8

The predicted job performance scores of Rodrigo, Maria, Ruben, and Blythe are greater than 60. Thus these applicants will be hired.

Appendix F
Commonly Used Formulas

FREQUENCY DISTRIBUTIONS
Ungrouped Frequency Distributions

$$rf \text{ of a score} = \frac{f \text{ of a score}}{N}$$

$$\%f \text{ of a score} = (rf \text{ of a score}) \times 100$$

Grouped Frequency Distributions

$$\text{size of class interval} = \frac{X_{\text{highest}} - X_{\text{lowest}}}{\text{number of intervals}}$$

$$rf \text{ of scores in an interval} = \frac{f \text{ of scores in interval}}{N}$$

$$\%f \text{ of scores in an interval} = \frac{f \text{ of scores in interval}}{N} \times 100$$

Percentile Rank

$$P_X = \left[\frac{cf_L + [(X - X_L)/i]fi}{N} \right] \times 100$$

Percentile Point

$$X_P = X_L + \left[\frac{P(N) - cf_L}{fi} \right] i$$

MEASURES OF CENTRAL TENDENCY

Median

$$Mdn = X_{.50} = X_L + \left[\frac{.50(N) - cf_L}{fi} \right] i$$

Mean

$$\overline{X} = \frac{\sum X}{N}$$

MEASURES OF VARIABILITY

Range

$\text{range} = X_{\text{highest}} - X_{\text{lowest}}$

Interquartile Range

$IQR = X_{75} - X_{25}$

Semi-interquartile Range

$SIQR = \dfrac{IQR}{2} = \dfrac{X_{75} - X_{25}}{2}$

Variance

Population Variance

$\sigma^2 = \dfrac{\sum (X - \mu)^2}{N_{\text{population}}}$

Sample Variance

$S^2 = \dfrac{\sum (X - \overline{X})^2}{N}$

Estimated Population Variance

Definitional formula: $s^2 = \dfrac{\sum (X - \overline{X})^2}{N - 1}$

Sum-of-squares formula: $s^2 = \dfrac{SS}{N - 1}$

Computational formula: $s^2 = \dfrac{\sum X^2 - \left[\left(\sum X \right)^2 / N \right]}{N - 1}$

Standard Deviation

Population Standard Deviation

$\sigma = \sqrt{\sigma^2}$

Sample Standard Deviation

$S = \sqrt{S^2} = \sqrt{\dfrac{\sum (X - \overline{X})^2}{N}}$

Estimated Population Standard Deviation

Definitional formula: $s = \sqrt{s^2} = \sqrt{\dfrac{\sum(X - \overline{X})^2}{N - 1}}$

or

Sum-of-squares formula: $s = \sqrt{\dfrac{SS}{N - 1}}$

Standard Error of the Mean

σ Known

$$\sigma_{\overline{X}} = \frac{\sigma}{\sqrt{N}}$$

σ Unknown

$$s_{\overline{X}} = \frac{s}{\sqrt{N}}$$

Standard Error of the Difference between Means

σ Known

$$\sigma_{\overline{X}A1 - \overline{X}A2} = \sqrt{\frac{\sigma_{A1}^2}{n_{A1}} + \frac{\sigma_{A2}^2}{n_{A2}}}$$

σ Unknown

$$s_{\overline{X}A1 - \overline{X}A2} = \sqrt{\left[\frac{(n_{A1} - 1)s_{A1}^2 + (n_{A2} - 1)s_{A2}^2}{n_{A1} + n_{A2} - 2}\right]\left[\frac{1}{n_{A1}} + \frac{1}{n_{A2}}\right]}$$

PROBABILITY

Probability (p) of Occurrence of an Event

$$p(\text{event}) = \frac{\text{number of occurrences of the event in a population}}{\text{total number of possible events in a population}}$$

z SCORES AND STANDARD SCORES

Single Score

$$z = \frac{X - \mu}{\sigma}$$

Standard Score

$$z = \frac{X - \overline{X}}{S}$$

or

$$z = \frac{X - \overline{X}}{\sqrt{\sum(X - \overline{X})^2/N}}$$

Sample Mean

$$z = \frac{\overline{X} - \mu}{\sigma_{\overline{X}}}$$

t TESTS

One-sample t Test

$$t = \frac{\overline{X} - \mu}{s_{\overline{X}}}$$

or

$$t = \frac{\overline{X} - \mu}{s/\sqrt{N}}, \quad df = N - 1$$

t Test for Independent Groups

Definitional formula: $t_{ind} = \dfrac{\overline{X}_{A1} - \overline{X}_{A2}}{s_{\overline{X}A1 - \overline{X}A2}}$

Computational formula: $t_{ind} = \dfrac{\overline{X}_{A1} - \overline{X}_{A2}}{\sqrt{\left[\dfrac{(n_{A1} - 1)s_{A1}^2 + (n_{A2} - 1)s_{A2}^2}{n_{A1} + n_{A2} - 2}\right]\left[\dfrac{1}{n_{A1}} + \dfrac{1}{n_{A2}}\right]}}, \quad df = N - 2$

t Test for Related Groups

$$t_{rel} = \dfrac{\overline{X}_{A1} - \overline{X}_{A2}}{\sqrt{\dfrac{\sum D^2 - (\sum D)^2/N_{pairs}}{N_{pairs}(N_{pairs} - 1)}}}, \quad df = N_{pairs} - 1$$

ANALYSIS OF VARIANCE

One-factor Between-subjects Design

Sums of Squares (Definitional Formulas)

$$SS_{Total} = \sum\sum(X - \overline{X}_G)^2$$

$$SS_A = \sum\sum(\overline{X}_A - \overline{X}_G)^2$$

$$SS_{Error} = \sum\sum(X - \overline{X}_A)^2$$

Degrees of Freedom

$$df_{Total} = N - 1$$

$$df_A = a - 1$$

$$df_{Error} = a(n_A - 1)$$

or

$$df_{Error} = N - a$$

Mean Squares

$$MS_A = \frac{SS_A}{df_A}$$

$$MS_{Error} = \frac{SS_{Error}}{df_{Error}}$$

F Statistic

$$F = \frac{MS_A}{MS_{Error}}$$

Two-factor Between-subjects Design

Sums of Squares (Definitional Formulas)

$$SS_{Total} = \sum\sum\sum(X - \overline{X}_G)^2$$

$$SS_A = \sum\sum\sum(\overline{X}_A - \overline{X}_G)^2$$

$$SS_B = \sum\sum\sum(\overline{X}_B - \overline{X}_G)^2$$

$$SS_{A \times B} = \sum \sum \sum (\overline{X}_{AB} - \overline{X}_A - \overline{X}_B + \overline{X}_G)^2$$

$$SS_{\text{Error}} = \sum \sum \sum (X - \overline{X}_{AB})^2$$

Degrees of Freedom

$df_{\text{Total}} = N - 1$

$df_A = a - 1$

$df_B = b - 1$

$df_{A \times B} = (a - 1)(b - 1)$

$df_{\text{Error}} = ab(n_{AB} - 1)$

Mean Squares

$$MS_A = \frac{SS_A}{df_A}$$

$$MS_B = \frac{SS_B}{df_B}$$

$$MS_{A \times B} = \frac{SS_{A \times B}}{df_{A \times B}}$$

$$MS_{\text{Error}} = \frac{SS_{\text{Error}}}{df_{\text{Error}}}$$

F Statistics

Source of Variation	F Ratio
Factor A	$\dfrac{MS_A}{MS_{\text{Error}}}$
Factor B	$\dfrac{MS_B}{MS_{\text{Error}}}$
Interaction of $A \times B$	$\dfrac{MS_{A \times B}}{MS_{\text{Error}}}$

One-factor Within-subjects Design

Sums of Squares (Definitional Formulas)

$$SS_{Total} = \sum\sum(X - \overline{X}_G)^2$$

$$SS_A = \sum\sum(\overline{X}_A - \overline{X}_G)^2$$

$$SS_S = \sum\sum(\overline{X}_S - \overline{X}_G)^2$$

$$SS_{A\times S} = \sum\sum(X - \overline{X}_A - \overline{X}_S + \overline{X}_G)^2$$

Degrees of Freedom

$$df_{Total} = N - 1$$

$$df_A = a - 1$$

$$df_S = n_A - 1$$

$$df_{A\times S} = (a - 1)(n_A - 1)$$

Mean Squares

$$MS_A = \frac{SS_A}{df_A}$$

$$MS_S = \frac{SS_S}{df_S}$$

$$MS_{A\times S} = \frac{SS_{A\times S}}{df_{A\times S}}$$

F Statistic

$$F = \frac{MS_A}{MS_{A\times S}}$$

TUKEY HSD MULTIPLE COMPARISON TESTS

For One-factor Between-subjects Designs

$$CD = q\sqrt{\frac{MS_{Error}}{n_A}}$$

For One-factor Within-subjects Designs

$$CD = q \sqrt{\frac{MS_{A \times S}}{n_A}}$$

For Simple Effects in a Factorial Between-subjects Design

$$CD = q \sqrt{\frac{MS_{Error}}{n_{AB}}}$$

STRENGTH OF EFFECT MEASURES

Eta Squared for t Test

$$\eta^2 = \frac{t_{obs}^2}{t_{obs}^2 + df}$$

Eta Squared for One-factor Between-subjects Analysis of Variance

$$\eta^2 = \frac{SS_A}{SS_{Total}}$$

or

$$\eta^2 = \frac{(df_A)(F_{obs})}{(df_A)(F_{obs}) + df_{Error}}$$

Eta Squared for One-factor Within-subjects Analysis of Variance

$$\eta^2 = \frac{SS_A}{SS_A + SS_{A \times S}}$$

Eta Squared for Two-factor Between-subjects Analysis of Variance

$$\eta^2 = \frac{SS_A}{SS_{Total}}$$ For factor A

$$\eta^2 = \frac{SS_B}{SS_{Total}}$$ For factor B

$$\eta^2 = \frac{SS_{A \times B}}{SS_{Total}}$$ For the interaction of factors A and B

NONPARAMETRIC TESTS

Chi-square Test for Independence

$$\chi^2 = \sum\sum \frac{(O_{rc} - E_{rc})^2}{E_{rc}}$$

$$\begin{pmatrix} \text{Expected} \\ \text{frequency} \\ \text{of a cell} \end{pmatrix} = \frac{(\text{Row marginal for cell})(\text{Column marginal for cell})}{\text{Total number of responses}}, \quad df = (r-1)(c-1)$$

Chi-square Test for Goodness of Fit

$$\chi^2 = \sum \frac{(O_c - E_c)^2}{E_c}, \quad df = c - 1$$

Mann–Whitney U Test

$$U_{A1} = n_{A1}n_{A2} + \frac{n_{A1}(n_{A1} + 1)}{2} - \sum R_{A1}$$

$$U_{A2} = n_{A1}n_{A2} + \frac{n_{A2}(n_{A2} + 1)}{2} - \sum R_{A2}$$

or

$$U_{A2} = n_{A1}n_{A2} - U_{A1}$$

Wilcoxon Signed-ranks Test

$$T = \text{smaller of } \sum(-R) \text{ or } \sum(+R)$$

CORRELATION

Pearson Correlation Coefficient

Definitional formula: $r = \dfrac{\sum(X - \overline{X})(Y - \overline{Y})}{\sqrt{[\sum(X - \overline{X})^2][\sum(Y - \overline{Y})^2]}}$

Cross-products formula: $r = \dfrac{CP_{XY}}{\sqrt{(SS_X)(SS_Y)}}$

Computational formula: $r = \dfrac{(N_{\text{pairs}})(\sum XY) - (\sum X)(\sum Y)}{\sqrt{[(N_{\text{pairs}})(\sum X^2) - (\sum X)^2][(N_{\text{pairs}})(\sum Y^2) - (\sum Y)^2]}}$

or

Standard score formula: $r = \dfrac{\sum(z_X z_Y)}{N_{\text{pairs}}}$,

$df = N_{\text{pairs}} - 2$ for all formulas

Coefficient of Determination

r^2

Spearman Rank-order Correlation Coefficient

$$r_s = 1 - \left[\frac{6 \sum D^2}{(N_{\text{pairs}})(N^2_{\text{pairs}} - 1)} \right]$$

REGRESSION

Equation of a Straight Line

$Y = bX + a$

Slope of a Straight Line

$$b = \frac{\text{change in value of } Y}{\text{change in value of } X}$$

or

$$b = \frac{Y_2 - Y_1}{X_2 - X_1}$$

Equation of Least-squares Linear Regression Line

$Y' = bX + a$

Slope of Least-squares Linear Regression Line

Deviational formula: $b = \dfrac{\sum (X - \overline{X})(Y - \overline{Y})}{\sum (X - \overline{X})^2}$

Cross-products formula: $b = \dfrac{CP_{XY}}{SS_X}$

Computational formula: $b = \dfrac{(N_{\text{pairs}}) \left(\sum XY \right) - \left(\sum X \right) \left(\sum Y \right)}{(N_{\text{pairs}}) \left(\sum X^2 \right) - \left(\sum X \right)^2}$

Correlation formula: $b = r \left(\dfrac{s_Y}{s_X} \right)$

Y-intercept of Least-squares Linear Regression Line

$a = \overline{Y} - b\overline{X}$

Standard Error of Estimate

Definitional formula: $\quad s_Y \cdot X = \sqrt{\dfrac{SS_{\text{Residual}}}{N_{\text{pairs}} - 2}}$

or

$$s_Y \cdot X = \sqrt{\dfrac{\sum (Y - Y')^2}{N_{\text{pairs}} - 2}}$$

Computational formula:

$$s_Y \cdot X = \sqrt{\left[\dfrac{1}{N_{\text{pairs}}(N_{\text{pairs}} - 2)}\right]\left[N_{\text{pairs}} \sum Y^2 - \left(\sum Y\right)^2 - \dfrac{\left[N_{\text{pairs}}\left(\sum XY\right) - \left(\sum X\right)\left(\sum Y\right)\right]^2}{N_{\text{pairs}} \sum X^2 - \left(\sum X\right)^2}\right]}$$

Correlation formula: $\quad s_Y \cdot X = s_Y \sqrt{\left[\dfrac{N_{\text{pairs}} - 1}{N_{\text{pairs}} - 2}\right](1 - r_{\text{obs}}^2)}$

References

Adams, J. M. (1986, November 11). Service jobs log best real earnings rise. *Boston Globe*, p. 69.

Addison, W. E. (1986). Agonistic behavior in preschool children: A comparison of same-sex versus opposite-sex interactions. *Bulletin of the Psychonomic Society, 24*, 44–46.

American Psychological Association. (1994). *Publication Manual of the American Psychological Association* (4th ed.). Washington, DC: Author.

Artis, J. B. (1993, January 28). A fat promise in the dark days of January. *Boston Globe*, p. 45.

Bausell, R. B. (1986). Health-seeking behaviors: Public versus public health perspectives. *Psychological Reports, 58*, 187–190.

Bellizzi, J. A., & Hite, R. E. (1987). Headline size and position influence on consumers' perception. *Perceptual and Motor Skills, 64*, 296–298.

Birth weight, secondary smoke linked. (1986, August 22). *Boston Globe*, p. 83.

Bond, C. F., Jr., & Anderson, E. L. (1987). The reluctance to transmit bad news: Private discomfort or public display? *Journal of Experimental Social Psychology, 23*, 176–187.

Borgia, G., & Gore, M. A. (1986). Feather stealing in the satin bowerbird (Ptilonorhynchus violaceus): Male competition and the quality of display. *Animal Behaviour, 34*, 727–738.

Bower, G. H. (1981). Mood and memory. *American Psychologist, 36*, 129–148.

Bradley, J. V. (1980). Nonrobustness in classical tests on means and variances: A large-scale sampling study. *Bulletin of the Psychonomic Society, 15*, 275–278.

Bradley, J. V. (1984). The complexity of nonrobustness effects. *Bulletin of the Psychonomic Society, 22*, 250–253.

Bradley-Johnson, S., Graham, D. P., & Johnson, C. M. (1986). Token reinforcement on WISC—R performance for white, low-socioeconomic, upper and lower elementary-school-age students. *Journal of School Psychology, 24*, 73–79.

Browning, J., & Dutton, D. (1986). Assessment of wife assault with the Conflict Tactics Scale: Using couple data to quantify the differential reporting effect. *Journal of Marriage and the Family, 48*, 375–379.

Buckalew, L. W., Daly, J. D., & Coffield, K. E. (1986). Relationship of initial class attendance and seating location to academic performance in psychology classes. *Bulletin of the Psychonomic Society, 24*, 63–64.

Cafardo, N. (1994, August 12). What they're forfeiting. *Boston Globe*, p. 41.

Caro, T. M. (1986). The functions of stotting in Thompson's gazelles: Some tests of the predictions. *Animal Behaviour, 34*, 663–684.

Carroll, J. L., & Shmidt, J. L., Jr. (1992). Correlation between humorous coping style and health. *Psychological Reports, 70*, 402.

Chances. (1985, December 31). *USA Today*, p. 4D.

Clarkson, P. M., James, R., Watkins, A., & Foley, P. (1986). The effect of augmented feedback on foot pronation during barre exercise in dance. *Research Quarterly for Exercise and Sport, 57*, 33–40.

Cosmides, L. (1983). Invariance in the acoustic expression of emotion during speech. *Journal of Experimental Psychology: Human Performance and Perception, 9*, 864–881.

Coulter, R. G., Coulter, M. L., & Glover, J. A. (1984). Details and picture recall. *Bulletin of the Psychonomic Society, 22*, 327–329.

Craik, F. I. M., & Tulving, E. (1975). Depth of processing and the retention of words in episodic memory. *Journal of Experimental Psychology: General, 104*, 268–294.

Crews, D. J., Shirreffs, J. H., Thomas, G., Krahenbuhl, G. S., & Helfrich, H. M. (1986). Psychological and physiological attributes associated with performance of selected players of the Ladies Professional Golf Association tour. *Perceptual and Motor Skills, 63*, 235–238.

Davidson, J. D., & Templin, T. J. (1986). Determinants of success among professional golfers. *Research Quarterly for Exercise and Sport, 57*, 60–67.

Davis, D. M. (1990). Portrayals of women in prime-time network television: Some demographic characteristics. *Sex Roles, 23*, 325–331.

Day, R. H., & Kasperczyk, R. T. (1984). The Morinaga misalignment effect with circular stimulus elements. *Bulletin of the Psychonomic Society, 22,* 193–196.

Dihoff, R. E., Hetznecker, W., Brosvic, G. M., Carpenter, L. N., & Hoffman, L. S. (1993). Ordinal measurement of autistic behavior: A preliminary report. *Bulletin of the Psychonomic Society, 31,* 287–290.

Doddridge, R., Schumm, W. R., & Bergen, M. B. (1987). Factors related to decline in preferred frequency of sexual intercourse among young couples. *Psychological Reports, 60,* 391–395.

Dudycha, A. L., & Dudycha, L. W. (1972). Behavioral statistics. In R. E. Kirk (ed.) *Statistical issues: A reader for the behavioral sciences* (pp. 2–25). Monterey, CA: Brooks/Cole.

Egli, E. A., & Meyers, L. S. (1984). The role of video game playing in adolescent life: Is there reason to be concerned? *Bulletin of the Psychonomic Society, 22,* 309–312.

Eisenman, R. (1987). Creativity, birth order, and risk taking. *Bulletin of the Psychonomic Society, 25,* 87–88.

Elgar, M. A., McKay, H., & Woon, P. (1986). Scanning, pecking, and alarm flights in house sparrows. *Animal Behaviour, 34,* 1892–1894.

Emling, R. C., & Yankell, S. L. (1985). First clinical studies of a new prebrushing mouthrinse. *Compendium of Continuing Education in Dentistry, 6,* 636–646.

Feaver, J., Mendl, M., & Bateson, P. (1986). A method for rating the individual distinctiveness of domestic cats. *Animal Behaviour, 34,* 1016–1025.

4 in 5 readers say everyone should be tested for AIDs. (1987, August 4). *National Enquirer,* p. 26.

Friedman, H. S., Tucker, J. S., Tomlinson-Keasey, C., Schwartz, J. E., Wingard, D. L., & Criqui, M. H. (1993). Does childhood personality predict longevity? *Journal of Personality and Social Psychology, 65,* 176–185.

Fudin, R., & Levinson, H. (1994). Note on 1993 salaries of major league baseball players. *Perceptual and Motor Skills, 78,* 1085–1086.

Gaito, J. (1977). Directional and nondirectional alternative hypotheses. *Bulletin of the Psychonomic Society, 9,* 371–372.

Gardner, P. L. (1975). Scales and statistics. *Review of Educational Research. 45,* 43–57.

Geban, O., Askar, P., & Özkan, I. (1992). Effects of computer simulations and problem-solving approaches on high school students. *Journal of Educational Research, 86*(1), 5–10.

Good, L. R., & Good, K. C. (1973). An objective measure of the motive to avoid success. *Psychological Reports, 33,* 1009–1010.

Gormly, J., & Gormly, A. (1986). Social introversion and spatial abilities. *Bulletin of the Psychonomic Society, 24,* 273–274.

Gross, W. C. (1993). Gender and age differences in college students' alcohol consumption. *Psychological Reports, 72,* 211–216.

Gurnack, A. M., & Werbie, D. L. (1985). Characteristics of youths arrested for drunk driving in two Wisconsin counties 1981–1984. *Psychological Reports, 57,* 1271–1276.

Gustafson, R. (1987a). Alcohol and aggression: A test of an indirect measure of aggression. *Psychological Reports, 60,* 1241–1242.

Gustafson, R. (1987b). Alcohol and the acceptance of social influence: A preliminary study. *Psychological Reports, 60,* 488–490.

Gwartney-Gibbs, P. A. (1986). The institutionalization of premarital cohabitation: Estimates from marriage license applications, 1970 and 1980. *Journal of Marriage and the Family, 48,* 423–434.

Haase, R. F., Waechter, D. M., & Solomon, G. S. (1982). How significant is a significant difference? Average effect size of research in counseling psychology. *Journal of Counseling Psychology, 29,* 58–65.

Homan, S. P., Topping, M., & Hall, B. W. (1986). Does teacher oral reading of test items affect the performance of students of varying reading ability? *Journal of Educational Research, 79,* 363–365.

Hughey, A. W. (1985). Further inquiry into the relationship between GPA and undesirable behavior in residence halls. *Psychological Reports, 56,* 510.

Ishee, J. H., & Titlow, L. W. (1986). Diurnal variations in physical performance. *Perceptual and Motor Skills, 63,* 835–838.

Jenkins, C. D., Zyzanski, S. J., & Rosenman, R. H. (1979). *Jenkins activity survey.* New York: Psychological Corporation.

Keppel, G. (1991). *Design and analysis: A researcher's handbook* (3rd ed.). Englewood Cliffs, NJ: Prentice Hall.

Kleinknecht, R. A., & Donaldson, D. A. (1975). A review of the effects of diazepam on cognitive and psychomotor performance. *Journal of Nervous and Mental Diseases, 161*, 399–411.

Kong, D. (1993, June 7). AIDS conferees disagree on best use of AZT. *Boston Globe*, p. 2.

Krantz, M. (1987). Physical attractiveness and popularity: A predictive study. *Psychological Reports, 60*, 723–726.

Langan, L. M., & Watkins, S. M. (1987). Pressure of menswear on the neck in relation to visual performance. *Human Factors, 29*, 67–71.

Lester, D. (1981–82). Spiritualism and suicide. *Omega—The Journal of Death and Dying, 12*, 45–49.

LeTourneau, J. (1976). Effects of training in design on magnitude of the Müller–Lyer illusion. *Perceptual and Motor Skills, 42*, 119–124.

Levy, P. F. (1983, June 7). Flog or shock all nonviolent criminals. *National Enquirer*.

Lewis, K. E., & Bierly, M. (1990). Toward a profile of the female voter: Sex differences in perceived physical attractiveness and competence of political candidates. *Sex Roles, 22*, 1–12.

Lhyle, K. G., & Kulhavy, R. W. (1987). Feedback processing and error correction. *Journal of Educational Psychology, 79*, 320–322.

Lindner, D., & Hynan, M. T. (1987). Perceived structure of abstract paintings as a function of structure of music listened to on initial viewing. *Bulletin of the Psychonomic Society, 25*, 44–46.

Martin, R. A., & Lefcourt, H. M. (1984). Situational humor response questionnaire: Quantitative measure of sense of humor. *Journal of Personality and Social Psychology, 47*, 145–155.

Maynard, I. W., & Howe, B. L. (1987). Interrelations of trait and state anxiety with game performance of rugby players. *Perceptual and Motor Skills, 64*, 599–602.

McCarthy, P. R., & Schmeck, R. R. (1982). Effects of teacher self-disclosure on student learning and perceptions of teacher. *College Student Journal, 16*, 45–49.

McCloskey, M., Washburn, A., & Felch, L. (1983). Intuitive physics: The straight-down belief and its origin. *Journal of Experimental Psychology: Learning, Memory, and Cognition, 9*, 636–649.

McElrea, H., & Standing, L. (1992). Fast music causes fast drinking. *Perceptual and Motor Skills, 75*, 362.

Mehegan, D. (1985, October 17). Ya pays ya money and …. *Boston Globe*, p. 2.

Meyer, G. E. (1986). Interactions of subjective contours with the Ponzo, Müller–Lyer, and vertical–horizontal illusions. *Bulletin of the Psychonomic Society, 24*, 39–40.

Mintz, L. B., & Betz, N. E. (1986). Sex differences in the nature, realism, and correlates of body image. *Sex Roles, 15*, 185–195.

Morrison, C., & Reeve, J. (1986). Effect of instructional units on the analysis of related and unrelated skills. *Perceptual and Motor Skills, 62*, 563–566.

Newburger, J. W., Takahashi, M., Burns, J. C., Beiser, A. S., Chung, K. J., Duffy, C. E., Glode, M. P., Mason, W. H., Reddy, V., Sanders, S. P., Shulman, S. T., Wiggins, J. W., Hicks, R. V., Fulton, D. R., Lewis, A. B., Leung, D. Y. M., Colton, T., Rosen, F. S., & Melish, M. E. (1986). The treatment of Kawasaki syndrome with intravenous gamma globulin. *New England Journal of Medicine, 315*, 341–347.

O'Brien, E. J., & Wolford, C. R. (1982). Effect of delay in testing on retention of plausible versus bizarre mental images. *Journal of Experimental Psychology: Learning, Memory, and Cognition, 8*, 148–152.

Ouellet, R., & Joshi, P. (1986). Loneliness in relation to depression and self-esteem. *Psychological Reports, 58*, 821–822.

Pedersen, D. M. (1979). Dimensions of privacy. *Perceptual and Motor Skills, 48*, 1291–1297.

Pedersen, D. M. (1987). Sex differences in privacy preferences. *Perceptual and Motor Skills, 64*, 1239–1242.

Pfendler, C., & Widdel, H. (1986). Vigilance performance when using colour on electronic displays. *Perceptual and Motor Skills, 63*, 939–944.

Pope says angels have intellect, free will. (1986, August 7). *Boston Globe*, p. 76.

Predebon, J. (1987). Familiar size and judgments of distance: Effects of response mode. *Bulletin of the Psychonomic Society, 25*, 244–246.

Provine, R. R., & Hamernik, H. B. (1986). Yawning: Effects of stimulus interest. *Bulletin of the Psychonomic Society, 24*, 437–438.

Reisberg, D. (1983). General mental resources and perceptual judgments. *Journal of Experimental Psychology: Human Performance and Perception, 9*, 966–979.

Roballey, T. C., McGreevy, C., Rongo, R. R., Schwantes, M. L., Steger, P. J., Wininger, M. A., & Gardner, E. B. (1985). The effect of music on eating behavior. *Bulletin of the Psychonomic Society, 23,* 221–222.

Roberts, R. E., Lewinsohn, P. M., & Seeley, J. R. (1993). A brief measure of loneliness suitable for use with adolescents. *Psychological Reports, 72,* 1379–1391.

Rotton, J., & Kelly, I. W. (1985). A scale for assessing belief in lunar effects: Reliability and concurrent validity. *Psychological Reports, 57,* 239–245.

Ruback, R. B., & Dabbs, J. M., Jr. (1986). Talkativeness and verbal aptitude: Perception and reality. *Bulletin of the Psychonomic Society, 24,* 423–426.

Russell, D., Peplau, L., & Cutrona, C. (1980). The revised UCLA Loneliness Scale. *Journal of Personality and Social Psychology, 39,* 472–480.

Senders, V. L. (1958). *Measurement and statistics.* New York: Oxford University Press.

Seretny, M. L., & Dean, R. S. (1986). Interspersed post passage questions and reading comprehension achievement. *Journal of Educational Psychology, 78,* 228–229.

Sherwood, J. V. (1987). Facilitative effects of gaze upon learning. *Perceptual and Motor Skills, 64,* 1275–1278.

Smith, J. E., Waldorf, V. A., & Trembath, D. L. (1990). "Single white male looking for thin, very attractive …." *Sex Roles, 23,* 675–683.

Spielberger, C. D. (1980). *Test anxiety inventory.* Palo Alto, CA: Consulting Psychologists Press.

Stahler, G. J., & Eisenman, R. (1987). Psychotherapy dropouts: Do they have poor psychological adjustment? *Bulletin of the Psychonomic Society, 25,* 198–200.

Standing, L., Lynn, D., & Moxness, K. (1990). Effects of noise upon introverts and extroverts. *Bulletin of the Psychonomic Society, 28,* 138–140.

Stigler, S. M. (1986). *The history of statistics: The measurement of uncertainty before 1900.* Cambridge, MA: Harvard University Press.

Sturgeon, R., & Beer, J. (1990). Attendance reward and absenteeism in high school. *Psychological Reports, 66,* 759–762.

The way we are. (1985, December 31). *USA Today,* p. 4D.

The wizards of odds (1989, June). *Aide Magazine,* pp. 9–13.

Thorson, J. A. (1993). To die with your boots on: Relative lethality of the states. *Psychological Reports, 72,* 843–854.

Tismer, K. G. (1985). Sex and age differences in personal and global future time perspectives: A replication. *Perceptual and Motor Skills, 61,* 1007–1010.

Tobacyk, J., Miller, M. J., & Jones, G. (1984). Paranormal beliefs of high school students. *Psychological Reports, 55,* 255–261.

Trinkhaus, J. (1982). Stop sign compliance: An informal look. *Psychological Reports, 50,* 288.

Trinkhaus, J. (1983). Stop sign compliance: Another look. *Psychological Reports, 57,* 922.

Trinkhaus, J. (1988). Stop sign compliance: A further look. *Perceptual and Motor Skills, 67,* 670.

Trinkhaus, J. (1993). Stop sign compliance: A follow-up look. *Perceptual and Motor Skills, 76,* 1218.

Tukey, J. W. (1977). *Exploratory data analysis.* Reading, MA: Addison-Wesley.

Unrug-Neervoort, A., Kaiser, J., & Coenen, A. (1992). Influence of diazepam on prospective time estimation. *Perceptual and Motor Skills, 75,* 993–994.

Villimez, C., Eisenberg, N., & Carroll, J. L. (1986). Sex differences in the relation of children's height and weight to academic performance and others' attributions of competence. *Sex Roles, 15,* 667–681.

Wang, A. Y., Thomas, M. H., & Ouellette, J. A. (1992). Keyword mnemonic and retention of second language vocabulary words. *Journal of Educational Psychology, 84,* 520–528.

Weinstein, L., & de Man, A. (1987). U.S. students do not know as much as foreign students about the world. *Bulletin of the Psychonomic Society, 25,* 202–203.

Weinstein, L., Prather, G. A., & de Man, A. F. (1987). College baseball pitchers' throwing velocities as a function of awareness of being clocked. *Perceptual and Motor Skills, 64,* 1185–1186.

Weiss, B. A., Kimmel, D., & Stein, J. (1993). Psychology of computer use: XXVII: Effect of computer use on depth perception. *Perceptual and Motor Skills, 77,* 175–178.

Wellens, A. R. (1987). Heart-rate changes in response to shifts in interpersonal gaze from liked and disliked others. *Perceptual and Motor Skills, 64,* 595–598.

Wiehe, V. R. (1986). *Loco Parentis* and locus of control. *Psychological Reports, 59,* 169–170.

Wong, J. L. (1993). Comparison of the Shipley versus WAIS—R subtests and summary scores in predicting college grade point average. *Perceptual and Motor Skills, 76*, 1075–1078.

Wood, D. R. (1986). Self-perceived masculinity between bearded and nonbearded males. *Perceptual and Motor Skills, 62*, 769–770.

Yarnold, P. R., Grimm, L. G., & Mueser, K. T. (1986). Social conformity and the Type A behavior pattern. *Perceptual and Motor Skills, 62*, 99–104.

You are what you use. (1976, February 1). *Forbes*, p. 8.

Zuckerman, M. (1979). *Sensation seeking: Beyond the optimal level of arousal*. Hillsdale, NJ: Erlbaum.

Zusne, L. (1986–87). Some factors affecting the birthday–deathday phenomenon. *Omega, 17*, 9–26.

Name Index

Subject Index